Byzantine Saints' Lives in Translation

II

Byzantine Defenders of Images

BYZANTINE DEFENDERS OF IMAGES

EIGHT SAINTS' LIVES IN ENGLISH TRANSLATION

Edited by Alice-Mary Talbot

Dumbarton Oaks Research Library and Collection

Washington, D.C.

BX
393
.B97
1998

Library of Congress Cataloging-in-Publication Data
Byzantine defenders of images : eight saints' lives in English
   translation / edited by Alice-Mary Talbot.
      p.   cm. — (Byzantine saints' lives in translation ; 2)
     Includes 4 selections from the Synaxarion of Constantinople, published in the
10th century.
     Includes bibliographical references and indexes.
     Contents: Life of St. Theodosia of Constantinople — Life of St.
Stephen the Younger — Life of St. Anthousa of Mantineon — Life of
St. Anthousa, daughter of Constantine V — Life of the patriarch
Nikephoros I of Constantinople — Life of Sts. David, Symeon, and George of
Lesbos — Life of St. Ioannikios — Life of St. Theodora the Empress.
    ISBN 0-88402-259-5 (alk. paper)
    1. Christian saints—Byzantine Empire—Biography. 2. Byzantine
Empire—Church history. I. Talbot, Alice-Mary Maffry. II. Series.
BX393.B97   1998
270.2′092′2
[B]—DC21   97-31611
                                               CIP

CONTENTS

GENERAL INTRODUCTION

During the eighth and ninth centuries in Byzantium, theological and popular opinion was strongly divided on the question of the admissibility of icons of Christ, the Virgin, and the saints. The Greek term for icon, εἰκών, included not only the narrow sense of the word, a depiction of a sacred figure on a wooden panel, but any divine representation in any medium, whether on cloth, wood, metal, parchment, fresco, or mosaic. Controversy over the production and veneration of these sacred images became a political as well as a religious issue between 726 and 843, when a series of emperors imposed on the empire a policy of iconoclasm, literally "breaking of images."[1] Debate over the iconic representation of holy figures was not a new phenomenon in the eighth century, however, but had in fact concerned Christians since the formative period of their religion and the development of Christian art and iconography.[2]

The Argument over Images

Discussion of the permissibility of Christian sacred images was prompted by the conflicting teachings of the Old and New Testaments. On the one hand, Christians had inherited the Judaic tradition of the prohibition of idolatrous imagery, specifically the Second Commandment (Ex. 20:4), which proclaimed: "Thou shalt not make to thyself an idol, nor likeness of anything, whatever things are in the heaven above, and whatever are in the earth beneath, and whatever are in the waters under the earth." This was interpreted by some Christian apologists, such as Eusebios of Caesarea and Epiphanios of Cyprus,

---

[1] The phenomenon of iconoclasm was not confined to the Byzantine Empire, but is attested in western Europe as well. It was a prominent feature, for example, of the Protestant Reformation in Northern Europe and of the French Revolution. Cf. D. Freedberg, "The Structure of Byzantine and European Iconoclasm," in Bryer-Herrin, *Iconoclasm,* 165–77; idem, *The Power of Images: Studies in the History and Theory of Response* (Chicago, Ill., 1989).

[2] N. H. Baynes, "The Icons before Iconoclasm," *HThR* 44 (1951), 93–106, esp. 93–95; E. Kitzinger, "The Cult of Images in the Age before Iconoclasm," *DOP* 8 (1954), 83–150.

as prohibiting any depiction of a sacred figure.[3] Other Christian writers, how-ever, dismissed the relevancy of the Second Commandment, making a strong distinction between pagan idols and Christian icons. They argued further that veneration of icons bore no resemblance to idolatry, since the faithful were not worshiping the material icon, but the sacred figure represented on the icon. In the words of the fourth-century Father Basil of Caesarea, "The honor given to the image passes to the original (πρωτότυπον)."[4] Yet other theologians defended the didactic role of icons, especially useful for the illiterate.[5]

Nonetheless, as the cult of images spread in the Byzantine world, espe-cially in the sixth and seventh centuries, it seems evident that many pious individuals blurred the distinction between image and prototype, and assigned magical properties to the icon itself.[6] Iconoclastic reaction may well have been a response to the perceived excesses in veneration of images and relics by icon-odules or iconophiles, the "servants" or "lovers of images."

The controversy that erupted in Byzantium in the early eighth century over the veneration of religious images was to be a dominant issue in the Byz-antine church for over a century until the restoration of icons in 843 under the empress Theodora. At stake were basic tenets of Christian theology, espe-cially the doctrine of salvation. The iconoclasts, attacking image veneration as an idolatrous practice, claimed that Christ, as divine, could not be circum-scribed. If one did depict Him in His human aspect, then he was guilty of separating His two natures.[7] The iconodules argued, on the other hand, that

---

[3] For the relevant texts of these authors in English translation, see Mango, *Art*, 16–18, 41–43. For discussion of these apologists, see H. G. Thümmel, *Die Frühgeschichte der ostkirchlichen Bilderlehre* [Texte und Untersuchungen zur Geschichte der altchrist-lichen Literatur 139] (Berlin, 1992), and Sister M. C. Murray, "Art and the Early Church," *Journal of Theological Studies* 28 (1977), 305–45.

[4] Basil of Caesarea, *Liber de spiritu sancto*, XVIII.45, PG 32:149C.

[5] Cf. the 6th-century Hypatios of Ephesus, *Miscellaneous Enquiries*, ed. F. Diekamp, *Analecta Patristica* [*Orientalia Christiana Analecta* 117] (Rome, 1938), 127–29. See also S. Gero, "Hypatius of Ephesus on the Cult of Images," in *Christianity, Judaism and Other Greco-Roman Cults: Studies for Morton Smith at Sixty*, ed. J. Neusner, pt. 2 (Leiden, 1975), 208–16. A similar argument was also stressed by John of Damascus in the 8th century; cf. *De imaginibus Oratio* 1, chap. 17, ed. B. Kotter, *Die Schriften des Johannes von Damaskos* 3 (Berlin-New York, 1975), 93; PG 94:1248C–D.

[6] Cf. Kitzinger, "Cult of Images."

[7] Cf. J. Meyendorff, *Byzantine Theology* (New York, 1983), 44.

the New Testament, with its teaching of the incarnation of Christ, superseded the prohibition of images in the Old Testament. As John of Damascus stated, since God was made flesh, He could be depicted.[8] If the iconoclasts claimed that Christ could not be circumscribed, then they were denying His humanity and the mystery of the Incarnation through which God became man in order to save mankind.

The First Period of Iconoclasm (726–787)[9]

In 717 Leo, a general of Syrian origins,[10] became Byzantine emperor as Leo III, and inaugurated his reign by leading the successful defense of Constantinople against an Arab siege. Some nine years later, in 726, Leo first declared that icons of Christ and the saints should be removed from public display.[11] About the same time, Leo ordered the destruction of the celebrated image of Christ that adorned the Chalke Gate, the entrance to the palace. This incident, subsequently embroidered, gave rise to legendary accounts of the heroic defense of the image by Theodosia and her companions (see Life no. 1), who became the first martyrs of the iconodule cause.[12]

The exact course of events between 726 and 730 is unclear; in any case Leo seems to have proceeded slowly in implementing his new policy. The iconodule patriarch Germanos I remained in office until 730, when he was forced to abdicate after Leo convened a formal meeting (*silention*) to proclaim his rulings against the public veneration of images. According to Germanos, Leo persecuted iconodules, especially monks, some of whom were driven into ex-

---

[8] John of Damascus, *De imaginibus Oratio* 1, chap. 16, ed. Kotter, *Die Schriften des Johannes von Damaskos,* 89; also PG 94:1245A.

[9] The following outline of historical events is based primarily on the surveys of C. Mango ("Historical Introduction" in Bryer-Herrin, *Iconoclasm,* 1–6) and W. Treadgold (*Byz. Revival,* 4–11, 50, 55, 75–89, 124–25, 199, 207–15, 221–22, 227, 230–32, 261, 264–65, 275–81, 310–12, 327–28, 375–76).

[10] Cf. Gero, *Leo III,* 1–12, who argues that the epithet "the Isaurian" applied to Leo derives from a later historical tradition, and that he was actually born in Germanikeia on the northwestern fringes of Syria.

[11] M. Anastos, "Leo III's Edict against the Images in the Year 726–27 and Italo-Byzantine Relations between 726 and 730," *ByzF* 3 (1968), 5–41.

[12] M.-F. Auzépy ("Chalcé," 445–92) has questioned the historicity of this incident. See below, Life of Theodosia, n. 2.

ile; his iconoclast supporters are also said to have destroyed both portable icons and monumental church decoration.[13]

Under Leo's son Constantine V (741–775) persecution of iconodules became much more severe; he came to be regarded as the arch-iconoclast by subsequent generations of Byzantines who attached to him the epithet of Kopronymos or "Dung-named."[14] It was Constantine who gave iconoclastic policy a sound theological foundation by sponsoring study of passages from the Scriptures and patristic literature that would support the abolition of religious figural imagery. In 754 a church council was held at Hieria, near Constantinople, which officially prohibited the installation or veneration of images of Christ, the Virgin, and saints, even in private. In the words of the *Acta,*

> We decree unanimously in the name of the Holy . . . Trinity that there shall be rejected and removed and cursed out of the Christian church every likeness which is made out of any material whatever by the evil art of painters. Anyone who presumes from now on to manufacture an icon, or to worship it, or set it up in a church or in a private house, or possesses it in secret, if he be a bishop, priest, or deacon, he shall be deposed; if he be a monk or layman, he shall be anathematized and deemed guilty under imperial law as a foe of God's commands. . . .[15]

The council specifically anathematized the iconodule spokesmen Germanos, John of Damascus, and George of Cyprus. One of the chief arguments of the *Definition* of iconoclast doctrine was that Christ, as divine, is uncircumscribable; anyone who depicts His fleshly nature separates His two indivisible natures, as did the Nestorian heretics. The council also argued that the only true image of Christ was the Eucharist.[16]

Constantine especially targeted iconodule monks and nuns, as at the double monastery of Mantineon where the abbess Anthousa and her nephew were tortured (see Life no. 3). In 765/6 the emperor reportedly imposed mar-

---

[13] See G. Ostrogorsky, "Les débuts de la querelle des images," in *Mélanges Charles Diehl* 1 (Paris, 1930), 235–55.

[14] The iconodules gave him this nickname either for having allegedly defecated while being baptized, or for the still more indecorous charge of coprophilia; cf. Gero, *Constantine V,* 171–74.

[15] I. D. Mansi, *Sacrorum conciliorum nova et amplissima collectio* 13 (Florence, 1767), 324DE, 328C; the translation is a slightly modified version of Mango, *Art,* 167–68.

[16] S. Gero, "The Eucharistic Doctrine of the Byzantine Iconoclasts and Its Sources," *BZ* 68 (1975), 4–22.

riage upon a group of abbots; they were also paraded through the Hippo-drome of Constantinople to be spat upon and cursed by the crowd.[17] In a similar incident of 771 Michael Lachanodrakon, general of the Thrakesion theme, is said to have assembled at Ephesos all the monks and nuns of the theme, and tried to force them into marriage; blinding and exile to Cyprus was the fate of those who refused.[18] Executions of unrepentant iconophiles like Stephen the Younger (see Life no. 2) seem to have occurred primarily in the 760s.[19] According to the Life of Stephen, many monks were imprisoned;[20] others abandoned monastic life. Some monasteries had their properties con-fiscated, others were left deserted.[21]

Since the depiction of sacred images was banned under Constantine V, the repertory of religious art was limited to the cross. The monumental mosaic crosses attested in churches such as St. Irene in Constantinople and the Koimesis in Nicaea are traditionally assigned to this period.[22] Elsewhere sa-cred art was replaced with secular imagery: the *vita* of St. Stephen the Younger relates that Constantine V had scenes from the life of Christ destroyed at the church of Blachernai, the principal Constantinopolitan shrine to the Virgin; he then converted it "into a storehouse of fruit and an aviary, for he covered it with mosaics [representing] trees and all kinds of birds and beasts, and cer-tain swirls of ivy-leaves [enclosing] cranes, crows, and peacocks." The same text goes on to describe how the scenes of the six ecumenical councils depicted on the Milion or central milestone in the capital were replaced with pictures of horse races and the emperor's favorite charioteer.[23]

Constantine V's eldest son, Leo IV, who succeeded him in 775, followed a much milder iconoclastic policy than his father, recalling iconodules from exile or releasing them from prison. He was acutely distressed, however, to

---

[17] Theoph. 437–38; Turtledove, *Theophanes,* 126.

[18] Theoph. 445; Turtledove, *Theophanes,* 132.

[19] Cf. Gero, *Constantine V,* 122–25.

[20] *V. Stephan. Jun.,* PG 100:1160c.

[21] On the persecution of monks and monasteries under Constantine V, see D. Pa-pachryssanthou, *Actes du Prôtaton* (Paris, 1975), 9–10.

[22] R. Cormack, "The Arts during the Age of Iconoclasm," in Bryer-Herrin, *Icono-clasm,* 35–44, esp. 35–41.

[23] *V. Stephan. Jun.* 1120c, 1172ab; the English translation is that of Mango, *Art,* 152–53. Gero (*Constantine V,* 112–13) is suspicious of the historicity of these texts.

learn that his wife, the Athenian Irene, secretly kept icons in her private quarters. In 780, soon after this discovery, which led to strained relations with his wife, Leo died under suspicious circumstances.

There has been considerable discussion of why icon veneration should have become such a controversial and politicized issue in the eighth century, and numerous theories have been adduced to explain the outbreak of iconoclasm at this particular time. Among the postulated causes, some of which are now discredited, are: 1) The new policy was influenced by Judaism or Islam.[24] 2) It was an attempt by the imperial authorities to curry favor with the population of Asia Minor, presumed to be iconoclast in sentiment.[25] 3) It reflected the imperial desire to gain the support of the army, again assumed to be iconoclast.[26] 4) The attack on icons was really a veiled attempt to combat the growing economic power of monasteries (a stronghold of iconodule support) by closing them down and confiscating their properties.[27] This theory has been subsequently modified by Peter Brown, who saw iconoclasm as an attempt to weaken the power of monasteries and especially of holy men who were seen as a threat to the authority of the ecclesiastical hierarchy and emperor.[28]

[24] For reassessment of these theories, see A. Sharf, *Byzantine Jewry from Justinian to the Fourth Crusade* (London, 1971), 61–81; O. Grabar, "Islam and Iconoclasm," in Bryer-Herrin, *Iconoclasm,* 45–52; S. Gero, "Contemporary Muslim Iconoclasm and Leo," in his *Leo III,* 59–84.

[25] Cf. H. Ahrweiler, "L'Asie Mineure et les invasions arabes," *Revue Historique* 227 (1962), 23, a position now revised in her "The Geography of the Iconoclast World," in Bryer-Herrin, *Iconoclasm,* 21–27. G. Ostrogorsky (*Studien zur Geschichte der byzantinischen Bilderstreites* [Breslau, 1929], 5, 25–28, 40) argued that the people of eastern Anatolia were influenced by monophysitic views and hence "hostile or indifferent to the Chalcedonian synthesis of the divine and the human in Christ and, consequently, to the showing of Christ in human form" (Brown, "Dark Age Crisis," 253). It should be noted, however, that several Anatolian bishops espoused iconoclasm in the early 8th century well before Leo's edict of 726; cf. S. Gero, "Iconoclasm in Asia Minor before 726," in his *Leo III,* 85–93.

[26] For refutation of this view, see W. E. Kaegi, "The Byzantine Armies and Iconoclasm," *ByzSlav* 27 (1966), 48–70.

[27] Cf. N. Iorga, *Etudes byzantines* 2 (Bucharest, 1940), 233–34, with response by G. Ostrogorsky, "Über die vermeintliche Reformtätigkeit der Isaurier," *BZ* 30 (1930), 399.

[28] Brown, "Dark Age Crisis," 295–300; in his words, "Iconomachy in action is monachomachy." For a response to the Brown thesis, see S. Gero, "Byzantine Iconoclasm and Monachomachy," *Journal of Ecclesiastical History* 28 (1977), 241–48, and J. Hal-

5) Iconoclasm reflected a genuine concern on the part of many Byzantines with the increasing devotion to sacred images.[29] 6) It was a response to the demoralization caused by recent disasters in the empire, such as the military successes of the Arabs in Anatolia and a devastating volcanic eruption at Thera (Santorini), which were taken to indicate divine displeasure with icon veneration.[30] 7) Adoption of an iconoclastic policy was a way of reasserting imperial authority which had been weakened by the growing importance of icon worship.[31]

The First Restoration of Icons (787–815)

When Leo IV died in 780, leaving a nine-year-old son, Constantine VI, the empress Irene became regent. In 784 she took advantage of her position to appoint as patriarch the layman Tarasios, who was sympathetic to the iconodule position. The two immediately began to lay the groundwork for an ecumenical council that would reverse the rulings of the iconoclastic council of 754. After an abortive initial session in Constantinople in 786, disrupted by iconoclast troops, the Seventh Ecumenical Council was convened in 787 at Nicaea, the site of the first ecumenical council in 325. Thanks to careful strategy and planning by empress and patriarch, the iconodule position prevailed and a set of decrees proclaimed the restoration of image veneration as official ecclesiastical policy. The iconoclast clergy was subjected to only mild punishment, and the controversy seemed to be at an end. Nonetheless, there is little evidence for the revival of iconic art during the reign of Irene and Constantine.[32]

Unfortunately for the iconodules, the thirty years following the reintroduction of icons were a low ebb for the empire. Irene, who came to be venerated as a saint for her restoration of images, was less successful as a temporal

---

don, "Some Remarks on the Background to the Iconoclast Controversy," *ByzSlav* 38 (1977), 161–62.

[29] Brown, "Dark Age Crisis," 285–88.

[30] Brown, "Dark Age Crisis," 252, 284–89; G. Ostrogorsky, *History of the Byzantine State* (Oxford, 1968), 162; Mango, "Historical Introduction," in Bryer-Herrin, *Iconoclasm,* 1–2.

[31] Haldon, "Background to the Iconoclast Controversy," esp. 180–84.

[32] See n. 41 below and Gero, *Constantine V,* 112 and n. 6; P. Speck, "Ein Heiligenbilderzyklus im Studios-Kloster um das Jahr 800," *Actes du XIIe Congrès international d'études byzantines, Ochride, 10–16 septembre 1961* 3 (Belgrade, 1964), 340.

ruler. Her struggle for power with her son Constantine VI culminated in 797 in his blinding, an operation which proved fatal. By some his downfall was seen to be divine retribution for his adulterous second marriage, a scandal that was to divide the Church for years after his death. On the battlefield the Byzantines suffered a disastrous defeat in 792 at the hands of the Bulgarians at Markellai; it was this battle which led to the spiritual conversion of St. Ioannikios (see Life no. 7). The Arabs' numerous raids into Anatolia twice forced Irene to conclude costly peace treaties with the Abbasids. Between 797 and 802 Irene held the anomalous position of sole empress, as the first woman to sit alone on the imperial throne. Despite her efforts to curry favor with her subjects through tax exemptions and abolition of trading duties, she was deposed in 802 by a treasury official, Nikephoros I (802–811), who promptly instituted economic reforms. In 811, however, Nikephoros was killed in battle with the Bulgarians, and his son and heir Staurakios was mortally wounded. Michael I Rangabe (811–813) was also no match for the Bulgarian khan Krum.

The Second Period of Iconoclasm

Leo V the Armenian,[33] who seized the throne in 813, may well have felt he had a divine mandate to return to the iconoclastic policy of Leo III and Constantine V, during whose lengthy reigns the Byzantines had successfully held foreign enemies at bay. Although upon his accession to the throne he had promised the patriarch Nikephoros I (806–815) to uphold icon veneration, Leo soon reversed his position. One of his first actions was to forbid the installation of images in the lower part of churches, where they would be accessible for acts of veneration. He also removed once more from the Chalke Gate the image of Christ that had been restored by Irene. In 814 Leo convened a committee of iconoclast scholars under the leadership of John the Grammarian to prepare a florilegium of scriptural and patristic passages that opposed religious imagery. He then convoked a church council in 815 to repudiate the Seventh Ecumenical Council and reinstate the doctrines of the council of 754. The patriarch Nikephoros I (see Life no. 5), who had led the opposition to Leo, was deposed and sent into exile, where he continued to write treatises in defense of the iconodule position.

---

[33] On Leo V, see Treadgold, *Byz. Revival,* 196–225; Alexander, *Nicephorus,* 125–47.

Leo exiled many bishops, abbots (including Theodore of Stoudios, the champion of the iconodules), and monks such as Symeon of Lesbos (see Life no. 6); some iconodules were imprisoned and flogged; others, like St. Ioannikios and Niketas Patrikios, fled their monasteries and wandered about to escape persecution.[34] Leo's primary support was from the army, which traditionally had favored an iconoclast policy. Nonetheless, it was one of his own generals, a native of Amorion, who conspired to assassinate Leo on Christmas Day 820 and succeeded him as Michael II (820–829).

Michael's reign provided a period of respite in the overt persecution of iconophiles; he revoked sentences of imprisonment and exile, and may even have permitted the painting of images of saints.[35] But as Theodore the Stoudite astutely recognized, "The winter is over, but spring has not yet arrived."[36] For at the same time Michael appointed an iconoclast patriarch, Antony Kassymatas, in 821, and made John the Grammarian, the leading iconoclast intellectual, tutor to his young son Theophilos.

Not surprisingly Theophilos became an ardent iconoclast. After succeeding his father in 829, at age sixteen, he renewed the attack on outspoken supporters of icons; in 833 he ordered the arrest of certain iconodule clergy and monks. Many monks were imprisoned, and a few were martyred, for example, the aged Euthymios of Sardis who died of a flogging in 831. In 839 the Palestinian brothers Theodore and Theophanes suffered the unusual punishment of having iambic verses tattooed on their foreheads.[37]

In 837, or more probably 838, John the Grammarian, who was considered the "evil genius" of the iconoclast intelligentsia, finally ascended the patriarchal throne.[38] Ironically, however, he achieved his long-awaited goal only to preside over the final years of iconoclasm, which was by this time a dying

---

[34] Cf. Life of Ioannikios (no. 7 below), Chaps. 19, 30; D. Papachryssanthou, "Un confesseur du second iconoclasme. La Vie du patrice Nicétas (†836)," *TM* 3 (1968), 319.

[35] Treadgold, *Byz. Revival,* 247 and n. 342.

[36] Fatouros, *Theod. Stud. Epist., ep.* 469.35–36.

[37] See *vita* of David, Symeon, and George (Life no. 6), below, Chaps. 23–24.

[38] The dates of his patriarchate are traditionally given as 837–843, but W. Treadgold has shown that he probably became patriarch in April 838; cf. W. Treadgold, "The Chronological Accuracy of the Chronicle of Symeon the Logothete for the Years 813–845," *DOP* 33 (1979), 178–79.

movement. Theophilos could not even enforce his views among members of his own family. His wife Theodora (see Life no. 8) secretly venerated icons throughout his reign, as did his stepmother Euphrosyne and his daughters. The terrible disaster of the Arab conquest of Amorion, the hometown of the Amorian dynasty, in 838 and the subsequent destruction of the city ended the myth of the invincibility of iconoclast emperors against foreign enemies. Theophilos fell ill at the news, and never totally regained his health, dying four years later at the age of 29. Hoping to save her husband from eternal damnation, Theodora circulated the pious fiction that he had repented on his deathbed, kissing an icon of Christ.[39]

The shallowness of support for the iconoclast position is further demonstrated by the almost immediate collapse of the iconoclast party after Theophilos' death in 842. Little more than a year later, on 11 March 843, a Constantinopolitan church council declared the restoration of image veneration, and the iconodule Methodios (843–847) replaced John VII on the patriarchal throne. Since that time the orthodox Church has celebrated the Feast of Orthodoxy on the first Sunday in Lent.

The abundance of *vitae* of iconophile saints has made difficult the choice of saints' Lives to be included in this volume; the approximately 75 surviving *vitae* and notices from the tenth-century *Synaxarion of Constantinople*[40] provide sufficient materials for several volumes of translations. The eight texts selected here fall into two groups: four brief synaxarion notices of saints from the first iconoclastic era, and four lengthy *vitae* from the second. The unequal pagination allotted to the two periods suggests the great disparity between the number of saints commemorated from the two eras; although the first period of iconoclasm (726–787) was much longer than the second (815–843), the saints who are recorded as having been persecuted by the ninth-century emperors greatly outnumber those who suffered at the hands of Leo III, Constantine V, and Leo IV.[41] The selection of texts reflects as well the paucity of preserved *vitae* of iconodule saints of the first iconoclastic era and the fact that not a single one of these Lives was actually written in the eighth century.

---

[39] See Life of Theodora below, Chap. 8.

[40] This figure (8 female saints plus 64 male saints) is based on the calculations of Kazhdan-Talbot, "Women and Iconoclasm," 393, 395–96.

[41] Cf. Kazhdan-Talbot, "Women and Iconoclasm," appendix A, 405–7.

Even during the thirty-year hiatus (787–815) between the two iconoclastic periods, only one *vita* of an iconodule saint was composed, that of Stephen the Younger (d. 764 or 765?) ca. 806. The sparseness of hagiographical compositions in the eighth century is yet another indication of the generally restricted level of literary activity during this period; moreover, the few Lives that were written eulogize holy men and women of earlier centuries rather than contemporary saints.[42] The ninth century, however, saw an efflorescence of iconodule hagiography, particularly after the permanent restoration of images in 843.[43] A similar phenomenon can be observed in the realm of art; no figural religious art survives from the years 787–815 (a period of limited building activity), whereas there was a resurgence in iconic depictions after 843, especially under Basil I (867–886) and Leo VI (886–912).[44]

This explains the paucity of eighth-century materials in this volume. We should have liked to include the *vita* of the martyr Stephen the Younger, "a jewel of the hagiography of the iconoclastic period,"[45] which provides such a detailed picture of the persecution of Constantine V, but the decision was made to exclude it because a new critical edition and French translation by M.-F. Auzépy is now in press. Stephen is therefore represented with a brief synaxarion notice.

The four *vitae* of ninth-century saints chosen for this volume eulogize an iconodule patriarch, an empress, and four saintly monks. The Life of the patriarch Nikephoros I, forced to resign his throne in 815 as a result of the second wave of iconoclastic persecution under Leo V, is generally regarded as one of the key works of iconodule hagiography. It is especially important because of its exposition of the Byzantine theory of images and justification of icon veneration in a lengthy debate between emperor and patriarch in the form of

---

[42] This point was emphasized by A. Kazhdan and L. Sherry in their *History of Byzantine Literature,* currently in preparation.

[43] Thus, three of the four *vitae* of 9th-century saints in this volume were composed in the 9th or early 10th century: the *vita Nicephori* probably between 843 and 846, the *vita Ioannicii* perhaps in 847, and the *vita Theodorae* after 867, probably during the reign of Leo VI (886–912).

[44] See n. 29 above and R. Cormack, "The Arts during the Age of Iconoclasm," in Bryer-Herrin, *Iconoclasm,* 35–36 (on St. Sophia in Thessalonike) and 40; idem, "Painting after Iconoclasm," in Bryer-Herrin, *Iconoclasm,* 147–63; and L. Brubaker, "Byzantine Art in the Ninth Century: Theory, Practice, and Culture," *BMGS* 13 (1989), 23–93.

[45] The phrase is that of Ševčenko, "Hagiography," 115.

a Socratic dialogue. The *Acta* of the three brothers from Lesbos, David, Symeon, and George, vividly describe the impact of iconoclastic policy on that Aegean island, and the exile and imprisonment of Symeon for his iconodule beliefs. Likewise, St. Ioannikios of Bithynia was forced to flee his monastery and wander in isolated regions to escape persecution by the iconoclasts.[46] His *vita* complements the account of the *Acta* of the brothers from Lesbos in its detailed description of events surrounding the restoration of icons under Theodora and the election of the patriarch Methodios in 843. The concluding *vita* in the book, the Life of the empress Theodora, also stresses the demise of iconoclasm with the death of Theophilos and the revival of image veneration.

Although four out of the eight selections deal with women, the total pagination devoted to female iconodules is a small proportion of the volume. This again reflects the imbalance in the hagiographical record of male and female saints of the iconoclastic era. As has been recently shown, very few iconodule women saints were commemorated in the *Synaxarion of Constantinople,* and full-fledged *vitae* survive for only two of them, the empresses Irene and Theodora.[47] The male saints are much more numerous in the *Synaxarion of Constantinople* than their female counterparts, and twenty-eight of the full-length *vitae* stress the iconophile views of their heroes. Nonetheless it is generally believed that women were in fact ardent supporters of icons, as demonstrated, for example, by the correspondence of Theodore of Stoudios;[48] thus it seemed appropriate to give them substantial representation in this collection.

The saints' Lives included in this volume take a variety of forms. In addition to the short synaxarion notices (some of which may be summaries of Lives now lost), one can find two *vitae* written in a mid-level style (those of the three brothers from Lesbos and of Ioannikios), one written in extremely high style replete with numerous classical allusions and unattested vocabulary (the Life of Nikephoros), and a *vita* that combines elements of a chronicle and an imperial oration (the Life of Theodora).

[46] Life of Ioannikios (no. 7 below), Chaps. 19, 30.

[47] Kazhdan-Talbot, "Women and Iconoclasm," 391–95. There is also a *passio* of the martyr Maria, an alternative version of the incident at the Chalke Gate in which Maria and a group of men are celebrated in place of Theodosia and her female companions; see Kazhdan-Talbot, ibid., 393–94 and n. 13.

[48] Cf. Kazhdan-Talbot, "Women and Iconoclasm," 396–400, and J. Herrin, "Women and the Faith in Icons in Early Christianity," in R. Samuel, G. S. Jones, *Culture, Ideology, and Politics* (London, 1982), 56–83, esp. 68–75.

The Lives of several of the saints featured here reveal that the dividing line between iconodules and iconoclasts was not hard and fast; even for champions of icon veneration there were gray areas of ambivalence, both in their personal careers and in their relatives and associates.[49] Thus, Anthousa of Mantineon (see Life no. 3), who was tortured under Constantine V for her iconophile position, ended up on good terms with the imperial family; the empress made generous donations to the monastery of Mantineon, and apparently named her daughter after the holy woman in thanksgiving for the baby's safe delivery. This very same princess Anthousa (see Life no. 4), although the daughter of the arch-iconoclast Constantine V, attained sanctity and was linked with the empress Irene, the restorer of image veneration in 787. Ignatios the Deacon, the hagiographer of the staunch iconodule patriarch Nikephoros (see Life no. 5), reveals at the end of his *vita* that he composed the work as atonement for his own lapse into iconoclasm and communion with the "heretics."[50] One version of the Life of St. Ioannikios (by Sabas) states that the saint, following in his parents' footsteps, was an iconoclast in his youth during his military service, but subsequently converted to iconophile views.[51] Peter's account (see Life no. 7) conveniently ignores this embarrassing episode in Ioannikios' past history, but does describe the deeply held iconoclastic convictions of Ioannikios' unnamed brother-in-law.[52] Finally, the empress Theodora (see Life no. 8) was married to the iconoclastic emperor Theophilos; although she reversed her husband's religious policy as soon as she assumed the regency for their young son, at the same time she reportedly sought absolution for Theophilos by promoting the fabricated tale of the emperor's deathbed conversion to image veneration.[53]

The *vitae* of Ioannikios and of the three brothers from Lesbos (Lives

---

[49] In this connection it is interesting to note that D. Freedberg gives the title "Ambiguity of Attitude" to one section of his article on "The Structure of Byzantine and European Iconoclasm"; cf. Bryer-Herrin, *Iconoclasm,* 175–76.

[50] *V. Niceph.* 215–17. On Ignatios, see Ševčenko, "Hagiography," 125, and n. 25 to the Life of Nikephoros, below.

[51] *V. Ioannic. a Sab.,* chaps. 2, 5.

[52] Life of Ioannikios by Peter (no. 7 below), Chap. 35.

[53] For further examples of iconodule women married to iconoclast husbands, attested in the correspondence of Theodore of Stoudios, see Kazhdan-Talbot, "Women and Iconoclasm," 399.

nos. 6 and 7) demonstrate that there were splits even among the iconodules, especially at the time of the Triumph of Orthodoxy in 843. Thus, the hagiographer Peter adopts a strong stance against the rigorist Stoudite monks who opposed any accommodation with the iconoclasts; his hero Ioannikios is portrayed as a fervent supporter of Methodios as the new patriarch. Likewise the author of the *vita* of the three brothers of Lesbos describes their difference of opinion over the question of the absolution of Theophilos, with Symeon adopting the more rigorous view, while George was more conciliatory.[54]

Despite the triumph of the cause of icons espoused by the iconodule saints, and their commemoration in official church compilations such as *synaxaria*, menologia, and the *Synodikon of Orthodoxy*, few of these holy men and women attained fully developed personal cults. Nikephoros and Theodora were recognized as saints for their leadership in the defense of images, rather than for more typical saintly qualities such as clairvoyance and miraculous powers. It is significant that the translation of the patriarch Nikephoros' relics to the church of the Holy Apostles in Constantinople was an act promoted at the highest level, by empress and patriarch, rather than the result of popular demand.[55] Although Ioannikios and David, Symeon, and George performed miracles during their lifetime, atypically no posthumous miracles are recorded for them, and we know very little of their commemoration in later centuries.[56] Ironically, of the saints included in this volume, it was Theodosia, the only one who was not a historical figure, to whose cult the Byzantines were most devoted. This is shown by the importance of her healing shrine and feastday in Constantinople, especially in the Palaiologan period.[57]

Four of our saints (Theodosia, Stephen the Younger, Nikephoros, and Ioannikios) became part of the standard iconographic repertoire of manuscript, panel, and monumental painting; surprisingly, however, the empress Theodora was not honored in art to the same extent that she received liturgical commemoration.[58]

One can conclude then that iconodule saints should not be placed into one homogeneous category, defined only by their common opposition to icon-

---

[54] Life of David, Symeon, and George (no. 6 below), Chap. 27.

[55] Cf. Introduction to the Life of Nikephoros, below, 38.

[56] It is perhaps significant that the *vita* of Ioannikios by Peter and the *Acta* of the three brothers from Lesbos survive in unique copies.

[57] For further details, see Life no. 1, 3–4.

[58] Cf. Introduction to the Life of Theodora, below, 356–57.

oclasm. They represent rather several types of sanctity: Nikephoros is a saintly patriarch and theologian, revered for his eloquent exposition of iconodule doctrine and brave confrontation with Leo V; Theodosia, Stephen, and Anthousa of Mantineon are martyrs or confessors who suffered mortal or severe wounds as a result of their iconophile convictions; Ioannikios and the three brothers from Lesbos are monastic saints, renowned for their asceticism, gifts of prophecy and miracle-working, in addition to their support of icons; Anthousa, daughter of Constantine V, is a pious princess who evidently defied her father to venerate images; the empress Theodora is an imperial saint whose authority enabled her to restore sacred images to church decoration.

It is important to keep in mind that the later hagiographic tradition magnified the degree to which iconoclasm was a dominant issue of the eighth and ninth centuries.[59] Perusal of the Lives of iconodule saints leaves the reader with the erroneous impression that the emperors of this period were concerned only with this controversy. The narrative histories of the ninth century, on the other hand, provide a valuable corrective, emphasizing rather the external threats to the empire from Arabs and Bulgarians, the development of the theme system, economic recovery, and legal reform. Nonetheless, the quarrel over images was an important chapter in the history of Orthodoxy and the relations between Byzantine Church and State; the eventual triumph of the iconodules was to determine the future direction of Byzantine art and confirm the major role of monks and monasteries in Byzantine society.

[59] Cf. the remarks of C. Mango in Bryer-Herrin, *Iconoclasm,* 6.

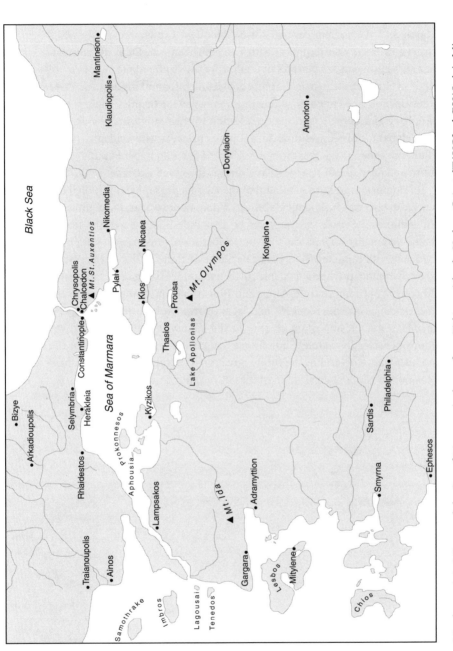

Northwest Asia Minor and the Sea of Marmara (redrawn from *Tübinger Atlas des Vorderen Orients* [TAVO], pl. BV18, Asia Minor: The Byzantine Empire, 7th–9th Century A.D. [Wiesbaden, 1988])

GENERAL BIBLIOGRAPHY

D. E. Afinogenov, "The Great Purge of 843: A Re-Examination," ΛΕΙΜΩΝ. *Studies Presented to Lennart Rydén on His Sixty-fifth Birthday,* ed. J. O. Rosenqvist (Uppsala, 1996), 79–91.

————, "Κωνσταντινούπολις ἐπίσκοπον ἔχει. The Rise of the Patriarchal Power in Byzantium from Nicaenum II to Epanagoga. Part I. From Nicaenum II to the Second Outbreak of Iconoclasm," *Erytheia* 15 (1994), 45–65; "Part II. From the Second Outbreak of Iconoclasm to the Death of Methodios," *Erytheia* 17 (1996), 43–71.

P. Alexander, *The Patriarch Nicephorus of Constantinople* (Oxford, 1958).

M. V. Anastos, "Iconoclasm and Imperial Rule, 717–842," in *Cambridge Mediaeval History* 4.1 (Cambridge, 1966), 61–104.

P. Brown, "A Dark Age Crisis: Aspects of the Iconoclastic Controversy," *English Historical Review* 88 (1973), 1–34.

A. A. M. Bryer, J. Herrin, *Iconoclasm* (Birmingham, 1977).

S. Gero, *Byzantine Iconoclasm during the Reign of Constantine V* (Louvain, 1977).

————, *Byzantine Iconoclasm during the Reign of Leo III* (Louvain, 1973).

A. Grabar, *L'Iconoclasme byzantin. Le dossier archéologique,* 2d ed. (Paris, 1984).

J. Haldon, "Some Remarks on the Background to the Iconoclast Controversy," *ByzSlav* 38 (1977), 161–84.

H. Hennephof, *Textus byzantinos ad iconomachiam pertinentes in usum academicum* (Leiden, 1969).

P. A. Hollingsworth, A. Cutler, "Iconoclasm," *ODB* 2:975–77.

A. Kazhdan, A.-M. Talbot, "Women and Iconoclasm," *BZ* 84/85 (1991/92), 391–408.

D. J. Sahas, *Icon and Logos. Sources in Eighth-Century Iconoclasm* (Toronto, 1988).

P. Schreiner, "Der byzantinische Bilderstreit: kritische Analyse der zeitgenössischen Meinungen und das Urteil der Nachwelt bis heute," *Settimane di Studio del Centro Italiano di Studi sull' alto medioevo* 34.1 (1988), 319–407.

D. Stein, *Der Beginn des byzantinischen Bilderstreites und seine Entwicklung* (Munich, 1980).

W. Treadgold, *The Byzantine Revival, 780–842* (Stanford, Calif., 1988).

.

NOTE ON THE TRANSLATION

The aim of the translators has been the production of a text that is close to the original Greek, yet at the same time readable and comprehensible. It has proved impossible to impose stylistic uniformity on the work of seven different contributors; hence, variations in style may indicate the taste of the individual translator rather than that of the hagiographer, with the exception of the Life of the patriarch Nikephoros, written in a very high style that is reflected in its translation.

Greek proper names and technical terms have been strictly transliterated for the most part, except in instances where a traditional latinized or anglicized form (e.g., Homer, Thebes, Constantinople) is well known. The anglicized form of Greek first names that are common in English (e.g., Mary, John, Peter) has also been adopted.

The use of pointed brackets (< . . . >) indicates the insertion of words to clarify the meaning of a phrase, for example, "the <previous> miracle," while square brackets ([. . .]) represent an additional phrase of identification, e.g., "the superior [Gregory]."

Scriptural citations are taken from the Lancelot Brenton translation of the Septuagint and from the King James Version of the New Testament.[1]

---

[1] The King James Version was chosen over the more accurate translation of the New Revised Standard Version, because its archaizing language harmonizes better with the Brenton translation of the Septuagint. In a few cases where the Brenton or King James translations are misleading, the translators have substituted their own rendering.

ACKNOWLEDGMENTS

I should like first of all to express my appreciation to the fine group of translators involved in the preparation of this volume; they set high standards for themselves, were cooperative in meeting deadlines and preparing revisions, and have become valued colleagues and collaborators. Let me also acknowledge the invaluable assistance of the members of the Advisory Board for the series, who helped to define the scope and contents of this book, and advised on the selection of translators. My Dumbarton Oaks colleagues Stephanos Efthymiades, Alexander Kazhdan, and Lee Sherry provided helpful advice on the translation and interpretation of difficult passages; I am also grateful to Lee Sherry and Stamatina McGrath for assistance with computer problems. I should especially like to express my gratitude and that of the translators for the painstaking review of the manuscript, particularly the translations, made by Alexander Alexakis and Lennart Rydén; they made many helpful suggestions for improvement of the translations and for emendations of the Greek text. As always, the staff of the Dumbarton Oaks Publications Office, especially Glenn Ruby, Robin Surratt, and Olga Grushin, and the copyeditor, Susan Higman, have carefully shepherded this volume through the publication process. I should also like to thank Sarah Gordon for her assistance with the indexing.

The translators and I warmly acknowledge the extensive use we have made of the *Thesaurus Linguae Graecae* (copyrighted by the *TLG* and the Regents of the University of California) and of the Dumbarton Oaks Hagiography Database (copyrighted by Dumbarton Oaks and the Trustees for Harvard University). Our searches in these two computerized *instrumenta studiorum* have made possible many of the citations of sources and parallels.

I should also like to express my thanks to the Centre of Byzantine Research of the National Hellenic Research Foundation, which has graciously granted permission for the translation of the Greek text of the *vita* of the empress Theodora that originally appeared in *Symmeikta.*

The National Endowment for the Humanities and Dumbarton Oaks have provided generous support for preparation of the translations. I am particularly grateful to the director of Dumbarton Oaks, Angeliki Laiou, who first suggested the project of a series of hagiographic translations, and to Henry Maguire, director of Byzantine Studies from 1991 to 1996, who has offered encouragement and advice.

LIST OF CONTRIBUTORS

Dorothy Abrahamse, who has published numerous articles on the hagiography of the Middle Byzantine period, is currently dean of the College of Liberal Arts at California State University, Long Beach.

Nicholas Constas, a specialist in patristics and historical theology, is assistant professor of patristics at Hellenic College–Holy Cross Greek Orthodox School of Theology in Brookline, Massachusetts.

Douglas Domingo-Forasté, associate professor of classics at California State University, Long Beach, has recently edited the letters and fragments of Aelian (Teubner).

Elizabeth A. Fisher, chairman of the classics department at the George Washington University in Washington, D.C., is the editor of the hagiographic orations of Michael Psellos (Teubner).

Denis F. Sullivan, associate professor of curriculum and instruction at the University of Maryland, College Park, is the editor and translator of the *vita* of St. Nikon ho Metanoeite.

Alice-Mary Talbot, director of Byzantine Studies at Dumbarton Oaks, previously edited and translated the correspondence of Athanasios I, patriarch of Constantinople, as well as an account of his posthumous miracles.

Martha Vinson is the editor and translator of *The Correspondence of Leo, Metropolitan of Synada and Syncellus.*

LIST OF ABBREVIATIONS

Scriptural Citations

Septuagint (all citations are based on the numbering of the L. C. L. Brenton edition, *The Septuagint with Apocrypha: Greek and English* [London, 1851])

Gen.   Genesis
Ex.   Exodus
Lev.   Leviticus
Num.   Numbers
Deut.   Deuteronomy
Josh.   Joshua
Judg.   Judges
Ruth
Ki.   Kings
              N.B.   1–2 Sam. in OT = 1–2 Kings in Septuagint
                      1–2 Kings in OT = 3–4 Kings in Sept.
Chr.   Chronicles (= Paralipomenon of Sept.)
Ezra
Esth.   Esther
Job
Ps.   Psalms (first number = Sept. numbering, bracketed number = OT numbering)
Prov.   Proverbs
Eccl.   Ecclesiastes
Song of Sol.   Song of Solomon
Is.   Isaiah
Jer.   Jeremiah
Ezek.   Ezekiel
Dan.   Daniel
Hos.   Hosea
Joel
Amos
Obad.   Obadiah

Jon.   Jonah
Mic.   Micah
Nah.   Nahum
Hab.   Habakkuk
Zeph.   Zephaniah
Hag.   Haggai
Zach.   Zachariah
Mal.   Malachi

Apocrypha

Macc.   Maccabees
Tob.   Tobit
Jdth.   Judith
Sir.   Siracides (Wisdom of Jesus ben Sirach, Ecclesiasticus)
Sap.   Wisdom of Solomon (Sapientia Solomonis)

New Testament

Mt.   Matthew
Mk.   Mark
Lk.   Luke
Jn.   John
Acts
Rom.   Romans
Cor.   Corinthians
Gal.   Galatians
Eph.   Ephesians
Phil.   Philippians
Col.   Colossians
Th.   Thessalonians
Tim.   Timothy
Tit.   Titus
Philem.   Philemon
Heb.   Hebrews
James
Pet.   Peter
John   epistles of John
Jude
Rev.   Revelation

Bibliography

AASS   *Acta Sanctorum,* 71 vols. (Paris, 1863–1940)
Afinogenov, "Great Purge"
           D. Afinogenov, "The Great Purge of 843: A Re-
           Examination," ΛΕΙΜΩΝ. *Studies Presented to*
           Lennart Rydén on His Sixty-Fifth Birthday,
           ed. J. O. Rosenqvist (Uppsala, 1996), 79–91
Afinogenov, "Κωνσταντινούπολις ἐπίσκοπον ἔχει: Part II"
           D. Afinogenov, "Κωνσταντινούπολις ἐπίσκοπον ἔχει.
           The Rise of the Patriarchal Power in Byzantium
           from Nicaenum II to Epanagoga. Part II: From
           the Second Outbreak of Iconoclasm to the Death
           of Methodius," *Erytheia* 17 (1996), 43–71
Alexander, *Nicephorus*
           P. J. Alexander, *The Patriarch Nicephorus of*
           Constantinople (Oxford, 1958)
AnalBoll   *Analecta Bollandiana*
Auzépy, "Chalcé"   M.-F. Auzépy, "La destruction de l'icône du Christ de
           la Chalcé par Léon III: propagande ou réalité?"
           Byzantion 60 (1990), 445–92
Basilics, ed. Scheltema et al.
           Basilicorum Libri XX, ed. H. J. Scheltema et al.,
           17 vols. (Groningen, 1953–88)
Beck, *Kirche*   H.-G. Beck, *Kirche und theologische Literatur im*
           byzantinischen Reich (Munich, 1959)
BHG   *Bibliotheca hagiographica graeca,* 3d ed., ed. F. Halkin
           (Brussels, 1957)
BHG Nov. Auct.   *Bibliotheca hagiographica graeca,* ed. F. Halkin, vol. 5,
           Novum Auctarium (Brussels, 1984)
Bibl.sanct.   *Bibliotheca sanctorum,* 12 vols. (Rome, 1961–70)
BMGS   *Byzantine and Modern Greek Studies*
Brown, "Dark Age Crisis"
           P. Brown, "A Dark Age Crisis: Aspects of the
           Iconoclastic Controversy," *English Historical*
           Review 88 (1973), 1–34, repr. in *Society and the*

Holy in Late Antiquity (Berkeley, Calif., 1982), 251–301

Bryer-Herrin, *Iconoclasm*
> A. Bryer, J. Herrin, ed., *Iconoclasm* (Birmingham, 1977)

BSC Abstr   *Byzantine Studies Conference: Abstracts of Papers*

BS/EB   *Byzantine Studies/Etudes Byzantines*

Bury, *Eastern Roman Empire*
> J. B. Bury, *A History of the Eastern Roman Empire* (London, 1912)

ByzF   *Byzantinische Forschungen*

ByzSlav   *Byzantinoslavica*

Cedr.   *Georgius Cedrenus,* ed. I. Bekker, 2 vols. (Bonn, 1838–39)

Christides, *Conquest of Crete*
> V. Christides, *The Conquest of Crete by the Arabs (ca. 824): A Turning Point in the Struggle between Byzantium and Islam* (Athens, 1984)

CIC   *Corpus Iuris Civilis,* 2d ed., ed. T. Mommsen, P. Krueger, et al., 3 vols. (Berlin, 1928–29)

Const. Porph., *De cer.*
> *De ceremoniis aulae byzantinae,* ed. J. J. Reiske, 2 vols. (Bonn, 1829–30)

Const. Porph., *De them.*
> *Costantino Porfirogenito. De thematibus,* ed. A. Pertusi (Vatican, 1952)

da Costa-Louillet, "Saints de CP"
> G. da Costa-Louillet, "Saints de Constantinople aux VIIIe, IXe et Xe siècles," *Byzantion* 24 (1955–56), 179–263, 453–511; 25–27 (1957), 783–852

Darrouzès, *Documents inédits*
> J. Darrouzès, *Documents inédits d'ecclésiologie byzantine* [Archives de l'Orient Chrétien 10] (Paris, 1966)

Darrouzès, *Notitiae*
> J. Darrouzès, *Notitiae episcopatuum Ecclesiae Constantinopolitanae* (Paris, 1981)

Darrouzès, *Offikia*   J. Darrouzès, *Recherches sur les* ὀφφίκια *de l'église byzantine* (Paris, 1970)

Darrouzès, "Le patriarche Méthode"
> J. Darrouzès, "Le patriarche Méthode contre les iconoclastes et les Studites," *REB* 45 (1987), 15–57

Delehaye, *Saints stylites*
> H. Delehaye, *Les saints stylites* (Brussels-Paris, 1923)

Demetrakos, *Lexikon*
> D. B. Demetrakos, Μέγα λεξικὸν τῆς Ἑλληνικῆς γλώσσης, 9 vols. (Athens, 1933–51)

DHGE   *Dictionnaire d'histoire et de géographie ecclésiastique*

Dict. Spir.   *Dictionnaire de spiritualité*

DOP   *Dumbarton Oaks Papers*

DuCange, *Glossarium*
> *Glossarium ad Scriptores Mediae et Infimae Graecitatis* (Leiden, 1688; repr. Paris, 1943)

Duffy-Parker, *Synodicon Vetus*
> J. Duffy, J. Parker, *The Synodicon Vetus* (Washington, D.C., 1979)

Dvornik, *Légendes*   F. Dvornik, *Les légendes de Constantin et de Méthode vues de Byzance* (Prague, 1933)

EEBS   Ἐπετηρὶς τῆς Ἑταιρείας Βυζαντινῶν Σπουδῶν

Efthymiadis, "Correspondence of Theodore"
> S. Efthymiadis, "Notes on the Correspondence of Theodore the Studite," *REB* 53 (1995), 141–63

EO   *Echos d'Orient*

Fatouros, *Theod. Stud. Epist.*
> G. Fatouros, ed., *Theodori Studitae Epistulae,* 2 vols. (Berlin-New York, 1992)

Genes.   *Genesii Regum libri quattuor,* ed. A. Lesmüller-Werner, H. Thurn (Berlin-New York, 1978)

Georg. Mon.   *Georgius Monachus, Chronicon,* ed. C. de Boor, 2 vols. (Leipzig, 1904; repr. Stuttgart, 1978, with corr. P. Wirth)

Georg. Mon. Cont.   *TheophCont* 761–924

Gero, *Constantine V*   S. Gero, *Byzantine Iconoclasm during the Reign of Constantine V* (Louvain, 1977)

Gero, *Leo III*   S. Gero, *Byzantine Iconoclasm during the Reign of Leo III* (Louvain, 1973)

GOrThR   *Greek Orthodox Theological Review*

Gouillard, "Synodikon"

     J. Gouillard, "Le Synodikon de l'Orthodoxie," *TM* 2 (1967), 120–35

GRBS   *Greek, Roman and Byzantine Studies*

Greg.   *Nicephorus Gregoras: Byzantina historia,* ed. L. Schopen, I. Bekker, 3 vols. (Bonn, 1829–55)

Hackel, *Byz. Saint* *The Byzantine Saint: University of Birmingham 14th Spring Symposium of Byzantine Studies,* ed. S. Hackel (London, 1981)

Halkin, "Saints Georges"

     F. Halkin, "Y a-t-il trois saints Georges, évêques de Mytilène et 'confesseurs' sous les iconoclastes?" *AnalBoll* 77 (1959), 464–69

Homer, *Il.*   Homer, *The Iliad*

Homer, *Od.*   Homer, *The Odyssey*

HThR   *Harvard Theological Review*

Hunger, *Lit.*   H. Hunger, *Die hochsprachliche profane Literatur der Byzantiner,* 2 vols. (Munich, 1978)

IRAIK   *Izvestija Russkogo Arheologičeskogo Instituta v Konstantinopole*

Janin, *CP byz.* R. Janin, *Constantinople byzantine: développement urbain et répertoire topographique,* 2d ed. (Paris, 1964)

Janin, *Eglises Centres*

     R. Janin, *Les églises et les monastères des grands centres byzantins* (Paris, 1975)

Janin, *Eglises CP* R. Janin, *La géographie ecclésiastique de l'empire byzantin, I: Le siège de Constantinople et le patriarcat oecuménique,* 2d ed. (Paris, 1969)

Joannou, *Démonologie*

     P. Joannou, *Démonologie populaire, démonologie critique au XIe siècle: la vie inédite de S. Auxence par M. Psellos* (Wiesbaden, 1971)

Joannou, *Discipline* P. Joannou, *Discipline générale antique, IIe-IXe s. I.1:*

Les canons des conciles oecuméniques
(Grottaferrata, 1962)

JÖB   *Jahrbuch der Österreichischen Byzantinistik*

Karlin-Hayter, "Etudes"

P. Karlin-Hayter, "Etudes sur les deux histoires du
règne de Michel III," *Byzantion* 41 (1971), 469–74

Karlin-Hayter, "Théodora"

P. Karlin-Hayter, "La mort de Théodora," *JÖB* 40
(1990), 205–8

Kazhdan, "Hagiographical Notes"

A. Kazhdan, "Hagiographical Notes. 7. The Exact
Date of the Life of David, Symeon, and
George," *Byzantion* 54 (1984), 185–88

Kazhdan, *List of Saints*

A. Kazhdan, *The List of Saints of the 1st–10th
Centuries in a Chronological Order* (unpublished
typescript, available at Dumbarton Oaks
Byzantine Library)

Kazhdan-Talbot, "Women and Iconoclasm"

A. Kazhdan, A.-M. Talbot, "Women and
Iconoclasm," *BZ* 84–85 (1991–92), 391–408

Koukoules, *Bios*   Ph. Koukoules, Βυζαντινῶν βίος καὶ πολιτισμός, 6
vols. (Athens, 1948–57)

Lampe, *Lexicon*   G. W. H. Lampe, *A Patristic Greek Lexicon* (Oxford,
1961–68)

Laurent, *Corpus*   V. Laurent, *Le corpus des sceaux de l'Empire byzantin,*
2 vols. in 5 pts. (Paris, 1963–81)

LCI   *Lexikon der christlichen Ikonographie,* ed. E.
Kirschbaum, W. Braunfels, 8 vols. (Rome-
Freiburg-Basel-Vienna, 1968–76)

Lemerle, *Byz. Humanism*

P. Lemerle, *Byzantine Humanism, The First Phase.
Notes and Remarks on Education and Culture in
Byzantium from Its Origins to the 10th Century,*
trans. H. Lindsay and A. Moffatt (Canberra,
1986)

Leo Gramm.   *Leo Grammaticus, Chronographia,* ed. I. Bekker
(Bonn, 1842)

Leutsch-Schneidewin, *Corpus*
>   *Corpus Paroemiographorum Graecorum,* ed. E. L.
>   Leutsch, F. G. Schneidewin, 2 vols. (Göttingen,
>   1839–51; repr. Hildesheim, 1958)
Liddell-Scott, *Lexicon*
>   H. G. Liddell, R. Scott, H. S. Jones, *A Greek-English
>   Lexicon* (Oxford, 1968)
Majeska, *Russian Travelers*
>   G. P. Majeska, *Russian Travelers to Constantinople
>   in the Fourteenth and Fifteenth Centuries*
>   (Washington, D.C., 1989)
Malamut, *Les îles*   E. Malamut, *Les îles de l'Empire byzantin* (Paris,
>   1988)
Mango, "Anthusa"   C. Mango, "St. Anthusa of Mantineon and the
>   Family of Constantine V," *AnalBoll* 100 (1982),
>   401–9
Mango, *Art*   C. Mango, *The Art of the Byzantine Empire, 312–1453*
>   (Englewood Cliffs, N.J., 1972)
Mango, "Ioannikios"
>   C. Mango, "The Two Lives of St. Ioannikios and the
>   Bulgarians," in *Okeanos* [=*Harvard Ukrainian
>   Studies* 7] (Cambridge, Mass., 1983), 393–404
Markopoulos, "Theodora"
>   A. Markopoulos, "Βίος τῆς αὐτοκράτειρας
>   Θεοδώρας," *Symmeikta* 5 (1983), 249–85
Markopoulos, "Georgios Monachos"
>   A. Markopoulos, "Συμβολὴ στὴ Χρονολόγηση τοῦ
>   Γεωργίου Μοναχοῦ," *Symmeikta* 6 (1985), 223–31
Menthon, *L'Olympe de Bithynie*
>   B. Menthon, *Une terre de légende. L'Olympe de
>   Bithynie* (Paris, 1935)
Moffatt, "Schooling"
>   A. Moffatt, "Schooling in the Iconoclast Centuries,"
>   in Bryer-Herrin, *Iconoclasm,* 85–92
ODB   *Oxford Dictionary of Byzantium,* ed. A. Kazhdan et
>   al., 3 vols. (New York, 1991)

Oikonomidès, *Listes*
> N. Oikonomidès, *Les listes de préséance byzantines du IXe et Xe siècle* (Paris, 1972)

Pach.
> *Georgii Pachymeris de Michaele et Andronico Palaeologis libri tredecim*, ed. I. Bekker, 2 vols. (Bonn, 1835)

PG
> Patrologiae cursus completus, series graeca, ed. J.-P. Migne, 161 vols. (Paris, 1857–66)

Phountoules, Οἱ ἅγιοι Γεώργιοι
> I. M. Phountoules, Οἱ ἅγιοι Γεώργιοι ἀρχιεπίσκοποι Μυτιλήνης [Λεσβιακὸν Ἑορτολόγιον, Α'] (Athens, 1959)

Phountoules, Οἱ ὅσιοι αὐτάδελφοι
> I. M. Phountoules, Οἱ ὅσιοι αὐτάδελφοι Δαβίδ, Συμεών, καὶ Γεώργιος οἱ ὁμολογηταί [Λεσβιακὸν Ἑορτολόγιον, Γ'] (Athens, 1961)

ps.-Sym. Mag.
> *TheophCont* 603–760

PW
> G. Wissowa et al., *Paulys Real-Encyclopädie der klassischen Altertumswissenschaft* (1893–)

REB
> *Revue des études byzantines*

Regel, *Analecta*
> W. Regel, *Analecta Byzantino-Russica* (St. Petersburg, 1891)

RegPatr
> *Les regestes des actes du patriarcat de Constantinople*, ed. V. Grumel, V. Laurent, J. Darrouzès, 2 vols. in 8 pts. (Paris, 1932–79)

Rhalles-Potles, *Syntagma*
> G. A. Rhalles, M. Potles, Σύνταγμα τῶν θείων καὶ ἱερῶν κανόνων, 6 vols. (Athens, 1852–59; repr. 1966)

RHR
> *Revue de l'histoire des religions*

ROC
> *Revue de l'Orient chrétien*

RQ
> *Römische Quartalschrift für christliche Altertumskunde und Kirchengeschichte*

Schilbach, *Metrologie*
> E. Schilbach, *Byzantinische Metrologie* (Munich, 1970)

Ševčenko, "Hagiography"
> I. Ševčenko, "Hagiography of the Iconoclast Period," in Bryer-Herrin, *Iconoclasm*, 113–31

Sophocles, *Lexicon*

> E. A. Sophocles, *Greek Lexicon of the Roman and Byzantine Periods* (New York, 1900; repr. New York, 1957)

Stephanus, *Thesaurus Linguae Graecae*

> H. Estienne, *Thesaurus Linguae Graecae,* 8 vols. (Paris, 1831–65)

SubsHag   Subsidia Hagiographica

SynaxCP   *Synaxarium ecclesiae Constantinopolitanae: Propylaeum ad Acta Sanctorum Novembris,* ed. H. Delehaye (Brussels: Société des Bollandistes, 1902)

Talbot, "Comparison"

> A.-M. Talbot, "A Comparison of the Monastic Experience of Byzantine Men and Women," *GOrThR* 30 (1985), 1–20

Talbot, *Holy Women of Byzantium*

> A.-M. Talbot, ed., *Holy Women of Byzantium: Ten Saints' Lives in Translation* (Washington, D.C., 1996)

Theoph.   Theophanes, *Chronographia,* ed. C. de Boor, 2 vols. (Leipzig, 1883–85; repr. Hildesheim, 1963)

TheophCont   *Theophanes Continuatus,* ed. I. Bekker (Bonn, 1838)

TIB   *Tabula imperii byzantini,* ed. H. Hunger, vols. 1– (Vienna, 1976–)

TLG   *Thesaurus Linguae Graecae,* CD-ROM produced by Department of Classics, University of California at Irvine

TM   *Travaux et mémoires*

Trapp, *Lexikon*   E. Trapp, ed., *Lexikon zur byzantinischen Gräzität* (Vienna, 1994–)

Travis, *Defense*   J. Travis, *In Defense of the Faith* (Brookline, Mass., 1984)

Treadgold, *Byz. Revival*

> W. T. Treadgold, *The Byzantine Revival, 780–842* (Stanford, Calif., 1988)

Treadgold, "Chronological Accuracy"

> W. T. Treadgold, "The Chronological Accuracy of the

Chronicle of Symeon the Logothete for the Years
813–845," *DOP* 33 (1979), 157–97

Tsames, *Meterikon*   D. G. Tsames, Μητερικόν, 7 vols. (Thessalonike,
1990–97)

Tsougarakis, *Byzantine Crete*

    D. Tsougarakis, *Byzantine Crete. From the 5th Century
to the Venetian Conquest* (Athens, 1988)

Turtledove, *Theophanes*

    H. Turtledove, *The Chronicle of Theophanes*
(Philadelphia, Pa., 1982)

v. Andr. Sal.   L. Rydén, *The Life of St. Andrew the Fool,* 2 vols.
(Uppsala, 1995)

v. Ant.   *vita Antonii,* PG 26:835–978

v. Ant. Jun.   *vita Antonii Junioris,* ed. A. Papadopoulos-Kerameus,
Pravoslavnij Palestinskij Sbornik 19.3 (1907),
186–216

v. Ath. Aeg.   F. Halkin, "Vie de sainte Athanasie d'Egine," in *Six
inédits d'hagiologie byzantine* [SubsHag 74]
(Brussels, 1987), 179–95

v. Const. Jud.   *vita Constantini Judaei, AASS,* Nov. 4:628–56

v. Dan. Styl.   *vita Danielis Stylitae,* in Delehaye, *Saints stylites,*
1–147

v. Davidis, Sym. et Georg.

    J. van den Gheyn, ed., "Acta graeca ss. Davidis,
Symeonis et Georgii Mitylenae in insula Lesbo,"
AnalBoll 18 (1899), 209–59

v. Eliae Jun.   G. Rossi Taibbi, *Vita di sant'Elia il Giovane* (Palermo,
1962)

v. Eliae Spel.   *vita Eliae Spelaiotae, AASS,* Sept. 3:843–88

v. Eustrat.   *vita Eustratii,* ed. A. Papadopoulos-Kerameus,
Analekta Hierosolymitikes Stachyologias 4 (St.
Petersburg, 1897), 367–400; 5 (St. Petersburg,
1898), 408–10

v. Euthym. CP   P. Karlin-Hayter, *Vita Euthymii patriarchae CP.*
[Bibliothèque de Byzantion 3] (Brussels, 1970)

v. Euthym. Sard.   J. Gouillard, "La vie d'Euthyme de Sardes (†831),"
TM 10 (1987), 1–101

v. Georg. Amast.   *vita Georgii Amastridos,* ed. V. Vasil'evskij, *Russko-*

vizantijskija issledovanija 2 (St. Petersburg, 1893), 1–73

v. Georg. Chozib.   vita Georgii Chozibae, ed. C. Houze, AnalBoll 7 (1888), 97–114, 336–59

v. Georg. Mytil.   I. M. Phountoules, Οἱ ἅγιοι Γεώργιοι ἀρχιεπίσκοποι Μυτιλήνης [Λεσβιακὸν Ἑορτολόγιον, Α'] (Athens, 1959)

v. Greg. Decap.   F. Dvornik, La vie de St. Grégoire le Décapolite et les Slaves macédoniens au IXe siècle (Paris, 1926)

v. Ignat.   vita Ignatii by Niketas David Paphlagon, PG 105:488–574

v. Ioannic. a Petr.   vita Ioannicii a Petro, ed. I. van den Gheyn, AASS, Nov. 2.1 (Brussels, 1894), 384–435

v. Ioannic. a Sab.   vita Ioannicii a Saba, ed. I. van den Gheyn, AASS, Nov. 2.1 (Brussels, 1894), 332–83

v. Iren. Chrysobalant.   J. O. Rosenqvist, The Life of St. Irene, Abbess of Chrysobalanton (Uppsala, 1986)

v. Luc. Styl.   vita Lucae Stylitae, in Delehaye, Saints stylites, 195–237

v. Macar. Pel.   I. van den Gheyn, "S. Macarii monasterii Pelecetes hegumeni acta graeca," AnalBoll 16 (1897), 142–63

v. Method.   vita Methodii, PG 100:1243–62

v. Mich. Sync.   M. B. Cunningham, The Life of Michael the Synkellos (Belfast, 1991)

v. Niceph.   vita Nicephori, in C. de Boor, Nicephori archiepiscopi Constantinopolitani Opuscula historica (Leipzig, 1880), 139–217

v. Niceph. Med.   F. Halkin, "La Vie de s. Nicéphore, fondateur de Médikion en Bithynie (†813)," AnalBoll 78 (1960), 401–25

v. Nicet. Med.   vita Nicetae Medicii, AASS, Apr. 1:xviii–xxvii (at end of volume)

v. Petr. Atr.   V. Laurent, La vie merveilleuse de Saint Pierre d'Atroa (†837) (Brussels, 1956)

v. Phantin. Jun.   E. Follieri, La Vita di San Fantino il Giovane (Brussels, 1993)

v. Sab.	*vita Sabae,* in E. Schwartz, ed., *Kyrillos von Skythopolis* (Leipzig, 1939), 85–200
v. Stephan. Jun.	*vita Stephani Junioris,* PG 100:1069–186
v. Taras.	I. A. Heikel, ed., *Ignatii Diaconi Vita Tarasii archiepiscopi Constantinopolitani* (Helsingfors, 1891)
v. Theod. Edess.	I. Pomjalovskij, *Žitie iže vo svjatych otca našego Feodora archiepiskopa edesskogo* (St. Petersburg, 1892)
v. Theod. Syc.	A.-J. Festugière, *Vie de Théodore de Sykéon,* 2 vols. (Brussels, 1970)
v. Theod. Thess.	S. A. Paschalides, Ὁ βίος τῆς ὁσιομυροβλύτιδος Θεοδώρας τῆς ἐν Θεσσαλονίκῃ (Thessalonike, 1991)
v. Theodorae imp.	A. Markopoulos, "Βίος τῆς αὐτοκράτειρας Θεοδώρας (*BHG* 1731)," *Symmeikta* 5 (1983), 249–85
v. Theoph.	E. Kurtz, *Zwei griechische Texte über die heilige Theophano, die Gemahlin Kaisers Leo VI.* (St. Petersburg, 1898)
v. Theoph. Conf.	V. V. Latyšev, *Mefodija patriarcha Konstantinopol'skogo Žitie prep. Feofana Ispovednika* (St. Petersburg, 1918)
Van den Gheyn, *Acta*	
	I. van den Gheyn, "Acta graeca ss. Davidis, Symeonis et Georgii Mitylenae in insula Lesbo," *AnalBoll* 18 (1899), 209–59
Vasiliev, *Byz. Arabes*	
	A. A. Vasiliev, *Byzance et les Arabes* 1 (Brussels, 1935); 2.1 (1968); 2.2 (1950)
Von Dobschütz, "Methodios und die Studiten"	
	E. von Dobschütz, "Methodios und die Studiten," *BZ* 18 (1909), 41–105
Zacos, *Seals*	G. Zacos, *Byzantine Lead Seals,* 2 vols. in 6 pts. [vol. 1 co-authored with A. Veglery; vol. 2 ed. J. W. Nesbitt] (Basel-Berne, 1972–84)
ZapANIst.-fil.	*Zapiski Akademii Nauk: Istoriko-filologičeskoe otdelenie*

Zepos, *Jus* J. and P. Zepos, *Jus Graecoromanum,* 8 vols. (Athens, 1931; repr. Aalen, 1962)

ZRVI *Zbornik radova vizantološkog Instituta*

1. LIFE OF ST. THEODOSIA OF CONSTANTINOPLE

introduction and translation by Nicholas Constas

Introduction

St. Theodosia, an iconodule martyr of the eighth century, is known primarily from a short notice in the *Synaxarion of Constantinople* under 18 July.[1] According to this notice, she was born in the imperial capital, and at the age of seven was placed in a convent by her widowed mother. Theodosia is presented as a staunch defender of sacred images, and is said to have commissioned costly icons of Christ, the Theotokos, and St. Anastasia the martyr. During the reign of the iconoclast emperor Leo III (717–741), probably in 726, Theodosia, "together with other pious women," attempted to protect the icon of Christ that was installed above the main entrance to the palace, called the Chalke Gate. The emperor had personally ordered the icon's destruction, and the pious women, for their act of militant defiance, were immediately put to death. Theodosia, as the principal dissenter, was singled out for a particularly violent execution.

Theodosia attained considerable popularity as one of the few true martyrs of the iconophile cause, but her historicity is suspect. Although subsequent iconophile literature attached considerable symbolic importance to the incident of the defense of the Chalke icon, none of the other extant sources (which are not entirely consistent) makes any mention of a nun called Theodosia among those protesting the icon's destruction.[2] The chronicler Theo-

---

[1] The text, translated below, is found in *SynaxCP* 828–30.

[2] These sources have recently been studied by Auzépy, "Chalcé," 445–92. Auzépy, in an opinion that has not found general acceptance, denies the Chalke icon's existence during the reign of Leo III, and argues that the entire incident was fabricated at the instigation of the iconodule patriarch Nikephoros I (806–815) in the interests of transforming "political repression into religious persecution" (p. 487). The inconsistencies in the sources are conveniently summarized on p. 463.

phanes, for example, mentions only anonymous "crowds" (οἱ ὄχλοι) of outraged Constantinopolitans.[3] Stephen the Deacon, in his Life of Saint Stephen the Younger, does note, however, that these dissenters were a group of "honorable women" (τίμιαι γυναῖκες),[4] while the letter of Pope Gregory II to emperor Leo III similarly commends the "zealous women" (γυναῖκες ζηλωτρίαι) who defied Leo's edict.[5] The incident is again described in a *synaxarion* notice for 9 August,[6] which substitutes a company of ten men[7] for the group of "pious women," and replaces Theodosia with a beautiful patrician called Maria.[8] Although the historical accuracy of some of these sources may be questionable, they are of interest because of the emphasis they place on the role of women in opposing iconoclasm.[9]

M. Gedeon, in his study of the festal calendar of the church of Constantinople,[10] reported the existence of an unpublished *vita* of St. Theodosia which he found in a twelfth-century Athonite manuscript (Koutloumousiou 109).[11] The text remains unpublished and is known only from the few passages tran-

---

[3] Theoph. 405.5–11; Eng. tr. in Turtledove, *Theophanes,* 97.

[4] *v. Stephan. Jun.* 1085C.12. The *synaxarion* notice for St. Theodosia reproduces verbatim the description of the Chalke Gate incident found in the *vita* of St. Stephen; cf. below, nn. 28 and 30. I. Ševčenko ("Hagiography," 115) notes that the *vitae* of "Germanos, that of Andrew in Krisei, that of Paul the Younger, perhaps the Lives of the Ten Martyrs, borrow situations, motifs, toponyms and whole phrases from the *Life* of Stephen."

[5] J. Gouillard, "Aux origines de l'iconoclasme: le témoignage de Grégoire II?" *TM* 3 (1968), 293.221. The letter, which is of dubious authenticity, shifts the scene from the Chalke Gate to the Chalkoprateia, and describes the icon as an Antiphonetes type. For an exhaustive treatment of the literature on these letters, see P. Conte, *Regesto delle lettere dei Papi del secolo VII, Saggi* (Milan, 1984), 46–79.

[6] The text, known as the *Passio ss. martyrum Constantinopolitanorum,* may be found in *AASS,* Aug. 2:434–37, 439–42; the Chalke episode is on p. 441c.

[7] Or nine, according to some manuscripts; cf. *AASS,* Aug. 2:428.

[8] Μαρία . . . εὐγενεστάτη καὶ ὡραία τῷ κάλλει, καὶ βασιλικωτάτου γένους καταγομένη. . . ; cf. *AASS,* Aug. 2:436E4–6.

[9] On which see J. Herrin, "Women and the Faith in Icons in Early Christianity," in R. Samuel, G. S. Jones, *Culture, Ideology, and Politics* (London, 1982), 56–83, esp. 68–75, and Kazhdan-Talbot, "Women and Iconoclasm," 391–408.

[10] M. Gedeon, Βυζαντινὸν Ἑορτολόγιον (Constantinople, 1899), 130–33.

[11] It may be worth noting that S. Lampros (*Catalogue of the Greek Manuscripts on Mount Athos* 1 [Cambridge, 1895], 284) describes Koutloumousiou 109 as a "collection of homilies by John Chrysostom, copied in the fifteenth century." Lampros' entry for

scribed by Gedeon. According to this version, after the incident at the Chalke Gate, Theodosia returned to her family convent (τῷ γονικῷ αὐτῆς μοναστηρίῳ) located near Skoteinon Phrear, and was martyred ten years later at Leomakellon under Constantine V (741–775).

The inclusion of a notice on Theodosia in the *Synaxarion of Constantinople* suggests that her cult was established in Constantinople by the tenth century. In 1200 the Russian pilgrim Antony of Novgorod saw the relics of St. Theodosia in an open silver reliquary in a nunnery in Constantinople (to which later Russian pilgrims gave the name of St. Theodosia), and noted that the relics were periodically carried in procession and effected miraculous cures.[12] The healing cult of St. Theodosia flourished especially in the Palaiologan period. The historian Pachymeres records the cure of a deaf and dumb boy at her shrine in 1306; the cure attracted such attention that the emperor himself attended an all-night vigil of thanksgiving at her church.[13] At about the same time the hagiographer Constantine Akropolites wrote a lengthy enkomion of the saint. He provides no new biographical material, but does give information on her posthumous cult, describing miraculous cures of his son-in-law and himself at the shrine.[14] Russian pilgrims of the fourteenth and fifteenth centuries also attest to the importance of her cult: her relics were carried in procession twice weekly, and hordes of pilgrims continued to seek healing at her church.[15] By 1301 the feastday of St. Theodosia had been changed to 29 May, evidently as the result of conflation with her homonym, St. Theodosia of Tyre.[16]

There is considerable confusion in the sources about the identity and location of the church in which Theodosia's relics were deposited. For our purposes it will be sufficient to note the conclusions of recent scholarship,

---

Koutloumousiou 19 (pp. 275–76), a "twelfth-century *panegyrikon* on saints and feasts for the entire year," seems closer to the manuscript described by Gedeon.

[12] Majeska, *Russian Travelers,* 349.

[13] Pach. 2:452–55.

[14] *Sermo in s. martyrem Theodosiam,* PG 140:893–936 (*BHG* 1774). On the hagiographic work of Akropolites, and on the cult of St. Theodosia around 1300, see A.-M. Talbot, "Old Wine in New Bottles: The Rewriting of Saints' Lives in the Palaeologan Period," in *The Twilight of Byzantium,* ed. S. Ćurčić, D. Mouriki (Princeton, N.J., 1991), 18. Another enkomion, by the 13th-century writer John Staurakios (*BHG* 1774a), remains unpublished.

[15] Majeska, *Russian Travelers,* 346–51.

[16] *SynaxCP* 715.52; Majeska, *Russian Travelers,* 350.

which situate the church in the Petrion quarter along the Golden Horn, but reject the traditional identification of St. Theodosia's church with Gül Cami.[17] In any case the church of St. Theodosia played a pivotal role in the dramatic final hours of Constantinople, which fell to the Turks on the saint's feastday, 29 May 1453. As the historian Doukas records, crowds of people attending services at St. Theodosia's that day were slaughtered after Turkish troops entered the city.[18]

The surviving images of St. Theodosia (with the exception of her picture in the *Menologion of Basil II*)[19] all date to the Palaiologan period. She is typically represented as a nun, either in an individual portrait, as in five icons at Mt. Sinai and a fresco at Prizren,[20] or in icons with multiple figures depicting the Triumph of Orthodoxy, as in the Feast of Orthodoxy icon of ca. 1400 recently acquired by the British Museum.[21]

Bibliography

Edition Used for Translation
(*BHG* 1774e) *SynaxCP* 828–30.

Secondary Literature
R. Janin, "Theodosia," *Bibl.sanct.* 12 (1969), 288–89.
G. P. Majeska, *Russian Travelers to Constantinople in the Fourteenth and Fifteenth Centuries* (Washington, D.C., 1989), 346–51.

---

[17] Majeska, *Russian Travelers,* 347 and n. 64. See also n. 39, below.

[18] *Michael Ducas. Byzantina Historia,* ed. I. Bekker (Bonn, 1834), 293–94.

[19] *Il Menologio di Basilio II* (Turin, 1907), 547–50.

[20] D. Mouriki, "Portraits of St. Theodosia in Five Sinai Icons," in Θυμίαμα στὴ μνήμη τῆς Λασκαρίνας Μπούρα (Athens, 1994), 213–19; G. Galavaris, "Two Icons of St. Theodosia at Sinai," Δελτίον τῆς Χριστιανικῆς Ἀρχαιολογικῆς Ἑταιρείας 17 (1993–94), 313–16; *LCI* 8 (1976), 454.

[21] D. Buckton, *Byzantium: Treasures of Byzantine Art and Culture from British Collections* (London, 1994), no. 140. There are excellent color plates and details, as well as some discussion on this icon in Robin Cormack, *Painting the Soul: Icons, Death Masks, and Shrouds* (London, 1997), pls. 11–13, discussion at pp. 62–63, esp. 63: "We know that the icon held by St. Theodosia of Constantinople is to be read as the image of Christ from the Chalke Gate of the Imperial Palace."

[SYNAXARION NOTICE OF ST. THEODOSIA
OF CONSTANTINOPLE]

On the same day[22] <we commemorate the martyrdom of> the holy ascetic martyr Theodosia. She was born and raised by pious parents from the God-protected Queen of Cities during the time of Theodosios of Atramyttion.[23] Her father died when she was seven years old, and her mother took the child and had her tonsured[24] in one of the convents of Byzantium.

Then her mother also died, bequeathing her entire fortune to the blessed <Theodosia>. After commissioning three holy icons of Christ, the most holy Theotokos, and the holy martyr Anastasia[25] of gold and silver, she distributed the remainder of her inheritance to the poor and the orphaned.

After a certain period of time, the impious Leo[26] deposed the most pious Theodosios and seized control of the empire. Immediately the wicked man deposed Germanos,[27] great among patriarchs, from the patriarchate with cudgels and swords because he refused to obey his ungodly decrees.[28] <Leo then>

---

[22] 18 July.

[23] Theodosios III was emperor from 715–717. He served as tax collector in his native city of Atramyttion (now Edremit on the northwest coast of Asia Minor), home to an important Byzantine naval base. When the rebellious Opsikion fleet landed there in 714, the rebels seized Theodosios and proclaimed him emperor. After a brief and reluctant tenure, he abdicated on 25 March 717, and entered a monastery. He died in Ephesos after 754. For further information, see *ODB* 3:2052.

[24] It is unlikely that Theodosia's tonsure entailed her final profession as a nun, for which candidates had to be at least sixteen years old; cf. "Nun" and "Tonsure" in *ODB* 3:1504, 2093–94.

[25] Probably the Roman martyr of the 3d century; cf. *BHG* 76x–78e and *BHG Nov. Auct.* 76x–76zd.

[26] Leo III, emperor from 717 to 741, founder of the Isaurian dynasty. In 726 he inaugurated imperial iconoclasm, on which see General Introduction, ix–x, and Gero, *Leo III,* 94–112.

[27] Germanos I, patriarch of Constantinople from 715 to 730; cf. L. Lamza, *Patriarch Germanos I. von Konstantinopel* (Würzburg, 1975), and Gero, *Leo III,* 85–93.

[28] Following the Life of St. Stephen the Younger (PG 100:1085c), the *synaxarion* notice conflates the outbreak of iconoclasm in 726 with Leo's deposition of Germanos in 730, thereby shifting the incident at the Chalke Gate to the patriarchate of Anastas-

hastened to remove and commit to the flames the holy and sovereign icon of Christ our God, the one fixed above the gates among which[29] <was one> called the Holy Chalke <Gate> because of this image.[30] When the <emperor's orders> were being carried out, and as the *spatharios*[31] stood upon the ladder endeavoring to strike down the holy icon with an ax, [829] the blessed Theodosia, together with other pious women, took hold of the ladder, cast the *spatharios* to the ground, and handed him over to death. Proceeding to the patriarchate, they threw stones at the impious Anastasios[32] the chief conspirator.[33] As a result, the other women <with the exception of Theodosia> were

---

ios (on whom see n. 32 below). This was probably done to obviate the question of Germanos' failure to protest Leo's edict of 726, and, at the same time, to distance him from the massacre of the pious women; cf. Gero, *Leo III*, 212–17 (= "The Destruction of the Chalce Image"); G. L. Huxley, "On the *Vita* of St. Stephen the Younger," *GRBS* 18 (1977), 97–108, esp. 98, and M.-F. Rouan, "Une lecture 'iconoclaste' de la Vie d'Étienne le Jeune," *TM* 8 (1981), 415–36, esp. 421. See also M. Anastos, "Leo III's Edict against the Images in the Year 726–27 and Italo-Byzantine Relations between 726 and 730," *ByzF* 3 (1968), 5–41.

[29] Reading αἵσπερ for οἵσπερ.

[30] This sentence has been taken almost verbatim from the Life of St. Stephen the Younger (PG 100:1085c). The Chalke (Χαλκῆ, or Brazen) Gate was part of the main vestibule leading into the Great Palace of Constantinople, so named either for the gilded bronze tiles of its roof, or for its bronze portals. On the image of Christ "Chalkites," see C. Mango, *The Brazen House: A Study of the Vestibule of the Imperial Palace of Constantinople* (Copenhagen, 1959), 108–42, 170–74; A. Frolow, "Le Christ de la Chalcé," *Byzantion* 33 (1963), 107–20; and Auzépy, "Chalcé."

[31] Lit., "sword-bearer," a member of the elite imperial guard. The apocryphal letter of Pope Gregory II to Leo III calls the soldier "Julian [or Jovian, in some manuscripts] the *spatharokandidatos*"; cf. Gouillard, "Grégoire II," 293.218–19.

[32] Anastasios, who had formerly served as *synkellos* to Germanos, embraced iconoclasm and was appointed patriarch by Leo after the deposition of Germanos in 730, i.e., four years after the destruction of the Chalke image; cf. n. 28 above. Anastasios remained in office until 754; cf. Grumel, *RegPatr* 2:343–44.

[33] The Greek text calls him Ἀναστάσιον τὸν φατριάρχην, a pun on πατριάρχης derived from the word φατρία, or conspiracy, and a favorite term of abuse for iconoclast patriarchs. See, for example, the *v. Stephan. Jun.* (PG 100:1112c), where the iconoclast patriarch is described as "unworthy of the *pi*, and rather deserving of the *phi*, for to the church he was more arch-conspirator (φατριάρχης) than patriarch (πατριάρχης)." Theophanes describes Anastasios as one who acted "as a conspirator, and not as a confessor" (ὡς φατριαστήν, καὶ οὐχ ὡς ὁμολογητήν); cf. Theoph. 407.31–408.1; Eng. tr. by Turtledove, *Theophanes*, 99.

immediately decapitated. The holy woman, however, was seized by a public executioner, savage and inhuman, who dragged her away[34] to the <Forum of the> Ox[35] and slew her with a horn.[36] Having thus fought the good fight,[37] they delivered their spirits into the hands of God. [830]

The *synaxis*[38] of <St. Theodosia> is celebrated in the holy monastery of the Savior, Christ the Evergetes.[39]

[34] The notice in the *Menologion of Basil II* reports that the saint was tied to the end of a rope by which she was dragged through the streets (PG 117:549B).

[35] The Forum of the Ox (Forum Bovis) was located on the Mese thoroughfare between the Arcadian and Taurian (or Theodosian) Forums, about 2 km from the Chalke Gate. The Forum was named after its central monument, a large antique bronze furnace in the shape of an ox's head taken from Pergamum. Another iconodule saint, Andrew of Crete, was also martyred here; cf. Janin, *CP byz.*, 69–72.

[36] Another version of the *synaxarion* notes that Theodosia was taken to a place near the Forum of the Ox by a soldier, who slit her throat with the horn of a ram (*SynaxCP* 827–828.48–50 [= *Synaxaria Selecta*, D]).

[37] Cf. 1 Tim. 6:12.

[38] A *synaxis* is a general term for a public liturgical gathering or religious service, and here refers to the eucharistic assembly held in honor of the martyr; see *ODB* 3:1992, and Lampe, *Lexicon*, s. v. B.5, 10.

[39] Not to be confused with the monastery dedicated to the Theotokos Evergetis located approximately 3 km outside the capital. The monastery of Christ Evergetes was located within the city and possessed an icon bearing the epithet of "Christ the Benefactor (Εὐεργέτης)"; cf. Janin, *Eglises CP*, 508–10. The *Synaxaria Selecta*, D (*SynaxCP* 827–828.51–52), however, notes that "her [Theodosia's] *synaxis* is celebrated in the monastery of Dexiokrates, where her relics are preserved." The text mentioned by Gedeon (see n. 10, above) similarly notes that immediately after her martyrdom, "the faithful interred Theodosia's body somewhere near Dexiokrates"; cf. Gedeon, Βυζαντινὸν Ἑορτολόγιον, 131. Following J. Pargoire, "Constantinople: l'église Sainte-Théodosie," *EO* 9 (1906), 161–65, Janin (*Eglises CP*, 87–88, 127–29) suggested that this discrepancy was the result of a 13th-century conflation of St. Euphemia of Petrion, St. Theodosia of Tyre, and St. Theodosia of Constantinople, all of whom had some connection with the monastery of Dexiokrates, or with churches in that quarter of the city. Gedeon (*op. cit.*, 131–33) suggested that the *synaxis* was first celebrated at the monastery of Dexiokrates, and then at the Evergetes, where Theodosia's remains had been later transferred. G. Majeska, who has studied the problem most recently, concludes that Dexiokrates and Christ Evergetes "were either contiguous or two parts of the same monastic complex" (*Russian Travelers*, 348).

2. LIFE OF ST. STEPHEN THE YOUNGER

introduction and translation by Alice-Mary Talbot

Introduction

Stephen is the best-known martyr of the first period of iconoclasm, thanks to the lengthy *vita* composed in his honor by Stephen the Deacon ca. 807.[1] Since a new critical edition and French translation by M.-F. Auzépy of this important source are in press, it was decided to represent St. Stephen in this volume through his brief notice in the *Synaxarion of Constantinople,* under 28 November, his day of martyrdom.

Stephen, born in Constantinople ca. 713, was baptized by the iconodule patriarch Germanos I. He became a monk on the holy mountain of St. Auxentios, where he lived as a solitary earning his living by copying manuscripts. Eventually he founded a monastery on the mountain that became a bastion of opposition to the iconoclastic policy of the emperor Constantine V. According to his *vita* the monks were forced to flee the monastery because of persecution. Stephen himself, who attacked the rulings of the Council of Hieria in 754, was arrested and imprisoned in the capital together with hundreds of other iconodule monks. In 765 he was put to death by being dragged through the streets, stoned, and beaten with clubs. The stoning is clearly an evocation of the violent death of his early Christian namesake, Stephen the First Martyr.

Stephen was a historical figure who is mentioned in both the *Chronographia* of Theophanes and the *Short History* of the patriarch Nikephoros I. The chronicle accounts, however, portray Stephen as being persecuted as a champion of monasticism rather than on account of his iconodule views.[2]

---

[1] PG 100:1069–186. His *vita* was written 42 years after his death, now placed by Mango in 765; cf. C. Mango, *Nikephoros, Patriarch of Constantinople. Short History* (Washington, D.C., 1990), 222. This date is also given by Gero, *Constantine V,* 123. The traditional date of his death is 764.

[2] Gero, *Constantine V,* 123–24.

As indicated by the *Synaxarion of Constantinople,* Stephen's feastday was commemorated in the tenth century at the church of St. Stephen the Proto-martyr. His cult continued throughout the Byzantine centuries, but his relics were divided up among different churches. In 1200 Antony of Novgorod de-scribes a procession on his feastday in which his head was carried to the site of the Praitorion where he had been imprisoned. In the Palaiologan period his skull is variously assigned to St. Sophia and the Peribleptos monastery, while his hand was preserved at Pantokrator, his body at Lips.[3]

Stephen is frequently depicted in mosaics, frescoes, and manuscript illu-mination as one of the great defenders of icons. He is usually represented as a relatively young man with black hair, and is often shown holding an icon.[4]

Bibliography

Edition Used for Translation
SynaxCP 261–63.

Secondary Literature
J. Gill, "The Life of Stephen the Younger by Stephen the Deacon: Debts and Loans," *Orientalia Christiana Periodica* 6 (1940), 114–39.
G. Huxley, "On the Vita of Stephen the Younger," *GRBS* 18 (1977), 99–107.
A. Kazhdan, N. P. Ševčenko, "Stephen the Younger," *ODB* 3:1955.
M.-F. Rouan, "Une lecture 'iconoclaste' de la Vie d'Étienne le Jeune," *TM* 8 (1981), 415–36.

---

[3] Majeska, *Russian Travelers,* 279–80, esp. n. 81.

[4] *LCI* 8:404 f and *ODB* 3:1955. See, for example, D. Mouriki, *The Mosaics of Nea Moni on Chios* (Athens, 1985), 156–58; C. Mango, E. J. W. Hawkins, "The Hermitage of St. Neophytos and Its Wall Paintings," *DOP* 20 (1966), 156–57 and fig. 41.

THE MARTYRDOM OF OUR BLESSED FATHER STEPHEN
THE YOUNGER

This man, born in the reign of Anastasios, also <called> Artemios,[5] during the patriarchate of the saintly Germanos,[6] was the offspring and nursling of the Queen of Cities [Constantinople], and the son of the pious John and Anna. After entering monastic life, he restrained all his bodily urges through fasting and other <forms of> mortification. When his abbot, the divinely inspired John, departed to his <eternal> repose, <Stephen> assumed his office, accomplishing the course of asceticism at the celebrated mountain of St. Auxentios.[7]

When Constantine Kopronymos[8] succeeded to the imperial <throne> after the death of his father Leo <III>,[9] striving to overshadow his father through his <own> wickedness, he rekindled the war against the holy and venerable icons, and condemned the pious monks to countless tortures and exiles. Among them was the blessed Stephen who defied him and whom <Constantine> imprisoned in the Praitorion[10] after <subjecting him to> much abuse. Other leading monks were also imprisoned there, including Peter[11]

---

[5] Anastasios II, emperor 713–715; his baptismal name was Artemios.

[6] Germanos I, iconodule patriarch of Constantinople 715–730; cf. n. 27 in the Life of St. Theodosia, above.

[7] Mt. St. Auxentios (modern Kayişdag in Turkey) was a holy mountain located just across the Bosporos from Constantinople, 12 km southeast of Chalcedon.

[8] On Constantine V Kopronymos, emperor 741–775, see General Introduction, x–xi.

[9] On Leo III, see General Introduction, ix–x, and n. 26 in the Life of St. Theodosia, above.

[10] The Praitorion was a building in Constantinople where criminal sentences were announced by the *praetor;* it also served as a prison (Janin, *CP byz.,* 165–69).

[11] Peter is perhaps the iconodule martyr alluded to in *v. Stephan. Jun.* 1165c–d, who died as the result of a vicious scourging with rawhide whips; he is called a recluse (ἐγκεκλεισμένον) at Blachernai. In Theophanes (Theoph. 442.18–22) Peter is described as a stylite who was executed in 767/8.

and Andrew[12] and their forty comrades, and three hundred others from different places; and some of them were deprived of their noses, others of their ears and eyes, [col. 263] yet others of their hands and beards.

After eleven months had passed and it was Stephen's turn to be sentenced, he was taken out of the prison and thrown to the ground and his feet were bound. He was then dragged off along the public road, while <people> threw stones at him and struck him with wooden clubs. As he was being dragged along, a certain *komes* Philommatios,[13] who was striving to please the emperor, hit him on the head with a huge wooden club so that he died immediately, as his brains poured forth from his shattered skull. The other executioners dragged his dead body along the street and abandoned it in the quarter of Pelagios.[14] Peter also departed to the Lord after enduring the many beatings inflicted upon him by the tyrannical emperor. And Andrew also gave up the ghost after being subjected to many outrages as he was being mercilessly dragged through the city at the tyrant's command. Their feastday is celebrated at the martyrion of St. Stephen in the Konstas quarter.[15]

---

[12] According to S. Gero (*Constantine V,* 122 and n. 39) this is a reference to Andrew the Kalybites, martyred in 761/2. He is not mentioned in the *vita* of Stephen the Younger, but does appear in Theophanes (Theoph. 432.16–21).

[13] In the *vita* of Stephen he is called Philomates (*v. Stephan. Jun.* 1176c); the *synaxarion* notice adds his title of *komes,* a term used for various officials in charge of the city walls, aqueducts, etc. (cf. *ODB* 1:484–85, 2:1139–40).

[14] A region of Constantinople used for the burial of criminals; cf. Janin, *CP byz.,* 167, 405.

[15] A church that contained the relics of St. Stephen the Protomartyr, probably founded in the 6th century. Ta Konsta (sometimes called Konstantianai or Konstantiniai) was a region of Constantinople supposedly named after the palace built by Constantine I for his son Constans; see Janin, *Eglises CP,* 474–76, and Janin, *CP byz.,* 372–73.

3. LIFE OF ST. ANTHOUSA OF MANTINEON

introduction and translation by Alice-Mary Talbot

Introduction

St. Anthousa, abbess of the monastery of Mantineon in Paphlagonia, is known from two sources: a short notice devoted to her in the *Synaxarion of Constantinople,* under 27 July, and some passages in the *vita* of one of her male disciples, Romanos the Neomartyr, who died at the hands of the Arabs in 780. The latter *vita* survives only in a Georgian version (which has been translated into Latin in modern times).[1] The *synaxarion* notice most probably represents a summary of a more extensive *vita,* no longer preserved; C. Mango suggests that the original *vita* was written toward the end of the eighth century,[2] a period of sparse hagiographical activity in Byzantium because of the iconoclastic controversy.

If, as Mango suggests, Anthousa founded the monastery of Mantineon "not later than ca. 740,"[3] she must have been born in the early part of the eighth century. The terminus post quem for her death is 771, the year in which she sent Romanos on the mission which resulted in his death.

Anthousa is of interest for several reasons: as the abbess of a large double monastery, as an iconodule nun who was tortured for her beliefs, and finally as an iconodule confessor who reportedly was able to mollify the rage of the iconoclastic emperor Constantine V. Double monasteries, that is, monasteries housing both men and women in separate but adjacent communities under the direction of the same superior,[4] were periodically condemned in Byzantium, for example, by Justinian I in 546 (novel 123.36), by the Second Council of Nicaea in 787 (canon 20), and by Patriarch Nikephoros I ca. 810. Man-

---

[1] Peeters, "S. Romain le néomartyr," 393–427.

[2] Mango, "Anthusa," 403.

[3] Ibid., 408.

[4] On double monasteries, see the Life of Nikephoros, below, 66–67 and n. 170; *ODB* 2:1392; and Talbot, "Comparison," 5–7, with further bibliography.

tineon was evidently one of the eighth-century double monasteries targeted by ecclesiastical legislation; the monks lived in a monastery on the shore of a lake, while the nuns resided on an island in the lake. From the *vita* of St. Romanos[5] we learn that the monks of Mantineon brought food to the nuns, so they never had to leave their island convent; in turn the nuns wove cloth to make habits for the monks, so that a true symbiotic relationship was established. The figure of nine hundred cited by the *synaxarion* notice for the total number of inhabitants of the monastic community is no doubt inflated. Anthousa seems to have been the superior of both monks and nuns, with her nephew serving as a deputy with special responsibility for the male division of the monastery. A parallel can be attested in the fourteenth century at the monastery of the Philanthropos Soter in Constantinople, presided over by Irene-Eulogia Choumnaina.[6]

The torture of Anthousa and her nephew described below is yet another example of the persecution of iconodule monastics that reached its peak during the reign of Constantine V. The *synaxarion* notice is particularly valuable, however, for its rare and graphic account of the torment of a *female* defender of icons; although women are reputed to have been ardent iconophiles, the sources rarely depict them as martyrs or confessors for the faith.[7]

Subsequently, however, the relationship between emperor and abbess seems to have drastically altered. Following Anthousa's interview by Constantine and her reassurance that the empress would safely deliver twins, the empress in gratitude made substantial donations to the monastery of Mantineon, and Constantine stopped attacking the abbess. The comment of the hagiographer that "virtue can tame wild beasts and make enemies into friends" suggests that there was in fact a fundamental change in attitude on the part of the emperor. And if indeed Constantine's daughter was named after the abbess Anthousa,[8] it would be yet another indication of a reconciliation between the two opponents.

---

[5] Peeters, "S. Romain le néomartyr," 410.

[6] On this monastery see R. Trone, "A Constantinopolitan Double Monastery of the Fourteenth Century: The Philanthropic Saviour," *BS/EB* 10 (1983), 81–87, and A. C. Hero, "Irene-Eulogia Choumnaina Palaiologina, Abbess of the Convent of Philanthropos Soter in Constantinople," *ByzF* 9 (1985), 119–47.

[7] See Kazhdan-Talbot, "Women and Iconoclasm," 391–95.

[8] See introduction to the next *vita*.

Although the presence of Anthousa in the *Synaxarion* indicates that she was commemorated in Constantinople in the tenth century, nothing is known of her cult and no iconographic image survives. One can hypothesize, however, that her cult continued at Mantineon at least until the mid-ninth century, when the nunnery is still attested.[9]

Bibliography

Edition Used for Translation
(BHG Nov. Auct. 2029h) *SynaxCP* 848–52.

Translations
(modern Greek) K. Katsanes in Tsames, *Meterikon* 2:124–31.

Secondary Literature
G. Huxley, "Women in Byzantine Iconoclasm," in *Les femmes et le mona-chisme byzantin,* ed. J. Y. Perreault (Athens, 1991), 13–14, 17.
R. Janin, "Anthuse," *DHGE* 3 (1924), 538.
C. Mango, "St. Anthusa of Mantineon and the Family of Constantine V," *AnalBoll* 100 (1982), 401–9.
P. Peeters, "S. Romain le néomartyr (†1 mai 780) d'après un document géor-gien," *AnalBoll* 30 (1911), 393–427.
E. Ruggieri, "Anthusa di Mantineon ed il canone XX del concilio di Nicea II (anno 787)," *JÖB* 35 (1985), 131–42.
M. Salsano, "Antusa di Costantinopoli [*sic*]," in *Bibl.sanct.* 2 (1962), 224–25.

---

[9] *Vita* of Eudokimos, ed. Ch. Loparev, *IRAIK* 13 (1908), 22.

[Synaxarion Notice for Anthousa of Mantineon]

On the same day[10] <is celebrated> the memory of the holy Anthousa who founded the most holy monastery of Mantineon.[11] She lived during the reign of Constantine Kopronymos,[12] <being born> of pious parents, Strategios and Febronia. [849] Yearning for purity almost from the time she was in her mother's arms, the blessed woman lived *in mountains and caves,*[13] in the words of the apostle, despising and rejecting all worldly affairs, embracing and desiring only tranquility.[14] In those days a certain monk and priest named Sisinnios[15] resided in the region of Mantineon and pursued every kind of virtue; and the blessed <Anthousa> was incited to emulate and imitate him. First of all she was molded and disciplined by him, and finally, after being commanded by him to enter into a heated oven,[16] she emerged from it unscathed and mastered other higher virtues, which brought her close to God. He foretold to her that she would found a large monastery and undertake the supervision of nine hundred monastics.[17] Then she received the tonsure and was bidden by that miracle-working old man to dwell on a small island in the lake near the village of Perkile.[18]

[10] 27 July.

[11] Mantineon, a region of Paphlagonia east of Klaudiopolis (modern Bolu); cf. K. Belke, *Paphlagonien und Honorias* [*TIB* 9] (Vienna, 1996), 249–51.

[12] On Constantine V Kopronymos (741–775), the most ruthless of the iconoclast emperors in his persecution of iconodules, see General Introduction, x–xi. His anti-monastic campaign became particularly relentless following the Council of Hieria of 754.

[13] Heb. 11:38.

[14] Lit., "hesychia."

[15] Not otherwise attested.

[16] For a parallel to this miracle, cf. *The Spiritual Meadow* of John Moschos, which describes a monk, George the Cappadocian, who entered a hot oven and cleaned it with his cloak (PG 87:2949B).

[17] It is impossible to determine whether the Greek genitive plural ἀδελφῶν refers to monks, nuns, or both. I have therefore chosen the gender-neutral term "monastics."

[18] Perkile is not elsewhere attested. L. Robert (*A travers l'Asie Mineure* [Paris, 1980], 138–46) suggested that the lake should be identified with Çagagöl, west of modern Gerede.

Thereafter the blessed <Anthousa>, devoting herself to a life of abstinence and other forms of asceticism, made herself into a dwelling place of the holy and consubstantial Trinity. For binding herself with iron <fetters> and wearing garments of haircloth, she was recognized by people of intelligence as being beyond flesh and the world. Once when she approached the great Sisinnios, she entreated him to build a church to the mother of the Mother of God.[19] After giving her much advice and instruction for a while, and most clearly revealing the future, he dismissed her, predicting the time of his own death. After about thirty nuns joined the holy <Anthousa> and the chapel was built and the events foretold by the old man hastened toward fulfillment, that marvelous and divine Sisinnios departed this life. And since the great Anthousa saw that the community was increasing in size, she erected two very large churches from the foundations, <dedicated> to the Mother of God and to the apostles. And she assigned the church of the Mother of God [850] to the nuns, and the church of the apostles to the monks.[20] And many men who were pricked by the goads of repentance and had formerly gone to the holy Sisinnios, now went to the great Anthousa, to be instructed and molded by her.[21]

Since she was filled with correct faith and justice, she rejected every new heresy. And as she became well known for this, reports of her reached even the emperors. And at that time, as has already been stated, Constantine <Kopronymos> the hater of Christ and iconoclast ruled tyrannically over the Roman Empire. And in his zeal to convert her to his own erroneous belief, he summoned one of those men who shared his views,[22] and said to him, "Go to this province, and persuade Anthousa to convert to our way of thinking. And if she is persuaded, well and good. If not, then torment her and make her yield to our laws, even if she is unwilling." Taking many other men with him, he

---

[19] St. Anna.

[20] C. Mango suggests that the double monastery was established ca. 740; see introduction, 13. The Georgian version of the *vita* of St. Romanos the Neomartyr adds the further information that the nuns lived on an island, while the monks resided on the lake shore; cf. Peeters, "S. Romain le néomartyr," 409.23–410.3.

[21] The *vita* of St. Romanos confirms that Anthousa was responsible for the direction of both monks and nuns, since it was she who sent Romanos on a mission connected with the affairs of the monastery; cf. Peeters, "S. Romain le néomartyr," 411.33–36.

[22] A variant version of the *synaxarion* notice (*SynaxCP* 850.54), even further compressed, calls this official a *magistrianos,* the equivalent of the Latin *agens in rebus;* cf. Sophocles, *Lexicon,* 726.

seized and collected large numbers of holy images, both on panels and on pieces of cloth; then he arrested the great <Anthousa> together with her nephew, who was at that time entrusted with the administration of the male monastery, and brought them for interrogation. The nephew was immediately lacerated for a long time with whips, and was encouraged by the holy woman to abide by his profession <of faith> and stand fast in the face of torture. And when he was about to pass away, he was released. But she was flogged with rawhide thongs with her arms and legs stretched out, and had numerous burning holy icons placed on her head, and fiery embers on her shoes so that her feet would be burned. But since she remained untouched through the grace of God, she was sent into exile.

Then, when the emperor was traveling through that province with his entire army, so as to summon the great <Anthousa> and examine her him-self,[23] as a result of her prayers blindness [851] bound him fast and prevented him from carrying out his designs against her. When queried by the emperor, she said to the empress,[24] who was experiencing a difficult pregnancy and was in mortal danger, that all would be well and she would give birth to one male and one female child.[25] And she foretold the mode and way of life of each <child>. When the empress heard this, she donated numerous villages and offerings to the monasteries under <Anthousa's> direction,[26] and the tyranni-cal ruler desisted from his attack on her. Thus virtue has the power of taming wild beasts and making enemies into friends.

Since as a result the holy <Anthousa> was magnified to an even greater extent and hymned on the tongues of all, many flocked to her, some for the sake of a blessing, others to renounce their secular life, and yet others to attain

[23] It seems likely that the main purpose of Constantine's journey was the campaign against the Arabs that he led in 756 or 757.

[24] Eudokia, who became the third wife of Constantine V in the early 750s. She bore five sons and one daughter.

[25] This daughter was named Anthousa after the holy woman who predicted her safe delivery; she was probably born in 756 or 757. Mango ("Anthusa," 408) suggests that the baby boy whose birth was predicted was a twin of Anthousa, and identifies him as Christopher or Nikephoros. Like her namesake, the princess Anthousa also came to be honored as a saint; the translation of her *synaxarion* notice is no. 4 in this volume.

[26] Eudokia's financial support of an iconophile double monastery is yet another ex-ample of the iconodule sympathies of women of the imperial family in defiance of the will of the emperor.

healing for the diseases with which each was afflicted. And among them was a certain man, a soldier by profession, who came with his wife after changing his clothes[27] to beg the great <Anthousa> for a child and to make an offering, if he should achieve his goal. After hearing from her the thoughts of his heart and having received assurance as to the purpose of his visit, he joyfully returned home. And if someone could count the sands of the seashore and drops of rain and measure the depth of the sea and the height of the sky and the breadth of the earth, he would be able to commit to writing the miracles that have been and will be wrought by the holy and great Anthousa. However, inasmuch as she was human, she had to taste death and to sleep the sleep of the just on the day of the martyrdom of the great martyr Panteleimon.[28] For this was her wish, to die on that day. And she was buried in the cell in which she lived, and continues to perform wondrous miracles, to the glory and praise of Christ our true God.

[27] It is unclear why the soldier "changed his clothes," i.e., exchanged his uniform for civilian dress. Mango ("Anthusa," 402 n. 3) suggests that during the iconoclast era soldiers were discouraged from associating with monks and nuns who were normally iconodule.

[28] A martyr who died in 305 in the persecution of Diocletian; his feastday is 27 July.

4. LIFE OF ST. ANTHOUSA, DAUGHTER OF CONSTANTINE V

introduction and translation by Nicholas Constas

Introduction

What little is known about the holy princess Anthousa is derived solely from short notices in *menologia* and *synaxaria*.[1] As the daughter of the ruthless iconoclast emperor Constantine V (741–775), Anthousa was styled by an encomiast as "fragrant fruit from a putrid root."[2] Although the *synaxarion* notices curiously say nothing of Anthousa's attitude toward icons, her association with the empress Irene and the patriarch Tarasios, as well as the fact that she became a saint, suggests that she was most probably iconodule.[3] It was of course poetic justice that the daughter of a man so violently opposed to the cult of the saints should herself be sanctified.

Princess Anthousa should not be confused with her older contemporary and namesake, St. Anthousa of Mantineon (see previous *vita*). Constantine V was married three times, and Anthousa was apparently born of his final union with Eudokia, who bore him at least six children. During a life-threatening pregnancy,[4] Eudokia was assured by Anthousa of Mantineon that she would safely deliver twins, one male and one female, which she did, probably in 756 or 757. Although the relationship between the two Saint Anthousas is enigmatic, it seems reasonable to assume that the female child was named An-

---

[1] In addition to the 10th-century *synaxarion* notice translated below (*SynaxCP* 613–14), a variant *synaxarion* notice of 1301 is preserved (*SynaxCP* 597–600), as well as a paragraph in the *Menologion of Basil II* (PG 117:409A–C).

[2] Μηναῖον Ἀπριλίου (Athens, 1977), 89.

[3] Anthousa may have been among the official recipients of the relics of St. Euphemia upon their return to Constantinople in 796; cf. F. Halkin, *Euphémie de Chalcédoine* [SubsHag 41] (Brussels, 1965), 103, as suggested by Mango, "Anthusa," 409, n. 31.

[4] In the *synaxarion* notice for Anthousa of Mantineon, the empress is described as δυστοκούσῃ καὶ μελλούσῃ θνῄσκειν; cf. *SynaxCP* 851.3 and above, 18.

thousa in honor of the holy abbess of Mantineon who predicted her birth.[5] Upon the instructions of the empress Irene, Anthousa's five siblings, all male, were forcibly ordained before Christmas Day 780; Constantine VI ordered them mutilated on 15 August 792.[6] Anthousa is thought to have died in 808 or 809.[7]

Bibliography

Edition Used for Translation
SynaxCP 613–14.

Translation
(modern Greek) K. Katsanes in Tsames, *Meterikon* 2:132–35.

Secondary Literature

U. V. Bosch, "Anthusa. Ein Beitrag zum Kaisertum der Eirene," in P. Wirth, ed., *Polychordia. Festschrift Franz Dölger* [= *ByzF* 1] (Amsterdam, 1966), 24–29.

N. DiGrigoli, "Antusa," *Bibl.sanct.* 2 (1962), 224.

R. Janin, "Anthuse," *DHGE* 3 (1924), 538.

C. Mango, "St. Anthusa of Mantineon and the Family of Constantine V," *AnalBoll* 100 (1982), 401–9.

[5] This chronology has been proposed by Mango, "Anthusa," 408.

[6] Theoph. 454.21–23, 468.11–13; Eng. tr. in Turtledove, *Theophanes,* 140 and 151.

[7] Mango, "Anthusa," 408.

[SYNAXARION NOTICE FOR ANTHOUSA, DAUGHTER OF CONSTANTINE V]

On this day[8] we commemorate the blessed Anthousa, who was the daughter of the emperor Constantine Kopronymos.[9] She refused her father's numerous attempts to compel her to take a husband. After his departure from this life,[10] she consequently found herself unconstrained and, distributing her entire inheritance to the poor, to churches, and to pious institutions,[11] she became the mother of many orphans, and the protectress of widows and orphans.[12]

The most pious Augusta Irene, by means of numerous supplications, frequently urged her to be associated with her, and reign together with her, but she in no way accepted this.[13] As often as she had occasion to be in the palace, <Anthousa> donned an imperial robe as an outer garment, under which, however, she wore a tattered hairshirt. Her diet was strictly ascetic, and she drank <only> water; in her eye was a tear, and upon her lips a hymn.

Consequently, she retired into monastic life, and was tonsured in the

---

[8] 12 April.

[9] On the iconoclast emperor Constantine V, see General Introduction, x–xi.

[10] Constantine V died on the feast of the Holy Cross (14 September) 775.

[11] Pious institutions (εὐαγεῖς οἶκοι) are a legal category of philanthropic establishments such as hostels, hospitals, poorhouses, and orphanages; cf. *ODB* 2:736.

[12] Cf. James 1:27: "Pure religion and undefiled before God and the Father is this, to visit the fatherless and widows in their affliction, and to keep oneself unspotted from the world."

[13] After the death of her husband Leo IV in 780, Irene, a devoted iconodule, ruled the empire as regent for ten years. In 790, the army refused her demand for control of the government over her son Constantine VI, who subsequently deposed her. Recalled from her exile in 792, Irene subsequently dethroned and blinded Constantine VI in 797. She reigned as sole monarch for five years until her political fall and exile in 802, becoming the first Byzantine female autocrat (see General Introduction, xiii–xiv). It is difficult to believe that Irene had any interest in sharing imperial power with anyone, and there is no other historical evidence to support the assertion of the *synaxarion* notice on this point; see, however, Bosch, "Anthusa," 24–29.

monastery of Eumenia[14] by the hand of the sainted Tarasios.[15] From that moment, neither she nor any of the nuns ever left the convent,[16] she was never absent from church, she never slacked <in her devotions>, nor was she negligent in her prayer. Her eyes never ceased to gush forth tears, her humility was immeasurable, she served all the sisters, she adorned the church, she fetched water, and in the refectory she stood by and served. Living out the span of her life in this manner, she departed for God with a cargo of virtue at the age of fifty-two.

[14] Janin (*Eglises CP,* 383) favors the variant reading of Homonoia (Ὁμονοία) found in an early 14th-century version of the *Synaxarion of Constantinople* (*SynaxCP* 598.57), but which is otherwise unknown. He suggests that the monastery was attached to the church of Homonoia in the Vlanga quarter of the capital, which is well attested.

[15] On Tarasios, patriarch of Constantinople from 784 to 806, see General Introduction, xiii.

[16] On cloistered nuns in Byzantium, see Talbot, "Comparison," 13–14.

5. LIFE OF THE PATRIARCH NIKEPHOROS I OF CONSTANTINOPLE

introduction and translation by Elizabeth A. Fisher

Introduction

The Career of Nikephoros

Ignatios' Life of Nikephoros informs us that its subject was born to Theodore and Eudokia at Constantinople but indicates no date of birth (*v. Niceph.* 142.5–12). However, the liturgical calendar of Constantinople notes that the patriarch Nikephoros I died in 828 at the age of seventy, implying that he was born in 758.[1] Nikephoros' father Theodore served the iconoclast emperor Constantine V Kopronymos (741–775) as a clerk *asekretis* (*v. Niceph.* 142.19–22), an office which placed him in the upper echelon of the imperial chancery where he was entrusted with the drafting of confidential documents.[2] Denounced to the emperor for venerating icons, Theodore maintained his faith in spite of torture, expulsion from office, and exile briefly to the northern Anatolian fortress of Pemolis(s)a/Pimolisa, then again to Nicaea in Bithynia until his death (*v. Niceph.* 142.24–143.24).[3] At the time of his father's death, Nikephoros had just begun his secondary education while training in the imperial chancery to follow his father's career (*v. Niceph.* 144.4–10).[4] Although Ignatios' Life of Nikephoros contains a fairly specific description of the sort of

---

[1] See Alexander, *Nicephorus,* 54 and n. 1, citing the *Synaxarion of Constantinople* (*SynaxCP* 725.14); H.-G. Beck's remark that Nikephoros was born "um 750" ("about 750") seems to be an approximate reference to this date rather than an alternative date, since Beck supplies no documentation for it (Beck, *Kirche,* 489).

[2] See *ODB* 1:204, and Prokopios, *Secret History,* chap. 14, 4, ed. J. Haury, G. Wirth, *Procopii Caesariensis opera omnia* 3 (Leipzig, 1963), 90.9–15.

[3] Theodore spent six years in Nicaea; see Alexander, *Nicephorus,* 56, citing the *Synaxarion of Constantinople.*

[4] In the 8th and 9th centuries, children began their secondary education at age eleven or twelve and concluded it by age eighteen (Lemerle, *Byz. Humanism,* 112). Nikephoros' father therefore died ca. 770 and was exiled ca. 763.

traditional education that the young Nikephoros probably received (i.e., biblical studies, grammar, rhetoric, astronomy, geometry, music, arithmetic, and philosophy—*v. Niceph.* 149.3–151.13), the school where Nikephoros studied is not specified. It is tempting to suppose that an imperial academy existed where future officials were educated as they apprenticed in their intended profession,[5] but there is no evidence of such a school in this period.[6] When Nikephoros eventually began his career as an imperial clerk *asekretis,* he probably served in the chancery of the iconoclast Leo IV (775–780) under the supervision of the first secretary (and future patriarch of Constantinople) Tarasios.[7] At the succession to the imperial throne of Leo's widow Irene and his minor son Constantine VI (780–797), the climate of imperial opinion changed in favor of venerating icons, and Nikephoros took a part in their restoration in spite of his relative youth and lay status. He accompanied Tarasios, now patriarch of Constantinople (784–806), to the Seventh Ecumenical Council at Nicaea (787) and was selected to read to the council the imperial proclamation reaffirming the veneration of icons as Orthodox worship practice (*v. Niceph.* 146.22–27).

Although Nikephoros' success in imperial service won him some fiscal responsibilities in addition to his chancery duties (*v. Niceph.* 147.15–17), he decided to renounce Constantinople and to undertake a solitary contemplative life in a rugged setting near the city, where he eventually founded a monastery (*v. Niceph.* 147.18–149.2). Nikephoros' motives for suddenly altering the course of his life are mysterious; he may have taken this dramatic step in 797 when the empress Irene blinded her son the emperor Constantine VI and resumed the throne herself (797–802).[8] Eventually Nikephoros, still a layman, submitted to imperial pressure from Irene's successor Nikephoros I (802–811) and returned to Constantinople as head of the city's chief poorhouse (*v. Niceph.* 152.14–18).

At the death of the patriarch Tarasios (806), the emperor Nikephoros began canvassing responsible lay and ecclesiastical opinion in search of a suc-

---

[5] Alexander, *Nicephorus,* 58.

[6] Lemerle, *Byz. Humanism,* 116.

[7] See Alexander, *Nicephorus,* 57–59, and Lemerle, *Byz. Humanism,* 149 with n. 86.

[8] See Alexander, *Nicephorus,* 63, who suggests that Nikephoros supported Constantine VI in this bitter feud and withdrew from court at her victory.

cessor to the patriarchate. Although it became clear that the monks of the powerful Stoudios monastery in Constantinople considered ordained clergy, abbots, stylites, and religious recluses the only acceptable candidates to succeed Tarasios,[9] the emperor Nikephoros I settled upon the layman Nikephoros as his favorite for the office and eventually persuaded the various factions promoting other candidates to support his choice (v. Niceph. 154.2–21). Thus the emperor gained the office of patriarch for Nikephoros, whom he then summoned to the imperial palace and admonished to accept this unsought honor. Reluctantly, Nikephoros agreed, on condition that he be allowed to take monastic vows (v. Niceph. 154.22–157.10). In quick succession, Nikephoros was ordained deacon (9 April), priest (10 April), and finally bishop of Constantinople (i.e., patriarch) on Easter Sunday (12 April 806). His rapid progress through ecclesiastical orders followed a precedent set by his immediate predecessor Tarasios, but the sudden promotion of a layman to the highest office of the eastern Church outraged the Stoudite monks and their supporters. Stoudite opposition to the ecclesiastical policies of the emperor Nikephoros and his patriarch Nikephoros stirred dissension within the Church as Nikephoros' patriarchate began.[10]

Ignatios' Life of Nikephoros does not so much as mention the so-called Moechian ("adultery") controversy which set the patriarch Nikephoros against the Stoudite monks, but the story is well attested in other sources.[11] In 795 the emperor Constantine VI had divorced his wife and entered upon a second marriage, adulterous in the eyes of the Church. The ceremony was performed by Joseph, oikonomos of the church of St. Sophia (i.e., cleric responsible for managing its properties) and abbot of the monastery of Kathara. Vigorous Stoudite protest eventually resulted in the excommunication of Joseph and in his deposition from the priesthood (ca. 797). Joseph then became a valuable functionary of the emperor Nikephoros; in 803 his negotiating skill neutralized a dangerous threat of rebellion. After Nikephoros became patri-

---

[9] See Alexander, Nicephorus, 67.

[10] See Alexander, Nicephorus, 69–70.

[11] For a full and well documented account of this controversy and its roots, see Alexander, Nicephorus, 80–101; see also D. E. Afinogenov, "Κωνσταντινούπολις ἐπίσκοπον ἔχει. The Rise of Patriarchal Power in Byzantium from Nicaenum II to Epanagoga," Erytheia 15 (1994), 55–65, and ODB 2:1388–89.

arch in 806, the emperor ensured that a synod of fifteen bishops would revoke Joseph of Kathara's excommunication and deposition from the priesthood. Confronted with continuing Stoudite resistance to communion with Joseph and with those who accepted him, the emperor engineered the condemnation of Stoudite leaders by a synod of bishops and exiled his opponents in 809. From exile Theodore, abbot of the Stoudios monastery, declared both emperor and patriarch heretics for allowing Joseph to remain a priest and communicant and thereby condoning the adulterous union he had solemnized. This bitter estrangement of monks from ecclesiastical hierarchy and emperor continued until the successor of the emperor Nikephoros, Michael I Rangabe (811–813), resolved it by reinstating the Stoudite exiles and acceding to their demands.

In the Moechian controversy the actions of the patriarch Nikephoros had been consistent with the anti-Stoudite aims of the emperor Nikephoros. The extent to which this firm-minded emperor controlled his patriarch's ecclesiastical policy is further illustrated by Nikephoros' tardiness in dispatching his letter of enthronement to the four other patriarchs of the Church, including Pope Leo III, patriarch of Rome. When Nikephoros finally sent this letter in 811, five years after his enthronement and after Michael I Rangabe became emperor, he pointed to his own unseemly and involuntary tardiness as evidence of the former emperor's coercive anti-Frankish and anti-papal policies.[12]

In the early period of his patriarchate, Nikephoros took several measures that demonstrated both his commitment to sexual purity in the Church and his opposition to heresy, moral high ground that the Stoudites claimed as their own in the Moechian controversy. The patriarch Nikephoros effectively suppressed the so-called double monasteries (i.e., closely associated communities of monks and nuns; see *v. Niceph.* 159.12–160.19), took a firm stand against the (adulterous) second marriage of a Byzantine governor in the Crimea (806–808; see *v. Niceph.* 160.22–30), and compiled a document for the emperor Nikephoros detailing the heretical beliefs of various sects within the empire (*v. Niceph.* 158.25–159.8). Synodal and imperial decrees imposed the death

---

[12] See Alexander, *Nicephorus,* 102–10, for a full discussion of the background and details of imperial policy toward the Frankish kings and the pope; the Life of Nikephoros refers only obliquely to Nikephoros' discomfiture at 162.2–10.

penalty upon the adherents of these sects (811) until Theodore of Stoudios convinced the emperor Michael I Rangabe to spare them.[13]

In 813 Byzantine troops led by Michael I lost a major battle to the Bulgarians. One of Michael's generals, Leo the Armenian, exploited this defeat by using the troops under his command to depose Michael and seize imperial power for himself (v. Niceph. 162.31–163.25). Before agreeing to officiate at Leo's coronation, the patriarch Nikephoros demanded signed assurance from Leo that his beliefs conformed to the orthodox (i.e., iconophile) position. Leo proposed fulfilling this demand after his coronation, which occurred 12 July 813.[14] As emperor, Leo V then embarked upon a resolutely iconoclastic course. He commissioned a special committee chaired by John the Grammarian to compile passages from scriptural and patristic writings that supported the iconoclasts' opposition to religious images.[15] Late in 814 Leo proposed removing those church images that were accessible to worshipers and was rebuffed by Nikephoros; Leo then precipitated an incident that gave him an excuse to remove Christ's image from the Chalke Gate of the imperial palace. In response, Nikephoros summoned a mass assembly of monks and bishops to meet in an all-night vigil on Christmas Eve at the church of St. Sophia, where they guaranteed their commitment to orthodox (i.e., iconophile) belief. At dawn Leo summoned the patriarch to the imperial palace to defend his views. At the conclusion of this private interview, the emperor admitted the court dignitaries supporting him as well as the monks and bishops supporting the patriarch in an emblematic confrontation between Church and State that resolved nothing.[16]

Nikephoros wrote to members of Leo's inner circle in an unsuccessful effort to enlist their help in persuading the emperor to abandon his measures

---

[13] See Alexander, *Nicephorus*, 99, as well as his "Religious Persecution and Resistance in the Byzantine Empire of the Eighth and Ninth Centuries: Methods and Justifications," *Speculum* 52 (1977), 238–64, especially 245 f.

[14] See Alexander, *Nicephorus*, 78, and *v. Niceph.* 163.26–164.19.

[15] *v. Niceph.* 165.20–30; the activities and membership of this committee are analyzed in detail by Alexander, *Nicephorus*, 126–28.

[16] See *v. Niceph.* 165.31–189.5, where these events provide the setting for a lengthy discussion of iconophile and iconoclast arguments in a dialogue between emperor and patriarch. Alexander (*Nicephorus*, 128–32) discusses the chronological problems connected with Leo's early pro-iconoclast measures and Nikephoros' response to them.

against iconophiles (*v. Niceph.* 189.19–190.14). Leo, however, was determined to persist. He banished some of Nikephoros' clerical supporters and persuaded others to join the ranks of his own followers, thus isolating the patriarch within the Church. Attempts by both the emperor and complaisant clergy to persuade Nikephoros to moderate his defense of icons were unsuccessful. The committee that had assembled Leo's florilegium of pro-iconoclast writings and the bishops and clergy who supported Leo's cause pressed Nikephoros either to debate publicly or to change his iconophile position (*v. Niceph.* 190.30–194.16). Nikephoros, however, declared that his opponents were unworthy of such a debate, emphatically refused to meet with them, and pronounced a sentence of deposition upon some of the clergy associated with them (*v. Niceph.* 194.17–196.1). Abandoning their demands for a public confrontation, Nikephoros' iconoclast enemies even plotted to murder the patriarch (*v. Niceph.* 196.13–197.17). At this point, Nikephoros submitted to the emperor his letter of resignation from the patriarchate, citing his own poor health and the evil that threatened to contaminate the emperor through the murderous plans of his supporters (*v. Niceph.* 197.21–198.18). Weakened by illness and escorted by soldiers, Nikephoros made his farewell visit to the great patriarchal church of St. Sophia on the first day of Lent, 815, then sailed across the Bosporos by night to his initial place of exile, the monastery of Agathos in Chrysopolis (*v. Niceph.* 198.19–201.3).[17]

After a brief stay in Chrysopolis, Nikephoros was forced by the emperor Leo to relocate at a greater distance from Constantinople, in the monastery of St. Theodore Teron, which Nikephoros had himself founded in the brighter days of his career (*v. Niceph.* 201.3–6). Nikephoros spent the final thirteen years of his life at this monastery, isolated and estranged from ecclesiastical affairs. When Michael II succeeded Leo V on the Byzantine throne (820), Nikephoros wrote the new emperor asserting the orthodoxy of iconophile doctrine; Michael II responded by prohibiting all discussion of icons and by offering to reinstate Nikephoros as patriarch only if he kept silent on the subject (*v. Niceph.* 209.12–210.12). In 821 Nikephoros received a visit from Theodore of Stoudios, who played a prominent role in focusing iconophile opposition after Nikephoros abdicated.[18] Although Theodore reports that the

---

[17] For a detailed discussion and chronology of the events surrounding the abdication of the patriarch Nikephoros, see Alexander, *Nicephorus,* 132–35.

[18] See Alexander, *Nicephorus,* 153–54.

meeting was cordial and unmarked by controversy, Nikephoros' biographer Ignatios does not even mention it. Virtually nothing is known of the final years of Nikephoros' life. While in exile he wrote various tracts defending his views (*v. Niceph.* 210.25–27) and received those who sought instruction from him, although his strength was impaired by the chronic and occasionally debilitating illness that beset him shortly before he abdicated (*v. Niceph.* 213.26–214.2). Nikephoros died in exile on 2 June 828.[19]

The Writings of Nikephoros

Nikephoros left behind a significant literary legacy. Two official documents survive from the years of his patriarchate, the synodal letter to Pope Leo III (811–812) and the *Apologeticus minor* (813–815), which admonished pro-iconoclast clergy to refrain from agitation on the subject of icons. In the essay *De Magnete* (814–815), Nikephoros officially protested against excerpts made from the obscure Christian apologist Makarios Magnes by a troublesome clique, evidently Leo's florilegium committee. Around 818–820, soon after Nikephoros abdicated and went into exile, he wrote two works directed to a clerical audience in refutation of specific iconoclast doctrines, the *Apologeticus atque antirrhetici* (with a florilegium of patristic texts supporting the veneration of icons) and the essay *Contra Eusebium et Epiphanidem;* an essay *Adversus Iconomachos* made the arguments in *Contra Eusebium* accessible to a more general audience. In the final years of his life (820–828), Nikephoros wrote the *Refutatio et eversio,* countering in detail the Acts and florilegium of the iconoclast Council of St. Sophia (815).[20]

Nikephoros' writings include historical as well as theological works. During his career in the imperial chancery, he wrote the *Breviarium*, a chronicle continuing the *Histories* of Theophylaktos Simokattes from the death of Mau-

---

[19] See F. Halkin, *AnalBoll* 76 (1958), 232, citing the *SynaxCP* 723–26 and the *menologia* entries collected by A. Ehrhard, *Überlieferung und Bestand der hagiographischen und homiletischen Literatur der griechischen Kirche* 1 (Leipzig, 1936–37), 643–57.

[20] For bibliography relating to Nikephoros' ecclesiastical and theological writings, see Beck, *Kirche,* 490–91, and Hunger, *Lit.* 1:344. P. Alexander discusses these works in some detail (*Nicephorus,* 162–88) and offers a topical summary of the *Refutatio et eversio,* which exists at present only in manuscript form (appendix, pp. 242–62). J. Featherstone's critical edition of this important work (*Nicephori patriarchae constantinopolitani Refutatio et eversio definitionis synodalis anni 815* [Leuven, 1997]) appeared too late to be consulted.

rice to the marriage of Irene and Leo IV the Khazar (602–769).[21] He also compiled a popular *Chronography,* or list of important dates from Adam to the accession of the emperor Michael II (820), which was translated into Latin (870) and old Bulgarian.[22]

Ignatios the Deacon as Hagiographer

The tenth-century lexicon known as the *Souda* describes the author of the Life of Nikephoros as follows: "Ignatios <was> a deacon and the *skeuophylax* of the Great Church <of St. Sophia> in Constantinople;[23] <he> became metropolitan <bishop> of Nicaea. A learned scholar, he wrote a Life of Tarasios and <one> of Nikephoros (the holy and blessed patriarchs), biographical accounts to be delivered at tombs, letters, satiric poetry <directed> against Thomas the Insurgent [i.e., Thomas the Slav] called 'the <writings> about Thomas,' and many other <works>."[24] This basic sketch can be supplemented with biographical data derived from Ignatios' own writings. He tells us that he was a pupil and protégé of the patriarch Tarasios (*v. Taras.* 423.1–16) and describes an educational curriculum in the Life of Nikephoros which he may have followed himself (*v. Niceph.* 149.3–151.13). At some point in his career, Ignatios joined the iconoclast cause, an association of expediency that probably accounted for his election as metropolitan bishop of Nicaea.[25] At the close of the Life of Nikephoros (*v. Niceph.* 215.13–217.27), a repentant

---

[21] See the translation by N. Tobias and A. Santoro, *Eyewitness to History: Patriarch Nikephoros of Constantinople* (Brookline, Mass., n.d.), and the critical edition and translation by C. Mango, *Nikephoros, Patriarch of Constantinople: Short History. Text, Translation, and Commentary* (Washington, D.C., 1990).

[22] See Alexander, *Nicephorus,* 157–62, and Hunger, *Lit.* 1:344–47.

[23] The *skeuophylax* was a clerical official (usually a priest), who supervised the sacred valuables and liturgical vessels belonging to a church and took a prominent place in both church ceremonial and ecclesiastical administration. In the 9th century the *skeuophylax* of the patriarchal church of St. Sophia enjoyed high prestige and was appointed by the emperor; see *ODB* 3:1909–10 and *v. Niceph.* 190.15–18.

[24] Text from C. de Boor, *Nicephori archiepiscopi Constantinopolitani opuscula historica* (Leipzig, 1880), 138.

[25] See C. Mango, "Observations on the Correspondence of Ignatius, Metropolitan of Nicaea," in *Überlieferungsgeschichtliche Untersuchungen,* ed. F. Paschke [Texte und Untersuchungen 125] (Berlin, 1981), 408–9.

Ignatios renounces this lapse from orthodoxy. This autobiographical passage suggests that Ignatios wrote the Life of Nikephoros sometime between 843 and 846, that is, after the restoration of icons created a climate in which iconophile sentiments could be expressed freely and before Nikephoros' remains were translated to Constantinople (846), an event which is not mentioned in the Life; further, the new iconophile patriarch Methodios (843–847) may have commissioned the Lives of both Tarasios and Nikephoros.[26] In his letters, Ignatios remarks that he voluntarily joined a monastic community on Mt. Olympos in Bithynia, probably after being deposed from his see at Nicaea.[27] In the mid-ninth century the monastic communities on Mt. Olympos nurtured authors and subjects for learned iconophile hagiography similar to Ignatios' Life of Tarasios and Life of Nikephoros.[28] Ignatios the Deacon may have belonged to that milieu. His letters reveal that later on, in 843, he was confined in the monastery of Pikridion at the head of the Golden Horn near Constantinople.[29] Although no precise information exists on the dates of Ignatios' birth and death, it is reasonable to place his birth ca. 770–780 and his death after 845.[30]

The Life of Nikephoros is remarkable among Ignatios' writings. Of the four saints' Lives attributed to him, the Life of Nikephoros is the longest and the most ambitious in literary style; it also contains Ignatios' intensely personal testimonial to the scar iconoclasm left in his own life. Ignatios wrote the Lives of George of Amastris and Gregory of Decapolis in a simple and direct style, which contrasts sharply with the literary level of the Life of Nikephoros. Since Ignatios claims to be a neophyte hagiographer in the Life of George of

[26] See von Dobschütz, "Methodius und die Studiten," 54; Ševčenko, "Hagiography," 123, 125 and n. 92; and S. Efthymiadis, "On the Hagiographical Work of Ignatius the Deacon," *JÖB* 41 (1991), 83. Ignatios may have hoped the *vita Nicephori* would persuade Methodios to exempt him from the mass deposition of iconoclast clergy (843); see Afinogenov, "Great Purge," 89–90.

[27] See Efthymiadis, "Ignatius the Deacon," 78–79.

[28] See S. Efthymiadis, "The *Vita Tarasii* and the Hagiographical Work of Ignatios the Deacon," Ph.D. dissertation, Oxford University, 1991, 34–40.

[29] See Mango, "Observations," 409.

[30] See *ODB* 2:984. For a full discussion of the extensive bibliography on Ignatios the Deacon, see W. Wolska-Conus, "De quibusdam Ignatiis," *TM* 4 (1970), 329–60, at 329–51.

Amastris, and since he makes no references to iconophile concerns, this Life may date from the iconoclast phase of Ignatios' career.[31] The Life of Tarasios displays the same stylistic pretensions as the Life of Nikephoros, but to a lesser degree; written in an artificial, archaic, and grammatically complex dialect of scholarly Greek, both these Lives contain frequent allusions to the literary works, realia, history, and mythology of classical antiquity. This difficult and allusive style typifies iconophile literature in the mid-ninth century and distinguishes it from the simple diction of the iconoclast authors.[32] At the same time, Ignatios supports his narrative with frequent and varied allusions to biblical figures and citations.

The Life of Nikephoros is more than a straightforward narrative of the saint's experiences. Ignatios opens his account as if delivering a eulogy at Nikephoros' tomb, even addressing his audience directly (e.g., "Gentlemen, had not . . ." [v. Niceph. 139.7]; "My good friends" [v. Niceph. 139.15]).[33] He embellishes his account of Nikephoros' early life with a unique summary of the curriculum in Byzantine higher education. Throughout the Life, Ignatios supplies speeches to explicate a point of view or to add dramatic impact to an important event. The most remarkable of these speeches is a lengthy interchange between the patriarch Nikephoros and the iconoclast emperor Leo V, cast in the form of a Platonic dialogue. Nikephoros plays the wise Socrates, lucidly explicating the theological basis for the veneration of icons, persistently pressing questions upon Leo, and ruthlessly demolishing his iconoclast responses. Finally, Ignatios closes the Life with an extended and traditional comparison (synkrisis) between his holy subject and the great figures of the Old and New Testaments. Mundane information such as the date and place of Nikephoros' death is never mentioned; instead, Ignatios concludes the Life by pouring out his own frustrations as a reconstructed iconoclast.

The Sanctification and Cult of Nikephoros

Nikephoros himself was by no means the typical Byzantine holy man who attained sanctity by enduring great physical privations, performing notable miracles, or suffering painful martyrdom. Instead, the patriarch Nikephoros undertook extraordinary labors to defend the Church's integrity in faith

---

[31] See Ševčenko, "Hagiography," 120–25; Efthymiadis, "Ignatius the Deacon," 78–79.

[32] Lemerle, *Byz. Humanism,* 120–68.

[33] First noted by von Dobschütz, "Methodius und die Studiten," 54.

and practice and to protect it against harmful intervention by heretical emperors. His feats of Christian achievement were intellectual and institutional in nature. He purified the Church by severely controlling double monasteries and defended the orthodox faith by speaking and writing in support of the veneration of icons despite opposition and eventual persecution from the highest levels of the empire. While others like Ignatios acquiesced to iconoclasm and enjoyed advancement within the Church hierarchy, Nikephoros retained his orthodox and iconophile convictions even at the cost of his lofty ecclesiastical office and his opportunity to play a public role in Constantinople. Although Nikephoros performed no miracles in the physical realm (such as healing the sick, averting natural disasters, etc.), Ignatios portrays him as possessing divinely inspired foresight, for example, when he senses the emperor Leo's imminent plunge into violent heresy (*v. Niceph.* 164.10–19) and when he forecasts the eventual downfall of Bardas, the arrogant young emissary from the same emperor (*v. Niceph.* 201.8–28).

Ignatios depicts Nikephoros throughout his long life as a lonely figure, supported by no congregation of fellow monks nor corps of close associates. At critical points in his career, Ignatios labels him αὐτουργός, "doing his work by himself," for example, when Nikephoros is installed as patriarch even though he did not seek the office (*v. Niceph.* 158.14) and when he crowns Leo as emperor (*v. Niceph.* 164.9). Ignatios intends to portray Nikephoros as an independent hero uniquely defined by his own actions within the Church and through conflict with his obvious opponents, the iconoclasts. To achieve this end, Ignatios ignores or suppresses any mention of situations involving Nikephoros and the Stoudite monks, who staunchly supported the iconophile cause but opposed Nikephoros in the Moechian controversy and took a public role defending icons after Nikephoros went into exile. To Ignatios, Nikephoros is a lonely and heroic figure, a tower of unshakable integrity in a bureaucratic, institutional, and intellectual landscape. It is not surprising that this image of the saint remained potent in literature and in art long after his death.

In spite of its length and difficult, archaizing style, the Life of the Patriarch Nikephoros by Ignatios survives in a surprisingly large number of manuscripts, several of which were copied relatively soon after the composition of the *vita.* One palimpsest manuscript dates from the ninth century (Vat. gr. 984), three manuscripts survive from the tenth century (Vat. gr. 1809,[34] Vat.

---

[34] De Boor based his edition of the Life of Nikephoros solely on this manuscript.

gr. 1667, Par. gr. 910), one from the eleventh century (Athos, Philotheou 8), one from the fourteenth century (Par. gr. 909), and two from the sixteenth century (Vat. gr. 707, Athen. gr. 191).[35] Ignatios' Life of the Patriarch Nikephoros evidently earned a place in the libraries of learned readers while the memory of iconoclast outrages was still vivid, and it retained its attractions as a work capable of inspiring and instructing its readers long after the horrors of iconoclasm had receded into the distant past.

Within the century after Nikephoros' death, vignettes drawn from his struggles against the iconoclasts appeared in deluxe illuminated psalters to accompany the text of Psalm 25 (26).[36] Nikephoros is portrayed as an elderly but vigorous man with a long white beard, halo, and bishop's robes as he treads upon John the Grammarian, exalts the image of Christ on a shield-shaped device, or confronts the iconoclast council of 815. These vivid images preserved and reinforced the memory of Nikephoros' career and also provided a particularly appropriate visual commentary on the words of the psalm: "Judge me, O Lord; for I have walked in my innocence. . . . I have not sat with the council of vanity, and will in no wise enter in with transgressors. I have hated the assembly of wicked doers; and will not sit with ungodly men. . . . Lord, I have loved the beauty of thy house, and the place of the tabernacle of thy glory. . . ."[37]

Similar scenes from the career of Nikephoros are associated with this psalm in psalters produced and illustrated in later centuries as well, demonstrating the tenacity of Nikephoros' reputation as a defender of the faith against God's enemies.[38] Illustrated *menologia* (i.e., collections of brief bio-

---

[35] Manuscripts enumerated by Efthymiadis, "*Vita Tarasii*," 124–25.

[36] See the two 9th-century psalters designated Moscow, Hist. Mus. Cod. 129 (the "Khludov Psalter"), fols. 23v and 51v (illustrating Ps. 51 [52]), and Athos, Pantokrator 61, fol. 16r, both discussed by K. Corrigan in *Visual Polemics in the Ninth-Century Byzantine Psalters* (Cambridge, 1992); see figs. 38 and 43 (Khludov Psalter) and fig. 111 (Pantokrator Psalter). I have compiled the portrayals of Nikephoros listed here from the Princeton Index of Christian Art at Dumbarton Oaks and from *LCI* 8:40–42.

[37] Ps. 25 (26):1, 4–5, 8.

[38] Cf. two 11th-century psalters (the "Theodore Psalter," London: Mus. Brit. Add. 19352, fol. 27v; and Vat. Barb. gr. 372, fol. 39v), one psalter of the 11th or 12th century (Vat. gr. 1927, fol. 41r), and one psalter of the 13th or 14th century (the "Hamilton Psalter," Berlin: Mus. Kupferstich Kab. 78.A.9, fol. 75v).

graphies of saints arranged according to the order in which their feastdays were celebrated in the church year) portray Nikephoros in his episcopal robes to accompany the entry for his feastday (2 June, the date of his death) or depict the festal procession which conveyed his remains to their final resting place on 13 March, the date of his translation.[39] A visual tradition separate from that represented by the psalters and *menologia* depicts three incidents from the career of Nikephoros as accompaniment to the Chronicle of John Skylitzes in the lavishly illustrated Madrid manuscript (Bibl. Nac. vitr. 26–2). Nikephoros appears leaving Constantinople by boat (fol. 20v), saluted during his sea voyage by a group of monks headed by Theophanes the Confessor (fol. 21r), and corresponding with the emperor Michael II about his restoration to the patriarchate (fol. 28v).[40]

Images of Nikephoros as a bearded bishop standing attentive in his episcopal robes also began to appear in programs of church decoration installed shortly after his death. The mosaics of the mid-ninth century in the patriarchal rooms at St. Sophia include Nikephoros among the bishops portrayed,[41] as do the frescoes in the ninth-century church at Kiliçlar in Cappadocia and the twelfth-century frescoes of the church at Asinou, Cyprus. This iconographic type of Nikephoros also survives with those of other great bishops of the orthodox Church portrayed in three Serbian churches decorated with fresco programs in the fourteenth century (Staro Nagoričino, Žiča, and Čučer). Thus Nikephoros' image appears in churches decorated at great expense under the patronage of the Church hierarchy or of rulers who wished to assert their orthodox connections. Like the deluxe manuscripts in which Nikephoros is depicted, these fresco programs attest his importance to the established Church and indicate the wealth at the disposition of those who honored Nikephoros by portraying him. A silver-gilt and sardonyx chalice of the tenth century now in the Treasury of San Marco, Venice (the "Chalice of the Emperor Romanos"), is rimmed with beading and small enamel plaques depicting

---

[39] E.g., Moscow: Lib. Synodal 183, p. 197, an 11th-century *menologion.*

[40] Cf. A. Grabar, M. Manoussacas, *L'Illustration du manuscrit de Skylitzès de la Bibliothèque Nationale de Madrid* (Venice, 1979), 29, 32.

[41] See R. Cormack, E. J. W. Hawkins, "The Mosaics of St. Sophia at Istanbul: The Rooms above the Southwest Vestibule and Ramp," *DOP* 31 (1977), 177–251, esp. 224–25, with figs. 41, 44, 45, and color fig. B.

Nikephoros and several other bishops and saints;[42] this costly eucharistic vessel reinforces the impression that commemoration of Nikephoros' image and deeds is associated with the very highest levels of Byzantine society.

Nikephoros' earthly remains became the object of official celebration and commemoration rather than of popular devotion and veneration. He was honored twice yearly at the Church of the Holy Apostles in Constantinople on 2 June (the day of his death) and on 13 March (the anniversary of his exile and of the translation of his relics). Major entries in the *Synaxarion of Constantinople* for these days mention the return of Nikephoros' relics at the instigation of the patriarch Methodios,[43] a story told in greater detail by Theophanes, presbyter and *hegoumenos,* in his "Oration on the Exile of the Sainted Nikephoros, Patriarch of Constantinople, and on the Translation of his Venerated Corpse."[44] According to Theophanes, Methodios gained approval from the empress Theodora to restore Nikephoros' body to Constantinople in 846 (p. 124, chap. 9 = 165AB, chap. 14), traveled himself with a retinue to the monastery of St. Theodore Teron where the remains of Nikephoros had lain for eighteen years, and addressed the coffin of Nikephoros "as if he were living." "Now grant yourself to us who long for you eagerly," prayed Methodios, "leave those here and move to your own <place> so that the people who love their father may joyfully receive your translated <body>, just as those in the past <received> that <of John Chrysostom>" (p. 125, chap. 11 = 165CD, chap. 15). After an all-night vigil and Eucharist, the ecclesiastical delegation conveyed the uncorrupted body of Nikephoros to the patriarch's waiting ship, an imperial trireme. In Constantinople, a torch-lit procession of nobles led by the child-emperor Michael III accompanied the coffin to the church of St. Sophia, site of Nikephoros' banishment from the city. On 13 March, a second torch-lit procession took the body through the city to the church of the Holy Apostles to commemorate and reverse Nikephoros' exile. Among the great

---

[42] Cf. D. Buckton, ed., *The Treasury of San Marco, Venice* (Milan, 1984), 129–33, cat. no. 10.

[43] *SynaxCP* 726.4–7 and 533–34.

[44] Published by Th. Joannou in Μνημεῖα ἁγιολογικὰ νῦν πρῶτον ἐκδιδόμενα (Venice, 1884; repr. Leipzig, 1973), 115–28; a Latin translation appears in PG 100:159–68. The following summary cites first the Greek text, then the Latin translation. The account of the translation of Nikephoros' relics is contrasted with the translation of the relics of Theodore of Stoudios by D. E. Afinogenov in "Κωνσταντινούπολις ἐπίσκοπον ἔχει: Part II," 68–70.

crowd assembled to watch this spectacle, some persons possessed by unclean spirits rushed forward with tears and blasphemous cries and were cured by the saint's presence. His body was then entombed at the Holy Apostles (p. 126, chap. 12–p. 127, chap. 13 = 166, chaps. 16–17), where he performed no further recorded miracles nor received any known devotions in popular cult. At the end, Nikephoros, patriarch of Constantinople, rested in peace among saints and emperors in the imperial city of his birth.

Bibliography

Edition Used for Translation

(*BHG* 1335) C. de Boor, *Nicephori archiepiscopi Constantinopolitani opuscula historica* (Leipzig, 1880; repr. New York, 1975), 139–217.

Related Texts

(*BHG* 1336) "Θεοφάνους πρεσβυτέρου καὶ ἡγουμένου λόγος εἰς τὴν ἐξορίαν τοῦ ἐν ἁγίοις Νικηφόρου πατριάρχου Κωνσταντινουπόλεως καὶ εἰς τὴν μετακομιδὴν τοῦ τιμίου λειψάνου αὐτοῦ," ed. Th. Joannou, Μνημεῖα ἁγιολογικά (Venice, 1884; repr. Leipzig, 1973), 115–28.

Secondary Literature

P. J. Alexander, *The Patriarch Nicephorus of Constantinople* (Oxford, 1958).

S. Efthymiadis, "On the Hagiographical Work of Ignatius the Deacon," *JÖB* 41 (1991), 73–83.

———, "The *Vita Tarasii* and the Hagiographical Work of Ignatios the Deacon," Ph.D. dissertation, Oxford University, 1991.

H. Hunger, *Die hochsprachliche profane Literatur der Byzantiner,* 2 vols. (Munich, 1978), 1:344–47.

A. Kazhdan, "Nikephoros I," *ODB* 3:1477.

C. Lardiero, "The Critical Patriarchate of Nikephoros of Constantinople (806–815): Religious and Secular Controversies," Ph.D. dissertation, The Catholic University of America, 1993.

Lexikon der christlichen Ikonographie, ed. E. Kirschbaum, W. Braunfels, 8 vols. (Rome-Freiburg-Basel-Vienna, 1968–76), 8:40–42.

C. Mango, *Nikephoros, Patriarch of Constantinople: Short History. Text, Translation and Commentary* (Washington, D.C., 1990).

———, "Observations on the Correspondence of Ignatius, Metropolitan of

Nicaea," in *Überlieferungsgeschichtliche Untersuchungen,* ed. F. Paschke [Texte und Untersuchungen 125] (Berlin, 1981), 403–10.

D. Stiernon, *Bibl.sanct.* 9 (1967), 871–74.

N. Tobias, A. Santoro, *Eyewitness to History: Patriarch Nikephoros of Constantinople* (Brookline, Mass., n.d.).

J. J. Travis, *In Defense of the Faith: The Theology of Patriarch Nikephoros of Constantinople* (Brookline, Mass., 1984).

W. Wolska-Conus, "De quibusdam Ignatiis," *TM* 4 (1970), 329–60.

THE LIFE OF OUR SAINTED FATHER NIKEPHOROS, ARCHBISHOP OF CONSTANTINOPLE THE NEW ROME, WRITTEN BY IGNATIOS THE DEACON AND SKEUOPHYLAX[45] OF THE MOST HOLY GREAT CHURCH OF ST. SOPHIA

Gentlemen, had not a time of tears brought me to the point of heartbreak and had not the pangs of grief dulled my soul's perceptions, my narrative would have flowed swiftly and smoothly,[46] fulfilling its eager desire to the best of its ability, although falling short of its subject.[47] But now, under the inexorable power of such sufferings, <my narrative> has experienced a sort of paralysis of the tongue regarding panegyric and has chosen to express lamentations; it has renounced giving generous praise and fallen completely <under the power> of despair. What is it then, my friends, that has hindered <my narrative>? What is it that has engendered despair, and what has caused turmoil and darkness to enter into my thoughts? My good friends, it is the departure and loss of a God-bearing father, the extinction of the radiant star of the Church, the defeat of the one proclaiming the only way to worship God, the silence of the great trumpet voice that roused <us> to the true faith, the concealment of the priceless treasure of spiritual teaching, the stilling of the lips winged to pursue the vain puffery [p. 140] of unbelief—the one in reality bearing the name of victory,[48] even if he, being a man, was conquered by death. This <tragic death> prompted the paralysis of my tongue for panegyric, this

---

[45] Ignatios held an important liturgical and administrative position as curator of the moveable properties contained in the church of St. Sophia and as head of a department which assisted him; cf. *ODB* 3:1909–10, s.v. "Skeuophylax."

[46] Cf. Plato, *Republic* 492c.

[47] The hagiographer's sense of inadequacy when confronted by the huge task of recording his saintly subject's virtues is a theme that often marks the beginning (and sometimes the end) of a saint's Life; see *ODB* 2:1387, s.v. "Modesty, Topos of." Ignatios returns to this theme in the final sentence of the Life of Nikephoros, which also contains two verbal echoes of this first sentence: προθυμίας recalling πρόθυμον and ὑπὲρ δύναμιν echoing ὅση δύναμις.

[48] A pun on the two elements of Nikephoros' name, νίκη- ("victory") and -φόρος ("bearing").

drove my narrative to speechlessness, this plunged my thoughts into incongruous lamentation. Therefore,[49] had I not feared the complaint <made against> unfeeling persons, <namely> about a son who chooses to be silent at the death of his father and disregards a great marvel that cannot be *hidden* with *the bushel*[50] of oblivion, <I would have behaved differently>; enveloped in a cloud of ignorance and forced back by a storm of sin like the ancient people <of Israel>, I would have persuaded myself not to approach *the mountain* of the man's virtues nor *to touch any part of it* with my unworthy attempt, thus revealing myself to be a *beast* in my audacity and being stoned *with stones* or struck *with darts*.[51] All the same, then, with singleness of purpose, with my heart burning deeply with desire, and with the knowledge that to do one's best is dear to God, I have descended[52] to the best of my ability into the depths of panegyric for the wholly praiseworthy father <Nikephoros>. But with the help of your intercessions to the Almighty, let it be possible for me to seize the *pearl hidden in* <that depth>,[53] to swim up <to the surface> without danger to my purpose, and to sell away that wealth undefiled to you[54] who desire <it>. For I would do him[55] [Nikephoros] an injustice if I did not repay <him> with words after receiving from him the resources for my speaking.

Now then, abandoning our song of mourning, let us proceed to the narrative, and display[56] to those who love goodness the life of the God-bearing

---

[49] I have restructured Ignatios' long and complex single sentence into two parts, believing that his Greek syntax could not be both replicated and comprehended.

[50] Cf. Mk. 4:21–22 (also Mt. 5:15 and Lk. 11:33).

[51] Cf. Ex. 19:12–13, where God promises death to any of the Israelites or their animals who approach Mt. Sinai while a fiery storm cloud marks God's presence there with Moses.

[52] Ignatios applies the experiences of Moses on Mt. Sinai to himself, recalling the fiery presence of the Lord (Ex. 24:17) and Moses' subsequent descent into the plain below the mountain (Ex. 32:15).

[53] Ignatios, imagining himself a pearlfisher, combines a reference to the pearl as symbol of Christian teaching (cf. Mt. 7:6) with an allusion to the parable of the man who sold his goods to buy the treasure hidden in a field (cf. Mt. 13:44).

[54] Reading ὑμῖν for the printed ἡμῖν.

[55] Reading αὐτὸν for the printed ἑαυτὸν.

[56] Although context requires a subjunctive form here, the printed προθήσωμεν represents either a rare lapse from classical usage on the part of Ignatios or a corruption in the manuscript.

man as if it were a picture of virtue in public <view>. For <his deeds> will serve to delight and benefit all who have given their passionate attention to the good and who love the doctrines of the pure faith, since they clearly exemplify the power of truth and cut out the sinews of [i.e., incapacitate] those who do not look for truth in the correct way. For <my narrative> will include and somehow call to mind not only his accomplishments in holy conduct and habits but also his *striving unto blood*[57] on behalf of truth itself. [p. 141] I wish to have and am pleased to have in my audience all the nurslings of the true faith and those for whom the Church has bared her own breast (that is, instruction in superior <doctrines>) and filled with perfect spiritual nourishment so that they might distinguish the good from the inferior. However, I reject and banish those who fell under the sway of unsound doctrine and offered mad opposition to the father [i.e., Nikephoros] as if in a vain attempt to *shake* thoroughly *the foundation*[58] of the Church while, as the prophet <says>, they entrusted *their* own *hope to falsehood.*[59] After adopting a malicious attitude toward him and after practicing every terrible <thing> imaginable against him, they would take no delight in praises of <Nikephoros> nor would they ever agree with those <praises>. Indeed, *godliness is an abomination to sinners,* as it seems to Solomon and to Truth.[60] For they were continuously pressed by the nets of <Nikephoros'> inescapable arguments as they ran around endlessly in a labyrinth of <his> refutations; constrained by their distress, they turned to evil actions, and like *dumb dogs* they do not stop *barking*[61] at the saint. For the depravity of heresy is relentless and unyielding: even if it is devoured ten thousand times over by refutations,[62] just as many times it responds shamelessly.

Therefore, my account avoids climbing the difficult heights of these <matters> and maintains a straight path, introducing the object of our

[57] Cf. Heb. 12:4. Ignatios paraphrases this sentiment at the close of the *vita* (217.28–29).

[58] Cf. Acts 16:26.

[59] Cf. Is. 28:15.

[60] Sir. 1:25. Ignatios confuses two apocryphal books of the Bible, the Wisdom of Jesus Son of Sirach (= Ecclesiasticus) and the Wisdom of Solomon.

[61] Cf. Is. 56:10.

[62] With his use of the terms ἐλέγχων and ἐλέγχοις in 141.15 and 19, Ignatios makes a punning reference to Nikephoros' *Refutatio et eversio* ("Ελεγχος καὶ ἀνατροπή). Thanks are due to A. Alexakis for this observation.

praise. Indeed, in my opinion it seems neither holy nor pious for those who choose to praise virtue to describe with admiring wonder the family, the distinction in life, the homeland, the wealth and <those categories in> which the rules of secular <literature> prescribe that narratives be constructed, <when the subject of the narrative> had no time for these <things> and took pride, as is fitting, only in the boasts of piety. For the one recognized through his deeds as an uncompromising[63] standard and rule of virtuous conduct does not follow the rules for sophistic disputations. However, knowing the fame of <Nikephoros'> earthly homeland and the high reputation of his parents before God is a road leading to gladness of heart, and it *makes the forehead* of our undertaking [p. 142] *shine from afar,* as a lyric poet said somewhere.[64] Come, therefore, let us portray for you his entire image in its heavenly and spiritual dimensions by sketching the man <starting> from his family and by outlining the events of his material life.

[Constantinople], the foremost city and Queen of Cities, brought him forth for her own through the agency of his truly God-fearing parents;[65] from his very cradle he was like a living spark which kindled the world and would quench the flame of ungodly heresy that was soon to be revived. His parents, now, had names which proved to be very appropriate, since Eudokia <"Good Repute">, joining in marital union with Theodore <"God's Gift">, brought forth Nikephoros, who was truly in good repute and God's gift; she nurtured this little plant into a heavenly tree. The father was so distinguished and famous in his devotion to God that he voluntarily accepted danger, exile, and beatings in witness to the truth. In my opinion, he was a prophecy of the deeds to be fulfilled in his son and a sort of prefiguration and image that both child and father would risk every danger for a similar faith, but not at the same time.

At that time when Constantine controlled the helm of the imperial government, <Theodore> happened to be acting as secretary and serving in the imperial chancery.[66] Like a second patriarch Abraham,[67] he was adorned with

---

[63] Reading ἀπαρέγκλιτος for ἀπαρέγκλητος.

[64] Pindar, *Olympian Ode* 6:3–4.

[65] Nikephoros was probably born in 758; see Introduction, 25.

[66] Theodore was an imperial secretary ("asecretis") under Constantine V (741–775); see Introduction, 25.

[67] Abraham followed God's commands to leave his home in Harran and caused the pharaoh of Egypt to suffer God's wrath on his account (cf. Gen. 12:1–20).

the pure light of the true faith and belief in God; because he revered Christ in His image as well as His immaculate mother and all the saints, he was bitterly denounced to <the emperor>, who exercised a tyrannical rule over the <faith>.[68] The <emperor>, a virtual enemy of the truth, became obsessed with a rumor he could hardly believe and ordered Theodore to come into his presence and to justify himself immediately concerning what the emperor had heard <about him>. Theodore appeared as if he had been summoned to a banquet, not called up for judgment, and demonstrated that the rumor was true in every respect. When his disposition [p. 143] became evident to the emperor and his unyielding resistance first caused the emperor's malice to smolder, then to burst into flame, <Theodore> was subjected to demeaning threats and beatings, like a condemned criminal. But when <Theodore's> judge saw that these tortures did not soften his resolve, he stripped him of his robe <of office> and his rank and consigned him to a relatively harsh exile.

After some time elapsed, <the emperor> had Theodore summoned from Pemolissa, for he had been sentenced to this fortress for his exile.[69] He ordered Theodore to appear in the palace in the confident belief, as I suppose, that as a result of hardship and torture he would have come to understand that <the emperor's> suppositions were the good. However, he found Theodore harder than steel in his resistance, superior to imperial threats and insolence, and more than ready for other even worse measures if he should encounter them. For Theodore rushed headlong after these <punishments>. He preferred to beautify himself with Christ's own stigmata rather than deviate from that ordinance of the Church which most opportunely affirmed that it is right to represent and reverence Christ, our true God, in His human form according to apostolic and patristic tradition. When the holy man loudly confessed his salvation and aligned himself with the party opposing the tyrannical emperor, he roused the emperor to further forms of torture. After <Theodore> endured this assault in the bravest manner imaginable, he was banished by the emperor to Nicaea in the province of Bithynia, where he lived out the remainder of his life in fear of God and provided to all an example of resistance on behalf of

[68] Or "over this <empire>."

[69] Pemolis(s)a/Pimolisa (modern Osmancik) in north-central Anatolia was a station on the main northern road from Constantinople eastward to Theodosiopolis (modern Erzerum). See A. Bryer, D. Winfield, *The Byzantine Monuments and Topography of the Pontos* 1 (Washington, D.C., 1985), 20 n. 25.

the true faith. Then he passed over to that <heavenly> rest and eternal life, to receive the rewards for his sufferings when he is judged for his deeds in life. Theodore's consort who lived with him according to divine law, a woman who manifestly loved both her God and her husband, followed her spouse in all circumstances—in dangers, in banishment, *in afflictions,* in [p. 144] <occasions for the armor> *of righteousness on the right hand and on the left,* in the words of the holy apostle,[70] that is to say, in <times of> both sorrow and pleasure. For as a married couple, they urged themselves on to greater <actions>, and were blended in spirit no less than united in body. After the blessed death of her husband, for some time Eudokia lived with her son who was just then undertaking his general education while working at his <secretarial> craft with hands and ink. For he had been selected as a secretary serving in the emperor's chancery [*mysteriois*] (for thus the Latin term <for secretary> "asecretis" should be translated, <as> "secret-ary").[71] <Eudokia> also saw <Nikephoros>, her torch-bearing luminary, installed in the lampstand of the patriarchate, and shining eternal *light on our path;*[72] until she was *old and advanced in years*[73] she very rightly enjoyed from her son the honor due to parents second only to God. She considered the changeable circumstances of life to be <fragile> as the threads of a spider's web and devoted herself to the arena of ascetic exercise,[74] covering herself with dust <in her struggles> against the Enemy, finally overcoming him, *finishing* with glory *the course* she had promised <to follow> and putting on *the crown* of immortality in death.[75] <In heaven> she joins the dancing throng of maidens in the bride-chamber and keeps her lamp tirelessly furnished with the oil of good deeds.[76] Child, how fortunate you are in parents who have been proclaimed such cham-

---

[70] Cf. 2 Cor. 6:4–7.

[71] For the translation of this passage, cf. Lemerle, *Byz. Humanism,* 148–49. Ignatios exploits a bilingual pun between his term for offices of the palace (τοῖς . . . μυστηρίοις, also at 142.21) and the Latin loan word used in Greek to designate an imperial secretary, ἀσηκρῆτις.

[72] Cf. Ps. 118 (119):105.

[73] Ps. 70 (71):18.

[74] I.e., she entered a convent (cf. Alexander, *Nicephorus,* 56).

[75] This passage recalls 2 Tim. 4:7–8.

[76] The reference is to the parable of the wise and foolish virgins, Mt. 25:1–13.

pions of piety! Parents, how fortunate you are in such a child who has attained moral virtue![77]

This account of the parents who nurtured this righteous man must now conclude, although it falls far short of what they deserve. However, it remains to relate how Nikephoros established himself on the foundation of virtue and *set the ways* [of the Lord] *in his heart,*[78] in the words of the prophet [David]. Still, the writer reels under the suspicion that he speaks in a manner unworthy <of his subject> although the fairminded reader does not even expect an account worthy <of that subject>. Therefore, in my own small and modest [p. 145] way, I shall muster my abundance of inadequacy and try to give my whole attention to some single part of Nikephoros' accomplishments. I shall try to make the whole known to you by means of a part, *like a lion by means of its claws.*[79]

Both the emperor and the imperial court looked upon him as a distinguished speaker and a sort of divine embellishment and glory, <regarding him even more highly than> Philip <regarded> the orator from Paiania.[80] For <Nikephoros> was not a garrulous fellow who declaimed a speech consisting of pure flattery in order to say what people wanted to hear and capture praise for himself. When a speech was made according to all the rhetorical formulae, he countered with a speech that avoided cultivating the audience with sweet and delicately refined expressions, and rather deliberated cogently the best course of action in a simple and relaxed <manner>. When he saw that a party of those who adhered to the true faith had suffered shipwreck due to those who then controlled the helm of the Roman Empire,[81] he calmed down the storm to the best of his ability. For in their arrogance <those rulers> set aside

[77] Perhaps reading εἰς ἀρετῆς ἐπίτευξιν for εἰς ἀρετὴν ἐπιτεύξεως, at the suggestion of L. Rydén.

[78] Ps. 83 (84):6 (version by translator).

[79] "It is possible to get to know a lion from its claws and a spring from a little taste" is the full form of this proverb, explained by the medieval commentator as "applicable to situations where one becomes acquainted with a whole thing from some small [indication of it]." Cf. Leutsch-Schneidewin, *Corpus* 2:409, no. 57.

[80] The Attic deme Paiania was the ancestral home of Demosthenes (384–322 B.C.), Athens' greatest orator. Demosthenes and Philip II of Macedon, father of Alexander the Great, maintained a relationship of mutual respect and antagonism.

[81] The Byzantines considered their empire to be the continuation of ancient Rome.

a tradition that the Church had inherited blamelessly from the beginning through apostolic and patristic ordinance, that is, I mean to say, the making and veneration of the holy icons. They seemed actually afraid to see that Christ is represented with distinctive physical features, and attacked that same beauty like swine.[82] They defiled every depiction of the God-man, of Christ, our true God, Who bore our weaknesses in His flesh; they defiled the likenesses of the bodies of Christ's entirely blameless mother and of the <saints>, who have pleased Christ of old; they decided to assemble in the Queen of Cities a local faction of bishops, or, to tell the truth, a Sanhedrin of Pharisees.[83] For while <the Sanhedrin> railed against Christ and brought upon itself the charge of killing God, these men had long since gained an enviable reputation for making war on Christ, because they looked askance at His bodily representation. They assembled no proof that conformed with the recommendations of Holy Scripture, but instead they stupidly snipped out excerpts from those utterances of the church fathers that opposed the <pagan> idols. [p. 146] By means of vague definitions, they misused what the Fathers were trying to say and shifted the boundaries of the Fathers' <exact meaning> in their writings. <In this way,> they wrote down their own loathsome and outrageous tenets.

But the time came when the balance of heavenly justice, which abhors all evildoers, terminated the lives and the offices of those who raged against the Church, or, rather, who stitched up evil in opposition to the holy faith which we profess. Then [Irene], whose name means "peace," together with her son Constantine, received the imperial scepter <that is conferred> from God as an inheritance from Constantine's father.[84] Irene was a mere woman, but she possessed both the love of God and firmness of understanding, if it is right to give the name of woman to one who surpassed even men in the piety of her understanding; she was God's instrument in His love and pity for mankind, reconciling into orthodoxy the perversity and dissension that insinuated itself

---

[82] The tendency of swine to trample pearls (and anything else of value) was well known to readers of the Bible (cf. Mt. 7:6).

[83] Ignatios equates the iconoclastic Council of 754 with the tribunal that condemned Jesus.

[84] At the death of Leo IV in 780, his widow Irene ruled as regent for their young son Constantine [VI], born in 771.

like a serpent into the Church at that time. Therefore she carried out the purpose of God, Who protects <us> still, and she decreed that an assembly of holy men[85] from the very ends of the inhabited world should gather in the metropolitan see of the Bithynian city of Nicaea in order to remove this pestilential disease. Tarasios, most holy patriarch of the Queen <of Cities>, presided over this assembly, and also present were the most blessed legates from Hadrian, <patriarch> of the older Rome,[86] from Politian, <patriarch> of Alexandria, from Theodoretos, <patriarch> of Antioch,[87] and from Elias, <patriarch> of Aelia <Capitolina>.[88] Nikephoros was honored above many of his contemporaries <by being chosen> to travel in company with these eminent prelates. He was entrusted with the imperial proclamation to that holy synod in which he announced the pure <form> of the faith to all. For this purpose he sat as a colleague with the holy council, even before <he himself had put on> his holy garment,[89] and proclaimed clearly as if from a high vantage point the ancient <practice of> making and venerating the holy images.[90] This was the first[91] struggle over <the proper> reverence to God accomplished by the blessed <man>. It was his first prize <gained> in contest, and <he won> a crown of victory that cannot be taken away, but is more precious by far than the <crowns> of wool, of wild olive, and of [wild] celery [p. 147] and <all the prizes> with which the ancients thought fit to reward

[85] The Second Council of Nicaea, 787.

[86] The Byzantines called Constantinople "The New Rome." Hadrian I was pope 772–795.

[87] Politian was patriarch of Alexandria ca. 767–801 (*DHGE* 2:366) or 768–813 (V. Grumel, *La chronologie byzantine* [Paris, 1958], 443); Theodoretos was patriarch of Antioch from sometime before 787–? (*DHGE* 3:699). Information about these patriarchal sees after they came under Arab domination is sometimes scanty, uncertain, and contradictory. See, for example, Ch. A. Papadopoulos, Ἱστορία τῆς Ἐκκλησίας Ἀντιοχείας (Alexandria, Egypt, 1951), 776–86, on the sources for the reign of Theodoretos, patriarch of Antioch.

[88] Elias II was patriarch of Jerusalem (Aelia Capitolina) at the end of the 8th century; his exact dates are uncertain (cf. Grumel, *Chronologie,* 452).

[89] I.e., "even before he took orders in the Church," or "while still a layman."

[90] For a slightly different translation of the passage from "Nikephoros was honored . . . the holy images" and commentary, see Alexander, *Nicephorus,* 60–61.

[91] Reading οὗτος α' (i.e., πρῶτος) with de Boor for the manuscript's οὗτος ὁ.

contestants.[92] That assembly of the church fathers, selected by God and inspired by the breezes of the Holy Spirit, now brought into the safe harbor of orthodoxy the ship of our faith. The garment of the Church was once again embellished with holy representations, and the labor pangs of heresy produced a stillborn offspring. Then the great Nikephoros brought forth the sounding board of victory and struck up a piercing <battle> tune of the <war god> Enyalios [Ares] against the opponents of the <true> faith. <Nikephoros> confirmed that Christ was uncircumscribed in His single and intangible divine nature, but circumscribed and capable of depiction in His tangible human nature <that is> compounded <with the divine>. <He asserted that> the representation in images would follow closely these <human traits>, so that we might escape the fantastical hallucinations of those who follow the tenets of Mani.[93] He continued to say these things and to hold these views as he went about his business <as *a secretis*> in the confidential imperial service,[94] as they say, and was involved in matters of the fisc.

Since <Nikephoros> understood very well the mystical[95] injunction that bid him to *take heed for himself* and to be devoted only to God[96] (for thus we separate ourselves from material <things> and are borne in this life toward God), he bent every effort to take <himself> away into the solitary contemplative life beloved <by monks>. He made entreaties and devised every sort of supplication to persuade those who drew him back into the turbulence of secular life to allow him to gain his purpose. Indeed he persuaded them, and achieved such of his desires as had not been accomplished. He cared little for the seething city center and all the activity swirling about in it, but crowned the

---

[92] Victors in the ancient Olympian Games were crowned with wild olive wreaths; wild celery leaf wreaths were awarded to victors in the Pythian and Nemean Games. Plato (*Republic* 398a) describes rewarding a poet with a garland of wool.

[93] Manichaeans believed in an essential opposition between Spirit, which was good, and Matter, which was evil.

[94] See Introduction, 26.

[95] "Mystical" (μυστικωτέραν) puns upon the "confidential" (μυστικῇ) service mentioned just above.

[96] An oblique reference to Jesus' commandment to his disciples at Mk. 12:29–30, "Hear, O Israel . . . thou shalt love the Lord thy God with all thy heart, and with all thy soul, and with all thy mind, and with all thy strength." The New Testament expression "take heed for [one]self" (cf. Lk. 17:3, 21:34; Acts 5:35, 20:28) frequently occurs in the hagiographical tradition applied to a saint's behavior before God.

glory of office with a wool fillet[97] <and renounced that recognition>, bidding farewell to all that enticed him to folly, excess, and undue physical comfort. He then went away to a ridge facing the Bosporos,[98] taking no more than Elijah's sheepskin <cloak>, that is, no more than poverty, to <the mountain which was> like Mt. Carmel <for him>.[99] Poverty truly constructs the first dwelling place for virtue; it [p. 148] bestows immortality upon the one who acquires it and who <thereby> eagerly embraces the angelic way of life. Thus <Nikephoros>, this rich merchant, took <poverty> as his partner for gain and loved it greatly, <more> than other men <love> the <precious> stones *of Ophir*[100] and the silks of China. He hastened off then to his new Mt. Carmel, so to speak, which revealed itself unlovely because of its harsh and uneven ground and completely barren for cultivation because of the steepness of the ridge; it was a thirsty <land>, not softened by any water, and unless rain water was brought to it, deprived <even> of that by virtue of its precipitous slope.

Why do I need to elaborate at great length upon the unpleasant <aspect> of the place and its inconvenience for dwelling in comfort? For anyone who is there and wishes to can test and examine the <particulars> of the site instead of just hearing about them, <learning> what sort of place it was and its later transformation. For <Nikephoros> stripped away its wild and uncultivated <character> like a rotting and ragged garment, and replaced its bar-

---

[97] Perhaps an allusion to the famous passage in Plato's *Republic* (398a) where the poet is reverenced like a holy person, anointed with fragrant oil, crowned with a wool fillet and dismissed from the ideal state because his talents are not appropriate to it. That the wool fillet conveyed extraordinary honor to its recipient is plain from the remark of the Neoplatonic commentator Proklos, who observed that Plato's poet received ritual treatment accorded to the gods in their temples (G. Kroll, *Procli Diadochi in Platonis Rem Publicam commentarii* [Leipzig, 1899], 42.5–7), and from Pausanias' comment (X. 24, 6) that untreated wool (strands) were placed upon the sacred "omphalos" stone at Delphi at the time of festivals.

[98] According to Nikephoros' *Letter to Pope Leo III* (PG 100:176A), his retreat was apparently near the Sea of Marmara not far from Constantinople; the text is uncertain (cf. Alexander, *Nicephorus*, 62 and n. 2). For the possible identification of the monastery he founded here, see notes 403 and 404 below.

[99] The Old Testament prophet Elijah received prophecy and power from the Lord on Mt. Carmel (3 Ki. [1 Ki.] 18:42) and took only a sheepskin cloak with him during his flight into the wilderness (3 Ki. [1 Ki.] 19:13).

[100] Cf. 3 Ki. [1 Ki.] 10:11.

renness with a reputation for fruitfulness, its aridity with the abundant rains of heaven. <He accomplished this> by enriching <the land> with an abundance of interconnected cisterns branching through the hollow rocks; he thus surpassed the delight of <King> Alcinous' audience hall and of Xerxes' golden plane tree, to the same extent that truth is more worthy of regard than mythical fictions.[101] Consecrated by martyrs' shrines that are completely decorated with <images of> their holy struggles, <the spot> imitates faithfully *the paradise of God,* as Scripture <says>.[102] For even before trying <to live there>, who would not admire <the site's> capacity to support a <saint's> way of life, and its convenience as a place to live? Then he appointed the place a monastery of holy men, <dedicated> to the unceasing praise of the Almighty. Together with them, he himself persisted day and night in prayerful and holy speech and in taking delight in a most excellent degree of temperate conduct. For he devoted himself to reading the Scriptures and to <secular> studies, refusing to accept <dainties from the> table of Syracuse[103] [p. 149] or even so much as to hear <of them>, and nourishing himself instead with a <diet> sufficient <only> to maintain life.

But since I have mentioned his studies, I consider it neither without charm nor a redundant digression also to remark upon both his exactitude and his excellence in these matters. For as well as studying Holy Scripture, he also acquired familiarity with secular <rhetorical education>, partly out of a desire to enhance the persuasive <quality> of his <own> teaching and partly out of a desire to expose the implausibility of <heretical> error. Now moral virtue requires the comprehension of what is just and unjust law, in order to measure out for listeners which of two alternatives is the right response <in a situation>; so also, it is fitting that a complete education brings to teaching a knowledge of each of these two areas, <secular and scriptural>. But God forbid that we regard the two <areas, secular and scriptural,> as alternatives

---

[101] Alcinous, king of the mythical Phaeacians, welcomed Odysseus in his fabulous palace (Homer, *Od.* 7:81–102). Xerxes, king of Persia, encountered a plane tree so beautiful that he decorated it with gold and assigned it a guard in perpetuity (Herodotus, book 7, chap. 31).

[102] Rev. 2:7.

[103] For this proverb, describing a luxurious banquet table, see Leutsch-Schneidewin, *Corpus* 2:213 (Macarius, 7.92).

<to one another>! For the handmaiden is not equal <in status> to the mistress; indeed, *the son of [the] bondwoman shall not inherit with [the] son* of the free woman (to cite the words spoken to Abraham <by Sarah>).[104] For it is clear even to those with only a modest knowledge of the art <of rhetoric> how great <an authority Nikephoros> was on grammar, its component parts, and the logical <principles> by which correct and incorrect writing is distinguished, by which the <classical> Greek language is governed, and by which metrical elements are brought into harmonious order. It is <no less> easy to see what a reputation he gained for sweet and gracious speech <as a performer> on the rhetoricians' many stringed lyres. For he steadfastly rejected the affected and verbose style that leads to aimless sophistic babble and chatter; he used a sweet and graceful style <observing linguistic> clarity and purity.

He also <was remarkable> in acquiring knowledge of the mathematical quartet, which is constituted of continuous and discrete wholes.[105] For <the objects of mathematics> are either subject to motion and constitute astronomy, or without motion and constitute geometry, or [p. 150] in relationship <to matter> and constitute music, or not related <to matter> and constitute arithmetic. <Nikephoros> attained such <a level of proficiency in these disciplines> through diligent study that he achieved first rank in them all, having learned one as if it were all, and all as if they were one. He tuned an elegant lyre, not the kind <used by> Pythagoras of Samos nor the clever <fellow> Aristoxenus, but <a psaltery> with 150 strings.[106] <Nikephoros> played this

---

[104] Abraham had two sons, Ishmael, born to the Egyptian slave Hagar, and Isaac, born to Abraham's wife Sarah (see Gen. 16; 17; 21:1–21). Isaac enjoyed special favor from God (see Gen. 17:19–21), while Ishmael grew up honored but in exile (see Gen. 21:10–21). Sarah's words at Gen. 21:10 are quoted almost verbatim by Ignatios.

[105] The so-called quadrivium of mathematical studies (arithmetic, geometry, music, and astronomy), complemented by the three branches of literary studies (grammar, rhetoric, and dialectic), composed the ideal of general education formulated in Hellenistic times and practiced through late antiquity; cf. H. I. Marrou, *A History of Education in Antiquity* (New York, 1956), 177, and Lemerle, *Byz. Humanism,* 150–54. The conception of mathematics presented here is based on Aristotle's *Categories* (cf. *Cat.* 4 b 20–5 a 26) and was elaborated by late antique commentators, e.g., ps.-Elias; cf. L. G. Westerink, *Pseudo-Elias (Pseudo-David). Lectures on Porphyry's Isagoge* (Amsterdam, 1967), 32 ff, esp. 36.

[106] Both Pythagoras (fl. 531 B.C.) and Aristoxenus (b. 375–360 B.C.) were noted musical theorists. A pun contrasts Nikephoros' familiarity with the psalter, which contains

<instrument> and protected his listeners <as> of old from Saul's disease.[107] He tamed the most savage tyrant,[108] who was strangled by the spirit of error and raged like an unrepentant drunkard against the Incarnation of Christ; he delivered the flock <of the Church> from this <tyrant's> destructiveness.

After <Nikephoros> had made distinct and thorough acquaintance with these four handmaidens of true knowledge [astronomy, geometry, music, and arithmetic], he proceeded directly and unerringly to their mistress, I mean to philosophy, and to the topics considered <in philosophy>.[109] For he examined what the definitions of <philosophy> are, how many <may be> reasonably <enumerated>, and what the particular nature of <each of> them is;[110] <he investigated> what sort <of thing> serves as a logical subject and what the <logical> predicate is, and whether it is predicated of everything or of nothing, or in general, and <other> similar <questions>. <He studied> what the elements <of proof> purport to clarify according to <philosophers>, and whether <"elements"> is a homonym [denoting things having the same name but different natures and definitions in the case] of physics and geometry

---

some 150 psalms (Alexander, *Nicephorus,* 57), with the inferior wisdom of these pagan savants. Ignatios may also refer to Nikephoros' skill in playing the Byzantine stringed instrument that descended from the ancient psaltery. The ancient instrument had seven strings in Pythagoras' time and as many as twelve in Aristoxenus'; the Byzantine psaltery could have as many as thirty or forty strings (S. Karakases, Ἑλληνικὰ μουσικὰ ὄργανα [Athens, 1970], 47–48 and pl. 35).

[107] The shepherd boy David soothed King Saul's madness by playing the harp (1 Ki. [1 Sam.] 16:14–23).

[108] The "tyrant" is probably Leo IV or possibly Constantine V (Alexander, *Nicephorus,* 57).

[109] I am grateful to John Duffy for his suggestions on the literary antecedents and translation of this vexed passage. It appears to be a list of chapter headings copied by Ignatios from an elementary textbook of logic and physics that has not been identified; see Alexander, *Nicephorus,* 57 and n. 3, and Lemerle, *Byz. Humanism,* 150–52. The topics and terminology derive from Aristotle's writings on logic (i.e., dialectic) and physics as presented and elaborated by such late antique commentators as ps.-Elias, Alexander of Aphrodisias, Simplikios, Philoponos, and Themistios. The study of logic was the basis of philosophical studies in Byzantium and constituted the first stage of a philosophical curriculum in Byzantine higher education. For an introduction to the principles of Aristotelian logic, see D. Ross, *Aristotle*[5] (London, 1953), 21–61.

[110] Philosophical studies traditionally began with the six standard definitions of philosophy.

alone, <or in other disciplines as well>. <He investigated> how many <kinds of> premisses <of a syllogism> there are, in what way they are convertible, <and> what the power of a contradiction <of a proposition is>; <he studied> what kinds <of terms> are attached in predication, what further specifications <there are>, what is analogous to the limitless as defined by <philosophers>, and how many modes of syllogisms <there are>. <He studied> the kind and number of figures <of a syllogism>, what sort is hypothetical, what sort is categorical, and in what way they differ; <he investigated> whether the <argument> *reductio ad impossibile* acts as proof in every <case>, <and> in what way and how frequently <these methods of argumentation> can be combined; <he studied> how one can draw a <syllogistic> conclusion and accomplish the reduction <of a syllogism>, <and> how a fallacious argument is formulated—what kind is sophistical and how it can be at once false and plausible. <He inquired into> what sort <of syllogism> has only one premiss, how the dialectical <syllogism> proves in as much as possible[111] things which are <not necessarily but> probably true, and what an argument by induction is in the case of things that are probably true. <He considered> the demonstrative <syllogism> and what sort of force it has [p. 151] to seek after truth from the weaker <arguments>. <He examined> which sorts of these <premisses> are problem<atic>, which are axiom<atic>, and which are so to speak like axioms, <and> what matter, mixtures, and combinations they admit of. <He studied> what the first principles of physics are and how they are indemonstrable; <he learned> what the state of being stationary is, in how many ways identity occurs, and that otherness occurs in the categories of place, relation, manner, and time. (However, the emanation of the <first> principles is continuous, and there are no definitions in this continuity.) <He studied> what motion[112] is what sort of instrumental <cause>, what is a generative <cause>, what is a predisposing one, and what sort is extruded <as a result>, and through what <it is extruded>, and at what point it converges by choice or by force. <He studied> what it is that retains the qualities <of a thing> and from what sort of negation those <philosophers> claim these things <come into existence> and if <they ever come into being> from the entirely nonexistent. <He inquired> how these things

---

[111] Reading διαλεκτικός for the printed λεκτικός and ἐνδεχομένως for the printed ἐνδεχόμενος (Lemerle, *Byz. Humanism,* 150 n. 93).

[112] Reading ἡ κίνησις with John Duffy for the printed ὁ κινήσας.

move into generation and substantification from their opposites, and how once again they are removed and destroyed by <those> opposites.

After investigating these and similar <topics> with the greatest possible degree of mental assiduity and perfect discipline, and tasting their benefits *with the <mere> tip of his finger*,[113] <Nikephoros> devoted himself to the much-honored practice of silently contemplating <God> and demonstrated a humility that raised him toward heaven. For perfect spiritual knowledge in a man is to attribute perfect mental apprehension to the Almighty with a thankful heart, and to know that he has not understood what creation is in essence. In this way, while he became <thoroughly> competent in his studies through the force of <his own> nature, the inclination of <his own> mind, and the assent of God's grace, he no less hastened toward the steps that lead to the divine virtues. For he did not consider distinction in those <learned endeavors> to be an obstacle to <his attaining> virtue, but he rather took an appropriate and orderly route to strive for success in both <learning and spirituality> and attained perfection in each.

He took as his consort chastity, which he cultivated in opposition to natural <inclination> by contenting himself with very little and by strict self-control, and he diminished the swelling and ungovernable passions that attack *the navel of the belly.*[114] He also achieved freedom from anger by virtue of his inborn gentleness and presented himself as totally mild mannered to everyone, [p. 152] thereby driving away the ugly countenance of anger. For the irrational temper <of the soul> that resembles a snake's found no place in him, but he rather exerted himself forcefully against only the serpent which caused <our> fall <in the Garden of Eden>. He set great store by voluntary poverty, which prepares a man to strive for the immaterial, but <did> not <store it> in the Cynic philosopher's barrel.[115] Rather, <like a river> constantly expanding with ever-flowing charitable contributions to the poor, he expressed his scorn for money and turned away from the way leading toward it. He made it his

---

[113] A proverbial expression found in Prokopios of Gaza (A. Garzya, R.-J. Loenertz, *Procopii Gazaei epistolae et declamationes* [Ettal, 1963], *ep.* 120.4), and Constantine Manasses (*Breviarium historiae metricum,* ed. I. Bekker [Bonn, 1837], 54.1207).

[114] I.e., the private parts; cf. Job 40:11.

[115] Diogenes of Sinope (ca. 400–323 B.C.) advocated a life of natural and unconventional simplicity achieved in the cheapest way possible. He soon gained legendary status as the practitioner of such bizarre disciplines as eating raw meat and living in a barrel.

proper practice to avoid ostentatious actions, gaining thereby a clear conscience and not only equipping *his right hand* for *almsgiving* but also confiding *knowledge* of this <deed> to *his left hand*,[116] so that he attained complete immunity from the diseased and insatiable craving for money.

As a result, <God's> grace, through the insistent pressure of the emperors [Nikephoros I and Staurakios], deemed <Nikephoros> worthy to supervise the largest poorhouse in the Queen <of Cities>, giving him advance training through this assignment and, as it were, handing over through a partial responsibility the governance of the universal church.[117] But as for these events and <the circumstances> attending them, let others tell the story, who have the love and desire to collect <Nikephoros'> superior deeds just as a bee <collects nectar> from a rose garden rich in blossoms, and who wish with words to hoard away the quality of these <deeds> in the sweetness of the honeycomb that is divine imitation. For I think that no one will ever be at a loss for <deeds of Nikephoros> like this, since they are numerous and magnificent and do not allow <us> to prefer one over another, for his every achievement was of the highest degree. But we shall leave off dragging the reader into a virtual state of nausea with our excessive speech and proceed, if God grants it, to the next <topic>.

<The patriarch> Tarasios[118] had been the Church's unsleeping torchbearer; he had steered the ship of faith well, caused it <to ride> above the surging seas of heresy, and in the best way possible brought it to harbor with its cargo of orthodoxy's goods. <Tarasios> now [p. 153] departed from the ephemeral <world> toward the better portion <of eternal life>;[119] he who was a Father <of the Church> joined the <church> fathers, he who took the office of patriarch in defense of truth <joined> the patriarchs, he who honored the divine in a blessed manner during his life <joined> the blessed ones,

---

[116] Cf. Mt. 6:3.

[117] The largest poorhouse in Constantinople was near the church of Sts. Archippos and Philemon in the Elaia region (above modern Galata). The Byzantine Church and State built and maintained poorhouses (*ptocheia/ptochotropheia*) throughout the empire, placing each under the supervision of an official who enjoyed considerable ecclesiastical prestige. After serving as director of the poorhouse mentioned here, Nikephoros became patriarch of Constantinople. Cf. D. J. Constantelos, *Byzantine Philanthropy and Social Welfare* (New Brunswick, N.J., 1968), 257–69, esp. 265–66.

[118] 784–806.

[119] 18 February 806. Cf. Alexander, *Nicephorus,* 65.

and he who imitated Christ, the chief shepherd, <joined> the true shepherds [i.e., bishops]. <For Tarasios> *called by name* and knew *his sheep*,[120] and frightened off the wolves with the staff of his words, shepherding <his flock> into the sheepfold of the correct confession of faith.[121] This heavenly man lived on earth but vied with the angels to the best of his ability; <now> even after placing in God's hands the reins of his priestly functions together with his irreproachable soul, he entreated God with pure prayer, as I think, that the worthy person should head the patriarchate and be proclaimed world famous herald of the Church that is near to Christ <Himself>. For <Tarasios> had labored and sweated much to cut out by the root the thorn of heresy growing in <the Church>, <to use> the guidance of the <Holy> Spirit to remove the obstacles in our path and the occasions for sin, to renew the good earth of faith with a spiritual plow, and to *sow* the symbols of Christ's Incarnation, which were handed down from God, not *in the wayside, on the rocks,* nor *among thorns,* but *upon ground good* and fruitful, and, as the parable says, *bearing an hundredfold.*[122] <Tarasios therefore>, even after death, desired and longed to see the one who would succeed him in his <task of> cultivation, and he was not disappointed in his request. For God, Who is always *found* by those who *seek,* Who *opens* the door unto those who *knock,*[123] and Who fulfills true requests, clearly indicated by His divine finger and by <the Holy> Spirit that the one worthy of holy anointing <as patriarch was> Nikephoros. <God> made His revelation quite clearly to the emperor of the time, who shared the name <Nikephoros>[124] and was without blemish in matters concerning the true faith.

In fact, <this emperor> was a most shrewd man, if ever anyone was. After much searching, he was able to install both as bridegroom and also as marriage broker for the widowed <Church> a man competent to *hold fast the faithful word as he hath been taught*[125] [p. 154] and to walk most prudently in the footsteps of the previous shepherd [Tarasios]. In order to do this, he

---

[120] Cf. Jn. 10:3.

[121] Cf. Jn. 10:3–15.

[122] Cf. Lk. 8:5–8 (also Mt. 13:3–8 and Mk. 4:3–8) and Gen. 26:12.

[123] Cf. Mt. 7:7–8 and Lk. 11:9–10.

[124] Emperor Nikephoros I (802–811).

[125] Tit. 1:9.

consulted with priests, monks, and those[126] members of the Senate whom he deemed notable and eminent, so that his <own> choice might also accord with the selection of the majority, which is most just and carries certainty through the assent of the Holy Spirit. Now it is impossible for mere humans to escape what is in accord with divine grace, but <these> men shattered <any> unanimous <decision> by disagreeing among themselves, and in a mosaic of votes for individual candidates,[127] each one drew forth not the person whom Heaven's influence sketched with divine foreknowledge, but rather the person whom each one's individual will fashioned and promoted. But the activity of <divine> intelligence brought to the emperor's mind a picture[128] of Nikephoros as chief shepherd <of the Church>, and <the emperor> pressed all <the others> to look to <Nikephoros>, recalling <to them> the glorious accomplishments of his virtues, his crucial <contribution> in both spiritual and secular writings, his humble and gentle character, and his purity *in conscience, void of offense toward* anyone.[129] All in all, the <emperor> deluged everyone's ears with a thick snowstorm of those imperial arguments; without any threat of force, he scooped them all into a unanimous vote <like fish> into a net. From that time, on every lip and on every tongue Nikephoros was proclaimed patriarch.

The emperor then dispatched men to <Nikephoros> to deliver the message that he should bestow his presence upon the Queen <of Cities> without any hesitation or delay. <Nikephoros> chose that *obedience* praised <in Scripture> over *the disobedience* which deserves blame[130] and, although unwillingly, he followed those who wished to conduct <him to the emperor>. When the emperor's quest had been accomplished and he could see the object

---

[126] Reading τοῖς τῆς for the printed τῆς.

[127] In using the extremely rare word ψηφολογέω ("make a mosaic"), Ignatios puns upon the more common verb ψηφοφορέω ("cast a vote"). The vocabulary that follows plays further upon the idea of visual representation (i.e., ὑπέγραφε "sketched," ἀνετυποῦτο "fashioned," ὑπεζωγράφει "pictured"). Alexander (*Nicephorus,* 67) translates "each one voted for his own candidate."

[128] Alternatively one could translate: "but the activity of his mind caused the emperor to conjure up a picture . . . ."

[129] Cf. Acts 24:16.

[130] Cf. Rom. 5:19.

of his desires with his very eyes, he is said to have had this conversation with
<Nikephoros>: "O man experienced in God's <ways>, if it were <my de-
sire> to disdain divine commands and to ignore their fulfillment out of sheer
indifference, <I could have done it>: there was a steeply sloping and *broad
way*[131] by which <it was possible> to choose as bishop for the Queen <of
Cities> some chance person who presented no qualification for the <patri-
arch's> tribune except the desire <to have it>. But [p. 155] <I am afraid>
because I have been admonished by Holy Scripture about the character required in one who will be ordained <bishop> and who must promote others
to this <office>—he must be lofty in virtue and unimpaired <in morality>,
one who *keeps* <true> *knowledge* with *his lips* and *bears in his mouth the law
he has sought,* and who is called *because of this a messenger of the Lord almighty.*[132] I fear that I shall incur punishment for indifference by ignoring that
holy admonition, and that I shall call down upon myself the curse threatened
<by God upon the disobedient>.[133] Now then, since God has commended to
your hands the priesthood and <given you> the reins in this heavenly contest,
do not reject the summons, but undertake the holy *race, looking unto* the common benefit.[134] For we are well aware that we have encouraged you, as your
teacher and ours, <the apostle> Paul <says>, not to make a show of *boxing
with the air* nor to *run without understanding.*[135] Rather, because you have already accomplished the *subjection of the body* in order to *preach to others,*[136]
let the *trial* <of your faith> also shine out more <brightly> *than gold.*[137] Do
not strive to pray alone to God for your salvation, *nor to seek your own*[138] in a
solitary manner of life, but rather strive *to obtain salvation for all.*[139]

"The Church is aptly considered a most beautiful bride; her obedient ear

---

[131] Cf. Mt. 7:13.
[132] Cf. Mal. 2:7.
[133] Cf. Deut. 11:26–28.
[134] Cf. Heb. 12:1–2.
[135] Cf. 1 Cor. 9:26.
[136] Cf. 1 Cor. 9:27.
[137] Cf. 1 Pet. 1:7.
[138] Cf. 1 Cor. 10:24.
[139] Cf. 2 Tim. 2:10.

is looped with the pearls of correct and unsullied doctrines, her head is encircled with a crown of delights gleaming with the writings of the <church> fathers as if with exceedingly precious gems, and there hangs from her neck a breast ornament like a crescent of pure gold, <symbolizing> the decrees of the seven divinely inspired <Church> councils. She is clothed in all glory from within, and <wears garments> embroidered with the holy and sacred images in accordance with the Gospels. Do not let a fellow of lecherous habits court <the Church> as his bride and corrupt the beauty of even her legitimate children by *sowing* the seeds of heresy as *tares* in her;[140] do not let him make a pretense of sound <orthodox> faith by <wearing> the fleece of a tame sheep, then lay bare *the wolf* [p. 156] of heretical belief *within* <himself>[141] and drive the flock into the mountains and places where the Lord cannot care for them. You have then Christ, *the lamb of God,*[142] our *true God,*[143] as your helper <in gaining> a shepherd's skill, and you have His cross as a staff to support the flock <in maintaining> correct doctrine. <Therefore> do not turn a deaf ear to your summons <from God> nor scorn our supplication, lest this bring God's wrath upon you."

The emperor's admonitions struck <Nikephoros'> mind like missiles launched from the heart, and he spoke saying, "O emperor, in my opinion the man worthy to care for the spiritual flock <of Christ> is one who has not closely associated himself with the world, but has a steadfast longing infused <within him> to grasp the vaults of heaven, where no carnal matter attaches itself.[144] <He should be one> who has not been shown liable to the prophets' threats against the shepherds[145] <but> is eager to *lay down his* own *life for his sheep* in imitation of Christ, *the chief shepherd* and sole high priest,[146] one who

---

[140] Cf. Mt. 13:25.

[141] Cf. Mt. 7:15.

[142] Jn. 1:29, 36.

[143] 1 John 5:20.

[144] Reading καθαπτούσης for the printed καταπτώσης. A. Alexakis has suggested an alternative emendation to καταπτοούσης.

[145] Ezekiel (Ezek. 34:1–10) and Jeremiah (Jer. 23:1–4) prophesied God's wrath against the leaders of Israel, chastising them as negligent shepherds who had failed to care for God's people and let them wander astray.

[146] Cf. Jn. 10:11 and 1 Pet. 5:4.

does not *approach the sheepfold* of the Church *through the side gate to kill and destroy* with *stealthy* teachings, but has taken care *for life* and salvation[147] and for *engendering the young* in the sheepfolds of faith.[148] <He should be one> who shares in every custom and step and glance and pursuit of those he shepherds, and who is adorned by his pastoral concern for the care of each <of them>, commending <his flock> on most occasions to the staff that raises them up and supports them <against> falling, but on some few occasions using the rod that smites without a blow and keeps the mind unharmed by any resultant suffering.[149] I am unprepared for this war, and unwilling to dispatch myself against unseen and irreconcilable soldiers who are constantly mustered <for battle>.[150] I am <mere> flesh, and am inadequate to take up spiritual weapons <against those> whose attack cannot be escaped even if one were to protect oneself on all sides to the greatest possible degree." [p. 157]

The emperor *interrupted him in answering,*[151] "Do not let any disputatious word or speech of yours balk at the holy yoke of Christ.[152] For the Word Himself, as I already said, will guard you while sharing your tasks as shepherd and vigorously helping you; He will provide you with every protection against the things which appeared as difficulties up until now." <Nikephoros>, who had always obeyed every divine <bidding>, no less obeyed this one. He begged the emperor as an immediate favor <to allow him> to exchange the clothing of a lay person for a monk's angelic way of life, adding more rigid discipline to discipline and adding a more laborious perfection to the labors he had already virtuously accomplished. <The emperor> assented and wisely decided that the hair clipped from that holy head <during tonsuring> should be collected by the hands of his son and co-emperor as if it were the solemn glory of the purple robes that clothed <the emperors>.[153] For it was necessary that the hair nourished at the summit of divine virtues should be guarded by

---

[147] Cf. Jn. 10:1, 10.

[148] A reference to Jacob's ingenuity in increasing his flocks, as described in Gen. 30:35–43, esp. 39.

[149] This reference to the bishop's "rod and staff" recalls Ps. 22 (23):4.

[150] Cf. Eph. 6:12.

[151] Homer, *Il.* 1:292.

[152] Cf. Mt. 11:29–30.

[153] Staurakios participated as Nikephoros' sponsor in the ceremony that made him a monk on 5 April 806 (cf. Alexander, *Nicephorus,* 68–69).

the most prominent of noble men, and one who was about to ascend to a bishop's honor needed to be distinguished by an outstanding honor. Then after <Nikephoros'> initiation as a monk had proceeded in accord with the prescriptions of the wise Dionysios,[154] and after his consecration in holy orders had proceeded step by step in the sequence <determined by> holy law,[155] his ordination to the sacred episcopal office immediately followed these <other orders>. When and how <that occurred> I am now about to explain.

The emperor assembled with his imperial council in the greatest of churches [St. Sophia], to celebrate the liturgy of the awe-inspiring <feast of> the Resurrection;[156] the sun's golden illumination which shone full <in> that holy place proclaimed the radiant light expected in eternity, and the whole company of clergy was assembled in their white robes. That was the time when <Nikephoros> hastened to <ordination by> the imposition of the <bishops'> hands[157] after taking into his <own> hands the holy document <professing> his faith, which he had already prepared and acknowledged in his heart and by his speech, and which he had read out to the clergy in his <diocese of Constantinople>. [p. 158] <Nikephoros> invoked this <profession of faith> as a genuine witness should he ever violate any of the declarations <made> in it, but <he asserted> that in this true and sincere act of service <to God> he stood ready for the terrifying and glorious <second> coming of our great God and our Savior. After the ceremony <of> his <ordination>

---

[154] A series of influential theological works were attributed to the unknown 5th-century author who claimed to be "Dionysios the Areopagite," St. Paul's disciple (cf. Acts 17:34). In the *Ecclesiastical Hierarchy* (PG 3:533A–C), pseudo-Dionysios prescribed a ceremony for the initiation of a monk in which the candidate stood with the officiating priest at the altar, professed his willingness to accept the monastic way of life, underwent tonsure, exchanged his secular garments for monastic ones, and received the Eucharist.

[155] The sequence of major clerical orders proceeded from deacon to priest, and finally to bishop. The rapidity of Nikephoros' progression through these orders was highly unusual, but not unparalleled (cf. Alexander, *Nicephorus,* 69).

[156] Easter Sunday, 12 April 806 (Alexander, *Nicephorus,* 69).

[157] In accordance with the first of the Apostolic Canons, three bishops were required to ordain the new bishop (i.e., patriarch) of Constantinople. Nikephoros was ordained by Nicholas, archbishop of (Cappadocian) Caesarea, by Thomas, archbishop of Thessalonike, and by Leo, metropolitan bishop of (Thracian) Herakleia, who was included in the ordination by tradition because the bishop of Constantinople had once been suffragan of the see of Herakleia (Alexander, *Nicephorus,* 69).

had been completed, <Nikephoros> deposited <the document> beneath the
holy table to sanctify it and to appoint it as a surety before God that he accepted its terms.[158] After divine inspiration accomplished his holy ordination,
the people cried, "Worthy!"[159] three times in worthy acclamation for this worthy man.[160] <Nikephoros> then ascended the holy vantage point of the <pa-
triarchal> throne, as if it were some extremely lofty peak, which the wondrous
<prophet> Habakkuk also declared a holy watch in a spiritual sense,[161] pro-
nouncing the good <blessing> of peace upon all the people, and receiving
<theirs> in return. Thereafter, he showed himself a willing officiant of the
holy Eucharist.

In this way God, Who measures out <His > *grace upon the humble,*[162]
decided that this man [Nikephoros] as a lover of spiritual ascent should above
all obtain the heights of the ecclesiastical <hierarchy>. After gaining <these
heights>, <Nikephoros> began to build on them in a way worthy of Scripture, and kept secure the foundations of the faith.[163] He found the Church
in a <peaceful> state, undisturbed by factional divisions, since the billows[164]
of heresy had been smoothed away by the assembly, which was, so to speak,
patristic.[165] He then moved across the vast sea of the Church in an unruffled

---

[158] In earlier centuries, patriarchs had been required to make public oral profession
of their faith as a part of their ordination. Under iconoclast emperors, written professions of faith were submitted by the patriarchs Anastasios (730–754) and Paul IV (780–
784). Examples of these documents survive from the 9th century (Alexander, *Nicephorus,* 69–70).

[159] Changing de Boor's punctuation, "ἄξιος ἐπὶ τῷ ἀξίῳ," to "ἄξιος" ἐπὶ τῷ ἀξίῳ.

[160] This form of the people's acclamation for a bishop dates from the early days of
the Church, for it is reported by the 4th-century ecclesiastical historian Eusebios of
Caesarea (*Historia ecclesiastica,* book 6, chap. 29, PG 20:588C) and by his 5th-century
successors Sokrates (*Historia ecclesiastica,* book 4, chap. 30, PG 67:544B), and Philostorgios (*Historia ecclesiastica,* book 9, chap. 10, PG 65:576C).

[161] Habakkuk portrays himself as a watchman determined to await the response of
God in a time of extreme evil and trouble (Hab. 2:1).

[162] Cf. 1 Pet. 5:5.

[163] Cf. Eph. 2:20.

[164] Emending the printed σκώμματα to κύματα with Nikitin (p. 18).

[165] A complimentary reference to the Second Council of Nicaea (24 Sept.–13 Oct.
787), which ended the first period of iconoclasm in the same city where the early Fa-

calm, and anticipated no unfavorable wind of heresy <blowing> over it. Therefore, zeal motivated him to turn his steps in a different direction, against the unbelieving and outlandish heresies which just then were celebrating their abominable rituals without a blush of shame for their own mad folly—I am referring to Jews, and Phrygians, and those who <followed> the oversubtle arguments of Mani and drank the potion of his unbelief.[166] For that reason <Nikephoros> presented a written document to the emperor <outlining> the basic tenets of their unnatural religion in great detail and <explaining> how <these tenets> would maim the whole society like gangrene if <these sects> [p. 159] were allowed to continue doing as they wished. He demonstrated <all this> in the treatise, reproaching the Jews for slaying the Lord, assailing the monstrous sophistry of the Phrygians, and striking a serious blow against the hallucination of the Manichaeans, so that the pollution <of these groups> would not proceed out of their mouths, but rather their guileful nonsense would be <only> whispered in obscure secrecy. For if the impious had been deprived of free speech by the authorities, they would have been unable[167] to do anything even in secret.[168]

Thus the[169] stormy seas of illegal heresies gradually abated, and the orthodoxy of our correct profession of faith came into the open under perfectly

---

thers of the Church had gathered for the first ecumenical council (First Council of Nicaea, 325).

[166] <Kata>phrygians or Montanists, followers of the second-century Phrygian preacher Montanus and his two female associates, emphasized the importance of these "new prophets" and their eschatological expectations, attacking the established Church, and practicing asceticism and celibacy. Manichaeans preached the dualistic struggle in the world between Light (spirit) and Darkness (matter); some Greek sources presented the heretical Paulicians as heirs of Manichaeanism because they regarded the Incarnation as a mere illusion. Cf. J. Gouillard, "L'hérésie dans l'Empire byzantin des origines au XIIe siècle," *TM* 1 (1965), 299–324, and N. Garsoian, "Byzantine Heresy: A Re-Interpretation," *DOP* 25 (1971), 85–113.

[167] Perhaps ἄν should be supplied before περιέστησαν.

[168] In 811 a decree of the permanent synod at Constantinople condemned Paulicians and the judaizing heretics of Asia Minor known as Athinganoi ("Untouchables"); the patriarch Nikephoros' report to the emperor on their teachings, which is unfortunately lost, led the emperor Nikephoros I to issue an imperial decree also condemning them (cf. Alexander, *Nicephorus*, 99 and 264).

[169] Reading <τὸ> τῶν.

clear skies and ensured Sabbath rest for God's Church. Since, however, external matters were going well for <Nikephoros>, he shifted his attention to matters within <the Church>, that is, to monastic discipline. For men who had chosen or requested permission to choose this heavenly way of life had thought fit to establish their monasteries somewhere near convents,[170] making the excuse, I should suppose, of kinship <with the nuns> or some other favorable sounding words <of explanation>. They avoided open cohabitation, but they could not entirely escape indulgence in sexual fantasies. For both *their possessions and goods were all held in common,* but in a different manner from what was said long ago concerning the faithful.[171] For in the case of those <early Christians>, the community was honored in virtuously selling their possessions, but in this case <the community> exerted its efforts to avoid virtuously selling <possessions> by wickedly holding everything in common. Also, there was some disorder in the highest <monastic> way of life, and everyone suspected sexual impurity in <monks> who professed chastity. Observing this situation, that most pure mind <of Nikephoros> tolerated no continuation <of it>, nor did he allow the sin to bring its stain upon the entire <Church> and drive it towards a passion for sensuous living. But he

[170] This passage concerns the so-called "double monasteries," consisting of a community of monks and another of nuns located in close proximity to one another and sharing the same superior and the same properties and income. Although forbidden by legislation of the emperor Justinian, such communities continued to flourish (as we can see above in the Life of St. Anthousa of Mantineon, 14) because they provided convenient means of sharing defenses and apportioning tasks and also enabled family and household members to enter religious life without estrangement from one another (see S. Hilpisch, *Die Doppelklöster, Entstehung und Organisation* [Münster, 1928], 16–18). Since they also provided occasion for their members to be tempted away from chastity, the Church continued to move against double monasteries. The Second Council of Nicaea (787) prohibited new foundations, and Nikephoros used his patriarchal authority to abolish double monasteries entirely, threatening with excommunication any bishop, abbot, or priest who tolerated them (Hilpisch, p. 22, citing J. B. Pitra, *Spicilegium Solesmense* 4 [Paris, 1858], 403, no. 104). See J. Pargoire, "Les monastères doubles chez les byzantins," *EO* 9 (1906), 21–24, where this passage is closely paraphrased. For additional bibliography, see *ODB* 2:1392, s.v. "Monastery, Double."

[171] According to Acts 2:44–45 and 4:32 the early Christian community held all possessions of its members in common, selling them and distributing the income according to the needs of the community and of individuals within it. Double monasteries did not alienate the goods and property bestowed upon them, but rather used the resulting income for the maintenance of the community and its charities.

used his supreme apostolic authority and selected out bishops who were vigilant in guarding <the Church> and had Phinehas' zeal <for the Lord> in their hearts.[172] [p. 160] He dispatched them as if upon a second <Gospel> mission <of preaching>,[173] <commanding them> to stab out polluting passion with the javelin of canon law[174] and to halt the destruction by their atoning act of preaching. They went to every <part of> the empire that suffered this illness, applying the remedies of salvation appropriately and hastening to induce the healing of deadly wounds. They separated the women's quarters far from men and fortified <the nuns> with an abundance of provisions so that they would not be distressed by lack of <provisions>, be reminded of their <former> lewd behavior, and <find> *their last state worse than their first* <form of> collective life.[175] <The bishops> separated out the men according to their own disciplines and monasteries, or rather, according to the sensory capacities of each one's soul, and persuaded <the monks> to flee headlong from cohabitation with women as if from the bite of a serpent, so that sensual indulgence would not peep through the window of their fantasies, let fly an arrow, and work injury to the soul. Thus the rams of chastity rightly led the holy flock of monks and brought safely to the chief shepherd <Jesus> the profit from their soul-gaining work as well as the interest commended <by the Lord>.[176]

<Moreover, Nikephoros> extended his concern <for this issue> into each and every city and region; if he found this disease <of lewd behavior> flourishing, he took pen and ink to remedy it. And he appears to have done some such thing in one of the Tauric Klimata.[177] For the man who was at that time governor over the local people was swallowed up by this base behavior

---

[172] The priest Phinehas, grandson of Aaron, assuaged God's wrath against the Israelites when he thrust his javelin through both an Israelite man and the Midianite woman fornicating with him (cf. Num. 25:7–15).

[173] Cf. Lk. 9:2, where Jesus sends his disciples on the original mission of preaching.

[174] The metaphor encourages the bishops to emulate Phinehas.

[175] Cf. Mt. 12:45; 2 Pet. 2:20. The otherwise unattested word συνάλισις apparently derives from συναλίζω, "collect, assemble."

[176] Cf. Mt. 25:14–30 and Lk. 19:12–27.

[177] This individual was Toparch of Gotthia, one of the Klimata (administrative districts) in the Crimean peninsula of the Black Sea. The incident took place between 806 and 808 (cf. Alexander, *Nicephorus,* 77).

and sought a divorce from his wife in order to introduce a mistress <into his household>. <Nikephoros> set himself the task of wiping from this man the shameful stain by confronting him with his sin through warning and threatening letters. <Nikephoros warned> that unless he was willing to stop this <course of action>, he would be liable with justice to <the punishments that Nikephoros threatened>. This was more or less how these matters stood.

Now the rules of the Fathers <of the Church> required <Nikephoros> to express in detail the purity of his own orthodox faith. [p. 161] In conformity with the canonical and ancient usage that bid him communicate the <particulars> of his faith to the <patriarchs who held> the apostolic thrones, he reported and confirmed this <faith> in his synodal letter of enthronement, then dispatched it to Leo, current pope of the <Church> of the Romans.[178] <Nikephoros' profession> was at once a denunciation of heterodox heresies and a monument of orthodox faith.[179] (If anyone would like to experience the man's skill with words, let him read this <letter to Leo> and he will have a full and significant understanding <of Nikephoros' stance> on holy doctrines.) That holy man Leo admired this <profession of faith>; he gladly received it, accepted it, and proclaimed it most openly together with the chief doctrines of St. Peter. For he [Nikephoros] set forth so lucidly in his <statement> the single nature and equal honor of the consubstantial Trinity[180] that he was in no way inferior to the preeminent theologians in his precision of thought. Thus he stated clearly and followed the ecumenical councils in pro-

[178] Leo III, pope 795–816. A newly elected patriarch customarily collaborated with the synod of Constantinople in sending a formal letter of self-introduction to the pope and to the other three patriarchs. Nikephoros' synodal letter to Leo III (PG 100:169–200), finally dispatched in 811, is his earliest surviving literary work (cf. R. M. Mainka, "Zum Brief des Patriarchen Nikephoros I. an Papst Leo III.," *Ostkirchliche Studien* 13 [1964], 273–81; P. O'Connell, *The Ecclesiology of St. Nicephorus I (758–828)* [Orientalia Christiana Analecta 194] [Rome, 1972], 68–78, and Alexander, *Nicephorus,* 106 and 163).

[179] There is a play on words in the Greek text between στηλίτευμα ("denunciation") and στήλη ("monument").

[180] "Consubstantiality" (*homoousia*) describes the relationship among the three persons of the Trinity (Father, Son, and Holy Spirit) as equal because none is created by or subordinate to any of the others; all are of the same "substance." The three persons are also described as sharing the divine "nature" (*physis*). The Council of Nicaea (A.D. 325) established these concepts in Christian doctrine.

claiming the *manifestation in these last times*[181] of one <member> of the holy Trinity, Christ, *our true God,*[182] through the perfectly pure and unblemished Virgin and Mother of God,[183] so that nothing pertaining to reverent worship was unstated. And as for the prayers to God and the intercessions <made by> both the holy Mother of God and the heavenly <angelic> powers, by apostles, prophets, famous martyrs, and all blessed and just men, as for their relics, which deserve to be worshiped, and their holy images, he declared <them all> worthy of honor, inasmuch as it was proper to honor and extol those who have thus lived their lives and thus been *magnified by God.*[184] Thus *worshiping* God alone had been properly accomplished *in spirit and in truth by the true worshiper,*[185] and thus his <celebration> of healthy worship had been mixed as a transparent <eucharistic> draft, not like some mottled *strong drink,*[186] but a com*mingl*ing of the symbols handed down by God[187] and [p. 162] a curative for every outpouring of befouled heresy that burst forth in

---

[181] Cf. 1 Pet. 1:20.

[182] Cf. 1 John 5:20. The christology of the seven ecumenical councils dominates Nikephoros' profession of faith, which closes his synodal letter to Pope Leo III (cf. PG 100:181–95).

[183] Applying the epithet "Mother of God" (Theotokos) to the Virgin Mary was hotly contested during the christological controversies of the 4th and 5th centuries. Its use was endorsed by the Council of Ephesos (431).

[184] Cf. Ps. 4:3. This passage resembles Nikephoros' discussion of the prayers of the saints and the proper veneration of saints in his synodal letter to Pope Leo III (PG 100:189c–D).

[185] Cf. Jn. 4:23.

[186] Reading καθά τι σίκερα ποικιλλόμενον with I. D. Polemis (*Diptycha* 6 [1994/95], 183) for the printed καθά τισι κεραποικιλλόμενον. Cf. Is. 5:22 and Lk. 1:15.

[187] Ignatios contrasts Byzantine and Roman eucharistic practice here. The Byzantine rite mixed only wine and water (both cold and hot) for consecration, elements that symbolized the blood and water flowing from the side of Christ after his crucifixion (cf. R. Taft, "Water into Wine. The Twice-Mixed Chalice in the Byzantine Eucharist," *Muséon* 100 [1987], 323–42), and which could be described as "most transparent" in appearance. The Roman rite added a particle of the consecrated bread to the water and wine in the eucharistic chalice (cf. J. A. Jungmann, *Missarum Sollemnia* 2 [Vienna, 1948], 377–78), giving the mixture an appearance that could be described as ποικιλλό-μενον, "mottled." This section on eucharistic practice does not correspond to any part of Nikephoros' synodal letter to Leo III as it survives.

a neighbor. Did, then, this great <Nikephoros> proclaim the summation of the true faith with only a bare profession? Was there no fervor in his profession? Or, if this is indisputable, did he keep the <profession> safe in his heart, far from dangers? Or even if he was hardened like steel by these <dangers>, did he prefer disapproval in God's sight by failing to speak? No indeed, but together with profession, zeal, and dangers, beneficial speech *sharper than any sword*[188] hovered over his mind, cutting off as is proper the thoughts of those who had arrogated tyrannical power over holy matters.[189]

The adversary [i.e., the Devil] who always envies the virtuous was watching <all> this. It is he who devises storm-tossed seas when things are at rest, and who hates calm seas and peaceful tranquillity with an implacable hatred; he weaves onto the imperishable garment of the <true> faith tattered rags of heresy. He was unwilling to see the Church and the empire calmly guided in serenity, but devised a disruption to match his own insolence and launched sudden warfare against both <Church and empire>. He did not forge sharpened arrows and swords, as is the habit of those who take arms against the bodies <of their opponents>, but <took> the *whet*stone of his wickedness and sharpened *the tongues*[190] of those who knew how to practice mischief. He roused up <those tongues> to marshal spiritual dangers and first of all took as his adoptive son Leo, the emperor just recently exulting in his tyrannical rule.[191] It was Leo who appeared <as> a chameLeon of many guises in his elaborate impiety,[192] who lost his senses from the very <moment of> his proclamation <as emperor>, and converted better <orthodox> men to his impi-

---

[188] Cf. Heb. 4:12.

[189] In this enigmatic passage, Ignatios implies that secular authorities had encroached in matters of ecclesiastical practice or doctrine. He may refer to the emperor Charlemagne who, from the Byzantine point of view, had improperly forced Pope Leo III to anoint and crown him, or to the emperor Nikephoros I, who had imposed upon the patriarch Nikephoros an unseemly delay in sending his synodal letter of enthronement to Leo III (cf. Alexander, *Nicephorus*, 106–10).

[190] Cf. Ps. 63 (64):3 and Ps. 139 (140):3.

[191] Leo V the Armenian, 813–820. Alternatively, one might translate "introduced as emperor Leo, just recently exulting in his tyrannical rule."

[192] Ignatios puns upon Leo's name and "chameleon," an animal proverbial for its ability to change its color (cf. Leutsch-Schneidewin, *Corpus* 2:90, no. 32; 129, no. 7; 719, no. 9; 779, no. 43). Before becoming emperor Leo did not specify his religious views (cf. Alexander, *Nicephorus*, 78). See also n. 155 above.

ous doctrines; it was as if he had oppressed ancient Israel in tribal <warfare> at the time of Moses, and now showed himself fiercer than <any> Amalekite towards the new Israel [i.e., the Church];[193] he was harsher than Sennacherib, more loathsome than Rabshakeh, and more shameful than Nebuzaradan, the slave to the stomach.[194]

As regards the emperor [Michael I Rangabe] who had given him a position of honor, [p. 163] <Leo> valued neither the honor nor its donor, but capitulated to the temptation to seize the throne. (For under <Michael>, <Leo> became chief administrator of the first regiment of soldiers belonging to the so-called themes.)[195] Now the emperor [Michael I] had organized a military campaign in Thrace against the Huns,[196] who were inflicting great damage on the towns in that <region>. In <the course of that war>, Leo became the chief agent of defeat for the whole army when he originated a shameful retreat.[197] Therefore the city <of Constantinople> received the emperor, who enjoyed none of the benefits of victory, while <Leo> corrupted the soldiers

[193] During the Israelites' desert wanderings from Egypt, the desert-dwelling Amalekite tribe attacked God's people, was defeated, and earned God's eternal enmity (cf. Ex. 17:8–16). Leo V is frequently given the sobriquet of Amalekite in 9th-century hagiography; cf., e.g., v. Ioannic. a Sab. 347a, 355b.

[194] King Sennacherib of Assyria (705–681 b.c.) sent his army against a rebellious coalition of states led by King Hezekiah of Judah, captured the fortified towns, and besieged Jerusalem. Sennacherib's chief officer Rabshakeh served as his spokesman in demanding Israel's surrender and threatening its utter destruction (4 Ki. 18:7–19). Nebuzaradan was an important Babylonian official and captain of the king of Babylon's guard; his title meant literally "chief cook" (ἀρχιμάγειρος), the source of Ignatios' dismissive reference to him as "slave of <the King's> stomach." In 586 b.c., Nebuzaradan punished the Israelites' unsuccessful rebellion by burning Jerusalem and its temple, deporting the Israelites to Babylon, and arresting Israel's chief leaders for execution (cf. 4 Ki. 25:8–21 and Jer. 47:1–6, 52:12–27).

[195] Michael I Rangabe (811–813) appointed Leo commander of the soldiers of the Anatolikon theme of west-central Anatolia. "Theme" designated both a territorial unit and the population of farmer-soldiers who protected it. Each theme was administered by a general (strategos) who possessed both civil and military authority.

[196] Ignatios uses an archaizing ethnic term to designate the Turkic Bulgarians ruled by Khan Krum (802–814) from his capital at Pliska.

[197] At the battle of Versinikia (north of Adrianople in Thrace) Byzantine troops were defeated by the Bulgarians (22 June 813) when a successful Byzantine attack turned to a retreat and rout reportedly initiated by Leo's troops from the Anatolikon theme. Michael I then fled to Constantinople, and Leo was acclaimed emperor by the army.

with speeches <encouraging> revolt. He pilfered and filched <their loyalty> with empty hopes, then insinuated himself into the imperial dignity by usurpation of power. Then the wretched man arrived at the Queen <of Cities> with great speed and appeared inside the walls, as he should not have done. He processed with traditional honors along the chief thoroughfare to the imperial palace, cutting off from his <due> dignity his predecessor <Michael>, who was adorned more with the simplicity of goodness than the <imperial> purple. When <Michael> realized that the brutish Leo was roaring and raging like a lion against the <imperial> power, he tore off his imperial robes, cut his hair, and began to wear <monastic> black instead of <imperial> gold. Taking his wife and children, he shut himself up in the holy precincts <of a church>.[198] At length and with difficulty, this <action> persuaded Leo not to proceed harshly against <his predecessor>. <Leo> did, however, consign him to exile quicker than <you could say the> word, and he himself hastily undertook placing the imperial diadem upon his <own> head.

Now Nikephoros, who bore God <in his heart>, observed this turn of events and noted that the man [Leo] held many opinions and was irresolute <besides>. He looked <for the opportunity> to bring Leo under the authority of the traditional written professions of faith. <Nikephoros> composed a document containing the creed of our blameless worship,[199] and <sent> several bishops to urge the emperor to sign it with his own hand. Although <Leo> said that he certainly agreed with the text <of the document>, he put off doing this until the <imperial> dignity of the diadem [p. 164] should pass to him; <he said> that he was ready to subject himself to the yoke of the Church as soon as he achieved <coronation>. But since <Leo> was driven by the sharp prodding of a mind <sunk in> utter darkness, he put <the blackness of> ink and <the sharpness of> a pen to bad use by placing his signature upon a heretical document even before his coronation. He thereby turned himself wholly over to the demons who drove him, rather than relying upon the <episcopal> fathers who were eager to lead him to salvation.

---

[198] Michael I Rangabe took refuge in the church of the Virgin in Pharos in the palace complex and was eventually exiled to the island of Plate in the Sea of Marmara (cf. Treadgold, *Byz. Revival,* 188–89).

[199] Leo not only neglected to sign the document on this occasion, but also refused to append his signature after his coronation; cf. p. 164.23.

<Leo> came then to the church of <St.> Sophia to receive the <imperial> diadem. At the very moment that the great high priest <and patriarch> was about to take independent action and proclaim <the imperial coronation>, the sleepless eye <of God>,[200] that enables us to see the future, deemed it right that the just <man Nikephoros> should form a more correct assessment of <Leo>. For after he had pronounced the blessing and elevated the <imperial> crown, when it was time to touch the head of <Leo> for consecration, the saint seemed to press his hand into thorns and thistles, and let go of the crown with the claim that he distinctly felt pain.[201] For that head, that pricked like a thorn[202] at the saint's touch, foretold <Leo's> egregiously harsh and unlawful treatment of the Church, which was about to erupt.

But <Leo> left, having received the imperial crown on his head, upon which <eventually> he also suffered the last blow <of his life> with <perfect> justice, since he had been contemptuous of just men.[203] On the second day, then, of <Leo's> reign, <Nikephoros>, who bore God <in his heart>, once again urged the newly consecrated emperor to sign the document <asserting> his orthodoxy, but <Leo> vehemently refused. For he had tainted the <imperial> purple with falsehood, and had fixed the mask of Proteus <over his face>, appearing to incline toward whomever he might encounter.[204] What false religion that soul <possessed>, making the foundations of

---

[200] "The sleepless eye" (ὁ ἀκοίμητος ὀφθαλμός) is a favorite form of reference to God in patristic writings (e.g., Athanasios, Basil of Caesarea, John Chrysostom, Themistios, etc.), evidently derived from the writings of the 1st-century A.D. author Philo Judaeus (*De mutatione nominum*, §40.4, ed. P. Wendland, *Philonis Alexandrini opera quae supersunt* 3 [Berlin, 1898], 163.20).

[201] In the Bible, "thorns and thistles" occur together in contexts of God's disapproval and punishment for disobedience or impiety (cf. Gen. 3:18; Hos. 10:8; Mt. 7:16; Heb. 6:8).

[202] Here ἀκανθοπλήξ must mean "that pricked like a thorn" instead of its more usual meaning, "pricked by a thorn" (cf. Trapp, *Lexikon*, s.v.), since it is evidently not the crown but Leo's head that pricks Nikephoros.

[203] Leo was beheaded by assassins at Christmas morning services in 820, probably in the palace chapel of St. Stephen; cf. Treadgold, *Byz. Revival*, 224 and n. 452 below.

[204] The mythical figure Proteus, the Old Man of the Sea, could swiftly change his shape into any living creature or into fire, water, or a tree (cf. Homer, *Od.* 4:417–18 and 456–58).

faith tremble! How that fellow's thoughts wandered out of control, distorting with false reasoning the doctrine <set forth in> the orthodox profession of faith! What a tangled mass of falsehood ensnared the simplicity of orthodox beliefs! For <Leo's> first struggle was not against rivals, nor against enemies who had then blockaded the city,[205] [p. 165] but he rather set his hand to <drawing up> a battle line against <God>, Who had entrusted <to him> the reins of authority by virtue of judgments that <God alone> knows. For as I have already said, <Leo> paid little or no attention to the enemy because he was incapable either of engaging <in battle> with them or of meeting them face to face, due to the devious plan for defeat that he had previously executed. Therefore <Leo> proceeded against the universal sovereign of the whole <of creation>, letting out the rope of every <sail> and <casting> every die[206] to have pictorial images in <God's> Church stripped away. For it was appropriate to honor the venerable <nature> of the practice and to cherish a traditional <form of> worship as ancient as Ogyges <and the Flood>;[207] it was fitting to apportion extra guarantees to the road thus trodden by God and pressed by the footsteps of the saints, and it was appropriate to be astonished at the resistance <to tampering with the images expressed> by <Nikephoros>, the shepherd who bore God <in his heart>. But <Leo> failed to notice the serpent of madness[208] and held fast to his purpose with a mind

[205] Ignatios refers to the Bulgarian siege of Constantinople led by Khan Krum after his victory at Versinikia. Bulgarian troops captured Adrianople and laid waste the countryside around Constantinople; the sudden death of Krum (814) prevented them from attacking the city itself.

[206] Ignatios combines two expressions meaning "exert every effort." The proverbial sailing idiom "let out every reef" (cf. Plato, *Protagoras* 338a), which is often expressed as "let go/shake every reef" (cf. Leutsch-Schneidewin, *Corpus* 2:86, no. 4 and 1:145, no. 62 with note), is combined with the idea of casting dice, i.e., of taking a desperate gamble (cf. Plutarch, *Coriolanus,* chap. 3).

[207] Ogyges was a mythical Greek king who ruled at the time of the primeval flood usually associated with Noah; his name became proverbial for extreme antiquity (cf. Leutsch-Schneidewin, *Corpus* 1:466, no. 42).

[208] The serpent (ὄφις) appears both in the Bible and in classical mythology as an ambivalent symbol; its negative aspects are clear in the biblical story of the temptation of Eve (Gen. 3:1–4) and in its identification with the power of evil (Lk. 10:19) and with Satan himself (Rev. 20:2). In Greek mythology, the Furies who drove Orestes mad had serpents for hair (cf. Aeschylus, *Choephoroi* 1048–62).

tarnished by his deceitful doctrine. Like that *servile* <king> Jeroboam,[209] <Leo> pushed aside every word *of the old men* and <every> *counsel* of the wise that brings benefit from encountering it. Instead, <Leo> turned to the anecdotes *of young men* and to tales of old wives, although they spoke <words inspired> not from heaven but from earth, because <their fantasies> promised length of days and victories to him if he would vomit out his impiety upon what had been established in the past.

<Leo> now collected for himself a committee,[210] who were all excluded from the holy liturgy by canonical penance,[211] and who were persuaded by the seductions of force <to join the committee> if they were unwilling. The apostate <Leo> with his radical ideas bid them put together a new faith, assigning them space in the palace and allocating them a stipend for delicacies as if they were swine. They were like that mythical <giant> Aigaion, glorying in the boldness of their ruler[212] as they rushed with utmost ferocity against almost every church, searched out books, and took them away; they doted upon the <books> that opposed <pagan> idols, since these supported their <own> purpose, but they burned the ones that advocated images, since these refuted their fanciful tales.

---

[209] Ignatios conflates Jeroboam, a religious innovator and usurper like Leo, with his rival Rehoboam, son of king Solomon. Rehoboam sought advice about keeping his kingdom from wise elders and from his own impulsive contemporaries; when he oppressed his people as his friends advised, he was deposed by Jeroboam (cf. 3 Ki. 12:6–20). Jeroboam directed his people to worship two golden calves at Bethel and Dan instead of visiting God's temple at Jerusalem (cf. 3 Ki. 12:28–30).

[210] In 814 Leo assembled a six-man committee of senators, ecclesiastical officials, and monks, charging them to compile an anthology (florilegium) of authoritative writings in support of the iconoclastic measures he was planning. The committee based its work on the anthology presented by the iconoclastic Council of Hiereia (754), probably working closely with Leo himself (cf. Alexander, *Nicephorus,* 126–28). I am grateful to A. Alexakis for suggestions on the translation of this passage.

[211] Reading ἀπείργετο for the printed ἀνείργετο. Although other sources do not indicate that any member of Leo's committee had been excommunicated, this imprecise accusation implies that they were all immoral persons.

[212] Aigaion (or Briareos), one of the hundred-armed giants, delivered Zeus, king of the gods, from imprisonment by all the other Olympian gods and sat at Zeus' side as a bodyguard to intimidate them (cf. Homer, *Il.* 1:396–406). With this simile Ignatios implies that Leo's committee was monstrous and that Leo himself was unpopular and dependent upon the help of others.

<Leo> also summoned the majority of bishops [p. 166] to serve as advocates for the <religious> speculations he had invented. When they arrived at the ports opposite Constantinople, they sent messages to the patriarch and were ferried across to him, not out of free choice <on their part, but> in conformity with prevalent custom. <These bishops> collided with the opposing force of imperial influence and, in bonds that were forced upon them, they were escorted to <face> the punishments <inflicted upon victims> by Echetos and Phalaris.[213] If, however, they agreed to the doctrine espoused <by the imperial court>, deliverance and release from <these> horrors were the immediate consequences. But if someone was compelled by the goading of truth to oppose somehow the impious <program>, he was condemned to prison, starvation, and hellish terrors that were no more bearable than the fantastical manifestations of <the ogress> Empousa.[214] So it was that <Leo> assembled the council of the second Caiaphas;[215] thus *Iannes and Iambres* vaingloriously contested against the new *Moses*.[216] So it was that our father Nikephoros, the star of the priesthood and of the whole world, was brought to nothing by those who originated the darkness <of error while serving> as the champions and advance party of the Antichrist. For while they threatened

---

[213] The proverb "The reign of Phalaris and of Echetos" indicated utmost tyrannical cruelty (cf. Leutsch-Schneidewin, *Corpus* 2:706, no. 78). Phalaris, who ruled in Sicily in the 6th century B.C., was reputed to roast his victims to death in a specially constructed bronze bull. Echetos, a mythical king of Epiros, cut off the noses, ears, and private parts of his victims, and fed them to the dogs (cf. Homer, *Od.* 18:85–87).

[214] Empousa was a figure of ancient folklore notable for her ability to assume various terrifying shapes (cf. Aristophanes, *Frogs* 293) and to devour her human lovers (cf. Philostratos, *Vita Apollonii* 4.25, ed. C. L. Kayser, *Flavii Philostrati Opera* 1 [Leipzig, 1870], 145.29–146.1).

[215] The Jewish high priest Caiaphas presided over the trial of Jesus before the council of scribes and elders (cf. Mt. 26:57–60).

[216] Jewish tradition ascribed the names Iannes and Iambres to the anonymous magicians who matched their skills against Moses at the court of Pharaoh (cf. 2 Tim. 3:8; also Ex. 7:11 and 22; 9:11). In the 9th century the prominent iconoclast John the Grammarian ('Ιωάννης) was nicknamed Iannes ('Ιάννης) by his iconodule opponents and pictured as Iannes in several marginal psalter illustrations; here, Nikephoros takes the role of Moses in opposing Iannes/John (I. Ševčenko, "The Anti-Iconoclastic Poem in the Pantocrator Psalter," *Cahiers Archéologiques* 15 [1965], 41–47). Iambres may be intended to represent John the Grammarian's ally, the bishop Antony of Syllaion (cf. Ševčenko, p. 47, on a similar allusion from a letter by Theodore of Stoudios).

to silence the teacher, they urged the function of teaching in the churches upon those who had not even attained the status of students; they hindered in its flow the river of his speech that proverbially *streams with gold*,[217] and felt no fear in knowingly commending the Church into the hands of those who had *dug* for themselves *a pit*[218] of destruction and did not possess the water of <spiritual> wisdom. They prevented the high priest <Nikephoros> from touching the holy table, and entrusted the inner sanctuaries of the holy <churches> to people who did not even have the right to enter the house of God. They shook the pillars of the Church as they pleased, and boasted that they propped it up with their empty and wavering chatter.

When God's servant Nikephoros observed these <events>, he devised every sort of supplication to God, entreating Him, summoning Him as an ally, and <beseeching> Him to preserve unblemished <purity> in His Church and to keep from defilement [p. 167] by the foul pollution of heterodoxy the genuine <believers> in the flock. For this <purpose>, <Nikephoros> summoned everyone, warning and exhorting them not to be contaminated with the leaven of heretics,[219] and commanding[220] them to avoid the alien and aborted offspring of <heretical> teaching like poison and like *the vipers' brood*.[221] "For," he said, "<the heretics> do not cause a physical bruise that can respond to a doctor's remedies, but they rather inject into the inner recesses of the soul a danger that rejects[222] superficial <treatment with> an absorbent bandage. Now, let us not yield to the present shift in the scales nor to the influence of the ruler. For even if heresy drags along both the emperor and a great swarm of evil-minded people attending him, their power will nevertheless not amount to anything, and they will not be reckoned a part of

---

[217] "Streaming with gold" (χρυσόρρειθρος) is a rare word applied by Nikephoros' contemporary Theodore of Stoudios to the teachings of John Chrysostom (cf. J. B. Pitra, *Analecta Sacra* 1 [Paris, 1876], p. 358, XI.1, and p. 656, LXXXII.5).

[218] The pit that the wicked dig for their own unwitting destruction is proverbial in the Old Testament (cf. Ps. 56 [57]:6; 93 [94]:13; Prov. 26:27; Eccl. 10:8; Sir. 27:26; Zach. 3:10).

[219] Cf. Mt. 16:6–12 and 1 Cor. 5:6.

[220] Reading ἐπέτρεπεν for the printed ἀπέτρεπεν.

[221] The opponents of Jesus and of John the Baptist are called descendants of vipers in the New Testament (cf. Mt. 3:7, 12:34, 23:33).

[222] Reading ἀναινόμενον for the printed ἀναινόμενα.

God's Church. For God does not take pleasure in a multitude, but rather exercises His providential care for the one who feels fear and trembling at His words, and He clearly indicates that <such a> one is the whole Church. Let us propitiate <God's> favor through our prayers; let us soften Him by entreaty in an all-night vigil; let us beseech Him that we not suffer what our persecutors are urging against us." He spoke thus, and the church contained <within> all who intended to celebrate the night-long service.[223]

When the emperor became aware of the <circumstances> of the hymn-singing, he was overtaken by cowardice and by fear of a revolution against him, for he was embarrassed about his relationship with the patriarch. Around cockcrow, in distress and vexation he sent a message to the church and made an accusation against the patriarch concerning this <assembly>, saying that <the patriarch> was responsible for civil disturbance. "When an emperor is bending every effort toward peace," he said, "you must not practice discord and dissension and pray that there be no peace. But since you have been caught in activities contrary to the emperor's wish, come to the palace at daybreak so that <the emperor> may himself make a clear determination concerning these matters." When the crowd heard this announcement, they demonstrated zeal to an unheard of degree. For there was no one who did not summon heartfelt tears of supplication and press the ruler [p. 168] of all <creation> to act as judge and preserve justice for the universal faith. When they finished praying, the all-holy <Nikephoros> called together the holy congregation, and standing in their midst, spoke thus:

"O assembly designated by God, not even in a dream vision is it right to see the Church <in the situation> in which she is today, nor to observe the terrible <measures> taken against her: instead of her <former> radiance she <now> puts on mourning and instead of her <former> profound peace she is <now> driven into turmoil. She who *feeds all the flock with* perfect *willingness*[224] submits unwillingly to the seizure of those she shepherds, and she who commands all men to be in agreement is divided by differing doctrines, <although it was she> *whom* Christ *hath purchased with His own blood*,[225] whom He kept *undefiled* by *any blemish*[226] or stain, and whom He surrounded

---

[223] This assembly occurred in December 814; other sources imply two such night vigils (Alexander, *Nicephorus,* 129).

[224] Cf. 1 Pet. 5:2.

[225] Acts 20:28.

[226] Cf. Eph. 5:27.

with apostles, prophets, martyrs, and all the spirits of <the> just, walling her round like a garden. But now we see <the Church> enduring what we pray we not suffer from our enemies, and this at the hands of those who pretend to belong to us, but in reality are entirely alien.[227] For today[228] with the image of Christ its archetype is also dishonored, if indeed *the honor <rendered> an image devolves upon its original;*[229] today the tradition that the Church guarded from the beginning in teachings and writings has been cut off and ended as much as <possible> by the enemies of truth, and <the Church> gives ear to a doctrine that she has not heard before. But we must not capitulate to the threats <of the enemy> nor relax our zeal in any way, but rather rise up in fact as if <this> were warfare in company with an ally, <truth>. For the enemies of truth are like those who exert themselves to swim raging rivers against the current. For those <swimmers> strive to make headway, but are carried off by the river unwillingly, while these <enemies of truth> chatter a thousand <kinds of> nonsense against <truth> but agree with it involuntarily. For truth is a thing invincible and all-powerful, [p. 169] which bestows great weight for both <victory and defeat>; it knows how to award a crown <of victory> on each side when it is honored, and how to conquer everywhere when war is conducted against it. With <truth>, even an unarmed man is invulnerable, and without it, even a heavily armed soldier is easily captured. Those against whom my words are directed bear witness to what I have said. For <these men> who strive to take no heed of the truth have become mere playthings in the hands of those who have learned the elements of proof; in themselves supplying sufficient evidence to contradict themselves, they are gorged with their own flesh like maniacs."

After <Nikephoros> *forcefully addressed the company*[230] in such words, he put a humble but holy garment upon his shoulders,[231] and then entered the

---

[227] I.e., the emperor and his supporters, who claimed orthodoxy as the basis for actions foreign and destructive to it.

[228] Nikephoros probably held two night vigils, which Ignatios conflates in his account. The emperor responded to the first by inciting his soldiers to stone the image of Christ placed over the Chalke Gate of the Great Palace, then removed the image under pretense of protecting it. Nikephoros held his second night vigil on Christmas Eve 814, then was summoned to the palace (Alexander, *Nicephorus,* 129, esp. n. 1).

[229] Basil of Caesarea, *Liber de spiritu sancto* 45 (PG 32:149c).

[230] Cf. Homer, *Il.* 3:213 and *Od.* 18:26.

[231] Probably the *omophorion.*

imperial audience hall accompanied by the entire congregation from the
church. The emperor did not greet him with the customary hand<clasp> and
kiss, which marks an attitude of sincere regard, but <rather> cast an ugly
and angry glance <at him>, then went first to take his imperial throne while
assigning a seat of secondary honor to the just <man Nikephoros>. What
<Nikephoros> then said to him in a discussion between just the two of them,
deluging the emperor in a blizzard <of arguments> from sacred writings,
will be related now, as the occasion demands. For that puny fellow who was
blockaded under his impiety thought that he could entrap the saint if he assaulted him alone without allies or weapons. Therefore, with wrath inflaming
his mind from its most profound depths, <the emperor> began speaking
thus: "Fellow, what is this disagreement you have engineered, or rather what
is this violent insurrection against the empire? For the one who attempts to
gather an assembly without our authority, to teach false doctrines, and to
fabricate accusations against superior <power> <does> nothing <other>
than throw himself against the salvation of all. For if our <imperial> power
had chosen a course of action to destroy orthodox teachings and had attempted, as you say, to disturb the ancient <tradition> of these <teach-
ings>, there would be both an issue and an occasion for drenching us in
reproof and for accusing us of heterodoxy. But since we are devoted to orthodoxy in these <doctrines>, choose to deflect any disagreement, and would
wish for everyone to be of one mind in the faith [p. 170], why do we seem to
do wrong in this, when we are eager to obtain peace for the Church? Do you
not see that a faction of considerable size worries greatly <about this ques-
tion>[232] and stands at variance with the Church over the painting and display
of the icons? Do you not see that they are bringing forward scriptural citations
prohibiting these <icons>?[233] If their proposals lie neglected and unexamined,
nothing prevents the concord of faith from dissolving into factions and from
seeking forever the <re>union of Orthodoxy and its complete healing. Therefore, we urge you to engage without any delay in discussion with those who
have doubts concerning these matters, and we have decided that <you> shall
convince <them> or be convinced <by them>, so that we who have come to

---

[232] Reading διενοχλεύει for the printed διενοχλύει. Ignatios refers here to the faction that included Leo's iconoclastic committee of excerptors. I am grateful to A. Alexakis for suggestions on the translation of this passage.

[233] These excerpts from Scripture and patristic writings are later dismissed by Nikephoros (cf. v. Niceph. 172.16–17).

understand what is justly expressed might stand <together> with justice and weigh out our judgment in its favor. But if you should not agree to do this, and should rather choose to pursue justice for yourself in silence, it is clear where your <case> will be settled."

Nikephoros, the star of truth, took up <the discussion> and replied, "O emperor, we have not crafted <measures> that aim at disagreement or discord, nor have we deployed our prayers <like> weapons against your sovereignty. For we are admonished in Scripture *to pray* for *kings,* not against them.[234] Neither have we caused the healthy scripture of the faith to deviate into diseased teaching of false doctrines, but we ask for the renunciation of such <heresies> because of the commandments to us from[235] <God>, the *leader* of *truth.*[236] But we know this, and we call upon you to know, that all men[237] with even a modicum of sense agree that peace is the foremost good; accordingly, anyone who disrupts this <peace> would be the chief cause of evils <falling> not only upon his neighbors, but even upon his own family. The very best ruler, then, is one who is by nature able to compose peace out of war. But you have decided to wage war against us without provocation when the affairs of the Church were well disposed. [p. 171] Although orthodox teachings that proclaim the cross of Christ shine forth—and neither east nor west nor north nor the sea <to the south> is beyond their radiance—nonetheless you have decided to raise up against <orthodox doctrine> some murky teaching from pernicious men. What Rome is it,[238] first called the seat of the apostles, that accords with you in rejecting the revered image of Christ? Rather, Rome joins us in laboring and rejoicing to honor that <image>. What Alexandria is it, venerable precinct of the evangelist Mark, that ever joined <you> in refusing to set up the bodily and material likeness of the Mother of God? Rather, Alexandria assists and agrees with us in this <point>. What Antioch is it, far-famed seat of Peter, the chief <of the apostles>, that concurs

---

[234] Cf. Ezra [2 Esdras] 6:10.

[235] Reading ἐκ <τῶν ὑπὸ> with the editor, de Boor; cf. 1 Cor. 13:6, where Christians are enjoined "<to> rejoice not in iniquity but . . . in the truth."

[236] Cf. Ps. 24 (25):5.

[237] Reading ἀνθρώπων for the printed ἀνθρώπον.

[238] Nikephoros surveys the principal patriarchal sees in order of their precedence in the Church. Representatives from the sees of Rome, Constantinople, Alexandria, Antioch, and Jerusalem were required for the pronouncements of a church council to be considered doctrinally valid (cf. *ODB* 3:1625–26, s.v. "Pentarchy").

<with you> in insulting the representation of the saints? Rather, Antioch shares with us the long tradition of honoring these <images>. What Jerusalem is it, renowned home of <James>, the *brother of the Lord*,[239] that conspires <with you> in destroying the traditions <handed down> from the <church> fathers? What priest among your subjects follows and supports you with spontaneous willingness and not under unwilling constraint? As for the ecumenical councils that have clarified the pure creed of our faith through <the power of> the Holy Spirit, which one <of them> has voiced agreement with you in these matters? For one who is stripped of the assent of these <councils> will be unable to weave a garment of established doctrines for the Church. But, emperor, do not extend your hand to the heresy that is lying prostrate; do not infuse a voice <raised> against the Church into a <heresy> rightly condemned to silence. By means of your voice let this <heresy>[240] be banished far away with its inventors, let it go to the crows, let it be sent off to <the bastards' gymnasium of> Cynosarges.[241] Let the magnificence of the Church remain forever without peer! No place under the sun, as your majesty has just said,[242] exerts itself to cause grief to this <Church> on account of the holy icons, none has ever cultivated confusion in place of settled order in <the Church>. On every side, <the Church> clearly enjoys tranquillity and stability [p. 172] and *prevails against* squalls and swells upon the sea and *against the* very *gates of hell.*[243] Do not discharge revolutionary teachings against established tradition, for these <teachings> customarily speak not <in> the <words> of the Lord, but at <their own> pleasure; these <teachings> are the aborted fetuses of <magicians> who *speak from the belly.*[244] We

---

[239] James, the "brother of the Lord" (cf. Mt. 13:55; Mk. 6:3) was traditionally considered Peter's successor as leader of the Church in Jerusalem (cf. Acts 15:13–21 and 21:18–26).

[240] Punctuating ἐμπνεύσειας· διὰ φωνῆς with V, and reading αὕτη for the printed αὐτή.

[241] The gymnasium of Cynosarges was located outside the walls of ancient Athens and designated for the use of those who were not pure-blooded Athenians. "Go to the crows" (i.e., "go to hell," cf. Leutsch-Schneidewin, *Corpus* 2:380, no. 65; 1:52, no. 77) and "go to Cynosarges" (cf. Leutsch-Schneidewin, *Corpus* 2:76, no. 56 [with note], 381, no. 66; 1:398, no. 24) are traditional terms used in insults and curses.

[242] Cf. *v. Niceph.* 170.3–4.

[243] Cf. Mt. 16:18.

[244] Cf. Is. 8:19.

know that you too were devoted to the unblemished faith before your coronation; if, however, some <point> of heterodox <teaching> has shaken your
vigilant orthodoxy, and if some reasoning which is able to taint its hearers has
thrust into your ears, prevailed upon you, and engendered temptation in you,
and further if you long to find release from this <temptation>, we guarantee
that we shall provide this <release> for you with the assent of God.[245] This is
our obligation, even the most compelling of all <our> obligations, to pull up
by the roots (should God grant <it>), those things[246] that occasion sin for
you. However, we acknowledge no necessity to open our mouth and discuss
<matters> of the <Holy> Spirit with those who lack the Spirit, even if we
should be brought to trial <as> responsible for[247] every <sort of> violence,
nor do we submit before the snippets <made> by those <heretics> from
scriptural and patristic writings. For long ago <these snippets> were also
refuted by many of the <church> fathers and perished."

Then the emperor hastened to say, "But do you not think that Moses
spoke truthfully and thoughtfully concerning these matters? You would not
doubt that the words of Moses were the words of God when he commanded
<us> *not to make an idol nor likeness,* not only of man, but in the following
simple and all-inclusive <terms>: not of the <creatures> that move in the
air beneath *heaven,* nor of those that live *on the earth,* nor of those that swim
in the waters.[248] How then can you create images and give honor to the
<things> that the lawgiver has forbidden?"

PATRIARCH:[249] Upon what a deep and vast sea of inquiry you are embarking
us, O emperor! It is a sea upon which many have often sailed, but none, so far

---

[245] Reading ἐπ᾿ ὀφρύσι with L. Sherry for the ms. ἐπιφρ**ύσει; Ignatios uses a short-
ened form of the Homeric idiom meaning "nod assent," ἐπ᾿ ὀφρύσι νεῦσε (cf. Homer,
Il. 1:528; *Od.* 16:164).

[246] Reading τὰ τὸ for τὸ τὸ, as suggested by L. Rydén.

[247] Reading αἴτιοι for the printed αἴτια.

[248] Cf. Ex. 20:4–5 and also Deut. 5:8.

[249] In reporting this portion of the interview between patriarch and emperor, Ignatios
adopts the form of a Platonic dialogue, casting the patriarch in the role of the wise
expositor and the emperor as his unenlightened interlocutor. For a discussion of the
purpose and forms of the Platonic dialogue, see F. H. Sandbach, "Plato and the Socratic Work of Xenophon," in *The Cambridge History of Classical Literature, I. Greek
Literature,* ed. P. E. Easterling, B. M. W. Knox (New York, 1985), 482–97.

as we know, has reached the harbor of <theological> exactitude. For some people indeed consider images an unnatural monstrosity and the offspring of <pagan> Greek [p. 173] error, and complain against the <images> to the unseen tribunal of the soul, and make common cause with the accusers. However, in encountering reality, they <suddenly> back water <in retreat> and even act contrary to their convictions. For <these same people> have icons in their churches, in their marketplaces, and in their homes, and some of them even have portable icons as their companions when they travel by land and by sea. There are other <people, however>, who immediately throw away the weapons of the soul at their first close engagement and turn their backs to the enemy <in retreat> when they are completely exhausted in the face of trouble; they do not honor the images of the prophets nor the forms of the apostles nor the pictures of the martyrs. But they have built churches that are free of all these <representations>, without figures and without images, and they raise up their suppliant prayers to the unseen and incorporeal God. But if you agree, let us not flag in this inquiry; let us not lose interest in the chase if we do not capture <the subject of our inquiry> with the <hunting> nets of truth when we encircle it and track it in our discussion. Then listen to my argument, full well wise and true, which you will accept and approve, if in reality you love Him Who Is [i.e., God] and long for the truth.

Do you not realize what sort of erroneous opinion about God spread among the souls of the Egyptians long ago, that they reduced the uncreated and immaterial glory of the Lord <God> to matter and form, then gave reverence to this <glory> in a man's human shape? For such were the famous Osiris, Typhon, Horos, Isis, and the list of other humans <regarded as> gods, whose life stories display and expose their self-indulgence, whose warfare <reveals> their arrogance, and whose deaths <reveal> their <human> character.[250] What, then? Did <the ancient Egyptians> place limits upon divinity at

---

[250] The specific source or sources for this passage is uncertain, but it resembles the interpretation of ancient Egyptian religion contained in the 1st-century B.C. *History* of Diodoros of Sicily. Diodoros' euhemeristic explanation of the gods' origin identifies them as mortals of extraordinary virtue who eventually came to be regarded as gods (Diod., book 1, chap. 13.1). Like Herodotos before him, Diodoros amalgamates the chief gods of Egypt into the Greco-Roman pantheon, calling the Egyptian god Set/ Seth by the name of the Greek monster Typhon (Diod. 1.13.4; Herodotus, book 2, chap. 144). Diodoros describes the war on behalf of civilization waged by Osiris, his death at the hands of his brother Typhon, the vengeance exacted by his sister-queen

this <point>, or was the divine nature also molded and formed by them into irrational creatures and the natures of animals? They even crouched on their haunches worshiping the dog[251] as a god, sang hymns to Apis as a young bull, to Hermes as a goat, and to Athena as a fish![252] With their irrational way of thinking, they proclaimed that irrational[253] <beasts were> gods! [p. 174] Now they also combined <beasts> with one another and fashioned some gods of multiple shapes and forms. They created the goat-footed <god> (this was Pan), and fastened the face of a dog onto someone (I think he was called Anubis, a composite <creature>, neither wholly a man nor completely a dog).[254] Am I lying as I relate these matters, or do you agree with <what I say as> the truth?

Isis together with his son Horos, and Isis' own death and burial (Diod. 1.17–22). The anonymous and widely popular medieval prose romance *Barlaam and Ioasaph* also recounts the adventures of these Egyptian divinities, remarks upon their human vulnerability, and lists the goat, calf, and dog in a catalogue of animals and plants considered divine by the Egyptians (cf. PG 96:1117B–C). I am grateful to R. A. Hadley and to L. Sherry for these references.

[251] Ignatios puns upon the word for "worship" (προσεκύνουν) and for "dog" (κύνα).

[252] Diodoros remarks upon the extraordinary veneration accorded by the Egyptians to many sacred animals (Diod. 1.83), mentioning the dog (Diod. 1.84.2; 87.2–3), the Apis bull (Diod. 1.84.4–85.5), and the goat honored at Mendes (Diod. 1.84.4) among other beasts. Since Herodotos (book 2, chap. 46) states that Pan was worshiped as part goat at Mendes, Hermes may have been confused with Pan in this passage. Greco-Roman writers on Egyptian religion generally identified Hermes with Anubis, the dog-headed god of the dead, or with Thoth, the ibis-headed creator (cf. H. Bonnet, *Reallexikon der Ägyptischen Religionsgeschichte* [Berlin, 1952; repr. 1971], 289–90, s.vv. "Hermanubis" and "Hermes Trismegistos"). The identification of Athena with a sacred fish may be a confused reference to Diodoros' remarks about the Syrian goddess Derceto of Askalon (a manifestation of Aphrodite Ourania), who possessed a fish's body and woman's head (Diod. 2.4.2 and Herodotus, book 1, chap. 105). A search of the *TLG* for "Athena" juxtaposed with "fish" yields only one passage, unlikely to be the source of this reference: Plutarch describes a hieroglyphic inscription including a fish in the temple of Athena at Sais (Plutarch, "De Iside et Osiride," chap. 32, in *Moralia* 363F).

[253] Reading τὰ with A.-M. Talbot for the printed τὸ.

[254] For Pan, see Herodotus, book 2, chap. 46. Anubis was the son of Isis and Osiris who wore a dog skin as he accompanied his father in war (Diod. 1.18.1); Anubis was also represented as the dog-headed guardian of Isis and Osiris (Diod. 1.87.2).

EMPEROR: You are speaking the truth.

PATRIARCH: When, then, <Moses> the lawgiver was leading out of Egypt the people commended to him by God, he wished to wipe off and cleanse away the deep stain that had sunk from <Egypt> into their souls, so that they would not think that the divine was in a man's human shape or in other animal forms. Accordingly, he made such recommendations and ordained such laws by saying, "Do not behave according to Egyptian custom, O men, nor taking absurd lessons from them let a likeness of God be consecrated among you from the <creatures> that fly in the air or move *on the earth* or swim *in the waters.*[255] For these things are not God, even if the Egyptians think <they are>, and that which cannot be seen must not be depicted in an image. For the divine is formless; it cannot be seen nor represented by figures; it is not something observable and recognizable to the eyes of men, but can be perceived only by the mind, should anyone ever be capable <of apprehending> it. For if <the divine is> the creator of all things, he cannot himself be one <thing> from the totality. And if he extends through all <things>, he cannot be confined within one <thing>." Therefore <Moses> the lawgiver prevented <his people> from making images in the case of God only. And that this was his clear <intention>, he himself shall reveal first to those who wish to understand the Scriptures correctly. For with the intention of offering a statement about God and of attributing the words to <God> alone, <Moses> adduced <the following commandment>, saying *"For thou shalt not bow down to them, nor serve them; for I am the Lord thy God, a jealous God."*[256] For it is an impious act of presumption and [p. 175] an absurd notion, if anyone[257] shall ever dare to take his notions from what he can observe and to fashion for himself the <One Who Is> beyond nature, substance, and understanding, Whom no one has seen, and <Whose> form and image no one is able to behold. The <pagan> Greeks impiously dared such things; in seeking God, they did not raise the eyes of their souls on high nor float in mind above the heavenly firmament and there investigate the object of their desire. Rather, they descended to earthly matter and poured out all their wisdom <here>

---

[255] Cf. Ex. 20:4; Deut. 5:8.

[256] Ex. 20:5; Deut. 5:9.

[257] Reading εἴ τις for the printed ἥτις.

below, <then> proclaimed that what appears <to the senses> is God. Now, if a man honors a ruler, celebrates a general, or admires a valiant hero and makes images of them, I see nothing wrong <in it>, should he represent with <painted> colors the one whom he praises in his soul and sees with his eyes. Only keep the thing <thus> produced from ever being honored as God in the manner of foolish <pagan> babblings and chatter! For this is what Moses prohibits, Christian law abhors, and God wishes to preclude; He says, "I shall not grant my glory to another."[258] Whoever understands the words of <Moses> the lawgiver in this way keeps the eye of his understanding without fault, and one who regards the unchangeable <God> with unchangeable reverence does not think that <God> can be compassed by form, nor color, nor location, nor age, nor by any such property of <physical> bodies that attract <our> attention visually. But he who once fixes himself upon <God's> incorporeal <nature> stands unmoved and calm regarding virtue and keeps his own thoughts untroubled and undisturbed. However, <take> one who hears <and interprets these words> in a different way, and in the laziness of his soul grows dizzy when confronted by the formless and <purely> intellectual; he loses his grasp upon the notion of God and wanders through the Plain of Oblivion[259] <like a reptile> creeping around earthly bodies.[260]

What then, if I shall demonstrate that those holy men who lived under <the law of> Moses did not keep this commandment nor avoid making images of the creatures of heaven and on [p. 176] earth or in the sea, if the scriptural passage be understood according to your <broad and> undefined notions?

---

[258] At Is. 62:8 God swears an oath similar in vocabulary and structure to this statement (εἰ ἔτι δώσω τὸν σῖτόν σου καὶ τὰ βρώματά σου τοῖς ἐχθροῖς). The content of God's statement here recalls his prohibition against idolatry (Ex. 20:4–5 and Deut. 5:8–9).

[259] Classical authors mention the Plain of Oblivion as a physical feature in the Underworld (cf. Aristophanes, *Frogs* 186, and Plato, *Republic* 621a); it became proverbial for the activities of feeble and incompetent persons (cf. Leutsch-Schneidewin, *Corpus* 2:758, no. 98).

[260] In *Timaeus* 92a, Plato uses the rare word ἰλυσπώμενα (corrected by a medieval scholar to Ignatios' εἰλυσπ-) to designate reptiles, which he considers creatures devolved from men of excessively mundane mentality.

EMPEROR: How <do you mean>? In what way <did they do that>?

PATRIARCH: Have you not heard, then, O emperor, that when Solomon built the temple <at Jerusalem> he contrived that <famous> *brazen sea*[261] inside the temple precinct, where the priests cleansed their hands *spattered with blood and gore?*[262] Upon what, then, did he elevate it? Did he not forge *twelve* brazen *oxen* and place them beneath the laver that extended over them?[263] How then did he keep the commandment, when he had made for himself the likeness of bulls among his works? By means of <these twelve bulls>, I think, <Solomon> signified that a band of apostles in equal number,[264] the wise plowmen of the Word,[265] would lift on high this world <like the> laver by reverently tilling <the fields of ministry> and would use the flowing stream of their teaching to cleanse and purify the hands of the priests, stained with the blood of sacrifices, so they might be released from that <defilement> and offer bloodless sacrifice to the Lord. What then, when <King Solomon> constructed elaborate and costly thrones, did he not place figures of lions upon them, fixing some on high upon the arms <of the throne> and fitting some lower down on its steps? And the lions were made of ivory.[266]

And why should I tell you these things about others? If <these things> mean <what I say>, one can demonstrate that even <Moses> the lawgiver himself did not follow his own commandments. Do you not know that <Moses> constructed a *propitiatory of pure gold* and set it on top of[267] the *golden*

---

[261] The "brazen sea" in Solomon's temple was a bronze lustral basin that was used by the priests to purify animals for sacrifice and to cleanse themselves after sacrificing (cf. 2 Chr. 4:2, 6). For a discussion of this term applied to the furnishings of Jewish and Christian worship, see Θρησκευτικὴ καὶ ἠθικὴ ἐγκυκλοπαιδεία 6 (Athens, 1965), 99, s.v. θάλασσα τῶν ἐκκλησιῶν. Ignatios paraphrases a text from the Septuagint (2 Ki. 8:8) that does not appear in Jerome's Vulgate or in English translations of the corresponding verse in 2 Sam. 8:8.

[262] Homer, *Od.* 22:402.

[263] Cf. 2 Chr. 4:3–4.

[264] Cf. Mk. 3:14.

[265] Cf. Trapp, *Lexikon,* s.v. βοεργάτης.

[266] Cf. 3 Ki. 10:18–20.

[267] Reading τοῦτο ἄνωθεν for the printed τοῦ τοἄνωθεν.

Ark <of the Covenant>[268] and, like Paul, understood "propitiatory" as our Savior and Lord?[269] And why? Did <Moses> not fashion *two cherubim above the propitiatory,* which *stretch forth their wings* to *overshadow* and protect it,[270] and which announced silently in wordless cry the hidden and unknowable divinity of Him Who would appear on earth? Do you not agree that these [i.e., the cherubim][271] are spiritual powers that dance in a circle around God up along the heavenly radiant <door> panels?[272] [p. 177] They rejoice[273] in their tranquillity and in the fullness of the knowledge that they have concerning the object of their desire. How <did it happen that Moses> the lawgiver, who, as you said, forbade images, made images of these <creatures>? And when <Moses> saw the people of Israel once collapsing in the wilderness (disaster <befell them when> snakes crept out from hidden places and attacked the travelers <like> weapons of death), he made that *serpent of brass* and raised it *upon a signal <staff>.*[274] When the opposing powers looked upon <the brazen serpent>, some [the snakes] were killed, while the <Israelites> who were imperceptibly bitten were suddenly delivered from their wounds. This therefore clearly signified, they say, my Jesus,[275] <for> when <the opposing parties> saw Him hanging on the tree of the cross, some perished and stopped breathing, and vomited forth and spat out the poison of evil they had collected against mankind. But we who gaze upon Him either entirely escape the fire-bearing darts launched by <the Enemy> or we are struck <by them> but

---

[268] The Ark consisted of a container with a cover or "propitiatory" ("mercy seat") upon it (cf. Ex. 25:10–11, 17; Ex. 38:1, 5).

[269] Cf. Rom. 3:25.

[270] Cf. Ex. 25:20, 38:6–8; also Heb. 9:5.

[271] Reading ταῦτα for the printed ταύτας.

[272] The doors of the sanctuary in Solomon's temple had leaves or panels decorated with cherubim, lions, and palm trees; these cherubim could be said to move around God and to contemplate him at close range (cf. 3 Ki. 6:34–35).

[273] Reading γανύμενα for the printed γανυμένας.

[274] When the Israelites complained of their hardships in their desert wanderings, God punished them by sending poisonous snakes to kill them. Moses interceded for the Israelites when they repented and was instructed by God to make a brazen serpent as a standard in order to cure those bitten by the snakes (cf. Num. 21:4–9).

[275] Cf. Jn. 3:14.

saved. Because <the Devil> knows the might of <Christ>, Who hung on the tree <of the cross>, and recalls the weapons discharged from there by <Christ>, the dragon chief of the snakes turns back, lamenting in fear the ever-new occasion of his ancient wound.

Do you see that it is not without risk to interpret the words of <Moses> the lawgiver in this ill-considered, <broad and> undefined way? But, do you know this, O emperor, if you happen to recall it, why <Moses> the lawgiver once raged against the people of Israel?

EMPEROR: I know that <he became angry> many times, but I don't know <the episode> to which you have just now referred.

PATRIARCH: When <the Israelites> crafted the golden head of a calf,[276] <Moses> raged against them with the greatest possible justification. For they forgot the wonders worked <by Moses> in Egypt, their passage through the *midst* of *the sea*,[277] the mass death of the *firstborn* <of Egypt>,[278] [p. 178] and the transformation of the elements;[279] as soon as <Moses> the lawgiver turned his back,[280] they proclaimed that the calf's head was a god. You don't think they committed any sin, do you, nor did <Moses> the lawgiver make this accusation against them, namely, that they simply happened to manufacture a calf?

EMPEROR: Why?

PATRIARCH: Because, if we should find fault with <the Israelites> on this account, we should also accuse Solomon, because he also fashioned his bulls.[281] The reason why we find fault with the men <of Israel>, and <Mo-

---

[276] Cf. Ex. 32:3–4.

[277] Ex. 14:21–22.

[278] Ex. 12:29–30.

[279] Among the miracles performed by Moses in Egypt was the transformation of water into blood (cf. Ex. 7:17–25) and of dirt into lice (cf. Ex. 8:16–19).

[280] Reading ἀπέτρεπε for the printed ἐπέτρεπε. Moses left the Israelites behind in the wilderness when he obeyed God's summons to the summit of Mt. Sinai (cf. Ex. 24:15–18).

[281] Cf. *v. Niceph.* 176.7–9.

ses> the lawgiver made accusation <against them>, is that they proclaimed the calf a god and impiously attributed to it their deliverance in Egypt. He did not prohibit simply making an image, then, but rather making a god's image. To <impart> this <lesson> Scripture also has recorded that <the Israelites> removed *the golden earrings of their wives* and wrought that golden head of the calf.[282] In my opinion, <the passage> implies in an allusive manner that the hearing <or ears> of those <Israelite> men received the genuine <or golden> teachings about God, then lapsed into different <and erroneous> doctrines, stripped themselves naked of the ornament <of true teaching>, and were deprived of the adornment bestowed upon[283] their ears <and understanding>.[284] But <Moses> the lawgiver, as Scripture itself says, *ground the calf, scattered* it *on the water,* and *made* the people <of Israel> *to drink it.*[285] What does this signify? When <Moses> saw, as I think, this <people> ignorant concerning the sin of idolatry and not comprehending the extent of the harm <in it>, he taught them by making his statement about <idolatry> concise, to the point, and easy to understand; he gave the people <of Israel these words> to drink, and placed <the words> in their hearts so that failure to recognize impiety would not readily befall <them>.

But while I am asking you questions, also tell me this.

EMPEROR: What, then?

PATRIARCH: Is it not customary for men also to make works of art <that> frequently represent shaggy lions that glare fearsomely, or wild boars with bristling hairs,[286] or horses racing in full view as if on a plain or in the mountains, or figures of birds that seem to twitter, so that many times <the artists> provide an experience of hearing the sound <of the animal portrayed>? And men sometimes paint these <animal figures> on walls [p. 179] and sometimes weave them onto garments; some <artisans> now mold <animals> of

---

[282] Ex. 32:2–4.

[283] Reading A.-M. Talbot's ἐμβληθέντα for the printed ἐκβληθέντα.

[284] Gregory of Nyssa offered a similar allegorical interpretation of this episode (*De vita Moysis,* PG 44:396c).

[285] Ex. 32:20.

[286] The lions and boars are described in terms recalling Hesiod, *Shield of Herakles,* 168–75.

bronze and of gold to provide joy and beauty, placing them in homes or setting them up in marketplaces. What, then? Have they caused injury to men or to human life with these, so long as they do not follow the sacrilegious nonsense of the <pagan> Greeks and give the name of God to the works they have made? But if some witless fellow persuaded by demonic error shall consider one of these <statues> a god, will we not immediately pelt him with stones, burn him with fire, or offer him to the jaws of ravening beasts?

Emperor, there is, then, one way of resolving rightly both to know and to understand that <Moses> the lawgiver both barred and forbade us to make images in the case of God only. And if we say this, neither will we find fault with those who long ago conducted themselves according to the law, nor do we fall into error as Christians by making images of the martyrs or of men who are otherwise blessed and by setting forth in a visible <representation> their <attributes>, which might not have been <actually> seen[287] <by the artist>. And, if anyone aspiring to piety believes me, he must explain and analyze this scriptural passage in this way, and he must reckon that there are two rules, so to speak, which cannot be violated nor confused.

EMPEROR: How and in what manner <should he do this>?

PATRIARCH: That one must not make images of a god, but if he should attempt some such thing, he must be subjected to the most extreme penalties as a subscriber to <pagan> Greek doctrines. But one must depict holy men, who exult in their free access to God and in the purity of <eternal> life, who somehow will be mediators for us and intermediaries to <God>, and bring to God our requests and return to us God's gifts. For there is no single manner of life for those who approach God or whom He honors. But their access <to God> is commensurate with their way of life, and <God's> response follows consistently upon their conduct. For *God exists eternally and has no beginning,*[288] while that which does not exist through eternity but came into exis-

---

[287] Lit., "showing by means of what appears what does not appear." Ignatios justifies the activity of artists who do not have the opportunity to depict their holy subjects on the basis of life models, death masks, or divinely inspired visions.

[288] In *Timaeus* 27 d6, Plato contrasts the material universe with "that which eternally exists and has no beginning." This definition was applied to God by the 3d-century Christian theologian Hippolytos (*De universo* 3.9, publ. W. J. Malley, "Four Unedited Fragments of the *De Universo* of the pseudo-Josephus Found in the *Chronicon* of George Hamartolus [Coislin 305]," *Journal of Theological Studies* 16 [1965], 15–16) and

tence later has received its beginning [p. 180] from Him Who Is [i.e, God]. And in accordance with this passage, everything that has ever come into existence would be termed subject to *God,* for what has come into existence would be rightly considered subject to Him Who has *made* it.[289] By virtue of one's relationship to God and the difference in degree of radiance <received> from Him, a different name and title is applied appropriate to the different character of those who approach <God>. For those who avoid sin because they fear punishment would be called *servants* of God, and they are indeed the sort of slaves in need of a whipping, who require beatings, imprisonment, and attendant threats so that they will not sin. But <others>, who incline toward goodness in hope of benefits to come, would not be called *house*hold servants[290] but rather would be paid hirelings of God, as one might say, who do what is needful for the sake of some profit and *hire.*[291] There are, however, some in turn who appear completely superior to these latter <hirelings> also as regards virtue, and who are eager for goodness not because they fear <some> anticipated punishment nor because they hope for future benefits, but they achieve virtue for its own sake; these men are filled with *the* undefiled *treasures of wisdom*[292] and would rightly *be called the sons of God,*[293] bearing the name *heirs of God and joint heirs with Christ.*[294] These men, inasmuch as they are human by nature, prefer to beseech God with their prayers on behalf of all mankind, not only while yet wandering this errant and disordered world, but above all then when they have stripped off the rags <of this earthly body> and shaken off the heavy weight of bones and dust; casting matter upon matter, in purity they will return without blemish to their good and gracious master.

---

repeated by pseudo-Justin Martyr (*Cohortatio ad gentiles* 22 E 4 [Morel]) and Eusebios (*Constantini imp. oratio ad coetum sanctorum* 3.1, ed. J. A. Heikel, *Eusebius Werke* 1 [Leipzig, 1902], 156.9–10). Ignatios proceeds to expand upon the original definition in the manner of Eusebios.

[289] Cf. Gen. 2:4–5.

[290] In Heb. 3:5–6 Paul drew a distinction between those like Moses who were servants of God (with only partial knowledge of his nature), and those following Christ who are of God's house.

[291] Cf. Mt. 20:1–13.

[292] Col. 2:3.

[293] Cf. 1 John 3:1.

[294] Rom. 8:17.

EMPEROR: What, then? Do <men> not share in the doctrines of the <pagan> Greeks when they create images of the humans you call blessed?

PATRIARCH: We must not simply make accusations against them in this way; we must consider and examine <the situation>.

EMPEROR: How <can they> as Christians create such images? How <can> they depict <human beings>?

PATRIARCH: They do endow what they depict with a share of the ineffable reality [p. 181] beyond reality, do they not?

EMPEROR: Absolutely not.

PATRIARCH: What? Are they honoring <the saints> as possessing <God>, the first and heavenly cause?

EMPEROR: No indeed.

PATRIARCH: But do <the icon painters> consider <the saints> mortal men?

EMPEROR: Yes.

PATRIARCH: What reason is there to complain, then, if we who know <the saints> as men portray them as men? But as for the name "God," which is exceptional and by its very nature cannot be assigned to <created> beings in its proper sense, we allow <this name to be assigned> to the reality which transcends all, because it alone is appropriate to Him alone. We shall not paint that <transcendent reality> in forms and images (for how shall we depict what we do not perceive with our eyes?), but we shall make use of images of martyrs and of men who are otherwise holy, not because we consider them gods (may we not thus deviate from what is proper!), but <because we consider them> faithful servants of God. <We do this> to repay them for <their spiritual> valor and also so that they, as attendants of the king, may bring on our behalf as our representatives the requests we are unable to make of the king because we are captive to our sins.

If you approve, let the issue be examined on the basis of human examples. Surely you agree that the Creator of this whole <universe> is a good captain and has provided calm seas for those who sail in this <world>, so that they might not be hastened along by men like unballasted cargo ships and go astray[295] among the stormy seas of their lives? <Has the Creator not> established the emperor as an image and representation of Himself on earth?

EMPEROR: Yes.

PATRIARCH: While the <emperor> is not God, he wishes to imitate God to the extent possible for a human being; since <the emperor> is both circumscribed <by mortal limitations> and also merely human, he extends his own presence through the state by appointing others as officials so that he may be present to all even when absent and also may instill[296] in his subjects an awe that is close <at hand> when he is far away. What, then? Will <the emperor> ever tolerate for us to address as emperors those whom he has commanded to rule, or to share <with them> the manner of address <proper to> him? [p. 182]

EMPEROR: Surely not.

PATRIARCH: But will he find fault with us, if we approach and make supplication to his appointees who are conducting the affairs <of government> according to his wishes? Will he find fault if we convey to him through them whatever requests we are unable to bring him <directly>?

EMPEROR: Not at all.

PATRIARCH: So it is then, emperor, that we must understand God. He is angry should we give to another a share in the honor <due to> God, but He commends us and is pleased, should we choose to give honor to His servants.

But the most wise <St.> Paul will also seem to you to be conversant with this doctrine, in his epistle to the Romans. He did not simply level an accusation against icons, nor find fault with those who have made use of them,

---

[295] Reading πλάζοιντο with Nikitin for the printed πλέξοιντο.

[296] Reading ἐπάγῃ for the printed ἐπάγει.

but <complained> that *they changed the glory of the uncorruptible God into an image made like to corruptible man.*[297] For in reality, these are bold men[298] and also stupid, who have neither seen the representation of God or His form and shape nor been able to conceptualize them, <but> honored as God only the things they saw. For they were born of the earth and sown[299] and uncultivated <by Gospel teachings>; they were slaves of sense perception and some were bodies, so to speak, without souls and sluggish <besides>. They were perplexed at how to attain understanding of the immaterial without <using> matter, and unable to proceed beyond the nature of what they could see. In this <passage> you will truly marvel at the apostle [Paul's] very appropriate meaning. For <St. Paul> clearly presents <the phrase> *they changed* as equivalent to <the meaning> that the ideas about God sown in our souls and the traditions <handed down> by the earliest men from the very beginning *knew the* one and *only true God,*[300] while the devotees of earthly wisdom brashly tore piety up by the roots with their unphilosophical philosophy and their illogical logic. They both changed those <ideas about God> and took another <direction>; by implanting seedlings of polytheism, they betrayed the truth they possessed and furnished *an image* for God *like to man and to birds,* etc.[301] For a person makes an exchange when he chooses what he does not possess instead of the reality that he possessed before. [p. 183] He would never choose to exchange what he did not possess.

EMPEROR: Is this what you were preaching, then, that we must accept the dictum of <Moses> the lawgiver in the case of God only, and that <Moses> forbade the making of images in this circumstance?

PATRIARCH: So I said, and I will never stop saying it.

---

[297] Rom. 1:23.

[298] Reading τολμητίαι for the printed τολμητέοι.

[299] Greek myths identified some early rulers like Erechtheus/ Erechthonios of Athens as born from the land their descendants ruled and labeled the Thebans "sown men" because the ancestors of their nobility sprang from the dragon's teeth planted by Kadmos. Cf. T. Ganz, *Early Greek Myth: A Guide to Literary and Artistic Sources* (Baltimore, Md., 1993), 233–39 and 468–71.

[300] Cf. Jn. 17:3.

[301] Cf. Rom. 1:23.

EMPEROR: What, then? Do you not *preach Christ* as *the true God?*[302]

PATRIARCH: Indeed I do.

EMPEROR: And do you not depict images of Christ?

PATRIARCH: Of course.

EMPEROR: How then, if you *preach Christ* as *the true God,* do you depict images of Christ, if <Moses> the lawgiver forbade depicting images of God?

PATRIARCH: Bless you, emperor! For the <argument> advanced by you will set forth the <true> doctrine more distinctly. Tell me, do you not *preach* that *Christ* is *true God* and true man?"

EMPEROR: So I do.

PATRIARCH: Once having become a man, is Christ not complete in like manner regarding this <human nature> and that <divine nature>, neither diminishing his own <divine> nature nor transforming <the human nature> that He assumed into the nature of divinity?

EMPEROR: Certainly.

PATRIARCH: But do you not agree and assert that we would never claim that Christ is first one and then another <person>? But rather we call the same <person> one in accordance with first one and then another <nature>, at once incapable of suffering and liable to suffering <and death>. This <attribute "incapable of suffering"> accords with His divine <nature>, while that <attribute "liable to suffering and death"> accords with His human <nature>. What, then? Is He not invisible and intangible and apprehensible <only> spiritually inasmuch as He is God, but perceptible to sight, to touch, and to the senses inasmuch as He is man? Do we not know that the one who is depicted is also truly God? For Christ even incarnate

---

[302] Cf. Acts 8:5 and 1 John 5:20. The emperor temporarily takes the offensive by assuming the role of interrogator.

<in the flesh> is truly God. But we do not depict Christ in His divine <nature>, nor do we dedicate images to Him in accordance with this <nature>, but we have made use of images inasmuch as <this> same <Christ> was man and appeared on earth. We do not elevate what can be seen and circumscribed <by endowing it> with the capacities of what can neither be seen nor circumscribed, lest we be cheated of our salvation, nor do we in turn make mad attempts to give form to what can be neither touched, seen, nor circumscribed in <Christ> by demeaning it with terms <particular> to touching, circumscribing, and seeing. But we rather know [p. 184] that both *the visible and invisible*[303] of the one Christ are present, <both that> which can be circumscribed and <that> which cannot, <and these qualities> neither <can be> separated <from one another> nor <are they> commingled <with one another>. Indeed, we have learned to attribute what pertains to each <nature of Christ> as has seemed right in the past in accordance with the particular qualities of the natures from which <Christ> exists. And the way in which images are painted will demonstrate this. For they depict <Christ> either *lying in a manger*,[304] or being nursed by His God-bearing mother, or in company with His disciples, or standing in the presence of Pilate, or *hanging on a tree* [i.e., the Cross],[305] or whatever else in like manner shows His presence on earth. Not one of <these> accorded with <the manifestation in> which He was God, but rather accorded with that in which the same <Christ> was man. For if He had never become a man, nor of His own free will assumed on earth the shape and form of a man, neither would these things be depicted nor would they have any occasion to occur in the case of <Christ>. But if *the Word was made flesh*[306] and appeared on earth, and if God, Who was before without flesh and without body, was seen as a man by men, we would not be doing wrong, as I see it, if we wish to reproduce pictorially what we have seen.

EMPEROR: And what are you willing to say about the pictorial representation of the angels? For you will not, I think, claim that painters know the shapes of angels by observation and depict them while looking at their form.

---

[303] Cf. Col. 1:16.
[304] Lk. 2:12.
[305] Gal. 3:13, quoting Deut. 21:23.
[306] Jn. 1:14.

PATRIARCH: While I do not assert that <artists> have seen the form or shape of angels nor create a painting as if they had seen them, <artists> do in my belief confer upon angels the form of men in compliance with Scripture.

EMPEROR: What is your reason for saying this?

PATRIARCH: Do you not know that Scripture somewhere tells of the angels <seen> by Abraham *by the oak* <*of Mambre*>, how Abraham *lifted up his eyes* and *beheld three men* standing near it?[307] What then? Did <God> not send the *angels in Sodom* with the appearance of *men?*[308] Therefore <painters> do not themselves invent their paintings as offspring of unreasoning presumption, but they depict in their pictures the sorts of <creatures> that were seen.

EMPEROR: And what reason might they find for adding wings to <angels>?

PATRIARCH: [p. 185] In my opinion succinctly <stated>, to avoid the presumption that <angels> are men in every respect, <the artists> made the distinction clear by the addition <of wings>. <When artists> portray <angels> with wings, they are not adding wings as an irrational theory, but are alluding to the angels' progress through the air, to their dwelling place in heaven with God, to their sudden descents from <heaven> among us, and to their swift returns to heaven from us. Now Moses once described[309] the form of the cherubim as having wings[310] (for <cherubim> are also angels, and, in the opinion of Dionysios [the Areopagite], in general they call angels the powers that are both celestial and also of the spiritual order).[311] Therefore, <artists> not unreasonably, I think, have made <angels> resemble the pattern <of the cherubim>. And now, emperor, we must keep those <considerations> in mind, and must guard fast in our souls the fact that a painting is in turn a created thing if we paint images of angels, and that I approach <the

---

[307] Cf. Gen. 18:1–2.

[308] Cf. Gen. 19:1, 5.

[309] Reading τυπωσαμένου for the printed τυπωσομένου.

[310] Cf. Ex. 25:20.

[311] Cf. pseudo-Dionysios Areopagite, *De caelesti hierarchia,* chap. 5 (PG 3:195c) for a similar definition of angels.

images> not as if the highest and primary essence were allotted[312] them (may I not be so insane as to think that a created thing is God!), but rather as if they were fellow slaves of our common master, who have obtained exceptional privilege to approach Him because they are wealthy in virtue.

Although the emperor was overwhelmed by his inability to formulate an answer, he managed with difficulty to speak in a faint and lifeless voice: "But those who hold opinions contrary to yours also cite a swarm of citations from the Fathers [of the Church].[313] Do not refrain from refuting <these passages> in direct confrontation with <your opponents> and us." And the holy father <Nikephoros> answered, "I have said it <before>, emperor, and I shall say it again—with all deference to your power, I shall present refutations for both scriptural and patristic texts, if God gives <me grace to do it>. But I will have no dealings with those who have thrust themselves out of the Church and *brought themselves under excommunication,*[314] for I would not wish to strip or remove anything from the definitions and signators of the <church> councils. If you would like clear evidence that I have held these opinions not only for a very long time and indeed do not now hasten to speak for myself alone, but that a great and by no means insignificant crowd of both bishops and monks treads the orthodox road of this profession of faith, [p. 186] only look—these men stand at the gates of your palace. If you should consent to their presence, you will learn even from their <own mouths> that they have no doctrinal disagreement with me."[315]

Then <the emperor> consented to their entrance. But he gave orders that they be escorted by the chief members of his retinue, who had swords hanging at their sides according to each one's rank; in his cowardice he thought he would frighten the fearless ones with military might. Then that holy multitude of the Church processed into the palace with its golden roof, exulting greatly in their immense enthusiasm and goaded by confidence as if prodded by God. And when they drew near *where* the tyrant *was* still *sitting,*[316]

---

[312] Reading κληρωσαμένοις for the printed κληρωσαμένους.

[313] Leo refers to the committee he assembled to compile a florilegium of quotations opposing images (cf. *v. Niceph.* 165.20–30).

[314] Cf. Philostorgios, *Historia ecclesiastica,* book 2, chap. 11 (PG 65:473A).

[315] The patriarch's request effectively closes Ignatios' account of the dialogue and motivates the emperor's next action.

[316] Homer, *Il.* 9:194.

they saw the patriarch offering opposing arguments in quite a loud voice, and smiting the emperor with argument as if he were <slapping> a baby at its birth <to make it take its first breath>. At this, they gained the courage to speak and thrust off from themselves fear and timidity.

The *lionhearted* <emperor> *scowled from beneath his brows* at them[317] and said: "Just as you <now> see, it is obvious to you and to everyone that God has appointed me to act as mediator over this spiritual flock with its glorious name and <that I have been> assigned to level and destroy through my energetic endeavor any stumbling block[318] that might be in <that flock>. Since, then, certain persons are even now engaged in discussing the nature and veneration of images and are citing scriptural passages that oppose these <images>, it is absolutely necessary to refute these <passages> so that what I have struggled <to achieve> might be accomplished. (Indeed, in every respect I struggle <to achieve> unanimity in peace for all persons, as you know.) It is absolutely necessary, then, to offer a conclusion <to the argument> to those who raise difficulties and present problems. For as regards these matters, [p. 187] I also formerly met with the patriarch, but now that I am in your presence, I enjoin you to provide a speedy resolution for the matters in contention. <Be careful> lest silent reluctance <on your part> provide grounds for accusations against you and prove to be a disadvantage by implying your disobedience." But the followers and fellow pastors of the excellent chief shepherd <Nikephoros> drew out their quivers <full> of scriptural passages to oppose Leo, <the man> with a beast's name and a wolf's heart. In turn they emptied out every shaft of refutation and left <the emperor> wounded all over his body. And rather than rehearse in detail the speeches each one made then, let me expound one speech from them all, as if to summarize them all.[319] It ran as follows.

"Emperor, *it is obvious to us and to everyone,* as you say, *that you have*

---

[317] The Homeric epithet θυμολέων ("lionhearted") is reserved for the great (and violent) epic heroes Heracles, Achilles, and Odysseus; the Homeric formula ὑπόδρα ἰδὼν ("scowling from beneath the brows") is frequent in both the *Iliad* and the *Odyssey.*

[318] Cf. Is. 57:14.

[319] Von Dobschütz ("Methodios und die Studiten," 57) suggests that Ignatios' anonymous speaker was in reality Theodore of Stoudios, who played a prominent role in other historians' accounts of the incident.

been appointed to act as mediator over Christ's greatest *flock*[320] in accord with
<divine> *judgments* that we do not *know.*[321] It is, however, well known to
those who know how to judge correctly that the balance of <the scale in the
matter here under> mediation has inclined from the very beginning toward
you. For a mediator is not one who tips <the scale> this way and that and
gives the decisive turn to whichever <cause> he favors, but rather he who
pays equal attention to those on each <side of the argument>. If then you
are eager to investigate and destroy any obstacles to the Church,[322] why have
you not displayed the turn of the scale impartially towards everyone? For anyone who wishes <to look> sees that the advocates of true doctrine are driven
out and suffer the same fate as criminals, while those who foster <ideas>
contrary <to true doctrine> enjoy your devoted affection and every <expres-
sion of> cheerful solicitude. Or do these men not dwell under roofs of gold,
while we are oppressed in the confines of prison?[323] Are they not allotted meals
from bountiful palace fare, while we are pinched by famine and sated with
poverty? Have they not been provided with every book for their researches,
while those who supply[324] these <books> to us are threatened with punishment? What spark of mediation can be recognized in these <circumstan-
ces>? What impartiality and equality before the law is practiced in these <cir-
cumstances>? [p. 188] What stability of mind prevails in perfect balance in
these <aforementioned> situations, and keeps their conscience on the right
<path>? Because we see these things and note that you are inclined to be
irresolute <in your opinions>[325] and that we have been condemned by default
even from the <time of the> first assault <against us>, we pay silent honor
to the sanctity of the universal Church, lest we be caught in a mire of blas-
phemy and defiled with doctrines that ceaselessly outrage the Incarnation of

---

[320] This passage replicates the emperor's own words above (186.17–20) almost exactly.

[321] Cf. Rom. 11:33–35.

[322] A paraphrase of the emperor's words above (186.20–21).

[323] Ignatios noted earlier that Leo provided accommodations in the palace for the
committee that excerpted pro-iconoclastic passages from patristic literature (165.20–
25), but imprisoned and starved the bishops who supported Nikephoros (165.31–
166.11).

[324] Reading ἐπιχορηγοῦσι for the printed ἐπιχορηγεῖν.

[325] Ignatios characterizes the emperor in similar terms at 163.27–28.

Christ. What person possessed of reason and wisdom will follow you in <your path> of universal destruction? For from the sun's <first> rays <in the east>, even as far as Gadeira and the Pillars of Herakles <in the west>,[326] the making of holy icons is revered; in reality <this practice> is clearly implied not by some <recent> notion from yesterday but by the coming of Christ among men. Thus we have been taught that *the prophets, apostles, and teachers* built upon this *foundation*[327] <of Christ>. Indeed, we have observed that emperors complied with and accepted the judgments <made> by them [i.e., the leaders of the Church], but we have by no means known <emperors> to fix through legislation decisions that have been canceled by the Church.[328] And we leave the conscience of our audience to make the judgment that these things are true, for in that terrifying court which cannot be deceived [i.e., God's judgment seat] the truth will crown those who praise it, but will reject the opponents of holy doctrines for their shameful falsehood and will drive them away."

Thus <Leo's> mind was thunderstruck by these and as many more <arguments>, and his ears were virtually deafened by the resounding <response> of those holy men. He suspected that they had now struck an uncompromising blow against him and that he had been made a public figure of unmistakable slander, so he took sudden and cowardly flight from his own argument and openly acknowledged his defeat. For he was not able to stretch out his hand <to help> his own argument, nor even to dare confronting the refutation of what he had said. This was indeed very understandable. For once arrogance has gained even a small <amount of> power <over a person>, it makes its captive completely unstable and drives him out of his senses. But at the same time he understood that he could be easily conquered [p. 189] by the close examination of his argument. For even that <fellow> knew that the truth is difficult to capture and impossible to conquer. Therefore, although

---

[326] The western boundary of the known world at the Strait of Gibraltar is designated here by terms familiar in proverbs (Gadeira, cf. Leutsch-Schneidewin, *Corpus* 2:661, no. 19) and in classical literature (the Pillars of Herakles are first mentioned by Pindar and Herodotos).

[327] A variation on Eph. 2:20.

[328] Nikephoros may mean that Leo has revived the decisions of the iconoclast council in Hieria, which prohibited using images in worship (754); the Second Council of Nicaea (787) overturned those decisions.

he mustered some irrelevant and nonsensical prattle designed to make those opponents <of his> submit, he was unable to reverse his own defeat and, under these circumstances, he threatened and expelled from the palace these men together with their spiritual leader <Nikephoros>. O, how the man turned to the worse <course of action>! O, how he fell from the better one! For from that moment, as the proverb says, he donned <Herakles'> lionskin against the Church[329] and openly conspired with persons armed against <the Church>. He dispatched into immediate exile those who were willing athletes contending to the best of their abilities; he dispersed them to various destinations and banished them somewhere far from the sheepfolds of the Church. Indeed, <the emperor> became convinced that he could capture the patriarch <Nikephoros> in the snare of heresy without ever striking a blow or, if this were not <possible>, that <Nikephoros> would voluntarily[330] forsake his leadership of the priesthood because he had no ally enrolled <among the> holy <clergy>. Thereafter <Nikephoros> endured in solitude the adversity of the times, while looking to his heavenly allies <in confidence> that they would support him in his solitude and bring him the greatest possible assistance in his perplexity.

When <Nikephoros> saw that the man denied upon oath the <articles> of the true faith and now revealed himself an unbeliever in matters pertaining to God, <Nikephoros> wrote to <Leo's> consort <appealing to her> as a woman.[331] He reminded her of correct <practice in> worship and <correct> belief among Christians, and <urged her to> persuade her emperor and consort to refrain from such a terrible undertaking. He wrote also to a man who was then treasurer of imperial funds and a close associate of Leo by virtue of both his outspoken candor and his arrogance.[332] <Nikephoros instructed him> not to contrive plans against the Church nor to set any tempest in motion <against it>, since <the Church> presently enjoyed peace and freedom

---

[329] I.e., he undertook a task of great magnitude; see Leutsch-Schneidewin, *Corpus* 2:29, no. 72 (with notes) and 75, no. 75.

[330] Changing the punctuation of the printed edition at 189.13 so that the comma precedes γνώμης instead of following it.

[331] Leo's wife was Theodosia, daughter of the Armenian patrician and rebel Arsaber (see Alexander, *Nicephorus*, 132 n. 5).

[332] This anonymous official was probably a *sakellarios* (see Alexander, *Nicephorus*, 132–33 n. 1).

from factional strife; rather, <Nikephoros encouraged him> at that time both to extinguish the conflagration kindled in the <Church> by those who deserved *everlasting fire* <in Hell>[333] and to soothe the emperor's ferocity. <Nikephoros> wrote also to the man who was then the chief imperial secretary (this was Eutychianos)[334] [p. 190] and who had taken part with the heretics in reading <and analyzing> the texts of the orthodox faith. <Nikephoros> warned him> that if he should *not cease to pervert the right ways of the Lord* but rather chose to journey <in the way of> *Elymas the sorcerer,* he would suffer bodily harm <inflicted> by the justice that oversees <all things> and he would suffer dreadful affliction in the resources <needed> for life.[335] <But> the threats overtook <Eutychianos> although he was impervious to admonition. For from that moment the entire lifespan measured out for the wretched man brought him unrelenting pain and presented him daily at the gates of death as a living corpse. This is how God treats those who have condemned the Church to an illness that none can cure.

But these useful guides for life supplied by the teacher <Nikephoros> and his wise admonitions did not improve the emperor. He directed his attention towards this one <goal> only, <namely> to force <the patriarch> out <of office> and weave a widow's garment of wool for the bride of Christ, <the Church>. Thus he entrusted the fiscal administration of the church <of St. Sophia> and <guardianship of> the holy furnishings that had been dedicated <there> to a man who held patrician rank[336] and made it known that the patriarch was without jurisdiction in these matters. For <Leo> never stopped shifting every stone, as the proverb <says>,[337] in order to shake the

---

[333] Cf. Mt. 18:8 and 25:41.

[334] Eutychianos, head of the imperial chancery (*protasekretis*), is probably identical to the fervent opponent of icons who served on Leo's committee compiling the iconoclastic florilegium (see Alexander, *Nicephorus,* 133 n. 2).

[335] Ignatios quotes Acts 13:10 and 13:8. Elymas, a sorcerer from Paphos, was blinded when he persisted in disparaging Paul and Barnabas before the Roman ruler of Cyprus (cf. Acts 13:6–12).

[336] This was Thomas, twice consul, whom Leo appointed *logothetes* and *skeuophylax* of St. Sophia, the patriarchal church. The latter office would have included supervision over the images in the church. See Alexander, *Nicephorus,* 133–34.

[337] This proverbial expression meaning "to take every measure to achieve one's object" reportedly originated with the oracle of Apollo at Delphi (see Leutsch-Schneidewin, *Corpus* 1:146, no. 63; 293, no. 42; 2:201, no. 4).

supports of the Church. O, how my narrative <would> prefer to spread a bed of silence over the events that ensued, not continuing to the point where <my tale> will end![338] How my narrative shows that it needs a physician itself even before it declares the details of the blessed <Nikephoros'> illness! For he was confined to his <sick>bed struggling for breath because some flux assaulted his body, and he was wrestling with the intractable <symptoms> of the disease. But nothing caused the just <man Nikephoros> so much pain as the insurrection contrived against the Church by her enemies. For he alone had to endure the struggle <against illness>, whereas the entire body of citizens was at risk because of this <insurrection>.

Then the committee that opposed the Church grew conceited; bloated with the rich fat of falsehood, it sought an open confrontation. [p. 191] Accordingly, <the committee> again persuaded the emperor, who was carried along by every breeze of heresy, to press the teacher <Nikephoros> to meet for a debate with them. <Leo> dispatched the empress' brother Theophanes, who was girded with the imperial sword,[339] on the <mission> to drag the patriarch into the murderous company of that conspiracy. <Nikephoros> used with <Theophanes> the explanation <he had articulated> before[340] and also now had his illness to support him in refusing to meet for a debate with the impious <committee>. "A shepherd," he explained, "does not arm himself against wolves <if he has been> deprived of his sheep, nor is he eager to battle wild beasts alone <if he> takes forethought for his own safety. However, by sealing up his flock in a safe sheepfold and by pushing far aside *the*

---

[338] A paraphrase of Euripides, *Hippolytus* 342.

[339] Theophanes held the rank of *spatharios,* or member of the imperial bodyguard. The empress Theodosia and Theophanes were children of Arsaber, a noble Armenian of patrician rank who was proclaimed emperor by a putsch of lay and clerical officials (808), overwhelmed by the emperor Nikephoros, and exiled to Bithynia. Arsaber's reputation for eloquence may have been inherited by his son (see Alexander, *Nicephorus,* 134 and *ODB* 1:186, s.v. "Arsaber," and 3:1935–36, s.v. "Spatharios").

[340] Leo himself had already pressed Nikephoros to debate with the committee which compiled the florilegium of writings supporting the iconoclast position (see *v. Niceph.* 170.9–13). Nikephoros had refused this earlier request because the committee members lacked the Holy Spirit and their florilegium had already been refuted (see *v. Niceph.* 172.13–17), meaning presumably in the version presented to the Council of Hieria (754).

fear where there is *no fear,*[341] he builds a fence against the devices of the wolves. How is it then, that after you have deprived me of my lambs and driven them by force from their rightful pasture, you challenge me to fight alone against you terrible beasts? This is not glorious <behavior> for one who possesses sheep! But if you wish to succeed in your delusions (for the <arguments> you repeatedly offer us are a delusion that does not partake in any truth), grant freedom of choice for each person in weighing <his decision>, let every man be master of his own purpose, let the prisons be unlocked, let those oppressed in bitter exile return, let your dungeon pits be opened up, and let those be delivered who are the victims of starvation, who are the playthings of thirst, and who take daily pleasure, as the Psalm <says>, in the *night* <which *was*> *light in* their *luxury.*[342] Let the whip make pause in lacerating the bodies of godly minded persons. So if these things should come to pass, if you should authorize liberty for each man, and if you will not allow violence to gain its own <end>—when the manifest enemies of the Church have been expelled as well as those to whom no shred of priesthood remains and who cannot therefore be admitted to an ecclesiastical inquiry—then we shall persuade ourselves to enter into discussion with the remaining <members of the com-mittee>—if indeed anyone will <at that point> remain, <God> forbid! [p. 192] For it is not right to enlist unholy persons to investigate holy mat-ters. Now as for those who pay honor to the dogmatic <decrees> of Con-stantine,[343] long since silent and <now> resounding <again>, let them ex-plain—who has conferred upon them a priestly dignity? On the basis of what sacramental ordination recognized by ecclesiastical canons do they claim to be enrolled in the rank of those who perform priestly functions? If then eccle-siastical discipline bears witness to the fact that they are unworthy, who will allow them to speak for the Church? Let these <considerations> be made known to the people who sent you, and if they should seem persuaded by our

---

[341] Reading οὗ <οὐκ>; cf. Ps. 13 (14):5 and 52 (53):5, where the evil and ungodly are described as having "fear where there was no fear."

[342] Cf. Ps. 138 (139):11.

[343] Under the direction of the iconoclast emperor Constantine V, the Council of Hieria (754) decreed any pictorial representation of God to be impossible. The Council of Hieria and its decrees were declared invalid by the Second Council of Nicaea (787) under the direction of the empress Irene.

arguments, look here, we are setting an <appropriate> time and place for those with whom it is fitting to debate. And the <appropriate> time for conversation and discussion is whenever it should please God for my illness to abate, and God should grant me to remain among the living! The place is the far-famed church of divine reason[344] in which God sits, deciding and elucidating with elegance the most just decisions that pertain to the universal faith."

The messenger [Theophanes] relayed these <words> to the ears of the <emperor> who had sent him, and he <also> revealed absolutely everything to those who agreed in their opposition <to the patriarch's views>. <The patriarch's words> stunned their tongues completely speechless and froze <their very> hearts, since <his words> concerned impossible conditions that could not be adequately accomplished. Thereupon they huddled together in consultation and spewed out for the emperor some such words as these against the <patriarch>, the bulwark of the Church, saying, "Under the terms enunciated <by the patriarch>, it is impossible for the decisions <made> by your imperial majesty and the judgments rendered by the permanent synod <of the patriarchate>[345] to achieve an outcome that accomplishes the goals of both parties. For if each individual were to have an opportunity to weigh his decision about where he wishes to turn,[346] if those condemned to exile were allowed to return, and if each and every person were to be master of his own choice without any constraint, then we would very rapidly be left naked and alone. For every opinion formed freely will follow <the patriarch> [p. 193] with the greatest possible alacrity, and we will be rendered helpless, especially <since> he has refused even to debate with our leaders. For this would cause an extraordinary upset in our <affairs>. Enough, then, of extending offers! Although we have now urged our third invitation upon him, he remains stubborn and has not met <our challenge>. But if you agree, let us use our synodal authority to set forth for him in writing clear <conditions> for the disobedient, <namely> that he respond to and defend himself against the charges which the synod has brought against him."

---

[344] I.e., the patriarchal church of St. Sophia, or "Holy Wisdom." The adjective διώνυμος is used by Ignatios of the Magnaura Palace in the *Life of Tarasios* (v. *Taras.* 400.28).

[345] Nikephoros' opponents refer to a decision (now lost) made by the permanent assembly of bishops in Constantinople, which discussed the business of the patriarchate (see *ODB* 1:697, s.v. "Endemousa synodos").

[346] Cf. v. *Niceph.* 191.19–20.

Then in shabby and lame prose, they composed a document to <Nike­phoros>, the Church's primate, which ordered him to attend upon those who had not been ordained <to ecclesiastical office> and to give them an accounting of his intentions. They loaded <this document> upon certain bishops and clergymen who had never been ordained and dispatched it to <Nikepho­ros>, the beacon of orthodoxy, providing as escort <to these emissaries> a vagabond and vulgar mob appropriate to the loathsome conduct of <those men>. When they stood before the gates of the patriarchate, the troubling news of their arrival was conveyed to the great patriarch. Since he was irritated at the very sight of these evil-minded men (for pure natures are such that they feel disgust at anything whatsoever that is foreign to the truth), he felt no inclination to enter into discussions with them. However, he was forcefully compelled against his will by a certain patrician[347] who was entrusted with guarding him and who promised not to send <the delegation> back without accomplishing <its mission>. <Therefore, Nikephoros> allowed them entrance after a long time and with great reluctance.

Once they were admitted, the intractable <nature of the patriarch's> illness inspired no respect in those wretches, but with their customary shamelessness they made a histrionic display of reading out the text of that illegal legal document <of theirs>.[348] It said: "Since the synod has received accusations against you, it demands that you appear in person and clearly defend yourself in order to answer these <accusations> beyond any doubt. Now before the [p. 194] harshness of the <synod's> judgment takes its course and makes you liable to deposition, change your views to those of the synod and of the emperor and join us in agreeing and declaring that the icons must be suppressed and renounced. You will be able to counteract the disgrace of the letters of accusation by <doing> this, rather than by persistently rejecting and disagreeing with those who charge that you are clearly guilty. This <accu-

---

[347] This patrician has been identified as Thomas by Alexander, *Nicephorus,* 134, and Afinogenov, "Κωνσταντινούπολις ἐπίσκοπον ἔχει: Part II," 54.

[348] This document was the summons issued to Nikephoros by the *endemousa synodos* (*v. Niceph.* 193.6–9). Ignatios calls the summons an ἄτομος τόμος (which I have translated "illegal legal document"), a punning reference to the legal nature of the summons and the illegal constitution of the synod which dispatched it (i.e., the synod included unordained members). I am grateful to A. Alexakis for elucidating the sense of this puzzling expression.

sation> can only be removed[349] by standing before <your accusers> and by giving an account <as regards> the substance of their charges." Those who were wolves instead of shepherds misdirected these abusive jokes against their chief shepherd <Nikephoros>, muttering through their teeth (for they were incapable of directly defying or addressing that most pure mind). *Covering* over their *shame* and humiliation[350] with silence, they gave him a hearing, *stopped* <though their *ears* were>,[351] because they wanted to hear the eloquent rejoinder he would utter, even though they were hostile to him.

Although <Nikephoros> was weakened by his illness, he took the initiative in speaking thus: "Who is it that hurls letters of accusation at us and entertains charges against us? Over which patriarchal see does he claim to preside? What pastoral authority does he hold that he subjects us to canonical restraints? If the helmsman who reverently steers the older Rome summons us, I shall come. If the holy preacher of Alexandria brings a charge against us, I shall attend upon him without complaint. If the holy shepherd of Antioch drags us to a court of judgment, I shall not be absent. If he who administers Jerusalem has summoned us to stand to account, I shall not fail to do it. But if *grievous wolves* intent upon distressing *the flock*[352] disguise themselves in a sheep's skin[353] and insult the shepherd, who would consent so much as to come into the sight of those upon whom the holy apostle [Paul] loaded a burden of judgment?[354] But if indeed, as your empty chatter <proposes>, we were to be associated with that doctrine of yours and of those in power, would we cleanse ourselves from the stain of accusations against us?[355] [p. 195] And what sort of position will be assigned to us if we are held liable for the misadministration <of our current office>, as you say, and have been convicted of transgressions against the canons? Who is it that would in a single day depose and rehabili-

---

[349] μὴ οὐχὶ here = εἰ μή (except), as in Demosthenes, *De falsa legatione, or.* 19.123.

[350] Cf. Ps. 68 (69):7.

[351] Cf. Ps. 57 (58):4.

[352] Cf. Acts 20:29.

[353] Cf. Mt. 7:15.

[354] Cf. Paul's farewell admonition to the elders of the Church at Ephesos, Acts 20:28–31.

[355] Reading an ironical question here, i.e., "will I ever get rid of (middle sense of ἀποτρίβω) the reputation for sedition?"

tate to prominence one who is unable to stand in a subordinate <position>? Or have you assumed that I am inexperienced and ignorant with regard to the investigation of divine matters, <so as>[356] not to understand what wrongdoing is for priests? But in fact impiety, which draws down into *a snare of hell*[357] those who are persuaded by it, is ready[358] to overlook these matters and simply to proceed into transgression. Keep away from me, then, <you> *workers of iniquity!*[359] Return *to* your *own vomit*[360] and turn back to the dens of your thievery![361] You will not take hold of those who have fixed their mind upon the rock of the orthodox confession <of faith>, nor will you cast down those who set themselves upon the heights of definitions made by the <ecumenical> councils. However, the heavy seas of heresy will break upon you without washing over the universal Church."[362]

The blessed man inveighed thus against those who were empty of intelligence but full of folly and then added these <remarks>: "If the loss of its shepherd left the <patriarchal> throne unprovided for, no one from among the whole number <of bishops> would be allowed to teach attractive <but> false notions, nor to hold a rival assembly <of the Church>, nor to move from foreign parts into territory that does not belong to him. However, <the Church> prides itself upon the presence of a shepherd and fortunately does not lack a protector; what argument then will deliver you from the punishment <specified by> the canons, since you wish to *build* a heretical doctrine *of wood, of hay,* and *of stubble upon* the *foundation of gold* and *of silver,* adorned with *precious stones*[363] (I mean <by "precious stones"> the teachings of the apostles and of the <church> fathers)? It would be just as regards those who fight ignorantly against clear and obvious <doctrines> both to declare you subject to a strict interpretation of the holy canons and also to subject you to

---

[356] Adding ὡς before τὸ μὴ.

[357] Prov. 9:18.

[358] Reading ἕτοιμος for ἕτοιμον as an attempt to make sense out of this sentence.

[359] Cf. Lk. 13:27 and 1 Macc. 3:6.

[360] Cf. Prov. 26:11; 2 Pet. 2:22.

[361] Cf. Jer. 7:11.

[362] Heresy is similarly likened to a storm at sea at 159.9–12; see also passages cited by Nikitin, p. 17.

[363] Cf. 1 Cor. 3:12.

the *everlasting chains*[364] as is most appropriate."[365] <Nikephoros> then read out to them the canon, bound them under a sentence of deposition <from their ecclesiastical positions> [p. 196], and ordered them out of the holy precinct. They, however, were like men driven under the lash, possessed by grief and madness. Joined by their entourage of cavorting[366] vagabonds, they anathematized both <Nikephoros> and Tarasios,[367] those steadfast pillars of the Church. The abominable fellows then not only proceeded through the streets in an unseemly fashion but also betook themselves immediately to the palace with their jests against the holy men,[368] disgorging before the emperor and his trash heap of heretics what they had heard and done <regarding Nikephoros>.

Then, when <those fellows> realized that they had been sentenced in conformity with strict interpretation of the canons and when they learned from[369] their own false messengers the severe <response> of that holy soul Nikephoros, their courage diminished and they willingly renounced any discourse with him. Taking an alternative false trail, they babbled about deposing the saint by force and planned removing him by secret murder. Had not a

---

[364] Jude 6.

[365] Eleven canons of the church councils specifically prohibited clergy from leaving their church or diocese without the written permission of their own bishop (collected in V. Beneševič, *Iohannis Scholastici Synagoga L Titulorum* [Munich, 1937], 73–76). Bishops were explicitly included under this prohibition (cf. 74.15–16), and those violating it were subject to deposition from their offices (cf. 73.15 and 75.3–4) and to excommunication (74.5). The problem of clergy and monks descending upon Constantinople to make trouble in the Church was specifically addressed and prohibited (76.1–9).

[366] The hapax word κωμολόγοις is formed from the elements λογ- (speak/collect) and κῶμος (band of revelers) or κώμη (village). Because Ignatios immediately complains that these persons "proceeded in an unseemly fashion" (196.6, ἐνασχημονοῦντες), κωμολόγοις apparently means "collected from a band of revelers."

[367] Tarasios, patriarch of Constantinople (784–806), restored the veneration of icons and abolished the first episode of iconoclasm at the Second Council of Nicaea in 787. Cf. Ignatios' remarks on his career at *v. Niceph.* 152.28–153.23.

[368] Cf. *v. Niceph.* 196.14–15, where τὸν ἅγιον refers to the holy <man> Nikephoros. Nikitin (p. 18) reads σκέμμασιν for the printed σκώμμασιν, citing its use on p. 166.1. Nikitin's emended version would be translated, "with their speculations on holy <matters>."

[369] Reading ἀπὸ with A.-M. Talbot for the printed ὑπὸ.

cleric devoted to Orthodoxy learned the exact details of the plot from truthful <informants>, laid <those details> bare, and hastened to provide <measures> for <Nikephoros'> safety, perhaps tragic ceremonies of lamentation would have been made to please funereal Charon even in our own time.[370] But when the bloodthirsty fellows were frustrated in this scenario (for divine Providence in heaven was casting its influence and protecting its servant <Nikephoros>), they did not flag in their eagerness to depose <Nikephoros> by force for the sake <of controlling> the <patriarchal> throne. They threatened death, torture, the removal of all treatment for his illness—but <Nikephoros> was unyielding; they deprived him of the devotion of lay people, that is the customary commemoration in the services of the Church.[371] For that terrifying monster <Leo> (let any reference to him as emperor be avoided!) <behaved> like the Jews and threatened the priests in this way: *if any man openly did confess that he* [Nikephoros] *was* patriarch, *he should be put out of the synagogue.*[372]

Already then, <Nikephoros> *dwelt* alone *in hope*[373] and [p. 197] God *made room for* him *in tribulation,* as most holy David <says>.[374] However, only in this <respect> was he not strong enough to bear up, <namely> in seeing his flock reject their chief shepherd and become subject to the wolves. What, my good friends,[375] should he have done at that time in the name of your salvation? What should he have accomplished? How long should he have swum against a flood of difficulties, refused to surrender <to them>, <opposed> submitting to an evil time? <How long should he have avoided> yielding to a very evil authority and to those who wielded it, so that he would

[370] I.e., Nikephoros would have been murdered and would still be publicly mourned in Ignatios' time. An otherwise unattested word obscures the meaning of this sentence. ἐχαροτυπήθη is apparently formed from the roots χαρ- (joy) or Χαρ- (Charon, conveyor of souls to the Underworld) and τυπ- (form, shape).

[371] As early as the 5th century, the deacon regularly read out a list of living and dead emperors and patriarchs (the "liturgical diptychs") during the celebration of the eucharist.

[372] Cf. Jn. 9:22. This may be a threat of excommunication.

[373] Cf. Ps. 4:8.

[374] Cf. Ps. 4:1.

[375] Reading the variant ὦ τᾶν instead of V's ὦ sequestered by de Boor. Ignatios addresses his own orthodox, iconodule audience whose beliefs Nikephoros had championed.

not fall into sin at least for his part? And in fact <Nikephoros> took thought for *them which despitefully used* him[376] and persecuted him, imitating his teacher Christ in this. But those <others> were not so virtuous, who indeed[377] very obviously took strenuous measures against the one who tried to show them kindness. For they did not give up *imagining vain things* against him[378] and threatening him with violent death until they had thrust him *outside the gate*[379] (I mean, of the Church) and condemned him to death with one accord, repeating the words of the Lord's parable, "*Come, let us kill him, and let us seize* upon *his inheritance.*"[380] For this reason, since he had certain prophetic gifts in his pure mind and perceived the <events> to come, <Nikephoros> saw that *their heart was hardened*[381] and already intended bloodshed; he sent a letter to the emperor which ran thus:

"Since I have come into such circumstances and am physically ill, the present occasion requires my humble self to refer these matters to your majesty, as a lover of justice. Up until now we have fought to the best of our ability on behalf of truth and orthodox belief; as far as we know, we neglected none of our obligations and were neither slow <to enter> into discussion with those who requested it nor <reluctant> to offer instruction to those who welcomed it. But after we had suffered all sorts of affliction, distress, and abuse because of this <as well as> disgrace, imprisonment, confiscation of property, and injury to those who attend upon us, as a final <insult> persons pretending to be bishops came and inflicted upon us disgrace greater than any previous [p. 198] by bringing along a common mob of ruffians <armed> with daggers and cudgels and setting them upon us. They themselves felt neither shame nor compunction in contributing every sort of insult. They neither took to heart the fear of God nor did they accord me any reverence as their former chief priest—even though I lay desperately ill and had nothing but breath <remaining to me>. For their part, the mobs anathematized not only me but

---

[376] Lk. 6:28.

[377] Nikitin notes (p. 18) that ποθεν serves to emphasize a relative clause in the classical usage of Demosthenes, Heliodoros, etc.

[378] Acts 4:25 = Ps. 2:1.

[379] Cf. Heb. 13:12.

[380] Ignatios compares Nikephoros' opponents to the unjust tenants who murdered the vineyard owner's son (i.e., Jesus) in Mt. 21:38.

[381] Mk. 6:52.

also my predecessor as chief priest [i.e., Tarasios], which was high praise and the greatest tribute to us. After all these evil doings we heard that the enemies of truth were preparing an ambush against us in their eagerness to set upon us and accomplish either our destruction or a violent and deadly attack against us. Therefore to prevent any untoward event or any sin redounding to your majesty (since no greater persecution can possibly be contrived against us, although we are unwilling and reluctant and under persecution from those who despitefully use us, it is absolutely necessary for us to vacate our <patri-archal> throne. And since God judges and directs our affairs, we render Him devotion and *give thanks* to <Him in> His goodness." [382]

<The emperor> with a mind steeped in filth interpreted <Nikephoros'> letter as the ultimate blow. With the sardonic smile of a madman, he added yet more violence to the violence he had already accomplished. For he assigned a military contingent to the patrician guarding Father <Nikephoros>,[383] who bore God in his heart, and ordered this man to expel *the child of light*[384] <from the patriarchal palace> during the middle of that very night. How <did> this <come to pass>? The military contingent and their actions resembled the armed band <which gathered> against Christ.[385] For those <in the Bible> implemented their blows and their plots against Christ only by night, and these <in Nikephoros' time> had night in league with them <when> they were convicted in a similar betrayal of their good shepherd <Nikephoros>. When <Nikephoros> observed that *his hour was come*[386] and that the *band of soldiers*[387] <leaped> upon him like so many darting gnats and locusts, he called for a light, arose from his bed, and instructed one of his regular <atten-dants> to provide him support [p. 199] (for the pain from his disease was still at its very peak, and the strength to control his body had declined). With his

[382] Cf. Eph. 5:20. Nikephoros' letter of abdication survives only as quoted here by Ignatios (see *RegPatr* 1.2–3 [1972 rev. ed.]:47, no. 401).

[383] Nikephoros' patrician watchdog had already pressured the patriarch into reluc-tantly receiving the delegation of iconoclast bishops (see *v. Niceph.* 193.22–25).

[384] 1 Th. 5:5.

[385] Jesus was apprehended at night in the Garden of Gethsemane by an armed band; see, for example, Mt. 26:36–47.

[386] Cf. Jn. 13:1.

[387] The soldiers (σπεῖρα) of Pontius Pilate taunted Jesus before his crucifixion; see Mt. 27:27–31 and Mk. 15:16–20.

left hand he propped up his weakness, as I mentioned, but with his right hand he grasped the holy incense burner and made fragrant the[388] chambers of those sacred inner rooms. He then proceeded into the famous gallery of the Great Church <of St. Sophia>,[389] where he had so many times earnestly entreated God with appeals <lasting> through the night. He lighted two wax candles, relinquished what <he was holding> in his hands, and raised himself above visible <reality> by casting his body face downward upon the ground while stretching his spirit straight up into heaven. "Thou, <O God>," he said, "great beyond measure and beyond all nature, the lord of all the wonders of creation and of wisdom beyond our comprehension, whose slight traces Thou revealest through these <wonders>;[390] <Thou>, the sole originator <of all things>, be present through Thy compassionate love of mankind by working great and lofty miracles in Thy Church, where Thou receivest the whole burnt offerings of the pure and undefiled <sacramental> mysteries, and where Thou hast thought it right to release from sin <all> those who present themselves[391] worthily to partake <of it>. I commend into Thy hand, all powerful even now, this <*Church*> that is *without spot* or *blemish*,[392] just as I received it from <Thy hand>, watched over it in reverence as best I could, and kept it fixed upon the rock of true belief. As a *place* and *tabernacle of Thy glory*,[393] <Thy Church> has preserved its all-beautiful majesty, conducted to Thee many *sons* and *heirs*[394] by means of holy baptism, and rendered countless multitudes fit for Thy compassion and favor through enduring repentance. To Thee, O Savior, I deliver this sacred trust, albeit with unworthy hands, and I give over to the *great deep of Thy judgments*[395] the disposition of the <Church's> affairs as seems best <to Thee>. A lion [i.e., Leo] howls against the <Church> as

---

[388] Reading τὰ for the printed τὰς.

[389] The gallery (a sort of mezzanine) that ran around three sides of the nave at St. Sophia contained spaces reserved for imperial use and communicated by passageways directly both to the Great Palace and to the patriarchal residence (see *ODB* 2:818–19, s.v. "Gallery," and 2:892–95, s.v. "Hagia Sophia").

[390] Reading ὑποφαίνεις for the printed ὑποφαίεις with A.-M. Talbot. See Rom. 11:33 for a similar thought.

[391] Reading ἑαυτοὺς for the printed ἑαυτοῖς.

[392] Cf. Eph. 5:27.

[393] Ps. 25 (26):8.

[394] Cf. Gal. 4:7.

[395] Cf. Ps. 35 (36):6.

he tries to seize and prepare for his own whelps an ample dwelling place. Let not Thy radiant and sleepless eye[396] disregard in slumber his insolence. Let <Leo> know to whom he has given offense and against whom he has behaved with uncontrolled and drunken violence. He has transformed the shepherds into brutal wolves; [p. 200] he has driven to savage disobedience the sheep who readily obeyed those who led them well. Snatch away from the error of his heresy the flock that has not been given him; let it be released from terrors and delivered from afflictions. <The Church> is the possession of Thy hand. May it not become prey to those who seek to devour it, but lead us by the hand as we cast ourselves upon Thy judgment and conduct us to the place where Thou pleasest to guide us. Thou seest, Lord, how great the violence <has been against us>.[397] Do not exclude us from the rewards arising from that <violence>;[398] do not rebuke us like unproven and unprepared shepherds. For to Thee only it is given to lead and shepherd <the Church> with full understanding. May we not be condemned for apathy on the grounds that through this <fault> we have betrayed our birthright of <Christian> teachings useful for life. For in the best offering we could make, we have also preserved these <teachings> unblemished for Thee, the *first born of every creature.*[399]

Farewell, <O church of the Holy> Wisdom, the manifestly uncompromising precinct of God's word; I give you the locks <that secured> the orthodox faith undamaged by the crowbars of heretics. Under the seal of the pure confession <of faith>, I have secured the teachings of the <church> fathers, and I have been wholly eager to entrust to you <those teachings>, that cannot be despoiled by heretical distortions.[400] Farewell, <O patriarchal> throne, that I mounted not without constraint and that I now vacate under even greater constraint. Farewell, O godly shrines of the martyrs adorned with images of <the martyrs'> struggles and of the Gospel;[401] foolish men will lay

---

[396] Cf. *v. Niceph.* 164.11 and n. 200.

[397] Reading ὅση with Nikitin (p. 18) for the printed ὅσην.

[398] I.e., martyrdom.

[399] Col. 1:15.

[400] Nikephoros refers to the florilegium of patristic and scriptural passages assembled by Leo's committee to support the iconoclast position.

[401] In the *Life of Tarasios,* Ignatios enumerates various torments of the martyrs depicted in churches, commending the emotional response they rouse in the beholder (see *v. Taras.* 414.10–416.28). He notes the trials of women as well as men (415.19), men-

polluted hands upon <these images>, but they will not steal away the retribution that threatens them from the unconquerable hand <of God>. Farewell, too, O great city of God [i.e., Constantinople], and those of your <inhabitants> whose mainstay is sound patristic doctrine; I have commended them to your <sheltering> wings and to God's, so that no winged creature of evil might remove them from your loving care."

After offering the first fruits of his prayerful and holy eloquence in this way, <Nikephoros> placed himself upon a stretcher and albeit with unwilling heart set forth upon his journey in the direction that *the violent*[402] wished to lead him. The sea [p. 201] spread wide her surface beneath him, received the just man in a light boat, and conveyed him to the monastery he had built <called> the <Monastery> of Agathos.[403] After being allowed to spend a brief amount of time there, <Nikephoros> was again transferred by those who had initiated violence, <this time> to the holy monastery of the great martyr Theodore, situated at a greater distance <from Constantinople> and also founded by <Nikephoros>.[404] For <his persecutors> could not endure seeing the just man established anywhere near their own foul conduct. Bardas, the close relative of <the emperor> Leo,[405] was sent on this <mission>. He

---

tions the first martyrs Stephen and Thekla (415.30–31), and cites the depiction of Christ's torments on the cross as he turns to arguments justifying pictorial representations in churches (416.3–28).

[402] Cf. Mt. 11:12.

[403] The identity of "Agathos" and the exact location of the monastery bearing his name are unknown. Janin infers from this passage that the monastery was on the Asiatic bank of the Bosphoros near Chrysopolis and perhaps slightly north of that city; see R. Janin, "L'Église byzantine sur les rives du Bosphore (Côte asiatique)," *REB* 12 (1954), 91–92.

[404] St. Theodore Teron ("the recruit") refused to deny his Christian faith, set fire to a pagan temple, and was condemned to death under the emperor Maximian (286–305). Nikephoros may have wished to honor his own father Theodore by dedicating a monastery to this saint of the same name. Although this monastery was Nikephoros' home for thirteen years until he died and was the site of several visits made to Nikephoros by Theodore the Stoudite, the exact location of the monastery is unknown (Janin, *op. cit.*, 96–98). One of the two monasteries mentioned here may be identical to the anonymous monastery on the Bosporos founded by Nikephoros when he first left his career at court (cf. *v. Niceph.* 147.30–148, and Alexander, *Nicephorus*, 148 n. 1).

[405] Bardas is described as an ἀνεψιός, a term designating a cousin in classical Greek, a nephew in Byzantine usage. Alexander (*Nicephorus*, 148) discusses the problems connected with the identity of Bardas.

arrived at the place, entered the <monastery> church,[406] seated himself on a chair, and summoned the great high priest <Nikephoros> to himself. Then, when the military escorts had hastily <made> this <man Nikephoros> stand before him, <Bardas> himself showed no semblance of respect toward that beloved holy presence. If nothing else, he was not even shamed by the proverbial injunction that so wisely proclaims, *Thou shalt rise up* before *the hoary head*.[407] <Bardas> simply kept his seat. Although <Nikephoros> viewed with suspicion the *flimsy intentions of the young man,* in the words of the poet,[408] he limited his reply to the following words: "O good Bardas, know by <observing> the misfortunes of others how to manage your own well." With these words, he surrendered to the will of those who led him away. O, what clairvoyant purity <of vision> the most saintly man possessed! He saw from afar what was approaching and brought together present and future <events>. For justice did not follow close upon the heels of the youth, but when four years' time had nearly galloped by, it brought him disaster. And if anyone particularly wants final confirmation of this <man's fate>, let him go and meet the man. In observing the sorry condition of <Bardas'> eyes,[409] he will very clearly understand the tragedy that has befallen him. But enough about these matters.

Leo, however, bestirred himself to search for a wolf rather than a shepherd and without much effort brought in this <fellow> who reeked of worldly concerns and was very much attached to the battle axe <proper to Herakles> the beefeater.[410] <Theodotos> paid attention only to his stomach [p. 202] and

---

[406] The Greek phrase, νηὸς ἐπιβάς, could also be translated "embarked upon the ship."

[407] Lev. 19:32.

[408] Reading αἰωρημένας for the printed ἐωρημένας. Ignatios paraphrases Pindar, *Olympian Ode* 8.61, κουφότεραι γὰρ ἀπειράτων φρένες, "The minds of men untried are flimsy rather" (trans. R. Lattimore, *The Odes of Pindar* [Chicago, Ill., 1947], 27), a verse he quotes more exactly in his *Life of Tarasios,* νεωτερικαῖς φρεσί, κατὰ τὴν <π>οίησιν (v. *Taras.* 408.35–36).

[409] I.e., Bardas was blinded, perhaps in 820 when Michael II succeeded Leo and caused many of the latter's family members to be mutilated (see Alexander, *Nicephorus,* 148).

[410] Leo appointed as Nikephoros' patriarchal successor the elderly Theodotos I Kassiteras, son of a prominent iconoclast family, who held the title *spatharokandidatos* (usually connected with the offices of notary, secretary, or subordinate judge) and whose patrician father had been general of the Anatolic theme in 765/6; see Alexander,

to the spicing of the sauces in particular;[411] he was a complete stranger to any intellectual experience but very well versed in crude and barbarous diction. To bypass in silence intervening <events>,[412] the barbarian <Leo needed> only one day to wash off <Theodotos> and give him a quick course of instruction.[413] <Leo then> installed him upon the awe-inspiring sacerdotal throne <of the patriarch>, publicly proclaiming him the shepherd of his own wolflike soul (but <assuredly> not of Christ's flock). Immediately after that, <Leo drew> both upon the bishops who had been won over by torture or by their own inclinations and upon revolutionary and impious teachers; he assembled a conference of <cawing> jackdaws and convened in the church <of St. Sophia> a council against the Church.[414] In <this council>, they spewed forth every falsified and excerpted literary passage that had been foolishly cited before,[415] and they took as their ally the Council in Blachernai haphazardly assembled by Constantine <V>, calling this <council of theirs> the ratification of that <council>.[416] And that was entirely appropriate. For their

---

Nicephorus, 136 and *ODB* 3:1936, s.v. "Spatharokandidatos." The epithet Βουθοίνης ("beefeater") recalls the mythological hero Herakles, notable not only for his feats of military prowess but also for gluttonous, drunken, and generally wild behavior.

[411] By remarking upon Theodotos' affection for luxuriously prepared food, Ignatios emphasizes the contrast between Theodotos' secular way of life and Nikephoros' holy one. Comparing Theodotos to Herakles "the beefeater" reinforces this contrast, for meat was prohibited in the diet of Byzantine monks and avoided by ascetics.

[412] Ignatios does not mention that Leo's first candidate for the patriarchate, John the Grammarian, was rejected by the *silention,* which consisted of the senate and the imperial advisory council. See Alexander, *Nicephorus,* 136.

[413] Ignatios may mean that Theodotos was rapidly ordained to the ecclesiastical orders subordinate to patriarch, not unlike Nikephoros' rapid progression from deacon to priest to bishop. See *v. Niceph.* 157.17–22.

[414] Presided over by the patriarch Theodotos, the council convened soon after Easter in 815 (see Alexander, *Nicephorus,* 137).

[415] The falsification of literary texts (βίβλων παραγραφαί) is listed among the misdeeds of the iconoclasts in the Life of Theodora, wife of Theophilos (*v. Theodorae imp.* 258.16–18).

[416] See Alexander, *Nicephorus,* 137 with n. 2. The iconoclast council of 754 met at the palace of Hieria in Chalcedon, concluding its meetings in the presence of Constantine V at the Church of the Virgin Mary in Blachernai. The acts of the council prohibited making or venerating images and were supported by an iconoclastic florilegium of passages from Scripture and patristic writings, which was later used by Leo's committee of excerptors. See Alexander, *Nicephorus,* 12 and 126.

own <proceedings> ratified in a similar fashion <that council> that had neither validity based on patristic authority nor participation from the apostolic
sees, as canon law prescribes;[417] <their council> sought to cheat the truth
with a lie. After issuing these decrees on the very first day of their corrupt
assembly, they adjourned. But on the following day they all flooded into the
same <place> to make a start on their doctrines of falsehood. On this day
they also revealed the harsh savagery of their wickedness.

And <only> observe their excessive brutality. They selected several of
the bishops who <adhered to> the Orthodox profession <of faith> whom
they thought to bring under their control on their first attempt.[418] Next, they
shredded <the bishops'> holy garments[419] into mere rags and commanded
them to stand bound <in chains> like prisoners in front of the gates of the
Great Church <of St. Sophia>. Then in a wild frenzy they uttered disjointed
and inarticulate shouts against <the bishops> like <so many> frogs, and
ordered them to be dragged through the midst of their assembly. When
[p. 203] <the bishops> drew near to the leaders of the evil <heresy>, shouted
<orders> commanded them to halt. But because <the heretics> saw that
<the bishops> endured the abuse unshaken (for they were like hard rocks
or deep-rooted oak trees),[420] <the heretics> intoned against them some such

---

[417] Byzantines regarded the patriarchs of Rome, Constantinople, Alexandria, Antioch, and Jerusalem as the successors of the Apostles on earth and termed their sees
"apostolic." Representation by these five sees was essential for a council to be considered ecumenical and its proceedings to be binding (see *ODB* 3:1625–26, s.v. "Pentarchy").

[418] Alexander (*Nicephorus,* 137 n. 3) infers from a remark of Theodore the Stoudite
that John, bishop of Sardis, was among their targets; Theodore wrote in a letter to
John, "Blessed are you, <because> on behalf of the Lord you were struck and abused
by the fists of the ungodly before Caiaphas' council" (Fatouros, *Theod. Stud. Epist.,*
ep. 157.12–14).

[419] The ἱερὰ ἀμπεχόνη ("holy garment") is a term for ecclesiastical clothing peculiar
to Ignatios' usage. Since in this passage and at 211.15–16 he applies it to the clothing
of bishops, ἱερὰ ἀμπεχόνη may refer to the *omophorion* or long stole worn only by
bishops. In *v. Niceph.* 146.28–29 and *v. Taras.* 399.5–6, on the other hand, the term is
ambiguous and could refer either to ecclesiastical garments in general or to the *omophorion* in particular.

[420] Ignatios uses a proverbial Homeric expression to signify hardihood and endurance (see *Il.* 22:126; *Od.* 19:163; Leutsch-Schneidewin, *Corpus* 2:158, no. 40 and note),
embellishing it with Sophocles' adjective (*Trachiniae* 1195) for the oak tree, "deep-
rooted."

childish and putrid words as, "How long have you relied on your own disobedience and refused to look at the virtue of the truth, rejecting a better understanding of reverence for the true word? Now then, if some shred of hard-
heartedness still clings to you, strip it away and reconcile with us and with our
holy council. Do not, because of a frivolous quarrel, betray what is justice[421]
for your throne and for your office."

Although <the bishops> were in the position of condemned men and
were assailed by blasphemous speeches from everyone <in attendance>, nevertheless they ignored every outrage and offense while making a response
much like this: "Our disobedience to you preserves our very willing obedience
to the truth, for obeying you distances us from the truth and deprives us of a
close relationship with God. On the other hand, we and however many hold
our opinion or have come to do so renounce allegiance with your council,
which continues to dissent concerning exact conformity with the holy councils
<of the Church>, insulting the holy images of Christ and His saints and con-
signing to anathema however many adhere to <that council>. For we follow
the inviolate and unalterable <dogmatic> decisions of the ecumenical councils, secure in both the holy premises and the conclusions <set forth by> the
God-bearing Fathers <of the Church>; we therefore accept and embrace the
sacred icons, condemning to anathema those who think otherwise. We have
rejected the <dogmatic> decisions of your faction, its premises, its conclusions, that are more confining than the <constraints of> geometrical theo-
rems, and the teachings placed in your minds,[422] as alien to the teaching of the
Church. For <your faction's council> considers insults <to be dogmatic>
decisions, [p. 204] some sort of synthesis of these <insults to be> premises,
and threats <to be> conclusions. If these <statements> were taken as the
propositions of some other syllogism, they would not conclude in threats but
in treasonous plots and their consequences. *Pride goeth before destruction.*[423]
We attribute to ourselves <pride> as well as destruction, and we also intend to
seek <to fulfill> the remainder <of the quotation> with God as our helper."[424]

---

[421] Plato uses this expression in *Laws* 907a.

[422] Lit., "the teachings placed above <your> temples." The *TLG* contains no parallel
for this singular expression.

[423] Prov. 16:18.

[424] The aphorism in its entirety is "Pride goeth before destruction, and folly before a
fall." The bishops assert their readiness to assist God in the inevitable fall of their
foolish oppressors.

So it was that these men who cherished the wisdom of the serpent[425] deep in their hearts stood speaking clearly in the midst of the foolish. But the <heretics>, like *the council* <assembled> against the first martyr Stephen, *stopped their ears*[426] and gave orders that the holy men be thrown face down upon the ground and that the vulgar mob tread upon their necks. They played out this childish drama like actors upon a stage, and in their blind madness <ordered the bishops> to get to their feet and walk in procession back again <through the assembly>; <they ordered> that <the bishops> be pummeled about the head with fisticuffs, drenched over the whole body with spittle, and expelled. In this way they reeled like unruly and unholy drunkards in a holy <place> against holy men. Because the <dinner> hour now summoned them to the table, <the heretics> used a cleric to speak in florid style on their behalf acclaiming the imperial <family> and consigning to anathema, as they imagined, the leaders of the orthodox faith. They then adjourned <the session>.

After <the council> had accomplished what they wished in their foolish hearts <to do> against the Church, they composed a <dogmatic> decision[427] standing at wide variance from the <dogmatic> decisions of the truth. In this <document> they recommended that the emperor affix his signature <to the effect> that <the document> was <doctrinally> pure. <The emperor> acquiesced to them (for he was fickle as regards God if ever anyone was);[428] when the resumption of the council was proclaimed, he returned to sit elevated on his throne as if he were on the platform <at the Odeon>,[429] while the defend-

---

[425] Cf. Mt. 10:16.

[426] Cf. Acts 6:12, 7:57.

[427] The evidence surviving for this synodal definition against the images is discussed by V. Grumel in *RegPatr* 1.2:56, no. 409. The synod endorsed the definition of the iconoclastic Council of Blachernai (754), condemned the image-restoring Council of 787, and renewed the prohibition against making images of Christ and the saints. A letter to King Louis the Pious of France from Emperor Michael II (820–829), Leo's successor, states that the Council of 815 ordered images located in the lower portions of churches to be removed but allowed those high up to remain.

[428] Ignatios made a similar complaint about Leo's irresolute faith at the time of his coronation; cf. *v. Niceph.* 163.27–28.

[429] Plays to be performed at the Athenian festival of Dionysos were introduced to the public at a *proagon* in the Odeon a few days before the actual performance. Playwright and actors appeared on a raised platform wearing garlands but without costumes or masks to describe the upcoming presentation; see E. Csapo, W. J. Slater, *The Context of Ancient Drama* (Ann Arbor, Mich., 1995), 105 and 109–10.

ers of falsehood also hurried to take their own seats. After the <dogmatic> decision with its many errors had been read out in the hearing of all and met with approval from almost all those present, <the council> urged each <participant> to endorse with his personal signature the declarations in <the decision>. [p. 205] When, moreover, they had accomplished this and joined together in blackening their names and titles with the ink <of their signatures>, they offered the customary acclamations to the imperial family and anathematized the luminaries of the Church, using the same cleric <as before>[430] to speak on their behalf. They then dispersed.

Under this <circumstance> the *sin-hating vengeance* <of God>[431] would not <display> an ocean of patience by closing its eyes to the derision of holy men but expedited and miraculously revealed how punishment is exacted. For <after only> a short <time> intervened, that cleric who served as spokesman <for the council> was overtaken by retribution upon his tongue <in the form of> a sudden torpor and numbness in the organs of speech. And note how harsh <was the retribution>. For when anyone mentioned the words of a psalm to him, his tongue was loosened and tended to its words. But if he happened into conversation with anyone, this <tongue of his> lay slack and in fetters; it mumbled some sort of inarticulate and meaningless lisping <sounds> and conveyed speech unintelligible to the listener. Thus was disciplined the tongue that had been most reckless against those *speaking wisdom with* their *mouth and* bringing forth *understanding in the meditation of* their *heart.*[432] Therefore it is appropriate to utter the holy verse, *Life and death are in the power of the tongue; and they that rule it shall eat the fruits thereof.*[433]

But it is enough to expose these <events> and the malice of those <heretics> as well as to reveal how close to God were the holy men. <Now> let the <narrative> concerning the council and the <events> related to it come to a close, for <the narrative> is sufficient to the point of inducing nausea in those who hear it. However, the dark and moonless night that devolved upon[434] the churches as a result of that <man Leo> must not fade away in

---

[430] See *v. Niceph.* 204.17–18.

[431] Cf. Esth. 8:13.

[432] Cf. Ps. 48 (49):3.

[433] Prov. 18:21.

[434] Reading ἐπεισπολήσασαν for the printed ἐπεισπολάσασαν, unless Ignatios is using a hapax verb ἐπεισπολάζω.

the depths of silence. For all the beautiful <images> of the Gospel and the martyrs which have been depicted of old had holes gouged in them <by the heretics>, who had no compunction in smoothing them over with plaster.[435] But I should try to describe how <the heretics> wickedly entrusted <the materialization> of their maliciously conceived idea to those who yielded to the heresy, while simultaneously keeping sound teaching unimpaired in the court of their conscience.[436] [p. 206] They often sprinkled their tears into the plaster mixture, because they were unable to bear the pain of defiling <the images>. For insolence against the holy images was permitted to any who were so inclined. Some joined in shattering[437] the shrines of the relics, while others ripped treasured holy garments into tiny shreds and threw them to the ground. Still others used axes to hack up paintings on wooden panels and burned them in the middle of the public square with utmost barbarity. Yet others fouled <the images> with cow dung, grease, and other <things with a> nauseating stench instead of the incense which <had scented them> before. One could see the dedications belonging to the holy churches trampled under foot like spoils of war, while <objects> too <holy> to touch or to see were dragged away by many profane hands and exposed as a spectacle for everyone. Shepherds were thrust from their churches and wolves were entrusted with the flock, those who urged the true word were driven out and those who hated holy Scripture [were installed in their place].[438] The guiltless were called to account as if guilty and rogues were seated on thrones[439] in their place. Clerics *had trial of cruel mockings and scourgings*[440] and remained in prisons with neither door nor window. The Nazarenes [i.e., monks] among us

[435] Lit., "smoothing them over with wet gypsum" (or "lime"—τιτάνῳ διαβρόχῳ). A diluted mixture of water and gypsum or lime would produce whitewash, a thicker one, plaster. Here, the reference to gouging the surface before applying the mixture suggests that plaster was applied.

[436] The translation of this very difficult sentence was suggested by A. Alexakis, who proposes substituting a period for the question mark at the end of the sentence and adding τοῖς before τῆς at 205.30.

[437] Correcting the printed συνέκλων to συνέκλων.

[438] The printed edition contains a lacuna here, which fortunately can be filled with reasonable certainty from context.

[439] Ignatios might mean either the thrones of bishops or the benches of judges, since either sense fits this context.

[440] Heb. 11:36.

were oppressed by tortures, hunger, thirst, long imprisonment, and hard labor. They remained firm under their sufferings even to the point of their last perils, some being executed by the sword, some bound up in sacks and sunk like stones into the waters. Women were stripped naked in the sight of men, stretched like criminals <in bonds> and flogged, but bore all <these tortures> for the sake of Christ with a manly spirit.

Leo, the enemy of truth, demonstrated the following <attitude> toward holy things and those who hold them in high honor. Who would not weep scalding tears over the treaties, of friendship no less, that <Leo> concluded with the neighboring Huns[441] in so shameful and inappropriate a manner? For he followed their <ancestral customs> and they [p. 207] followed ours, thus ratifying the agreements with one another.[442] In <the course of confirming> them, the emperor of the Romans could be seen pouring <a libation of> water upon the earth from a cup with <his own> hands, turning the pack-saddles of the horses upside down all by himself, grasping the triple-stranded reins, lifting up grass on high, and invoking curses upon himself by all these <things should he break the treaty>.[443] The pagan nation <of Huns> on the other hand <could be seen> touching our sacred symbols with unlawful hands and swearing by the power of <those symbols>.[444] Do these <events> not spring from sheer barbarity? Are they not obvious madness and blindness

---

[441] I.e., the Bulgarians; see *v. Niceph.* 163.4 and n. 196.

[442] In 816 Leo concluded a 30-year peace treaty with the Bulgarian khan Omurtag (814/5–ca. 831), son of Krum, that set the boundary between Byzantine and Bulgarian territory, temporarily evacuated border fortresses, returned Slav fugitives to Bulgaria, and exchanged prisoners (cf. *ODB* 3:1526, s.v. "Omurtag"). Ignatios describes with disapproval an alteration in the procedure by which the customary oaths ratifying a treaty were sworn by each party according to its own customs and divinities. In this episode, Leo himself subscribed to pagan practices as well as contaminating Byzantine usages by allowing them to unbelievers. See D. A. Miller, "Byzantine Treaties and Treaty-Making: 500–1025 A.D.," *ByzSlav* 32 (1971), 56–76, esp. 74–76.

[443] The 10th-century source included under the name of Theophanes Continuatus describes the Byzantines swearing only upon their weapons and a dead dog. Whatever the actual Bulgarian usage may have been, both accounts serve to blacken the reputation of Leo V. See V. Grumel, "Sur les coutumes des anciens Bulgares dans la conclusion des traités," *Izvestija na Bulgarskoto istoricheskoto druzhestvo* 14–15 (Sofia, 1937), 82–92.

[444] Grumel (p. 89) understands these to be the consecrated bread and wine of the Eucharist; treaty oaths were also sworn on the cross and on the Bible (see Miller, "Byzantine Treaties," 75–76).

against Christ? Do they not induce God's righteous censure? Prodigious and extraordinary manifestations provided further evidence <of heaven's displeasure> during that time, <namely> *thrusting* out of the earth *and shaking, which break the heart* (as the prophet <says>)[445] and which bury cities and all their people, famines sowing every despair *upon the face of the earth,*[446] and farmers gathering grain in sacks using not sickles but their hands, while the heavens let flames fall like rods <of chastisement>, bringing utter dismay to those who watched, and the sea remained barren, abounding in great waves and billows instead of in supplies of fish.[447] Indifference to kin and household spread everywhere, producing internal strife in every land and city. For it happens that from then even until now the terrible malady of internal disasters [i.e., civil strife] has prevailed.

But the evil <caused by> that fellow <Leo> did not diminish nor stop at this. Instead, it grew ripe and active, threatening an eruption of distressing activities. <Leo's evil> *whetted the sword*[448] of insurrection against him. <It arose> not in the midst of battle nor in foreign <lands> nor in hostile territory (for <in that case> some feeble pretext for praise might be attributed to the wretched man, as one who fought for his fatherland), but rather <the insurrection arose> at home and in familiar <surroundings> and while his <affairs> were favorably disposed, as he thought. And in fact <Leo> held in prison under guard and in chains the man through whom the insurrection was brought painfully to birth.[449] <Michael the Amorian> was waiting until the imminent struggle <scheduled for> our Savior's birthday should be accomplished and until he should exactly assess his <own> situation.[450]

---

[445] Cf. Nah. 2:11 (10).

[446] Cf. Gen. 7:23, etc.

[447] Ignatios normally uses the word ὀψώνιον to refer to cooked delicacies (see *v. Taras.* 402.16–17; 403.6–7); here it must mean "fish," which is also a variant meaning of ὄψον; cf. Liddell-Scott, *Lexicon,* s.v. 3.

[448] Ps. 7:12.

[449] Leo arrested Michael the Amorian in December 820 for treason and condemned him to death, although Michael had served as Leo's commander of the imperial guard and had been elevated by him to patrician rank. He was proclaimed Emperor Michael II (820–829) after his co-conspirators assassinated Leo in church on Christmas Day. See *ODB* 2:1209–10 and 1363, s.vv. Leo V and Michael II.

[450] I have interpreted the "struggle of Christmas Day" as an allusion to the impending murder of Leo V. A. Alexakis suggests a different interpretation of the sentence, making Leo V the subject of διασκέψαιτο and translating "and <Leo> should

<Leo's> head, which had been crowned against [i.e., to the detriment of] the Church [p. 208], and his hand, which had been extended to destroy orthodox teachings, justly suffered an act of violence from the sword of <his> armed men and bodyguards;[451] in the middle of the holy church,[452] the weakling *gasped out the soul*[453] that had dishonored many churches of the saints.

But if it is agreeable <to my audience>, let us add a few <words> to our narrative, not exulting in his fall but rather feeling distress at the turn of events. What is this, O <man> excessively proud and arrogant, who both breathed storms upon us and blew a dragon's <blast> against the Church? How did that spirit fly away, that contrived a tempest of persecution and thundered against the faithful in complete madness like Salmoneus with his ox-hides?[454] To what end have come the sorcerers' <rites> into which you, or you with others, were initiated?[455] You tried to conceive years of royal rule, but gave birth to aborted fetuses that died young. How <did it happen that> the sword's blow against you was not prophesied by those Grammarians who

---

make an exact decision about him [i.e., the date of Michael's execution, originally scheduled for Christmas Eve but then postponed]."

[451] On the occasion of Leo's coronation, Ignatios forecast Leo's beheading in similiar terms; see *v. Niceph.* 164.20–23 and n. 203, above.

[452] W. Treadgold (*Byz. Revival,* 224–25 and n. 307) discusses the conflicting evidence for the location of Leo's murder and justifies the generally accepted opinion that it occurred in the palace chapel of St. Stephen (see, for example, Alexander, *Nicephorus,* 183). Like Ignatios, the historians Genesios and Theophanes Continuatus fail to specify the church in which Leo was murdered. The *v. Davidis, Sym. et Georg.* (chap. 16, 229.21–22; see below, 83) identifies it as the palace chapel of St. Stephen, while Niketas David Paphlagon in the *v. Ignatii* (PG 105:493AB) incorrectly locates Leo's murder in the church of the Virgin of Pharos.

[453] Homer, *Il.* 22:467.

[454] A paraphrase of Gregory Nazianzenos' description of the emperor Julian (PG 35:673B). Salmoneus was a mythical king of Elis and the son of Aeolos, eponymous ruler of the Aeolians in Thessaly (see Apollodoros, *Library of Greek Mythology* 1:7.3). Salmoneus presumed to imitate the thunder and lightning of Zeus by casting torches from his chariot while driving full speed with dried hides and bronze pans tied behind it. Zeus punished this mad impiety by destroying Salmoneus and his city with real thunderbolts (see Apollod. 1:9.7).

[455] Ignatios accuses Leo of sorcerous activities apparently because of his close association with John the Grammarian, alluded to immediately below.

spoke from the belly[456] and took money to measure the length of your imperial rule and to bellow to you about long <years of> prosperity? How did the Spektases and Hamazaspeses,[457] the best examples of the threat you <posed>, overlook[458] the ugly spectacle now visible and the disgrace of your bloody wounds? Where is your diadem belonging to the royal purple, that you accepted from the <hands of the> Church before cutting off her crown? How <can you be> dead today <when you were> swaggering <only> yesterday? How <can you be> studded with wounds <now> when formerly <you raged> unchecked against holy <men and objects>? Where are your intrigues against the great shepherd <Nikephoros> and your dreamlike and deluded inquiries, that you abandoned as incomprehensible? For in spite of much labor and effort, your probing intellect was unable to come close to so much as one report bringing <anything> sufficient to taint <Nikephoros>. However, since <Leo> cannot take a turn in answering for himself, let us leave this lifeless <body> defiled by disgrace to be bathed in drops of blood, while we advance to the next stage of our narrative. [p. 209]

Following <Leo> the imperial diadem adorned the prisoner <Michael II>, who expected to be stripped of his official regalia as well as deprived of life itself.[459] <Michael> rose up, so to speak, from the depth of prison to wear a crown instead of chains. He tipped victory to <his own> side and gained mastery over the one who had hoped to become master <of the empire>.[460] After settling the imperial power upon himself and slightly mitigating the evil

---

[456] Seers and fortunetellers were referred to as "ventriloquists" (ἐγγαστρίμυθοι, lit. "belly speakers"); see, for example, the famous witch of Endor, who conjured a vision of victory for King Saul (1 Ki. 28:7–19). Ignatios uses John the Grammarian as a convenient representative of Leo's close associates and exploits the persistent reputation for sorcery associated with John, a learned man who may have conducted experiments in ancient Greek science (see Lemerle, *Byz. Humanism,* 154–56 and 166–67). Ignatios earlier made a distant allusion to John as a sorcerer at 166.12.

[457] The senator and patrician John Spektas belonged to Leo's six-member florilegium committee, which apparently included as well an Armenian named or nicknamed "Hamazaspes." See Alexander, *Nicephorus,* 127.

[458] Reading παρέβλεψαν with Alexander (*Nicephorus,* 127 n. 3) for the printed παρέβλαψαν.

[459] Ignatios puns on ζώνη (the belt worn in official regalia) and ζωή (life).

[460] Leo's heir apparent may have been his son Symbatios/Constantine, who had represented his father at the iconoclast Council of 815. See Alexander, *Nicephorus,* 137.

prevalent before <his reign> to the extent that those <iconodules> in prison and in distress could fantasize of liberty in their dreams, <Michael> secretly nursed <the flame> of the dead <Leo's> purpose. Like a fish he was caught in the nets of heresy and perished in its unsound doctrines.

With his eminently perceptive intelligence, the great Nikephoros observed these <developments> and <understood> that the tail of heresy had not perished together with the coils of the serpent [Leo V], but continued to twitch and only pretended that its life was dead. <Nikephoros therefore> set himself the task of <using> his pen <under the guidance> of the <Holy> Spirit to give written notice of orthodox doctrines to the newly crowned emperor. He placed before <Michael's> eyes his fetters and <God>, Who had delivered him; he <recalled> the disgrace and destruction of the tyrant <Leo> whose lawlessness <was all> in vain, and his death in the very place where he had sinned.[461] <Nikephoros> sketched for <Michael> the representation of the holy images, which was a true <inheritance> handed down from the Fathers <of the Church>; <he asserted> that <doctrinal> certainty was not conferred by an innovative [i.e., heretical] discovery of yesterday, but <that such certainty> has been honored in reverence from the time when the apostolic trumpet made the splendor of the <Gospel> proclamation ring loudly round the inhabited world.

<Michael> marveled at the sagacity of <Nikephoros> and admired exceedingly the precision of his discourse, even though <Michael> was uninitiated in such matters to the very highest degree, since his family's lack of education bestowed upon him an inheritance of ignorance in abundant supply.[462] He is said to have responded something like this to those men who brought the letter: "Those clerics who were <engaged> in doctrinal investigations before our <time> will be required to make an accounting before God of whether [p. 210] they rendered their decrees well or not. We, however, prefer to maintain the Church on the <course> in which we found her traveling. We

---

[461] Probably a reference to the iconoclasts' sin of desecrating church images. Leo died in the palace chapel of St. Stephen (see *v. Niceph.* 208.3 and n. 452 above), which he had probably redecorated in the course of purging the images.

[462] Since Michael II was born to a humble family in the Anatolian fortress town of Amorion (modern Hisar), he could not have enjoyed the benefits of a rhetorical education such as might have been available in urban centers.

confirm this <decision> more precisely: that no one should be so bold as to open his mouth <to express> a free opinion for or against the icons. Let the Council of Tarasios, the one of Constantine long ago, and the one convened recently under Leo[463] depart <from public discussion> and remain remote; let a profound silence as regards any mention of icons be introduced through the whole <empire>. As for you and your eagerness to speak and write about these things—if you wish to exercise leadership over the Church as regards this doctrine, be ready to display complete silence for the rest <of your life> concerning the existence and veneration of icons."[464]

Then when news of the emperor's ridiculous <statements> reached the ears of the blessed father <Nikephoros>, he placed no value upon them nor had he any intention of taking them into consideration, but he persisted in his former solid and exact conformity <with orthodoxy> by demolishing the silly arguments of his opponents with the methods and proofs of logical argumentation. He included as the seventh among the ecumenical councils[465] the council <presided over> by Tarasios, famous among the all-praiseworthy Fathers <of the Church>. He demonstrated that both Constantine's slanderous doctrines against the holy icons <in 754> and those of Leo <that had> confirmed <them in 815> were obsolete, and he held <Leo> up as an object of ridicule to all. To those who had any concern <at all> for blameless worship and faith, he maintained that the mad folly of the <iconoclasts>, who made accusations against <true> Christians,[466] was the worst of all heresies.

Totally engrossed in divine doctrines, <Nikephoros> reasoned and taught thus, filling the whole world with his untainted opinion concerning

---

[463] Constantine VI and Irene convened the Second Council of Nicaea (787) that affirmed the use of icons under the presidency of the patriarch Tarasios. The Council in Hieria summoned by Constantine V (754) had condemned icons, a doctrinal stance reaffirmed by the synod called by Leo V in Constantinople (815).

[464] Perhaps Michael implies here that a cooperative attitude on Nikephoros' part might effect his reinstatement as patriarch.

[465] Nikephoros includes the Second Council of Nicaea (787) as one of the doctrinally definitive councils of the Church and pointedly omits the earlier iconoclast Council in Hieria (754) from that number.

[466] The adjective Χριστιανοκατήγορος was frequently applied to iconoclasts by their opponents; see *v. Ignat.,* PG 105:493A, 516A–B; *v. Theod. Edess.* 45.7–8; *v. Greg. Decap.* 54.1; *v. Niceph. Med.* 414, chap. 10.14–15.

divinity and to the best of his ability tracing the footsteps of those men of noble nature who <lived> under <both> *the Old* and *the New Testament*.[467] Emulating Abraham's faith,[468] his mind burning with this <faith> and <his> *home-born* <*servants*>[469] armed like those others by the force of his words, he clearly plundered and subdued the kings who raged against the Church, and he redeemed this Church like a second Lot from being led away captive into heresy.[470] [p. 211] He achieved and surpassed Isaac's obedience to *God, the father of all*,[471] up to the point of <shedding his own> blood, for <unlike Isaac> he was sacrificed through a multitude of trials, but <like Isaac> he did not actually become a whole burnt offering by <shedding his own> blood.[472] <Nikephoros>, however, was a priest who sacrificed the true and bloodless sacrifice <of the Eucharist> and clearly begot *sons and heirs of God*[473] by the Church, wedded to him in a spiritual sense like another Rebecca.[474] Anointed with Jacob's great reputation among shepherds, he did not increase his flock with ignoble <animals> but with notable and rational creatures, proclaiming aloud that <his flock> was *blessed by the Lord since* his *coming*.[475] <Nike-

---

[467] Cf. 2 Cor. 3:6, 14.

[468] Instead of supplying concrete information about the final years of Nikephoros' life, Ignatios adopts a device often used by hagiographers at the close of a saint's *vita*, an extended *synkrisis* or comparison of the saint with notable figures of the faith from both the Old and the New Testament.

[469] Cf. Gen. 14:14.

[470] When King Chodollogomor (i.e., Chedorlaomer) of Elam and his allies defeated a coalition of kings that included the king of Sodom, Abraham's nephew Lot was captured. Mustering his household, Abraham pursued the forces of Chodollogomor, defeated him, and rescued Lot. See Gen. 14:1–16.

[471] Cf. Eph. 4:6.

[472] Isaac, son and heir of Abraham, accepted his father's will to the point of lying bound on the altar as a blood sacrifice demanded by God; at the last moment, God sent a ram to substitute for the sacrifice of Isaac. See Gen. 22:1–13.

[473] Cf. Gal. 4:7.

[474] Isaac married Rebecca late in life and fathered two sons from her, although she had been barren. See Gen. 25:20–27.

[475] Cf. Gen. 30:30. Under the care of Jacob the herds of his father-in-law Laban increased greatly. Nikitin (p. 18) points out that this sentence very closely resembles a line from Ignatios' *Life of George of Amastris* (*v. Georg. Amast.*, chap. 38, p. 60).

phoros> not only resembled Joseph in his good judgment but also even surpassed him in his spiritual as well as his physical beauty, because <Nike-
phoros> preferred not only *his cloak* but also his holy garment[476] to be pulled
off by the Egyptian woman of this era (I mean the heresy with its vulgar language) that lusted after him and dragged him toward intimacy with forbidden
doctrines.[477] He demonstrated the forbearance of Job and his patience toward
his opponents[478] while living a holy life under duress; rather than *scraping*
away the boils of abuse with *a potsherd,*[479] he scrapped[480] the prattle of his
opponents, that dragged <men> toward folly. <Nikephoros> followed Moses' model[481] of leadership when he conducted the people out of *Egypt's dark-*
ness,[482] <i.e.,> heresy's foolish discourse, that nourishes its believers with *gar-*
lic and onions,[483] namely, with foul-smelling teachings. In the salty brine of
the Red <Sea>, that is of harsh teaching, <Nikephoros> washed from <his
people> their distasteful and very malodorous burden. <He led them> to the
land abounding in *milk and honey*[484] by conveying <to them> the sweetness of
divine doctrines, which is pure, genuine, and replete with pleasure. He inher-

---

[476] The clergy's distinctive ἱερὰ ἀμπεχόνη is also mentioned at *v. Niceph.* 146.28–29
and at 202.26; see n. 419 above.

[477] Ignatios compares Nikephoros, stripped of his patriarchal office by iconoclasts,
to Joseph, who steadfastly resisted the shamelessly seductive advances of Petephres'
(i.e., Potiphar's) wife and fled, leaving his clothing in her hands (cf. Gen. 39:6–13).

[478] The righteous and pious man Job suddenly and undeservedly lost his wealth and
his family, then broke out in painful boils (Job 1–2, 8). His friends afflicted him with
long speeches, incorrectly assuming that Job suffered because he was guilty before God
(Job 4–27).

[479] Cf. Job 2:7–8.

[480] "Scrape"/"scrap" is an attempt to replicate Ignatios' wordplay ὀστράκῳ (potsherd, ostrakon)/ἐξοστρακίζων (ostracize).

[481] Reading κανόνι for the printed κακόνι. Moses led the Israelites out of bondage
in Egypt, through the parted waters of the Red Sea, and on a prolonged period of
wandering toward the borders of the land promised them by God (Ex. 13:17–18:27 and
Num. 10:11–34; 13).

[482] Cf. Ex. 10:21.

[483] Cf. Num. 11:5.

[484] Cf. Ex. 3:8, 17, etc.

ited Aaron's[485] <position of> respect among priests, without having a Moses to interpret matters respecting God; instead, <Nikephoros> continually conversed <with God> *face to face*[486] through the holy words of <his prayers>. Nor did he *go into* the sanctuary <wearing> a *tire* [i.e., a turban], *a shoulderpiece,* and *bells* which sounded each year,[487] but [p. 212] striking <a chord upon> the twelve-stringed lyre of the apostles,[488] he entered the holy of holies more frequently <than Aaron did and> unfolded to all the *manifestation* of holy Scripture[489] with great clarity. Stamped upon him was Joshua's generalship and steadfastness against enemy assaults, <although> he did not check the lights <of heaven in their course> in order to *execute vengeance* on <his foes>.[490] Rather, by day and by night he made assaults upon God with his entreaties,[491] until He showed compassion upon the enemies of truth *washed in* their own *blood.*[492] <Nikephoros> will be extolled with Phinehas for slaying fornicators,[493] for <Nikephoros> also used *the goads* of just men's *words*[494] like a *javelin* to *pierce through*[495] those who *went a-whoring in departing from the Lord,* as the prophet warned,[496] and who wished to hide Chaldaean *seed*

---

[485] Reading τὸ for the printed τὸν with Nikitin, p. 18. Aaron, the brother of Moses and his companion in the events of the Exodus, also symbolized the power and sanctity of the high priesthood (e.g., at Ex. 28:1, 4, and 40:13).

[486] Cf. Ex. 33:11.

[487] Cf. Ex. 28:4, 29–31.

[488] A musical image originating in John of Damascus' *De hymno trisagio epistola* 14 (PG 95:48ʙ).

[489] τὴν τῶν θείων λογίων δήλωσιν may be a wordplay on the reference to Aaron's shoulder-piece or ephod at Lev. 8:8, ἐπέθηκεν ἐπὶ τὸ λογεῖον τὴν δήλωσιν.

[490] Cf. Josh. 10:13. Joshua accepted leadership of the Israelites from Moses and led them in the conquest of the Promised Land. In answer to Joshua's prayers, God made the sun and moon stand still until the Israelites vanquished the Amorites in battle (Josh. 10:12–14).

[491] Ignatios plays upon the similarity of sound between ἐντεύξεις ("entreaties") and παρατάξεις ("lines of battle").

[492] Cf. 3 Ki. 20:19.

[493] Cf. Num. 25:5–9. Ignatios had earlier paralleled Nikephoros' actions to Phinehas' because he suppressed licentiousness in double monasteries (see *v. Niceph.* 159.31).

[494] Cf. Eccl. 12:11.

[495] Num. 25:7–8.

[496] Hos. 1:2.

in the fields of the Church freshly plowed by the apostles.[497] Following in the footsteps of David, who spent his youthful years before he was anointed <king> in herding sheep, <Nikephoros> cared for spiritual sheep and *broke the cheek-teeth of the lions*[498] and of the bears, <that is> of the heretical tongues that roared against Christ's flock and raged with uncontrolled insolence. He embraced the solitary and contemplative <way of life practiced by> Elijah and John <the Baptist>, both before and after his holy installation <as patriarch>.[499] He had little to do with cities, <but> had great respect for these <ascetics, Elijah and John>, for he knew that solitude in the presence of God purifies the soul and releases it from every earthly concern; this was also the reason that he practiced a virtuous readiness for disputation, speaking out in the presence of emperors and neither doing anything out of shame nor concealing anything out of a desire to please.

Which one of those magnified in grace did he not imitate, tracing their steps in virtue? <Nikephoros> demonstrated the noble nature and fervent faith of Peter, the bulwark of the apostles and of the Church, and took into account Paul's *care* on behalf of *all* <things> and his labor in *that which cometh upon* one *daily.*[500] <Moreover>, he regarded any *rest* to be of lesser importance than the suffering that came upon <him> for God, contenting himself with everything that could bring forth the highest degree of *tribulation.*[501] He experienced as much <time> as Paul in prison, and more. It befell one such as Paul to be under guard in a succession <of prisons> as he moved from one place to another and [p. 213] disclosed the full power of the Gospel. A single, unchanging prison <befell Nikephoros>, however, from the time he agreed to renounce his <patriarchal> throne until his final <reward> gloriously replaced this <prison>. <Nikephoros> embodied the scrupulous <at-

---

[497] Cf. Mt. 13:24–30. According to the parable of the tares sown amid the wheat, enemies secretly added weed seed to the king's plowed fields; here, the "Chaldaean seed" probably refers to iconoclast doctrine, which suggested the dualistic ideas of the Chaldaeans because it resisted associating material objects with spiritual essence.

[498] Ps. 57 (58):6.

[499] For the meaning of ἀνάδειξις as "accession" or "installation <in office>," cf. ἀναδεῖξαι = "ordain" in Ignatios' *v. Georg. Amast.* 31.15, and in the *Life of Theodore of Stoudios,* PG 99:248D, chap. 11.

[500] Cf. 2 Cor. 11:28.

[501] Cf. 2 Th. 1:6–7.

tention> paid to apostolic <preaching>⁵⁰² by the other disciples of the word
and disclosed clearly to all men the life-giving utterances handed down by
God in their teachings about the hidden mysteries. He was a fellow confessor
with the martyrs who endured dangers for the sake of truth, for he preferred
to bear every disgrace rather than endure anything unworthy of the truth.
<Nikephoros> was in no way inferior to the illustrious Fathers <of the
Church> who lived before, during and after the approved councils <of the
Church>, nor in addition <was he inferior> to all those eminent men
through whom the Church enriched her glorious reputation concerning the
divine. In a holy manner befitting sacred things, <Nikephoros> imitated each
one in every respect inasmuch as possible, his mind guided by the pure radiance of the priesthood through care and practice attuned and in harmony
with divine things. He then dedicated his soul as an acceptable sacrifice to
<Christ>, the foremost *great high priest.*⁵⁰³

However, since <Nikephoros> was human and owed service to the inexorable <laws> of nature, he accomplished through death the departure from
his body to God, which departure should be considered not death but
<rather> a passage to a greater life and <heavenly> portion. There⁵⁰⁴ *the
Church of the firstborn, which are written in heaven,*⁵⁰⁵ celebrates in song and in
dance the eternal feastday. With them, <Nikephoros> leads a chorus and like
an angel echoes the holy <cry> of holiness, <for> he has inherited a share in
<God's> promises equal to theirs.⁵⁰⁶ <Nikephoros'> final lingering illness⁵⁰⁷

---

⁵⁰² Reading κηρυκείαν accepted from inferior mss. in the printed edition.

⁵⁰³ Heb. 4:14.

⁵⁰⁴ Alexander (*Nicephorus,* 155) understands the cryptic phrase ἐν ᾗ to be a reference
to the day of Nikephoros' death (i.e., "on <the day on> which the Church . . . celebrates the long-lasting feastday," interpreted by Alexander as Passover=Easter, or 5
April). Nikephoros actually died on 2 June 828 in the 13th year of his exile (*SynaxCP*
725.16–17); cf. n. 19 in Introduction, above.

⁵⁰⁵ Heb. 12:23.

⁵⁰⁶ Cf. Heb. 6:12, where Christians are described as κληρονομούντων τὰς ἐπαγγελίας,
"those who inherit the promises," and Rev. 4:4–11, where the worship of the elders in
heaven is described as they encircle the throne of God and respond to "Holy, holy,
holy" sung to God by the gospel writers.

⁵⁰⁷ Since Nikephoros survived for thirteen years in exile (Alexander, *Nicephorus,*
155), this unspecified illness was apparently acute at its onset (cf. *v. Niceph.* 190.23–26)
and debilitating for periods of time (192.12–14), but not immediately fatal.

overtook him in the eleventh month of the eighth year of his holy and blameless patriarchate. He knew perfectly well that the boundaries of death stood nearby, but at that time he received with a glad heart <the death> he had dreaded [p. 214] in former times because he feared it would come swift and unforeseen. He then awaited <death> with great gladness and with gratitude to the One that bound him while bringing deliverance by loosing him from the unholy, and that will unite him in heaven with the <divine> judgments that his conduct justified.[508] On the days of his illness, then, <when he was> strong and without symptoms, he did not give up <providing> every sort of instruction to those who came <to him>. He intended them to refrain from the confusion of the heretics, which *dries up the bones* of the soul and, as the prophet says,[509] *destroys the hopes* of those who cleave to it, and to cling instead to the single teaching and faith that the seven revered ecumenical councils <of the Church> elucidated and ratified. The universal Church reverently embraces <this faith>, conveying to God every hope of the faithful and making them grasp the object <of their desire>. For as you know, the devout faith of the Fathers <of the Church> does not permit itself to be blunted by empty innovation,[510] but rather is customarily strengthened by the orthodox[511] <teaching> of the apostles.

Thus <Nikephoros> uttered these sayings beneficial to life and many more as well from the treasure of his divinely endowed wisdom. He supported the hearts of his faithful listeners with spiritual bread,[512] so to speak; after he said in the hearing of those who had gathered around him, "*Blessed be the Lord, Who has not given us for a prey to their teeth,* but has *delivered us* and *broken the snare*,"[513] he commended his blessed and holy soul into the untouchable hands of God. No words can describe how much grief, dejection, and pain he left behind in those of a godly mind, but it was easy to understand by

---

[508] Or, "unite him with the divine judgments that God deemed right," a variation on the common construction οἷς οἶδε κρίμασι; see, for example, *v. Niceph.* 165.1–2.

[509] Ignatios combines and slightly paraphrases Prov. 17:22 and 11:7.

[510] Ignatios is using a word that literally means "empty cutting" as a pun upon καινοτομία ("innovation") and κενός ("empty").

[511] The adjective literally means "straight cutting," a continuation of the pun in κενο/καινοτομίαις.

[512] Cf. 1 Cor. 10:3.

[513] Ps. 123 (124):6–7.

<simple> observation what a great occasion for unrestrained rejoicing <his death> gave those of a wicked mind. For they were like jackals and foxes and any other creature notable for cowardice that are unable to bring themselves to look upon lions as they leap and very much prefer in general not to hear their roar <even> from afar, least of all when <that roar> contributes to <the lion's act of> noble daring. Thus the cowering creatures of heresy cringed at the leonine confidence of the saint's tongue while he yet lived, and [p. 215] quaked in terror at the fierce and wondrous holy roaring from his heart. Since they were oppressed by deep discomfort both at their actions against <Nikephoros> and at <the crimes> of which they were convicted in the presence of the truth itself, they did not find it easy to emerge from the evil to which they had descended. When that holy tabernacle <of Nikephoros' body> went by means of burial to lodge in a better tabernacling <in heaven>[514] and when the words of that holy tongue yielded to silence, it was as if <his opponents> rushed up into some watchtower of joy, washed from themselves all the pretense <accomplished by> mist and darkness, and, as the saying <goes>, *with head uncovered*[515] laid bare the subtle nonsense they had been declaiming, which will be scattered, I feel sure, by the luminous radiance of the father's words and will progressively devolve into nothingness.

Finally, as an epilogue I shall pour out before you, invincible <Nikephoros>, the <story> of my own defeat and lapse,[516] in hopes that I shall move your fatherly compassion and love to mercy and induce you to act as my mediator, protector, and intercessor before God. O guardian of the divine tabernacle and spiritual teacher most lucid in mysteries <of the faith>, it is you who walk with a <holy> company in the halls of the heavenly hierarchy, you who have been deemed worthy to approach the imperishable portion and undefiled mansions <of heaven>, you who partake fully of the good things prepared for those who have gained supremacy in virtue through action and spiritual contemplation.[517] By interceding most diligently before <God>, the only *husbandman* of souls,[518] demonstrate that my earthly, barren, and mate-

---

[514] Cf. 2 Cor. 5:1.

[515] I.e., brazenly; cf. Leutsch-Schneidewin, *Corpus* 2:65, no. 81 with note.

[516] The printed τὸν demands either a noun that must be supplied from context (e.g., λόγον "story") or the emendation τὰ ("the <things>").

[517] Cf. 1 Cor. 2:9.

[518] Jn. 15:1.

rial life is fit to grow <nourishing> grain rather than <useless> rushes by uprooting every wretched thorn bush that opposes good <spiritual> health. Since I was stolen away by force and sullied by receiving communion <with heretics> but was not *defiled* with them in the court of <my own> *conscience,*[519] grant that I may cleanse myself with tears of repentance and bitter penance, and deem me worthy once again to walk the road of truth, for on the whole I need only be corrected rather than [p. 216] educated <in the faith>. For <using> the irrefutable precepts and models that you have harmoniously enunciated, I have steadied my mind firmly upon the foundation of apostolic and patristic utterances, and as God is my witness I have maintained doctrinal purity unshaken, preserving it clearly as a sort of seed in *the sensitive powers of* my *heart.*[520] May you, who have great powers in the presence of God, not consider this unworthy defense of my conduct to be some sort of flattery and a motive for absurd babbling, but rather to be the fruit of a suffering heart and the contrition of an agonized soul. May I find that you have left <to me> an occasion and opportunity[521] <to gain> remission <of my sins>, <for I fear> being oppressed by <the weight of> my utter fall <from grace>, smitten by incurable despair, and thrown aside like <Esau> of old, who exchanged his *birthright* for a trifling gratification because he did not supply a commensurate sacrifice for his father's table.[522] For I am persuaded that I shall suffer to no small degree on account of this lapse, but that I *shall be beaten with many stripes* because I *knew* the *Lord's will and did not* do it,[523] and that I shall weep belated tears without end because I have *not found repentance although* I have *sought* it.[524] Now stretch out your helping hand to me, <Father

[519] Cf. 1 Cor. 8:7.

[520] Jer. 4:19.

[521] Ignatios introduces a wordplay with τόπον ("occasion") and τρόπον ("opportunity").

[522] Ignatios compares his own situation to that of Esau, who sold his rights as eldest son (τὰ πρωτοτόκια) to his brother Jacob for a bowl of soup (cf. Gen. 25:29–34), then lost the blessing of their father Isaac when Jacob fulfilled Isaac's request for a savory meal before Esau did (cf. Gen. 27:30–40). Ignatios hopes that his biography of Nikephoros will be an offering sufficient to compensate for his folly in exchanging his birthright of true faith for worthless heresy.

[523] Cf. Lk. 12:47.

[524] In Heb. 12:16–17, Paul parallels the story of Esau to the experience of those who fall from God's grace through their sins and later try to repent with ineffectual tears.

Nikephoros>, and draw forth one submerged by the billows of unbelief. *Let not the waterflood* of heresy *drown me, nor let the* yawning *deep* of a doctrine alienated from the truth *swallow me up; neither let the well* which has gushed *foul* and deadly *dregs shut its mouth upon me.*[525] On my behalf appease the Judge Who joins the heavenly powers in rejoicing *over one* condemned man *that repenteth* more *than <over>* a far greater number of *just persons <which need no repentance>.*[526] Be guarantor of my intentions before the Lord and make plain *to the One Who knew all <*my deeds*>* even *before* my *birth*[527] that I did not rush to <Mt.> Itabyrion's <heights> of heresy[528] with a willing purpose nor was I captured by the *snares* <set> upon it and by the *traps* difficult to escape.[529] Rather, hemmed in by threats that were sharp although in partial decay[530] and prevented from every avenue of escape, I was wickedly taken captive by the nets of those who hunt souls. On account of this, the sharp wound <felt> at prayer makes me suffer extreme pain and great distress as well as establishing my place [p. 217] among the condemned. <Use,> however, your prayers like a curative lint dressing to heal over what is hard to cure[531] and difficult to lead up into the well-known and smooth track of faith. <Take care> lest the inflamed wound prove difficult or even entirely impossible to heal because you have been long negligent in your healing supervision.[532] Let me not stand in some place far from your saving help nor be judged

---

[525] Ignatios quotes Ps. 68 (69):15, adding his own interpretive phrases and a reference to Hab. 2:15 (i.e., ἀνατροπὴν θολερὰν, *foul . . . dregs*).

[526] Cf. Lk. 15:7.

[527] Cf. the apocryphal book of Susanna, 35 (Septuagint version) or 42 (Theodotion version).

[528] In the Septuagint Mt. Tabor is called "Itabyrion" only at Jer. 26 (46):18, where it is cited for its conspicuous height, and at Hos. 5:1, where it is identified as a spot for hunting. Both references inform this passage.

[529] Cf. Rom. 11:9.

[530] Following the printed edition in sequestering ἡ σκῆψις, which appears in only one manuscript.

[531] Ignatios used the metaphor of the curative lint bandage (μότωσις) applied to an ailing soul earlier at 167.7.

[532] During the period of his exile, Nikephoros apparently chose to take no role in the issues addressed in secret by the adherents of Orthodoxy, as, for example, did Theodore of Stoudios. Ignatios may refer particularly to Nikephoros' failure to specify any mechanism for restoring to the Church repentant iconoclasts like himself; cf. Alexander, *Nicephorus*, 148–54, esp. 153.

to have no share in your holy profession <of faith> nor be *cast out* from your life-sustaining teachings *bound hand and foot,* like the one who *had not* a worthy *garment* at the wedding feast.[533] Hard pressed by starvation engendered[534] in me, not from <lack of> bread and water, but <from lack of> hearing the word spoken in <liturgical> greeting by the orthodox Church,[535] let me not be neglected like the Canaanite woman *bowed down* by a long illness,[536] and let me not make my requests for the *consolation* of those following *Christ*[537] like that woman did who *cried* in vain *after* <Jesus>.[538] But <take> the scraps from the holy *table* of your words to nourish me like some famished *dog,*[539] and free me from the bondage of my assent to unbelief, if I shall somehow be able to see aright and hear from your kind advice that I so desired the <words> "*Thy faith hath made thee whole* in the sight of God."[540] Lo, *I have put away*[541] being a Canaanite and I have cast aside whatever doctrine belongs to Canaanite thinking. I assent and submit to your teaching, useful for life; I abhor and reject every alien, strange, and unsound thought that dwells apart from the abode of the Church. For to think like you is *to think soberly,*[542] and to take one's place with you brings an intimate relationship with God.

These are the characteristics of your unattainable spiritual life, in a sort of summary form; these are your[543] struggles in <life> for the sake of the true faith *unto blood;*[544] these are the glorious achievements of your *confidence toward God*[545] on this account. O venerable soul equal to the angels, receive

---

[533] Mt. 22:11–13.

[534] Reading γεωργηθέντι for the printed γεωργηθέν τι.

[535] Possibly an allusion to an excommunication of Ignatios? Alternatively, one might translate, "the word of orthodox address of the Church."

[536] Cf. Lk. 13:11.

[537] Cf. Phil. 2:1.

[538] Cf. Mt. 15:23, where Jesus rebuffs a Canaanite woman who seeks his help. In his distress, Ignatios attributes Canaanite origins to the wrong woman in this passage.

[539] Cf. Mt. 15:27.

[540] Mt. 9:22.

[541] Cf. 1 Cor. 13:11.

[542] Cf. Rom. 12:3.

[543] Reading <τὰ> ἀγωνίσματα to parallel τὰ γνωρίσματα and τὰ αὐχήματα.

[544] Heb. 12:4.

[545] 1 John 3:21.

favorably our eagerness to undertake[546] <a task> beyond our capability because we trusted in the training you gave us, while you show mercy and sympathy to the uncouth style of our narrative[547] in the knowledge that praise is not to be expected when one gains one's end, but mercy is gratefully <received> when one fails <to do so>.

---

[546] Perhaps reading ἐγχειρήσασι for the printed ἐγχειρήσαντας.

[547] Ignatios follows the example of many Byzantine authors in closing his work with a modest apology for its literary inadequacies (see *ODB* 2:1387, s.v. "Modesty, Topos of"). To the reader who has struggled with Ignatios' learned and convoluted text, his criticism of it as "uncouth" seems rather disingenuous.

6. LIFE OF STS. DAVID, SYMEON, AND GEORGE OF LESBOS

introduction and notes by Dorothy Abrahamse
translation by Douglas Domingo-Forasté

Introduction

The *vita* (or *Acta*) of David, Symeon, and George of Lesbos tells the story of three brothers whose lives spanned much of the iconoclast period. According to the anonymous author, the three brothers were born to a pious couple in Mytilene, the major city of the island of Lesbos, and were eventually buried together in the monastery of the Theotokos near the city. Their lives encompassed several styles of asceticism and took them to the mainland of Asia Minor and to Constantinople. The biography has been of particular interest to scholars because of its vivid descriptions of the impact of the second period of iconoclasm on Lesbos and its account of the restoration of icons by the empress Theodora; it is widely used in analyses of the events of the first half of the ninth century. The date of composition and historical value of the text, however, remain a matter of controversy.

The first section of the biography (Chaps. 3–9) describes the ascetic career of the oldest brother David, who ostensibly lived from 717/8–783/4.[1] David resided as a solitary ascetic in the region of Mt. Ida in the Troad on the mainland opposite Lesbos. After thirty years of isolation, he was ordained to the priesthood by the bishop of Gargara and founded a monastery dedicated to Sts. Kyrikos and Julitta. He died at the monastery after training his young brother Symeon and passed the monastery on to him; he never returned in life to Lesbos.

---

[1] We have calculated these dates from the following chronological indications supplied by the author: David was ordained in his "forty-sixth year," i.e., at the age of forty-five, in the "twenty-second year" of Constantine V (741–775), i.e., 762 (Chap. 7), and must therefore have been born in 717/8. He died at age sixty-six (Chap. 9), i.e., in 783/4. Van den Gheyn, the editor of the *Acta,* computes his dates as 716/7–783/4 (pp. 210–11).

The story of Symeon, whose dates can be reckoned as 764/5–844/5,[2] is the most detailed and dramatic part of the work. After David's death, Symeon returned to Lesbos to erect a pillar near the south harbor of Mytilene. He lived there as a stylite until the iconoclast bishop of the island attempted to set fire to his column and exiled Symeon and his followers to the island of Lagousai off the coast of Asia Minor in 820. The biography then shifts to Symeon's life as an iconophile leader, as he descended from his column ca. 823 and sailed to Constantinople, where he was imprisoned by the emperor Theophilos and eventually, ca. 829, exiled to the island of Aphousia. In 843, according to the biography, he was invited by Theodora to the imperial palace to discuss the restoration of icons. The biography portrays Symeon as the empress' chief adviser in selecting Methodios as patriarch, and includes a debate between the saint and the iconoclast patriarch John the Grammarian. Symeon's miraculous powers were demonstrated above all through prophecy; he performed few healing miracles.

The third brother in the story is George (763/4–845/6); his life was closely bound up with that of Symeon, who was actually his younger brother, despite the order in which the brothers are presented in the story.[3] George was tonsured by Symeon and took over direction of his brother's monasteries in Asia Minor when Symeon went to Constantinople about 823. According to the biography, in 843 George was invited by his brother to Constantinople, where he supported the moderate faction of the clergy led by Methodios. George refused Theodora's offer of the bishopric of Ephesos, but agreed to return to Mytilene as bishop. The account of his short tenure as bishop, like earlier

[2] According to the author's chronology, Symeon was brought to David's monastery by his mother at age eight (Chap. 9), when David was 55 (i.e., in 772/3). Therefore Symeon must have been born in 764/5. He returned to Lesbos after his brother's death (Chap. 10) and was exiled at the beginning of Michael II's reign (Chap. 17). Symeon went to Constantinople at the time of the revolt of Thomas the Slav (Chap. 18), was imprisoned with other iconophile leaders "immediately" after Theophilos assumed the throne in 829, and was exiled to Aphousia with other iconoclast leaders (Chap. 23); he returned to Constantinople in 843. Symeon died on Lesbos in 844/5 at the age of eighty, one year after returning to the island with his brother George (Chap. 33). Van den Gheyn (p. 211) gives his dates as 764/5–843.

[3] George's dates are derived from the fact that he was appointed bishop of Mytilene in 843/4 at the age of eighty (Chap. 31). He is described as older than his brother Symeon in Chap. 11. In Chap. 8 Symeon is called the "last" (i.e., youngest) son of Konstanto.

incidents in his story, is filled with miraculous donations of food and supplies to the people of the island. The identity of the eldest brother, David, is otherwise unknown. Since his career was spent entirely in the Mt. Ida region and his body was transferred to the tomb of Symeon and George at an unknown date after their death (Chap. 37), it is possible that his cult came to be associated with theirs, and with Lesbos, long after the events in the *vita*. Modern scholars have suggested that George's identity has been confused with another (or possibly two other) St. George, who was a bishop of Lesbos in the eighth and ninth centuries and an iconophile confessor.[4] The Life of this St. George, which survives in a tenth-century manuscript and in synaxarial entries, appears to describe a different person.[5] Symeon the Stylite, however, was an authentic iconophile hero. The earliest version of the *Synodikon of Orthodoxy*, dating from the late ninth century, includes a Symeon the Stylite in the small group singled out for blessing, and he is mentioned in a letter of the patriarch Methodios I. It is almost certainly this ascetic who is the subject of our biography.[6]

The *vita*, preserved in a single fourteenth-century manuscript probably of Lesbian origin,[7] is written in a "middle-level" style, with some classical allusions and rhetorical figures and abundant Scriptural quotations. Neither text nor manuscript give any clues about the identity of the unknown author, other than the fact that he was familiar with Lesbos. The three brothers are commemorated on 1 February,[8] but are not remembered as a group in any surviving liturgical calendars or collections of saints' Lives, suggesting that

---

[4] See the discussion in Chap. 10, n. 119 and Chap. 15, n. 188.

[5] The *vita* (*BHG* 2163) was edited by I. M. Phountoules, Οἱ ἅγιοι Γεώργιοι, ἀρχιεπίσκοποι Μυτιλήνης [Λεσβιακὸν ἑορτολόγιον, Α′] (Athens, 1959). See *SynaxCP* 589–90, 687, for the synaxarial entries.

[6] See Chap. 27, n. 348.

[7] Cod. Flor. Bib. Med. Laur. XXI plutei IX (ff. 12ʳ–63ᵛ); described in A. Bandini, *Catalogus codicum manuscriptorum Bibliothecae Mediceae Laurentianae varia continens opera graecorum patrum* 1 (Florence, 1764), 425–26. According to the editor of the text, the manuscript also includes an *akolouthia* for the commemoration of the saints for 1 February that shows signs of constant use, for these folios are filled with wax and dirt and damage, while the others are relatively clean. The *akolouthia* is also preserved in a 16th-century manuscript from Lesbos; see Phountoules, Οἱ ὅσιοι αὐτάδελφοι, 5–8.

[8] The commemoration date of 1 February is identified in the *akolouthia* that accompanies the *vita* in the single surviving manuscript.

their cult was restricted to Lesbos or that the *vita* was a late compilation. No traces of the cult of the three saints remain today, and no relics or icons of the brothers are known.[9] The *Acta* also present chronological problems and inaccuracies that have cast doubt that the work as we now have it could be an early composition. The ages of the three brothers span a period of 150 years, and the author's chronology makes it biologically improbable that the mother described in the text could have given birth to all three brothers.[10] The text also includes references to buildings that did not exist in the ninth century and vocabulary unattested in other ninth-century compositions.[11] These problems have led several scholars to consider the *Acta* a late work or a piece of fantasy.[12]

Other sections of the biography seem, however, to present valuable and apparently contemporary information. Incidents set in Mytilene include accurate details of local topography and information on the relations between the island of Lesbos and the nearby mainland of Asia Minor. Descriptions of important events include some plausible details, names and places not found in other sources.[13] Despite their circumstantial glorification of Symeon's role,

---

[9] Traces of the cult of the saints are described by I. Phountoules, "Ἡ τιμὴ τῶν λει-ψάνων καὶ τῶν τάφων τῶν Λεσβίων ἁγίων," *Lesbiaka* 5 (1966), 31–36.

[10] See the comments of Ševčenko ("Hagiography," 117), who notes that the mother would have had to bear David at age twelve or fourteen and Symeon and George in her mid-fifties!

[11] E.g., references to the monastery of Peribleptos (Chap. 27 and n. 347) built in the 11th century, and the church of the Savior Christ in Chalke (Chap. 30 and n. 399), built in the 10th century. The text also appears to confuse the place of exile for several iconophile leaders (Chap. 24 and n. 305). Vocabulary that may be anachronistic includes the term μονύδριον, used five times in this *vita* and virtually unattested before the thirteenth century; cf. n. 225, below.

[12] I. Ševčenko ("Hagiography," 117) states: "As they stand now, the *Acta* are of late making." F. Halkin described the Life as "une Vie fantaisiste," noting its chronological inconsistencies and episodes similar to the Lives of Antony the Younger and Ioannikios the Great; cf. F. Halkin, "Un ménologe de Patmos (ms. 254) et ses légendes inédites," *AnalBoll* 72 (1954), 15–34; idem, "Saints Georges," 464–69.

[13] For example, the site for the murder of Leo V in St. Stephen's chapel in the palace (see Chap. 16 and n. 212) is unattested elsewhere. The inclusion of Sergios Niketiates among the heads of the imperial council (Chap. 28) was noted by H. Grégoire, who characterized the life as "<un> texte d'un très vif intérêt" and "<une> vie . . . contemporaine et *bonae notae*" ("Études sur le neuvième siècle," *Byzantion* 8 [1933], 517).

the *Acta*'s accounts of the imperial decision to restore icons, the synodal process, and the election of Methodios provide more extensive treatment of these topics than any other hagiographical source. Scholars impressed by these vivid portrayals cite evidence to demonstrate that the author must have been a contemporary.[14]

Close reading of the text leads to a compromise solution, the hypothesis that the *vita* is in fact a layered composition that integrates separate works and traditions about three individuals whose relics came to be deposited together in the tomb at the monastery of the Mother of God in Mytilene. That David's Life represented a tradition only loosely connected to Mytilene or to Symeon and George is suggested not only by the structure of the text itself, but by the existence of an eleventh-century *akolouthia* addressed solely to the brothers Symeon the Stylite and George.[15] Similarly, the narrative about George contains contradictions and awkward transitions that suggest compilation.[16] Symeon's story itself takes place in two loosely joined segments, first describing his career as stylite and then as iconophile champion. The relationship of these traditions to the final narrative can only be understood through a detailed analysis of the structure, language, and sources of each section of the text. The terminus post quem of composition is certainly after 863, the date of the victory of Petronas over the Arabs;[17] the unknown date when David's relics were transferred to Mytilene would be another. The death of Bardas in 865 has been proposed as a terminus post quem, but this date is problematic.[18] Although the *vita* as it now exists appears to be a compilation of several independent traditions, it may indeed preserve early reflections of ninth-century events within a compilation of the eleventh century or later. There can be no question that the vivid narrative, with its portrayal of local culture and portraits of three very distinct saints, is, in Grégoire's words, "a text of very lively interest."

---

[14] A. Kazhdan ("Hagiographical Notes," *Byzantion* 54 [1984], 186–87), cites the author's use of the formula "up to now" as evidence for early composition. See also n. 430, below.

[15] Phountoules, Οἱ ὅσιοι αὐτάδελφοι, 9–10.

[16] George's childhood and early training are not mentioned; he visits a twin sister never mentioned elsewhere (Chap. 12); there is a reference to an earlier vision that is not included in the text (Chap. 31 and n. 422).

[17] See Chap. 31, n. 428.

[18] See further discussion in Chap. 31, n. 430.

Bibliography

Edition Used for Translation

(*BHG* 494) J. van den Gheyn, "Acta graeca ss. Davidis, Symeonis et Georgii Mitylenae in insula Lesbo," *AnalBoll* 18 (1899), 209–59.

Other Editions

I. M. Phountoules, Οἱ ὅσιοι αὐτάδελφοι Δαβίδ, Συμεὼν καὶ Γεώργιος οἱ ὁμο-λογηταί [Λεσβιακὸν Ἑορτολόγιον, Γ'] (Athens, 1961).

Secondary Literature

Anonymous, "Nota in vitam ss. Davidis, Symeonis et Georgii," *AnalBoll* 18 (1899), 368.

P. Bertocchi, *Bibl.sanct.* 4 (1964), 519 f.

S. Efthymiadis, "Notes on the Correspondence of Theodore the Studite," *REB* 53 (1995), 141–63.

H. Grégoire, "Études sur le neuvième siècle," *Byzantion* 8 (1933), 517–20.

F. Halkin, "Un ménologe de Patmos (ms. 254) et ses légendes inédites," *Anal-Boll* 72 (1954), 15–34.

———, "Y a-t-il trois saints Georges, évêques de Mytilène et 'confesseurs' sous les iconoclastes?" *AnalBoll* 77 (1959), 464–69.

A. Kazhdan, "David, Symeon and George of Mytilene," *ODB* 1 (1991), 589.

———, "Hagiographical Notes," *Byzantion* 54 (1984), 185–88.

D. Michailidis, "Trois notules sur les saints de Lesbos," *AnalBoll* 89 (1971), 145–47.

I. M. Phountoules, Οἱ ἅγιοι Γεώργιοι ἀρχιεπίσκοποι Μυτιλήνης [Λεσβιακὸν Ἑορτολόγιον, Α'] (Athens, 1959).

———, "Ἡ τιμὴ τῶν λειψάνων καὶ τῶν τάφων τῶν Λεσβίων ἁγίων," *Lesbiaka* 5 (1966), 26–36.

The Life and Conduct of and Narrative about our Thrice Blessed and Inspired Fathers David, Symeon, and George, Those Lights Shining in Ancient[19] and Terrible Times

Give your blessing, Father.[20]

1. For some \<authors\> men's battles and wars against each other provided a starting point for their narratives, \<as did\> plans and stratagems and brave deeds against each other and trophies, so that time would not obscure their deeds; and the truth has convicted most of these \<works\> of \<being done\> as a favor or because of hatred.[21] For other men myths and fables \<encouraged\> the collection of narratives and their arrangement, \<fables\> that conceal the falsehood of the mythographers or demonstrate the plausibility of the poets.[22]

---

[19] The description of the events as taking place "in ancient" (ἐν παλαιοῖς) times demonstrates distance from the events of the narrative. It is possible that the title was added some time after the composition of the text; if, however, it is contemporary with the rest of the text, the description of the events as taking place in "ancient and terrible times" must be a sign of late composition.

[20] A formulaic expression uttered by the monk who read aloud in the refectory during communal meals seeking the abbot's blessing on his reading. We thank A. Alexakis for providing this information.

[21] The *prooimion* of the *vita* presents some difficulties in translation. The problems in this section of the text appear to derive not only from its rhetorical nature, but also in part from the text as transmitted, and emendation may be required. We express our gratitude to A. Alexakis and L. Rydén for suggestions on improving our translation of this section.

An alternative translation for the final phrase of the first sentence of the *prooimion* would be "and truth has revealed most of these \<events\> in a way that arouses pleasure or hatred."

[22] See E. Bundy, *Studia Pindarica I–II* (Berkeley, Calif., 1962), 4–26, and W. H. Race, *The Classical Priamel from Homer to Boethius* (Leiden, 1982), for the priamel; this use of an introductory foil was a standard literary topos from the time of Sappho and Pindar. The rhetorical contrast between "myths and stratagems" and the "truth" is found in the *prooimia* of several other mid-Byzantine hagiographical texts; some 9th-century examples are the *vitae* of John the Psichaite, Theophylaktos of Nikomedeia, and Nicholas of Stoudios, and Theodore of Stoudios' *Oration on Plato of Sakkoudion.*

But for those[23] who have labored for the sake of the history of these <events> and the truth <there is> great grace and approval for having provided[24] for <our> lives a memorial to the lives of good and fine <deeds>, [p. 212] so that those who read <these stories> hereafter may not fall into the same pitfalls from either lack of wisdom or from laziness, but may cling to right counsels and actions. But I do not know why any rational person would praise the compilers of myths and fables for their undertaking, unless he also heaped laughter upon them, since they leave their treatises as an indelible monument of their own[25] foolishness. And the more these <latter> men honor the myths with linguistic refinement, the more those <former> ones[26] condemn the foolishness and shamelessness of the compilers. But as for me who set the truth above all, whose eager intention it was to write about[27] blessed and revered men who have displayed on earth an angelic life and manner of living, and who am eager to do so, the assignment seemed heavy and burdensome, so that my mind reeled <when confronted> with such laborious struggles. And I would never have embarked upon this task of my own volition, for I was extremely reluctant[28] and fearful, since I was aware of my personal weakness with words. But since you bound me with chains[29] and divine injunctions, and not once, but even twice and three times you compelled me, though I begged[30] you <not to> and was unwilling to do this <task> and refused, <may you> pardon those things that escape my grasp because of ignorance as well as all the matters that our account does not manage to cover and therefore prefers to pass over in silence and leaves to more capable indi-

---

[23] Reading τοῖς for τῆς.

[24] Perhaps παρεσχημένη should be emended to παρεσχημένοις.

[25] Reading αὐτῶν for αὐτῆς, as proposed by A. Alexakis and L. Rydén.

[26] ἐκεῖνοι may refer to the historians who are contrasted with the mythographers at the beginning of the Life or to rational people.

[27] Sc. περὶ or perhaps read δεδειγμένην for δεδειγμένων and translate: "to write the life and angelic conduct manifested on earth by blessed and revered men."

[28] Reading ηὐλαβούμεθα for ἡβλαβούμεθα.

[29] To be understood metaphorically.

[30] L. Rydén has proposed emending ἐκλιπαρήσαντας to ἐκλιπαρήσαντες and translating "and not once, but even twice and three times you entreated me and compelled me, though I was unwilling. . . ."

viduals.[31] Rather by entreaties to our blessed men [i.e., David, Symeon, and George] and petitions to God may you assist me, though I have hesitated up to now to undertake <this task>, because of my reverence for these men and not because of audacity. May God lead this account, God from Whom *every good gift and every gift*[32] comes. So now then we must begin the narrative.

2. Lesbos is an island, one of the Cyclades, being part of <the district of> the Aegean Sea, not far removed from the Hellespont, closer to the Asian continent than to the European.[33] On this island is situated the city of Mytilene,[34] the progenitor of our completely blessed and thrice-happy fathers, I

---

[31] The author's protestation of his "weakness with words" is a common topos referring to lack of literary skill. The author does not identify who has compelled him to write, as is frequently the case where a text is commissioned by a successor abbot in the saint's monastery. Claims to "ignorance" and "silence" in hagiographical *prooimia* are often an indication that the writer did not have firsthand information on his subject. In claiming that he omits materials about which the account "prefers to keep silent," the author may also refer to conflicting materials and traditions available to him, or a desire to keep his narrative to a reasonable length so as not to overwhelm his readers.

[32] James 1:17.

[33] Lesbos is located off the coast of Asia Minor opposite the Troad and Pergamum; at its closest point, the distance from the mainland is approximately 10 km. The island is not particularly close to the Hellespont, as the author claims. In antiquity (Strabo), as in modern times, it was not considered part of the Cyclades archipelago, a term restricted to the islands that circled Delos. Byzantine authors seem to have expanded the terminology of Cyclades to include most Aegean islands. Lesbos (Mytilene) is also identified in Byzantine texts (e.g., Const. Porph., *De them.* 83.24) as forming part of the "Aeolides" or "Sporades"; at least one other 9th-century text (a miracle of St. Nicholas) describes Lesbos as a Cycladic island; cf. Malamut, *Les îles,* 1:41.

The description of Lesbos as "part of the Aegean Sea" identifies it as belonging to the governmental unit of the Aegean Sea, whose status in the mid-9th century is unclear. According to the Uspensky Taktikon, dated by Oikonomides to 842–843 (Oikonomidès, *Listes,* 46–47), Lesbos was under the control of a *droungarios* (Oikonomidès, *Listes,* 53.18); but the *Acta* of David, Symeon, and George suggest that by mid-9th century it was a theme under a *strategos;* see Chap. 32 and n. 440. The author's relatively extended description of Lesbos is curious if the text was a local product intended for a Lesbian audience, for whom no such identification would be needed!

[34] Mytilene was the major center of Lesbos in the Byzantine period, as in antiquity and modern times, and Byzantine texts frequently called the entire island "Mytilene." In the 8th and 9th centuries it was an autocephalous archbishopric; by the 10th century it had been raised to metropolitan status; cf. Darrouzès, *Notitiae,* Not. 1.51, 1.58, 7.678.

mean David, Symeon, and George. Their parents bore an additional four children; <of these last four> one pair they left in the world for a continuation of their family line, while the other pair, along with the three luminaries mentioned, they offered as a pure *sacrifice* [p. 213] *to God;*[35] <this pair>, though also embracing the solitary life, was as far outshined by the above-mentioned triadic group [David, Symeon, and George] as the stars are by the sun.[36] As for those responsible for the physical birth of the divine men, the husband was called Hadrian, the wife Konstanto; while not undistinguished in their family heritage (although men who follow God must not cling to earthly wealth and family), they were particularly distinguished in their virtue, even if they did hold second place to their children <in this respect>. Their lifestyle was that prayed for by Solomon,[37] both self-sufficient and such that they were neither burdens to those around <them> because of poverty, nor, because of the amount of their wealth, were they puffed up and arrogant toward their neighbors, but were greatly distinguished by their piety.[38] And such[39] were <the virtues> of their parents; as for the divinely inspired virtuous deeds and admirable works of the offspring, I will briefly relate them with the *Lord working with me;*[40] I have collected <information> here and there in the name of truth itself, some <data> from old writings, other <data> from God-loving and virtuous men who served as disciples to those holy fathers themselves, *dutifully from the very beginning*[41] and continuously, and I have not heard them from rumor.[42]

[35] Rom. 12:1.

[36] One of these children is presumably the recluse Hilaria, mentioned in Chap. 12 as George's twin sister. The other is unknown.

[37] Prov. 30:8, 9.

[38] The obligatory account of the birth and family of a saint almost always used this topos of distinction in virtue rather than rank in cases where a saint's background was not aristocratic. The description of the family as "self-sufficient" probably does not reflect any specific social or occupational status for the family.

[39] ἐν τούτοις.

[40] Mk. 16:20.

[41] Cf. Lk. 1:3.

[42] Here the author makes the apparently contradictory claim that his sources include both "old writings" and the oral reports of disciples. That would indicate that the biography was written within the lifetime of at least one disciple, who could have been a young monk in 844 and an old man when the reports were collected, but probably in

3. So once when that marvelous woman was carrying in her womb her first-born child, the all-blessed David, and was going into the baths,[43] a certain inspired monk who also could see the future was seated among a large number of soldiers on the street and was instructing them[44] about salvation and divine teachings; when he saw her going by, he stood up suddenly and with reverent silence did obeisance.[45] And when, on her way back home, he very reverently rendered her the same honor a second time, the soldiers sitting with him were very surprised and inquired anxiously, "Why in the world have you given such a double honor to that woman, holy father?"[46] And he said, "Look at this holy woman, brothers; by the providence of God a company of great holy men and most genuine servants of God will be born <of her>, and the fetus she now carries in her womb will be the way and the beginning and the leader of the offspring who succeed him[47] as well as a light for the wilderness and a

---

the 9th century. The use of "old writings" (ἐκ παλαιῶν συγγραμμάτων) would then have to refer to sources from the early 9th century that were used in compiling the first sections of the *vita*. In any case, the sentence is an important indication that the author compiled his text from multiple sources of varying age.

[43] This passage implies that the author considered the use of public baths by women a normal feature of daily life. Early Christian writers (e.g., Gregory of Nazianzos, PG 36:575B) inveighed against the sinfulness of baths and the dangers inherent in their use by women, and some recent works have argued that public baths had virtually disappeared by the 9th century; cf. C. Mango, "Daily Life in Byzantium," *JÖB* 31.1 (1981), 327–53, and A. Berger, *Das Bad in der byzantinischen Zeit* [Miscellanea Byzantina Monacensia 27] (Munich, 1982), 42–44, 56–72. Nevertheless, there are references in other Lives as well that suggest that women continued to use public baths in the 9th century. As a young girl, the future empress Theophano was taken to the baths late in the day to avoid being seen in public (*v. Theoph.*, chap. 6); an invalid girl in Thessalonike used the baths therapeutically after a bout with smallpox (*v. Theod. Thess.* 230.9–10).

[44] Reading αὐτοῖς for αὐτοῦ with Phountoules.

[45] Obeisance or *proskynesis:* a Byzantine gesture of veneration for the emperor, for holy men, or in prayer (*ODB* 3:1738). Manuscripts portray the act as the assumption of a prostrate position, but it could take various forms.

[46] Prophecies of future sanctity to a pregnant mother are a common theme. A similar theme of recognition by others can also be found in the Life of George of Amastris (*v. Georg. Amast.* 8.9–10.9), where the saint's mother prays in church while pregnant; men see her there, but "do not honor her other than as a woman." At home, they have visions at night of murderous men. When they discover the cause to be their failure to honor the woman, they run to her and throw themselves at her feet to ask her pardon.

[47] Reading μετ' αὐτὸν for μετ' αὐτοῦ, with Phountoules.

brightly shining star for his compatriots; for among all pregnancies her womb has been hallowed."[48] *When they heard these things, they glorified* [p. 214] *God*[49] and loudly reported her fame all over so that from that time forward she was recognized on the whole island as famous and honored.

4. As soon as <this baby> had just poked his head out from his mother's womb, he was dedicated to the Lord as a holy person, just like that great and wondrous Samuel,[50] having been consecrated even before birth, just like a second Jeremiah.[51] When he had been weaned and become a young boy, he was entrusted by his parents to a teacher to learn the "holy letters";[52] when he was nine years old in bodily age, and had acquired a basic education[53] and had learned the divinely inspired songs of the prophet his namesake [the Psalms of David], *he was subject*[54] to his parents. Once when he was grazing the flocks[55] with other boys of his own age, suddenly fiery lightning and terrifying

---

[48] Cf. Lk. 1:42.

[49] Acts 11:18.

[50] 1 Ki. 1:28. Infant consecration to God, on the analogy of Samuel who was dedicated to Jehovah after weaning, is another standard topos of hagiography. See, for example, the contemporary Life of Peter of Atroa (*v. Petr. Atr.*), chap. 2: "When his mother weaned him, she took him to the church, in fulfillment of her vow, and presented him to the bishop, thus returning in thanks to God her first-born son as another Samuel."

[51] Jer. 1:5.

[52] τὰ ἱερὰ γράμματα is the standard phrase used in hagiography to describe elementary education. It seems to combine the sense of "holy letters," i.e., learning the alphabet, and using the Bible, especially the Psalms, as the first reading material. See R. Browning, "Literacy in the Byzantine World," *BMGS* 4 (1978), 48, where he cites this text and defines τὰ ἱερὰ γράμματα as meaning the *propaideia* (preparatory education, the elementary curriculum) and the Psalms. For further discussion, see Talbot, *Holy Women*, 126 n. 47.

[53] The author's description of a "basic education" (προπαιδεία) as consisting of learning Scriptures with an individual teacher is typical of the iconoclast period. The formal school system that Byzantium had inherited from the ancient world disappeared after the 7th century, and there is little evidence of provincial schools during this period. As a shepherd son of "self-sufficient" parents, David's education in the Scriptures probably would have involved memorization rather than reading. See Browning, "Literacy," 39–54; "Education," *ODB* 2:677–78; Moffatt, "Schooling."

[54] Lk. 2:51.

[55] Like his namesake, David is a shepherd boy when he receives God's call through a prophet; cf. 1 Ki. 16:11–13.

thunder and violent rain appeared. While all the other shepherd boys scattered here and there and thought first of their own safety, this blessed young man gathered the sheep under a tree and stood in their midst frightened and getting wet from the rain. Then suddenly he looked and saw standing on his right in the garb of a monk a very old and venerable man, clothed with much glory. And the <boy> stood there watching him in speechless awe. Almost immediately the man who had appeared drove away the fear within his soul and suddenly turned the heaviness and gloom of the storm into springtime brightness; and with a gentle voice and soothing countenance he kindly said to the boy, "David, my child, why are you afraid and distressed?" And the <boy> answered, "I am afraid, most holy father, because of the fearful[56] event that has occurred and I grieve because my uncle is at home dying." And the <monk> answered him, "Courage, child; the man whom you say is nearing his end, he will be healed, but your paternal uncle, though not even sick, will die immediately. But as for you, our Lord and God has called you through me to be His genuine servant and true slave, and on account of you your four siblings, *which should be born*[57] after you. But hurry and go to that mountain on the opposite shore and you will find me[58] comforting you." But the boy said to him, "But as for yourself, my lord, who are you?" And the monk said, "I am Antony, the slave of Christ and the leader of the community of the wilderness."[59] And after saying this, he showed him with his hand Mt. Ida opposite Lesbos and made the sign of the cross over him; then after he had embraced him and filled him with courage, he suddenly disappeared. [p. 215]

5. *And when the evening was come*[60] he went back home with the sheep;

---

[56] Reading φοβερὰν for φοβερὸν, as proposed by L. Rydén.

[57] Cf. Ps. 77 (78):6.

[58] Reading με for μὲν, as suggested by L. Rydén.

[59] The Egyptian saint Antony the Great (ca. 251–356) is portrayed throughout the biography as the patron of David, and his *vita* is the literary model for the description of David. The Life of Antony by Athanasios of Alexandria established the model of the hermit monk and served as the most popular prototype for Byzantine hagiographers, directly and as referred to in later sources. For the phrase "leader of the community of the wilderness," cf. *v. Ant.,* chap. 14 (PG 26:865B): "And so, from then on, there were monasteries in the mountains and the desert was made a city by monks, who left their own people and registered themselves for the citizenship in the heavens" (trans. R. C. Gregg, *Athanasius: The Life of Antony and the Letter to Marcellinus* [New York, 1980], 42–43).

[60] Mt. 27:57. KJV has "even" for "evening."

and since everyone was grieving because of the man who was at death's door, he himself predicted what had been announced <to him> and concealed only his own <imminent> flight.[61] So while he put an end to the old dirge, he brought in its place a new and not unfamiliar one. For just before dawn he *arose and ran*[62] to the harbor and found a boat ready to cross to the place that had been pointed out to him; he got into it and fulfilled the bidding <of the vision>, eagerly hastening to bring it to fruition just as *good, rich ground*[63] does to seed that has been scattered <on it>. And when he had bid farewell to his native land and parents and the acquaintances time had provided and had made the journey across, he removed himself from *the toils* of this world *as a doe.*[64] He ran all the way to Mt. Ida and settled there so that this very place that the <ancient> Greeks claimed in myth to be the home of Zeus[65] might accurately be called the abode of a divine man and the sacred precinct of holy souls. There the noble <David> displayed endurance of many trials and tribulations, though he was still an adolescent (for he was sixteen years old). He lived in the desolate wilderness and mountains for thirty years[66] and ate wild greens that grew naturally from the earth and acorns he found lying about, with <only> pure spring-fed streams to drink from; and he grew out the hair of his body as a garment[67] and had as his brush-covered home rough

[61] Middle Byzantine hagiographers frequently began the account of a saint's training with a flight from home. In some texts the theme is explicitly identified with a family's opposition to a child's monastic vocation because of the need to carry on responsibilities of lineage, military obligation, and marriage. On this, see A.-M. Talbot, "The Byzantine Family and the Monastery," *DOP* 44 (1990), 119–20, 126–27.

[62] Lk. 23:12.

[63] Cf. Lk. 8:8.

[64] Prov. 6:5.

[65] The author has not confused the Mt. Ida of the Troad with the birthplace of Zeus, Mt. Ida of Crete. Rather, his familiarity with local myth and possibly Homer (*Il.* 24.290–91, 308) permits him a fortuitous contrast between Idaian Zeus, who had a small home (οἰκητήριον) there, and the genuine divine, David. That the name of the mountain range remained unchanged from the classical period is confirmed by the 5th-century *Synekdemos of Hierokles* (PW 9.1:862–64).

[66] If the author's chronology is accurate (see Introduction), this flight to the mainland would have taken place about 733. His thirty-year stay in the wilderness would have lasted until around 763.

[67] Descriptions of hermit life in the wilderness very frequently describe saints wearing hair shirts, but the claim that David grew his own hair out to use as a garment is unusual; no other lives of 9th-century male saints include this topos. It may derive from

caverns and caves among the rocks; and having put to flight with all his might our ancient enemy [i.e., the Devil] and his company, and having been distinguished with some incredible divine visions, he put on the monastic habit.[68]

6. For one day while he was sleeping it seemed to him that in his dreams he saw an exceedingly beautiful and altogether magnificent church, the kind that human nature is not able to imitate on earth; it was filled with priests, monastic and celibate,[69] who were offering the bloodless and *spiritual sacrifice*[70] to God, and no one of those we call the laity appeared among them at all. And the blessed one [David] tried to go within and to share with them the divine and eternal mysteries; for he had longed for many years to partake of the sacraments, but *those steadfastly continuing*[71] to guard the church would not allow him <in>.[72] While he was weeping and [p. 216] lamenting without

---

the popular legend and image of St. Onouphrios, a 5th-century Egyptian hermit who was described as "naked and hairy," and portrayed with a long white beard and covered with hair; cf. *Bibl.sanct.* 9:1187–200; *ODB* 3:1527.

[68] The description of David's severe ascetic life in the wilderness follows the model of early hagiography, based in turn on Elijah, John the Baptist, and Christ, beginning with a retreat to the desert (*xeniteia,* on which see V. Laurent in *v. Petr. Atr.* 79, n. 4), followed by a return to civilization, ordination, and the foundation of a community. The absence of an ascetic master under whom the saint begins his training is unusual among middle Byzantine saints' Lives. The descriptions of his diet of plants and home in a cave are standard for this stage of monastic training. The use of ancient models to describe stages of ascetic formation in eremitic and cenobitic biographies is discussed by B. Flusin, "L'Hagiographie monastique à Byzance au IXᵉ et au Xᵉ siècle," *Revue Bénédictine* 103 (1993), 31–50.

[69] παρθένων; cf. Lampe, *Lexicon,* s.v. II. The beginning of Chap. 6 describing David's dream vision of a "ναὸν . . . πεπληρωμένον ἀνδρῶν ἱερέων, μοναχῶν καὶ παρθένων, καὶ τὴν ἀναίμακτον . . . λατρείαν τῷ Θεῷ προσφερόντων" can be interpreted in two ways. If the participial phrase λατρείαν . . . προσφερόντων is taken in the narrow sense of "offering the Eucharist," then the phrase μοναχῶν καὶ παρθένων must be taken in apposition to ἱερέων as translated above, since only priests could celebrate the liturgy. The vision's reference to "celibate priests" would distinguish these priests from ordinary parish priests, who, in orthodox practice, would be allowed to marry. If προσφερόντων has a more generic sense of "participating in the liturgy," then the phrase ἱερέων, μοναχῶν καὶ παρθένων could be translated "priests, monks, and nuns."

[70] Rom. 12:1. KJV translates "reasonable service."

[71] Acts 1:14, 2:42; Rom. 12:12, 13:6.

[72] This passage reflects an inherent problem for isolated hermits, that they could not partake of the eucharist unless they were ordained, because no priest would be available to celebrate the liturgy. David, who developed his asceticism on his own without the

restraint, he saw an exceedingly noteworthy individual come from the sanctuary and say, "Why are you weeping like this, David, sir? If you wish to come in here with us and join us, go away and become like one of us." And <David> said, "Let me come in, father, and let me be thought worthy of the life-giving communion, and I will do what you command." But the man speaking to him answered, "No, son, no!" And that was the end of the vision.

When <David> awoke, he marveled to himself at what he had seen, and begged God persistently, if it was acceptable to Him, to confirm its truth with a second vision. Indeed on that same day at high noon when the sun was lighting the earth with its bright rays, all at once the sun hid its brightness; and it became dark and a storm completely concealed the mountains there. And though the holy man was gripped by overwhelming confusion and was not able to find the way to walk because of the mist, he *blindly*[73] continued along the mountain ridges; and lifting up his eyes to heaven and stretching out his hands, he besought help from on high; then as he glanced around, he saw on his right flashing forth on the next ridge a brilliant radiance greater than the rays of the sun; and taking heart he ran to see the sight. And as he drew near he saw standing in the middle of that light a huge young man, whose beauty defied all description. And <David> fortified himself with the sign of the life-giving cross and spoke to <the young man> who had appeared, asking, "My lord, who are you?" And <the young man> said, "Do not be afraid; I am an angel of God, and I have been sent to you"; and <David> immediately threw himself on the ground and begged to be blessed. But the angel answered him, "I will not bless you unless you assume the habit of the monastic life. Go away, tonsure your hair, and then come here and I will bless you." And with these <words the angel> departed from him.[74]

7. After <David> thanked the Lord for his clear and unmistakable as-

---

guidance of a master, had not even been tonsured by an abbot at the time of his vision. In presenting a divine commandment for David to conform to the sacraments of the church, the vision reflects the enduring tension between the ascetic freedom of the hermit and the institutional constraints of cenobitic monasticism and the sacraments of the church.

[73] Lk. 10:31. KJV translates "by chance."

[74] In narrating David's vision of the difficulty of acceptance into a monastic community after his years of solitary asceticism, the hagiographer appears to reverse a more common pattern where eremitic asceticism is seen as superior to communal monasticism; cf. A. Kazhdan, "Hermitic, Cenobitic, and Secular Ideals in Byzantine Hagiography of the Ninth Centuries [*sic*]," *GOrThR* 30 (1985), 479.

surance and marked the place, he went down from the mountain when he was forty-five years old; and he came to the bishop of Gargara,[75] a blessed man filled with the Holy Spirit who had hidden himself in the country because of fear that beset him of persecution from [p. 217] the iconoclast heretics; for it was the twenty-second year of the reign of Constantine Kopronymos;[76] and when he revealed to him [the bishop] the divine commandments, <David> received from him the all-holy habit and ordination to the priesthood.[77] And spending fourteen days with the bishop of God he was taught by him the mysteries of the monastic life and the precepts of the priesthood; then he ran back to the above-mentioned place, longing to enjoy the appearance and blessing of the angel. When he drew near the place, he glanced ahead and saw the object of his desire already awaiting his arrival. And in fact after he approached and had been both blessed and at the same time *empowered*,[78] he was ordered by the angel to build to the glory of God in that very place a chapel dedicated to the holy martyrs Kyrikos and Julitta[79] as well as a monastic community. And after giving this <command the angel> disappeared.

---

[75] Reading Γαργάρων for Γαλγάλων, with Phountoules. The city of Gargara, located on the coast opposite Lesbos, appears in classical sources (PW). It also appears in the lists of the *Synekdemos* of Hierokles and the *Notitiae Episcopatuum;* cf. W. Ramsay, *Historical Geography of Asia Minor* (London, 1890), 106, 118. The bishop Nikephoros of Gargara who is listed as an attendee at the Council of Nicaea in 787 must have been a successor of David's tonsurer; see J. Darrouzès, "Listes épiscopales du Concile de Nicée (787)," *REB* 33 (1975), 28.

[76] The "22nd year of Kopronymos," i.e., Constantine V (741–775), places the event in 762. The author's chronology here reflects the events described in the Life of Stephen the Younger: Stephen and other monks fled Constantinople after the iconoclastic Council of Hieria in 754, but widespread and public persecution of iconophiles and monks began in 765 with the martyrdom of Stephen the Younger; cf. Alexander, *Nicephorus*, 13–17; Gero, *Constantine V,* 121–29.

[77] Ordination to the priesthood was forbidden before the age of thirty; formal education or training was not required, but prior to ordination to the office, priests were expected to be familiar with orthodox doctrine and the canons; cf. "Priest," *ODB* 3:1718. This account of David's ordination after a very brief training with a bishop has many hagiographic parallels, and probably reflects a real practice of the ordination of ascetics and monks after nominal training with a bishop.

[78] Cf. Eph. 6:10; Phil. 4:13.

[79] According to the legend known by the 6th century, Kyrikos and Julitta were a mother and her three-year-old son martyred under Diocletian at Tarsus. Their cult was widespread in Asia Minor; cf. *Bibl.sanct.* 10:1324–28.

\<David\> fell to the ground, performed obeisance to God and said, "*Thy will be done,*[80] Lord"; he \<then\> began the work, collecting stones and the \<materials\> required for a house \<of God\>. And when he had finished it in a short time with the help of God and the cooperation of those who loved Christ, and after he had dedicated it, he took up residence there and \<again\> began the ascetic lifestyle[81] as \<he had done\> from the time he was still young, *forgetting those things which are behind and reaching forth unto those things which are before*[82] in accordance with the apostolic command; and worshiping the Lord with prayers and fasts and ceaseless hymns day after day, and living the spiritual and angelic life on earth, he soon obtained disciples and fellow combatants.

8. In the tenth year after the founding of the monastery, and in the fifty-sixth year of his life,[83] his God-pleasing mother heard reports about him and where he was living (for his praiseworthy father Hadrian had departed to the better and blessed life, after living seventy-two years); and she, setting aside her feminine weakness and as if unmindful of[84] her advanced years, took her last child, I mean the famous Symeon,[85] whose great fame is sung by all (for, like the great Moses, he was a lad *fair*[86] to see),[87] and crossed to \<David\> [p. 218] since she had longed to see her first and dearest son for a very long

---

[80] Mt. 6:10; Lk. 22:42.

[81] Literally, "wrestling-school," παλαίστρα.

[82] Phil. 3:13.

[83] I.e., in 772/3.

[84] Reading ὥσπερ ἐπιλαθομένη for ὡς περιεπιλαθομένη, with Phountoules.

[85] A. Alexakis has brought to our attention the way in which the introduction of Symeon evokes a passage from Theodoret of Cyrrhus' Life of Symeon the Stylite the Elder; cf. P. Canivet, A. Leroy-Molinghen, *Théodoret de Cyr. L'histoire des moines de Syrie* 1 (Paris, 1959), 159: Συμεώνην τὸν πάνυ, τὸ μέγα θαῦμα τῆς οἰκουμένης. . . .

[86] Ex. 2:2.

[87] This allusion to Symeon's fame may be more than hagiographical rhetoric; unlike David, Symeon the Stylite is referred to in iconophile texts of the early 9th century as one of the leaders of the monastic resistance. Notably, the *Synodikon of Orthodoxy* (the liturgical document drawn up to be read on the Feast of Orthodoxy) includes the name of a Symeon the Stylite among the defenders of icons; cf. Gouillard, "Synodikon," 53.132, 146–47. See also the introduction to this *vita,* above, and notes to Chaps. 26–29, below. The author probably was aware of sources for Symeon's Life that extended beyond Lesbos.

time. When she had sailed to the mainland and inquired of the local inhabitants about the monastery of her beloved <son> and the path leading to it, immediately a disciple sent by the holy man was there ready to become her guide for the trail and her escort. For he [David] had learned from God about the presence of his mother and had sent out the disciple, saying, "Go to the seashore, child, and you will find there an old woman with a teen-aged boy on the verge of manhood who has taken the trouble to come here on our account. Take her with you and lead her to us." And when in fact she arrived at his dwelling, the blessed one went out to meet her, bestowing the honor due a mother according to the commandment of the Lord that declares explicitly, *"Honor thy father and thy mother."*[88] When she saw him, she was nearly ready to die from the overwhelming joy, for she fainted and fell to the ground as though dead.[89] But <David> stretched out his hand to her, and raised her from "the dead," addressing her and embracing her as a son would. When she recovered she addressed words such as these to him, *"You are the first of my children*[90] and the fruit of my youth, O God-like and very spiritual son; and now through you[91] I offer to the God Who begets all things my last son and the seal of my old age, and your sibling and brother from the same womb; receive him and train him rightly for divine contests and ascetic exercises[92] as you know how <to do>." And when she had said this, she remained there a few days longer, bade him farewell and <then> set out for her homeland; and not much later she departed to the Lord, having lived seventy-three years in all.[93]

---

[88] Ex. 20:12.

[89] Reading <νεκρῷ> οὐδὲν διενηνοχυῖα, or the like, as suggested by A. Alexakis.

[90] Gen. 49:3.

[91] διὰ σοῦ here echoes διὰ σὲ of p. 214.26–27, where St. Antony the Great predicted that the foursome, i.e., Symeon and George and the other two lesser lights who embraced the monastic life (Chap. 2), would become true servants through David.

[92] Literally, "wrestling matches," παλαίσματα.

[93] Family chronology poses a problem: the mother of the saints, who is seventy-three, brings Symeon, the "youngest brother," who is identified as "on the verge of manhood" (πρόσηβος—presumably a teenager), and as a "lad" (μεῖραξ). As Ševčenko ("Hagiography," 117) notes, if this is to be believed, the mother of the saints must have been a biological marvel—she could not have been less than fifty-five at his birth. If the text of the following chapter is sound, where Symeon is said to be eight years old at his adoption by his brother, she would have given birth at sixty-five! Chronological incon-

9. Since he had been called forth as a servant, the very thing he was also ready to do, and had obeyed God, Symeon was given by his mother to his first brother and second father, the blessed David, when he had already completed his eighth year; <Symeon> was taught by him and learned the most holy psalter and everything that pertains to the monastic rule. When he was twenty-two years old, he was tonsured and enrolled in the company of the monks.[94] Then he nobly arrayed himself *against the principalities* and the *powers* of the [p. 219] *ruler of this world*[95] and crowned himself with trophies in regard to these <enemies>; when he was already finishing the twenty-eighth year of his life, by the divine judgment of his personal mentor he, aided by the all-holy Spirit, received the anointing and honor of the priesthood at the hand of the aforementioned very blessed bishop <of Gargara>.[96] Two years after the ordination of his brother, when the divine David was now about *to depart*[97] to the Lord and exchange the *tabernacles*[98] here for the heavenly ones, where he had possessed a *citizenship*[99] from his very infancy, so to speak, he summoned the divine Symeon and said, "My spiritual child[100] and brother by

---

sistency is one of the factors that led Halkin ("Saints Georges," 468) to doubt the authenticity of the text. See the discussion of chronology in the introduction to the *vita,* above, 143–47.

[94] Although Byzantine monasteries did not follow western practices of serving as schools for children, the concept of Symeon's placement in the ascetic community of his brother as an eight-year-old child has antecedents. Cyril of Scythopolis' *Life of Sabas,* which served as a model for the portrait of George, places his entry into a monastery at age eight; this figure is derived by combining information from chaps. 2 and 6 (*v. Sab.* 87.19–25, 90.5–19). Most other 9th-century saints' Lives, however, place entry into a monastery no earlier than the teenage years. The distinction between entry into a monastery and tonsure as a monk, at age twenty-two, accords with Byzantine monastic practice; although there was no single minimum age for tonsure, it averaged around eighteen. Standard bibliography is cited in the articles "Monasticism" and "Monk," *ODB* 2:1392–94, 1395–96, and "Tonsure," *ODB* 3:2093–94.

[95] Cf. Eph. 6:12.

[96] See Chap. 7, n. 75, above.

[97] Cf. Phil. 1:23.

[98] Cf. 2 Pet. 1:14.

[99] Phil. 3:20. KJV translates as "conversation."

[100] "Spiritual child": the standard monastic career involved training of a would-be ascetic under an ascetic master. The terminology of spiritual kinship was commonly

birth, I *have finished my course,*[101] *am hastening to die,*[102] and, look, after three days I will be departing from this world just like all who <dwell> upon the earth; but do you give *dust to dust*[103] and return to our homeland with haste, for it is in need of extraordinary assistance." When he heard these words, the holy Symeon groaned a deep groan from the bottom of his heart, beat his breast and face with powerful blows and, as he soaked his cheeks with gushing bitter tears, said to him, "You, dearest father, as you <rightly> say,[104] are departing from human existence, but to whom[105] do you leave me completely orphaned and bereft?" And he [David] said in reply, "My child and brother, do not grieve so immoderately, as *those who have no hope,*[106] and *break mine heart;*[107] for you have Christ Who bears and provides for all things fighting together with you in all things (for you must suffer much for His name's sake), and together with Him you also have my guide and teacher, the great Antony, the treasure of the wilderness and the light of the inhabited world; for often he visited me when I was suffering in the wilderness and never ceased to fill me with divine grace and power, especially on the yearly anniversaries of remembrance of his all-glorious and eternally revered death, which, as you also

---

used to demonstrate that bonds between ascetics replaced family ties, or, in this case, adoption by a brother. Spiritual fatherhood is described by I. Hausherr, *Spiritual Direction in the Early Christian East,* trans. A. P. Gythiel (Kalamazoo, Mich., 1990), and H. J. M. Turner, *St. Symeon the New Theologian and Spiritual Fatherhood* (Leiden, 1990). The real kinship between David and Symeon, reflecting the role of monasteries as family enterprises, is one of the most common features of 9th- and 10th-century saints' Lives. Some immediate parallels: Eustratios of Agauros, who ran away to join the monastery of his three uncles; Euthymios the Younger, who entrusted the supervision of two monasteries he had built to his grandson and granddaughter; John the Psichaite, who entered monastic life with his father and brothers. Cf. A.-M. Talbot, "The Byzantine Family and the Monastery," *DOP* 44 (1990), 119–29.

[101] 2 Tim. 4:7.

[102] Cf. Gen. 25:32.

[103] For these words from the burial prayer, see J. Goar, *Euchologion sive Rituale Graecorum* (Venice, 1730; repr. Graz, 1960), 437.

[104] Symeon agrees that his elder brother David is correct to address him as "spiritual child" by acknowledging David as "father."

[105] Reading τίνι for τινί, with Phountoules.

[106] 1 Th. 4:13.

[107] Acts 21:13.

know, I have never failed to observe in a worthy manner from the time I founded the monastery with the approval of God.[108] So *go and do thou likewise,*[109] *quit you like a man* in Christ and *be strong;*[110] *the grace of* our *Lord Jesus Christ and the love of God* the Father *and the communion of the Holy Ghost be with you.*"[111] And a voice came down from above which the blessed Symeon and some of the brothers standing around were also deemed worthy to hear, <a voice that spoke> as follows, "And *with thy spirit.*"[112] When he had prayed for them all and had received the undefiled and life-giving mysteries [the Eucharist] from [p. 220] the holy hands of his brother by birth, had embraced them all and completely sealed his pure and most holy body with the sign of the venerable cross, he said, "Lord, *into Thy hands I commend my spirit,*"[113] and *both lay down in peace and fell asleep,*[114] having lived sixty-six years in all.[115]

10. The all-blessed Symeon, together with the brethren who were there, reverently prepared for burial that most honored body that had endured many

---

[108] Antony: see vision in Chap. 7. The anniversary of Antony's death was commemorated on 17 January (*SynaxCP* 397–98). The annual commemoration of the death date of a patron saint was traditionally the most important ritual event of a monastery. Here, Antony, personal patron of David, is revered in addition to Kyrikos and Julitta, to whom the foundation is dedicated.

[109] Lk. 10:37.

[110] Cf. 1 Cor. 16:13.

[111] 2 Cor. 13:14.

[112] 2 Tim. 4:22.

[113] Lk. 23:46.

[114] Cf. Ps. 4:8.

[115] The last moments of an abbot were traditionally a public ritual act, as the dying man, surrounded by the community, received the Eucharist, made the sign of the cross, and said farewell to his followers. Hagiographers generally portrayed the death of a saint as the moment of triumph for the individual that proved his sanctity, signifying a smooth passage of the soul into heaven, although the mourning of the community for the loss of their father is also standard. For contemporary hagiographic parallels, see D. Abrahamse, "Rituals of Death in the Middle Byzantine Period," *GOrThR* 29 (1984), 125–34. A brief outline of the theology of death and dying and relevant bibliography can be found in the article on "Death," *ODB* 1:593–94. The author's chronology would place David's death at age sixty-six in 783/4. Note that he does not delay his death until the third day, as he predicted.

contests, and laid it to rest within the divine church; <then>, after the completion of the forty days,[116] he went to the land of his birth. Since he had
already received a greater anointing and gift,[117] he judged that he was ready
to strip down for more intense labors and exertions; and this in fact he did.
For when he reached his homeland, he erected for himself a column at the
holy sanctuary of the all-pure Mother of God called Molos,[118] located at the
south harbor. <This was done> while George was bishop of the island,
<George> who is <now> among the saints, and was a confessor during the
time of Leo the Isaurian's <reign>.[119] There he undertook ascetic exercises in

---

[116] Byzantine funeral ritual involved a forty-day mourning period. Liturgical prayers
were said on the third, ninth, and fortieth days after death to accompany the soul in
the stages of its ascent to heaven. Cf. bibliography in previous footnote; see also G.
Dagron, "Troisième, neuvième et quarantième jours dans la tradition byzantine: temps
chrétien et anthropologie," in *Le temps chrétien de la fin de l'Antiquité au Moyen Age*
(Paris, 1984), 419–30, and Koukoules, *Bios* 4:208–11.

[117] Cf. 4 Ki. 2:9; the phrase evidently means that just as Elisha had received a greater
"portion of the spirit" than Elijah, so had Symeon received a greater anointing (see
Chap. 9) than his brother David. Note the pun on χρίσματος (anointing) and χαρίσμα-
τος (gift).

[118] Mytilene is located on a promontory between two harbors, one still known as the
"south harbor." The geographic identification of the landmark here is an important
indication of the author's knowledge of the city, and suggests that the text was in part
a local production. The church of the Mother of God called Molos is otherwise unknown. Phountoules (Οἱ ὅσιοι αὐτάδελφοι, n. 50) suggests that it must be located in
the city of Mytilene, at the south harbor. The term *Molos* is probably not a corruption
of "Molyvos," the later Byzantine name for Methymna, at the northern end of the
island of Lesbos, as the editor of the text suggests (van den Gheyn, *Acta,* 220, n. 4),
since it is clear from later incidents in the story (Chaps. 32, 37) that the church was
located in Mytilene; cf. Malamut, *Les îles,* 1:275, n. 36. It is more likely to be the Greek
word μῶλος, meaning "mole, pier, breakwater"; cf. Demetrakos, *Lexikon,* s.v. 2.

[119] Since Leo III (the Isaurian) ruled from 717 to 741, the author's chronology would
imply that a St. George, bishop of Lesbos, had been a confessor more than forty years
earlier. This saint George cannot be identified with the George who is one of the three
heroes of this biography, since the latter lived into the restoration of orthodoxy in 843.
A second reference to a St. George, bishop of Mytilene and confessor under Leo V, is
made below in Chap. 15. Synaxarial notices of a St. George, bishop and confessor, exist
in several menologia under two separate dates of commemoration, and a Life of a St.
George, bishop of Mytilene and confessor who died in exile under Leo V, must have
been written by the 10th century, when it was copied in a menologion. I. Phountoules,

no way inferior to his earlier ones, but greater and more perfect and nearly exceeding human capacity. Remembering the deeds of Symeon the Elder, the one in the enclosure,[120] he communicated the following plan to the <monk> who served him, after binding him with irrevocable oaths not to divulge the

editor of the 10th-century *Life of St. George,* conjectures that there were three separate St. Georges, bishops of Mytilene, in the 8th and 9th centuries: a confessor under Leo III, a confessor under Leo V, and the brother in this story; cf. Phountoules, Οἱ ἅγιοι Γεώργιοι, 20–29. While it is possible to conjecture that there could have been two St. Georges of Mytilene, it seems most unlikely that there could have been three! Neither Halkin ("Saints Georges"), nor Kazhdan ("Hagiographical Notes," 186), accepts the existence of three. If the author's chronology is to be taken seriously, Symeon's column must have been erected sometime after David's death in 783/4; George the Confessor would have returned from exile many years earlier to serve as bishop of the island; he could not have been there in 787, when Mytilene was represented at the Council of Nicaea by Bishop Damianos. The seal of an iconophile bishop of Mytilene named Michael is also preserved, dated to the period 750–850, and probably to the years 787–815 (Zacos, *Seals,* 1.2, no. 1341). To accept the author's chronology, we would have to posit the existence of four iconophile bishops serving Mytilene between 782 and 815. It is possible that the biographer of this text or a later copyist confused Leo III (the Isaurian) with Leo V (the Armenian), and that the Bishop George the Confessor mentioned here was bishop after 787, a confessor under Leo V, and the same saint mentioned in Chap. 16, the synaxarial entries and the *vita* included in the 10th-century menologion. In any case, the reference reflects a confused tradition passed on by the author.

[120] Symeon the Elder: Symeon Stylites the Elder, a 5th-century saint, lived in the neighborhood of Antioch and was the earliest of the Byzantine "stylite" saints who spent their ascetic lives on the top of a column that they had erected. This identification of Symeon as "the one in the enclosure" (τοῦ παλαιοῦ Συμεὼν τοῦ ἐν τῇ μάνδρᾳ) is found in several synaxarial notices of commemoration for Symeon the Elder (*SynaxCP* 3.12, 846.1). The hardship Symeon and later stylites endured as they stood exposed to the elements, combined with their ability to practice extreme asceticism in public, contributed to the popularity of this model of asceticism. The chapters describing the life of Symeon of Mytilene are clearly based on the short *vita* of Symeon Stylites the Elder included in the 5th-century *Historia religiosa* of Theodoret of Cyrrhus (*Théodoret de Cyr. Histoire des moines de Syrie,* ed. P. Canivet, A. Leroy-Molinghen 2 [Paris, 1979], 158–215). Symeon Stylites the Elder spent three years enclosed in a hut atop a column (chap. 7), ate only once a week (chap. 5), fasted for the forty days of Lent (chap. 9), and chained his foot to the wall of his column, in emulation of Jeremiah who put an iron collar around his neck (chaps. 10, 12). Other stylites are referred to in 9th-century texts, indicating the continued allure of the practice: Antony the Younger is said to have asked advice from a stylite named Eustratios in the neighborhood of Attaleia before running away to become an ascetic (*v. Ant. Jun.* 202); the Life of Gregory the

daring plan to anyone.[121] <This monk was> the most blessed George, his actual brother (for he had tonsured <George> and enrolled him in the company of the monks, and, through the laying on of hands of the most holy bishop mentioned above, elevated him to the honor of the priesthood).[122] He [Symeon] ordered three *yokes* [collars] *of iron*[123] to be made, one of which he decided to put around his waist, the other two he put around his ankles, so that his calves would be glued to his thighs [in a kneeling position] and would always remain completely attached, [p. 221] and so that he would live in such a confined space that both his stomach and genitals would become wholly subservient to the ruling power of his mind.[124] For the noble man [Symeon] knew well the force of the *crooked serpent*[125] that could be *in the navel of the belly,*[126] and because of this in the beginning he consumed only bread and water once a day (even of this a very small amount and <consumed> only after sunset), and then he <ate> every other day, and often even extended his fast to a week; for he displayed such a rigorous and prolonged fast that he went without food during nearly all the days of holy Lent, no doubt a strange

---

Dekapolite includes two references to a stylite ascetic in Thessalonike (*v. Greg. Decap.* 60.8, 67.1—the same person?). References to stylites throughout the Byzantine period are collected in Delehaye, *Saints stylites,* cxvii–cxliii. Two seals of stylites from the Middle Byzantine period have been preserved (Laurent, *Corpus,* 5.2, nos. 1301–2).

[121] The translation of this passage as it stands in the printed text presents great difficulties. We have adopted the solution proposed by A. Alexakis, namely to move the phrase τοῖς τῶν δεσμῶν ἀλύτοις ἀσφαλισάμενος μηδενὶ τὸ θαρρηθὲν ἐξειπεῖν (p. 220.25–26) to p. 220.23, following τοιάνδε. For similar metaphorical use of δεσμοί as "binding oaths," see *Acta,* p. 212.15.

[122] The first reference to the third of the three brothers. Later sections suggest that George was older than Symeon by one or two years. This is the only reference to George's introduction to monasticism and ascetic training, and his relation to his parents or to David is not mentioned elsewhere.

[123] Jer. 35:13.

[124] ὁ αὐτοκράτωρ νοῦς, a phrase also found in such disparate sources as the Acts of the 42 Martyrs of Amorion, in *Skazanija o 42 amorijskich mučenikach,* ed. V. Vasil'evskij, P. Nikitin (St. Petersburg, 1905), 27.25; Meletios, *Hypothesis ad opus De natura hominis,* ed. J. A. Cramer, *Anecdota Graeca e codd. manuscriptis bibliothecarum Oxoniensium* 3 (Oxford, 1836), 2.25; and the *Doctrina Patrum de incarnatione verbi,* ed. F. Diekamp (Münster, 1907), 307.6.

[125] Is. 27:1.

[126] A euphemism for the sexual organs, cited from Job 40:11; see *v. Niceph.,* n. 114.

and bizarre report and apparition, but to those who have dedicated themselves to God a normal and natural one, since the grace of the all-holy Spirit strengthens one's nature beyond nature. You will hear <of this> later.

11. His clothing was a single rough garment woven from hairs. Once in wintertime, when the blessed George was bitterly frozen with the cold, his teeth were chattering uncontrollably, and he was suffering and feeling pain in his heart and abdomen, he went up the ladder without being seen; and he looked inside through a window[127] and saw his brother [Symeon] chained and sleeping deeply as a very large eagle covered his whole body with its wings and kept him warm.[128] Suffering terribly in his liver from the unbearable cold, <George> lay flat on his face at death's door; and he saw through the window what looked like a man named Prokopios, a healer by profession, with a sharpened sword in his hand;[129] and when <Prokopios> had made an incision and inflicted pain and shown him [George] the bloodied sword, he <suddenly> disappeared. And when the wondrous man [George] checked himself carefully, he found no wound at all, but his very unwholesome blood had

---

[127] Depictions of stylites generally show their columns with an access ladder, such as is frequently described in the Lives of stylite saints, as here. This passage suggests that Symeon's column included a small shelter with a window at the top, as some other columns evidently did. See "Stylite," *ODB* 3:1971, and "Styliten," *LCI* 8:411–13.

[128] The Life of George of Choziba describes a demon in the form of an eagle who spreads its wings over the saint to block the breeze (*v. Georg. Chozib.*, chap. 13).

[129] The identity of Prokopios is ambiguous. We have interpreted it to describe a vision of a healing saint, because Prokopios disappears immediately after curing George. It could, however, describe a real healer. Legends of the early Christian martyr Prokopios were widespread and extensive in Byzantium. At least two versions of the legend were known in 9th-century Byzantium. In one version, Prokopios is identified as a lector and exorcist before his martyrdom; in the second, he was a soldier convert to Christianity. This version was quoted in the second Council of Nicaea in 787, and would explain the sword in Prokopios' hand. Short versions of both legends are included in *synaxaria* (*SynaxCP* 245–46, 805–8). See also *Bibl.sanct.* 10:1159–66; H. Delehaye, *The Legends of the Saints* (New York, 1962), 101–18. We have not been able to find a literary reference to Prokopios as a healer (ἀκέστορα), but a hematite amulet in the British Museum invoking St. Prokopios suggests that he was viewed as a healing saint; cf. C. Bonner, *Studies in Magical Amulets, Chiefly Graeco-Egyptian* (Ann Arbor, Mich., 1950), 223 and cat. no. 334. We thank H. Maguire for bringing this reference to our attention.

drained out all at once through his nostrils, and the blessed man [George] was delivered from his affliction.[130]

Again another time at midday when <Symeon> was seated and holding the holy Scripture in his hands and reading aloud the divine words,[131] a great rumble suddenly occurred on the column. The holy man thought it was an earthquake and looked up; and someone standing exceedingly tall appeared to him reaching up to the roof <of his hut> and holding in his hand an iron staff; and he threatened <Symeon> greatly, saying, "In truth you have wrestled with many, but now you will not escape me." And <Symeon> said in reply, "I am just a lowly human, but I have a strong God able to defeat you and your followers." And when <Symeon> made the sign in Christ and blew on him, he immediately disappeared.[132] And why is it necessary to enumerate in detail the holy man's brave deeds, [p. 222] how many struggles against

---

[130] The passage is somewhat confusing, since the Greek text includes no proper names for guidance. Our thanks to L. Rydén whose interpretation we have followed.

[131] This reference to Symeon's reading of the Bible is the first of several instances in which reading and writing play a significant role in his biography. The description of his education in David's monastery does not include the standard primary education in reading and writing, but the author clearly knew a tradition in which Symeon wrote and read. Reading in antiquity and the early Middle Ages was generally reading aloud; the verb used here (ὑπαναγινώσκοντος) may mean "reading aloud" specifically; cf. Lampe, *Lexicon,* s.v. ὑπαναγιγνώσκω. Western medievalists have conjectured that silent reading was developed in monasteries in the 12th and 13th centuries; cf. C. Radding, *A World Made by Men* (Chapel Hill, N.C., 1983), and B. Stock, *The Implications of Literacy* (Princeton, N.J., 1983). A good discussion of current theories of orality and literacy as they apply to Byzantium can be found in M. Mullett, "Writing in Early Medieval Byzantium," in *The Uses of Literacy in Early Medieval Europe,* ed. R. McKitterick (Cambridge, 1990), 156–85, esp. 156–72. See also *Byzantine Books and Bookmen* (Washington, D.C., 1975), and E. Patlagean, "Discours écrit, discours parlé. Niveaux de culture à Byzance aux VIIIe–XIe siècles," *Annales. Economies, Sociétés, Civilisations* 34 (1979), 264–78.

[132] Biographies of stylites generally included accounts of struggles between saints and demons on top of the saints' pillars. The form taken by this demon, who appears as a "huge man," is similar to descriptions in the Lives of Abraamios of Krateia and Daniel the Stylite. Symeon's exorcism of the demon by blowing on him is also found in other hagiographical accounts. Further discussion of the forms of demons and their exorcism with extensive hagiographical references can be found in Joannou, *Démonologie,* 10–40.

demons he displayed and how many revelations from God he received, and how many healings and miracles God granted through him for his fellow countrymen and fellow Christians? For he himself stood between heaven and earth just as if <he were> a new vision, separate from that which is below and mingling with that which is above.[133]

As for this man's brother, the one who preceded him in order of birth, but followed him in the spiritual rank and order, his most legitimate brother George, the most fertile cultivated *field*[134] of Christ, he did not at all fall behind, nor was he found wanting in regard to the divine struggles and toils of his mentor. Not at all, but it was possible to see this wondrous pair, sung among all as worthy of love, as that great Moses and Joshua son of Nun, or (to speak more truly) as Elijah the Tishbite and Elisha.[135] For just as the latter destroyed the pride of many tyrants and kings that *exalteth itself against the knowledge of God*[136] and cast down the boldness of many demons, so also did these <heroes of ours>, as the coming account will make clear a little later to those clearly[137] desiring to have understanding in the Lord. For that wondrous and truly merciful[138] soul, George, would get up at night and go to the mountain to chop wood and carry it back on his shoulders and secretly place it at the doors of those who were infirm; for he had a very big body and very powerful physical strength, just like that man <considered> great and renowned among the monks, the most holy Sabas, whose life <George> strove after and emulated precisely.[139] For the blessed one said to himself,

---

[133] This sentence summarizes the concept behind stylite asceticism. The stylite was thought to be literally an intermediary between heaven and earth, removed from earth yet able to be reached by his followers. His literal closeness to heaven is seen as angelic. See the recent descriptions of the symbolism of the pillar by R. Doran, *The Lives of Simeon Stylites* (Kalamazoo, Mich., 1992), 29–36.

[134] 1 Cor. 3:9 (KJV translates "husbandry"). There is a pun on George (Γεώργιος) and field (γεώργιον).

[135] A reference to Elisha's role as servant, disciple, and eventual successor to Elijah (4 Ki. 2:1–18) and Moses' designation of Joshua as his successor (Deut. 31:1–8). See also n. 117, above.

[136] 2 Cor. 10:5.

[137] Reading ἀριδήλως for ἀριδήλοις with Phountoules.

[138] Reading ἐλεήμων for ἐλεείνων with Phountoules.

[139] The portrait of George in this chapter is modeled on another hagiographical classic, the 6th-century Life of Sabas by Cyril of Scythopolis (*v. Sab.*, chap. 8). Sabas, like

"George, you are a pack animal; bring the necessities and the basics *to the least of the brethren*[140] of your Lord, just as the holy psalmist teaches when he says, '*I became brutish before thee. Yet I am continually with thee.*'"[141] And he persevered in such work[142] for thirty-three years.

One night while doing the same task and singing the Psalms of David with his mouth (for this was the custom of the blessed man in accordance with the words of the prophet, "*I will bless the Lord at all times. His praise shall be continually in my mouth*"),[143] a troop of demons coming up on him from behind began to stone the holy man, shouting and uttering unnatural cries of some sort. And when the holy man reached the approach to the so-called Great Bridge,[144] the shouting and the phantoms themselves[145] increased in intensity even more so that he heard an articulate voice saying, "Come out, Himeres,[146] come out."[147] [p. 223] And this was, as it seemed, a most wicked demon who had been appointed to lie in wait at the bridge and to frighten many passersby both day and night and to drown them. When the holy man with his load was in the middle of these <demons>, one <of them> grabbed him forcefully and tried to throw him into the stream. The holy man, stricken

---

George, was "of good height and physical vigor," and as a young monk carried wood and water daily. He was a muleteer, and his regimen involved singing psalms. Cyril's compositions were among the most influential hagiographical models for later writers.

[140] Cf. Mt. 25:40.

[141] Ps. 72 (73):22–23.

[142] Reading διακονίᾳ for διανοίᾳ with Phountoules.

[143] Ps. 33 (34):1.

[144] The *kastron* of Mytilene, today connected to the city by a causeway, was once separated from it by a canal. Malamut (*Les îles,* 1:275) believes the "Great Bridge" connected the mainland of Lesbos to the island on which the *kastron* was located.

[145] Reading αὐτῶν for αὐτοῖς. Alternatively, αὐτοῖς could be retained as a dative of agent and the phrase translated, "the shouting and visual phenomena were increased by them."

[146] Reading Ἱμερῆ for Ἱμερή.

[147] Demons are commonly represented as shouting to saints to taunt them or resist exorcism, but we have been unable to find another reference to the name "Himeres" or, as the text reads, "Himere." Demons are frequently associated with rivers (Joannou, *Démonologie,* 12, 18) and their attacks often take the shape of stone throwing (ibid., 17). The Norse troll who lurks under bridges does not seem to have a common Byzantine equivalent.

with dismay, threw off his load and began to fight more forcefully with the phantom. And the struggle was a violent one that continued until dawn; <but> when the wicked spirit realized that it was powerless against the servant of God, it struck the jaw of its opponent [George] with its fist; but filled with divine aid and strength by the One [Christ] Who was slapped in the face at the time of His suffering for our salvation,[148] <George> threw the accursed <demon> to the left side <of the bridge> and drowned it in the depths <of the river>. So from that time until now by the grace of God there is safe passage <across the bridge> for all.

12. The blessed man [George] again picked up his load and placed it <at the door of the person> whom he had intended <to help>; he <then> made his way to his sister Hilaria.[149] For she was a holy virgin also who lived for the sake of the Lord as a recluse[150] in a very small cell at the shrine of the theologian and evangelist John;[151] she had been born a twin to this man [George], was tonsured by the divine Symeon and was served by the blessed George. When she saw that her brother's nose had been knocked out of line by the demon's blow, she was very upset. As soon as she learned the reason <for it>, she quickly sent him to the great Symeon. And when he [Symeon] saw him, he jokingly said, "Where have you just been, gladiator?[152] What happened to your face? Come near me." He then made the sign of the cross over him and restored him to health. This <miracle> was a sign that our divine father George remained in obedience while exercising the virtue of mercy. For al-

---

[148] Mt. 26:67, 27:30; Mk. 14:65, 15:19; Jn. 18:22.

[149] This episode is the only reference to Hilaria, or to a twin sister of George, in the text. Hilaria may be one of the "pair offered to God" by the parents of David, Symeon, and George, referred to in Chap. 2, or further evidence that a separate tradition about George has been incorporated into the text.

[150] ἐγκεκλεισμένη. The term "enkleistos" was used for monks or nuns who enclosed themselves in cells for seclusion. The practice existed as early as the 4th century. That women, as well as men, were recluses in the 9th century is evident from two letters of Theodore of Stoudios addressed to "the recluse Euphemia" (Fatouros, *Theod. Stud. Epist., epp.* 387, 413). See also references in the Life of Theodore of Edessa (*v. Theod. Edess.* 61.1–3; 62.24–25; 91.7–8) and *ODB* 1:699–700, s.v. "Enkleistos."

[151] We are unable to find other references to a Byzantine shrine of John the Theologian near Mytilene. The relative proximity of Lesbos to the major Byzantine shrine to John, at Ephesos, makes it likely that his cult would be popular on the island.

[152] μονομάχος.

though he performed[153] such <charitable acts> at night, he [George] was never absent from nocturnal services with the monks and abbot by night, coming into the Lord's <house> first of all and leaving last of all. He was extraordinary in his endurance of vigils and all-night stations. On one occasion on the Holy Saturday when he was offering the bloodless sacrifice [the Eucharist] to the Lord and, having finished, was taking off the holy vestments, he accidentally hit the lamp[154] with his hand and spilled it [the lamp oil] over his head; and the wondrous Symeon, on seeing this,[155] commanded him not to move at all from the spot where he was standing. And indeed this most meek man [George] did this [Symeon's bidding], rejoicing in the Lord and exalting Him from his soul. For he spread out [p. 224] his hands to heaven, fixed his two feet together, and chanting the psalter verse by verse he completed that whole divine night and Easter Day without eating and *stood upon his watch like the most wondrous Habakkuk.*[156] Self-control[157] became such a sought-after possession for him that for thirty-three whole years he did not taste bread or anything cooked with fire, only fruit, legumes steeped in water, and raw vegetables, and he drank <only> a little bit of water. And for three other years he did not even taste any water, but when he was oppressed by the heat and unquenchable thirst, especially in summertime, he would go into the sea up to his knees and find a little relief.

13. Once when there was a famine on the island, the great George was assigned to load grain on a donkey and go to the mill; and he did this very quickly, leaving not more than a cup of grain lying in the <monastery> granary. But two poor men met him as he was returning and fell down <at his feet>, begging him for a little flour; and he gave them not the amount they

---

[153] Reading περαίνων for παραίνων with Phountoules.

[154] φωταγωγός: cf. Demetrakos, *Lexikon,* s.v. 3.

[155] Reading ὃ Συμεὼν for ὁ Συμεὼν with Phountoules.

[156] Hab. 2:1. Liturgical vigils, requiring the monk to avoid sleep, were a regular part of monastic ritual. All-night vigils were held on the eve of major feastdays. Liturgical typika of the 10th and later centuries describe the psalms and hymns included in the ἀγρυπνία on Easter eve. The ability to remain standing, unmoving, in all-night vigil was seen in hagiography as one of the marks of sanctity; see "Vigil," *ODB* 3:2166.

[157] ἐγκράτεια. The discipline of self-control in eating and a regime of years of extreme diet was a mark of ascetic discipline. Compare, for example, the description of Peter of Atroa's diet: for eighteen years, he exerted self-control by eating no bread, wine, cheese, or oil, and living on only vegetables and greens (*v. Petr. Atr.* 147.32–34).

asked him for, but an amount they did not <even> hope for, putting a bag of three *modioi*[158] on the back of each one. Since they were too weak to carry it and were staggering[159] this way and that because of their terrible hunger, and were continually stumbling to the ground <under the weight of it>, the loving disciple of the compassionate Lord took pity on them and <also> gave them the donkey. And carrying his staff on his shoulders, as he was accustomed, and singing the psalms with his tongue he journeyed on to his ascetic arena [i.e., the monastery]; upon arrival <at the monastery>, he fell down before the superior[160] begging for forgiveness and lying prostrate <on the ground>. And bidding him stand up, he [the superior] inquired, "You didn't lose the donkey, did you?" And he said, "Not at all, father, but I gave it to those in need." And he [the superior] called him a lover of display[161] and a *man-pleaser,*[162] censured him and let him go. But it would be too much for me to write what sort of abuses and gibes his fellow brethren hurled at him, because they were deprived of the necessary <provisions>. But he [George] remained silent and endured everything stoically; and withdrawing a little to the south stairs, he fell to his knees and implored God to arrange an expedient <outcome>. Before three hours had gone by, lo and behold, a complete stranger came up to him as he was praying, bringing along two donkeys. One was loaded down with <twice> baked bread and other bread that was soft [i.e., fresh] and still warm, the second with wine and legumes and cheeses; and [p. 225] taking hold of his [George's] hand and leading him to the church of the Savior[163] opposite <Symeon's> column, where the animals also were standing, he [the unknown benefactor] departed from him not even saying his name. And the great man [George] fell to the ground and did obeisance to the Lord Who provides all things and expressed his great gratitude; he <then> began

---

[158] The *modios* was a Byzantine measure of grain, varying according to usage, with an equivalency of somewhere between 13 and 17 liters; cf. *ODB* 2:1388.

[159] Reading μετοκλαζόντων for μετοχλαζόντων with Phountoules.

[160] The superior, evidently not Symeon, who appears as the spiritual director for George in these chapters, is not mentioned elsewhere.

[161] Reading φιλενδείκτην for φιλεκδείκτην with Phountoules.

[162] Eph. 6:6; Col. 3:22.

[163] The church of the Savior is unknown outside this text; this is a further sign of the author's local knowledge.

to carry on his back and distribute to his fellow <monks> the generous and *good gifts*[164] of the Lord; and speaking cheerfully to them <he said>, "Look, you were extremely upset over one donkey, <but now> you have two instead. When you want to, load them up." The great Symeon, seeing God's swift repayment, sent up hymns of thanksgiving with gladness, while the brethren repented of the reproaches they had spoken earlier and groveled at the feet of the holy man weeping and begging forgiveness.

And lo and behold, five days later a ship that had set out from Smyrna[165] docked at the column; and the sailors tied the hawser to the column and disembarked from the ship in order to pray in the church and receive the prayers of the holy fathers; and they [the sailors] also gave them a letter[166] from one of the Christ-loving inhabitants of the city of the Smyrnans that detailed a gift for the sake of a blessing and absolution from his sins: five hundred *modioi* of grain and one hundred of legumes and one hundred gold coins.[167] The blessed men gave thanks to the Lord and repaid those who brought <the provisions> with prayers and kindly hospitality; and after receiving the blessed gifts, they

---

[164] James 1:17.

[165] Smyrna, modern Izmir, became the major port on the western coast of Asia Minor and one of the most important provincial cities in the Byzantine Empire by the 10th century, when it was a center of the Thrakesion theme and also the capital of the theme of Samos. It became a metropolitan see by the 10th century. The city was closely connected by sea to the nearby islands of Lesbos and Chios, and this story of donations arriving by boat is an indication of the role of Mytilene in the economy of the "region" of Smyrna. Although its focus is on a later period, H. Ahrweiler's study, "L'histoire et la géographie de la région de Smyrne entre les deux occupations turques (1081–1317)," *TM* 1 (1965), 1–204, contains a great deal of useful background information on Smyrna in earlier periods.

[166] ἀποστολή, literally "payment" (Liddell-Scott, *Lexicon,* s.v. 4), is evidently used here in the sense of a written document of goods presented by the Smyrnans. It could be a manifest of the cargo in the ship (cf. F. Preisigke, *Wörterbuch der griechischen Papyrusurkunden aus Ägypten* 1 [Berlin, 1925; repr. Wiesbaden, n.d.], col. 195), a list of the goods to be donated (these latter two meanings not documented), or a written request for the saints' prayers.

[167] A gift of 500 *modioi* of grain and one hundred of legumes would have been a substantial donation. The *nomisma,* the gold coin of the Byzantine currency system, minted at 72 to the pound of gold, has been estimated by W. Treadgold (*Byz. Revival,* 36) as worth "eighteen days' wages for a laborer" in this period.

dismissed them in peace.[168] They [the holy men] distributed more than half of the grain and legumes to the poor, and deliberated among themselves about the gold coins, <deciding> to buy a field as a means of support and a retreat for the *unashamed workmen*[169] of the Lord's vineyard. But they did not decide to do this on the spur of the moment or in a random fashion before they received *full assurance*[170] from God. In fact, when the two <monks> had completed an all-night prayerful vigil about such a purpose, after the close of prayer the two luminaries and famous fathers saw in a dream a man wearing the monastic and angelic habit say to them, "Bring into fruition immediately the God-pleasing plan that you have decided on. *Blessed are ye of the Lord Who made the heaven and the earth;*[171] may He make you *honored in all the earth*[172] because of the purity of your hearts.*[173] For I am Antony <the Great>, the servant of Christ." And with these words he departed. Upon awakening they revealed to each other what they had seen; and believing that the vision was divine, they [the monks] bought a field called Komekos [or: Komekon] about three miles from the city.[174]

14. <So> these holy and blessed men were living in this manner [p. 226] and practicing asceticism in accordance with God on that small and insignificant rocky shore.[175] <Once during this time> when the people were offering their evening prayers to the Lord in the church of the holy and famous martyr Theodora (the one located on the bank of the lower harbor),[176] as they were

---

[168] Cf. the words of the liturgical dismissal, ἀπολύεσθε ἐν εἰρήνῃ; see Lampe, *Lexicon*, s.v. εἰρήνη, k.1.

[169] 2 Tim. 2:15.

[170] 1 Th. 1:5.

[171] Ps. 113 (115):15 = Ps. 113 (114):23.

[172] Zeph. 3:19.

[173] Cf. Mt. 5:8.

[174] According to Phountoules (Οἱ ὅσιοι αὐτάδελφοι, n. 71) the location may be the village now called Koumko, which is about this distance above the city.

[175] Reading βράχῳ for βράχει.

[176] The "lower harbor" still exists in Mytilene, and a probable location for the church could be identified. There is no obvious candidate for the "famous" martyr Theodora: *synaxaria* include the commemoration of a Theodora who was martyred in Alexandria with Didymus, and of St. Theodoras who were not martyrs. Two episcopal seals of Mytilenian bishops of the 11th and 12th centuries contain on the obverse an invocation to "Ἡ ὁσία Θεοδώρα," with an image of a female

saying the final "Lord, have mercy" and were all together lifting up their hands and eyes to heaven, the cross attached to the ciborium over the holy altar[177] was sucked up with a great whistling <noise> and reached <the conch of> the apse; and then having turned upside down, it was piteously transplanted to a hole in the floor, and remained unmoved of its own accord[178] in such a position. When this unbearable and most fearful sight was witnessed by the very faithful people, the church was filled with many tears. For many hours they shouted "Lord, have mercy" with loud cries and were unwilling to leave the church (for they suspected that complete destruction from the wrath of God would immediately strike the island); but finally the assembly broke up. <Then> wailing and mourning, they all swiftly arrived at the column and told the fathers in detail the portentous vision that they had seen.[179] And the all-blessed Symeon interpreted it, as if he had received assurance from on high, and said to them in the midst of his tears, "Brothers and fathers, it is not as you assumed, that the country will experience complete extermination, but in these days a God-hating and God-opposing emperor will arise, who will destroy the adornment of the house of the Lord, I mean the venerable and holy icons, and will throw them to the ground. *Go in peace*[180] and *the will of the Lord be done.*"[181] A few days later a pig whose ears had been

---

saint holding a cross in her right hand (Laurent, *Corpus,* 5.1, nos. 754, 755). These seals and the account of George's investiture as bishop in the church (below, Chap. 32 and n. 443) make it clear that this was the episcopal church of Mytilene. Phountoules (Οἱ ὅσιοι αὐτάδελφοι, n. 72) identifies Theodora of Alexandria as the dedicatee of the church, but notes that there is now a church of "the holy Theodores" in the city. Laurent, quoting correspondence from Phountoules, notes a reference to the church of St. Theodora in an unpublished document of the 11th or 12th century, but also his statement that the cult of Theodora had disappeared by 1700; cf. Laurent, *Corpus,* 5.1, no. 755.

[177] The ciborium was a domed structure resting on four or six pillars that stood above the altar of a church or the tomb of a saint. Ciboria were frequently topped by a cross. Cf. "Ciborium," *ODB* 1:462.

[178] παρ᾽ ἑαυτοῦ.

[179] An accident to a cross was a clear portent of disaster to be read by a saint. A similar passage in the Life of Theodore of Sykeon described his interpretation of processional crosses shaking wildly; Theodore predicted that "great tribulations and disasters will menace the world" (*v. Theod. Syc.,* chap. 127).

[180] Mk. 5:34; James 2:16.

[181] Acts 21:14.

cropped[182] and tail docked on account of certain damages and disruptions <it had caused>, and was notorious and known throughout the city, somehow found open the doors of the above-mentioned holy church of God, came inside the holy sanctuary, climbed the stairs, and sat upon the priestly throne. And though the church's attendants saw this polluting <animal> and tried to scare it away, the unclean <beast> never moved from the throne until they expelled it bloodied and dead from the divine precinct as an abomination.[183] And with one accord the crowd rushed back again to God-bearing Symeon, reporting the unholy event. As though moved by God, he immediately said, "Have faith, my children; this[184] pig [p. 227] represents the bishop about to take up residence in our land by the permission of God, and prefigures the <fate> that will befall him." And it did so happen.

15. When the beast-named man [Leo V] tyrannically appropriated the scepter, in a similar fashion within a few days a beast-named and beastly mannered bishop [Leo] assumed the diocese of Lesbos.[185] Since all in the island

---

[182] An anonymous scholar (*AnalBoll* 18 [1899], 368) and Phountoules (Οἱ ὅσιοι αὐτά-δελφοι, n. 76a) have identified another, more extended version of this story in manuscripts of the 11th and 12th centuries: "Concerning the sow who sat on the *synthronon* of the metropolis of Mytilene, in the church of the holy Theodora," from E. von Dobschütz, *Christusbilder* (Leipzig, 1899), 225**–26**. As pointed out by A. Alexakis, the mutilation of the pig in the *Acta* is clarified by a passage from this tale: ὗς . . . , ἥτις καὶ τὰς τῶν πλησίων ἄρουρας καὶ τὰ λήια συνεχῶς παραφθείρουσα καὶ τὴν ὑπὲρ τῶν ἠδικημένων ποίνην ὑποστᾶσα ὠτότμητός τις ἐπεφύκει καὶ κωλοβόκερκος . . . ("A pig. . . , who was constantly damaging the tilled fields and crops of the neighbors and was subjected to punishment for the satisfaction of its victims, had its ears cropped and tail docked"). In the 1950s and 60s this custom was still alive in some rural areas of Greece.

Similar episodes, Phountoules notes, can be found in the same collection: "About the dog who sat on the *synthronon* of the monastery of Sts. Sergios and Bacchos" (223**–25**), and in Nikephoros Gregoras (Greg. 1:385) where the story of an intrusive pig takes place in Hagia Sophia.

[183] Symbolic of the uncleanliness associated with pigs, demons appear in the form of swine in several hagiographic texts (Joannou, *Démonologie,* 12). Animal irruptions into churches were regarded as pollution and portents in other hagiographic sources, as in the *vita Ignatii* (PG 105:548D–549A) where a water buffalo entered Hagia Sophia, or when Irene of Chrysobalanton had to purify her convent chapel from the pollution caused by a mouse found on the altar (*v. Iren. Chrysobalant.,* chap. 17).

[184] Reading αὕτη for αὐτὴ, with Phountoules.

[185] The epithets "beast-named" (θηριώνυμος) and "beastly mannered" (θηριότρο-πος), puns on the name "Leo" (meaning "lion"), were frequently used in iconophile

were orthodox and nourished on the divine milk of the divinely inspired scriptures[186] and watered and increased[187] by the holy teachings of the holy men, <that is> of George, the most blessed bishop (whom that most unlawful man [the emperor Leo] also condemned to exile in the <Thracian> Chersonese until his death)[188] and of our all-righteous and holy fathers Symeon and George, they [the inhabitants of Lesbos] intensely loathed this arch-heretic [the new bishop]; everyone rejected him and considered him a counterfeit, and ran to the holy fathers to receive the holy and awful mysteries [i.e., the Eucharist] from their sanctified hands.

As the heresy against the holy icons ruined nearly the entire world,[189]

---

texts to refer to both Leo III and Leo V. Here they are also applied to the newly appointed bishop of the same name.

[186] Cf. 1 Pet. 2:2.

[187] Cf. 1 Cor: 3:6.

[188] See Chap. 10, n. 119. There is doubt about the author's identification of bishop George's place of exile. St. George, bishop of Mytilene and confessor under Leo V, whose Life and *synaxaria* are known from 10th-century manuscripts, was exiled, according to these sources, in "the islands in a circle" (ἐν ταῖς κύκλῳ νήσοις); cf. *v. Georg. Myt.* 40.9. Phountoules believes that the "islands in a circle" were not the Cyclades as one might expect, but should be located in the Propontis, near Constantinople, because this was the most common place of exile, and that the reference to Cherson as a place of exile in this passage is borrowed from other texts (Phountoules, Οἱ ἅγιοι Γεώργιοι, 22–23). The term *Cherson* was associated with two localities in Byzantine times: the Thracian Chersonese and the Tauric Chersonese (and city of Cherson) in the Crimea. Although most iconophiles were exiled to the islands adjacent to Constantinople, Lives of iconophile saints do include references to both Chersoneses as places of exile: John the Psichaite (ed. P. van den Ven, *Le Muséon* 21 [1902], 118.16–17) to the Crimean Cherson, and Nicholas of Stoudios (*vita Nicolai Studitae*, PG 105:912B) to the Thracian Chersonese. No other sources include a George of Mytilene among the exiled. In the reign of Leo V, the Crimea was under the control of the Khazars, and was not returned to Byzantine suzerainty until the reign of Theophilos. In classical and early Byzantine texts the Tauric Chersonese was a common place of exile, and a legend of iconophile exile here may have grown from this fact; cf. "Chersonesos," *PW* 3:2242–70; "Chersonnèse," *DHGE* 12:636–38.

[189] Leo V began his attempt to return the empire to iconoclasm in 814 and convened a council in 815 that proclaimed image worship a heresy once again. The extent of his success outside Constantinople was mixed, but hagiographical texts and the letters of Theodore of Stoudios reveal the conviction of the Stoudite abbot that persecution was widespread and that numerous bishops had converted to iconoclasm or held communion with iconoclasts. See P. Alexander (*Nicephorus*, 140–47), who revises earlier scholarly assessments that 9th-century persecution of iconophiles was limited to Constantinople.

then this very mighty Symeon, on the one hand longing for martyrdom, and on the other stirred up with love for God, *putting* his column not in hiding nor *under a bushel* but as though *on a candlestick,*[190] shed the light of orthodoxy over all. Therefore <Leo> the bishop of Lesbos, like a beast, stirred up into madness against him [Symeon] Leo [the emperor], who had at that time seized the reins of the empire as a tyrant,[191] and Theodotos who in a similar manner had assumed the patriarchate like a bandit.[192] And the guardians of unholiness first decided to try to weaken the holy man with deceptive words through writings, as was appropriate <for liars>. When this, though done repeatedly, resulted in a complete failure, his [Leo's] anger, suffusing his heart, overflowed against the blessed one [Symeon]. And in fact a servant was sent from the emperor <with orders> either to drag him away wherever he wished or to mercilessly burn up the holy man on his column, imitating Nebuchadnezzar of old, from whom he traced his line of descent,[193] or rather overshadowing him in the magnitude of his offenses. For the former [Nebuchadnezzar] became filled with divine knowledge through the providential care of the *messenger of great counsel*[194] for the children [the three Hebrews in the fiery furnace],[195] while he [Emperor Leo], after His [Christ's] descent <to man> and sojourn among mankind and [p. 228] His teaching of piety, was insolent to-

---

[190] Mt. 5:15; Mk. 4:21; Lk. 11:33.

[191] Leo V the Armenian became emperor in 813 upon the abdication of Michael I Rangabe, who had fled the battlefield following the disastrous defeat of the Byzantine forces by the Bulgars at Versinikia. Leo, *strategos* of the Anatolikon theme and commander of a major part of the engaged troops, was suspected of treachery, but the sources indicate that Michael's decision to abdicate was voluntary, and that Leo's accession to the throne had wide support. Although similar language is found in most iconophile saints' Lives, the *Acta*'s description of Leo's "tyrannical seizure" of the throne does not reflect the fact that his predecessor, Michael I, came to the position in similar circumstances, and that Leo's own murder by Michael II's forces in 820 was a far more violent seizure of power. For details, see Alexander, *Nicephorus*, 75–80; Treadgold, *Byz. Revival*, 183–89.

[192] On Theodotos Kassiteras, appointed patriarch by Leo V in 815 following the forced abdication of the patriarch Nikephoros and the emperor's initial steps to restore iconoclasm, see Life of Nikephoros, above, n. 410.

[193] A reference to the tradition, included in several chronicles (Genes. 21.39–41; *TheophCont* 6.4–8; ps.-Sym. Mag. 603.3–9), that Leo's mother was of Assyrian descent.

[194] Is. 9:6.

[195] Dan. 3.

ward His holy image. And what is more, the tyrant who had been dispatched [i.e., Leo's emissary], in exceeding the <effrontery> of Ahab, spoke to the true imitator of Elijah and very eager zealot for holiness [Symeon] and said, *"Art thou he that perverts the house of Israel?"*[196] But he [Symeon] replied, "Not I, but your accursed emperor." And he [the emissary], recognizing the man's steadfastness and intransigence and boiling over with anger, ordered the inhabitants of Mytilene to gather wood from the mountain and to burn him at the stake in accordance with the emperor's order. And Christ's true disciple and imitator, obedient to his own teacher and with a desire for martyrdom wishing *to depart to his longed-for Christ and to be with Him,*[197] was not at all distressed at the orders, not one bit, nor did he try to forestall them, but ordered his own disciples to provide generous meals to the servants <acting> unwillingly as woodcutters. When the wood and a quantity of dry sticks had been collected, the emperor's emissary ordered his servants to set fire to the wood. And when this was done quickly and the flame rose on high, while everyone was gushing forth tears and exceeding the echo of thunder with wailing and beating their breasts, <the emissary> ordered the blessed one to come down from the column. And <Symeon> said with a gentle voice, "Child, I am not master of the flesh that I have had for a long time by the grace of God. *I will not disobey nor dispute*[198] those who wish to lead me down or do any other thing to me." But as they led him down from the column against his will and he [Symeon] began to sing the Amomos,[199] they were

[196] 3 Ki. 18:17.

[197] Cf. Phil. 1:23.

[198] Is. 50:5.

[199] A reference to Ps. 118 (119), which begins Μακάριοι οἱ ἄμωμοι. The psalm's opening words, "Blessed are the blameless," and its theme of innocent suffering, humility, and the love of the law and God's commandments are appropriate for the situation. Thus, Symeon may sing the Amomos to signify that his obedience to authority, despite his innocence, represents acceptance of God's will. The longest psalm, it had a special role in Byzantine liturgy. The Amomos was part of the morning office (*Orthros*) of the chanted cathedral service for Sundays (the *Asmatikos Orthros*). Later it became incorporated into the funeral liturgies for both laymen and monks, and was sung on other special occasions, such as the tonsuring of a monk. Since Symeon is portrayed here as expecting his own death and predicting that of the imperial representative, the singing of the Amomos as a funeral dirge would be symbolically appropriate. No early manuscripts of funeral rites survive, so it is difficult to tell whether this passage could refer to 9th-century practice; musical manuscripts of the Amomos do not date before

astounded at the <iron> collars with which he had shackled himself[200] and exchanged their insane madness for wonder. And not just <they>, but also their leader became frightened and was seized with chills and a violent[201] fever and was paralyzed throughout his entire body. And one could see a strange and marvelous sight; for in one moment of time, the wolf became a sheep, and like Paul he was tamed;[202] and he who a moment before had been violent and very bold and gripped by arrogance was calling upon the pitiful and humble man, the one living with the angels, and was begging that his life be spared, groveling at the knees of the holy man in a pitiful fashion. And he [Symeon] said, "Do not fear, child. For should you obey me and repudiate the heresy and become a devotee of the holy icons, not only will you not die in another land, but, after living in your homeland and departing from here in peace, you will even *be considered worthy of the kingdom* of heaven."[203] And when he [the emissary] promised with a sincere heart to do these things, the holy man said to him, "*Let this be for you* [p. 229] *a sign.*[204] You will not depart from <this> life until you receive my servant with a letter."

16. Not much later it was announced that the tyrant [Leo] had come to his end and been deprived of his reign and life with a pitiful and violent death. For once when God-loving men were sitting with the holy man at the column and conversing, they spoke <as follows> about this impious man: "Have you seen, father, what a lawless emperor God has made to live long because of our sins?[205] He subjects the orthodox to continuous banishments, he has deposed the most holy patriarch Nikephoros,[206] and after flogging the most blessed Euthymios, bishop of Sardis, he exiled him to the island of Thasos;[207] he has

---

the 14th and 15th centuries. See D. Touliatos-Banker, *The Byzantine Amomos Chant of the Fourteenth and Fifteenth Centuries* (Thessalonike, 1984), 22–26, 50–55, 100–117.

[200] Cf. Chap. 10, above.

[201] Reading λάβρῳ for λαύρῳ.

[202] Acts 9.

[203] Cf. 2 Th. 1:5.

[204] Lk. 2:12.

[205] Or "how God has granted long life to such a lawless emperor?"

[206] On Nikephoros, patriarch of Constantinople from 806 to 815, see Life no. 5 in this volume.

[207] Euthymios (754–831), metropolitan of Sardis, was a leader in the restoration of icons in 787 who lived on to become one of the most prominent opponents of the iconoclast policy of Leo V and of his successor Theophilos. The Life of Euthymios

condemned the great Theophanes to live in Samothrace,[208] and has relocated our shepherd and most holy bishop [George] to the Chersonese,[209] promoting in his place a most wicked beast both in name and manner of living and, to say it succinctly, has skewered many and countless holy and orthodox people with afflictions and various tortures. So what do you say, holy one, what? Encourage us your children." And opening his mouth our divine father Symeon said nothing scriptural[210] but a country saying known by all: "Endure patiently, brothers, for the squeals of swine <come> around the Kalends."[211] Which in fact happened; for during Christmastide in the church of Stephen the first martyr, the one within the palace, in the place named Daphne, during

---

written by the 9th-century patriarch Methodios describes Leo's attempt to gain the support of Euthymios and identifies his place of exile as the island of Thasos, near the Strymon (*v. Euthym. Sard.* 35.194–95). Euthymios is also mentioned as a prominent opponent of iconoclasm in two other hagiographical texts, the Lives of Theophylaktos of Nikomedeia (ed. A. Vogt, *AnalBoll* 50 [1932], 78.1) and Niketas of Medikion, chap. 35 (*AASS,* Apr. 1:xxv).

[208] Theophanes (ca. 760–ca. 817) is best known as the author of the chronicle that serves as the major surviving narrative source for the history of the 7th and 8th centuries. He also founded a monastery at Sigriane in the Propontis, opposed Leo's condemnation of icons, and became a confessor for the faith when he died in exile in the northern Aegean island of Samothrace in 817. His biography, like that of Euthymios of Sardis, was written by Patriarch Methodios.

The list of exiles in this passage is interesting in part because it omits the name of Theodore of Stoudios, one of the most famous of Leo's opponents.

[209] See the discussion in Chap. 15, n. 188.

[210] γραφικόν.

[211] φωναί is the correct reading (*pace* D. Michailidis, "Trois notules sur des saints de Lesbos," *AnalBoll* 89 [1971], 147, who emends to φοναί) as a passage in the *vita* of Irene of Chrysobalanton (*v. Iren. Chrysobalant.* 62.25) demonstrates, comparing the screams of demons to the squeals of swine being butchered (χοιρείων ὥσπερεὶ φωνῶν). Michailidis identifies the saying with the common folk practice in Greece, still observed in the 20th century in places including Lesbos, of slaughtering a pig for the Christmas feast on Christmas Eve; see also Koukoules, *Bios* 5:54–55. Swine were raised regularly and pork was an important part of Byzantine diet, although it was considered coarse peasant food; cf. the entries "Livestock," *ODB* 2:1242–43; "Swine," *ODB* 3:1979–80.

The Kalends was a Roman festival celebrating the new year that was denounced by John Chrysostom and other early Christian writers, but continued as a popular festival with carnival tone in Byzantine times. Although it was condemned by the 7th-century Council in Trullo, it was still known in the 12th century; cf. "Calends," *ODB* 1:367–68. The practice of singing carols known as *kalanda* has continued into the modern period (G. Megas, *Greek Calendar Customs* [Athens, 1958], 27–28).

the night he [the emperor Leo V] was cut to pieces limb from limb and departed to gloomy darkness.[212]

The tyrant's lieutenant [the emissary] at that time in Lesbos left the island in poor health, and after reaching the imperial city took to his bed in his home and became seriously ill. When the doctors were predicting his death as a result of their familiarity with <reading> pulses[213] and advised making burial preparations, he himself with firm state of mind considered it [their prognosis] of little importance, saying, "I know whom[214] I have been deemed worthy to meet though I was unwilling and did not desire it. I recognize the end of my time previously predicted to me [p. 230], and how true were his promises." But the godly minded Symeon after his descent from the column, since he was being harassed by the heresiarch bishop of the island, had relocated to a tiny islet lying right at the mouth of a small gulf on which the church of the gloriously triumphant martyr Isidore also stands.[215] And the blessed one, remem-

---

[212] Chronicle accounts of Leo's death (Georg. Mon. 788.12–15; Leo Gramm. 210.13–19; ps.-Sym. Mag. 618.18–619.2, 619.7–10; with later elaborations in Genes. 18.45–19.82; and *TheophCont* 38.14–40.13) describe Michael's conspiracy and the Christmas Day killing, but do not identify the church. St. Stephen's chapel in the Great Palace is named only in this text. Located in the Palace of Daphne, the oldest part of the Great Palace complex, the chapel of St. Stephen was a traditional site for imperial coronations and weddings; cf. Janin, *Eglises CP,* 473–74, and Janin, *CP byz.,* 113, citing Const. Porph., *De Cer.* 1:8.21, 628.5. This detail is probably an accurate addition to our knowledge of the event; cf. Treadgold, *Byz. Revival,* 224 and n. 307.

[213] Pulse lore (sphygmology) was a basic technique of the medical tradition of Galen, and Byzantine medical writers copied and expanded treatises on pulses that were part of the basic medical training of doctors; cf. "Medicine," *ODB* 2:1327–28. The benign reference to doctors in this text is interesting, for a common *topos* in hagiography was the success of saints in curing cases that doctors were unable to treat, while antipathy to medicine is commonly expressed in these texts. Many hagiographical references to doctors in middle Byzantine saints' Lives are collected in A. Kazhdan, "The Image of the Medical Doctor in Byzantine Literature of the Tenth to Twelfth Centuries," *DOP* 38 (1984), 43–51.

[214] Cf. 2 Tim. 1:12.

[215] According to Phountoules (Οἱ ὅσιοι αὐτάδελφοι, n. 97), the small rocky island in the gulf of Gera, called St. Isidore, still contained in 1961 a chapel to the martyr Isidore of Chios and the remains of ancient buildings, a cistern, and two small columns. In 5th-century passion accounts Isidore is described as a sailor from Chios who was martyred by decapitation during the reign of Decius; in the 5th century, some of his relics were taken to Constantinople where they were placed in a chapel near the church of St. Irene. His cult was widely popular in the Mediterranean (*Bibl.sanct.* 7:960–68).

bering his promise to the above-mentioned man [the emissary],[216] wrote a letter, gave it to one of his disciples, and sent him on the double. When the monk
reached the great city [Constantinople], he searched for the man's house and
made known his arrival through the gatekeeper. When <the emissary> heard
<the news>, he rejoiced and called together his friends and relatives; after
giving them a final embrace, he opened the letter of the holy man in front of
them; and when he had read it, he performed obeisance and laid it upon his
chest. Then, as all were watching, he gave up his spirit, taking the letter with
him as a resplendent mantle and a magnificent shroud.[217]

17. After the murder of Leo, as the holy man was contending in the Lord
on the aforementioned little island along with his fellow <monks>, Michael
[II the Amorian] received the scepter of the empire. He bore no resemblance
to the aforementioned [Leo] in cruelty (for no other man[218] was his equal), but
was a man who totally enjoyed the pleasures of the belly and displayed in a
human body a nearly beastlike behavior and lifestyle. Nevertheless he allowed
<people> to worship and do reverence as each one wished, acting and rea-
soning illogically when he said, "I hold fast <to my faith> just as I have
received it,[219] but let everyone <else> do what seems good to him."[220] Since
the emperor was declaring and issuing such decrees, when the above-

---

[216] Cf. Chap. 15.

[217] This passage reflects the importance of the letter as a public document in Byzantium. Letters were literary documents following classical form, intended to be read
aloud to an audience. The public deathbed forms a dramatic setting for the reading of
this letter. Letters were delivered privately by messengers, who were also expected to
deliver an oral message to the recipient. In the 9th century, letters would probably still
have been written on papyrus and delivered in rolls; see "Epistolography," *ODB* 1:718–
20, for further bibliography, and Mullett, "Writing in Early Byzantium," 172–80, for an
argument that in the middle Byzantine period letters were personal as well as rhetorical
documents. The large letter collection of Theodore of Stoudios is evidence for monastic
use of the literary genre. The hagiographer's description of Symeon's education (Chap.
9, above), however, is not congruent with the practice of literary epistolography.

[218] Reading ἀνθρώπων for ἀγῶν, with Phountoules.

[219] Placing καθὼς παρέλαβον within quotation marks.

[220] Michael II the Amorian is described as coarse and uncultured in all chronicle
accounts of his character (George the Monk, Symeon the Logothete, Genesios, Theophanes Continuatus). These sources emphasize his humble background, lack of education, coarse looks and stammer, but describe him as abstemious, with connections to
the ascetic heresy of the Athinganoi (Treadgold, *Byz. Revival,* 226, n. 308). Our author's
description of Michael as a pleasure-loving gourmand, which does not appear in other

mentioned bishop [Leo of Mytilene] saw that all the orthodox were daily flow-ing together like a river to him [Symeon], he could not tolerate the divine revealer Symeon, but was struck with acute pangs of jealousy. Since he was unable to harm the man of God because of the imperial decree that was in force, what did he do? He ran off to Constantinople and, approaching his own bishop [the patriarch Theodotos], feigned a resignation from his own <episco-pal> throne, saying, "In truth, the stylite is bishop in the diocese assigned to me, not I." By saying this and <even> [p. 231] more than this <Leo> per-suaded the unholy patriarch to report these charges against <Symeon> to the emperor. When he [the patriarch] had in fact done this, he received a judgment against the holy man that <allowed him> [the bishop] to exile him on his own authority wherever he wished.[221] So he [the bishop] quickly sailed from the capital and came to his own city; he <then> condemned the holy man to a small, uninhabited island named Lagousai.[222] But the blessed one was joy-

---

accounts, would be more appropriate for Michael III (842–867) than Michael II. Mi-chael's attempt to remain neutral on the question of icons is repeated in all sources. The quotation of Michael's statement on his wish to follow the doctrines he had re-ceived, but to let others maintain their beliefs, probably refers to a public statement in a *silention* (a solemn ceremonial gathering in the presence of the emperor), quoted in different language in Symeon the Logothete (Leo Gramm. 211) and George the Monk (Georg. Mon. 792). J. B. Bury (*Eastern Roman Empire,* 111–14) and W. Treadgold (*Byz. Revival,* 230–31 and notes) discuss the chronology of negotiations and a meeting with Theodore of Stoudios and his followers that appears to be the occasion for this state-ment. Our author, whose sympathies and information seem to lie with the opponents of Theodore, is either suppressing the role of the monks of Stoudios, or following a chronicle source similar to George the Monk and Symeon the Logothete.

[221] No other sources refer to actions of Theodotos Kassiteras after the death of Leo V, and chronicle accounts emphasize Michael's amnesty for exiled iconophiles early in his reign. Theodotos died around January 821, soon after Michael's accession.

[222] The island of Lagousai is identified by Phountoules (Οἱ ὅσιοι αὐτάδελφοι, n. 103) and van den Gheyn (*Acta,* 231 n. 1) as the modern Tavşan Adasi, mentioned in Pliny's *Natural History* and located off the coast of the Alexandrian Troad; cf. also PW 12:465, s.v. Λαγοῦσαι. What follows, however, must cast doubt either on this identification, since the Troad was not part of the Thrakesion theme in the 9th century, or on the author's knowledge of the boundaries between the Thrakesion and Opsikion themes in the 9th century. Mention of Smyrnan donations suggests that the island may have been located off the Asia Minor coast further south. The name is a common one, but none of the alternate sites called Lagousai and known in classical sources seems to be a possible identification.

ous[223] in all things and in noble fashion endured in unyielding exultation. He moved from his homeland to exile in the fifty-fourth year of his life;[224] he took <along> his seven disciples and set out, leaving his own brother, I mean the most blessed George, as the supervisor and leader of the small monastery[225] established by him in Mytilene. So he departed to the island mentioned above and built a column about ten cubits[226] <high> and climbed onto it. Even this <exile> was the arrangement and forethought of the all-powerful and manifold wisdom <of God>, so that the light of orthodoxy might shine also in the theme of the Thrakesians through the tongue and resolute teaching of the blessed man.[227] For before two years had elapsed all those in authority and positions of honor started coming to the great Symeon for a blessing and confession of their personal sins, not only those nearby and reasonably close, but even those who lived far away; as a result certain people from the church of the Smyrnans brought valuable possessions to him for the building of monasteries for souls [people] which came into being with the help of God and still stand today.[228]

---

[223] Reading ἄσμενος for ᾄσμενος.

[224] I.e., in 817/8, according to the author's chronology.

[225] μονυδρίου—not to be found in the lexica of Liddell-Scott, Lampe, Sophocles, or Du Cange. A *TLG* search records this diminutive form of μονή (cf. λογύδριον and variants λογίδιον, λογίδριον) only in the 14th-century authors Nikephoros Gregoras (Greg. 1:80.13, 114.1) and George Pachymeres (Pach. 2:133.14), and twelve times in 14th-century inscriptions from Mistra. It does not appear in other Lives of 9th-century saints. E. Trapp kindly informs us that the files for his *Lexikon* contain only one pre-13th-century use of μονύδριον, in an act of the Athonite monastery of Xenophontos for 1089. The appearance of the word in this text is either a very early attestation, if, indeed, the Life is a 9th-century composition or, alternatively, evidence of later composition or redaction.

[226] πῆχυς, a measure of length, varying between 46.8 and 62.5 cm; cf. *ODB* 3:1614. Symeon's column would have thus been somewhere between 14 and 19 feet high.

[227] This comment implies that Symeon's exile to the island of Lagousai brought him into the Thrakesion theme in western Asia Minor for the first time. Mytilene and Lesbos were under the *droungarios* of the Aegean Sea (mentioned in the mid-9th century in the Taktikon of Uspensky); Oikonomidès, *Listes,* 46–47, 53.18, 57.10. This passage must have been written when Lesbos was part of a separate theme of the Aegean Sea; cf. Chap. 2 and nn. 33 and 440.

[228] μέχρι τοῦ νῦν: an indication of some indeterminate distance between the author's writing and the events, as well as knowledge of the location.

So when the previously mentioned Michael [II] was ruling the imperial government, great and difficult trouble arose from the land for Christians; it already had its beginning when the tyrant Leo lived among men, but developed into great trouble for the Christian people at the time of Michael. This <man> was Thomas,[229] who at the time of the blessed Irene [p. 232] served in the rank of *protostrator*[230] to the general of the <theme of> Anatolikon,[231] <a man> named Tourkos.[232] <Thomas>, who was afraid <of being driven

[229] The revolt of Thomas the Slav, which was one of the central events of the reign of Michael II, receives extensive treatment in all the chronicle accounts of his reign. Other hagiographical sources (the Lives of Theodore of Stoudios by Michael, of Gregory the Dekapolite, and Antony the Younger) also give evidence that the rebellion caused widespread disruption in the empire. P. Lemerle ("Thomas le slave," *TM* 1 [1965], 255–97) has demonstrated that the sources contain two accounts of Thomas' origins and the reasons for his rebellion: one legendary, deriving from propaganda produced by Michael II and preserved in a contemporary letter to the emperor Louis the Pious, and a second, with a more favorable assessment of Thomas, that appears in the 10th-century chronicles of Genesios and Theophanes Continuatus and is based on a lost source. The second tradition appears to be a more probable account. Our author derives his information on Thomas from the propagandistic tradition of Michael II. It is noteworthy that he does not mention the important role Lesbos played in the revolt; in 821, Thomas assembled his fleet in Lesbos for the siege of Constantinople (Genes. 26.89–27.6; *TheophCont* 55.18–21).

[230] The office of *protostrator* involved accompanying the commander when he was on horseback and supervising grooms, stables, and perhaps chariots. In the 9th century, it was held most often at the imperial level, but there are other references to *protostratores* of theme generals. Because of their physical proximity to the emperor or commander, the position was an important one and often served as a starting place for people who went on to higher office. The chronicle of Genesios identified the three future leaders, Leo, Michael, and Thomas, only as "under the orders" of Bardanes; Theophanes Continuatus identifies Leo, Michael, and Thomas as "spear carriers and servants," probably part of his bodyguard, and a much more likely position. The author of the *Acta* has apparently promoted Thomas to an office unlikely for a young soldier and uncommon in the early 9th century.

[231] The Anatolikon theme was one of the original themes of Asia Minor; in the early 9th century it included a large area of south-central Asia Minor, with Amorion as its capital.

[232] Bardanes Tourkos was *strategos* of the Anatolikon theme in the reign of the emperor Nikephoros I; he is probably to be identified with the Bardanes who supported the empress Irene in 797 as *strategos* of the Thrakesion theme. In 803 he was appointed *monostrategos* (sole general) of the five eastern themes and allowed himself to be proclaimed emperor. According to the story in Genesios and Theophanes Continuatus, the future emperors Leo V and Michael II, as well as Thomas the Slav, all got their

out> because of some shameful and inappropriate assaults and deeds he had committed,[233] left behind his fatherland and <religious> faith and lord and defected to the Arabs. During the reign of the emperor Nikephoros[234] he seemed to behave himself for a while and continued to do so during <the reigns of> Staurakios[235] and Michael[236] and through much of <the reign of> the tyrant Leo.[237] But at the death of <Leo> he assembled an army by deception and gifts, promised the Arabs that he would make the Romans subject to them, and appeared at the theme called Armeniakon.[238] When Mi-

---

start under him, but when he was *monostrategos* rather than general of the Anatolikon theme. See "Bardanes Tourkos," *ODB* 1:255; Lemerle, "Thomas le slave," 264; W. Kaegi, Jr., *Byzantine Military Unrest, 471–843* (Amsterdam, 1981), 245–47.

[233] The letter of Michael II claims that Thomas the Slav, while in service to one of the most important patricians in the empire, seduced his wife and fled to the Arabs when his misdeed was discovered (Lemerle, "Thomas le slave," 256). Genesios, in the second of two contradictory accounts of the rebel's origins, claims that Thomas "placed himself under a certain patrician—'the already named Bardanes'—and was accused by him of adultery 'which Nikephoros, the then emperor, had incited him to because of his jealousy of Bardanes, on account of his merits'" (Lemerle, "Thomas le slave," 266). Theophanes Continuatus also preserves two accounts of the story, writing in one that in Constantinople Thomas served an unnamed senator whose wife he attempted to seduce, and, when discovered, fled to the Arabs (Lemerle, "Thomas le slave," 270). Lemerle believes that this and the following details about the background of Thomas are legendary: "Thus we take as legendary . . . : the sojourn of Thomas in Constantinople in service of a patrician whose wife he seduces; his flight for this reason to the Arabs, his stay of twenty-five years with them, his abjuration, his pretense of being Constantine VI, his revolt as early as the reign of Leo V. All this is intended either to blacken his character or to conceal the circumstances of the accession of Michael II" (Lemerle, "Thomas le slave," 284, translation mine).

[234] Nikephoros I, 802–811.

[235] Staurakios, son of emperor Nikephoros I, ruled 28 July–1 October 811.

[236] Michael I Rangabe, 811–813.

[237] Leo V, 813–820. This passage implies that Thomas fled to the Arabs in the reign of Irene and remained there until some later period in Leo's reign. The letter of Michael II claims the same chronology; Genesios and Theophanes Continuatus say that he remained in Arab territory for twenty-five years (Lemerle, "Thomas le slave," 256, 266, 270).

[238] The Armeniakon theme was another of the original themes of Asia Minor, comprising much of eastern Anatolia, with its capital in Amaseia. Like the Anatolikon theme, its troops frequently were involved in rebellions during the iconoclast period. Its location on the eastern border of the empire made the Armeniakon of particular strategic importance during this period.

chael[239] had already ascended the throne, he [Thomas] took bold action and advanced and decided to make an attempt on imperial power; <all the> while he pretended to be both a guardian of orthodox dogmas and a reverer of the holy icons.[240] In fact he even called himself the emperor Constantine[241] the younger, the one who was blinded, the son of the blessed Irene, and spread the rumor that someone else had suffered <the blinding> in his place. So this man [Thomas] was plundering and destroying Christian <territory> like a madman; for friends and brothers were fighting against each other employing swords and spears, bending bows and openly plundering and killing each other.

18. When this disaster befell the entire state of the Christians with God's permission, the people of Africa[242] (they are from the western part of the world) first made a small challenge <to the emperor's authority>. When they saw that the emperor and his troops were fighting[243] in the east and campaigning[244] and that they were almost completely occupied there,[245] <the Arabs> built a few ships and were raiding here and there the islands which were undefended and had no suspicion whatsoever[246] of enemy <attack>; they took captive their inhabitants, men, women, and children, mercilessly plun-

---

[239] Michael II, 820–829.

[240] The *Acta* and one other hagiographical source (the *vita* of Theodore of Stoudios by Michael) claim that Thomas was "thought to be" or "pretended to be" a supporter of icons, but no other source mentions icons as a factor in his rebellion; cf. Lemerle, "Thomas le slave," 262.

[241] Constantine VI, the son of Irene and Leo IV, emperor from 780 to 797. After Leo's death Irene ruled as regent during Constantine's minority, but later in his reign he deposed her and spent most of the rest of his reign in opposition to his mother. Constantine's blinding took place in 797 after a coup instigated by Irene against her son—a fact not mentioned by our hagiographer; cf. Treadgold, *Byz. Revival*, 103–10. Thomas' role as an imposter is also mentioned in the anti-Thomas accounts.

[242] I.e., Arabs from northwest Africa; see nn. 247 and 248 below.

[243] Reading πολεμησάμενον for παλαμησάμενον.

[244] Reading ἐκστρατεύοντα for ἐκστρατεύονται with Phountoules.

[245] This clause might refer to the campaigns Michael fought against the remaining supporters of Thomas in Thrace after the rebel's defeat in 823.

[246] Reading οἱασοῦν for οἵας οὖν.

dering and seizing their property.[247] And as the passage of time seemed to wear down the emperor with the hardships from the insurgent and caused him to forget about the west, [p. 233] right at that moment that small and paltry band of Africans and Mauretanians went forth in countless number, and violently ravaged and destroyed the islands and coastal areas.[248]

When he saw or, to speak more properly, foresaw these <events>, our inspired father Symeon left his column and was compelled by his friends and disciples to sail to Byzantium <to seek safety>. Perhaps he was also prompted by <the words of> the divine Spirit as in the vision of the blessed

---

[247] The date of the Arab raids on Crete and the Cyclades is disputed; at some time between 823 and 830 a group of exiled Spanish Arabs, who had settled in Egypt under the leadership of Abū Hafs, occupied Crete and raided the Cyclades islands. The occupation of Crete by the Arabs lasted until 961, and opened up other Aegean islands to Arab attacks. Several 10th-century chronicles (Genes. 32.81–90; *TheophCont* 73.5–78.3; Leo Gramm. 212; ps.-Sym. Mag. 621.20–624.8) connect Michael's involvement in the civil war with Byzantine inability to resist the invasions, dating the attack to 821–823. Contemporary Arab sources, however, assign dates of 825–826 or 827–828 to the attacks, and some accounts date the invasion even later; cf. Christides, *Conquest of Crete,* 85–86. Christides has argued (pp. 86–88) that the 10th-century Byzantine sources should be followed for an early date for the raids, citing the inability of the Byzantines to mount a defense against the small number of ships used by the Arabs. His arguments remain controversial, and many recent critics retain the traditional chronology; see, for example, Treadgold, *Byz. Revival,* 248–57 and notes; Malamut, *Les îles,* 1:72–77. D. Tsougarakis (*Byzantine Crete. From the 5th Century to the Venetian Conquest* [Athens, 1988], 30–41) argues that the Arab conquest of Crete was a gradual process that cannot be dated precisely. This passage in the *Acta* follows the accounts of Genesios and Theophanes Continuatus fairly closely, and may have been derived from one of them or from their source.

[248] Raids of Africans and Mauretanians (Μαυρούσιοι): Mauretania (*ODB* 2:1318–19) was generally considered the part of North Africa extending from the Numidian border to the Atlantic, and would not have included either Egypt or the Aghlabid territory from which the attack on Sicily was launched; the term refers to the Moorish origins of the exiles who took Crete. Two other hagiographical texts of the period refer to the raids: Gregory the Dekapolite was unable to sail from Ephesos to Constantinople because of Mauretanian raiders who disrupted shipping (*v. Greg. Decap.* 53.20); Athanasia of Aegina's first husband was killed in the attacks of "Mauretanian barbarians" on Aegina (*v. Ath. Aeg.* 181.1–3). Neither of these passages can be dated closely enough to provide evidence for the chronology of the beginnings of the Arab raids on the Aegean; see C. Mango, "On Re-reading the Life of St. Gregory the Decapolite," *Byzantina* 13 (1985), 637, who does not accept the early dating proposed by Christides.

apostle Paul, namely, "*Come over into Macedonia, and help us*";[249] because the all-blessed one said in regard to himself, "*I am not seeking mine own profit, but the profit of many, that they may be saved.*"[250] In fact he even summoned his brother, I mean the great George, from their homeland and entrusted to his hands the souls and property and possessions which he had acquired from God in the Thrakesion theme and made him superior and chief shepherd and put him in charge of everything.

19. The holy man *was rolled away*[251] from his column with violent force like a stone from a mountain into the midst of the encampment of the godless iconoclasts. Strengthened by the divine Spirit he set out to fight alongside the persecuted truth and to light up completely the darkness of ignorance that existed in Byzantium and the misty storm of heresy with the sparks of orthodoxy. Sailing past the great city of Constantine, he landed in a village that was miserable and poor, but was also the abode of that famous Niketas the Great, he who was quite truly the conqueror[252] of demons and superior of Medikion.[253] <Symeon> had for a long time, from divine foreknowledge as I see it, desired <to know him>. He met him *face to face*[254] and lived with him and there distributed to the poor *according as each had need*[255] the <offerings>

---

[249] Acts 16:9.

[250] 1 Cor. 10:33.

[251] Cf. Mt. 28:2.

[252] νικητής, a pun on Νικήτας.

[253] Niketas of Medikion (ca. 760–824), successor to Nikephoros as abbot of his foundation of Medikion in Bithynia, was one of the iconophile monastic leaders of the second iconoclastic period. His biography and letters from Theodore of Stoudios make it clear that Niketas was sent into exile on the island of Glykeria near Constantinople during the reign of Leo V; although offered amnesty by Michael II, he remained in Glykeria for a while, wandered from place to place, then finally bought a *metochion* at an unspecified locale, somewhere to the north of Constantinople, where he settled until his death in 824. The information provided by the *Acta* here is accurate as A. Alexakis has shown ("A Florilegium in the Life of Nicetas of Medicion and a Letter of Theodore of Studios," *DOP* 48 [1994], 197). The author also knows about the exorcisms of demons that are emphasized in the Life of Niketas by his disciple Theosteriktos (*AASS*, Apr. 1:xvii–xxviii [at end of volume]).

[254] 1 Cor. 13:12.

[255] Cf. Acts 4:35.

collected from the faithful. For as he had sailed by light boat along the coast of the Propontis and especially the regions of Sigriane and Kyzikos, in which most of the true servants [i.e., disciples] of the divine man [Niketas] were living under wretched conditions, from the Aegean Sea to the Black Sea[256] [p. 234] he *fulfilled the course*[257] of piety and service, imitating the disciples of Christ with his teachings and Stephen the first martyr[258] in his care of the poor.

But <now> I come to the narration <of a story> that I almost omitted. For while the blessed man [Symeon] had not yet revealed himself to the masses, but was still keeping his virtue under wraps, as was his custom, the One Who manages and guides everything for the best with divine judgment brought into the open and *divulged*[259] his virtue in the following manner. A certain pious woman had been left <a widow> with two daughters along with much wealth and a conspicuous lifestyle. <The daughters> ordered their lives with piety and were equipped by the teachings and admonitions of their mother and had already reached maturity. The older of these in age determined to devote herself to divine studies and also to poetry and grammar and the metrical works of the divine fathers; and she yearned for the monastic life.[260] But her mother, since she saw that the heir of the family shone in beauty

---

[256] The author here describes a route that would appear to lead to Medikion, which was located close to the shore on the southern coast of the Sea of Marmara (Propontis), east of Kyzikos and Theophanes' monastery near Sigriane (between Kyzikos and the Rhyndakos river), rather than to Niketas' place of exile in Glykeria in the gulf of Tuzla (between Nikomedeia and Constantinople, on the north shore of the Propontis). For description of the remains of Medikion and the location of Sigriane, see C. Mango and I. Ševčenko, "Some Churches and Monasteries on the Southern Shore of the Sea of Marmara," *DOP* 27 (1973), 240–42.

The term *Pontos* is translated here as referring to the southern coast of the Black Sea, rather than the provinces known by that name at different times; see also the *vita* of Theophylaktos of Nikomedeia (ed. A. Vogt, *AnalBoll* 50 [1932], 73.10–11: πρὸς τῇ εἰσβολῇ τοῦ Πόντου) for parallel use of the term. Neither location would have taken Symeon into the Black Sea, as the author indicates.

[257] Acts 13:25.

[258] Acts 6–7.

[259] 2 Cor. 2:14. KJV translates "causeth to triumph."

[260] From what follows, it appears that Febronia lived somewhere in Constantinople or its environs. The account suggests that this girl (whom we later learn was called Hypatia and took the monastic name Febronia) was educated by her mother (ταῖς τῆς

and loveliness of body and soul, because of her desire for the continuation of the family line urged and tried to persuade her <to agree> to a lawful marriage. For love and especially worldly <love> are not able to look toward the better things. But the girl was upset and distressed at this <prospect> since she wanted to present to God her beauty of soul and body uncorrupted by human intercourse. <Her mother> continued to make even stronger appeals and arguments, enumerating many <potential> suitors and promising the girl to marry her to whichever one of these she wished. But <the girl>, strengthened by the divine Spirit, shook off the drops of her mother's words as a solid rock does drops of water.

Finally one night when the second watch[261] had passed and the girl was engrossed in her studies, she saw an astonishing apparition, huge in size, fearful in appearance, with gray hair and shining clothes. The girl was shocked at this vision and became mute. And she who previously had possessed an eloquent and articulate tongue was condemned to mute silence. But since the

μητρὸς παιδαγωγίαις . . . καταρτιζόμεναι); she then progressed to learning that included the study of grammar (γραμματικῇ) and poetry (ποιητικῇ), traditionally part of the secondary and advanced curriculum of secular education consisting of grammar, rhetoric, then philosophy and other subjects. The subjects are linked with the study of "metrical works of the holy fathers"—presumably hymnography and liturgical poetry. The education claimed for Febronia is rare in any 9th-century hagiography, and can be best compared with the education of Michael the Synkellos in Jerusalem: "After he was completely educated in the letters of preliminary training, . . . he was sent by the order of the patriarch who had tonsured him for lessons in grammar, rhetoric, and philosophy; . . . not only these subjects did he learn, but what is best of poetry and astronomy as well" (trans. Cunningham, in *v. Mich. Sync.* 47–49). Other parallels are the training Tarasios' disciple received from him in various meters (*v. Taras.* 423.5–8), and the description of the education of the patriarch Nikephoros I (above, 52–56). See also Lemerle, *Byz. Humanism,* 111–17; Moffatt, "Schooling," 89–92. Most saints' Lives of the period claim a more limited education in "holy letters" (τὰ ἱερὰ γράμματα) for their heroes; this is the case in the accounts of two women saints, Athanasia of Aegina and Theodora of Thessalonike (Talbot, *Holy Women,* 142 and 167; Moffatt, "Schooling," 89–90). Theodore of Stoudios' correspondence with aristocratic laywomen is evidence that an educated female laity existed in this period; for an analysis of Theodore's correspondents, see Kazhdan-Talbot, "Women and Iconoclasm," 391–408. As evidence for the content of women's education, however, Febronia's story should be taken with caution.

[261] Following ancient tradition, the night hours were divided into four *vigiliae,* or watches.

vision had revealed to her the doctor for her illness and guide for her soul, the terrified girl awoke her mother. But she uttered no sound to her nor spoke with words, but *broke her heart*[262] with gestures and groans. When night ended and the sun, the charioteer of the day, had appeared to complete his own course from dawn to evening, <the girl> *asked for*[263] *a writing tablet*[264] and revealed the vision to her perplexed mother. This was what <she wrote>: "Symeon, who had his [p. 235] feet and loins bound with collars for the sake of Christ, has just left his column and is residing on the left side of Byzantis <as you go> toward the Euxine [Black] Sea near Pegai."[265] When the mother heard this, she eagerly rose up and took her daughter and attendant servants and maids with her, as was her custom; and she reached the place that had been revealed <to her>. The blessed one was sitting by the sea and working on a fishing net with his hands, while reciting with his mouth the inspired sayings of David [the Psalms].[266] And as he gazed <out to sea>, he saw the pious woman seated in a boat with her daughter and making toward the shore. So <Symeon> called one of his disciples and said, "Look, the child Febronia is coming to us with her mother. So hurry to meet them and bring them back to us." <The disciple> quickly obeyed his order and, with him leading the way, they came to the holy man. When he saw them, he said, "Welcome, my child Febronia!" Upon hearing these <words> her mother was perplexed, for no one of them was called by any such name.[267] So she [the mother] fell at his feet and with many tears offered to the God-bearer in a pitiful manner the words addressed to Christ by the Canaanite woman[268] and by the father of the

---

[262] Acts 21:13.

[263] Reading αἰτήσασα for αἰτήσουσα, with Phountoules.

[264] Lk. 1:63. Wood or ivory tablets, often filled with wax, which were incised with styli, continued to be used in the middle Byzantine period; cf. *ODB* 3:2205–6, s.v. "Writing Tablets."

[265] The suburb of Pegai was probably located on the northern shore of the Golden Horn, in the location of modern Kasimpaşa; cf. Janin, *CP byz.,* 463–64.

[266] "Working on a fishing net and reciting the sayings of David": The passage is certainly biblically inspired (cf. Mt. 4:21), if not a direct quotation. There is no earlier reference to Symeon as a fisherman although ascetics frequently did handwork.

[267] As we learn subsequently, the girl's baptismal name was Hypatia.

[268] Mt. 15:22: "And, behold, a woman of Canaan came out of the same coasts, and cried unto him, saying, 'Have mercy on me, O Lord, thou son of David; my daughter is grievously vexed with a devil.'"

epileptic.[269] But <Symeon> raised her up and made a prayer over the girl and told her to remain with him for seven days. So each day <the girl> received the immaculate mysteries [the Eucharist] from the hands of the holy man and she alone poured water on his hands as he did the <ritual> washing.[270] The seventh day came round and the holy man was about to offer to God the bloodless and spiritual sacrifice. He wanted his hands washed and called to the girl, "Febronia, my child." And she herself immediately answered with a clear and articulate voice, "What do you want me to do, master?" From that time on she was freed from the *string of her tongue,* and she was <able to> *speak plain*[271] and praised God along with her mother and her relatives and all those who heard and saw her. <From then on> that God-loving and most faithful woman [the daughter] threw away all human and fleshly thoughts and in a brief moment turned her mind to better and divine things; and she spoke from the heart the words of that famous Shunamite woman to Elisha, saying to the blessed man, *"As the Lord thy God lives, and as thy soul lives, I will not leave thee."*[272] So <Symeon> moved by God [p. 236] followed her together with his own disciples, and when he [Symeon] went into her house that amazing girl Febronia embraced him and said, *"This day is salvation come to this house."*[273] The blessed one <then> tonsured her and clothed her mother and the two sisters and the more outstanding of their maidservants with the monastic habit, making their house a holy monastery of virgins;[274] he gave her the name of Febronia, who distinguished herself in the ascetic habit, instead of Hypatia,[275] for she was educated and had great experience in the Scriptures.

[269] Mt. 17:15: "Lord, have mercy on my son; for he is lunatick, and sore vexed; for ofttimes he falleth into the fire, and oft into the water."

[270] The ritual washing of hands by the priest during the liturgy.

[271] Mk. 7:35.

[272] 4 Ki. 4:30.

[273] Lk. 19:9.

[274] The "house monastery" of pious women and their servants living in their house as in a monastery was a popular ideal for women, modeled after the ideal expressed in the Life of Makrina by Gregory of Nyssa; see J. Herrin, "Public and Private Forms of Religious Commitment among Byzantine Women," in *Women in Ancient Societies: An Illusion of the Night,* ed. L. Archer et al. (London, 1994), 181–203.

[275] Hypatia of Alexandria, the Neoplatonist teacher who was renowned for her beauty, asceticism, and learning, was the subject of invectives on the part of Cyril of Alexandria and was eventually murdered by a mob in 415; see *ODB* 2:962, and the recent study by M. Dzielska, *Hypatia of Alexandria* (Cambridge, Mass., 1995).

20. God made *this beginning of miracles*[276] through the holy Symeon in the imperial city. After this miracle was reported all over (for the woman was of the nobility and shared senatorial blood), all the orthodox of the palace and the senate[277] came running without hesitation to the holy man. They confessed their sins and distributed their money generously and were completely trained and instructed in piety <by Symeon>. <A certain> Stephen, the son of the most pious patrician Basil,[278] who was celebrating a feastday of martyrs

---

Febronia's namesake, St. Febronia, was an early Christian martyr of Persia whose cult became popular in the Byzantine Empire after the 7th century; see *Bibl.sanct.* 5:508–9, and S. P. Brock, S. A. Harvey, *Holy Women of the Syrian Orient* (Berkeley, Calif., 1987), 150–76. The long and colorful synaxarial account (*SynaxCP* 769–72) mentions her superior education (she surpassed "all with her in spiritual training and understanding and reading of scripture" (τῇ τῶν γραφῶν ἀναγνώσει), but the story of her martyrdom makes no further reference to learning as an attribute, and there is no reference to secular education that would include grammar and metrics. The change of name has a symbolic meaning, as the secular learning of Hypatia is replaced by the spiritual conventual life of Febronia. Ironically, the pagan name Hypatia would be a much better indication of the girl's learning than that of any likely Christian heroine.

[276] Jn. 2:11.

[277] The senate of Constantinople (σύγκλητος), created by Constantine I as a conscious counterpart to the Roman senate, survived to the end of the Byzantine Empire. In the 9th century, its duties were ceremonial and provided a solemn venue for imperial enactments and audiences. The senatorial class was a defined aristocracy in some periods of Byzantine history, but in the 9th century it would have comprised those individuals who held high civilian offices and their families. The term is frequently used, as it is here, more generally to define the ruling class of the capital.

[278] The rank of patrician (*patrikios*) was an honorific title that retained distinction in the 9th century; most known holders of the title in this period were generals, members of the imperial family, or sons of military leaders. No references to a patrician Basil from the reign of Michael II or his immediate predecessors are included in Guilland's listing of patricians (R. Guilland, "Contribution à la prosopographie de l'Empire byzantin," *Byzantion* 40 [1970], 317–60). Theodore of Stoudios wrote to a patrician Basil, offering condolences on the death of a son John, probably in 819 (Fatouros, *Theod. Stud. Epist., ep.* 398 and notes). Seals of patricians named Basil from this period include one of a Basil, *sakellarios* and *patrikios* (Laurent, *Corpus*, 2, no. 748, dated to the 8th-9th c.), and Basil, *patrikios, praepositos, chartoularios* of the imperial *vestiarion*, and *sakellarios* (Zacos, *Seals*, 1.2, no. 1777). Phountoules suggests that Basil's son Stephen might be identified with Stephen the *asecretis* who became a disciple of Michael the Synkellos (Phountoules, Οἱ ὅσιοι αὐτάδελφοι, n. 133). This Stephen was an iconophile layman who became a confessor under Theophilos; see *v. Mich. Sync.* 74–77 and notes.

on his own estate, invited the holy man to a banquet.[279] When <Symeon>
arrived, that pious man asked the holy man to bless the large jar <of wine>
that was being doled out to the poor as was the custom. When <Symeon>
made the sign of the cross over the wine jar and said, "Blessed is our God
forever," such a rush of air was produced by the wine jar that the lid flew off
to a distance of three cubits away[280] and, though the <servants> in attendance
filled fifty-two smaller containers, even so the wine did not decrease, but overflowed like a river; and the wine jar is still now called blessed by the neighboring inhabitants in amazement at the miracle.[281]

21. When many locusts were descending upon the outlying parts of Constantinople, as they did once in Egypt,[282] and were completely destroying the
whole crop, the aforementioned very God-loving Stephen went to visit the
holy man. And he secretly took the water that dripped from <Symeon's>
hands when he washed up at mealtime, put it in a pitcher, and sprinkled it on
his own fields.[283] By the grace of God and through the intercessions of the

---

[279] Byzantine banquets were held in private homes as well as in the imperial palace,
and clergymen and monks with special relationships to aristocrats were included on
occasion; cf. *ODB* 1:250–51. This story is the setting for a common topos—the miraculous multiplication of wine—with its origins in the biblical account of the wedding at
Cana (Jn. 2:1–11). If the author's story is credible, it would indicate that Symeon was
able to play a very public role as an iconophile holy man in Constantinople during the
reign of Michael II.

[280] Depending upon the length assigned to the cubit or *pechys* (cf. n. 226, above), 3
cubits equals about 4.5 or 5.5 feet.

[281] Miracles of overflowing wine, based on the biblical miracle, are among the most
common deeds of saints. A similar miracle is performed by George in Chap. 32. The
reference to the wine jar's survival "to the present" is a common proof of a miracle in
hagiography. Since a wine jar could survive indefinitely, the passage does not give evidence of the author's chronological relation to the story.

[282] Ex. 10:4–19.

[283] Items that came in contact with a saint's body were frequently considered to have
miraculous powers. A parallel example is found in the Life of Thomaïs of Lesbos, chap.
11, where a eunuch named Constantine is cured of paralysis and quinsy by anointing
himself with the "washwater" (ἀπόλουμα) from the saint's hands; cf. Talbot, *Holy
Women,* 310–11. The Life of Elias Spelaiotes describes miracles effected by sprinkling
the water in which the saint's staff had been washed on afflicted pilgrims or giving it to
them to drink; cf. *v. Eliae Spel.,* chap. 81. The miraculous healing power was thought
to be transmitted by previous contact with the body of the saint or his possessions, and
could effect cures without the presence of the saint or the relics. For the term ἀπόλουμα

holy man the water put the locusts to flight as from a whip, and it kept the crop unharmed so that they [the fields] supplied produce many times greater than in prior years. [p. 237]

22. After the emperor Michael defeated the insurgent Thomas, he first gouged out his eyes, and then inflicted on him a painful death.[284] <On the one hand> the effrontery of civil war was extinguished, but the race of the Arabs was at its peak. <At the same time> the persecution of the orthodox abated a bit in those days; for this emperor harmed none of the holy men except for the great and divine Methodios, archdeacon of the holy patriarch Nikephoros, because he [Methodios] had departed to Rome in secret.[285] The emperor, incited by the heresiarch patriarch,[286] ordered that this man of blessed memory [Methodios] be flogged extensively in his sight with whips, and then he shut him in a very small cell [lit., "tomb"] with a very narrow opening through

---

see Sophocles, *Lexicon,* and Trapp, *Lexikon,* s.v. For a parallel from 6th- or 7th-century Egypt, see *Beyond the Pharaohs,* ed. F. Friedman (Providence, R.I., 1989), no. 159, where a papyrus that mentions water in which saintly monks had washed their feet is being preserved as a kind of relic.

[284] The chronicles (ps.-Sym. Mag. 621.17–19, Georg. Mon. 797.10–16) describe Thomas' death as gruesome (amputation of hands and feet and impaling his body) but do not include our author's claim that his eyes were gouged out. Phountoules (Οἱ ὅσιοι αὐτάδελφοι, 62, n. 135) notes that the 12th-century author Constantine Manasses follows the *Acta* in his verse chronicle.

[285] Methodios I, patriarch of Constantinople from 843 to 847, was one of the major iconophile figures of the 9th century. A native of Syracuse, he served as archdeacon during the patriarchate of Nikephoros, and attended the synod that condemned the patriarch in 814. Methodios' stay in Rome is mentioned in chronicles (Genes. 59–60; *TheophCont* 159.5–6) and in the anonymous *vita* of Methodios (PG 100:1248A), where it is suggested that he went to Rome as an emissary of Nikephoros to Pope Paschal I. Theodore of Stoudios wrote a letter to Methodios during his stay, asking him to seek assistance from the pope for iconophiles (Fatouros, *Theod. Stud. Epist.,* ep. 274 and commentary). Methodios returned to Constantinople in 821 as bearer of a papal letter from Paschal; see *v. Euthym. Sard.,* introduction, 12. For an introduction to the life and works of Methodios, see the entries by D. Stiernon in *Bibl.sanct.* 9:382–92 and *Dict. Spir.* 10:1107–9.

[286] Antony I Kassymatas was appointed patriarch of Constantinople by Michael II in 821, following the death of Theodotos Kassiteras; see n. 221, above. He was a member of the committee that prepared an iconoclast florilegium in 814 and worked closely with John the Grammarian, who became his successor; see *ODB* 1:124–25 and n. 39 in the Life of Theodora, below.

which they passed food and water to him only on rare occasions and left him with two other conspirators in a very secure underground prison. These two <other> men died after a short passage of time, because they could not endure the darkness and stench of the underground cell, and further the unbearable fierceness of the lice. And so that noble Methodios of supernatural endurance remained alone, protected by the all-powerful right hand of the Most High. For what creature of the flesh could endure such a painful and unbearable punishment as this blessed one did in that dark underground cell?[287] For it had no light at all. The hordes of mice infesting it because of the stench of dead bodies gravely injured and wounded the man of God who was buried alive [because he was in a "tomb"]; <yet> this man of superior strength, though his hair fell out from his head,[288] endured five years of suffering in this awful imprisonment.[289]

This was the situation <when> the emperor departed the life of men,

[287] We have punctuated with a question mark here, following Phountoules. The rest of the paragraph also follows his punctuation.

[288] A sign of psychological torment; cf. modern Greek: "τοῦ ἔπεσαν τὰ μαλλιὰ (ἀπὸ τὴν στενοχώρια)."

[289] The sufferings of Methodios form an extended story in several accounts of the period, with varied and often contradictory details that are analyzed by Gouillard (v. Euthym. Sard. 12–16). The Acta agree with the Life of Methodios that the imprisonment of Methodios began under Michael II, not in the reign of Theophilos, as the Chronicle of pseudo-Symeon Magistros suggests (ps.-Sym. Mag. 642–43). In his Life of Euthymios, Methodios adds crucial information that makes it possible to conclude that he was imprisoned in 821 in a small prison in a convent on the island of St. Andrew near Cape Akritas, in a cell built twenty-four years earlier to hold a prisoner who remained as Methodios' cellmate. According to the Life of Methodios, his co-prisoner's crime was attempted usurpation; ties developed between the two during their mutual imprisonment. Although Methodios describes the bad air that made it impossible to chant psalms, the vermin, and the tomblike character of the prison, the Acta's story of rotting bodies appears to be a romanticization. According to Gouillard, Methodios also explains the reason for this severe punishment; his crime was not just iconophile resistance. Libelli (anonymous popular pamphlets) predicting the deaths of Leo V and Michael II were circulated several months before the death of each emperor; although Methodios was in Rome at the time of the first, and imprisoned when the second appeared, he was suspected of authorship of each. Gouillard believes that the Acta, which claim that Methodios' imprisonment lasted five years, may help to date to the years 829–834 the period of increased persecution following the appearance of the second libellus.

<but> left behind a seed of impiety for the Christians, the savage and God-hating[290] Theophilos.[291] After he assumed the throne, he immediately launched a grievous and unbearable persecution against the pious and orthodox. For he ordered all the church's [p. 238] orthodox bishops and the superiors of the monasteries to be confined in iron chains in the Praitorion along with our sanctified father Symeon, while he considered how to put them to death.[292] He had also confined earlier the spokesman of God and confessor Euthymios, the bishop of Sardis;[293] <Euthymios> had firmly stood up to him face to face and boldly called him in public an apostate and a godless man.[294] So he

[290] The author uses ironic wordplay to characterize a man named Theophilos ("lover of God") as God-hating (θεομισής). A convinced iconoclast who reversed his father's policy of nonintervention against iconophiles, Theophilos was described in similar language in other iconophile sources; see, for example, v. Method. 1249D: he is ἐθνόφιλος (lover of foreigners); v. Theodor. imp., chap. 7.1, ἀφίλου Θεῷ ("no friend of God"); v. Mich. Sync. 72.21: χριστομάχος (Christ-battling).

[291] Michael II died in 829 of kidney disease, leaving the throne to his sixteen-year-old son Theophilos, who reigned until 842. Chronicle sources written in the Macedonian period (867–1025) present a much more positive picture of the reign of Theophilos, who was remembered for his building program, patronage of learning and culture, reform of the army, and energetic pursuit of campaigns against the Arabs. For the reign of Theophilos, see Treadgold, Byz. Revival, 263–329; J. Rosser, "Theophilos (829–842): Popular Sovereign, Hated Persecutor," Byzantiaka 3 (1983), 37–56.

[292] This statement demonstrates both hagiographic exaggeration and chronological confusion. Clearly, imprisonment of iconophile leaders was selective, and hagiographical texts make it clear that most iconophile church leaders survived by staying away from the capital. According to Methodios' Life of Euthymios of Sardis (v. Euthym. Sard., chap. 13), Theophilos arrested Joseph of Thessalonike, brother of Theodore of Stoudios, and Euthymios of Sardis in 831 on suspicion of producing libelli prophesying his death. Joseph was imprisoned in the hospice of Sampson and Euthymios exiled to the island of St. Andrew. Mass persecutions and arrests did not take place until 833, following a new iconoclast synod and an imperial edict against iconophiles; cf. Treadgold, Byz. Revival, 436, n. 386, who cites the sources. On the Praitorion, see synaxarion notice for Stephen the Younger, above (Life no. 2), n. 10.

[293] On Euthymios, see nn. 207 and 292, above.

[294] The Life of Euthymios has the following chronology: Euthymios, who was living in a retreat at the beginning of the reign of Theophilos, was arrested in 831 in connection with the prophetic libelli; he was brought into the presence of the "princeling/serpent (βασιλίσκος)" for a face-to-face interrogation that consisted of demands that he identify his visitors. On his refusal, Euthymios was exiled to the island of St. Andrew

delayed bringing him back into his presence since he feared the man's noble-minded resistance. The day after the feast of Christ's nativity he sent the patrician Kosmas[295] to the blessed man and ordered him to lacerate his [Euthymios'] body with lashes until his soul departed his body. And that is what happened. For as the blessed man was being mercilessly beaten and was praying on behalf of his murderers, he committed his all-righteous and holy spirit into the hands of God. He was a very old man who had lived a full eighty years and was offered to Christ as a genuine priest and martyr, truly a most honorable birthday gift [in honor of Christmas].[296]

23. When this holy man [Euthymios] had died in this manner from the flogging, Theodora, the wife of the emperor,[297] upbraided him [Theophilos]

(v. Euthym. Sard., chap. 14). The saint's imprisonment was for suspicion of inciting rebellion rather than for his iconophile views. The synaxarial notice of Euthymios, however, does portray two confrontations in which the saint spoke boldly to the emperor in support of icons, declaring anathema on anyone who did not revere the image of Christ in an icon, which led to his exile and imprisonment in Akritas (SynaxCP 345). The Acta of the three brothers are clearly closer to this later summary than to Methodios' apology in the vita of Euthymios.

[295] The Acta are the only source to mention the imperial representative by name. According to Methodios' Life of Euthymios (v. Euthym. Sard., chap. 18), three officials were sent to the island to conduct the interrogation of Euthymios: a logothetes (logothete of the drome, the imperial official responsible, in the 9th century, for protection of the emperor and collection of political information), a kanikleios (private secretary to the emperor), and a manglabites (a member of a special imperial guard). All three positions were filled in the 9th century by men of standing who might hold the rank of patrician. No patrician Kosmas is recorded in any of these positions.

[296] The account of the Life of Euthymios describes the torture of the saint, including 120 lashes with a whip, that Methodios claims to have heard in his cell. The saint's death, following the beating, on 26 December 831 (v. Euthym. Sard. 49.398–99 and n. 104) at the age of seventy-eight, made him a martyr. Methodios' account claims that the intent of the imperial representatives was to obtain information and submission through torture rather than to create a martyr.

[297] For the empress Theodora, see the final vita in this volume. Theodora's faith in icons is a theme in chronicle accounts of the 10th century (TheophCont 91–92; ps.-Sym. Mag. 629–30); none of these accounts, however, mentions Theodora's reaction to the death of Euthymios, nor is there any reference to Theodora in Methodios' Life of Euthymios. This story must come from a later period when legends of Theodora, the restorer of icons, had developed.

without restraint, calling him another Licinius[298] for Christians, and said, "God is going to abandon you since you, too, are so fiercely destroying His servants." Upon hearing these words, he abated his great ferocity, but did not completely leave off from his mad rage against the holy men. <For> the patriarch John[299] easily swayed him since he was readily influenced. Thus when he wished to drown the fathers confined in the Praitorion, he held off from this act because of the opposition voiced by the Augusta [Theodora]. But he led them out of the prison, inspected them all in person, and asked which one was the stylite (for he had <heard> a great and extraordinary report about him). When he was pointed out by the guards, <the emperor> looked grimly at <Symeon> and said, "O Lord, what a man this is, half-severed and half-dead, who ignores the decrees of my imperial power and considers my laws foolish nonsense!" And he immediately ordered him to be stripped and commanded that the body of the thrice-blessed man be mercilessly flogged with 150 lashes.[300] <Then> he condemned the holy man to banishment on the island

---

[298] Licinius was created Augustus of the West in 308 with Galerius as his counterpart in the East. Although Licinius may have played a role in the publication of Galerius' Edict of Serdica in 311, was for a time the ally of Constantine, and even issued his own edict of toleration in Nikomedeia in 313, Christians connected Licinius' accession with the last order for a general sacrifice to the gods in the Great Persecution of 303–312 and particularly reviled him. Licinius' attempt to reinstitute persecution in 322–323 to secure pagan support for his final conflict with Constantine also contributed to his status as a proverbial persecutor.

[299] John the Grammarian was appointed patriarch of Constantinople by Theophilos in 837 (or more likely in 838; cf. Treadgold, "Chronological Accuracy," 178–79), following the death of Antony Kassymatas. Although he was an iconophile monk in his early years, John became the chief intellectual force in Leo V's revival of iconoclasm. He headed the florilegium committee that collected texts to support iconoclasm; in Michael II's reign he became the tutor of Theophilos. He was known as a scholar and debater, and is portrayed in almost all hagiographic texts of the period as the chief opponent of iconophile saints. See the article "John VII Grammatikos," *ODB* 2:1052 for further bibliography, and, for John's learning, Lemerle, *Byz. Humanism*, 154–68.

[300] Accounts of personal interrogation of imprisoned iconophile saints by Theophilos are a *topos* in the literature of this period: cf. *v. Macar. Pel.*, chap. 13; *v. Method.*, chap. 7; *v. Mich. Sync.*, chap. 19; and the synaxarial account of Hilarion of Dalmatos (*SynaxCP* 733–734.45–48). These scenes derive in literary form from the "epic passions" of early Christian martyrs, as analyzed by H. Delehaye in *Les passions des martyrs et les genres littéraires* (Brussels, 1921).

of Aphousia.[301] [p. 239] He also ordered that the fathers with him and the chief disciples, the pair of brothers, citizens of the holy city [Jerusalem], I mean Theodore and Theophanes the poets,[302] first be beaten and <then> he had inscribed on their foreheads with tattooing the following verses:

> When all long to run to the city [Jerusalem]
> Where the all-holy feet of the Word of God
> Stood as a government[303] of the world,
> These men were seen in the holy place
> As worthless vessels of superstitious error.
> And so since there from wrong belief
> They did many terrible, shameful things with impious thoughts,
> They were banished from there as apostates.
> And though they fled to the city of the empire [Constantinople],
> They did not abandon their lawless stupidity.
> Therefore with their faces inscribed as evil-doers,
> They are condemned and driven forth again.[304]

---

[301] Aphousia (modern Avşa Adasi) is one of the Prokonnesos islands, located in the Sea of Marmara west of the Kyzikos peninsula. In 833 Theophilos exiled to the island a group of iconophile leaders, including Hilarion of Dalmatos (*SynaxCP* 733–734.48), John of Kathara (*SynaxCP* 633–634.35–38), Makarios of Pelekete (*v. Macar. Pel.* 159.26), and the brothers Theodore and Theophanes (*v. Mich. Sync.*, chap. 14 and note). For a description of the island and its monasteries, see Janin, *Eglises Centres,* 200–201. No other sources mention the presence of a Symeon among the exiles on Aphousia.

[302] Theodore and Theophanes, known as the *Graptoi* ("inscribed"), were the most colorful victims of the persecution of Theophilos. The two brothers, originally from Palestine, were disciples of Michael the Synkellos. They were exiled by Leo V, and later summoned for interrogation and beating by Theophilos. When they refused to answer, the emperor ordered their foreheads to be tattooed with twelve iambic verses. The saints were subsequently sent into exile, where Theodore died. The story clearly caught the imagination of hagiographers and chroniclers, for it is repeated in many sources. The earliest and fullest account appears to be the anonymous Life of Michael Synkellos. For an analysis of the sources for their story, see M. Cunningham's introduction to the text, *v. Mich. Sync.,* especially pp. 7–17, and the notes to chaps. 17–24.

[303] The reading of σύστασιν ("support") found in other versions in lieu of σύστημα used here makes sense, but does not scan. The alpha in σύστασιν is short, whereas it should be long in this position in iambic trimeter.

[304] The words of the iambic verses quoted here are virtually identical with the lines in the *v. Mich. Sync.,* chap. 20. According to its editor, M. Cunningham (*v. Mich. Sync.* 157 n. 145), the verses, with a few textual variations, also appear in the chronicles of

24. He had these <words> tattooed on the foreheads of the holy men and exiled them with the rest of the fathers to the above-mentioned island of Aphousia.[305] Unified and strengthened by the Spirit, that holy and reverent [p. 240] company of fathers considered the blessed Symeon their chief leader in all things. He made his dwelling near a swift stream by the sea, haunted by evil demons. At noon <these demons> would fiercely threaten passersby with the result that none of the islanders could go along that road at that hour. Once the saint settled there, not only were the violent and unclean spirits dispelled, but also the place became an abode of the divine Spirit; for he erected a very lovely church there to the all-pure Mother of God and through the entreaties of the father the place is proclaimed to this day as an abode of holy ascetics and God-bearing men.[306]

A neighbor of this small monastery,[307] an acquaintance of the saint named Leo, came to him bringing along his youngest son, George. <This George> was afflicted with a hernia, and <his father came> seeking his advice and blessing to have his child castrated. The blessed one, seeing his suffering, was filled completely with tears at the child's misfortune and brought forth from the depths <of his soul> a breath of groaning to the Lord, the doctor of all, and concurrently with that intense[308] breath of the holy man (O, who would not have been astonished?) the young man's tumor shrank and the swol-

---

George Monachos, Theophanes Continuatus, pseudo-Symeon Magistros, and Zonaras; see also n. 3 on p. 239 of the *Acta*.

[305] The *Acta* are in error here; the brothers were probably exiled to Apameia in Bithynia after their tattooing, although one source says that they remained in prison in Constantinople. Their exile to the island of Aphousia probably took place at the beginning of the reign of Theophilos, and it was from there that they were brought to Constantinople for interrogation; cf. *v. Mich. Sync.*, chaps. 14, 18.

[306] In 1895 M. Gedeon (*Proikonnesos* [Constantinople, 1895], 61–63) noted the existence of a modern church of the Theotokos on Aphousia with "ancient rustic columns" outside; cf. Phountoules, Οἱ ὅσιοι αὐτάδελφοι, n. 152. Janin (*Eglises Centres*, 200–201) cites several groups of ruins on the island on the evidence of Gedeon's book, but does not mention the church of the Theotokos, perhaps because Gedeon wrote before the text of the *Acta* was published. The Lives of the other saints exiled on Aphousia mention neither the foundation of a monastery nor the presence of a Symeon.

[307] Changing punctuation, with Phountoules, to read ἀναδείκνυται. οὗ δῆτα σύνεγγυς. . . .

[308] Reading περιπαθεῖ for περιπατεῖ, with Phountoules.

len mass, that shortly before reached down to his knees, soon diminished unexpectedly in size and was restored to its natural <state of> health. When the boy's father and the bystanders saw this <miracle>, they were thoroughly amazed and gave glory to God.

<Once> when there was a famine in the land and there was[309] no grain in the monastery except for the daily bread that was being set out in the refectory[310] for the brethren's meal, the blessed one peeked out of his cell at the gatehouse and saw the crowd of poor people standing <around>. They were expecting their regular grain allotment and were in distress,[311] for the appointed hour <for distribution> had already gone by. <So Symeon> summoned the man entrusted with this duty and said indignantly, "Why are the <poor> brethren <being forced to> stand around so long? Are you not aware that it is written 'Cursed is the man that does the works of the Lord carelessly'?"[312] When he replied[313] that this neglect of duty was not the result of any personal laziness <on his part>, but because there was nothing except that day's bread set on the table for the brethren and <that sufficient> only for modest alleviation <of their hunger>, <Symeon> said, "While there is <still> bread, run quickly and pick up all the <loaves> on the table. Pay the appropriate debt to the <poor> brethren of the Lord[314] and let His *will be done*[315] in regard to the monks." When he [p. 241] did <Symeon's> bidding with much haste and had dismissed the poor people, the monks looked extremely unhappy because they were deprived of their daily meal. But when not even[316] a full hour had passed, lo and behold, a cargo ship with sails unfurled[317] sailed in front of the monastery and dropped anchor. It had been sent to the blessed one from the capital by lovers of Christ, and was full of flour and <twice> baked bread and all sorts of legumes and grain and wine and

---

[309] Reading προσόντος for προσιόντος, with Phountoules.

[310] Or "on the table."

[311] Reading ταλαιπωρουμένων for ταλαιπωρούμενον.

[312] Jer. 31 (48):10.

[313] After ῥαθυμίας Phountoules adds τὴν τοιαύτην φήσαντος ῥαθυμίαν omitted by van den Gheyn.

[314] Cf. Mt. 25:40.

[315] Acts 21:14.

[316] Reading οὔπω for οὔτω, with Phountoules.

[317] Reading διαπεπετασμένοις for διαπεπετασμένη.

cheeses and salted fish and fruit and vegetables.[318] When the great Symeon saw this together with all his associates and the venerable pair of the Graptoi [the "inscribed ones," Theodore and Theophanes], they all gave thanks together to <God>, the provider of wealth.

25. This <was the situation of> the blessed man Symeon after his journey from the theme of the Thrakesians to the imperial city because of his zeal for piety, when he had also left his brother George, as has been mentioned before,[319] and established him as a guardian as well as[320] a teacher of piety for the holy monasteries established by him both in that land and in their homeland of Mytilene. During this time <that Symeon> was refuting, contending, being beaten for the sake of piety, being banished, and working miracles, God glorified him since he struggled so hard on behalf of His image. As for his wondrous brother George (for let the story come back to him), did he not also contend <in a manner> not unworthy of his brother who had entrusted him

---

[318] The miracle illustrates several basic features of Byzantine diet. Bread was the staple food, to the extent that it was identified as a meal. It could be made of wheat, barley, or occasionally millet, depending on social class and regional agriculture. According to one estimate (E. Patlagean, *Pauvreté économique et pauvreté sociale à Byzance* [Paris, 1977], 46, 52), daily bread consumption in the late Roman Empire averaged three to six pounds, but declined to 1.5 pounds by the 11th century (A. Kazhdan, "Two Notes on Byzantine Demography of the Eleventh and Twelfth Centuries," *ByzF* 8 [1982], 118); see "Bread," *ODB* 1:321. The role of the monastery as distributor of grain as an act of philanthropy, replacing the bread dole of the Roman Empire, is well illustrated here. The miracle describes a regular daily distribution to a local public that must have formed part of the monastery's regular almsgiving. Miraculous distributions of food in times of famine are one of the most common *topoi* in Byzantine hagiography, and they probably reflect not only biblical precedents, but the actual importance of monasteries in the local economy. For the concept of philanthropy and almsgiving, see D. Constantelos, *Byzantine Philanthropy and Social Welfare,* 2d ed. (New Rochelle, N.Y., 1991); J. Herrin, "From Bread and Circuses to Soup and Salvation: The Origins of Byzantine Charity," Davis Center Seminar paper, 1985. The cargo delivered by the miraculously arriving ship lists most of the ingredients of the Byzantine diet, emphasizing greens, cheese, fish, and wine as accompaniments to bread, with the notable absence of olive products. See "Diet," *ODB* 1:621–22; M. Dembińska, "Diet: A Comparison of Food Consumption between some Eastern and Western Monasteries in the 4th to 12th Centuries," *Byzantion* 55 (1985–86), 431–62.

[319] In Chap. 18, above. Reference to George's direction of Symeon's monasteries in the Thrakesion theme as well as Mytilene.

[320] Reading ταυτῷ for ταύτῳ, with Phountoules.

with responsibility for the rules of guardianship, or did he [George] neglect the doctrines and teachings of piety? By no means, but in fact he <contended> in a manner that made him worthy of selection by his teacher and brother, and worthy of his appointment by God for the sake of the support of the right doctrines. For the bishop of Lesbos,[321] as has been said before, who was indeed a persecutor of piety and a teacher of impiety, breathed out persecution on the orthodox in the city of Mytilene and the province around it to such a degree after the expulsion of the blessed Symeon that he heedlessly ordered that the pious institutions[322] and holy monasteries of the orthodox be sold lock, stock, and barrel, and he also sold the monasteries under <the direction of> the blessed George together with their immovable properties[323] on a pretext of raising cash. When he had received the purchase price for these <properties>, he attacked them [the monks] suddenly, removing this wondrous man [George] along with his spiritual flock from the monasteries and forcing them to live in cramped quarters in an insignificant and very small village named Myrsinas.[324]

While he was living there a man [p. 242] named Hesychios (his rank was *protonotarios* of the Thrakesians)[325] wrote down on paper[326] a confession of his sins, secured it with a lead seal,[327] and sent it to this hallowed man so that

[321] See Chap. 15, above.

[322] εὐαγεῖς οἶκοι: philanthropic institutions that provided charity to the poor, the sick, or the old. The term could include hospitals, almshouses, or orphanages; cf. *ODB* 2:736.

[323] The lands and buildings of a property, as opposed to its animals or furnishings.

[324] Phountoules (Οἱ ὅσιοι αὐτάδελφοι, n. 158) and Malamut (*Les îles,* 234–35) identify Myrsinas (Myrsina?) with a site near the gulf of Gera in Lesbos, where a monastery of the Panagia Myrsiniotissa was constructed in the 12th century.

[325] In the 9th century, *protonotarioi* were attached to the administration of themes and held responsibility for civil administration in the theme; cf. Oikonomidès, *Listes,* 315.

[326] χάρτης is a term used to describe various kinds of writing material, and in the 9th century could refer either to papyrus or to parchment. Paper, which was introduced from the Arab world and gradually came to replace parchment, was not commonly used in Byzantium until the 11th century; cf. *ODB* 3:1579. In antiquity the term χάρτης commonly referred to papyrus, which was still available in parts of Byzantium in the 9th century, but disappeared soon thereafter; cf. "Papyrus," *ODB* 3:1581–82.

[327] Byzantine documents were closed with lead seals used to authenticate the identity of the sender and preserve the integrity of correspondence. Lead was one of the most common materials used for seals, and thousands of these seals survive. They ordinarily

through his boldly spoken prayers he might be deemed worthy of the Lord's forgiveness for them. After he [George] received it, he kept it with him for twenty days and then sent it back again to Hesychios with the seal intact; for he confessed that he was inadequate to such an undertaking and that this work was most fitting for God alone. When <Hesychios> received the document with much groaning and tears, he opened it and miraculously found that, by the grace of the all-holy Spirit, it was completely blank.[328] When the reverent man saw this unexpected <turn of events>, he was astonished by the extraordinary <character> of the miracle and seized with amazement[329] in his heart; and from happiness he poured out hot tears to God and appropriately gave thanks also to His servant [George].

Another man, one of those in power and <a member> of the aristocracy,[330] a very true, longtime friend of the fathers, fell ill with a terrible sickness and was approaching the end of his life; and he informed the blessed <George> that he should not delay coming to visit him. So <George> ordered the donkey to be saddled and after mounting <the animal> set out, although for the <entire> time of his life up to now he had used his feet instead of a pack animal, saying that he always had his own body in his possession as a slave.[331] When he came to the ill man, he got off his donkey and went in to greet him. While he was conversing with the sick man and offering <him> consolation, the donkey, which was tied in the courtyard, kept on braying disruptively; this disturbed the sick man a great deal. When the great <George> realized that <the sick man> was severely annoyed and the rea-

---

contained a monogram of the owner's name and title and an invocation to a saint, the Virgin, or Christ; after the restoration of icons, many included images. Surviving seals are one of the most important sources for administrative history and prosopography of Byzantium; cf. "Seals and Sealings" and "Sigillography," *ODB* 3:1859–60, 1894–95.

[328] Note the similarity to the miracle in Chap. 16, where another letter is the saint's means of forgiving sins. The stories are a good indication of the importance of written documents to the author or the society that developed the tradition of the saint.

[329] Reading θάμβει τε for θαμβεῖται, with Phountoules.

[330] τις τῶν ἐν τέλει καὶ εὐπατριδῶν. The author uses generic terms for rank and good family that are common in hagiography. They also reflect the fluidity of the aristocracy in the 9th century, a period when many new families rose to prominence. See E. Patlagean, "Les débuts d'une aristocratie byzantine et le témoignage de l'historiographie," in *The Byzantine Aristocracy: IX to XIII Centuries,* ed. M. Angold (Oxford, 1984), 23–43.

[331] Cf. 1 Cor. 9:27. This theme returns to the characterization of George in the early sections of the biography, where he is described, in imitation of St. Sabas, as a "pack animal" carrying necessities for his brothers; cf. Chap. 11 and n. 139.

son <for it>, through his traveling companion he privately commanded the donkey, "Brother, stop your cries until we leave here." And <the donkey> received the command as a rational <creature would> and took care to maintain an unbroken, deep silence. <Then> the blessed one made a prayer in the name of Christ for the suffering man and immediately restored him to health. Such were the tales about George and his virtuous deeds[332] after his brother's departure.

26. When the emperor Theophilos died,[333] the blessed Symeon (for let the account return to him again) was still in the same place of exile to which he had been condemned, Aphousia, as was stated <above>.[334] On the very night the emperor was about to die, <Symeon> saw him in a dream in [p. 243] most piteous civilian garb[335] saying to him in a suppliant manner three times, "O monk, help me!"[336] Upon awaking, he [Symeon] revealed the death of the emperor to his companions. When this report spread clearly everywhere, the pre-eminent men of the orthodox leapt from the caves of their lengthy exile and, like lambs freed from the pursuit of wolves <that reach> green pastures and springs of water, they confidently ran together to Byzantium from all over with rejoicing and much thanksgiving.[337] So a letter from the pious empress [Theodora] reached the father Symeon, urging him to come quickly to the

---

[332] Reading κατορθώματα for καθορθώματα.

[333] The emperor Theophilos died of dysentery in 842 at age twenty-nine.

[334] See Chap. 24.

[335] ἐν ἰδιωτικῷ καὶ οἰκτίστῳ σχήματι: portraits of Theophilos in manuscripts and on coins show him in imperial regalia, consisting of crown and purple *chlamys* (long garment) with gold *tablion,* and, on coins, holding the imperial orb and scepter; see "Insignia," *ODB* 2:999–1000; "Chlamys," *ODB* 1:424. Stripped of his ritual attire, he is a pitiful figure.

[336] The word καλόγηρος, which appears four times in the *Acta,* can be translated either as "venerable one" or "monk"; see also *Acta,* 243.21, 246.8, and 248.13.

Early chronicles offer no hint of repentance from Theophilos, but later sources (ps.-Sym. Mag. 650–51 and *TheophCont* 152–54) also include material suggesting deathbed remorse for his persecution of iconophiles; cf. Treadgold, *Byz. Revival,* 327 and n. 452. Here the author uses the passage to set the stage for Symeon's eventual concession to Theodora's wish to exempt Theophilos from post-mortem condemnation, in Chap. 28. Cf. also Chap. 8 of the *vita* of the empress Theodora, at the end of this volume.

[337] A rhetorical *topos* common in hagiography as, for example, in the Life of Michael the Synkellos, using different imagery: "the living monuments of Christ returned from the various districts and cities, just as wholly delightful flowers from spring meadows" (trans. Cunningham, *v. Mich. Sync.,* chap. 25).

Queen <of Cities> along with those fathers who shared his exile.[338] He sent a courier with a letter to his brother, the great George, urging him to come to him with great haste; he himself began the journey to Byzantium with many other divine fathers. During the voyage between Prokonnesos and Herakleia,[339] while he was sleeping in a small boat, he saw the great and wondrous Antony <the Great> walking on the sea, wearing golden sandals on his feet and holding a golden staff in his right hand[340] and walking swiftly.[341] He said to him, "Antony, holy father and true servant of God, where are you going?" He <replied> to him, "To establish orthodoxy in Byzantium and to *prepare a place*[342] for you and your companions in the quarter of Kanikleiou.[343] So be

[338] Several early sources demonstrate that the restoration of icons was preceded by a conference between Theodora and her officials and the monastic leaders of the iconophile opposition. Gouillard ("Synodikon," 121 ff) gives a careful analysis of these texts, emphasizing the overall chronology that can be derived from early sources, especially the late 9th-century author of the account of the transfer of the relics of Patriarch Nikephoros I. This passage in the *Acta* is the only source to suggest that Theodora initiated the events with a letter to Symeon and other monks. The 10th-century chronicles of Genesios and Theophanes Continuatus, reflecting a Stoudite tradition, place the initiative on a petition of monastic leaders led by the Stoudites; cf. *TheophCont* 149–50; Genes. 56–57.

[339] Prokonnesos (modern Marmara), west of Kyzikos, is the largest island in the Sea of Marmara (cf. *ODB* 2:1730–31) and would have been an obvious stopping point on the route of travel from the nearby small island of Aphousia to the capital. Herakleia in Thrace (modern Marmara Ereğli), which lies opposite Prokonnesos on the north shore of the Sea of Marmara, is the site of important road junctions (cf. *ODB* 2:915). This story, along with other references, provides valuable information for shipping and travel routes in the region of Constantinople.

[340] Add χειρὶ after δεξίᾳ, as in Phountoules.

[341] Compare the earlier appearances of Antony to David and Symeon (Chaps. 4, 9, 13), in which Antony is described as wearing monastic garb. This vision suggests the imagery of a mosaic or manuscript illumination with its allusion to golden sandals and staff.

[342] Jn. 14:2.

[343] The quarter of Kanikleiou, located on the shore of the Golden Horn, received its name from the office of the *kanikleios,* imperial private secretary, held by Theoktistos, the imperial official who masterminded the restoration of icons, and whose residence was here; see "Kanikleios" and "Theoktistos," *ODB* 2:1101 and 3:2056, and n. 68 in the *vita* of the empress Theodora, below. Kanikleiou is also mentioned as the location for the meeting in the 10th-century chronicle of Genesios (Genes. 57:78) and in the *Synodicon Vetus* (Duffy-Parker, *Synodicon Vetus,* chap. 156.4), probably composed in the late 9th century.

of good courage and hurry because it really is as I have told you, O monk." Immediately he woke up and described his vision to his companions, who were filled with courage and extraordinary zeal and sent up thanks to God. Moreover, when his brother, the God-bearing George, in response to his brother's message, was sailing near the shore at a place called Psalidion,[344] he seemed to see in a dream Spyridon,[345] famous among the saints, walking from the shore to his ship; he climbed aboard, greeted and embraced him. And he [George] said, "Why have you come here, my lord and most holy father?" And Spyridon <replied>, "I am coming to share your struggle in the synod that is about to be organized in Byzantium."[346] [p. 244]

27. When all the orthodox bishops and monks had assembled in the great city [Constantinople], the empress received them graciously and ordered that they be lodged for the time being within the palace in the <place> called Peribleptos;[347] but she kept this twin pair of brothers Symeon and George

[344] This is the only known reference to Psalidion. Janin (*CP byz.*, 453) thought it was probably a site to the west of Constantinople, while Phountoules (Οἱ ὅσιοι αὐτάδελφοι, n. 164) suggests that it might alternately designate an otherwise unknown location in Lesbos.

[345] Spyridon was a 4th-century bishop of Trimithous on Cyprus. The legend and miracles of Spyridon were popular in Byzantium; his relics were transferred from Cyprus to Constantinople at some point after the mid-seventh century. At the beginning of the 10th century they were venerated in the chapel of St. Peter at Hagia Sophia. Spyridon's appearance in the *Acta* may symbolize the restoration of his cult in Constantinople; cf. P. van den Ven, *La légende de S. Spyridon, évêque de Trimithonte* (Louvain, 1953), *143–*47. Spyridon is mentioned in only one other *vita* of a 9th-century saint: through his icon he instructed Constantine the Jew to go from his monastery on Mt. Olympos to Cyprus (*v. Const. Jud.* 635B).

[346] The author here describes the assembly that restored icons as a synod (σύνοδος), but no official acts have survived, and the event clearly lacked the stature of the Council of 787. The *Synodicon Vetus* (chap. 156) describes the meeting as a "divine and sacred local synod." A document circulated in the late 9th century as the "Decretal of the Synod of Michael and Theodora his mother" has been shown by Gouillard to be a forgery ("Synodikon," 161–63, 291–98).

[347] This passage is ambiguous. Phountoules (Οἱ ὅσιοι αὐτάδελφοι, n. 165) suggests that the term *Peribleptos* refers to an otherwise unmentioned wing of the palace, following the reasoning of the first editor of the text, van den Gheyn, who understood the text to mean "inside the imperial palace, in the place then called Peribleptos" (*Acta*, 244 n. 3), but confessed to lacking evidence for the existence of a specific part of the palace with that name.

along with the wondrous Methodios with her in a private chamber, frequently conversed <with them>, and invited them to dine with her.[348] When the emperor was on his deathbed, he had repented, if not entirely, of his departure from piety and his persecution of the orthodox, and ordered that sixty pounds of gold be distributed to the disabled and the poor, and <ordered> another <distribution> of the same amount to those living as hermits *in the caves and the mountains*[349] and those sentenced to exile by him. <Now> that pious empress who loved her husband, but loved Christ even more,[350] declared her personal purpose to these three holy men [Symeon, George, and Methodios], and revealed it openly, saying: "O holy and God-bearing fathers, with a pious heart I wish to restore to the Church of God its appropriate adornment, and for this reason I have ordered your most blessed assembly to gather before us from the ends <of the earth>. But I also bring one request to you, a trifle in your eyes and indeed very easy <to grant>; for you as His priests and pure

---

Ševčenko ("Hagiography," 118, n. 36) inserts a comma after βασιλείων and translates the passage as "The empress, having gladly received them inside the Palace, ordered that they should for the time being be lodged in the so-called Peribleptos." If we accept this translation, then Peribleptos could refer to the monastery of that name; it was not founded, however, until the 11th century (Janin, *Eglises CP,* 218–22), and this reference would thus be evidence of late composition or emendation of the *Acta.* The Peribleptos monastery was located far from the palace, in Psamathia in the southwest part of the city.

[348] This passage has probably telescoped a period of informal discussion between Theodora, her advisers, and monastic leaders that may have extended over several months; cf. Gouillard, "Synodikon," 123–25. The author is clearly intent on magnifying the role of Symeon and George as central to the plan for restoration of icons. A Symeon the Stylite is mentioned in several documents as one of the monastic leaders of the restoration: in the *Synodikon of Orthodoxy* he is blessed along with Ioannikios, Hilarion of Dalmatos, Theodore of Stoudios, and "Isaac the miracle worker" (Gouillard, "Synodikon," 52–53 and 146–47); Methodios cites Ioannikios, Hilarion, and Symeon in a homily (Darrouzès, *Documents inédits,* 296.5) defending his policy to former iconoclasts. George is not mentioned in any other source. Other sources also plead the case for their heroes as advisers to Theodora as she shaped the restoration of icons; the Stoudites, for example, are promoted in Theophanes Continuatus (*TheophCont* 148–49).

[349] Cf. Heb. 11:38.

[350] φίλανδρος, μᾶλλον δὲ φιλόχριστος: a pun not only on the piety of the empress, but on the terminology used to describe her husband Theophilos as "God-hating"; cf. Chap. 22 and n. 290, above.

worshipers and servants have the power from God to bind and to loose whatever you wish,[351] not only the sins of those who are examined in this life, but
also those who have already been taken away by death.[352] Now I also beseech
you not to condemn to anathema[353] my husband who was also your emperor,
but to receive him in the spirit of concession as faithful and orthodox. For I
am persuaded that you also have the power, if only you are willing, <to do
this>. For, look, he even left you and your associates a token of his favor in his
will as he was departing <this life>." And that most gentle pair of moderate
temperament,[354] I mean Methodios and George, were silent as they considered

[351] Cf. Mt. 16:19, 18:18.

[352] Theodora here uses the passage from Matthew to apply to all clergy, claiming that
it gives them the power to grant posthumous absolution from sins. The *Narratio de
Theophili imperatoris absolutione* (ed. Regel, *Analecta*, 30–31), a legendary text, sets
Theodora's conversation with Methodios alone after his appointment as patriarch. She
also asks him to "implore the merciful and compassionate God about Theophilos . . .
that He would pardon his sins. . . . For I know from the holy gospels that you have
been granted by God the power to bind and loose. . . ." In this version of the legend
Methodios claims that such forgiveness is beyond his powers, but orders a general fast
and calls together an assembly of "all the orthodox people" for fasting, vigils, and
prayers on behalf of Theophilos. Byzantine patriarchs, of course, did not claim apostolic power derived from Mt. 16:19, since their see had no legend of foundation by
Peter. Inasmuch as condemnation or absolution of heretics in Byzantium was the responsibility of church councils, the request should probably be read as an issue Theodora intended to bring to the attention of the monastic leaders assembled as a synod.

[353] Anathema was an ecclesiastical censure or malediction for heresy or mistaken
belief pronounced solemnly at a church council. It did not involve precise punishment,
as did excommunication, and could be pronounced on both deceased and living figures.
The *Synodikon of Orthodoxy* includes a list of anathemas (with the phrase "Anathema
to . . .") carefully balanced with statements of blessing ("may their memory be eternal. . .") for the synod of 843; see "Anathema," *ODB* 1:89; Gouillard, "Synodikon,"
48–56, 146–53. As A. Alexakis has pointed out, however, in a private communication,
in fact no Byzantine emperor was anathematized in the *Synodikon* or by any synod.

[354] μετριόφρων: Methodios was identified with the moderate faction of church leaders, who had supported the patriarchs Tarasios and Nikephoros in their policy of accommodation in the iconophile restoration of the early 9th century (the reign of Irene)
against the rigorist Stoudite monks. The factional quarrel was renewed when Methodios became patriarch and proclaimed a policy of purifying former iconoclast clergy,
a policy that was opposed by the Stoudites. Although there are no reliable sources that
identify the absolution of Theophilos as the subject of a quarrel, it is apparent from
the early *vita* of Ioannikios by Peter (cf. Chaps. 69–70, in Life no. 7, below) that

with great anxiety what answer they should give. But the divine Symeon, who was hotter than fire and [p. 245] *sharper*[355] at stabbing *than a sword,* wavered not one bit nor was he at all fearful, but very angrily shouted that famous apostolic dictum, *"His money perish with him.* For he has neither *part nor lot*[356] with the pious and orthodox, since he was a desecrater of the holy and fought against God. The divine was hateful to him while he was alive, and it is clear that this is also <true> now that he has departed." When he had said these things about her late[357] <husband>, the empress was seized with grief and filled with hostility; she irately ordered these men and their associates to be expelled from the palace and said the following angry words: "Since you have come to this conclusion, *depart from me.*[358] For as I received and learned from my spouse and husband, I will rule with a firm hand.[359] *You will see.*"[360] So the fathers departed not only from the palace, but also from the city, and the whole band of confessors and exiles followed Symeon, since they held the same beliefs as he did and chose *to die with him.*[361] Only <the following indi-viduals> along with George approved of the empress' purpose and wished to see it accomplished, since with deep understanding they were concerned for

---

moderate-rigorist quarrels broke out again as soon as the restoration of orthodoxy began to be put in place; cf. Darrouzès, "Le patriarche Méthode," 15–57; V. Grumel, "La politique religieuse du patriarche saint Méthode," *EO* 34 (1935), 385–401. It is significant that no Stoudite is mentioned by our author.

[355] Cf. Heb. 4:12.

[356] Acts 8:20–21.

[357] Phountoules queries the reading μακαρίου, "blessed," and emends it to μακ-αρίτου, "deceased." Alternatively, as suggested by L. Rydén, one could read παρὰ for περὶ and translate "when this had been said thus by the blessed man."

[358] Mt. 25:41.

[359] Theodora's claim to rule firmly is echoed in *v. Mich. Sync.,* chap. 25, describing her "manly nobility."

[360] Mt. 27:25.

[361] Cf. Jn. 11:16. No other sources describe a secession of monastic leaders before the appointment of a patriarch; cf. Gouillard, "Synodikon," 124–25. Methodios, how-ever, refers in a letter to the fact that Symeon, Hilarion of Dalmatos, and Ioannikios later took a hard line on the readmission of iconoclasts to orthodoxy (see Methodios, *Diaskepsis,* quoted by Niketas of Herakleia, in Darrouzès, *Documents inédits,* 296) and that may be reflected here. The claim that the exiles would face death is certainly mis-placed or the product of rhetorical exaggeration even for the reigns of Theodora's pre-decessors.

the common salvation: they were Methodios, John called Katasambas,[362] and Ioannikios, who was like an angel preeminent among the hermits at that point in time on <Mt.> Olympos.[363]

28. When the leader of the heresy who was still laying claim to the <patriarchal> throne [John VII the Grammarian][364] learned that the fathers had left the palace and the city in disunity and disaccord, he rejoiced greatly; and he emptied his extensive coffers to <bribe> the clergy and all those of the same mind as he and urged them to fight with him like bandits to retain control of the patriarchal throne. When he had devised this mischievous plan and carried it out, the madman went to the Augusta [Theodora], demanding and imploring that she arrange a disputation with the orthodox concerning <the evidence of> the Scriptures, and that the leadership of the church should be unambiguously assigned to the winning party. This <idea> pleased the empress and she agreed without hesitation.[365] And the men of God, George and Methodios, took along Sergios Niketiates,[366] Theoktistos,[367]

[362] John Katasambas (also called "Kakosambas") is attacked in the biography of Ioannikios as an enemy of Ioannikios and Methodios because of his alliance with the Stoudites; cf. Chaps. 69–70 and n. 499 of his *vita* by Peter in this volume.

[363] On Ioannikios, see his Life by Peter, no. 7 in this volume. In Chap. 69 one can find his prediction of the election of Methodios and allusion to a letter from the saint; see also chaps. 46–47 in the *vita* of Ioannikios by Sabas. The *vita* of Michael the Synkellos (*v. Mich. Sync.*, chap. 26) claims that the election of Methodios was determined by sending an embassy to Ioannikios for a prediction.

[364] John VII, chief architect of the second iconoclastic period (see Chap. 23, n. 299). John is presented in most sources as the villain of the story, and his deposition and punishment are treated with vivid imagination. Thus, the *vita* of Michael the Synkellos describes him as "deranged" (*v. Mich. Sync.*, chap. 25); in Theophanes Continuatus and Genesios (as in the *Acta*, Chap. 30) he attempts to commit suicide or simulates an attack against himself (*TheophCont* 150.21–151.17; Genes. 57.81–58.14).

[365] Reading ἀμελλητὶ for ἀμελητὶ as suggested by L. Rydén.

[366] Sergios Niketiates was identified by H. Grégoire ("Études sur le neuvième siècle," *Byzantion* 8 [1933], 515–20) as one of the admirals in command of the Byzantine fleet at Damietta; he is called Ibn Qatuna in Arab sources. Under the name Sergios Magistros he is also the subject of a synaxarial entry, which describes him as the founder of the monastery of the Virgin known as the "Monastery of Niketiates" in the gulf of Nikomedeia; he died in Crete as supreme commander of the Byzantine fleet (*SynaxCP* 777).

[367] On his deathbed Theophilos designated Theoktistos (who held the rank of *magistros* and the position of logothete of the drome) as regent for Michael III and adviser to Theodora. Although Theoktistos held key positions under both Michael II and

Bardas,[368] and [p. 246] Petronas,[369] very orthodox men who happened to be leaders of the senate,[370] and did not stop insistently begging and imploring Symeon to assent to the Augusta's request and not to abandon in darkness the church of God, which was being pitifully excited to Bacchic frenzy by the devil. Symeon was abashed at their words because of the virtue inherent in these men and their prominence; and when he also considered the entreaty of the emperor Theophilos, whom he had seen in a dream on Aphousia, as he said three times, "O monk, help me,"[371] he agreed to do this as if pricked by God. So they proceeded to the empress and reported the father's most sincere assent to her request. She was filled with exceeding joy and ordered both parties [the iconophile and iconoclast] to assemble at Kanikleiou and to have the debate with each other based on the divine Scriptures.[372] When this occurred and the whole phalanx of the iconoclasts in its first and only assault could not

---

Theophilos, later sources credit him with masterminding Theodora's restoration of icons and the election of Methodios to the patriarchate (*Georg. Mon. Cont.* 811.7–16; *TheophCont* 148; Genes. 56.41). He was also instrumental in reviving secular learning (Lemerle, *Byz. Humanism,* 186–90). Theoktistos was killed in 855 at the orders of Bardas when Theodora was dethroned; cf. "Theoktistos," *ODB* 3:2056, and Life of Theodora, below, n. 68.

[368] Bardas, Theodora's brother, played a central role in her reign and later that of Michael III, after he made possible Michael's coup against his mother. Bardas was later responsible for many of the cultural achievements of the mid-9th century, such as the mission of Constantine and Methodios to the Slavs and the patronage of scholars involved in the revival of secular learning; see "Bardas," *ODB* 1:255–56. Bardas is also mentioned as one of the political powers behind the restoration of icons in the 10th-century chronicle of Theophanes Continuatus (*TheophCont* 148). He was assassinated by Basil I in 866.

[369] A younger brother of Theodora, Petronas served in military roles under Theophilos and Theodora, and joined his brother Bardas in the conspiracy against Theoktistos in 855; cf. "Petronas," *ODB* 3:1644–45. The *vita* of Antony the Younger describes his close affiliation with the saint in later years; see F. Halkin, "Saint Antoine le Jeune et Pétronas le vainqueur des Arabes en 863," *AnalBoll* 62 (1944), 187–255. Petronas died around 865 while returning from a campaign.

[370] See Chap. 20, n. 277.

[371] See Chap. 26, above.

[372] The restoration of icons and repudiation of the iconoclast Council of 815 required patristic evidence to refute the arguments of the iconoclasts. One early source, the priest Theophanes' account of the transfer of the relics of the patriarch Nikephoros I, describes the council as follows: "<Theodora> . . . ordered that they support their position with regard to the truth through patristic citations, as demonstrated in various

withstand the force of the thrice-blessed Methodios in his arguments from the Scriptures, they completely threw away their shields and immediately deserted <the battlefield>.[373] At that point the leader[374] of the priests of the Great Church [Hagia Sophia] took all the clergy with him and came to father Symeon at Kanikleiou; he fell on his knees before him and reviled the heresy from his heart and condemned it along with the heresiarch to anathema. When he heard about these <developments>, the bishop of the church [Patriarch John VII] was at his wits' end; he was filled with fear and terrible confusion.

29.[375] But clinging to the heresy inherent[376] in him, he persuaded the Augusta <to let him> debate Symeon separately in her presence. He thought

---

books. She <then> commanded that the whole body of the Church assemble in a specified palace building, and that it proclaim their decision very clearly to the multitudes. Such an innumerable crowd gathered, not only those who had maintained a sound opinion in the time of impiety, but also most of those who had consorted with the opposite party, or had been chosen by them as priests and rulers of the church; and the <latter> suddenly changed their minds and subjected to anathema those who had fought against the images." Cf. the "Logos of Theophanes the Priest and Abbot on the Exile of Nikephoros the Holy Patriarch of Constantinople, and on the Translation of His Venerable Relics," in Μνημεῖα ἁγιολογικά, ed. Th. Ioannou (Leipzig, 1884), 123, and analysis in Gouillard, "Synodikon," 125–26.

[373] Although no documents have survived from the synod of 843, the acts of the councils of 787 and 815 give an idea of how arguments would have been developed. The iconophile leaders would have presented and debated a selection of passages from scripture and the church fathers (florilegia) and argued their validity against the arguments of the iconoclast Council of 815, the most recent doctrinal statement on icons. For an account of the way florilegia were assembled and used by councils, see P. Alexander, "The Iconoclastic Council of St. Sophia (815) and Its Definition (*Horos*)," *DOP* 7 (1953), 35–66, and "Church Councils and Patristic Authority," *Harvard Studies in Classical Philology* 63 (1958), 493–505, and, most recently, A. Alexakis, *Codex Parisinus Graecus 1115 and Its Archetype* (Washington, D.C., 1996). It seems clear that Methodios led the theological debate, but iconoclast leaders who attended did so to ask for acceptance rather than to put up resistance. John the Grammarian did not attend. See Gouillard, "Synodikon," 126–27.

[374] ἐξάρχων is probably a term for the *oikonomos* of the Great Church, the cleric appointed to administer the affairs of the patriarchal church; see "Oikonomos," *ODB* 3:1517.

[375] Following Phountoules, we have begun paragraph 29 at this point.

[376] Reading ἐνούσης for ἐνούσης.

that since <Symeon> lacked general education,[377] he would destroy him with his glib tongue and the sophisticated form of his arguments and his multifaceted cleverness and would reduce his opposition to nothingness.[378] He was cheated of his expectation, however. For when they both came together in the presence of the Augusta, before anyone began the debate, it happened that God brought about an extraordinary and wondrous <event> worthy of report [p. 247] that exposed[379] the evil and baseness lurking in the dark recesses <of the patriarch's soul>, while the blessed <Symeon revealed> the virtue in his simple character and his accomplishments. For Michael, that is the young emperor,[380] who was still quite a little lad, while playing next to his mother and sitting beside her, kept pointing out the patriarch with his finger and calling him "bad grandfather" with lisping baby talk.[381] Even though <the patriarch> was familiar and well known <to Michael>, when he wished to be near him, <the boy> pushed him away and shook him off; but <he kept calling> Symeon "good" and clearly enjoyed being near him; he would joy-

[377] ἐγκύκλιος παίδευσις: the education that succeeded primary education, most likely in this period undertaken from approximately ages 11 to 17. This training could include secular (classical) as well as religious education. Subjects probably included grammar, rhetoric, and philosophy, the classical trivium that would have served as the foundation for theological debate. See Lemerle, *Byz. Humanism,* 112–13 and n. 88.

[378] A *topos* that probably had as its model the Life of Antony the Great, which featured debates between Greek philosophers and Antony, described as illiterate and educated in the Scriptures alone; cf. *v. Ant.,* chaps. 72–80.

[379] Reading δημοσιεῦον for δημοσιεύοντος with Phountoules, and placing a comma instead of a period after θαυμάσιον, so as to continue sentence from Chap. 28 (in van den Gheyn ed.) into Chap. 29.

[380] Michael III was born 19 January 840, and reigned from 842 to 867. Since the year of the convocation is 843, he would have been about three years old at the time of the episode. For Michael's birthdate, see C. Mango, "When Was Michael III Born?" *DOP* 21 (1967), 253–58. The *Acta* are thus more accurate than some of the chronicles, which allege that Michael was about five at the time of the convocation.

[381] The phrase "bad grandfather" (πάππος) is evidently meant to indicate that the toddler Michael recognized John the Grammarian's wickedness, in spite of the latter's intimate relationship with the family, and preferred the unfamiliar and forbidding Symeon. "Grandfather" is apparently used here in a generic sense for an old man, for although John was related to Theodora through the marriage of her sister Kalomaria to John's brother Arsaber (*TheophCont* 175.3; ps.-Sym. Mag. 647.10), he was not a member of the immediate family.

fully grasp his knees with both hands and gently fix his gaze upon his face, and reveal to his mother the loving disposition of his soul toward the holy man. This seemed strange to those present there and <they realized> that it was not without the forethought of God that a baby still babbling and cherished in his mother's arms should appear to embrace and talk to and take pleasure in a strange and unfamiliar <man> who presented a disagreeable appearance to children because of his ascetism and his garb. But to his mother, the empress, and the assembled crowd this wonder seemed ordained of God, while the face of the unholy patriarch was filled with immeasurable shame.

Then Symeon directed his speech toward the patriarch, saying, "Let the orator[382] speak, if you have something to say from divine inspiration. For I am *rude in speech, yet not in knowledge,*[383] and am inexperienced in all sophistry and *enticing words.*[384] For *our help* and strength *is in the name of the Lord Who made heaven and earth.*"[385] And he [John VII], who a short time before had spoken *great words* and bragged and *magnified* his own *tongue* and boasted that his own *lips were*[386] under his control, was cut off[387] in mid-sentence like a country bumpkin; the result was that those present with the empress were greatly amazed at such an unexpected sight and sent up praise to God Who so magnified His servant. Then the Christ-loving and pious empress said to Symeon without hesitation, "Go, father, and with God's help take counsel with people of like mind to you about a worthy bishop of the church [patriarch] and cast your votes

---

[382] ῥήτωρ. Byzantium retained public roles for trained orators, especially in the church. Sermons, ceremonial speeches, and theological debates followed rules of rhetoric derived from classical models. Rhetoric remained the basis of Byzantine education during the 8th and 9th centuries, and John was only one of several patriarchs known for their skill in rhetoric. In a world where oral communication still predominated, spoken rhetoric was the art cultivated by the educational system. Symeon's subsequent quotation from Corinthians reinforces the contrast between the skilled rhetor and the inspired ascetic. See "Rhetoric," *ODB* 3:1788–90, and Lemerle, *Byz. Humanism,* chap. 4.

[383] 2 Cor. 11:6.

[384] Cf. Col. 2:4.

[385] Ps. 123 (124):8.

[386] Ps. 11 (12):4.

[387] Reading ἀπελήφθη for ἀπελήθη.

together."[388] And the divine man, rewarding the empress and her children with prayers, said, "See here, most excellent mistress, in consideration of [p. 248] God's love for mankind, we, too, accept your husband, our emperor, among the pious as orthodox, nor will we ever condemn him to anathema. But with regard to this man," referring to the patriarch, "he simply will not be driven from his throne until he makes an attempt upon his life."[389] When these <words> had been said by the holy man, that famed heretic left the palace without farewell and breathing rage. But the Augusta was filled with great joy because of the assurance she received from Symeon about her own husband's salvation; so she sent him away with appropriate recognition to take counsel with those of like mind about what needed to be done.

As the great man [Symeon] left and was going along the street, a certain poor beggar addressed him loudly, "Are you listening, sir?" And he said, "Yes." And <the beggar> said, "Know that no one will topple the patriarch from his throne except for this monk who is passing by."[390] And he indicated <Symeon> with his finger. When the father heard these words from God,[391] he said to his companion named Theophilos,[392] "Did you hear what the beggar said?" And he said, "Yes, master, not I alone, but also many others." And the

---

[388] Compare the *vita* of Michael the Synkellos, where Theodora is said to have asked Michael to accept the patriarchal position and, upon his refusal, to have sought Ioannikios' advice on an appropriate candidate. (*v. Mich. Sync.,* chaps. 25–26); according to the Life of Ioannikios by Sabas, the saint predicted the ascent of Methodios to the patriarchate (*v. Ioannic. a Sab.* 371c–372a); according to the Life of Methodios, although "many great and holy men were proposed, only Methodios was approved" (*v. Method.,* chap. 10; PG 100:1253b). The chronicle account of Theophanes Continuatus places the selection of Methodios with Theodora's advisers Theoktistos and Bardas (*TheophCont* 151.9–22). While the story of Symeon's influence is unlikely to be historical, the text shares with other hagiographical accounts an attempt to emphasize that Methodios was not merely an imperial candidate, but the selection of the monastic leaders. The stories may reflect the versions of the supporters of Methodios against their Stoudite opponents, as well as imperial need to assure monastic support for Methodios.

[389] After ἐξελαθήσεται add ἕως οὗ αὐτόχειρ ἑαυτοῦ γενήσεται as in Phountoules. This is a prediction of John's faked attempt at suicide; see Chap. 30, below.

[390] The beggar is apparently referring to Symeon, whose prophecy results in Theodora's dismissal of John VII (cf. *Acta,* 250.10–14).

[391] Reading ἀθεεὶ for ἀθεὶ.

[392] This individual is not mentioned elsewhere in the biography.

father said to him, "Know, father Theophilos, <that> as Gideon heard in the camp of Midian one man explaining to another his dream and its interpretation,[393] in the same way the Lord according to His dispensation has entrusted to this brother [the beggar] to reveal what will happen so that we having heard may be all the more zealous."

When he came to the Kanikleiou quarter, he explained to all his people the unexpected miracles wrought by God in the palace, how the eloquent patriarch had had his tongue muzzled by divine forethought and was not even able to dispute with him, and how "the empress moved by God entrusted us with God's help to elect the patriarch." When the priests and monks present and the whole rest of the enormous crowd heard <this>, all as from one mouth raised one voice of glory and praise to God so that the shout resounded for a great distance. To the great one [Symeon] they said, "Holy father, we have you after God as a guide and unshakable tower of dogma. Whomever God indicates to you,[394] we will all follow him and we will accept the decision as from God." And he said to them, "To me, all-holy and God-gathered congregation, [p. 249] it seems that no one exceeds in honor the confessor, father Methodios, both in wisdom and the excellence of his virtue and his good deeds on behalf of piety. That's how it seems to me, brothers, but express frankly your opinion." Upon hearing this, the multitude shouted with one voice by acclamation, "<You have spoken> not from yourself,[395] but God in you, father, has spoken this. So let this[396] decision remain irrevocable, with God's help." When the blessed man had greatly thanked God for the people's unity of thought and had said, "*Let the name of the Lord be blessed, from this present time and for ever,*"[397] he ordered an all-night service of hymnody to the Lord to be held on the coming night.

30. At dawn he took that great phalanx of people and they raised on high

---

[393] Reading σύγκρισιν for σύγκρυσιν; cf. Judg. 7:13–15. Before a battle against the Midianites God ordered Gideon to sneak into the enemy camp, where he overheard one soldier report his dream to another. In the dream a loaf of bread rolled into the Midianite camp and smashed a tent. The second soldier interpreted the bread to be "none other than the sword of Gideon, son of Joash, a man of Israel: for God has delivered Midian and all the host into his hand."

[394] Reading ἐπινεύσῃ σοι for ἐπινεύσησοι.

[395] ἀφ᾽ ἑαυτοῦ: third person reflexive used for second; cf. Liddell-Scott, *Lexicon,* s.v. II.

[396] Reading αὕτη for αὐτὴ.

[397] Ps. 112 (113):2.

with their hands the all-holy icon of our Lord and of the Mother of God who bore Him and openly carried it through the street in public <procession>;[398] they gathered at the church called by the all-glorious name of our Savior, Christ,[399] and from there they made known their arrival to the empress. She delayed not at all but went down into the so-called Magnaura[400] and saw that

---

[398] The ceremonial procession of Methodios, which symbolized the public announcement of the restoration of icons, took place on 11 March 843, the first Sunday in Lent. It became the central act in the annual commemoration of the Triumph of Orthodoxy. The procession is mentioned in several accounts of the event, and its description in the *Book of Ceremonies* dates from the time of Michael III, with revisions in the 10th century ("De Ceremoniis," *ODB* 1:595–97). By the end of the 9th century, the annual procession led from the church of the Theotokos at Blachernai to Hagia Sophia. The church of the Virgin at Blachernai was symbolic both of early events in the history of Byzantium and of the triumph over iconoclasm. The basilica of the Virgin was located in the northwest corner of the city of Constantinople, outside the Theodosian walls and near the Golden Horn. It became the most famous shrine to the Virgin in Constantinople after the "Virgin's Robe" was brought there from Palestine in the 5th century. In the iconoclast period, the basilica at Blachernai was the site of the final session of the iconoclast Council of Hieria in 754 that promulgated the decree against images. An icon of the Virgin at the church figured prominently in public ceremonies of the 7th century: in 626, the icon of the Virgin of Blachernai, carried in procession by the son of the emperor Herakleios, was credited with saving the city from the Avar siege. The *vita* of Stephen the Younger also describes a miraculous icon of the Virgin in the church: the mother of the saint prayed there for the conception of a child, addressing a miraculous icon of the Virgin that was venerated on Friday evenings; cf. *v. Stephan. Jun.* 1076B, 1080B. The *Acta* do not mention the church of Blachernai, but center the description of the procession on an icon, which the author may have identified with the church. Other accounts (Genes. 60.77–79; *TheophCont* 160.2–9) do not identify any particular icon with the event; the *Narratio de absolutione Theophili* claims that icons were set up again in Hagia Sophia at the end of the ceremony (Regel, *Analecta,* 38–39). Since any miraculous icons associated with the church would have been removed, and no tradition before the 11th century describes the miraculous preservation or finding of the early icon of the Virgin, it is likely that this detail is an anachronism. Detailed analysis of the sources for the procession can be found in Gouillard, "Synodikon," 129–38.

[399] The allusion to the church of the Savior Christ is almost certainly anachronistic, if it refers to the chapel of Christ in Chalke, which seems likely. This chapel, part of the main vestibule of the imperial palace, was not built until the 10th century; see Janin, *Eglises CP,* 529–30; "Chalke," *ODB* 1:405–6; Gouillard, "Synodikon," 132; and n. 403, below.

[400] The basilica at the edge of the Great Palace that was the reception hall for foreign ambassadors and for imperial addresses to the people; cf. "Magnaura," *ODB* 2:1267–68.

angelic throng and learned from Symeon <the name of> the bishop [patri-
arch] who had been elected; and she ratified their decision and ordered that
they celebrate the divine mystery in the church of God and invited them to
dine with her in the palace.[401]

As the procession confidently traversed the street between the Milion[402]
and the so-called Chalke Gate[403] and shouted loudly in exultation "Lord, have
mercy," the patriarch [John VII], stunned by the sound, learned the reason for
it from his attendants: that the multitude was escorting Methodios with a brilliant procession <complete> with icons and that he [Methodios] had been
appointed patriarch and they were proceeding into the palace. He was driven
out of his mind [p. 250] and, since he was alone in a cell of the *katechoumena*,[404]
and despairing of his rule <as patriarch>, he stabbed himself in the side at
the rib with a little knife with which he trimmed his nails—but not in a vital
place; and he shouted loudly, "Come quickly, I am being violently murdered
by the murderous iconiates" (for that's what he usually called those who venerated icons). His attendants had run there quickly and asked, "Where are the
murderers?" But when they examined the precipitous drop from the window

[401] In the description in the *Book of Ceremonies* the celebration of the Triumph of
Orthodoxy closed with a banquet in the patriarchal palace; cf. Const. Porph., *De cer.*
1:156–60, and Gouillard, "Synodikon," 130–31.

[402] Located in the central Augustaion square in front of Hagia Sophia, the Milion
was the initial milestone of the empire, from which led the Mese, the major avenue of
Constantinople. A monumental structure, like a triumphal arch, adorned with imperial
statues, it was a stopping point for imperial processions; cf. Janin, *CP byz.*, 103–4.

[403] The Chalke Gate, the entrance to the Great Palace, had symbolic as well as imperial significance as a destination for the procession. The bronze gate (named either for
its bronze roof or doors) was the location of public events connected with imperial
policy about icons. Leo III's first public act in opposition to the veneration of icons
was the removal of the icon of Christ that was located on the facade, in 726 or 730; see
Life of St. Theodosia, above. The icon was restored by Irene and removed again by
Leo V in 817. In addition to the bibliography cited above in n. 399, see C. Mango, *The
Brazen House* (Copenhagen, 1959), and Auzépy, "Chalcé," 445–92.

[404] In early Christianity, catechumens were candidates for baptism who attended separate services and were segregated from full participants in the services. Although the
separate service for the catechumenate was compressed into a single service with the
introduction of infant baptism, church galleries were still known as *katechoumena* after
the 7th century; see "Catechumenate," *ODB* 1:390–91. John was apparently in the bal-
cony of Hagia Sophia.

to which the coward pointed and saw no one at all, finding only the little knife with blood on it, the fool was convicted of making an attempt on his own life out of his love of power.[405] When word of such an unholy deed spread throughout the city and came to the ears of the Augusta and orthodox people, they remembered Symeon's clear prophecy,[406] and the empress dismissed the thrice-wretched man from the patriarchate and the city against his will and exiled him.[407] And rejoicing in the Lord with the orthodox throng (for it was Cheese-eating Sunday),[408] she dismissed them in peace and said, "Go, honored fathers, and during the first week of Lent which is just now here, let each of you propitiate God with prayers and fasts, as is customary, and on Sunday let all of you come together in prayerful procession in the Great Church of God [Hagia Sophia] and fulfill the will of God." Taking their leave and making customary prayers for the empress, they went home rejoicing. On the first Sunday of Lent, they gathered in the most holy church of God and installed Methodios in the high priestly and lofty throne, and appointed Symeon *synkellos* of the patriarchate with the assent of the Augusta,[409] and they gave him the monas-

---

[405] Variations of this story are included in several 10th-century chronicles (*Theoph-Cont* 151.2–9; ps.-Sym. Mag. 648.10–649.3; and Genes. 57–58).

[406] See above, Chap. 29: "But about this man," referring to the patriarch <John>, "he simply will not be driven from his throne until he makes an attempt upon his life."

[407] The next few sentences are a restatement of the events just recounted in Chaps. 29–30; they suggest that the author was following two sources for his account and described the expulsion of John and election of Methodios twice as he followed them.

[408] The Sunday preceding Lent. Lent originally lasted six weeks, but was extended by a pre-Lenten fast known as "Cheesefare Week" so that it would include forty days of fasting; cf. "Lent," *ODB* 2:1205–6.

[409] The term *synkellos* (lit., "cell-mate") denoted an adviser to a patriarch. By the 10th century the office was an imperial nomination and generally denoted the successor-designate to a patriarch; cf. "Synkellos," *ODB* 3:1993–94; Darrouzès, *Offikia*, 17–19. The author's reference is problematic, since the Life of Michael the Synkellos and his *synaxarion* notice claim that he was appointed to the office by Methodios at the command of Michael and Theodora and held it until his death in 846 (*v. Mich. Sync.*, chap. 27; *SynaxCP* 324–26). S. Efthymiadis ("Correspondence of Theodore," 153 and n. 53) has recently suggested (on the basis of a law of Herakleios limiting the number of *synkelloi* to two) that Methodios appointed both Symeon and Michael as *synkelloi*, and notes a seal of a 9th-century abbot of Sts. Sergios and Bacchos who was also a *synkellos*.

tery of Sts. Sergios and Bacchos[410] as a residence for his disciples and a retreat for him; and they proclaimed and decreed as doctrine the setting up and veneration of the holy icons.

31. When the affairs of the Church were by the forethought of God prospering as they should, the great Methodios summoned Symeon and entreated and advised him concerning his brother George,[411] whom he wished to appoint as bishop of Ephesos.[412] [p. 251] And <Symeon> said, "If he is willing, I have no objection." This settled, each departed to his assigned abode. When Symeon communicated the patriarch's wishes to his brother, however, he found the blessed man reluctant and difficult to persuade because of his humility; for the man of God [George] averred that he was unworthy and unequal to such a very great ministry. So <Symeon> immediately informed the patriarch of his brother's refusal. But the godly minded Methodios, prompted by God in this <matter>, could not bear to keep quiet <about this>, but shared the situation with the empress. She received the report with <some> pleasure [because of his humility and her opportunity for a ruse] and summoned the wondrous pair of brothers; and she employed soothing and gentle words with

[410] The monastery of Sts. Sergios and Bacchos, founded by Justinian and Theodora and located near the palace of Hormisdas, was the scene of iconoclast trials. John the Grammarian was appointed abbot by Leo V in 814, and texts and letters describe it as the location of his interrogations of the chronographer Theophanes, Theodore of Stoudios, Plato of Sakkoudion, and one of Theodore's disciples; cf. Janin, *Eglises CP*, 451–54. There is no other record of a Symeon as abbot of the monastery.

[411] This sentence marks a transition from Symeon to George, who reappears in the story, and may reflect the author's attempt to make a transition between two sources: a Life of a Symeon, stylite and confessor, centered in Constantinople, and a Lesbos-centered account of bishop George, whose activities in the capital so far included only taking a more moderate view than his brother Symeon regarding Theodora's desire to rescue the memory of Theophilos from anathema (Chap. 27, above).

[412] Methodios, as patriarch, would appoint metropolitan archbishops, with the consent of the empress. Ephesos was one of the leading metropolitan sees of the empire, and at the end of the 8th century it still had thirty-nine subordinate bishoprics attached to it. Several of its 9th-century bishops are known, including Theophilos the Confessor, a correspondent of Theodore of Stoudios who died after 829; Mark, sent on an embassy to Louis the Pious in 833; Theodore; and Basil, who attended the Council of 869. It would be natural to expect that this important appointment would go to a strong iconophile capable of playing a leading role in the church, and that Greek education in religious letters would be expected. See "Ephèse," *DHGE* 15:554–61; P. Culerrier, "Les évêchés suffragants d'Ephèse aux 5e–13e siècles," *REB* 45 (1987), 139–64.

them. Addressing Symeon she said, "Why, father, have you refused the request of the patriarch about the see of Ephesos?" She introduced this <notion> cleverly. And when he [Symeon] figured out the stratagem (for if anyone was ever shrewd, he was), <he said>, "Because I am sinful and beneath it."[413] She quickly <replied>, "It is written: '*Instead of thy fathers children are born to thee.*'[414] So, look, let your brother accept the ministry in your place." The most gentle and humble George was grievously afflicted by her words and openly rejected <the offer>. But the Christ-loving, in fact God-loving, empress <said> to him, "But if you run away from the see of Ephesos, you will at least not desert <the bishopric> of your homeland; for I will compel you *to obey*[415] those in authority even if you are unwilling and it is not to your liking." <George> fell to his knees and in a gentle and calm voice implored her, saying that he declined the lofty bishopric of Ephesos because he was a country person and uneducated;[416] and <he declined> that of his homeland because of its wretched poverty so that it was not even able to pay its taxes because of its deep misfortune. But she seized upon this excuse and said, "I will find a remedy for all the misfortunes of your homeland." And immediately she summoned the *logothetes tou genikou*[417] and ordered that it be confirmed with an imperial decree that no taxes should be demanded from Lesbos as long as this Father George continued among the living as bishop. She gave him in

---

[413] ποδῶν ὑστερεῖσθαι: The derivation of this idiom is not clear; it may mean "losing the use of (Liddell-Scott, *Lexicon*, s.v. ὑστερέω, IV) his feet," i.e., being unable to walk well, or "being inferior to the feet," an allusion to 1 Cor. 12:15, 21, 22, meaning "unworthy."

[414] Ps. 44 (45):16.

[415] Tit. 3:1.

[416] ἄγροικος καὶ ἀγράμματος: the description could mean that George was illiterate, or that he lacked the secondary education in grammar and Greek usage, religious or secular, that would be expected of the archbishop of a major see. The brief account of George's training with his brother Symeon and the bishop of Mytilene (Chap. 10) makes no reference to his education. The author's comments here suggest that education (or perhaps literacy) was not thought necessary for a provincial bishopric like Mytilene in the mid-9th century.

[417] Reading γενικὸν for γενικῶν. The *Genikon* was the imperial department responsible for the assessment of land taxes, and was headed in the 9th century by a *logothetes*, one of a number of high fiscal officials who headed the centralized departments of the imperial bureaucracy. See "Logothetes" and "Genikon," *ODB* 2:1247 and 829–30; R. Guilland, "Les logothètes," *REB* 29 (1971), 11–24.

addition three thousand blankets[418] and the same number of tunics and fifteen pounds of gold and, of silver coins, drachmas[419] weighing two pounds, and copper coins[420] weighing three <pounds>[421] from her husband's property left to her for the relief of the poor, saying, "Give these things to the poor [p. 252] of your homeland and do not refuse a leadership of mankind that profits the soul." When he [George] saw the sincere appeal of the Augusta and her abundant and truly imperial provision of the necessities <of life>, and when he remembered the vision of the Mother of God that had appeared to him the previous night, which had commanded him beforehand not to refuse the patriarch and the empress,[422] he decided to accept the see of his homeland. So he

[418] σαγία: small "blankets" or "cloaks"; cf. Liddell-Scott, *Lexicon,* s.v. Here it must mean "blanket," since the same items are described on p. 253.27 as νυκτερινοῖς ἐνδύμασι, "nighttime blankets."

[419] δραχμάς: No 9th-century saint's Life or other Byzantine literary text refers to the Byzantine silver coin, the miliaresion, as a drachma, a silver coin of ancient Greece; however, drachma is the standard Greek translation for the Roman denarius, a silver coin of approximately the same weight (about 4 g), but one not minted since the reign of Constantine the Great. The use of the term drachma here may be explained as either an archaism, a regular feature of this author's style, or as a deliberate attempt to distinguish the heavy (about 3.4 g) miliaresia introduced by Theophilos early in his reign from his later coins of the traditional weight (2.27 g). For a discussion of the coinage of Theophilos, see P. Grierson, *Catalogue of the Byzantine Coins in the Dumbarton Oaks Collection and in the Whittemore Collection* 3.1 (Washington, D.C., 1973), 406–51, pls. XXII–XXVII, and idem, *Byzantine Coins* (Berkeley, Calif., 1982), 172–87 and plates; also, S. Boutin, *Monnaies des empires de Byzance* (Maastricht, 1983), nos. 533–34, for examples of the solidus (nomisma) and miliaresion. The miliaresion was exchanged at the rate of twelve to the gold solidus and the copper (not bronze) follis at twenty-four to the miliaresion.

[420] Reading φόλλεις for φόλεις.

[421] Note that Theodora's donations are described by weight (two or three pounds) rather than monetary value or numbers of coins, even though the silver and copper is distributed in coins. In the early 9th century, three pounds of gold would have been the annual salary for a turmarch, a provincial commander of approximately 5,000 soldiers, according to W. Treadgold, *The Byzantine State Finances in the Eighth and Ninth Centuries* (New York, 1982), 99. Theophilos was known for his wealth and the issuance of gold nomismata and redesigned copper coins (folleis); cf. Treadgold, *Byz. Revival,* 283–89.

[422] No vision of the Mother of God by George has been mentioned earlier in the text. In contrast, in sections dealing with Symeon, the author is careful to present visions and prophecies in detail and return to their fulfillment later in the text as evidence for Symeon's holiness (for example, his dream of Theophilos asking for mercy;

was sent to the bishop [i.e., patriarch] Methodios by the empress and installed <as bishop> at the age of eighty.[423] After the anointing, when a horse was brought to him to ride, he took hold of the saddle[424] and <saying>, "Woe to the monk seated between two curves!"[425] (that is what he called the curved <parts> of the saddle), the blessed one refused to ride but made the journey on foot, as was his custom, to his residence. This <incident> caused many to be astonished and to marvel at the man's humility and incited them to divine love and imitation of him.

<Then> Petronas, the empress' brother, summoned him, supposedly for <an act of> kindness, and laid bare the complete confession of his deeds, and as atonement for his sins gave eight pounds[426] of gold to the holy man and three hundred tunics and the same number of blankets.[427] The blessed <George> prayed for the forgiveness of his sins and predicted and prophesied

---

the beggar's statement that John the Grammarian would attempt suicide before he resigned). Was George's vision described in a section of the biography now lost, or not used by the author?

[423] This chronology would place George's birth in approximately 763. In Chap. 8, the author describes Symeon's adoption by his brother David in 772; he was then eight years old (Chap. 9) and his mother's youngest child. George is said to be older than Symeon (Chap. 11) and a twin to Hilaria (Chap. 12).

[424] ἐφεστρίδος.

[425] Or "whores" (κουρβῶν). The author makes George pun on two senses of κούρβα and implicitly derides riding and luxury as being as inappropriate for monks as prostitution. For a parallel use of κούρβα in a hagiographical text as part of a saddle, see Delehaye, *Saints stylites,* 47. See also the lexica of Liddell-Scott, Sophocles, and Du Cange, s.v. κούρβα. In modern Greek slang κουβάς means "whore," in Russian slang *kurva* means "whore"; the Russian is a relatively mild general obscenity that can be used of a man. George puns on two homophonic Greek borrowings from Latin, the first probably a femininization of *corvus* (obscene), meaning "fellator" (C. T. Lewis and C. Short, *Harper's Latin Dictionary* [New York, 1907], s.v. II.4.C), and the second, more properly applied to a curved saddle, the adjective *curvus.* The first vowel of either might possibly be represented as ου. See Ševčenko, "Hagiography," 118 n. 34, and E. Kriaras, Λεξικό της μεσαιωνικής Ἑλληνικῆς δημώδους γραμματείας, 1100–1669, 3 (Thessalonike, 1982), 334, for a full discussion, bibliography, and related lexical entries.

[426] A pun on λύτρου, "atonement," and λίτρας, "pounds."

[427] On Petronas, see above, Chap. 28, n. 369. In the Life of Antony the Younger (ed. F. Halkin, "Saint Antoine le Jeune et Pétronas le vainqueur des Arabes en 863," *Anal-Boll* 62 [1944], 215–17), Petronas is cured by the saint after an illness and visions of a demon who claims ownership of his soul. The saint then becomes a spiritual father to Petronas.

his victory over and total annihilation of the Assyrian [i.e., Arab] Amer that would occur at a later time by divine decision.[428] When Bardas[429] learned that his brother had done this deed because of his love for God, he was fired with zeal and asked George to come to him without delay. And so the great one also went to him and received a confession of his deeds [sins], and took for distribution to the poor ten pounds of gold and three hundred tunics and the same number of woolen blankets. And as he shared <Bardas'> table he prophesied the summit of the highest office which would soon be granted <to him> and his final certain death in this <position>.[430]

----

[428] In September, 863, Petronas led the Byzantine army that defeated the forces of Umar, emir of Melitene, at Po<r>son. The battle was a major victory for Byzantium in its attempts to retake the offensive against the Arabs and establish its eastern border. The predictions of holy men are associated with the event in several sources: Antony the Younger predicted the victory to Petronas when the imperial orders to campaign were received (Halkin, "Antoine le Jeune," chap. 15); the chronicle of Theophanes Continuatus includes in its account of the campaign the predictions of John, a monk from the monastic center of Latros, that the Byzantines would win the battle (*TheophCont* 180.13–181.2). These prophecies are said to have taken place close to the battle rather than twenty years earlier, as is the case in the *Acta*. If the *Acta* are a late composition, their author could have known and used either story as a model for George's demonstration of holy prescience. The victory at Po<r>son in 863 has been considered a terminus post quem for the composition of the biography, since the author must have known the outcome of the battle to include the prediction (Kazhdan, "Hagiographical Notes," 187).

[429] See above, Chap. 28, n. 368.

[430] τὴν ἐπὶ ταύτης τελευταίαν ἀσφαλῆ τούτῳ κατάλυσιν. The interpretation of this passage is very important for the dating of the composition of the text. In 855 Theodora's brother Bardas conspired with Michael III to seize power, by dethroning Theodora and having Theoktistos arrested and killed. He was given several high offices by Michael (then about fifteen years old) and in 862 was crowned as caesar, a title ordinarily reserved for the emperor's sons. Bardas was assassinated, in turn, by Basil I in 866, a deed in which Michael is considered by many to have been compromised. George's prophecy for Bardas is that he will reach the highest office (τῆς ὑπερτάτης ἀρχῆς) and what we have translated as "a final certain death in <the office>" (τὴν ἐπὶ ταύτης τελευταίαν ἀσφαλῆ τούτῳ κατάλυσιν). This translation makes the prophecy a foretelling of the assassination as well as the promotion of Bardas, and would give the year 866 as a terminus post quem for the composition of the text. The author would be, in this case, following the standard practice of putting in the mouth of the saint a prophecy of an event he knew to have happened.

A. Kazhdan has used the same passage to argue that the text was written *before* 866,

<Then> after making the customary prayer for him, he left for his own home.

32. Since everything <had turned out>[431] well, it was necessary for the holy pair of Fathers who were brothers no less in their souls than in their bodies, having justly and evangelically [p. 253] run the race of confession in Constantinople[432] and having supported the church of God and restored piety in an orthodox manner, to go also to their homeland and to secure it in orthodox dogmas and to sanctify it and illumine it with miracles. <So> they bade farewell to the Augusta and the patriarch and embarked on an imperial warship[433] that the empress kindly provided for them. They were tearfully seen off at their departure by all the members of the senate and the clergy who could not endure losing them. <But> they prayed for them all and *bid farewell* to all *with a holy kiss*[434] and sailed off to their homeland.

When they got there [Mytilene] and the warship had put into the harbor,

---

and that the passage should be translated as "a final *safe* end" ("Hagiographical Notes," 188). The word ἀσφαλῆ can have both meanings, and most often means "safe," but it would be out of character for an author to put a prediction of the manner of death in the mouth of a saint unless he could be certain it would be fulfilled. Thus, we believe that the sentence should be taken to demonstrate that the author wrote *after* the assassination of Bardas. Although the "sins" confessed by Bardas in this passage would have taken place after George's visit with him, the author may have had them in mind. Parallel uses of the word κατάλυσις to mean "death" can be found in the *vitae* of Peter of Atroa (*v. Petr. Atr.* 89.13); Tarasios (*v. Taras.* 398.34); and Theodora of Thessalonike (*v. Theod. Thess.* 224.31 [= *Translatio et miracula,* chap. 16.31]).

[431] Add ἐγένετο or the like.

[432] Symeon's exile from Constantinople as a confessor is described in Chap. 23. George, however, was not in Constantinople during the reigns of Michael and Theophilos, but joined Symeon only at the news of the impending restoration of orthodoxy (Chap. 26).

[433] *dromon:* the two-masted ship, usually with one bank of rowers, that was the main warship of the Byzantine navy. It carried as many as 230 warriors, and could be used to launch Greek fire or to fire catapults; cf. "Dromon," *ODB* 1:662. Note that the holy brothers made their earlier voyages in small merchant boats. The author's description is undoubtedly meant to convey the esteem that the brothers now enjoyed, and an imperial desire to demonstrate government authority to the island. Imperial warships probably were used on occasion to herald the arrival and demonstrate the significance of an official to a provincial capital. It is unlikely that the bishop of a relatively minor see would in reality be given such ceremonial transportation.

[434] 1 Cor. 16:20.

the people learned of the arrival of the God-bearing men. <Then> one could see rivers of people flowing down from the city into the harbors—<people of> every age, of every type, men, women and children, government officials, members of the clergy—all in festal attire and carrying palm branches in their hands. They carried the icons of the saints and of the Lord's cross[435] and made the air smoky with torches and perfumed oil, and welcomed and escorted the holy men with hymns and songs; and they all longed to revel in that sweet sight of the holy men and in the celebration <of their coming>.[436] And so as the city made this procession for the holy men, eventually they arrived at the church of the all-pure Mother of God (where the noble men had angelically performed their ascetic exercises)[437] and celebrated the Feast of her [Mary's] Birth.[438] There the great <George>, truly their shepherd, welcomed the multi-

---

[435] It is not clear what is meant by the τοῦ κυριακοῦ σταυροῦ εἰκόνας. Perhaps it is a reference to icons of the Crucifixion or to cruciform icons, of which examples survive only on Sinai; cf. K. Weitzmann, "Three Painted Crosses," in *Studies in the Arts at Sinai. Essays by K. Weitzmann* (Princeton, N.J., 1982), pt. XIV.

[436] This passage offers an excellent description of an *adventus*—the ceremonial arrival of a bishop, relics, or imperial official in a city. The ceremony, which went back to late antiquity, involved distinct features described here: the populace went outside the city (here, to the harbor) to welcome the official, who was greeted with lights, incense, and ceremonial hymns or liturgies. Icons and ceremonial crosses were probably regularly carried in such processions in the 9th century, but here, where the event celebrates the return of icon veneration to the city, the inclusion of icons would have been especially symbolic. The official then went in procession to a church or shrine; cf. "Adventus," *ODB* 1:25–26; S. MacCormack, *Art and Ceremony in Late Antiquity* (Berkeley, Calif., 1981). The best-known ceremonies were imperial, and they are reflected in their greatest elaboration in the *Book of Ceremonies*. Saints' Lives of the 7th century, especially the Life of Theodore of Sykeon, describe *adventus* ceremonies involving the welcome of bishops to provincial cities in Asia Minor as a demonstration of the symbolic importance of an official's presence and authority in a city. This passage provides valuable evidence of the continuity of the ceremony in the provinces in the middle Byzantine period.

[437] From the context here and in Chap. 10, it is clear that the church of the Mother of God (Theotokos) was the brothers' monastery, located close to the site of Symeon's column near Molos; see n. 118 above.

[438] The Feast of the Birth of the Virgin was celebrated as one of the Great Feasts of the Orthodox church on 8 September in the liturgy of Constantinople. The celebration involved an all-night vigil on the eve of the ceremony and a liturgy on the festival day; see "Birth of the Virgin" and "Great Feasts," *ODB* 1:291, 2:868–69. This passage demonstrates that the Constantinopolitan liturgy was followed in Lesbos. The holy man's use of the festival as an occasion for public charity would have reinforced his

tude with holy words of teaching and fortified them with prayers; he approved of their eager reception of them and the procession and thanked them, generously bestowing upon the poor the silver and gold and daytime tunics and nighttime blankets, and then sent them all home in peace; for it was grape harvest time.[439]

When the day of veneration of the life-giving Cross arrived, <the day> on which the Church of God has ordained to the pious that they should all celebrate a festival of the venerable Wood [i.e., the Cross] elevated by the hands of the priests, the commander[440] of the island wanted to perform the investiture to the bishop's throne and the installation of the wondrous George; <so> through heralds he proclaimed that everyone should come at the festival of the Elevation <of the Cross>.[441] Therefore [p. 254] the people flowed in such

---

authority in the island and role as economic provider for the people; see n. 318, above, on charity and distribution of food and necessities.

[439] Wine was the staple beverage of the Byzantine Empire, and grapes a major crop in many parts of the empire. Grape harvesting and wine production are frequently illustrated in Byzantine manuscripts and mosaics depicting autumn.

[440] στρατηγός, a term normally referring to the commander of a theme. As mentioned above (n. 33) the administrative status of Lesbos in the mid-9th century is uncertain. Oikonomidès (*Listes,* 47 and n. 19) uses this passage as evidence that the Aegean Sea, which was certainly a theme by the 10th century (Const. Porph., *De them.,* chap. 17, line 22), had attained that status by 843. Four *droungarioi* and three *strategoi* are known from seals dated to the 9th or early 10th centuries; cf. Zacos, *Seals,* 1:1887, 1969, 2360, 3167; 2:122, 232, 243.

The fact that the commander is represented as ordering the ceremony of installation is significant in indicating the role of the imperial government in the oversight of the provincial church in Byzantium. Contrary to the situation in western Europe, the investiture of bishops did not become an issue for a church-state controversy in Byzantium.

[441] The Feast of the Elevation of the Cross, celebrated on 14 September, became one of the central liturgical events of the rite of Constantinople, where it was associated with the relics of the wood of the True Cross. In Hagia Sophia in the middle Byzantine period the feast was preceded by four days of veneration of the wood relics, and followed by a weeklong ritual of observance. Following a solemn vigil, the feast was celebrated with a ritual that involved a patriarchal procession with the relic and its elevation to the four corners of the Earth followed by a patriarchal banquet. The feast symbolized the Cross as the means of universal salvation. Since the iconoclast emperors emphasized veneration of the Cross as the only legitimate icon, the feast may have gained importance during this period. This passage reflects the importance that the rite held in a provincial bishopric not known to have possessed relics of the Cross; thus, it indicates the generalization of the feast as a central liturgical event of the church calendar; cf. "Cross, Cult of the," *ODB* 1:551–53.

streams that the place was too cramped for their numbers. They <then> held an all-night festival with their shepherd in the church of the Mother of God in which he was lodged.[442] At daybreak the commander and his retinue, dressed in their finest, along with the multitude escorted the bishop with torches (as was appropriate) and hymns to the shrine of the martyr Theodora,[443] raised the man of God to the rank of bishop in accordance with the canons and installed him.[444] <Then> angels were heard singing the Trisagion[445] to the Lord and receiving the people's praise and acclamation of the saint that reached high as heaven, and they also rejoiced with them and shared in the celebration.

Finally, after the bloodless and *spiritual sacrifice*[446] had been performed and the solemnization of the sacred rites for the holy man, as was required, the disciple of the peaceful Christ blessed them all, and also said and gave the blessing "Peace to all." Then he addressed all the people, <saying>, "Brothers and fathers in the Lord and dear children, after receiving the holy gifts [the Eucharist], come here to this vineyard" (indicating a small <one>) "that belongs to the church of God and is near it and do each of you enter and take a bunch of grapes as a gift." <This was to be the> first miracle that God showed to the people through him after his installation, <demonstrating> what sort of *husbandman*[447] the <newly> installed <bishop George> would

---

[442] He was lodged no doubt in the monastery. For this meaning of κατήχθη, cf. *Acta*, 244.3–4.

[443] See above, Chap. 14, n. 176. The church of Theodora was the metropolitan church of Mytilene, and the procession from George's monastic church of the Theotokos to the shrine of St. Theodora is a symbolic one.

[444] The ordination of a bishop takes place during the liturgy and is performed by a consecrating bishop. Central moments in the ceremony include a profession of orthodox faith, an abjuration of heresy, and reception of the episcopal vestments and pastoral staff before the *trisagion* is sung. The bishop-elect is then consecrated, clothed with the episcopal tunic (*sakkos*) and stole (*omophorion*), and acclaimed as "worthy" (ἄξιος) by the congregation. The bishop is enthroned after exchanging the Kiss of Peace with his consecrators; cf. C. Jones et al., *The Study of Liturgy* (New York, 1978), 318–20.

[445] The Trisagion or "thrice holy hymn" was the Byzantine term for the Sanctus, sung as a central portion of the Eucharist. The Trisagion was also frequently used as a processional chant in Constantinople. The term is further used for the troparion sung at the beginning of the Eucharist; cf. "Trisagion," *ODB* 3:2121. It is not surprising that this central liturgical expression should be described as an angelic hymn.

[446] Rom. 12:1. KJV translates as "reasonable service."

[447] Cf. 2 Tim. 2:6, a pun on George (Γεώργιος) and husbandman (γεωργός).

be for his flock. For though the vineyard happened to be quite small and was not expected to supply even one leaf <apiece> to the multitude, when they all came following the instructions of the holy man, O what a miracle, they departed each with one bunch of grapes. They returned home rejoicing and praising God for all they had seen and enjoyed. Three days later the blessed man, accomplishing miracle upon miracle, ordered some of the clergy to collect <the grapes> that the people had left in the vineyard and put them in a wine vat. Then he sent for his brother Symeon and asked him make a prayer over the wine vat. When Symeon saw the wine vat <almost> empty of grape bunches and realized the small amount of gleaned grapes that had been put in, he smiled a little and said jokingly to his bishop and his brother, "You need more grape crushers, brother, for this amount." But George, the servant of God, asked his brother for a prayer and ordered two men to tread in the vat while he himself stood by and sang psalms of David. [p. 255] O Thy wondrous miracles, Christ, Who grants the *desire* of those who hope in Thee![448] For one could <then> see such streams <of juice> pouring and flowing from the vat that not only did they fill the storage jars one-hundredfold, but there was also enough in abundance for every container that each member of the clergy and the poor happened to bring. This <miracle> was no less spectacular than the miracles of Elijah for the woman of Sarepta with regard to the oil flask and water jug.[449]

33. The wondrous and truly blessed Symeon, after the journey from Byzantium to his homeland, *finished the course* well[450] and *kept the faith,*[451] helping his brother for one year and advising him on the proper course of action. He was then ordered to leave this world, and was deemed worthy <to hear> the voice and <see the> apparition of an angel that said, "Symeon, forget earthly <affairs> and leave these things and come to us, as the Lord commands." So he called for his brother and shared with him the substance of the vision, <thereby> filling his <brother's> soul and heart with immeasurable despondency. But as he [Symeon] was breathing his last, seeking to relieve his brother's despair,[452] he said to him, "This is the decision of the Lord, my

---

[448] Cf. Ps. 144 (145):19.

[449] 3 Ki. 17:8–16.

[450] Reading καλῶς for κακῶς.

[451] 2 Tim. 4:7. Compare the description of the death of David in Chap. 9, where the same scriptural passage is used.

[452] Reading ἀθυμίας for εὐθυμίας, with Phountoules.

friend. And in fact I am going away *to prepare a place for you,*[453] as the Lord has revealed to me; and I will see you soon when the Lord calls you. So *be courageous and strong*[454] and care for and shepherd this holy flock that has been entrusted to you in a manner worthy of Him Who has honored you; and drive far away from it the *grievous wolves*[455] of heresies[456] and pursue them." With these last words Symeon sustained his brother, and embraced him; and then, saying, *"Into thy hands,* Savior, *I commend my spirit,"*[457] he gave his body to the earth, but his spirit to the Lord with a procession of angels. When word of his demise had spread everywhere, the people of the island gathered together and cried bitter tears and wailed over their loss; they encircled his honored body that had endured many labors and escorted it with weeping and songs and funeral dirges to the monastery of the Theotokos, where they buried it in a blessed and fitting manner.[458]

34. But that wondrous and most faithful shepherd of the Lord's sheep, George, though deprived of his fraternal partner and now left alone, did not stop supporting and benefitting and ministering to his flock by means of almsgiving and teachings and miracles. [p. 256] <For example,> a certain friend living in the region of the so-called Gothograikia[459] succumbed to a very severe

---

[453] Cf. Jn. 14:2.

[454] Deut. 31:6 et passim.

[455] Acts 20:29.

[456] This may be a reference to remaining iconoclast sympathizers, or to quarrels between the monks of Stoudios and the allies of Methodios over the acceptance of repentant iconoclasts into the clergy. The Life of Ioannikios by Peter includes Ioannikios' warning of heresies arising after 843; cf. *v. Ioannic. a Petr.,* chaps. 69–70, and below, 338–44.

[457] Lk. 23:46.

[458] The account of the public mourning and burial rites for Symeon should be compared with the monastic death scene described for David in Chaps. 9 and 10. Note also that the *Acta* do not give a date of death or remembrance for Symeon, David, or George.

[459] Gothograikia was traditionally identified as the area of northwestern Asia Minor (in the Opsikion theme) where Goths had been settled in late antiquity. Gothograikoi were still an identifiable group in the entry of the Chronicle of Theophanes for 715 (Theoph. 386.6). Goths are known to have lived in other parts of Asia Minor, but no Gothograikia is known in Lesbos, although the setting of this story on "the island" is specifically mentioned at 256.10–11. A. Alexakis has suggested emending the text to read ἐκ τῶν τῆς . . . ὑπάρχοντος μερῶν ("hailing from the region of the so-called Gothograikia") in place of ἐν τοῖς . . . ὑπάρχοντος μέρεσι to make sense of the passage.

illness; since his doctors despaired of his recovery, he had sent word begging the holy man not to delay coming to him. This wondrous soul [George] was both truly very compassionate and ready for good works, for he took no heed either of the cold weather or the late hour; but while those who had come to get him and those who out of love were eager to accompany him held back in a cowardly manner on account of the continuous rain and storm, he delayed not at all and encouraged them with words. And <so>, though very violent rain and lightning and thunder and thunderbolts assailed the whole extent of the island for two days and as many nights, an angel, which everybody saw, appeared to him and his companions and completely sheltered them; and he traveled the <road> to his friend without delay and with eagerness. And his companions appeared to everyone at his friend's house <to have arrived with> dry <clothes> and related the wondrous deeds of God along the road. When he arrived at his friend's house, he found him already breathing his last and the funeral songs for him beginning. The great <George> took the dying man's hand and made a prayer over his head and opened his eyes and made to sit up the man who shortly before was <all but> dead. He [the dying man] took hold of the holy man's cloak and looked at him, observing his beautiful face full of divine graces. Then sitting up he did obeisance with the appropriate reverence and delight and kissed him. The divine man <then> shared the divine and undefiled mysteries with him; and after ordering a table to be set and having dined with him, he restored his friend to health and said to him, "Don't be afraid of death for the moment. *Take heed to thyself,*[460] my friend, for after seven years you will arrive at the place where I will finally go; and let us see each other whenever the Lord wishes." The man, intelligent as he was, understood the meaning of [George's] words and gave thanks to God and to His servant. And when he had said, "*Let the name of the Lord be blessed,*"[461] and, "*His will be done,*"[462] he did obeisance on the ground. And in fact it happened later[463] just as the holy man predicted.

35. The fame of his miracle working was reported not only on the island under his jurisdiction and his homeland, but also in the cities on the other islands and mainland, and everyone was talking about and amazed at the di-

---

[460] Gen. 24:6 et passim.

[461] Ps. 112 (113):2; Job 1:21.

[462] Acts 21:14.

[463] Phountoules added ὕστερον, omitted by van den Gheyn in his transcription of the manuscript.

vinely inspired man's miracles and [p. 257] virtuous deeds. So the Smyrnans,[464] who before the man's installation had not been excluded from his miracles, inasmuch as they were his long-time friends and associates, thought that it was partly an indication of their bad luck and partly their insufficient love of God that after the installation they had not enjoyed his presence and the sight of him and his sweetness and his blessing; <so> they sent ambassadors who begged and beseeched him to spend time among them. Since he was truly an imitator of the Lord's love of humanity and very ready for good works, he did not refuse or delay, but ignored his old age and his bodily weakness resulting from his labors and exertions on behalf of piety.[465] Nor did he worry about such an expanse of sea, but considered one <point> alone, how he might support and help the souls of people who hungered for the correct word of God; and so he sailed to them not as one summoned, but of his own free will.

36. When he reached the city of the Smyrnans and had been received and welcomed by the very souls and hands of all and had sown the divine seed of orthodoxy as was necessary, he inspected and put in order the two monasteries which he had established there[466] and remained a few days. One night an angel appeared to him announcing his departure from his earthly body in this world, saying, "The King is calling you so that He may give you rest from your many labors."[467] That soul, truly loving his homeland and his brethren, was both very concerned for his flock and mindful of it in their hour of need. "I beseech you," he said to the angel, "let me go <first> to my land to equip my brethren" (talking about his own flock) "for piety since they are unequipped, and there *the will of the Lord be done.*"[468] When the blessed man said this to the bearer of the divine message [the angel], the divine angel gave him the <kiss of> peace and departed, saying, "It will be *as thou hast said.*"[469] Upon awakening, he bade farewell to everyone, both his rational sheep [people] and their

---

[464] See Chaps. 13 and 17 for earlier references to the saints' connections with Smyrna.

[465] I.e., his sufferings as a result of iconoclast persecution.

[466] The establishment of the monastery at Lagousai is described in Chap. 17. In Chap. 25, Symeon leaves in George's care "the monasteries" he had established in the Thrakesion theme. It is likely that one of these was the monastery of Kyrikos and Julitta founded by David near Mt. Ida (Chap. 7).

[467] Cf. Rev. 14:13.

[468] Acts 21:14.

[469] Gen. 18:5.

shepherds, his acquaintances and friends. After being escorted to the sea <shore> by everyone, since they were reluctant to separate from him (as one might expect), he said to all within earshot, "Farewell, brothers, and remember us always. For I will no longer come to this place in the flesh." When he had embraced them all for the last time and had given his blessing, he got into the boat[470] and sailed to the land of his birth; the Smyrnans, filled with tears at his departure, sat for a long time on the beach looking out toward the boat and lamenting. When [p. 258] he came to anchor on the soil of his homeland, it is not possible to describe with what pleasure and joy his flock received his arrival. For the whole island assembled longing to enjoy the sweetness and the sight and blessing of their good Father and shepherd.

37. He had finished <his voyage across> the great sea of holy Lent and had given himself even more to ascetic exercises and self-control, because it was the week of the salvific Passion of the Lord; it was the solemn and great Holy Thursday, on which the mystical lamb of God is sacrificed by the hands of priests and shared with those worthy of it, and all were gathered together in the church. After the imitator and apostle of the Lord had washed the feet[471] of many, the great bishop of God and sacrificer had celebrated the divine liturgy and distributed the immaculate mysteries with his own hands to the deserving. He then returned to his cell to rest his battered and withered body. While he was sleeping, there stood beside him two men in white garments whose beauty seemed beyond every glory of the human face.[472] With reverence and at the same time joy they said to him, "The King is calling you so that you may celebrate with us in His house the august day of God's resurrection." He woke up and understood what the command of the vision meant and ordered all the clergy to assemble along with the entire populace of the city. When these <people> had all gathered, the great father came into their midst and gave them much instruction about the orthodox faith; he commanded them to hold fast to the correct church traditions to the end,[473] and explained

---

[470] πορθμεῖον: a ferry or boat used to cross a strait.

[471] Cf. Jn. 13:14. In imitation of Christ's washing the feet of the disciples during the Last Supper, bishops and abbots washed the feet of twelve clergymen as part of the liturgy of Holy Thursday; cf. *ODB* 3:2190–91.

[472] Cf. Mt. 28:3; Mk. 16:5; Jn. 20:12. Angels traditionally appear in visions clothed in white garments; see Talbot, *Holy Women,* 151 n. 55.

[473] The passage emphasizes both George's pastoral role as bishop and guardian of orthodoxy in his diocese, and the fear of renewed heresy that is reflected earlier in the text and in several other *vitae* of iconophile saints.

to them at length about the <Day of> Judgment. Finally he revealed to them the foreshadowing of his departure from life, saying, "No more, children, will I celebrate Easter with you, for indeed the Lord has already called me, and tomorrow, whenever He wishes, I will go to do obeisance before Him." Of course everyone was shocked by this announcement and raised a great funeral dirge along with wailing.[474] All the people of the city and the island streamed together, bewailing the loss of their father and longing and desiring to be deemed worthy of his blessing. When the evening of the wondrous Holy Saturday had already arrived, the blessed one departed to the Lord for Whom he longed,[475] and many extraordinary miracles occurred at that hour. So both the clergy and civil officials and the citizens and the army—not even the general [p. 259] was missing from among them—divided by ranks,[476] and transported that holy and wondrous body in the hands of the priests. They escorted it in splendor with torches and psalms and fragrant perfumes to the august church of the Mother of God where the wondrous man had performed those ascetic exercises; and after honorable funerary rites they buried it. Some years later the remains of the great David were also transferred by Christ-loving men from Ida to Lesbos and placed in one coffin with his two brothers,[477] so that

[474] θρῆνον σὺν οἰμωγῇ μέγαν. The public ritual lament of funeral dirge, weeping, and beating the breast formed part of the funeral services for public figures like bishops and ascetics; cf. "Funeral," *ODB* 2:808–9.

[475] On 28 March 845 or 18 April 846. Phountoules (Οἱ ὅσιοι αὐτάδελφοι, n. 229) suggests that the trip to Gothograikia and the visit to the Smyrnans would have been difficult to accomplish in the same year, and prefers 846 as a date for George's death. But if A. Alexakis is correct, his trip to the "man from Gothograikia" seems to have been a short one, on the island of Lesbos; cf. n. 459 above.

[476] The description mirrors the language used to identify George's welcome to the island and, in emphasizing the official presence of the entire city, identifies one way social divisions were ascribed to middle Byzantine society. This description identifies the populace by function—the clergy (οἱ τοῦ κλήρου), civil officials (οἱ τῶν ἐν τέλει), citizens (οἱ τῆς πολιτείας), and soldiers (ὁ στρατός)—rather than by class, and emphasizes the fluidity of Byzantine social structure. The "ranks" (διατάξεις) in which they joined the funeral procession should be compared to functional "orders" rather than social classes; cf. "Class Structure," *ODB* 1:468–69, and bibliography cited there.

[477] This passage is the first time that all three brothers are explicitly connected in the text. The date of David's burial together with Symeon and George is otherwise unknown, and it is possible that his body and cult were translated to Mytilene long after the death of George. The association of the three saints in a common tomb in the

the same men whom one sanctified womb had brought into the world, one miracle-abounding tomb might also display, adding to the glory of the Father and the Son and the Holy Spirit, of the one Godhead and kingdom, for Whom glory and honor and veneration are appropriate, now and always, forever and ever. Amen.

---

church of the Mother of God may have been the impetus for the writing of the biography to document the cult of remembrance observed by the monastery.

7. LIFE OF ST. IOANNIKIOS

introduction and translation by Denis F. Sullivan

Introduction

Ioannikios was born in the village of Marykaton, north of Lake Apollonias in Bithynia; one version of his *vita* (by Sabas) places his birth in 754/5,[1] the other (by Peter) in 762. The later date seems more likely.[2] His name, a diminutive of Ἰωάννης (John), was apparently a boyhood appellation;[3] his family name was Boilas.[4] His parents set their son to tending swine and provided him no formal education; he learned to read only later in life after he entered a monastery.

As a young man Ioannikios joined the army in the imperial regiment of the Exkoubitors and, according to the version of his life by Sabas (chap. 2), became an iconoclast,[5] but subsequently converted to orthodoxy (chap. 5). He participated in the battle of Markellai (792), where his experience of the slaughter of so many of his comrades by the Bulgarians was apparently a turning point in his life. He left the army, almost certainly as a deserter,[6] and

---

[1] According to the *v. Ioannic. a Sab.* (333B), Ioannikios was born in the fourteenth year of the emperor Constantine V, who ascended the throne in 741.

[2] See Mango, "Ioannikios," 398–401.

[3] See van den Gheyn, *AASS*, Nov. 2.1:333 note d.

[4] For the likely Slavic origin of the family see S. Vryonis, "St. Ioannicius the Great (754–846) and the 'Slavs' of Bithynia," *Byzantion* 31 (1961), 245–48, and Ph. Malingoudis, "Σλαβικὰ ὀνόματα ἀπὸ τὴ βυζαντινὴ Βιθυνία," *Hellenika* 31 (1979), 494–96.

[5] See also W. E. Kaegi, "The Byzantine Armies and Iconoclasm," *ByzSlav* 27 (1966), 48–70, esp. 60–61.

[6] The version by Peter (Chap. 7) indicates that Ioannikios, following a visit to his parents, was about to return to his army unit, but went instead to the monastery of the Agauroi on Mt. Olympos. Peter also comments (Chap. 2) that Ioannikios "flew away from the earthly army" and (Chap. 72) that "he left the temporal army." Mango ("Ioannikios," 401) concludes that Peter's chronology makes it likely that Ioannikios deserted;

entered the monastery of Antidion on Mt. Olympos in Bithynia; after two years he became a hermit[7] on the same mountain. He subsequently gained fame for his prophetic gifts, especially his ability to predict the approaching death of others, and his ability to kill snakes and dragons, accomplishments that render Ioannikios virtually unique among his contemporaries. While other saints predict their own death and perhaps that of one or two others,[8] Ioannikios predicts the death of ten other people including emperors and other high officials, as well as his own; his slaying of or encounters with seven snakes and dragons[9] is without precedent in ninth-century *vitae*. He is also depicted as having the ability to levitate, as being transfigured, becoming invisible at will, controlling wild animals, and in a few instances curing illness, gifts more commonly found in other ninth-century Lives.

During the second period of iconoclasm (815–843) Ioannikios moved frequently both within the Mt. Olympos region and to wilderness areas of Lydia, to flee persecution as well as to seek solitude and avoid glorification by

---

see also J. Haldon, *Byzantine Praetorians* (Bonn, 1984), 327. A. Alexakis (in a private communication) notes that independent confirmation is to be found in the *kontakion* composed to Ioannikios by the saint's contemporary, the patriarch Methodios (see J. Schiro, *Analecta Hymnica Graeca III: Canones Novembris* [Rome, 1972], 134–45), in which wording similar to Peter's is found and where Ioannikios is specifically called ῥίψασπις (line 86). Joseph the Hymnographer, in his hymn to Ioannikios, also comments: τὴν ἐπίγειον ἀπεβάλου στρατιάν (Μηναῖα τοῦ ὅλου ἐνιαυτοῦ [Rome, 1889], 44:14–15).

[7] Curiously, Peter never mentions any formal tonsure of Ioannikios. The version of his life by Sabas (chap. 13) does state that he became a regularly tonsured monk, but only at age 53. For doubts about Sabas' account of Ioannikios' tonsure, see Mango, "Ioannikios," 404, who suggests that the abbots on Mt. Olympos may have refused to tonsure Ioannikios because he was a deserter.

[8] Cf., for example, Peter of Atroa, who predicts his own death (*v. Petr. Atr.,* chap. 82) and that of two others (chaps. 29 and 53).

[9] For a list of other "dragon-slayers," see C. Walters, "The Thracian Horseman: Ancestor of the Warrior Saints?" *ByzF* 14 (1989), 657–73, esp. 661, to which should be added F. Halkin, "Sainte Elisabeth d'Héraclée, abbesse à Constantinople," *AnalBoll* 91 (1973), 251–64, esp. 258–59 (for Eng. trans., see Talbot, *Holy Women,* 122–35), and Eusebius, *Vita Constantini* 3:3 (ed. F. Winkelmann, *Eusebius Werke* 1:1 [Berlin, 1975], 3–151). Generally on the δράκων in biblical and patristic contexts, see N. Kiessling, "Antecedents of the Medieval Dragon in Sacred History," *Journal of Biblical Literature* 89 (1970), 167–75, and A. Quacquarelli, *Il Leone e il Drago nella Simbolica dell'Età Patristica* (Bari, 1975).

men. He was criticized by his contemporary Theodore the Stoudite, however, for dwelling "in the wilderness and the mountains" while others were being arrested and flogged.[10] The last iconoclast emperor, Theophilos, died in January 842. More than a year later the iconoclast patriarch John VII Grammatikos was deposed and replaced by the iconodule monk Methodios, and the first Triumph of Orthodoxy celebrated (11 March 843). Ioannikios is depicted in the sources as recommending and predicting Methodios' elevation and subsequently supporting his policies. Ioannikios died on Mt. Olympos shortly after the restoration of icons, on 3 November 846.

The *Life of Ioannikios* is preserved in two early versions written by the monks Peter and Sabas (each of whom claims to have known him personally), as well as in a later Metaphrastic revision. The precise relationship between the versions is not absolutely clear. The editor of the texts in the *Acta Sanctorum,* J. van den Gheyn,[11] argued that Peter's version was earlier and revised by Sabas, a view followed by E. von Dobschütz,[12] V. Laurent,[13] F. Dvornik,[14] C. Mango, and D. Afinogenov.[15] Dvornik and Mango suggest that the motivation for Sabas' version may have been to eliminate Peter's open hostility to the Stoudite monks; Mango adds that, by changes in chronology, Sabas may have sought to absolve Ioannikios of the charge of desertion from the army.[16] Alexander Kazhdan,[17] however, suggests that the two monks may have written independently, basing their work on oral tradition.

Peter, a monk of the Agauroi monastery on Mt. Olympos, cites (Chaps. 12, 40, 46, 54, 62) as the source of his information his abbot Eustratios, Ioannikios' closest friend for fifty years. Peter also indicates that he writes at the direction of Eustratios (Chap. 12) and twice speaks of his writing as an "obligation" (ὑπόχρεων, Chaps. 3, 62). He generally calls his work a "treatise"

[10] *Theodori Studitis Praepositi Parva Catechesis,* ed. E. Auvray (Paris, 1891), 141.45–46.

[11] *AASS,* Nov. 2.1:316–17.

[12] Von Dobschütz, "Methodios und die Studiten," 99–100.

[13] V. Laurent in *v. Petr. Atr.* 15–16.

[14] Dvornik, *Légendes,* 127–28 n. 1.

[15] Afinogenov, "Great Purge," 85.

[16] Mango, "Ioannikios," 401.

[17] In his unpublished *List of Saints,* no. 263, which may be consulted at Dumbarton Oaks.

(πραγματεία), but in the final chapter also calls it a "funerary composition" (ἐπιτάφιον σύνταγμα). The relationship between Peter and Eustratios in the authorship of this *vita* of Ioannikios is not completely clear. Peter says (Chap. 12) that he was prompted by Eustratios "to compile" (καθυποτάξαι)[18] the treatise and that he will "repeat . . . also all I have heard from him" (ὅσα τε παρ' αὐτοῦ ἠκούσαμεν, ταῦτα πάντα καὶ ἀναγγελοῦμεν). In Chapter 62 he indicates that he will complete his narrative with only the descriptions of Ioannikios' miracles that Eustratios has "narrated" to him (μόνοις τοῖς ῥηθεῖσιν ἡμῖν παρὰ τοῦ ἡγιασμένου Εὐστρατίου). Peter also says (Chap. 68) that he "compiled this treatise" (ἐμοῦ. . .πραγματείαν. . .συντάξαντος). But in Chapter 54, Peter apparently says that Eustratios "composed the treatise" (Εὐστρατίῳ . . .πραγματείαν. . .ἀναταξαμένῳ), Peter's term here perhaps echoing Luke 1:1, ἐπειδήπερ πολλοὶ ἐπεχείρησαν ἀνατάξασθαι διήγησιν. The same verb ἀνατάξασθαι is also used in the *vitae* of Elias the Younger and Luke the Stylite to describe the activity of the authors of those works.[19] Thus Eustratios himself may have put something in writing,[20] but it is not absolutely certain, and the precise distinction among the terms καθυποτάξαι, συντάξαι, and ἀνατάξασθαι is difficult to determine. It is, however, notable that Peter on four[21] occasions specifically indicates some kind of *oral* communication to him from Eustratios. It thus seems best to acknowledge the significant role of Eustratios in

[18] The translation of καθυποτάξαι is difficult. Liddell-Scott gives "subject" and "= καθυπογράφειν," Lampe, *Lexicon,* s.v., gives "subject," "subjugate," or "subjoin, append." For the first meaning see, for example, Joseph the Hymnographer, who uses the verb to describe Ioannikios' taming of wild animals through subjugating the passions: ὅθεν σοι εἰρήνευσαν ἄγριοι θῆρες καθυποτάξαντι πάθη ψυχῆς δυσκάθεκτα, Ἰωαννίκιε (Μηναῖα τοῦ ὅλου ἐνιαυτοῦ 2 [Rome, 1889], 46.31–32). Perhaps Peter's choice here reflects his role in coordinating and putting in final form (? "subjugating") Eustratios' information, the immediate context perhaps suggesting the military metaphor and the term also influenced by Peter's later use of ἀνατάξασθαι and συντάξαι. As an alternative might καθυποτάξαι in the sense "subjoin, append" (= καθυπογράφειν) be used to describe Peter's role as subordinate to Eustratios in the creation of the *vita*?

[19] *v. Eliae Jun.* 3.14 and *v. Luc. Styl.* 199.11.

[20] Mango ("Ioannikios," 393) suggests that Peter "may have had before him a memoir or set of notes composed by Eustratios" and (p. 394 n. 4) translates ἀναταξαμένῳ as "set in order," citing the passage from Luke. Van den Gheyn translates the same term with "mandavit."

[21] In addition to the two instances cited above, see also Chaps. 40 (ἔλεγεν . . . Εὐστράτιος) and 46 (ἔλεγεν . . . Εὐστράτιος).

the composition of this *vita* of Ioannikios, but to leave open whether he left something in writing or was a source of oral history.

Peter is apparently writing not long after Ioannikios' death; in mentioning that Ioannikios was quite tall, he says to his audience (Chap. 49) "as you all know" (ὡς ἴστε πάντες), suggesting that his listeners too had seen Ioannikios. He also, however, uses the phrases "up to this time" (μέχρι τοῦ νῦν, Chap. 41), "even now leads a good life" (καὶ νῦν εὐβιοῦσα, Chap. 58), and "even to this day" (μέχρι τῆς σήμερον, Chap. 59) to describe individuals who had met Ioannikios, and says (Chap. 71) that miracles at Ioannikios' grave are effected "up to this day" (μέχρι τῆς σήμερον), all indicating some passage of time after Ioannikios' death. More uncertain is whether the patriarch Methodios, who died on 4 June 847, was still alive when Peter wrote, as Mango argues.[22] Peter describes Methodios as "among the saints" (Chap. 70) and as "among the martyrs" (Chap. 69), terminology suggesting that the patriarch was already dead by the time Peter completed his composition. Mango's arguments that Peter was writing before April 848 are more persuasive. The bishop Peter of Syl(l)aion, whom the hagiographer Peter describes as still in office, τὸν νυνὶ μητροπολίτην (Chap. 68), was apparently removed by late 847 or early 848,[23] while Naukratios, abbot of Stoudios who died on 18 April 848, is, as Mango notes, "censured without any indication that he was dead at the time" (Chaps. 57, 69).[24] Thus it seems likely, though not certain, that Peter was writing in part at least after the death of Methodios and in toto before that of Naukratios, and certainly not later than 852–853. One might speculate that the first anniversary of Ioannikios' death on 3 November 847 would accord with an initial declamation of the text and might be an appropriate point to refer to the *vita* as an *epitaphios*.

The other early version of Ioannikios' *vita* is by the monk Sabas of the St. Zacharias monastery at the foot of Mt. Olympos; he is apparently also the

[22] Mango, "Ioannikios," 394.

[23] Mango, "Ioannikios," 394 and n. 5. Mango follows V. Grumel (*RegPatr* 2:445) in accepting a date of 847 or 848 for the deposition of this bishop Peter by Methodios' successor Ignatios, due to Peter's participation in a group, led by Gregory Asbestas, which opposed Ignatios' reversal of Methodios' policy toward the Stoudites. Grumel also records other views which place the deposition as late as 852–853, to which add V. Ruggieri, F. Nethercott, "The Metropolitan City of Syllion and Its Churches," *JÖB* 36 (1986), 133–56, specifically 147.

[24] Mango, "Ioannikios," 394 n. 5.

author[25] of the Life of Peter of Atroa and wrote his version of the *Life of Ioannikios* at the request of his abbot Joseph. Sabas' text includes many of the same incidents found in Peter's version, but has significant differences in chronology, provides some additional details and incidents, while omitting other incidents recorded by Peter. Sabas treats iconoclasm, Theophilos, and the Stoudites in a radically different manner. Peter's claim to use "eyewitness" information provided by Eustratios and the apparent priority of his version were the factors leading to the selection of his treatise for the translation given in this volume.

Peter's stated purpose in writing is to provide his audience with knowledge of Ioannikios' conduct, ascetic struggles, and manly deeds, in the belief that such knowledge will be beneficial to "those who are pious and have achieved perfect mental discipline" (Chap. 3). His presentation does indeed provide such standard descriptions, but he also sets them in a distinctly political context. Following the Triumph of Orthodoxy the new iconodule patriarch Methodios faced two extremely divisive issues, the treatment of heretical iconoclast clergy and schismatic opposition to him by the monks of Stoudios.[26] Writing in this heated political atmosphere, Peter, as noted above, presents Ioannikios as strongly supporting Methodios, who was elevated on condition that the deceased emperor Theophilos not be subject to anathema with the other iconoclasts. Methodios strongly defended the views of his iconodule predecessors, the patriarchs Tarasios and Nikephoros I, as well as the authority of the patriarch over the monks. Notably Peter's description of iconoclasm is largely limited to the reign of Leo V (Chap. 18), he speaks only of "the heresy," not "the iconoclastic heresy" as does Sabas, and he makes few mentions of icons;[27] he also never mentions Theophilos, whom Sabas more than once de-

---

[25] See V. Laurent in *v. Petr. Atr.* 9–13.

[26] For a recent examination of Methodios' treatment of the iconoclasts and the origin and nature of the Stoudite schism, with earlier bibliography, see Afinogenov, "Κωνσταντινούπολις ἐπίσκοπον ἔχει: Part II," 79–91.

[27] Peter's association of Ioannikios with the cross, which is more prominent than in Sabas' version, is also interesting in this context. In addition to depicting Ioannikios as working miracles with the sign of the cross or his cross-bearing staff, which Peter in Chap. 29 calls the "victorious weapon of the life-giving cross," Peter narrates (Chap. 68) that Ioannikios gave him "a wooden cross made by his own hands and beautifully carved." The cross, particularly as a symbol of military victory, was often connected

scribes in pejorative terms. Perhaps the most striking aspect of Peter's presentation is his virulent criticism of the Stoudite monks,[28] whom he calls arrogant sowers of scandal (Chap. 36), self-serving venom-tongued critics of saints, and fabrications of the devil (Chap. 57), co-conspirators in subornation of perjury against Methodios (Chaps. 69–70), and "most abominable" (Chap. 70). His hostility to the Stoudites is perhaps also reinforced in more subtle ways. In Chapter Five, for example, he has Ioannikios save the life of the emperor Constantine VI on the battlefield. This emperor's subsequent divorce and remarriage led to a bitter division between the Stoudites (who considered the remarriage adulterous) and the emperors, and to imperial persecution of the Stoudites. The story of Ioannikios' battlefield valor (i.e., saving the "adulterer") is apparently untrue and "modeled" by Peter on a similar incident in Theophanes' *Chronographia.*[29] He also depicts (Chap. 36) Ioannikios granting a friendly reception to Joseph of Kathara, the priest who performed this second marriage, and predicting Joseph's pious death, a prediction that scandalized the Stoudites present. Moreover, he refers to both Constantine VI and the emperor Nikephoros I, who also was opposed by the Stoudites due to his restoration of the deposed Joseph of Kathara, as "most pious" (Chaps. 5, 14).[30] One other aspect of Peter's presentation deserves mention. At a number

---

with the emperors and the iconoclasts; see Gero, *Leo III,* 37, 114–23; J. Moorhead, "Iconoclasm, the Cross and the Imperial Image," *Byzantion* 55 (1985), 165–79; A. Kazhdan, "'Constantin Imaginaire.' Byzantine Legends of the Ninth Century about Constantine the Great," *Byzantion* 57 (1987), 196–250; A. Kazhdan, "Kosmas of Jerusalem: 2. Can We Speak of His Political Views?" *Le Muséon* 103 (1991), 329–46. Perhaps this association is another aspect of Peter's rhetorical attempt to counter the Stoudites by linking Ioannikios with imperial imagery.

[28] F. Dvornik (*Légendes,* 127) aptly comments: "Cette biographie, en certains endroits, devient presque un pamphlet contre les Studites."

[29] See D. Sullivan, "Was Constantine VI Lassoed at Markellai?" *GRBS* 35 (1994), 287–91. I would add to the arguments presented there, regarding the continuing political importance of the Moechian controversy in the mid-9th century, the translation of the remains of the patriarch Nikephoros to the church of the Apostles in Constantinople on 13 March 847, an event opposed by the Stoudites based, in part, on their view that Nikephoros had condoned Constantine VI's "adultery" (see Bury, *Eastern Roman Empire,* 182, and Dvornik, *Légendes,* 125).

[30] Van den Gheyn (*AASS,* Nov. 2.1:345 note e, 394 note b) suggested that the use of the epithet for Nikephoros is simply traditional. It is surely significant, however, that

of points he presents his subject as a "new Moses," in three instances specifically comparing Ioannikios to Moses on Mt. Sinai entering into "the darkness <where God was>."[31] He also describes (Chap. 10) Ioannikios as leading the people "out of Egypt,[32] that is out of the transitory and dark life." Presumably Peter is here defending Ioannikios' choice of a hermit's existence during the iconoclastic persecution by likening it to the withdrawal from his people of a major Old Testament figure, while at the same time suggesting that Ioannikios' example had positive effects on society. Sabas also compares Ioannikios to Moses, but does not specifically refer to the "darkness" of Exodus.

As Mango[33] notes, Peter is not an elegant writer, but did on occasion "aspire to an elevated style," even using the dual on two occasions. His difficult introductory paragraph is one good example of such aspiration. Generally, however, his writing is more characteristic of the middle style,[34] with its paratactic structure and use of citations taken almost exclusively from the church fathers, particularly Athanasios, Basil, Gregory of Nazianzos, Gregory of Nyssa, and John Chrysostom, as well as the Old and New Testaments. The few possible classical references in his text could easily have been derived indirectly.

Ioannikios is frequently mentioned in other *vitae* and writings of the ninth century and was often referred to as "the great," indicating a prominence and influence that, particularly for a hermit, was rare among his contemporaries. He was indeed a "star" of the ninth century. Theodore the Stou-

---

Sabas does not use it of Constantine VI and uses only εὐσεβοῦς of Nikephoros, while Peter uses the superlative of both.

[31] Ex. 20:21.

[32] For a similar comparison, see J. Manek, "The New Exodus in the Books of Luke," *Novum Testamentum* 2 (1958), 8–23. For other examples of a "new Moses" connected with the victorious cross, cf. Eusebius, *Vita Constantini* 1:12 and 38–40 (ed. F. Winkelmann, *Eusebius Werke* 1:1 [Berlin, 1975], 3–151); see also Gero, *Leo III,* 37; Moorhead, "Iconoclasm, the Cross and the Imperial Image," esp. 174; and A. Kazhdan, "Kosmas of Jerusalem: 2. Can We Speak of His Political Views?" *Le Muséon* 103 (1991), 329–46, esp. 332.

[33] Mango, "Ioannikios," 395.

[34] For the characteristics of the middle style, see I. Ševčenko, "Levels of Style of Byzantine Prose," *JÖB* 31.1 (1981), 289–312, specifically 291.

dite addressed a letter[35] to "Ioannikios the hermit" in which he described seeing him as "transfigured like Moses" (λαμπρυνθεὶς μωσαϊκῶς), an interesting parallel to the comparison found in the *vitae* of both Peter and Sabas. He is mentioned in fragments of the letters of the patriarch Methodios.[36] He is also mentioned in the *vitae* of the ninth-century saints Athanasia of Aegina; Constantine the Jew; David, Symeon, and George; Eustratios; Euthymios the Younger; Ignatios the Patriarch; Michael the Synkellos; Peter Patrikios; and the empress Theodora, wife of Theophilos; as well as the tenth-century *vita* of Irene of Chrysobalanton.

Ioannikios was buried in the monastery of Antidion on Mt. Olympos in Bithynia. Of his subsequent cult not a great deal is known, which is somewhat unexpected given his initial prominence. Van den Gheyn notes[37] that Ioannikios is included in the *Menologion of Basil II* as well as in the *Synaxarion of Constantinople;* that Joseph the Hymnographer (ninth century) composed a *theotokion* in his honor;[38] that his feastday was celebrated in the monastery of St. Kallistratos in Constantinople;[39] that in the year 1200 Antony of Novgorod mentioned seeing the skull of Ioannikios in the Constantinopolitan church of the Forty Martyrs of Sebasteia; and, that John Komnenos in his Προσκυνη- τάριον τοῦ Ἁγίου Ὄρους (Athens, 1701) reported, after his visit in 1700, that the skull was then numbered among the relics in the Athonite monastery of the Pantokrator. One might add that three other hymns were written for Ioannikios in the ninth century, by the patriarch Methodios, George of Nikomedeia, and Theodosia the Melode, and that two later kanons are also known.[40]

[35] Fatouros, *Theod. Stud. Epist., ep.* 461.

[36] Darrouzès, "Le patriarche Méthode," 54.

[37] The references, including the relevant texts of the *Menologion* and the *Synaxarion,* are gathered by van den Gheyn, *AASS,* Nov. 2.1:311–13.

[38] This kanon is employed for the *orthros* of Ioannikios' feastday on November 4; for the text, see the Μηναῖα τοῦ ὅλου ἐνιαυτοῦ 2 (Rome, 1889), 39–47.

[39] See also Janin, *Eglises CP,* 275–76.

[40] For the text of these three 9th-century hymns, see J. Schiro, *Analecta Hymnica Graeca III: Canones Novembris* (Rome, 1972), 111–45, with commentary at 568–72, and for discussion, especially of Theodosia, E. C. Topping, "Women Hymnographers in Byzantium," *Diptycha* 3 (1982–83), 102–7 and "Theodosia: Melodos and Monastria," *Diptycha* 4 (1986–87), 384–405. For the later kanons, see Topping, "Theodosia," 387 n. 4.

Ioannikios is usually depicted as a monk with medium-length beard, and is sometimes associated with a representation of a mountain.[41] Images of him are to be found in the *Menologion of Basil II,*[42] in the Theodore Psalter,[43] at Hosios Loukas,[44] in three manuscripts of the Metaphrastian Menologion,[45] and in the early thirteenth-century Serbian church at Mileševa.[46] He is also mentioned in the eighteenth-century "Painter's Manual" of Dionysius of Fourna.[47]

The version of the *vita* of Ioannikios by Peter survives in only one manuscript, Paris, Coislin 303 (fols. 304–53), dated to the tenth or eleventh century; the version by Sabas is found in four manuscripts, Paris gr. 1519 (eleventh century), Vienna Caes. Aug. 5 (eleventh century), Vaticanus gr. 807 (twelfth century), and Vaticanus gr. 1256 (fifteenth century). The survival of Peter's text in a single manuscript may reflect the more controversial nature of his presentation.

Peter's version of the *vita* of Ioannikios is included in this volume for the light it sheds on forms of monasticism on Mt. Olympos during the second period of iconoclasm, on the heated political conflict between the patriarch Methodios and the monks of Stoudios following the Triumph of Orthodoxy, and for the interesting depiction of a former iconoclast and a hermit, who was criticized by his contemporaries for failing to face the persecution directly and

---

[41] A. Kazhdan, N. P. Ševčenko, *ODB* 2:1005–6; see also L. Mariès, "L'irruption des saints dans l'illustration du psautier byzantin," *AnalBoll* 68 (1950), 153–62, specifically 160.

[42] *Il Menologio di Basilio II* 2 (Turin, 1907), 158.

[43] S. Der Nersessian, *L' illustration des Psautiers grecs du moyen âge, II. Londres Add. 19.352* (Paris, 1970), fig. 282.

[44] C. Connor, *Art and Miracles in Medieval Byzantium* (Princeton, N.J., 1991), 24 and fig. 37.

[45] N. Ševčenko, *Illustrated Manuscripts of the Metaphrastian Menologion* (Chicago, Ill., 1990), 65, 126–27, 170.

[46] S. Tomeković, "Les saints ermites et moines dans le décor du narthex de Mileševa," in *Mileševa dans l'histoire du peuple Serbe,* ed. V. Djurić (Belgrade, 1987), 51–67, esp. 53 and nn. 30 and 58 and fig. 3. See also N. L. Okunev, "Mileševo. Ein Denkmal der serbischen Kunst des 13. Jahrhunderts," *ByzSlav* 7 (1937–38), pl. XXIV.

[47] P. Hetherington, *The 'Painter's Manual' of Dionysius of Fourna. Translation and Commentary* (London, 1974), 60.

for predicting the day of a man's death. The *vita* also provides valuable specifics on political figures and events and rural life in the ninth century.

Bibliography

Edition Used for Translation

(BHG 936) J. van den Gheyn, *Acta Sanctorum Novembris* 2.1 (Brussels: Société des Bollandistes, 1894), 384–435, with Latin translation. The version of Sabas (BHG 935) precedes that of Peter, 332–83.

Secondary Literature

D. Afinogenov, "Κωνσταντινούπολις ἐπίσκοπον ἔχει. Part II: From the Second Outbreak of Iconoclasm to the Death of Methodios," *Erytheia* 17 (1996), 43–71.

———, "The Great Purge of 843: A Re-Examination," in ΛΕΙΜΩΝ: *Studies Presented to Lennart Rydén on His Sixty-fifth Birthday*, ed. J. O. Rosenqvist (Uppsala, 1996), 79–91.

V. Grumel, "Joannice le Grand," *Catholicisme* 6 (Paris, 1967), 896–97.

A. Kazhdan, N. P. Ševčenko, "Ioannikios," *ODB* 2:1005–6.

O. Lampsides, "Das Wunder des heiligen Ioannikios in der Kirche des Evangelisten Johannes in Ephesos," *AnalBoll* 100 (1982), 429–30.

C. Loparev, "Vizantijskija žitija svjatych VIII–IX vekov," *Vizantijskij vremennik* 18 (1911), 70–92.

P. Malingoudes, "Σλαβικὰ ὀνόματα ἀπὸ τὴ βυζαντινὴ Βιθυνία," *Hellenika* 31 (1979), 494–96.

C. Mango, "The Two Lives of St. Ioannikios and the Bulgarians," *Okeanos, Harvard Ukrainian Studies* 7 (1983), 393–404.

B. Menthon, *Une terre de légendes, L'Olympe de Bithynie. Ses saints, ses couvents, ses sites* (Paris, 1935).

J. Pargoire, "Quel jour S. Joannice est-il mort?" *EO* 4 (1900–1901), 75–80.

J. van den Gheyn, "Un moine grec au IXe siècle, s. Joannice le Grand, abbé en Bithynie," *Études religieuses publiées par des Pères de la Compagnie de Jésus* 50 (1890), 407–34.

E. von Dobschütz, "Methodios und die Studiten," *BZ* 18 (1909), 41–105, esp. 93–100.

S. Vryonis, "St. Ioannicius the Great (754–846) and the 'Slavs' of Bithynia," *Byzantion* 31 (1961), 245–48.

L. Rydén, "New Forms of Hagiography: Heroes and Saints," in *The 17th International Byzantine Congress. Major Papers* (Washington, D.C., 1986), 540–41.

LIFE OF OUR MOST BLESSED AND HOLY FATHER IOANNIKIOS WRITTEN BY PETER, A MONK

Father, give your blessing.

1. The constitution of the <nature> of all us mortals was allotted by the all-wise Creator to consist of the soul and the *spiritual essence*[48] and the *concurrence of the elements*[49] that is the flesh, while the beauty of perfect virtuous conduct, pious faith, and *the keeping of God's commandments*[50] <can be> mastered.[51] For neither is the body alive when deprived of the soul[52] nor indeed will *keeping of the commandments* without orthodoxy in any way benefit man. For as the soul is to the body, such is orthodoxy to spirit. Therefore the man whom we now praise became through his pious life a precise guardian and *fulfiller*[53] of this pure *keeping of the commandments* and of the blameless and orthodox faith. Like some excellent and precise painter,[54] imitating the lives

---

[48] Cf. pseudo-Athanasius, *Quaestiones ad Antiochum ducem*, PG 28:608.9–10: ἡ μὲν τοῦ ἀνθρώπου ψυχή ἐστιν οὐσία νοερά.

[49] Cf., e.g., Gregory of Nyssa, *Dialogus de anima et resurrectione*, PG 46:24B, 84D.

[50] Cf. 1 Cor. 7:19.

[51] This difficult introductory sentence apparently contrasts ἔλαχεν ("was allotted") with κρατύνεται ("<can be> mastered"), i.e., the first is given by God to all humans, the second is achieved by human action. The translation follows van den Gheyn. If the genitives could be taken as equivalent to instrumental datives, however, a possible translation might be: "<its> beauty is strengthened by perfect virtuous conduct, pious faith, and the *keeping of God's commandments*."

[52] The genitive ζωῆς, if not in apposition to ψυχῆς, is difficult to parallel with καθίσταται; presumably it is used in the literal sense of "come into the state of life." Van den Gheyn renders "in vita positum est," literally, "is placed in life."

[53] The term "fulfiller" (πληρωτής) suggests a successor of Moses, a theme used of Ioannikios at a number of points in the *vita;* on this interpretation, cf., for example, J. Daniélou, *Grégoire de Nysse. La Vie de Moïse*, 3d ed. (Paris, 1968), pt. 2, sec. 148: ὁ πληρωτὴς τοῦ νόμου καὶ Μωϋσέως διάδοχος.

[54] For a similar analogy, see Gregory of Nyssa, *De Vita Moysis* (as in previous footnote), pt. 2, sec. 313: ὥσπερ τις ἀνδριαντοποιὸς ἐπιστήμων, ὅλον ἑαυτοῦ τὸν ἀνδριάντα τοῦ βίου ἐξεργασάμενος ἀκριβῶς, and pt. 2, sec. 316: ὅταν γένη τῶν σῶν καρδιῶν λαοξόος, ὥστε ἐν ταύταις παρὰ τοῦ Θεοῦ τὰ θεῖα λόγια ἐγχαράξαι.

and ways of our blessed fathers who went before him and were admired and heralded for their virtues, he engraved them on the tablets of his heart[55] with ideas written in gold.[56] While he fell just short of some, he most ardently rivaled and competed with others; sometimes [p. 385] he even outstripped them, if I dare to say so in the words of[57] the Theologian.[58] Like some ever-shining sun with the illuminations of his virtues he revealed himself to our generation as if shining from another firmament by his pure life. Thus now that you have heard these *gateways, so august and immense,*[59] of lofty conduct and are inflamed by divine love, you are eager that both the man's conduct, which is admirable and totally wondrous, and his name be made known to you. But indeed, if you desire to hear of his ascetic struggles and manly deeds, and in addition his life from the beginning and its conclusion, in death, let me first tell[60] <you> the name he was called,[61] and then, as it thus gives power <of speech> to our humble self, I will narrate events one by one, to the best of my ability.

2. This <man> is Ioannikios, who was distinguished in ascetic contests and renowned, the *faithful servant*[62] of God, *the heavenly man and earthly angel,*[63] and a delightful workshop of Christ. This <man> is Ioannikios, who rightly secured *the feet of his mind*[64] in the unshakable *rock which is*

---

[55] Cf. 2 Cor. 3:3.

[56] On "writing in gold (χρυσογραφία)," a specialized technique "used occasionally for whole manuscripts and regularly for epigrams, titles and initials, and also for special documents, the foreign letters, in the imperial chancery," see I. Hutter, "Decorative Systems in Byzantine Manuscripts, and the Scribe as Artist: Evidence from the Manuscripts in Oxford," *Word and Image* 12.1 (1996), 4–20, esp. 4–5. The reference here is, of course, metaphorical.

[57] Reading ᾗ for ἤ.

[58] See Gregory of Nazianzos (officially designated "the Theologian" by the Council of Chalcedon), *In laudem Athanasii* (or. 21), PG 35:1085B: Τούτων Ἀθανάσιος, τοῖς μὲν ἡμιλλήθη, τῶν δὲ μικρὸν ἀπελείφθη, ἔστι δὲ οὓς καὶ ὑπερέσχεν, εἰ μὴ τολμηρὸν εἰπεῖν.

[59] Cf. Basil of Caesarea, *Homiliae in Hexaemeron, Hom.* 2, chap. 1.4–5 (ed. S. Giet, *Homélies sur l'Hexaéméron,* 2d ed. [Paris, 1968], 138).

[60] Reading εἴπωμεν for εἴπομεν.

[61] Ioannikios' name is used eight times in the following chapter.

[62] Cf. Heb. 3:5 (used of Moses).

[63] Cf., e.g., John Chrysostom, *De poenitentia,* PG 49:291.1–2.

[64] Cf. John Chrysostom, *Expositio in Psalmum IV,* PG 55:48.6–7, who defines "thoughts" (λογισμοί) as "the feet of the mind."

Christ,[65] and strove to be elevated to heaven, in order to see Him more brightly. For he beheld each day the Lord *on his right hand,* as the psalmist David says,[66] and took care not to be *moved* by the attacks of the <evil> spirits tyrannizing him on either side, but already *reaching forward*[67] even more perfectly through the contests he accomplished, which indeed he did not fail to meet. This <man> is Ioannikios, who slipped into the *darkness*[68] of divine grace and like Moses on the mountain received tablets, not with his hands, but with his mind, with the finger of the spirit, and gave laws to the people through his actions. And after leading them through the darkness of life, that is the mundane sea, he brought them into the promised land, like Joshua, son of Naue,[69] and preserved them expertly. This <man> is Ioannikios, who cried out and heralded loudly from the peak of Mt. Olympos,[70] as in the midst of people and tyrannical emperors, that the incarnate Christ should be represented in images, and he never was fearful or ashamed. This <man> is Ioannikios, who put to flight the phalanxes of the invisible enemy, nobly enduring much severe cold and heat and *waiting for the Lord.*[71] This <man> is Ioannikios, who by the brilliance of his achievements was worthily called *more beautiful than the sons of men.*[72] This <man> is Ioannikios, who scorned the delights of the world and *counted them but dung,*[73] and flew away from the earthly army to embrace the better one. And he followed Christ, served Him, and was loved by Him, and rightly rested in the true *bridal chamber* of His glory and *led* eternal *choruses.*[74] This <man> is Ioannikios, who lived a prophetic life and saw distant things

[65] Cf. 1 Cor. 10:4.

[66] Ps. 15 (16):8.

[67] Cf. Phil. 3:13.

[68] Ex. 20:21: "Moses approached the darkness where God was" (εἰς τὸν γνόφον οὗ ἦν ὁ Θεός). Ioannikios is also said to enter this *darkness* (γνόφος) below at Chaps. 10 and 72. For the interpretation of the darkness as representing the ultimate inaccessibility of God to human comprehension, see Gregory of Nyssa, *The Life of Moses,* trans. A. Malherbe, E. Ferguson (New York, 1978), chaps. 162–69 and pp. 176–77, n. 191.

[69] I.e., the successor of Moses; see Josh. 1:1 ff.

[70] Bithynian Olympos, southeast of Prusa, a holy mountain and monastic center; see *ODB* 3:1525 and Janin, *Eglises Centres,* 127–91.

[71] Cf. Ps. 39 (40):1.

[72] Cf. Ps. 44 (45):2.

[73] Phil. 3:8.

[74] Cf. Mt. 25:1–13 and pseudo-John Chrysostom, *De salute animae,* PG 60:737.15.

as quite near and was deemed worthy, so to speak, of prophetic utterance and *apostolic blessings and healings*[75]—to an extent unequaled by anyone else I know—and became a fount of grace and receptacle of the all-holy Spirit.

3. And lest I go on at too great length[76] (I am not capable of praising the virtues of the all-blessed man—for I hesitate to speak, since even of those who recall <his deeds> more perfectly, who would be able to weave his praises?), to the best of my power of speech I will embark upon the aforementioned treatise to which I am obligated.[77] For even though I am unworthy of and poor in the gift of speech, I will reach out boldly toward the riches undeservedly. But nonetheless <the story> will be told, even if inadequately,[78] since *the prattlings of children are dear to their fathers*[79] and *our best efforts are dear to God.*[80] I will add even this, lest anyone suspect that I write falsehood and fabrication; [p. 386] for it is customary to defile what is useful with disbelief. For what gain is there to me from lying, if I support others, but show myself subject to the judgment of the Holy Spirit, as stated by the prophet David?[81] For what is said <here> is not myth, as it seems to the impious and faithless, but full of truth and packed with benefit, as it is for those who are pious and have achieved perfect mental discipline. I will begin from here, invoking God the source of every beginning.[82]

4. This most famous and divine man, the light of the wilderness[83] and all-shining pillar of monks, was called forth *not by men or through men,*[84] but by

---

[75] Cf. 1 Cor. 12:9.

[76] Cf. pseudo-John Chrysostom, *In natale domini nostri Jesu Christi,* PG 61:763.63–64: ἵνα μὴ ἐν τῷ προλόγῳ μηκύνω τὸν λόγον.

[77] I.e., he was commissioned to write by his abbot Eustratios; see Introduction, 245–47.

[78] Reading ἀποδεόντως for ἀποδέοντος. Or else maintain the original reading, and translate, "even though <I am> inadequate <to the task>," as suggested by A. Alexakis.

[79] Cf. John of Damascus, *Laudatio sancti Joannis Chrysostomi,* PG 96:764.9–10.

[80] Cf. Gregory of Nazianzos, *or.* 7, chap. 17 (PG 35:776B); *or.* 43, chap. 82 (PG 36:604D).

[81] Perhaps he is alluding to Ps. 1:5?

[82] There is a play on words between ἄρξομαι and ἀρχή.

[83] On the use of the term ἔρημος for "any wild, uninhabited region," see *ODB* 1:613, s.v. "Desert."

[84] Cf. Gal. 1:1.

divine grace from <heaven> above. His <home>land was the province[85] of the Bithynians; he was born in the village called Marykaton.[86] His father's name was Myritzikios, his mother's Anastaso.[87] From them then was born the star of the day, the all-bright sun, the illustrious Ioannikios. After he was piously weaned and passed beyond childhood to adolescence[88] and came to the age of young manhood, he first joined the army, and was assigned to the eighteenth company of the God-protected regiment of the Exkoubitoi.[89] He performed there every military duty well, surpassing all in intellect and strength; and he appeared to everyone as a pleasant and most attractive man, not only because of the blossoming gracefulness of his youth and for the splendor of his handsomeness, but already also because of his steadfastness and discipline and his praiseworthy demeanor and the great asceticism[90] of his conduct.

5. In those times the nation of the Huns, that is the Bulgarians,[91] moved to war against us Christians. And in response <a campaign> was launched against them by the scepter-carrying and most pious emperor named Con-

---

[85] On Bithynia, in northwest Asia Minor, opposite Constantinople, see *ODB* 1:292. It was initially part of the Opsikion theme, then in the mid to late 8th century divided between Opsikion and Optimatoi.

[86] Marykaton was located, according to Sabas (chap. 2), on the north shore of Lake Apollonias (for which see Janin, *Eglises Centres,* 153–54 and his map [p. 130] and below, n. 280). The village is also mentioned in the life of Paul the Younger (*AnalBoll* 11 [1892], 215) who lived in another village nearby, and by Cedrenus (Cedr. 550.14).

[87] Their family name was Boilas according to Sabas' version of the Life (chap. 6). For its possible Slavic origin see S. Vryonis, "St. Ioannicius the Great (754–846) and the 'Slavs' of Bithynia," *Byzantion* 31 (1961), 245–48.

[88] The word ἔφηβος is not elsewhere attested as an adjective and, if adjectival, the phrase "adolescent childhood" (applying the classical meaning) is odd. As an alternative, perhaps ἐφ᾽ ἥβην should be read for ἔφηβον, translating "childhood leading to adolescence."

[89] The Exkoubitoi were one of the regiments (*tagmata*) composed of professional soldiers, stationed at Constantinople. For a discussion of their role in the iconoclastic controversy, see W. E. Kaegi, "The Byzantine Armies and Iconoclasm," *ByzSlav* 27 (1966), 48–70, esp. 60–61 for Ioannikios. This passage is evidence that the Exkoubitoi were divided into at least eighteen companies (*banda*), on which see J. Haldon, *Byzantine Praetorians* (Bonn, 1984), 280.

[90] For the use of φιλοσοφία as "asceticism," see Lampe, *Lexicon,* s.v. B.5.b.

[91] The description of Bulgarians as "Huns" is apparently here an archaizing ethnic designation; see *ODB* 2:957–58.

stantine,[92] the son of the most blessed and orthodox empress Irene.[93] When both <armies> were drawn up at a place called Markellai,[94] there was a clash between them, and the Christians were defeated on account of our sins and turned their back to the enemy; and as the enemy was pursuing from behind and exacting severe casualties, even the emperor himself, after being lassoed by some device, was captured, dragged off, and held by those impious men. When he saw this, that most noble Ioannikios, impelled by divine zeal and, to speak with the prophet, *girded with strength*[95] [p. 387] from on high, courageously leapt into their midst and severing that snare (which I would call a diabolical contrivance) most quickly with a sword, miraculously saved the emperor;[96] he was himself protected by divine grace, scattering the enemy here and there as he went through their midst, preserved unharmed. When he withdrew a little from the battle and was making his way forward with seven other comrades, he saw in turn one of the aforementioned pagans making a stand and mercilessly slaughtering the Christians passing through there. For since, as I see it, a narrow defile, the aforementioned[97] pass, presented itself, the

[92] Constantine VI, emperor (780–797); see *ODB* 1:501–2.

[93] Irene, wife of Leo IV, sole empress (797–802), a devoted iconophile; see *ODB* 2:1008–9.

[94] Markellai was a fortification on the Byzantine-Bulgarian border; in 792 Constantine VI was defeated there by the Bulgarian khan Kardamos; see *ODB* 2:1300.

[95] Ps. 17 (18):32.

[96] Mango ("Ioannikios," 401, n. 22) has suggested that Peter exaggerated in having the saint save the emperor's life; the version by Sabas (chap. 6) says a "grandee" (ἕνα τῶν μεγιστάνων), not the emperor, was saved. For Peter's likely "borrowing," from the *Chronicle* of Theophanes (Theoph. 1:217 f), of the story of saving a lassoed emperor and its link to his anti-Stoudite rhetoric (he has Ioannikios save the life of the "most pious" emperor whose "adulterous" second marriage led to a major rift in the Church, particularly between the Stoudite monks and the patriarchs [*ODB* 2:1388–89, s.v. "Moechian Controversy"]), see Introduction to this *vita*, 249, and D. Sullivan, "Was Constantine VI Lassoed at Markellai?" *GRBS* 35 (1994), 287–91.

[97] The "aforementioned pass" here, τῆς εἰρημένης διαβάσεως, presumably refers to the "pass" implied in the participle διερχομένους ("passing through") in the previous sentence. Διαβάσεως is apparently in apposition to and explaining the term translated "narrow defile," κλεισούρας, which can mean (1) a defile, (2) a strongpoint or fortification guarding such a defile, and is also used to refer (3) to a territorial unit (on this last see *ODB* 2:1132). For a similar combination in the sense of a strongpoint above a pass, see Theophylaktos Simokattes, *Historiae* (ed. C. de Boor, revised P. Wirth [Stuttgart, 1972]) 7:14.8: οἱ βάρβαροι τὰ ἐχυρώματα τῶν διαβάσεων περικάθηνται· κλεισούρας τῇ

<soldiers> going in that direction could not proceed in any other way except that one. Immediately then he called upon God for assistance and, taking courage in the hope of his faith more than in arms, advanced most courageously against the accursed wretch, and guiding his sword with his hand against that lawless neck, like David of old against Goliath,[98] he bravely cut off the man's wretched head. So he crowned himself with a great victory that saved <many lives> and won painless and secure passage thenceforth for those passing through there.

6. He continued his journey in tears, contemplating the disaster and defeat that had occurred and filled with deepest grief. And coming to a lofty place he looked opposite and saw Mt. Olympos.[99] As soon as he beheld it, he immediately dismounted from his horse and stood in prayer. Directing[100] his eyes to heaven and spreading his hands upward to form a cross,[101] he called to his aid and assistance the gracious power of God and the

---

πατρίῳ Ῥωμαῖοι φωνῇ ἀποκαλεῖν ταῦτα εἰώθασιν. The version of Sabas (338A) says more simply that the enemy stood ἐπὶ μιᾶς στενῆς . . . διαβάσεως.

Alternatively one might translate, "since a narrow defile intervened in their aforementioned passage," but I can find no parallel to παρεμπίπτω being followed by a genitive.

[98] 1 Ki. 17:51.

[99] Ioannikios' itinerary following the battle of Markellai here and in the next chapter is problematic. Leaving Markellai (on the Byzantine-Bulgarian border) he journeyed (τὴν ὁδὸν διήνυεν) and saw a Mt. Olympos, where he prayed to the Theotokos and offered to give himself to the mountain (ἐπὶ τὸ ὄρος τοῦτο ἐμαυτὸν ἐκδώσω). Then he "completed the entire span of the road" (τὸ πᾶν τῆς ὁδοῦ διάστημα διανύσας) and came to Constantinople, next went home (to Marykaton in Bithynia) to visit his parents, then to the Agauroi monastery beside Mt. Olympos. The second Olympos is clearly the monastic mountain in Bithynia, but, as Constantinople lies between Markellai and Bithynia, is the first Mt. Olympos the same Bithynian mountain? Presumably so, particularly given Ioannikios' offer of self-dedication to the mountain, and since in the version by Sabas (chap. 7) the Olympos where Ioannikios prays is specifically identified as that in Bithynia. Yet Ioannikios' initial movement from Markellai to Olympos in Peter's version remains strange. A. Kazhdan (in his forthcoming *History of Byzantine Literature*) suggests that the first Olympos in Peter's version may be that in Thessaly.

[100] Reading τό τε for τότε.

[101] Perhaps in imitation of Moses, Ex. 17; cf., for example, John of Damascus, *Expositio fidei*, ed. B. Kotter, *Die Schriften des Johannes von Damaskos* 2 (Berlin, 1973), chap. 84.80: χεῖρες σταυροειδῶς ἐκτεινόμεναι καὶ τὸν Ἀμαλὴκ τροπούμεναι. The specific reference to a crosslike posture in prayer is also found in at least one other saint's *vita*; cf. the Life of Sabas the Younger, ed. I. Cozza-Luzi, *Historia et laudes ss. Sabae et Macarii* (Rome, 1893), 16.11: χεῖρας τείνας σταυροειδῶς.

defending protectress of the world and only bridge and salvation of the human race, the most venerable and most glorious mother of our God. And with groans and tears he spoke as follows in supplication: "Mother of the Word and virgin, *accept <this> vile petition* unworthily offered *from a vile mouth*[102] and do not cast aside one who wishes to be saved, but open for me the door of Thy compassionate mercy and guiding me to repentance be my helper and protection and guide, my harbor and succor and salvation. For from this time I make Thee the surety of my soul and, taking courage in Thee, I will give myself to this mountain and I will offer myself totally and completely and dedicate myself to Thee and to our God Who was born of Thee. And as I have placed all my hope in Thee, O queen, do not abandon me."

7. When he said these and additional <words> and offered his prayer, he mounted his horse and within a few days completed the entire span of the road and reached Constantinople. And after he made petition and supplication in all the venerable churches and offered his prayers to the Lord, he flew from the imperial city. He departed to his fatherland to garner his parents' blessings and spent a very brief time there with them. And just as he was about to return to his military unit—at the urging of God's love, I believe—he took leave of his parents or, to speak more correctly, renounced them, and giving them a final embrace and most rightly receiving their blessings, he again mounted his horse and made the journey he desired; he reached the monastery called Agauroi,[103] that is situated beside Mt. Olympos.

8. After he was received most joyfully by the <monks> there and given most generous hospitality, as is customary for those who serve God, he begged also to see the superior[104] of the monastery. When he achieved his request and fell at that great man's holy feet, [p. 388] he importuned him tearfully to point out to him a place for solitary contemplation, where he might serve God without distraction. The father saw his good intention, but knew that it would be

---

[102] John Chrysostom, *In parabolam de filio prodigo,* PG 59:519.8.

[103] On the monastery of Agauroi, "The Eunuchs" (Peter always uses the plural τῶν Ἀγαύρων, but it appears elsewhere as "Agauros" and "Augaros") on Mt. Olympos, a monastery known from other sources, see A. Hergès, "Le Monastère des Agaures," *EO* 2 (1898–99), 230–38; Janin, *Eglises Centres,* 132–34; and K. Ringrose, "Monks and Society in Iconoclastic Byzantium," *BS/EB* 6 (1979), 130–51, esp. 147 and 149 n. 61.

[104] The version of the *vita* by Sabas (chap. 8) indicates that his name was Gregory; see also Janin, *Eglises Centres,* 132–33.

unreasonable <to expect> someone not previously trained in ascetic struggles nor endowed with every virtue to attain, at the very beginning, the loftiest <goal of> solitary contemplation. And so <the superior> gave him good and most praiseworthy counsel, and urged him to go <first> to a monastic community and practice humility; then, so <trained>, to give himself to the athletic arena of solitary contemplation. When the father saw him persuaded by the advice, he blessed him and pointed out the road leading to Atroa;[105] he bade him journey to the monastery called Antidion,[106] and there to achieve great <personal> benefit through acceptance of a menial position.

9. After he obtained the father's blessings and wearily traveled the long road, he came to the aforementioned monastery. It happened, in accordance with the foresight of God, that the head[107] of the monastery met him; and indeed he began to ask him who he was, and from where he came and why he had come to the monastery. Ioannikios, the elect and predestined of God, answered: "The reason I am here, father, is to renounce all the earthly and mundane things of this life, lest I lose the eternal blessings of heaven." When he heard these <words> the *good shepherd*[108] admitted him to the monastery, instructing him in the sacred letters;[109] for he was not yet educated. By carefully teaching him every service and monastic discipline he [the superior] made him an *approved workman*[110] for God. After completing there a period of two years, he was prodded in his heart with, so to speak, golden goads by the desire for blessed contemplation and pressed the superior to let him go. And the one held <him> fast, the other made urgent entreaty. Finally the all-wise <father>, persuaded by his pleas, summoned him and embraced him in his

---

[105] The plain at the foot of Mt. Olympos, southwest of Prusa, and site of several monastic communities; see *ODB* 1:228 and Janin, *Eglises Centres,* 151. The version of Sabas (chap. 8) indicates that Ioannikios first came to a village of Kastoulo in the plain of Atroa, then went to a monastery called Telai, where he received education in basic literacy, before reaching Antidion.

[106] The monastery of Antidion on Mt. Olympos, where Ioannikios began his cenobitic monastic life and where he was buried, is known exclusively from his *vitae.* For his burial there see below, Chap. 71 and, generally, Janin, *Eglises Centres,* 135–36.

[107] The version by Sabas (chap. 9) gives his name as John.

[108] Cf. Jn. 10:11.

[109] On τὰ ἱερὰ γράμματα, see n. 52 to the Life of David, Symeon, and George, above.

[110] Cf. 2 Tim. 2:15.

arms and kissed that blessed neck. And after he bathed him abundantly[111] with tears, he entrusted him to the hands of God and sent him off with many other prayers. [p. 389]

10. With faith and prayer as his breastplate and holding the prayers of the all-blessed <father> in his hand like arrows, <Ioannikios> courageously went forth to war against the unseen enemy. He went up to mountain peaks and, after wandering through them, came to Mt. Agaurinon[112] very near <the dependency> of St. Kosmas.[113] Again therefore making his presence known to the head of the Agauroi <monastery>, he begged to see him. When <the superior> heard <his entreaty>, he immediately went up <to him> and after a prayer began asking why he had come. And so he learned that he came for solitary contemplation; this blessed Ioannikios pointed out the cave and supplicated him to have a tiny shelter constructed in it; immediately that hallowed man [the superior] ordered two of the brethren, Eustratios[114] and Theophylaktos, to carry out his request. After this was accomplished this blessed man bade farewell to the brethren and entered into the spiritual darkness.[115]

---

[111] Reading here (and below in Chaps. 62 and 68) with the manuscript, and at the suggestion of L. Rydén, καταχρηστικῶς for van den Gheyn's conjecture καταχριστικῶς. The choice requires a meaning ("excessively," "abundantly") for the frequently attested adverb not given in the lexica, but one recorded for the related noun, while the conjectured adverb καταχριστικῶς is not elsewhere attested. It is perhaps worth noting that, while van den Gheyn emends in all three cases, he translates the first two with "inungendo," and "inuncti," but the last with "abundanter."

[112] A spur of Mt. Olympos and apparently the same as Mt. Trichalix, mentioned below in Chap. 11; see Janin, *Eglises Centres,* 188–89, and Mango, "Ioannikios," 402.

[113] Peter below (Chap. 56) describes a plague of caterpillars as attacking the dependency of the Agauroi monastery dedicated to Sts. Kosmas and Damian. The same story is told by Sabas (chap. 32), who describes the metochion as dedicated to St. Kosmas. The metochion is also mentioned in the *Life of Eustratios* (*v. Eustrat.,* chap. 13); see Janin, *Eglises Centres,* 134.

[114] Eustratios was to become Ioannikios' closest friend and later superior of the Agauroi monastery; Peter, the author of the *Life,* also a monk of Agauroi, names Eustratios as the source of much of his information about Ioannikios (Chaps. 12, 46, and 54). Eustratios' own *Life* (*BHG* 645), in large part derived from the *Life of Ioannikios* by Sabas (see von Dobschütz, "Methodios und die Studiten," 100, n. 6), was edited by A. Papadopoulos-Kerameus, *Analekta Hierosolymitikes Stachyologias* 4 (St. Petersburg, 1897), 367–400.

[115] For the darkness and the relation to Moses, see above, n. 68.

There he petitioned God with prayers and fasting and diligently continued for thirteen years; he too received, like Moses of old, divine law and heavenly and prophetic gifts; he prophesied future events as if present and led many out of Egypt, that is out of the transitory and dark life, to the brilliant and heavenly abode and transported them to a better existence. Thus he became famous everywhere and many came to him, like a swarm of bees. That contemplative mind, *made* just *a little lower than angels,*[116] could not endure being disturbed by interaction with humans, but wished to live immaterially and purely and without distraction and to converse by himself with God alone. And so he decided to hide himself totally from men; and taking with him Peter and Sabas and Antony,[117] holy contemplative men, who symbolized the consubstantial Trinity,[118] he left for the region <of the theme> of the Thrakesioi.[119]

11. He spent some time there with them, until, as I believe, the despondency[120] to which humans are subject crept over the spiritual men and <Ioannikios> made them return to their former abode. That most noble man was left alone and decided to hide himself completely in the further regions of the wilderness. And while beseeching God most fervently to guide him in an expedient manner, he was overcome by weakness <and fell> into a semblance of sleep. He was advised in a dream by an angel, like that illustrious Joseph,[121] not once, but twice, and ordered to return to that mountain from which he had fled, so as not to conceal himself, since God had arranged this for the salvation and benefit of many. He knew not how to arch his neck against God, but to yield readily to His commands; he obeyed the angelic oracle that came

[116] Heb. 2:9.

[117] Certain identification of the three individuals mentioned here is not possible. Van den Gheyn (*AASS,* Nov. 2.1:391, notes e–g) suggests (a) that this Peter may be St. Peter of Atroa, (b) that it is possible to conjecture that this Sabas was the author of the other version of the Life of Ioannikios, and (c) that it is uncertain whether this Antony may be identified with the Antony mentioned in the version by Sabas (chap. 36). Sabas does claim (chap. 44) that Ioannikios related to him a vision of the death of Peter of Atroa, but for doubts about Sabas' veracity see Mango, "Ioannikios," 394 and n. 6.

[118] Presumably they symbolized the Trinity, because there were three of them.

[119] For the Thrakesion theme of western Asia Minor, which included Ionia, Lydia, and parts of Phrygia and Caria, see *ODB* 3:2080 and Oikonomidès, *Listes,* 348.

[120] On despondency (ἀκηδία), a state of listlessness found in monks, see *ODB* 1:44–45.

[121] Mt. 1:20, 2:12–22.

from God and returned again, not to the cave in which he had lived, but to other very rugged places of crags and abysses called Trichalix.[122] And there he thought to escape <the attention of> everyone, [p. 390] but since, according to the words spoken by God, *"A city that is set on a hill cannot be hidden. Neither do men light a lamp and put it under a bushel but on a lampstand, and it giveth light unto all that are in the house,"*[123] so also this man shone forth by his good works and became then even more famous than before. For the oft-mentioned most holy superior, when he learned of his arrival, went up to him most eagerly. <The superior> blessed him, or rather, to tell the truth, was himself blessed by him [Ioannikios], and both men gave thanks to God. And <the superior> again ordered his two subordinates, Eustratios and Theophylaktos, to build a cell for the blessed man and to obey him most humbly in all his bidding; with these words he departed.

12. The God-inspired Ioannikios was greatly devoted to and loved the most devout Eustratios, more than anyone else. This was not unreasonable; for he knew that this man would later be entrusted with the helm of leadership[124] and be proclaimed as father of many spiritual sheep. Whenever something confidential or important occurred to him, that holy soul reported it all to the wondrous Eustratios. And indeed I was prompted by no other than this divine man to compile[125] this holy and beneficial treatise. Since I feared the danger of disobedience but, to tell the truth, was overcome by our father's orders, I have moved my foot *more expansively*[126] and overreaching myself, so to speak, have fulfilled the commission with great anxiety, although unworthily, if I may say it, and in an untutored manner. And I am going to repeat to you also all that I have heard from him. You all know the man, how from the beginning to the end he followed the saint, how he was dignified by both

---

[122] Sabas (chap. 10) indicates that Trichalix was the "mountain of the Agauroi monastery," hence a spur of Mt. Olympos and apparently the same as the Mt. Agaurinon mentioned above by Peter in Chap. 10 (see n. 112). It is also mentioned in the *Life of Eustratios;* see Janin, *Eglises Centres,* 188–89.

[123] Mt. 5:14–15.

[124] I.e., would become superior of the Agauroi monastery as he did during the reign of Theophilos; see Janin, *Eglises Centres,* 133.

[125] For the roles of Peter and Eustratios in the composition of the *vita,* see Introduction, 245–47.

[126] Cf. Gregory of Nyssa, *In sanctum Ephraim,* PG 46:849.26.

his words and deeds so that one could almost say that he illuminated in angelic imitation all the land of the Bithynians and quietly guided and brought it to <safe> harbor by his enlightening injunctions. But now I must return to the goal of my story.

13. While the cell was being built, as mentioned, those engaged in the task suddenly raised their eyes and saw a herd of wild goats grazing; one of them, quite large, handsome, and fat, approached them, apart <from the others>. While they were considering whether it was possible to catch him and make him into a very fine wineskin, the great and most clairvoyant Ioannikios became aware <of their thoughts and> said to one of the brothers, Sabas by name: "Go, brother, and catch the animal and bring him to me." Immediately then the brother carried out his bidding and led the animal, not by compulsion but willingly, to the blessed man; and he set it before him not constrained, but totally free. <The saint> filled his hand with salt and offered it to the animal, which most gratefully took the salt. Likewise <the saint> filled[127] a cup[128] full of the clearest[129] water and offered it; <the goat> eagerly drained it off,[130] as if from some fine spring or *flinty rock*[131] gushing forth streams of water. As the brothers stood in amazement, the saint smiling gently said: "Will this one, then, brothers, make a wineskin?" When they replied, "Certainly," the blessed man said, "Since the deed was accomplished by the grace of Christ, let this <animal> go unharmed." And he again bade the aforementioned Sabas to take the animal by the horns and lead him to some place and let him go. This was indeed the first miracle of that prophetic and angelic man. [p. 391]

14. You will <now> learn the nature of the second <miracle>. In those times, as mentioned earlier, the nation of Bulgarians again moved to war, and the most pious emperor who then wielded the scepter of the empire, Nike-

---

[127] Reading πλήσας for πλήρη.

[128] The Greek term translated here (and below in Chap. 22) as "cup" is βαυκάλιον. On the evolution of its meaning, see A. Leroy-Molinghen, "Du κώθων au βαυκάλιον," *Byzantion* 35 (1965), 208–20 and J. S. Palmer, *El Monacato Oriental en el Pratum Spirituale de Juan Mosco* (Madrid, 1993), 392. Additional examples of the word are listed in DuCange (s.v.) and add *v. Eliae Spel.* 862, chap. 36:13–16, 873, chap. 61:22–24; *v. Mich. Sync.* 52:13; *v. Petr. Atr.* 54.9, 14.

[129] Reading διειδεστάτου for δι' ἡδεστάτου, as suggested by A. Alexakis.

[130] Reading ἀπαρύεται for ἀπαρρύεται.

[131] Deut. 8:15.

phoros[132] by name, campaigned against them. When this occurred, the so-called co-parents-in-law[133] of the emperor, taking the opportunity, went to the blessed man in the company also of the revered Eustratios, the best friend of the blessed man. And when they had seen him and received his blessing, they asked him also to pray most earnestly for the emperors. Since he knew what was about to happen, that most pure mind replied: "I have prayed already on behalf of the emperors,[134] my children, and I will pray now on behalf of the emperor."[135] They were stung by his obscure <statement> and remained speechless; for none of them comprehended what was said, except Eustratios alone, since he was a shrewd man. The saint looked at him and nodded <to him> to be silent, and <then>, turning again to the others, dismissed them with a blessing. As they went down the mountain, they sought to learn quite precisely from the most devout Eustratios what was <the meaning of> the statement. And he said: "So that you may see that, with God's consent, the emperor has fallen in the battle;[136] for this reason he said to you, 'I have already prayed for the emperors <and> I will pray now for the one who is going to be proclaimed emperor.'" The men were gravely shaken, overcome by anxiety and fear; they whipped on their horses and very quickly completed their journey. Upon their arrival near Pylai,[137] they

---

[132] Nikephoros I, emperor (802–811); see *ODB* 3:1476–77.

[133] The term συμπένθεροι should mean "co-parents-in-law," and hence refer to the parents of either Nikephoros' son-in-law Michael Rangabe (who married his daughter Prokopia) or those of his daughter-in-law Theophano of Athens, the wife of his son Staurakios. The subsequent reference to Staurakios as the γαμβρός (a term that ranges in meaning from "in-law" generally to "son-in-law," but also "brother-in-law" or "father-in-law") of these same people would perhaps suggest that the parents of Theophano, a relative of the empress Irene, are referred to here. Peter's designation of the term συμπένθεροι as "so-called," Sabas' use (chap. 15) of the generic term "relatives" (συγγενῶν) for them, and the use of γαμβρός by both Sabas and by Theophanes the Confessor to refer to Michael Rangabe in relation to Staurakios (i.e., "brother-in-law"), however, suggest the fluid nature of these relational designations and make specific identification tenuous. I have therefore translated γαμβρός below simply as "in-law."

[134] I.e., Nikephoros and his son Staurakios, who had been crowned co-emperor in December 803; see *ODB* 3:1945–46.

[135] I.e., Staurakios on the death of his father.

[136] Nikephoros was killed in battle by the Bulgarian forces under Krum on 26 July 811; see Treadgold, *Byz. Revival,* 172–74.

[137] Reading Πυλῶν, following a suggestion of A. Alexakis. For Pylai, a port on the Sea of Marmara and regular place of embarkation to Constantinople, see *ODB* 3:1760,

heard that pitiful and sorrowful news, the death of the emperor,[138] as was mentioned, being cried out by all. With fear and lamentation they completed the remainder of their journey by sea and came to anchor in the imperial city.

15. So that the words of the prophecy might be fulfilled, Staurakios, the son of Nikephoros, succeeded to the empire. While he was guiding the empire, the aforementioned in-laws of the emperor were again possessed with an uncontrollable desire to see the blessed man and especially to seek to learn whether or not their in-law's reign would be a long one. [p. 392] They were absorbed in these thoughts, but found no opportunity to fulfill their hearts' desire. One day, as they were going to the palace, they met the most reverent Eustratios on the street (for he had been sent by his superior to the imperial city on some business). As soon as they recognized him, they greeted him most sincerely and, after embracing him with both arms, hastened to return to their home with him. After they provided him with wax candles and incense and other gifts and petitioned him, they sent him to learn from the saint most precisely the future of their in-law and to inform them. He departed <from Constantinople> and first spoke to that best of shepherds[139] concerning the mission entrusted to him, and then, after obtaining his blessing, went to the blessed man [Ioannikios]. When he had presented himself to him and obtained his blessing, <Eustratios> gave him the gifts and sought to learn what would happen to the emperor. That high-minded and heavenly person, after being pressured for some time and not wishing to distress the <other> man in any way, opened his mouth only after long delay, and answered with a parable, as tears flowed down his cheeks: "O most beloved Eustratios, let it be known to you that like a *bird* sitting *on some spreading branch*[140] of a plant and singing sweetly, when a hawk suddenly appears and most quickly seizes him, in such a brief time will this man's reign be snatched away." And this is what happened, for the very brief duration of his reign[141] is not

---

and for a tentative location see the map of Janin, *Eglises Centres,* <xviii>. This seems more likely than van den Gheyn's πυλῶν, referring to the "gates" of Prusa, the first city they would be likely to reach after leaving Mt. Olympos, particularly as they are said to have "completed the remainder of their journey by sea."

[138] 26 July 811.

[139] I.e., his abbot.

[140] Cf. Sap. 17:18.

[141] 28 July to 1 October 811.

unknown, but quite well known to all. Michael,[142] who was <to be later> distinguished by his monastic rank,[143] succeeded to the empire. And you will learn subsequently how this <Michael> was overpowered by Leo,[144] a man of savage name[145] and savage temperament, and had his empire stolen away.

16. The son of Tourkos,[146] Bryenes by name, made it a habit to visit the saint frequently and obtain his prayers. On one of his frequent visits, the God-inspired man said to him: "Lord Bryenes, does your cousin[147] know how to herd sheep?" Upset at the question, <Bryenes> replied: "How could this man guard sheep, father, when he is entrusted with a military command? For it would be completely improper and incongruous." The most admirable <Ioannikios> spoke as he did, since he foresaw that this <cousin> would later be emperor,[148] and that he would be a wolf not a shepherd, and would tear to shreds the flock of Christ and the God-woven tunic of the church of God.[149] Nevertheless the blessed man remained silent, prayed for <Bryenes> and sent him off. After some time the Bulgarian nation rose to war again[150] against the

---

[142] Michael I Rangabe, emperor (811–813). He was married to Staurakios' sister Prokopia and had survived the battle that cost Nikephoros and eventually Staurakios their lives; see *ODB* 2:1362.

[143] Michael became a monk after being deposed (11 July 813) by Leo.

[144] On Leo V the Armenian, emperor (813–820), who restored iconoclasm, see General Introduction, above, xiv–xv.

[145] I.e., Leo = lion. For this type of punning on the name of a bad character and specifically Leo V, see the Life of David, Symeon, and George, above, n. 185, and *v. Mich. Sync.* 145–46.

[146] Tourkos is Bardanes Tourkos, *strategos* of the theme of Anatolikon (802–803); see *ODB* 1:255.

[147] For discussion of the term (ἐξάδελφος) Peter uses to describe the relationship of Bryenes to Leo, see D. Turner, "The Origins and Accession of Leo V (813–820)," *JÖB* 40 (1990), 171–203, esp. 177, where he suggests that Leo's father Bardas was a brother of Bryenes' mother Domnika. Mango, however ("Ioannikios," 400 n. 17), comments "Leo's father was the brother or, at any rate, a close relative of Bardanes Tourkos." The version by Sabas uses the term ἀδελφιδός to describe the relationship and adds that Bryenes was a senator (συγκλητικός).

[148] I.e., Leo V.

[149] For this metaphor, see n. 520 in Chap. 70.

[150] I.e., A.D. 813.

Christians; it happened that that most vile <cousin>, as he was military commander of the theme of the Anatolians,[151] went forth to oppose
them[152] together with the most blessed and pious and orthodox emperor lord
Michael. Thereafter, with God's permission, <Leo> drove out the Christ-
loving man [Michael] from the imperial rule and himself tyrannically[153] seized,
as has been said, the diadem of the empire.

17. The aforementioned Bryenes remembered the words spoken by the
saint, and especially when he saw the fulfillment of that prophetic utterance
he explained them all to the tyrant. But he [Leo] said: "Go quickly and please
inquire also precisely how long our reign will be[154] and return and report to
me; for if he examined so well events before our rule, how much more will he
know what is to follow." As Bryenes was carrying out his bidding and was
about to approach the saint's cell, the blessed man became aware of his arrival
and said to the most excellent Eustratios who was there with him at that time:
"I want you to know, dearest Eustratios, [p. 393] that the chameleon[155] tyrant,
who became emperor because of our sins, is stirring up a terrible persecution
against the church of God; indeed he has even sent Bryenes whom we know
so well to learn from us his future. But arise and go to meet him and, after
addressing him sternly <and> with wise words, let him come to me." When

---

[151] On the Anatolikon, one of the original themes of Asia Minor with its capital at
Amorion, see *ODB* 1:89–90.

[152] I.e., at Versinikia, north of Adrianople, 22 June 813; see *ODB* 3:2161.

[153] For the traditional view of Leo's accession as emperor, see Bury, *Eastern Roman
Empire,* 26–30; for the view that Peter's statement reflects iconodule bias see Turner,
"Leo V," 192 and n. 110 and 201 where he concludes: "Leo, however, did not usurp the
throne, but accepted it in the face of the willing abdication of the emperor Michael I
and after pressure from the army, the patriarch and the Senate."

[154] Leo's concern with the length of his reign is also reflected in the story that a monk
Sabbatios led him into iconoclasm with the promise of a long reign; cf. *TheophCont*
26–28 and Genes. 10.24 ff.

[155] The Scriptor Incertus, *De Leone Bardae* (ed. I. Bekker, *Leonis Grammatici Chronographia* [Bonn, 1842], 341.3–7) says: καθάπερ ὁ λόγος ὑπογράφει τὸν χαμαιλέοντα
ἐναλλάττειν τὰς μορφάς, οὕτως καὶ αὐτὸς ποτὲ μὲν ὡς χρηστολόγος καὶ ἄριστος φαινό-
μενος, ποτὲ καὶ τοὐναντίον, ὅπερ καὶ δικαίως ἐπωνομάσθη Χαμαιλέων ὑπὸ ἁγίου ἀν-
δρός (i.e., the patriarch Nikephoros I). The term "chameleon" literally means "ground
lion," a play on Leo (=lion). As Symeon Magistros (ps.-Sym. Mag. 603.3–4) says of
the emperor Leo V, "He was short in stature (and so called chameleon)." See also *v.
Niceph.* 162.24 and PG 100:570 n. 37.

the most devout Eustratios had gone just *a bow-shot away*,[156] he met the man; and <Bryenes>, feigning the customary greeting, inquired if he had heard from the saint anything concerning the tyrant. And <Eustratios> replied: "He will be a great enemy of God and will severely upset the church of God; but proceed and learn <for yourself> most clearly from the just man." <Bryenes> appeared before the saint and knelt on the ground with both knees; after receiving a blessing from the saint he rose and eagerly sought to learn about the wretched <emperor>. The blessed man employed rather grave words and explained all <the tyrant's> wickedness in summary fashion. When that one [Bryenes] feigned <ignorance> and said it was not so, the blessed man in turn replied: "As you have heard, so will it be, and as you have heard, so will you report." <Bryenes> took his leave of the saint and, returning to the emperor, reported all that was said. The tyrant, severely shocked and most especially astounded that the persecution had not escaped notice, said to his emissary: "What did you learn about the length of our reign?" He <replied>: "I pressed him severely, but he told us no more than you have heard." When he learned this, the tyrant said: "I don't think he is ignorant of that <fact>; so hasten quickly and, after questioning <him>, give us a full report." The man made the journey in haste but learned nothing other than what he had <already> heard; and so he returned again unsuccessful to the emperor.

18. Leo the tyrant, whose name indicates his savagery,[157] at first contrived to hide the deceit of his mind, as if by a curtain; using treachery and falsely fabricated piety and faith, he thought therewith to deceive, I believe, the majority of the simpler folk. <But> just as a bad tree cannot bear good fruit, <his nature> became manifest to all through his bad fruits.[158] When he realized that he did not escape detection, he revealed his nefarious purpose and displayed openly his impiety and, upholding the teachings of Mani,[159] the wretch dared to remove every beneficial and iconographic image of Christ our

---

[156] Cf. Gen. 21:16.

[157] See n. 145.

[158] Cf. Mt. 7:17–18, 12:33; Lk. 6:43.

[159] The use of the term Manichaeans as a synonym for iconoclasts in the 8th and 9th centuries has been shown by N. Garsoian, *The Paulician Heresy* (The Hague, 1967), 197–204. She suggests that it was based on the iconoclastic rejection of matter and the Incarnation.

God Who revealed Himself as God and man, and of His most glorious mother and all the saints. And after he exiled[160] the divine patriarch[161] and replaced him with a shameful and nefarious one,[162] he put in chains every sanctioned congregation, priestly and monastic, so to speak, and of pious laity. Some he gave over to drowning[163] in the dead of night;[164] he cruelly[165] slit the throats of others, some he subjected to punishments and floggings and fetters of torture racks, others he sent to prison bound in iron chains; and some he treated in a kindly and gentle manner, while others he crushed with hunger and thirst. Sometimes he deceived the simpler folk and won them over to his position, either wearied by fear of torture, or deceived by the glory of the transitory and fleeting <nature of> life. Not sated with this, the tyrant began to despoil those living for the Lord *in deserts and in mountains and in dens and caves of*

---

[160] Reading ὑπερωρίσας for ὑπερορήσας.

[161] Nikephoros I, deposed 13 March 815; see his *vita* earlier in this volume.

[162] Theodotos I Kassiteras (815–ca. Jan. 821), from the iconoclast family of Melissenoi. He presided over the local council of Constantinople of 815, which officially reestablished iconoclasm; see *ODB* 3:2054 and Life of Nikephoros, above, n. 410.

[163] I do not find ποντοφορήτους attested elsewhere, but a word of parallel formation, ποταμοφόρητος, "carried off by a river," is attested in Liddell-Scott, *Lexicon*, s.v. The translation is supported somewhat by the use of the phrase ἐν θαλάσσῃ ποντοῦσθαι to refer to drowning in a list of punishments of iconodules in the earlier and influential Νουθεσία γέροντος περὶ τῶν ἁγίων εἰκόνων (ed. B. Melioranskij, *Georgij Kiprianin i Ioann Ierusalimlianin* [St. Petersburg, 1901], vii, 18). For a contemporary reference to punishment by drowning under Leo V, see Fatouros, *Theod. Stud. Epist.* 2:408, no. 275:53–54 (εἰσὶ δὲ οἳ καὶ σακκισθέντες ἐθαλασσεύθησαν ἀωρίᾳ), and the related comments of Bury, *Eastern Roman Empire,* 74–75. For other examples of punishment by drowning see *v. Nicet. Med.* xxiv, chap. 29; *v. Niceph.* 206.22–23; the *vita* of Theophylaktos of Nikomedeia, ed. F. Halkin, *Hagiologie byzantine* (Brussels, 1986), 171.1; *v. Euthym. Sard.* 35.193; *v. Davidis, Sym. et Georg.* 238.24; and the *vita* of the Forty-Two Martyrs of Amorion, ed. V. Vasil'evskij and P. Nikitin, *Skazanija o 42 amorijskich mučenikach* (St. Petersburg, 1905), 24.29.

[164] Reading ἀώρως for ἀόρως which is unattested. The translation "in the dead of night" is prompted by P. Henry's translation of the passage from a letter of Theodore of Stoudios cited in the above footnote as "some were tied up in sacks and thrown into the sea at night (ἀωρίᾳ)"; cf. P. Henry, "Theodore of Stoudios: Byzantine Churchman," Ph.D. dissertation, Yale University, 1968, 310–11. Van den Gheyn, who retains ἀόρως, translates "ut secreto in mare mergantur." L. Rydén suggests emending ἀόρως to ἀοράτως and translating "secretly."

[165] Reading ἀνηλεῶς for ἀνειλεῶς.

the earth[166] and sent everywhere officials full of impiety. He gave them the following order: if they found certain people kissing the icon of Christ, but they were <subsequently> persuaded to renounce its veneration, they would be deemed worthy of mercy; otherwise they [p. 394] should be killed in various ways with different forms of punishments. And especially if they were able to arrest and send the blessed man to him in chains, they would receive no ordinary honors and promotions. Agitation and fear then possessed everyone and everything was full of cries and lamentation. For father handed over child to <certain> death, and children their fathers, and brothers brothers and friends friends and, simply put, great grief possessed the whole land.

19. Since the blessed man knew that they would also search for him, he moved to the mountain called Alsos;[167] and there he outspokenly proclaimed the word of truth, building also venerable churches in the name of our lady the Mother of God and the holy chief apostles Peter and Paul and the military martyr Eustathios.[168] But let no one, who hears that our blessed father ran away, assume that he feared the tyrant or death; for he was a wanderer through the world and rejected all its delights, and moreover gave up his *mother and father and sisters*[169] for the Lord; he feared neither death nor the anger of the tyrant, but heard the apostle saying, *"Give place unto wrath,"*[170] and again the Lord in the divine Gospels advising, *"But when they persecute you in this city, flee ye into another"*;[171] so he fled, at the same time restraining his overboldness. The Lord Who guards the souls of His saints and *keeps them from the hand of the sinner*[172] also preserved him by His divine grace and saved him

---

[166] Heb. 11:38.

[167] Mt. Alsos (mentioned below, see Chap. 41) is apparently the same as Mt. Lissos, which is also mentioned below (see Chap. 39), and Mt. Lisos in the version of Sabas (for the identification see Mango, "Ioannikios," 402). Sabas (chap. 14) says: ἐπὶ τὰ τῆς Λυδίας τοῦ ἄλσους ὄρη καὶ ἐν κάστρῳ τῷ Λισῷ παρακειμένῳ τόπῳ, Χελιδόνα καλουμένῳ . . . , suggesting a location in Lydia southwest of Mt. Olympos; see also Janin, *Eglises Centres,* 150, and below, n. 292.

[168] The martyr and saint executed under Trajan (*BHG* 641–43); see *ODB* 2:753 and below, Chap. 22.

[169] Cf. Mk. 10:29; Mt. 19:29.

[170] Rom. 12:19.

[171] Mt. 10:23.

[172] Ps. 139 (140):4.

for the salvation [p. 395] and benefit of many people who are saved. But since we have made mention of the holy and venerable churches, we will also describe in so far as we can the reason for their construction.

20. A certain thoroughly evil and terrible man, Gourias by name, was a deceiver of people and magical[173] seer, and, in the words of the apostle, trained by the devil as and <truly> being *a vessel for the wrath of destruction*.[174] He undertook the solitary life, not in truth, but as a falsehood and pretense; and he feigned to have a semblance of piety, but totally rejected its essence. This most abominable man could not bear that the name of the saint, our most divine father, was invoked and echoed <everywhere>, celebrated by all and deservedly praised. This malignant wretch, this misanthrope, was overcome by the passion of envy;[175] he came to kill the blessed man in a crafty manner, like another serpent.[176] So, mixing the poison of treachery with humility, the lover of falsehood begged with lamentable lies to become, ostensibly, a disciple of the great man of God. He reasoned, although this was quite rash and in vain, that if only he might obtain the invitation to join the saint, he could destroy him in <one of> two ways. For either he would frighten[177] or terrify him with the abuse and terror of the *rebellious powers*[178] who assisted him in his magic and would drive him away; or, if defeated in this, he would take refuge in another magical technique. Combining[179] deadly mixtures of potions in food or drink and offering them surreptitiously,[180] he would suddenly rob him of his life; and he [Gourias] all alone would capture from men the glory

---

[173] On magic in Byzantium, see the articles "Magic" and "Magicians" in *ODB* 2:1265–66, and H. Maguire, ed., *Byzantine Magic* (Washington, D.C., 1995).

[174] Cf. Rom. 9:22: σκεύη ὀργῆς κατηρτισμένα εἰς ἀπώλειαν.

[175] On the intensity of rivalry among ascetics with specific discussion of this passage, see A. Kazhdan, "Hermitic, Cenobitic and Secular Ideals in Byzantine Hagiography of the Ninth through the Twelfth Centuries," *GOrThR* 30 (1985), 473–87, esp. 481–82, and D. Abrahamse, "Magic and Sorcery in the Hagiography of the Middle Byzantine Period," *ByzF* 8 (1982), 3–17, esp. 10–11.

[176] Cf. Gen. 3.

[177] Reading δειματώσας for δειγματίσας.

[178] B. Pruche, *Basile de Césarée. Sur le Saint-Esprit,* 2d ed. (Paris, 1968), chap. 20, sec. 51.40–41.

[179] Reading συμμίσγων for συσμίγων.

[180] Reading λεληθότως for λεληθότος.

of highest fame as a solitary anchorite. In the ignorance of his benighted mind he did not comprehend that the power of Christ is invincible but, to speak with the prophet, he was deaf, like *an asp that stops her ears,*[181] and did not heed the God-inspired voice that cried out most clearly to the apostles and to our father who is second in holiness <only> to the apostles: "*I beheld Satan as lightning fall from heaven; behold I give unto you power to tread on serpents and scorpions, and over all the power of the enemy*";[182] and, "*if they drink any deadly thing it shall not hurt them.*"[183] Since he [Gourias] was *walking in the darkness,*[184] he did not understand these God-inspired words, but he came, as mentioned, to the saint, his heart filled by Satan with other terrible notions. But our divinely inspired father was not at all ignorant of his evil deceit, but indeed, as I think, rather desired to expose him and to reveal the rot and weakness of that mind bloated with magic, and <to show> that by God's grace he [Ioannikios] would suffer no <harm> from partaking of the magic potions; but indeed that, protected by heavenly Providence, he would put to flight the prince of darkness and spirits of evil[185] and demonstrate their weakness. And so <Ioannikios> accepted him, ostensibly, as a disciple and entrusted him with the rank of assistant.

21. The son of the Devil most gladly settled in and immediately tried to begin his magical practices. And so one day—it was late at night— he went out of the cell before dawn and, going to a spooky place, summoned to his side in full armor the demonic phalanxes who worked with him. These were transformed into a multitude of horse and foot soldiers in iron armor; they seemed to hold bows and arrows and quivers and stood in a circle around him. When that abominable magician saw them, he was greatly emboldened and urged them to go to war against the blessed man. As they immediately marched out at his order, the arrows in the quivers of the <soldiers> who carried them made a loud noise.[186] [p. 396] When they were a short distance from the cell, they drew up into formation, and began to shout and launch a thick <hail of> arrows against the saint. Our most holy father, to speak with

[181] Ps. 57 (58):4.
[182] Lk. 10:18–19.
[183] Mk. 16:18.
[184] Is. 9:2.
[185] Cf. Eph. 6:12.
[186] For the ominous sound of arrows in a quiver, cf. Homer, *Il.* 1:45–46.

the scripture, was *confident as a lion*[187] and in no way frightened,[188] but lifting his holy palms to heaven, called to his aid *the Lord* Who is fearsome in war and *mighty.*[189] And he chanted from the psalms as follows: "*The Lord is my light and my Savior, whom shall I fear? The Lord is the defender of my life, of whom shall I be afraid?*[190] *Though an army should set itself in array against me, my heart shall not be afraid. Though war should rise up against me, in this I am confident.*"[191] He made the four-part[192] sign of the cross in the air with his hand and immediately caused all that demonic multitude to disappear. He <then> began again to sing psalms as follows: "*My persecutors and mine enemies they fainted and fell,*[193] verily *Let their sword enter into their own heart and their bows be broken,*"[194] and "*Some glory in chariots, some in horses, we will glory in the name of the Lord; they are overthrown and fallen, but we are risen and have been set upright.*"[195] After he sang very many other <psalms> similar to these and prayed intensely, he fell silent.

22. After the hater of monks failed in these <efforts>, he next rested his hopes on another kind of magic. Finding an opportune moment, he ground up a compound of various poisons and mixed them together in honey and milk. He <then> filled a cup[196] with the mixture and offered it to the saint. Our all-blessed father stretched out his hand and, making the life-giving sign of the cross as was his custom, drank it confidently. That deceitful and

[187] Prov. 28:1.

[188] Reading δειλανθείς for δηλανθείς.

[189] Cf. Ps. 23 (24):8.

[190] Ps. 26 (27):1.

[191] Ps. 26 (27):3.

[192] The Greek here is τετραμερῶς. Cf. Basil, *Commento al profeta Isaia,* ed. P. Trevisan, 2 vols. (Turin, 1939), 11:250.16: Τετραχῇ γὰρ διαιρεῖται τοῦ σταυροῦ τὰ μέρη, ὥστε ἕκαστον ἀπονεύειν πρὸς τὰ τέσσαρα μέρη τοῦ κόσμου. Εἴτε οὖν ἵνα πάντα τὰ μέρη διὰ τῶν μερῶν τοῦ σταυροῦ οἰκονομηθῇ πρὸς σωτηρίαν; and Gregory of Nyssa, *Oratio catechetica magna,* ed. J. Srawley, *The Catechetical Oration of Gregory of Nyssa* (Cambridge, 1903; repr. 1956), 32:55: τοῦτο διὰ τοῦ σταυροῦ διδασκόμεθα, τετραχῇ τοῦ κατ' αὐτὸν σχήματος διῃρημένου, ὡς ἐκ τοῦ μέσου, καθ' ὃ πρὸς ἑαυτὸν συνάπτεται, τέσσαρας ἀριθμεῖσθαι τὰς προβολάς.

[193] Ps. 26 (27):2.

[194] Ps. 36 (37):15.

[195] Ps. 19 (20):7–8.

[196] See n. 128 above.

wretched magician was filled with joy, thinking and hoping that <the saint> would die very quickly; he was elated and haughty, as if he had obtained his hope. Did he prevail as he planned or did he kill the saint? Perish <the thought>! On the contrary he was deceived in his hope and most clearly exposed as having broken the law in vain. For after <Ioannikios> drank the poison, as mentioned, and was suffering severe internal pain, he petitioned God Who loves men to save him from that deadly magical intrigue. He had recourse in sleep from the pains that beset him <and> saw a most handsome man wearing military attire, who stood beside him and held in his right hand a healing remedy; he urged him to *take* and *eat*[197] it and recover his health. The saint asked him to indicate who he was and as whose emissary he had come. This man announced that he was the soldier Eustathios[198] sent by God to aid and protect him; at the same time he also pointed out the remedy he held in his hand, <saying> that if he should *take* and *eat* it, he should no longer fear being harmed or injured by any of the various magical potions that might be offered to him. The blessed man took this <remedy> and swallowed it in one gulp. Suddenly he awoke and, though he looked this way and that, he saw no one, but suffering and riven with severe stomach pain he was forced to vomit; he turned his mouth toward the ground and spewed forth the poison with a copious amount of blood. <Thus> relieved of his pains, he praised God Who had saved him through St. Eustathios. And <indeed> as soon as he had thoroughly discredited and shamed that magician and driven him away, he immediately erected a holy church in the name of the holy martyr Eustathios. And when he made it into a monastery,[199] he tonsured many there and offered them to the Lord, so that to the present time the number of those living there is about seventy. After he appointed one of them, indeed the most devout man,[200] as superior, he delegated and entrusted the supervision <of the monastery> to him, while he himself again undertook <solitary> contemplation. [p. 397]

---

[197] The words are reminiscent of the Eucharist; cf. Mt. 26:26.

[198] See above, n. 168.

[199] The version of Sabas (chap. 49) indicates that the churches and monasteries of both Eustathios and the Theotokos were officially consecrated only after the Triumph of Orthodoxy; see also Janin, *Eglises Centres,* 150.

[200] The version of Sabas (chap. 49) indicates that the superior of St. Eustathios at the time of its official consecration (ca. 844–845) was named Makar; Janin (*Eglises Centres,* 150) considers him "le premier higoumène."

23. Some days later he perceived in a dream a spring rising toward the east and a multitude of blind sheep going to the spring. As soon as they came into contact with and touched the water they regained their eyesight and departed in good health. As the blessed man marveled and pondered what this might mean, he saw a man dressed in white[201] pointing and saying to him: "This spring at which you look in wonder, Ioannikios, is <that> of the Mother of God, and whoever approaches it with blind eyes, and takes and washes with the water, will see with the eyes of the mind[202] and be saved." The blessed man awoke trembling and, although he went to the place he had perceived <in his vision>, he did not find the spring he had seen. He observed, however, that the place was very beautiful and well-situated, and since he considered that it would be most pleasing for the Mother of God to immediately dwell there, he erected a venerable church in her name. And he made this a monastery and led forth many from the blindness[203] of life; he tonsured them and dispensed *the light of the knowledge of Christ*[204] to all who came and especially made their way to it. He built another church in the name of the holy chief apostles Peter and Paul and made this, too, a monastery, and in both he appointed excellent superiors and composed holy rules and regulations.[205] After he delivered <the monasteries> over to them, he himself again undertook the loftiest contemplation as before. This was the reason for the construction of the venerable houses of God that we have described for you in some detail <and> to the best of our ability.[206] Since therefore enough has been said about them, let us move on to another miracle.

24. One day when the sky was cloudy and loud thunder was already rumbling because of the collision[207] and extension of the clouds, a blast of fire

[201] This description of angels is often used in hagiography; see *ODB* 1:97, and Talbot, *Holy Women*, 151 n. 55.

[202] Cf. Basil of Caesarea, *Homiliae in Hexaemeron, Hom.* 2, chap. 1.5–6 (ed. S. Giet, *Homélies sur l'Hexaéméron,* 2d ed. [Paris, 1968], 138).

[203] Cf. Rom. 11:25.

[204] Cf. 2 Cor. 4:6.

[205] For the establishment of administrative and behavioral regulations by a monastic founder, see *ODB* 3:2132, s.v. "Typikon, Monastic."

[206] The Greek here, κατὰ τὸ ἡμῖν θεμιτόν, should literally mean "as 'lawful' [or 'right'] for me," but this seems strong in the context. I have followed van den Gheyn's "quam pro viribus nostris." The same usage occurs below in Chaps. 62 and 66.

[207] Reading ἐπιπλήξει ("striking together"; see Demetrakos, *Lexikon,* s.v.) for ἐπιπλήσει. Cf. Aristotle, *Meteorologica* 369a: οὕτως γὰρ καὶ ἐν τοῖς νέφεσι ἡ γιγνο-

appeared with a fearful rushing noise, heading for and threatening one of[208] the venerable churches. At this sight the blessed man stood in prayer and stretched his hands toward heaven, begging that the threat of the fire might gradually abate.[209] *The God of miracles,*[210] *He Who honors those who honor Him,*[211] *He Who performs the desire of those that fear Him, He Who hears their supplications* [p. 398] *and saves them,*[212] very quickly heard His own servant and preserved the church unharmed in the following way. The fire approached the holy house like a ship's sail filled by wind and walled it around like an arch for a long time. All who had congregated there observed the sight and thought that the church would be totally reduced to ashes by the fire. <But> by divine power the fire was dispersed in all directions and finally vanished, and the venerable house shone forth safe and sound through the aforementioned prayer of our God-inspired father. All those who were present there at that time and saw this incredible miracle sent up hymns of thanksgiving with one voice and glorified God.

25. There was a cave near these venerable churches, to which the saint used to go and pray. When the aforementioned Eustratios went to the blessed man, as was his custom, and told of the terrible misfortune of the <icono-clastic> persecution that persisted, the blessed man in turn arose and went to the cave to pray. As he stayed there for a long time, the revered Eustratios wondered why he was taking so long. And so he arose and approached the cave to see <what was happening>. He beheld the blessed man in prayer, not standing on the ground, but suspended in the air two cubits[213] above the earth,

μένη τοῦ πνεύματος ἔκκρισις πρὸς τὴν πυκνότητα τῶν νεφῶν ἐμπίπτουσα ποιεῖ τὴν βροντήν.

[208] Reading ἐφ᾽ ἕνα for ὑφ᾽ ἕν.

[209] Reading ὑπολωφῆσαι for ὑπολοφῆσαι.

[210] Cf. Ps. 76 (77):12; the full epithet is found in Gregory of Nazianzos, *Funebris oratio in Laudem Basilii* 7.2:1–2 (ed. F. Boulenger, *Grégoire de Nazianze: Discours funè-bres en l'honneur de son frère Césaire et de Basile de Césarée* [Paris, 1908], 70), and else-where.

[211] Cf. 1 Ki. 2:30.

[212] Ps. 144 (145):19.

[213] Two cubits (*pechyes*) is slightly less than one meter. For examples of someone observing a saint levitating, see L. Rydén, *The Life of Andrew the Fool* (Uppsala, 1995), lines 416–17 and 1313–14, and C. and R. Connor, *The Life and Miracles of Saint Luke of Steiris* (Brookline, Mass., 1994), chap. 7, and for bibliography on the phenomenon

totally illuminated brighter than the sun. He [Eustratios] was astonished at the sight and fearful lest he should in any way interrupt the saint<'s pray­er>. <So> he walked off quietly and returned <home>, thinking he had escaped notice. A little later the saint also came. Our all-wise father did not reproach him right away, but one day, many days later, when they were again conversing, the blessed man said to him: "It is not good, beloved Eustratios, that a person standing in prayer should be spied on by another."²¹⁴ <Eustrat­ios>, realizing that he had not escaped notice, said in his own defense, "Father, I did not come to spy on your prayer but, on account of the length of time that had elapsed, I came to inquire the reason for it." The blessed man <said>: "And indeed I am aware <of this>, noble Eustratios, but nevertheless it is good to do all things circumspectly." He was able to offer no answer²¹⁵ to this <but> made obeisance and received pardon.

26. While the saint still remained there and the <iconoclastic> persecution persisted, it so happened that a child was sent by his parents to draw water. When the child had carried out their bidding and was about to return home, he saw some men, dark in appearance,²¹⁶ who approached him and said: "Child, you have not taken the right road; at this point turn left toward us, that we may show you the road." <Now> these *workers of the darkness*²¹⁷ wished to lead the child to the precipice and kill him. The <child> assumed that they were speaking the truth and followed them. When he came near the precipice, <however>, the saint suddenly appeared to the child. As soon as they perceived the saint's presence, the entire demonic multitude threw themselves down over the precipice with cries of lament. <Thereupon> the saint gave the child his hand, guided him to the road, and sent him on his way with

---

their note at chap. 7, line 17, to which add the article on "Levitation" in *The New Catholic Encyclopedia* 8:683–84. See also *v. Iren. Chrysobalant.* 77 n. 4.

²¹⁴ The version by Sabas (chap. 21) elaborates on the reason for Ioannikios' admonition, adding "lest the one praying be led astray by the demon of vainglory."

²¹⁵ Reading ἀντειπεῖν for ἀντεπεῖν.

²¹⁶ Demons are often depicted as of dark complexion, a view that "took shape in the Egyptian milieux subjected to the savage raids of Nubian tribes . . . but color awareness never implied racial prejudice"; see *ODB* 2:733, s.v. "Ethiopians," and R. T. Meyer, *St. Athanasius: The Life of Saint Antony* (Westminster, Md., 1950), 109 n. 35.

²¹⁷ John Chrysostom, *In magnam feriam,* ed. R. Trautmann and R. Klostermann, "Noch ein griechischer Text zum Codex Suprasliensis," *Zeitschrift für slavische Philologie* 13 (1936), 339.3.

a blessing. When the parents asked the child why he took so long to return, the child told them everything: how he was led astray by the demons and forced to the precipice and how he was miraculously rescued through the saint's protection. And when they heard this, they gave thanks to God and His servant.

27. A woman fell victim to a *spirit of fornication*[218] and was inflamed throughout her body by passionate sexual desire—it was, one might say, like fire—[p. 399], but she resisted it with a strong resolve to give the victory to chastity. Finally she was overcome and driven distraught by mad desire; she tore her clothes and combed out her braids and let her hair hang indecently; she wandered in the wilderness like a wild boar and made her home <there>. Thus one could see an extraordinary marvel, a rational nature acting like an animal. <But unlike wild beasts> she did not partake of the food animals eat, but unsparingly ate her own flesh. Her appearance was animal-like and totally transformed. She glowered with her eyes, fearful and terrifying; she *gnashed her teeth*[219] and lacerated[220] her inwards with her hands, and filled the earth with streams of blood, as she cried out in various voices. For sometimes she barked like a dog, then she bellowed like a bull, and sometimes she brayed like an ass; at other times she hissed violently like a snake. After she continued in this frenzied state for some days, the woman was guided by the power of God to come upon the saint who was in the wilderness. When the saint saw her and recognized the activity of the evil demon who hates what is good, with pleas of supplication he urged God Who loves humanity that she regain with good health the same[221] guiding and ruling reasoning power of a rational nature. The Lord Who loves humanity and is compassionate, *Who will have all men to be saved and to come unto the knowledge of the truth,*[222] *Who does not desire the death of the sinner, <but> that they turn about and live,*[223] was swayed by the petitions of His servant. Taking pity on <a human

---

[218] Hos. 4:12. For examples of the "spirit of fornication" in hagiography, see A. Kazhdan, "Byzantine Hagiography and Sex in the Fifth to Twelfth Centuries," *DOP* 44 (1990), 131–43, esp. 141, where this passage is discussed.

[219] Mk. 9:18.

[220] Reading κατατέμνουσα for κατατείνουσα.

[221] Reading ταὐτῷ for ταῦτῷ.

[222] 1 Tim. 2:4.

[223] Ezek. 18:32 (Codex A).

being in> His own image,[224] whose senses had been deranged from their rational and natural state by unnatural irrationality, He restored the woman's health. When therefore the woman came to her senses and saw the saint standing before her, she threw herself at his feet, <saying> with cries of lamentation: "Pity me, father, the sinner beyond all <others>, one who has not the least rational control, but has totally destroyed *the temple of her body,*[225] subjecting herself to profligacy, becoming a plaything of the demons. Pity me who have been changed from a rational nature to that of the animals. And since you see me totally humiliated and consuming myself and destroying all my dignity, relieve the burning erotic madness that resides in me and make supplication so that the dew of chastity may be sent to me. Lift from me the heavy collar of fornication and bind me by your supplications with the bridle of self-control. Steer the ship of my soul, that is buffeted by the winds of fornication, and bring me to the harbor of freedom from passion. Aid wretched me as I am tossed by <my> many sins and passions, and secure me to the rock of Christ's commandments. I know that all is possible for you through God *Who strengtheneth you,*[226] and nothing is impossible for you. Therefore I beg you not to reject me, for I am in dire straits; but moved by my humble tears purify me and guide me to self-control, as Christ did of old for the blessed and praised prostitute."[227] When the saint heard these <words>, he was moved with feelings of compassion, for he too very greatly loved humanity. Raising his eyes to heaven and sending forth a groan from deep within, he said to the woman: "Woman, take courage, and in the name of Jesus Christ, the son of God, be[228] healthy from this very day. For from now on your battle will be mine and Christ will free you in the future from passion, but it will be active in me as He permits it." The woman was suddenly cured as he spoke and freed from the passion of sexual dementia; she returned to her home healthy, [p. 400] praising and honoring God. And thereafter regulating her life chastely and piously, she dedicated herself totally to the Lord.

28. Our blessed father, as mentioned, took the battle upon himself and with tears and prayers and fasting supplicated God to be freed from such a

---

[224] Cf. Gen. 1:26.

[225] Cf. Jn. 2:21.

[226] Cf. Phil. 4:13.

[227] Lk. 7:37–39, 44–50.

[228] Reading ἔσο for ἔστω.

great affliction. The demon was unable to withstand <him> even for a moment but, struck by the saint's prayers as if by an arrow, cried out in a loud voice: "O, <what> violence, <what a> terrible blow! O, <how> I am now burned by the fire of this evil old man.[229] For I am not strong enough to impede him for <even> a short time from his discipline." Then with plaintive words he next said: "Let me go, and do not torture me any longer; do not still harm me, I adjure you by God the Most High, because I cannot bear to behold the divine glory of God residing in you." The saint said: "Why are you thus in such a rush and haste and why do you wrangle and shout unintelligibly? Wait for a week and then depart from me." The demon responded: "Do not hold me any longer and do not deliver me to the eternal fire, I implore you." Then after that day passed and at about the first watch of night the saint was dozing, the demon transformed himself into a huge bear[230] and attacked the saint, emitting a loud growl. The saint stretched out his hand and seized the fur on its head and dragged it to himself by force; the demon in turn responded in a human voice: "Woe, woe is wretched me." Then the saint signed himself with the sign of the life-giving cross and rebuked[231] the demon; suddenly he was delivered from the battle <against passion> and caused <the demon> to disappear.

29. When he became well known to all there[232] and report of him spread everywhere, <one> night he arose and, eluding everyone and especially *those who sought his life,*[233] hastened again to Mt. Olympos. By the providence of God Who loves humanity he happened to come near a certain village. When its inhabitants learned of the saint's presence, they all went of one accord to meet him and, after a prayer, threw themselves at the saint's feet and wailing in a pitiful voice supplicated him to give them a helping hand. Through his prophetic gift he was <already> aware of their request <but>, as if he did not know, asked what they wanted. They said: "Because of our sins a very

[229] The Greek here, κακόγηρος, is a pun on the word καλόγηρος, meaning "monk." For the same word play see V. Laurent, in *v. Petr. Atr.* 200 n. 1.

[230] For encounters with bears in saints' Lives, see *v. Phantin. Jun.* 45 n. 39. The encounter described here is unusual in that a demon has assumed the shape of a bear. For a friendly encounter with a bear, see below, Chap. 51.

[231] Cf. Ps. 67 (68):30.

[232] I.e., Mt. Alsos; see n. 167 above.

[233] I.e., his persecutors; cf. Mt. 2:20; Lk. 17:33; Rom. 11:3.

large dragon who lives nearby us has made our road impassable and, whenever it encounters our cattle, it seizes them and gulps them down whole." Our most exceedingly compassionate father took pity on their tears, <saying>: "Brothers, be patient and the Lord *will show mercy on you*."[234] Then he proclaimed that they should fast for seven days and earnestly entreat God about this <matter>. After the completion of the days of fasting the saint took in his hand the victorious weapon, the life-giving cross that he carried on his travels, and those small or, better said, lofty garments of hair that he wore and <with which> he covered his private parts. *Girt in pure faith rather than a breastplate*,[235] he went barefoot,[236] and washed[237] his *beautiful feet*,[238] *to ransom the people*[239] of God. And he began to chant from the psalms as follows: "*He that dwells in the help of the Highest*,"[240] and, "*Thou shalt tread on asp and basilisk, and thou shalt trample on the lion and dragon*,"[241] and the rest of the psalm. Then he approached the cave and, making *the Most High his refuge*,[242] he ordered the evil beast to come out. When <the dragon> emerged and drew near the blessed <Ioannikios>, it opened its most terrifying mouth and tried to devour the just man, while everyone stood at the scene [p. 401] crying out,

[234] Cf. Ps. 17 (18):50, 108 (109):21, etc.

[235] Cf. Eph. 6:14.

[236] Gregory of Nazianzos, *In sanctum pascha* (*or.* 45), PG 36:649, says, γυμνοποδεῖν, ἵνα φανῶσιν οἱ πόδες ὡραῖοι τῶν εὐαγγελιζομένων εἰρήνην ("to go barefoot in order that the feet of those proclaiming the good news of peace may appear beautiful"). He adds, however, "Let the one fleeing Egypt and the things of Egypt wear sandals (ὑποδεδέσθω) for safety otherwise and against scorpions and snakes." The barefoot Ioannikios here apparently displays great confidence in the protection of faith.

[237] Cf. Homer, *Od.* 19:387, the only other attestation of the form ἐξαπενίσατο, of Eurykleia washing Odysseus' feet. Ioannikios' washing of his own feet here is unusual and apparently a purification prior to the encounter with the dragon. For the usual Christian washing the feet of another as an act of humility, see O. Hofius, "Fusswaschung als Erweis der Liebe: Sprachliche und sachliche Anmerkungen zu Lk. 7,44b," *Zeitschrift für die Neutestamentliche Wissenschaft und die Kunde der älteren Kirche* 81 (1990), 171–77.

[238] Cf. Rom. 10:15.

[239] Cf. Ps. 110 (111):9.

[240] Ps. 90 (91):1.

[241] Ps. 90 (91):13.

[242] Ps. 90 (91):9.

"Lord, have mercy." The blessed man fearlessly invoked the three persons and single nature of the life-giving Trinity and with his miracle-bearing weapon made the sign <of the cross> three times over the beast, instantly killing it. Thereupon the people there who had received <such> mercy gave thanks to God and His blessed <servant>.

30. And so the blessed man, as mentioned, reached Mt. Olympos. Since the <iconoclastic> persecution still persisted, he concealed himself in a rugged place known only to Eustratios. While he was staying there, the most admirable Eustratios went to visit him. When he told of the tumult and fearful storm of the persecution, the blessed man said to him: "Noble-souled[243] Eustratios, do not be distressed. For in a *little season*[244] the Lord will take pity on His heritage." For the blessed man knew that the impious <Leo> would soon die[245] and *in the very entrance of the temple,*[246] to speak with the Scriptures, and that *early will that sinner and worker of lawlessness be slain <and> destroyed out of the city of the Lord.*[247] "Nevertheless, noble Eustratios," <he said,> "go to the house of lord Niketas Lygdenos[248] and remain there until such time as you hear something; <then> come report to me." He carried out his bidding and three days later <news of> the abominable death of the most impious <Leo> was spread all about and was on everyone's lips. Lord Eus-

[243] Reading περισσόψυχε for περίψυχε.

[244] Is. 26:20.

[245] Leo V was assassinated at the dawn service on Christmas morning, 820, apparently in the palace chapel of St. Stephen. For discussion of the source statements on the location, see Treadgold, *Byz. Revival,* 421 n. 307, the Life of Nikephoros, above, n. 452, and the *v. Davidis, Sym. et Georg.,* n. 212.

[246] Ezek. 8:16.

[247] Cf. Ps. 100 (101):8.

[248] The Greek Λυγδηνοῦ (ms. Λυγδινοῦ, which means "of white marble," or "marble-white <in color>") is uncertain. Van den Gheyn (404 note d) observes that in the lexicon attributed to Zonaras Λυγδηνός is defined as "from Lygde" (Λύγδη), which is said to be a place name (ὄνομα τοῦ τόπου). Van den Gheyn questions whether a person would be so designated. Sabas (chap. 25) calls this Niketas only "a pious layman." Van den Gheyn (358 note g) observes that a number of laymen named Niketas are attested for the period, e.g., in the letters of Theodore the Stoudite are to be found Niketas, a *patrikios,* and Niketas, a *spatharios* (see Fatouros, *Theod. Stud. Epist., epp.* 27, 476, and 520).

tratios came to the blessed man and told of all that had happened and with
<the saint> sent up praise to God.

31. Another <time> the aforementioned Niketas again came to the
blessed man for his blessing, taking with him the sanctified Eustratios. And
indeed he was blessed by the saint; and after he was first filled with ambrosial
and spiritual nourishment and divine words and beneficial advice, as considerable time passed, the saint bade him to partake also of physical food. <Now
there lived> nearby the saint a most devout man who practiced solitary contemplation, named Elias. The blessed <Ioannikios> bade this man to serve
them. As the meal was in progress, opening his mouth the saint said to the
sanctified Elias: "Pray, lord Elias, that you are not suddenly overtaken by
death in a worldly place." <Elias> replied to him: "When I have lived for so
many years in the wilderness and never approached [p. 402] worldly places, do
you fear that I will die in them? This is impossible, father, impossible." The
saint repeated it a second time and <then> fell silent. When the meal was
completed, the aforementioned Niketas received a blessing and returned to
his own <home>, while the most devout Eustratios continued to stay with
the saint. The next day at dawn the God-pleasing Elias arose and went to the
blessed man; he asked for his blessing to be allowed <to go> to the hot
springs,[249] on the grounds of some bodily ailment. The blessed man said to
him: "Brother, I want you to remain in your cell and to go nowhere, because
it is not beneficial for you." But he persistently asked to be allowed <to
go>. After the saint forbade him not once but twice to no avail, he finally
gave his blessing and let him go. The beloved Eustratios knew what was going
to happen to the man through the saint's true prophecy. For as a result of his
intelligence he knew from the very words and signs and parables of the saint
what was going to take place. Then he himself made an excuse that he had
some business near the hot springs and asked <Ioannikios'> blessing to be
allowed to go. The saint said: "Yes, <but> I exhort you, dearest Eustratios,
to return quite quickly before evening and not to be otherwise occupied."
When the two men parted, the most devout Elias had already reached the hot
springs and had lowered both his feet into the bubbling source of the hot

[249] On the hot springs near Prusa, which were also frequented by Byzantine emperors, see Janin, *Eglises Centres,* 175 n. 3, and C. Texier, *Asie Mineure* (Paris, 1862), 116
and 123–25.

water. He went into a severe faint and was carried away half dead by some bystanders; and he collapsed <into bed>[250] in the house of a woman called Leopardina. Eustratios, who was beloved by God, had completed his business and was traveling along the road leading to that house. He heard some voices and groans being emitted and peeped over the perimeter fence[251] to observe the <source> of the cries. He saw Elias lying down and, as mentioned, groaning in pain. Remembering the father's prophecy, he [Eustratios] said to himself: "Look, <there's> the place that the father predicted." Then going in to the sick man, he said to him: "Please, sir, leave here quickly, lest you be overtaken in this place in accordance with the <saint's> prophetic utterance and lose the benefit of your labors." Upon hearing these <words>, <Elias>, remembering the words spoken by the father, bade <them> with most awful oaths to carry him out of there in short order. Then he was transported to one of the dependencies[252] of the Agauroi monastery,[253] the one named for St. Agapios,[254] where he lay down <to rest>. About the sixth hour of the night, in accordance with the true prophecy, he entrusted his *spirit* into the *hands* of God and *gave up the spirit*.[255] After his body was placed on a wagon, he was conveyed to the monastery that he had previously indicated.[256] The saint, knowing of his demise, went down and embraced that venerable vessel [i.e., Elias' corpse]. And so when the customary singing of the psalms was completed, they entrusted his remains to a proper grave and praising God parted from one another.

32. As the saint was returning and hastening through the mountains to

[250] For καταπίπτω with the meaning of "to lie down," cf. *Eranos* 30 (1932), 106. I am indebted to L. Rydén for this reference.

[251] The term τρόχου, translated here as "perimeter <fence>," normally means a "wheel." For its use as a "wall" or "fence," see T. Nissen, "Unbekannte Erzählungen aus dem Pratum spirituale," *BZ* 38 (1938), 351–76, esp. 359.2 and 375, and L. Rydén, *The Life of Andrew the Fool* 2 (Uppsala, 1995), 138 line 1907 and p. 325, n. 7.

[252] Smaller monastic establishments, called *metochia,* were often subordinate to larger ones; see *ODB* 2:1356–57.

[253] For the monastery, see above, n. 103.

[254] Janin (*Eglises Centres,* 132) briefly comments on this dependency, mentioned as a *proasteion* in the *Vita of Eustratios.*

[255] Cf. Lk. 23:46.

[256] The version by Sabas (chap. 25) indicates that this was the monastery called Kellia, on which see Janin, *Eglises Centres,* 160–61.

reach his cell, it so happened that he drew near an area cleft by a ravine. By diabolic activity the iron cross he held in his hand was snatched away and fell into that fearful ravine. Since, because of its inaccessibility, it was impossible for him to descend <into the ravine> to recover <the cross> that had fallen, what did he do? Standing in prayer he tearfully supplicated God to regain it. The Lord of saints, *the One Who works great* miracles, *glorious and marvelous ones, of which there is no number,*[257] anticipated the petition of His servant. And the symbol of the cross that had been snatched from his hand suddenly was dragged up from the subterranean chasms and [p. 403] rose up into the air, <and the Lord> gave it into the saint's hands. He received it and, kissing it with his holy lips, gave thanks to God.

33. Near the saint's cell there was a cave in which a multitude of evil spirits lived. And so our father Ioannikios wished to purify the place so that those who came there might be kept safe. Taking courage in the power of God he went to live in the cave for a specified <number of> days. When he went in, all that demonic multitude formed ranks against him, and emitted many shouts and indecent words. For some of them hurled insults at the blessed man, others threatened <him>, some attacked <him> in various ways, while others hastened to withdraw from there. Sometimes they encouraged one another to raze the very cave from its foundations. The saint spread his hands to heaven and supplicated God that these <demons> might be driven away. After <his> prayer, when he began to sing a psalm, *"Let God arise and let His enemies be scattered, let them that hate Him flee from before Him,"*[258] that demonic phalanx, as if driven invisibly by a whip and transformed into crows, all flew off and, escaping through a hole of the cavern, vanished with much lamentation. And from that day there was great safety for those passing by there.

34. Theodotos the *kandidatos*,[259] called Sellokakas, had a pure faith in the saint. Taking his daughter, who was totally feeble and paralyzed, he went

[257] Job 5:9.

[258] Ps. 67 (68):2.

[259] This term was originally used for members of a unit of the imperial bodyguard and subsequently "connected with subaltern offices in the army and in the civil service"; see *ODB* 2:1100. The version by Sabas (chap. 27) describes a similar and apparently the same miracle as occurring for the "daughter of an <unnamed> senator" (συγκλητικοῦ . . . θυγάτριον).

to the blessed man, and indeed was deemed worthy to enjoy that angelic sight. He placed his daughter before the blessed man's feet and, crying out with words of supplication, said: "Have mercy, father, on a girl paralyzed in all her limbs on both <sides of her body> on account of my sins; take pity on me who have run to your saintliness with faith, restore my daughter to me whole and healthy by your pure prayers to God. Have mercy on me, O disciple and servant of Christ, and do not send me away unsuccessful, humbled, and humiliated. May I obtain aid and succor from you, may I with everyone obtain salvation from you, may I obtain the riches of your healing gifts. So therefore healing my daughter in imitation of the Lord, send me off to herald the powers and miracles of God that are accomplished through you." Swayed by these words the saint (for he was really exceedingly compassionate) bade that the girl be lifted up and carried to him. When this was done, the saint tearfully made the sign of the life-giving cross over the girl three times, speaking as follows: "In the name of Jesus Christ, Who *heals all manner of sickness and all manner of disease,*[260] *arise and walk.*"[261] As soon as he spoke the girl's *feet and anklebones received strength*[262] and, as her limbs were mutually <and> wondrously strengthened, she arose and leapt up before all, and going to the saint she fell at his feet. The saint prayed for and blessed her and restored her in good health to her father; the father taking her returned home with joy, sending up glory and honor to the God of all.

35. This miracle-worker and prophet of our generation had a brother-in-law[263] who was deeply heretical, for he believed in and adhered to the foul dogmas of the God-hated and most loathsome Kopronymos.[264] The father often admonished this man and counseled him to make a change for the best, <but> was not able to alter his innate quality or permanent condition[265] of

---

[260] Mt. 4:23.

[261] Mt. 9:5.

[262] Acts 3:7.

[263] The Greek term here is γαμβρός. As Peter notes above (Chap. 19) that Ioannikios had sisters, the translation "brother-in-law" is appropriate here.

[264] On the emperor Constantine V (741–775), see General Introduction, x–xi.

[265] The terminology here (ποιότητα . . . ἕξιν) seems to reflect philosophical concepts ultimately drawn from Aristotle; cf. L. Minio-Paluello, *Aristotelis Categoriae et Liber de Interpretatione* (Oxford, 1949), 15b:18.

evil. He still persisted in his most shameful <ways> and with blasphemous words attacked the saints and our holy <monastic> habit.[266] [p. 404] For the all-wretched man in no way accepted the intercessions of the saints, nor indeed did he venerate their holy relics,[267] but even did not cease subjecting to babbling nonsense the monks among us who imitate the angels. Since he saw that the man was incorrigible and wished to cure him through some edifying punishment, the blessed man said: "Brother, let us both make an agreement as follows, and let whichever of us has the wrong faith lose his eyesight and so be converted to the better faith." When <the other> agreed to this, he went blind as he spoke. The saint said: "What do you say to this, brother? Will you not now fulfill <the agreement> and turn in pure repentance to the orthodox and blameless faith, or will you still persist in the lawless admonitions and teachings of that anti-Christ and most evil Kopronymos?" He replied: "I both have persisted and will persist for eternity <in my beliefs>." The saint drove him away with loathing and not many days later the man fell gravely ill and died wretchedly. And indeed more pitiful was that the wretch departed into eternal darkness deprived of his eyesight.

36. It happened once that <some> of the prominent fathers agreed to visit the saint. There were metropolitans, the all-saintly John of Chalcedon,[268] and Peter,[269] the most saintly metropolitan of Nicaea; <and> monastic supe-

[266] The Greek here (σχήματος) surely refers to the monastic habit and, given the next sentence, this seems the appropriate translation. Van den Gheyn, however, translates "illum, qui pro nobis incarnatus apparuit," i.e., as a reference to the incarnate Christ. For the latter usage see Lampe, *Lexicon,* s.v. σχῆμα, 3. According to the *vita* of Stephen the Younger (PG 100:1112A), Constantine V declared war on the monastic habit and called it the "habit of darkness" (σκοτίας . . . τὸ σχῆμα).

[267] These first two accusations (denial of the intercessions of the saints and rejection of their relics) accord with similar accusations made against Constantine V; see G. Dagron, "L'ombre d'un doute: l'hagiographie en question, VIe–XIe siècle," *DOP* 46 (1992), 59–68, specifically 65. Dagron also provides useful comments on the nature of saintly "interventions" (πρεσβεῖαι).

[268] The version by Sabas (chap. 28) adds that his surname was Kamoulianos. He is known from other sources, particularly the letters of Theodore the Stoudite. See Fatouros, *Theod. Stud. Epist.* 1:300, n. 536, and Efthymiadis, "Correspondence of Theodore," no. 8 ("John, Bishop of Chalcedon"), 155.

[269] Peter of Nicaea is known from other sources, particularly the letters of Theodore the Stoudite. See Fatouros, *Theod. Stud. Epist.* 1:219, n. 256.

riors, the most holy Clement,[270] Theodore the Stoudite,[271] Joseph[272] the former steward[273] of the Great Church together with his brother, and many other superiors. So in all they numbered one hundred or even more. On account of the difficult <access> to the mountain they were not able to go up to the saint, <but> assembled together in the dependency of the Agauroi <monastery>, in which the all-sacred church of St. Elias[274] is venerated. They <then> sent word to the blessed man through the most devout Eustratios to come down for the sake of the Lord and give them his blessing. When he had come down and was about to draw near them, those men arose and went to meet him to make obeisance. After a prayer, they all sat together [p. 405] on the ground and began to discuss with one another <the question> which of the virtues is loftier. One proposed love, another prayer, another charity, yet another hospitality, another fasting; all said different things. As there was serious disagreement, they urged the blessed man to resolve the question that beset them. Our humble-minded and angelic father Ioannikios, after considerable urging by them, answered after some time in a gentle voice: "As I see it, holy fathers, there is no other virtue loftier than humility." They nodded assent and

[270] Clement is presumably the abbot Clement mentioned in the letters of Theodore the Stoudite. See Fatouros, *Theod. Stud. Epist.* 1:407, n. 799, and Efthymiadis, "Correspondence of Theodore," no. 5 ("The Studite Clement"), 148–49.

[271] The famous theologian, monastic reformer, and saint (759–826); see *ODB* 3:2044–45.

[272] For the identification of this Joseph with Joseph of Kathara, who performed the second "adulterous" marriage of Constantine VI in 795, igniting the Moechian ("adultery") controversy, see Mango, "Ioannikios," 395 and n. 9. Mango comments that Peter's identification and description of him are more specific and more favorable than that of Sabas (chap. 28) who says he was "steward of the church," not "of the Great Church" (i.e., Hagia Sophia in Constantinople), and makes no mention of his generosity to the poor before his death. For doubts about the identification see von Dobschütz, "Methodios und die Studiten," 95 n. 3, and Janin, *Eglises Centres,* 189 n. 1. For a recent review of Joseph's career, see P. Niavis, "Ἰωσήφ, Ἡγούμενος τῆς Μονῆς τῶν Καθαρῶν (†825)," Βυζαντινὸς Δόμος 4 (1990), 85–98. On the Moechian controversy, see *ODB* 2:1388–89.

[273] The steward (*oikonomos*) was "a cleric, usually a priest, responsible for managing the property, income and expenditure of a see or religious foundation"; see *ODB* 3:1517, s.v. "Oikonomos."

[274] For a review of monasteries so dedicated and referred to elsewhere, see Janin, *Eglises Centres,* 151–52, and M. Cunningham in *v. Mich. Sync.* 164 n. 182.

making obeisance grew quiet. A short time later they all arose and invited the saint to join them in a meal. And indeed accepting their invitation the blessed man went with them to the lunch.[275] When therefore all had taken their places at the lunch, our father, opening his holy mouth, said to the former steward of the Great Church, the lord Joseph, before all: "Some time ago when you desired to see us, it was not possible for us to present ourselves to you; for perhaps it was not then the will of God. Now, however, I both see you and in the presence of all the fathers urge you to set your affairs in good order and always look each day to the hour of your death. For the time of your death has already come." He [Joseph] agreed to carry out earnestly all that had been said and making obeisance to the saint sat down.[276] The Stoudites were scandalized at this, for they are always accustomed to concoct scandal and to consider themselves superior to anyone else. Thus in no small measure they found fault with the blessed man in their thoughts, adding even this in their mind: "Who knows <the day> of each man's death but God alone?"[277] The saint therefore, knowing their thoughts, remained quiet for the time being. But after they finished their drink, he summoned them individually and giving voice to their thoughts shocked them severely and put them to shame; he instructed them not to be so rashly ready for evil nor, *beholding* in advance *the motes in others' <eyes>, to* <fail to> *consider their own beams.*[278] And addressing them sternly with other beneficial words, he had them kneel on the ground and cry out, "I have sinned," <asking for> forgiveness. The blessed man <then> had them rise and forgave and dismissed them. <As for> the aforementioned Joseph, he distributed all his possessions to the poor and, in accordance with the saint's prophetic utterance, departed to the Lord, after living eighteen days <longer>.

37. It happened once that the blessed man went down to the monastery

---

[275] The term ἄριστον, translated here as "lunch," was used in monastic circles to refer to the first and perhaps only meal of the day; see *ODB* 1:170.

[276] Reading συγκαταθέμενος for συγκαθέμενος.

[277] The version by Sabas (chap. 28) cites as the basis of their complaint Job 3:23A (Codex Alexandrinus): Θάνατος γὰρ ἀνδρὶ ἀνάπαυσις, οὗ ἡ ὁδὸς ἀπεκρύβη ἀπ᾽ αὐτοῦ. For Byzantine concern with the question of whether the human lifespan was fixed in advance by God, see C. Garton, L. Westerink, *Germanos: On Predestined Terms of Life* (Buffalo, N.Y., 1979), esp. xiv–xxvi.

[278] Mt. 7:3; Lk. 6:42.

of the great Isaac,[279] the one named Agros, and there he prayed and kissed the saint's tomb. While returning he came to the island called Thasios[280] to the great Daniel.[281] The sanctified Daniel, when he learned of the saint's arrival, went out to meet him with all the holy brotherhood under his authority and received him with honor as a prophet of God. Then, in the belief that he [Ioannikios] was sent from God because of the misfortune that beset them (for a most fearful dragon was living in one part of the island—indeed, there was a countless multitude of snakes all over the island), the great Daniel therefore took good counsel and taking with him all the brotherhood threw himself at the saint's feet and supplicated him to drive out the beast through his prayers. Yielding to their supplication the saint bade them strike the wooden sounding board[282] and urged the brothers to enter the church and, by keeping sleepless vigil from evening till dawn with hymns of praise and prayers, to supplicate God about their <dire straits>. After this was done, <Ioannikios> took in his [p. 406] hand the venerable cross that guided him and advanced alone against the beast. When he was above the cave where the dragon lived, he petitioned God throughout the night to drive away the most evil dragon. When the dragon became aware of the saint's presence, it began to shake everything there with powerful contortions and loud hissings. At about daybreak, when the sun was already coming up and everyone was watching, <the dragon>, as if driven by fire, threw itself into the lake and, after crossing it

---

[279] "Isaac" here refers to the famous Theophanes the Confessor; the version by Sabas (chap. 31) speaks of the "Sigrianian monastery of saint Theophanes, the one called Agros." We learn from the *Life of Theophanes* by Methodios (ed. V. Latyšev, *Mefodija patriarcha Konstantinopol'skogo Žitie prep. Feofana Ispovednika* [St. Petersburg, 1918], chap. 4) that Isaac was the name of Theophanes' father, a noted general, and that Constantine V imposed the name on Theophanes: οὐκ ὀνομασθεὶς οὕτως ἐν τῷ βαπτίσματι, ἀλλὰ φιλοπατόρως τῷ τοῦ Ἰσαύρου μιαρῷ Κωνσταντίνῳ ἐπικληθεὶς Ἰσαάκιος. For Theophanes and his monastery Megas Agros, on the mountain of Sigriane, on the southern shore of the Propontis, see Janin, *Eglises Centres,* 195–99, *ODB* 3:2063, and the Life of David, Symeon, and George, above, n. 208.

[280] The version by Sabas (chap. 31) indicates that this island was "at the northern part of Lake Apollonias." See Janin, *Eglises Centres* (153–54) and his map (130) for its location on the route from Sigriane to Olympos.

[281] Janin *(Eglises Centres,* 154) notes that this Daniel is not attested elsewhere and that the modern *akolouthia* composed in his honor is based on the *Life of Ioannikios.*

[282] On the *semantron* (here a long piece of wood that would be struck with a hammer) used in monasteries in preference to the bell, see *ODB* 3:1868.

and coming to the shore, it vanished.[283] And when the brothers saw this incredible miracle, they sent up praise to God and rendered honorable reverence to the saint.

38. When the saint returned again up to the mountain, there came to him Antony, the former superior of Elaiobomoi,[284] with his steward Basil. After the blessed man received and blessed them, he said[285] to the most devout superior: "Lord Antony, will you convey to the metropolitan of Nicaea, named Inger,[286] whatever <message> you should hear from us?" Since he knew the severity of the man [i.e., Inger], he replied: "No, father." The father turned from him and looking at Basil asked: "What do you say, Basil?" He replied fearfully: "Whatever you bid me, master, I will convey it to the man in full." Our divine father <said>: "You will give him the following message: 'If you wish to see the face of God, leave your metropolis and hasten to repent. For your death has already drawn near and see that you do not lose <the benefit of> your labors.'" So the saint spoke and dismissed the men with a blessing. Basil went to Inger, in accordance with the father's bidding, and reported to

[283] The version by Sabas (chap. 31) adds that he was accompanied by a multitude of other snakes (σὺν πλήθει τῶν ἄλλων ὄφεων).

[284] This monastery ("Olive Altars") may be the same as both Heliou Bomon and Elegmoi, which are first mentioned in the 10th century and situated near the modern Kurşunlu, and may have been founded by the patriarch Methodios. Sabas (chap. 30, 360A) also calls it Ἐλαιοβώμων (ms. Ἐλαιοκώμων), while the Metaphrastic recension (PG 116:69B) records τῶν τοῦ Ἡλίου βωμῶν. For views on the forms of its name and identifications, see Janin, Eglises Centres, 142–44; C. Mango, "The Monastery of St. Abercius at Kurşunlu (Elegmi) in Bithynia," DOP 22 (1968), 169–76, specifically 174; ODB 2:910–11 (s.v. "Heliou Bomon"); and M. Cunningham in v. Mich. Sync. 164–65. Janin, Eglises Centres (143 n. 5) dates this meeting 820–824.

[285] Reading εἴρετο for ἤρετο.

[286] Van den Gheyn (AASS, Nov. 2.1:364, n. 1) and Janin (Eglises Centres, 143, n. 5) comment that Inger is not attested elsewhere. He must have succeeded the metropolitan of Nicaea Peter who is mentioned above at Chap. 36. J. Pargoire ("Saints iconophiles," EO 4 [1900/1], 353–54) notes that while the iconophile Peter died in 826, he was deposed and replaced earlier by the iconoclast Inger; see also C. Mango, "Observations on the Correspondence of Ignatius, Metropolitan of Nicaea," Texte und Untersuchungen zur Geschichte der altchristlichen Literatur 125 (1981), 403–10, specifically 406, who dates Inger's death "in or shortly after 825." C. Mango ("Eudocia Ingerina, the Normans, and the Macedonian Dynasty," ZRVI 14/15 [1973], 17–27, specifically 18–19) also comments on the Scandinavian origin of the name and suggests that his Christian name is omitted in order to brand him as a barbarian as well as a heretic.

him everything that he had been ordered. <Inger> was swayed briefly to repentance but, misled again by the glory of the transitory and corruptible life, he disregarded <the saint's> words. Then, fifteen days later as he sat on his throne, he breathed his last without saying a further word or setting his affairs in order. At the very same hour the saint, who knew <of his death> by his gift of clairvoyance, summoned the most admirable Eustratios, and weeping bitterly said: "Be[287] aware, brother Eustratios, that the wretched Inger has just died unrepentant without heeding [p. 407] our word<s>. We are not to blame, for we had warned him beforehand, but he himself will garner the fruits of disobedience, since he did not renounce the heresy,[288] but died in his sin."

39. And so since our God-inspired father Ioannikios had become renowned in the world, and a great multitude of men came to him to learn from him what was necessary and beneficial for their souls, indeed then each one garnered sufficient benefit from his all-holy mouth as if from the mouth of God and returned glorifying God. <The saint>, inasmuch as[289] he strove *to live purely with the pure*[290] and viewed the multitudes that kept coming as an impediment to his life of virtue and contemplation, but I believe also shunning the empty glory of men, secretly departed from the place where he was. He moved to the so-called Ktemata[291] that are beyond the aforenamed Lissos,[292]

---

[287] Reading ἔσο for ἔστω.

[288] The version by Sabas (chap. 30) is more explicit in twice stating that Inger was an adherent of the "icon-fighting heresy."

[289] Reading ἅτε for ἄτε.

[290] John of Damascus, *Homilia in sabbatum sanctum*, PG 96:640.45.

[291] Sabas (chap. 13) places the cave "in a place called τὰ Κρίταμα" (other mss. read Κρίματα and τακρίταμα) and indicates it was near τὰ Μητάτα and the river Gorgytes. I have found no attestation elsewhere. Mango ("Ioannikios," 402) places it "in Mysia, in the general area of modern Balikesir." Peter's term κτήματα may mean "(landed) possessions," "estates."

[292] Peter has actually not previously mentioned a "Lissos." Mango ("Ioannikios," 402) plausibly suggests that the correct reading here should be Alsos (i.e., the mountain in Lydia first mentioned by Peter in Chap. 19), noting that the error can be readily explained by similarity of the uncial letters in each term. The error has apparently been picked up in the text of Sabas (chap. 14), who mentions a *kastron* of "Lisos" (ἐν κάστρῳ τῷ Λισῷ), on which Janin (*Eglises Centres,* 150 and n. 1 and cf. 164 n. 6) comments: "On lira évidemment: mont Alsos de Lydie."

on the river called Gorgytes,[293] to a cave there that was truly quite hard to reach and inaccessible, uttering that phrase of the prophet that says: *"For Thou, Lord, only hast caused me to dwell securely."*[294] He found a huge rock lying there and ordered that a chain be made six fathoms in length and, after binding himself with the chain, he fastened the chain[295] to that very large rock. Thus bound in iron and sorely distressed and practicing mortification, he endured for three full years in such travail. And so when the three-year time period was completed and he rendered to God the vow that he began (I mean indeed that of the confinement, for he made this agreement with God), he broke the bonds and went off to visit an all-wondrous old man.[296]

40. He was about to cross the Gorgytes River, for the old man was on the other side of the river. As he raised his eyes the venerable Ioannikios saw in the middle of the river a truly most fearful dragon that held back the water[297] by uncoiling its enormous bulk and in no way allowed it to flow, until gradually the current rose over that huge body and so was borne violently down<stream>. When the saint saw and truly marveled that the beast was so large, he returned to his cave and supplicated God for the destruction of the dragon with fasts and sleeping on the ground and all-night vigils and numerous prayers. And, so to speak, receiving from Him <the power> to destroy the beast and given assurance, he took up a pick-axe,[298] left his cave and went

[293] Menthon (*L'Olympe de Bithynie*, 17) and Janin (*Eglises Centres*, 148–50) identified the Gorgytes with the modern Ainessi Dere, a tributary of the Nilufer. Mango ("Ioannikios," 402 n. 23) casts strong doubt on the identification.

[294] Ps. 4 (5):8.

[295] A fathom (*orgyia*) was 1.87 meters; hence the chain was about eleven meters long. The use of chains as a means of mortification and as a way of sharing the lot of less fortunate members of society was employed by a number of saints; for examples see R. Browning, "The 'Low Level' Saint's Life in the Early Byzantine World," in Hackel, *Byz. Saint,* 117–27, specifically 124. For a symbolic use of a chain, see *The Life of Saint Nikon,* ed. and trans. D. Sullivan (Brookline, Mass., 1987), chap. 37, p. 128.34–36.

[296] Sabas (chap. 14) indicates that the old man was the "great George," who is not otherwise known (see van den Gheyn, 346 note r).

[297] For the association of dragons with the impounding of water, see S. Thompson, *Motif-Index of Folk-Literature* 1 (Bloomington, Ind., 1955), 194–95, A1111.

[298] Reading ἀξινορύγιον for ἀξινορόγιον. On the term see Trapp, *Lexikon,* s.v., who defines it as "Spitzhacke, Spaten," Koukoules, *Bios* 5:269, who gives εἶδος τσάπας, and J. Haldon, *Constantine Porphyrogenitus: Three Treatises on Imperial Military Expeditions* (Vienna, 1990), 199 n. (C)130, who translates as "a widebladed pick-axe" and adds other citations.

to the place where the beast was accustomed to come out and bask in the warmth of the sun. After observing it from a distance, therefore, he went in front of it and came near. When the most evil beast saw Ioannikios, the servant of God, it opened its mouth wide and seemed <ready> to swallow him. <The saint> raised his eyes to heaven and, taking power from on high, lifted the iron tool in his hand. And he crashed it forcefully down on the head of this <beast> and wounded it. And immediately the beast was destroyed by the power of God. The man of God, the sanctified and renowned Eustratios, said that the servant of God Ioannikios also killed through prayer an evil viper that lived in that cave for many years.

41. And so the all-blessed man departed from the cave and moved to the mountain called Alsos,[299] on which he <had> erected the aforementioned all-wondrous church of the military martyr Eustathios.[300] The man who had obtained *citizenship in heaven*[301] hastened to construct <there> a cell to receive and shelter his all-holy body. Therefore he outlined the site and sketched <the design> of its construction[302] and also told the builders to work carefully; he himself ventured into the more remote wilderness. When the work was completed [p. 408] and evening came, they all fell asleep. An evil viper <then> emerged, <driven> by diabolic compulsion,[303] that bit on the temple a workman named Pardos, and fled. When the man felt the pain and woke up, he cried out in a loud voice. And so everyone woke up and inquired[304] why he cried out so violently. He said that he had unbearable pain in his head, but had no idea at all what had happened to him. As the venom spread through his head and all his body and caused dark discoloration and great swelling all

---

[299] For Alsos, see above, nn. 167 and 292.

[300] For Eustathios, see above, n. 168.

[301] Phil. 3:20.

[302] The precise meaning of the phrase here, τὸν χῶρον οὖν σχηματίσας καὶ τὸ τεκτόνημα διαγράψας, is unclear. The saint apparently indicates directly on the ground the planar dimensions of the building, but precisely what he sketches (? elevation) is questionable. For discussion of this and related passages in the context of Byzantine approaches to building design, see R. Ousterhout, "Byzantine Hagiography and the Art of Building," *BSC Abstr* 19 (1993), 80–81, and his forthcoming book on Byzantine architectural construction, *Byzantine Masons at Work.*

[303] Peter's term here for "compulsion," συνέλασις, is attested elsewhere only as a gloss.

[304] Reading πυθομένων for πειθομένων.

over his body, it brought the man to the very brink of death. The holy Ioannikios knew from God what had happened, even in the <distant> place where he was. He left there and reached the builders in the morning at about the third hour. As soon as the men saw the saint, they threw themselves at his feet, supplicating him to take pity on the victim <of the snakebite>. The <saint>, taking the man, withdrew about a stone's throw away from them, and stood in prayer, raising his hands to the heaven like a cross. After the prayer he touched with that holy finger of his the place where he had been bitten and made[305] the sign[306] of the honored cross. And immediately that fearful swelling ruptured and all the noisome venom flowed out. The man who was cured glorified God Who provided him the cure through His servant Ioannikios[307] and resumed his work unhindered as before. And the aforementioned Pardos has been preserved up to this time in a long life and proclaims to all the power of God and the cure effected for him through the saint; and he narrates it vividly so that all his listeners glorify God and praise His servant Ioannikios.

42. Our holy father Ioannikios once had a desire to travel to the regions of the Thrakesioi[308] and to go and pray in the all-sacred church of the apostle and evangelist John the Theologian.[309] And so he took to the road and began his journey. He became exhausted due to the lack of provisions, the sun's heat (for it was the last[310] month <of the year>) and the length of the journey. When he saw a chapel by the road, he turned aside to it and went inside. And, lo and behold, a man and his wife arrived bringing an offering. When they were inside the chapel, raising their eyes they suddenly saw the saint, his face shining like the sun (for our God-bearing father Ioannikios was truly angelic,

---

[305] The verb here, διεχάραξε (lit., "incised"), is ambiguous. As no knife is mentioned, it is difficult to tell whether the saint simply made the sign of the cross with his finger or actually cut into the skin to release the poison. Sabas (chap. 20) says ῥήξας καθάπερ ξίφει: "he ruptured it *as if* with a sword."

[306] Reading τύπον for τόπον.

[307] Reading Ἰωαννικίου for Ἰωαννίκιον.

[308] On the theme of Thrakesioi, see above, n. 119.

[309] As Sabas (chap. 12) notes, this was the church of Saint John in Ephesos. On the church, see *ODB* 1:706 (s.v. "Ephesus").

[310] That is, August, as the Byzantine calendar began in September; see *ODB* 1:448, s.v. "Chronology."

if anyone is); and in fear they turned quickly back. The saint said to them: "Stay, children, and do not be afraid, for I am *a man with like passions as you*.[311] Therefore draw near me and you will realize that I am not a spirit as you suspect, but a creation of God." Obeying the saint's bidding, therefore, and turning around, they threw themselves at his honorable feet, begging him to pray for them. And after the saint prayed for them, they returned home with joy praising God. After this they took some bread and other foods and brought them to the saint. He took just a very little from all <they brought> and regained some strength. He <then> questioned them about the road and bade them to say what route he should take. They replied: "By no means, holy man, should you make the journey by night, for an impassable river lies near here that is barely fordable in a certain place by those who are familiar <with it>, even during the daytime. But since you are unfamiliar <with the river>, you will in no way find the correct route, if you make haste to cross it by night. For if you should attempt to do this, you will surely end up totally submerged under the waters." <Ioannikios> seemingly nodded assent and saying that they gave good advice, dismissed them with a blessing. He himself immediately arose [p. 409] and took to the road. And when he arrived near the river he stood in prayer. After the prayer he stretched out his hand and, sealing the waters with the sign of the cross, did not divide them in two, as Elisha <did> with the mantle of Elijah,[312] but by the power of God caused their fluid nature to become firm and walked on <them>. And he hurried over them as if walking on dry <land> until he stood on the other side of the river on the shore and, after sending up a hymn to God, again continued his journey.

43. He arrived then at the all-revered church of the apostle and evangelist John. As he had no desire to enter along with the crowd streaming in there, he begged the man responsible[313] for the church to permit him to enter privately at night. This man totally refused to relent and told him, if he wished <to go in>, to enter with all <the others> and pray. Since the blessed man did not

---

[311] Cf. Acts 14:15.

[312] 4 Ki. 2:8. Presumably the example of Elisha dividing the Jordan is chosen here, rather than Moses dividing the Red Sea, because Ioannikios is also crossing a river. As the "new Moses" he of course walks on the water like Christ, rather than dividing it. For a similar comparison of both Moses and Elisha to Christ, see *Photii Bibliotheca*, ed. I. Bekker (Berlin, 1824), cod. 222, p. 183.

[313] Presumably the ἐκκλησιάρχης or sacristan; see *ODB* 1:682.

agree <to this>, for a third day[314] <the man> shut the doors in his face and departed. Our noble and patient father Ioannikios was in no way despondent, but stood outside somewhere near the foregates of the church and for three days, never lying down, begged God to obtain his request. And indeed after the third day, as evening fell, all the gates were locked up as usual by the holder of the keys. And on that night the apostle and theologian John appeared before his eyes in a vision and asked him what he wanted. When <Ioannikios> said he was there to pray, but was kept out by the keeper of the keys there, <John> bade him to follow him and to go[315] wherever he wished. With the apostle proceeding <before him>, he walked behind until they both came to the locked gates. The locks were suddenly broken together with the bolts[316] and *the gates were lifted up*[317] and furnished them unobstructed access.[318] The saint's guide remained visible as far as the chancel barriers[319] of the holy sanctuary, but after entering <the sanctuary> he disappeared from view. Our holy father Ioannikios rendered his prayers to God and many thanks to the saint [i.e., John]. He <then> left the church and upon his departure the gates were again locked and restored to their previous <condition>.[320] He returned and again went to the same mountain called Lissos.[321]

[314] The Greek here, ὡς ἐπὶ τρίτης ἡμέρας, is somewhat difficult. The ὡς ἐπὶ may be used in combination (cf. below 423c ὡς ἀπὸ) or perhaps ὡς is intensive from the demonstrative sense "thus," "so," hence "for, indeed, a third day."

[315] The infinitive here (ἀποφέρειν) may perhaps be used intransitively (cf. Trapp, *Lexikon*, s.v., "sich erstrechen, sich hinziehen") and Ioannikios would then be the subject of both infinitives, as translated. And yet, since St. John is then said to be leading, can Ioannikios be literally said to be "going where he wishes"? Van den Gheyn translated, "ille sequi se iussit, eum quo vellet ire ducturus," although the combination "ire ducturus" cannot be justified from the Greek except through an assumed ellipsis.

[316] Reading ῥωμανησίων for ῥωμανισίων. On locking systems in Byzantium, see *ODB* 2:1125, s.v. "Keys."

[317] Cf. Ps. 23 (24):7: ἄρατε πύλας, οἱ ἄρχοντες ὑμῶν, καὶ ἐπάρθητε, πύλαι αἰώνιοι. . . .

[318] For a similar miracle, see *v. Petr. Atr.*, chap. 3. For the gates of a prison miraculously opening, see below, Chap. 62, and Acts 16:26.

[319] On the chancel barriers (here κιγκλίδων, lit., "grills"), the screens separating the nave from the sanctuary, see *ODB* 3:2023–24, s.v. "Templon."

[320] For the story of Ioannikios in the church of St. John in Ephesos repeated in a later text, see O. Lampsides, "Das Wunder des Heiligen Ioannikios in der Kirche des Evangelisten Johannes in Ephesos," *AnalBoll* 100 (1982), 429–30.

[321] For Lissos (= Alsos) see above, n. 292.

44. It happened once that our miracle-worker father Ioannikios went to the holy monastery called Kounin.[322] At that time a very large gathering of fathers and most devout monks was there to celebrate in the monastery the annual feastday. When those holy worshipers had completed the customary kanon[323] and divine liturgy, they hastened to partake also of physical food. When all the guests were seated, they ordered[324] the blessed Ioannikios, as a stranger and unknown <to them>, to sit at the last place. During the meal, one of the nuns there,[325] who was troubled by an unclean spirit, suddenly had a fit. Foaming <at the mouth> and gnashing her teeth she stood behind the servant of God. Violently scourged and overwhelmed by the demon, she cried out and proclaimed that saint by name. Upon hearing this, that holy assembly fell at the saint's feet and begged forgiveness, for their ignorance, I believe. And when this was done, they in turn importuned him to drive out the unclean spirit through his prayer. Our truly humble-minded father Ioannikios told the fathers that it was rather they who should pray, calling himself a sinner with earth-bound mind,[326] while they <were> lofty and heavenly. For they say that some of them were honored with the dignity of priesthood. They replied that [p. 410] since he had received the gift of miracles from God it was reasonable that he should make the prayer. Since there was very great disagreement between them, <Ioannikios> heeded <their arguments> and was persuaded, inasmuch as there were so many of the fathers. Focusing his mind on heaven he stood in prayer. And after the prayer, as soon as he sealed the suffering <woman> with the sign of the cross, the unclean spirit that rent and tore her asunder departed from her. And the woman regained her health and all there with her glorified God and His saint.

45. When therefore this bright lamp shone forth as a result of the variety of his miracles and report of him was spread everywhere, he decided, so he thought, to conceal himself by migrating to wild regions, the lairs of savage

---

[322] Kounin is not mentioned by Sabas and is not otherwise attested; for discussion and a 13th-century monastery of similar name, see Janin, *Eglises Centres,* 164.

[323] On this hymnographic form, see *ODB* 2:1102.

[324] Reading ἐπέτρεψαν for ἐπέστρεψαν.

[325] The phrase suggests that Kounin may have been a nunnery, as this nun appears to be one of the residents, rather than one who came with the "fathers and . . . monks." Cf. below, Chap. 50 (413в), ὁ ἐκεῖσε μοναχὸς ὤν, of a monk of the Antidion monastery.

[326] The Greek word γεήφρων is unattested elsewhere; cf. οἱ τὰ ἐπίγεια φρονοῦντες in Phil. 3:19.

beasts. But he was not <able to> escape notice; for wherever he went, the grace of the Spirit made him manifest. Going therefore to the place called Chelidon[327] and penetrating into the innermost depths of the wilderness, he found a cave <in an area> without any <source> of water and spent some time there. For he always rejoiced to live in harsh places in order to mortify his flesh with fasting and thirst, with cold and nakedness. After some time he decided to erect a chapel in that very place and in the cave. And so he summoned workmen for the construction of the building. As they inspected the site, they had qualms about the construction as there was no water; for our blessed father Ioannikios fetched water for himself from a distance. Since he saw that these men were worried, he said to them: "Do not be vexed about this; but let us cast our hopes on the Lord[328] and as His goodness bids, <so> will He do with us." Withdrawing a little apart from them therefore and secretly stretching his hands toward the heaven, he begged God that water be provided in that dry place. Christ our God, Who observes the hearts of all, *and performs the desire of them that fear Him and hears their supplication,*[329] immediately fulfilled the request. And water came forth that continues even up to now; by it also many cures are effected so that the prophetic verse is fulfilled: *And there will be a channel of water in a thirsty land.*[330] When the chapel was completed, he made it a monastery for the salvation of many and the benefit of souls wishing to be saved.

46. Departing from there he next moved to the cave called Marsalenon[331] very near Chelidon.[332] And going inside he found a most terrifying dragon whose length, as the most holy Eustratios told me (and he was informed by the saint), was sixty cubits.[333] At the sight of this <dragon>, the saint was

---

[327] Chelidon is mentioned by Peter below in Chap. 46 and by Sabas (chaps. 14 and 23). The first reference in Sabas places it in Lydia; see Janin, *Eglises Centres,* 150, and Mango, "Ioannikios," 402 and n. 24.

[328] Cf. Ps. 54 (55):22 and John Chrysostom, *In epistulam ad Ephesios, cap. VI, hom.* 22 (PG 62:158).

[329] Ps. 144 (145):19.

[330] Is. 35:6.

[331] Peter has Μαρσαληνὸν, Sabas (chap. 20) Μαρσαλινῷ. I do not find the name attested elsewhere; cf. Janin, *Eglises Centres,* 150.

[332] For Chelidon, see n. 327.

[333] Since a cubit (*pechys*) is 46.8 cm, the dragon would have been about 28 meters long.

quite frightened and begged God fervently for the destruction of the beast. And indeed when the prayer had been sent up, the beast was killed by an unseen <agency> and destroyed, and the saint left the cave singing God's praises. As he was on his way to the region of Kountouria,[334] a nun of distinguished <family> was making a journey in the opposite direction[335] with her daughter. And indeed while <they were> on the road, *the spirit of fornication,*[336] with God's permission, entered into[337] and agitated her daughter terribly. The girl could not endure the fiery <passion kindled in her by> the demon; yielding herself <to it> she cried out indecently to her mother. When the mother saw her daughter totally overwhelmed, she said with pitiful lamentation: "Woe, woe, my child, why do you cry out thus indecently and shamefully? Remember, my child, the good and holy nurture with which I raised you from a tender age, in fear of the Lord and in meditation on the Holy Scriptures, and <how> I guided you to maturity, most devoutly with God. Remember those holy virgins[338] who in the undefiled beauty of virginity adorned their lamps with the oil of good works [p. 411] and entered in triumph with the bridegroom. Remember, child, the fearful <Day of> Judgment, and that unending fire that will burn and punish to the ages of ages all who foolishly surrender themselves to ephemeral and corrupting pleasure and live profligately. Remember, my child, the joy of the saints and that unspeakable glory in which will abide those who do not corrupt *the temple of the body*[339] nor defile the soul that is unified with the body. Verily, my child, I exhort you to cease from the indecent impulse of irrational <animals>, and let us both stand here in prayer and the Lord will fully grant us His mercy, driving from us the evil spirit." When the mother gave this and further admonition to her daughter, she was struck still more by the insane passion and could not bear at all to listen to her mother's advice, but cried out shamelessly: "O mother,

---

[334] The place name is given as Κουντουρία (Kountouria) by Peter, while Sabas (chap. 10) describes the mountains of Κουνδουρία (Koundouria) as located to the west of Lycia and east of Asia, near Myra (πέλοντα πρὸς δύσιν Λυκίας καὶ πρὸς ἀνατολὴν διακείμενα τῆς Ἀσίας, πλησίον Μύρων).

[335] Literally, "from there to here."

[336] See above, n. 218.

[337] Reading ἐπεισφρήσαν for ἐπισφρίσαν.

[338] Mt. 25:1–13.

[339] Cf. Jn. 2:21.

either let me go out into the world and fulfill my desire or I will kill myself." The mother was in dire straits and, throwing herself upon God, begged with loud cries and groans that strength be sent to them from on high, and that either invisibly, I mean by the protection[340] of an angel, or visibly through some servant of His, the furnacelike fire that had come upon her daughter's body be rapidly quenched. And indeed as the mother was engaged in her cries and petition, she raised[341] her eyes and saw our thrice-blessed father Ioannikios walking from the other direction and going toward Kountouria,[342] as mentioned. Running up <to him> she zealously took hold of his feet and washed his feet with her tears, like that blessed prostitute of old,[343] begging him to take pity on her and her daughter. In amazement at her faith he ordered her to rise and bade[344] her relate the cause of her lament. After she narrated what had happened, the saint took the girl's right hand and touched it to his neck, crying out: "O child, may your battle be <transferred> to me from now on, and may you be[345] healed from your scourge by the grace of God." The girl immediately regained self-control and was delivered from her battle and with her mother joyfully sang God's and the saint's praises and hereafter they completed their journey in peace.

47. That most bitter battle made an abrupt shift and impaled the saint like a stake,[346] oppressing him exceedingly. He gave himself over to fasting and vigils and sleeping on the bare ground and all-night prayers; but despite his supplication to God, he found no relief at all for the time being. God, I believe, permitted this in order to purify His blessed man by fire. After he was constrained by the travail for many days, he fell into a sea of despair. He knew that in the caves thereabouts lived a large snake that had been transformed from a sack[347] into its animal shape. He said to himself: "It would be better,

---

[340] Reading ἐπιστασίας for ἐπιτασίας.

[341] Reading ἐπάρασα for ἐπάρας.

[342] See n. 334.

[343] Lk. 7:37–39.

[344] Reading ἐπέτρεψεν for ἐπέστρεψαν.

[345] Reading ἔσο for ἔστω.

[346] The Greek is σκόλοψ, which may also mean a "thorn," a possible translation here; cf. 2 Cor. 12:7: ἐδόθη μοι σκόλοψ τῇ σαρκί.

[347] The interpretation of the Greek here (ἀσπίδα . . . ἐκ σάκκου . . . μεταβληθεῖσαν) is uncertain. Given the frequent references to Moses, one is reminded of the story of

O wretched Ioannikios, for you to go and have your body eaten by the physical serpent, than to yield to sin and have your soul become food for the spiritual serpent." With these words he approached the snake. When he drew near it, he grasped its head with both his hands and shook it violently, provoking the beast to rage against him. The <creature> was filled with frenzy and hissed loudly against the saint. However, he neither harmed nor hurt the saint, <but> rather with the protection and aid of God <the burden of> that violent and terrible battle was lifted and finally abated. And giving thanks to God the saint joyfully resumed his journey singing psalms. [p. 412]

48. On another occasion—it was wintertime, but as[348] often is the case in those days, and especially during the so-called halcyon days,[349] there was steady calm <weather> and the sun was then naturally rising to the south and emitting somewhat less light because it was not at the zenith, but toward the lower part <of its path>—the saint went out of his cell to warm up and at the same time to walk about. He had gone some distance from his cell when suddenly a great storm fell upon him. He was unable to return <to his cell>, <but> was terribly beset by the storm in the midst of the mountain, as if he were on the high seas. Begging God to save him, he looked about this

---

the transformation of Moses' staff into a snake (Ex. 4:17, 7:15 and cf. J. Daniélou, *Grégoire de Nysse. La Vie de Moïse,* 2d ed. [Paris, 1955], pt. 1:24: τοῦ δράκοντος τοῦ ἐκ τῆς Μωϋσέως βακτηρίας μεταβληθέντος, and pt. 2:26: τῆς εἰς ὄψιν μεταβληθείσης βακτηρίας). Emendation to βακτηρίας, βάκτρου, or ῥάβδου, however, seems unlikely and presumably Peter wrote σάκκου. Perhaps there is a reference to a snake's slough, but Euripides, *Iphigeneia in Tauris* 288, uses χίτων, *Physiologus* (ed. F. Sbordone [Milan, 1936; repr. Hildesheim, 1976], 38:3) uses τὸ γῆρας. There are no parallels for such a use of σάκκος in the *TLG,* and to describe the snake as "transformed" from a slough seems strained.

The word σάκκος is used of the monastic habit (see, for example, *v. Ant. Jun.* 191.2, 198.25, 199.5, 203.25 and 215.7–8, and *Physiologus, op. cit.,* 253.7, of the "dry frog" compared to monks) and particularly for those practicing extreme asceticism (see *ODB* 3:1830). Given Peter's strong anti-Stoudite rhetoric, his description of the Stoudites in Chap. 57 as "venom-tongued," and the fact that the name of the original Stoudite house was Σακκούδιον, perhaps Peter is engaging in wordplay here.

[348] Reading οἷα for οἴα.

[349] The halcyon was a symbolic or mystical bird identified with the kingfisher. The halcyon days, fourteen traditionally calm days at the winter solstice, when the halcyon lays and hatches her eggs, were first mentioned by Simonides (ed. D. L. Page, *Poetae Melici Graeci* [Oxford, 1962], 508, p. 240). See D'Arcy Thompson, *A Glossary of Greek Birds* (Oxford, 1936), 46–51.

way and that and, seeing that there was a cave close by, gladly turned aside to it. When he reached the entrance to the cave, he saw something like fiery embers lying in its innermost part. This was actually a dragon, whose eyes were like blazing fire. <The saint> did not realize this but, as I have said earlier, thought it was a fire. He very gladly gathered leaves that were lying in the cave and filled both hands <with them>. He <then> went in and spread them on the dragon's eyes. When this happened, the beast thrashed about violently and wanted to attack the saint. But it was unable to do so, for divine grace gave <the saint> total protection and guarded him. The saint saw this and rather quietly[350] withdrew and sat down in another part of the cave. And he remained there with the dragon until the storm abated. Then emerging unharmed, he traveled back to his cell singing God's praises. [p. 413]

49. When the saint was living in the most holy monastery of Antidion,[351] he once ordered his most devout assistant, whose name was Theophilos, to take a mattock[352] and excavate a sufficient distance out from his cell to create a pathway. For <he lived>, as I have often said, in an area that was almost inaccessible. When this was done, the saint took his assistant Theophilos and went out for a walk with him. After they passed through the shady forest of the mountains, they came to a place that was bare of trees and sunny. The aforementioned disciple, the sanctified Theophilos, raised his eyes and saw the brothers of the monastery coming up and with them a very large number of poor people who customarily came to the saint and were ministered to by him. Noting <this>, he told the great man to return. But the saint, who was bent with old age and unable to walk further, turned around with difficulty and stood still right where he was. When the visitors drew near them, they all saw the disciple Theophilos and all made obeisance to him. But they did not see at all the saint, who was standing with his disciple in the <same> place, even though, as you all know, he was quite tall in stature. As they passed, the

---

[350] Reading ἠρέμα for ἡμέρα, as suggested by L. Rydén.

[351] On the monastery, see above, n. 106.

[352] On the Greek term here, σκαπάνη, see Suda, sigma 537, 1: Σκαπάνη - σκάφιον, ὀρύγιον, δικέλλιον, ὁ παρ' ἡμῖν τζόκος λεγόμενος; Koukoules, *Bios,* 5:269, who says ἡ δίκελλα, ἣν ὁρίζουσιν ὡς σκαπάνην; and A. Bryer, "Byzantine Agricultural Implements: The Evidence of Medieval Illustrations of Hesiod's *Works and Days,*" *Annual of the British School of Athens* 81 (1986), 45–80, specifically 70, where it is translated as "mattock." For parallels in hagiographic texts, see *v. Ant. Jun.* 203.14, *v. Theoph. conf.* 12.18, and *vita* of Theodore of Stoudios, PG 99:241D.

saint said to his disciple: "O Theophilos, take blessed bread[353] and distribute it to the poor people, because great need has compelled them to come here." After he did this and distributed provisions to each person, Theophilos was asked by the brothers why he was standing there alone and for what reason. He said that he was not alone, but was standing with the saint. They affirmed under oath that they saw no one else but him[354] and jointly gave thanks and glorified God.

50. Once some men came from a distance to see our saintly father Ioannikios and arrived at the monastery of Antidion.[355] And indeed *by chance*[356] they met one of its monks, the sanctified Paul, who was going out to obtain wood for burning lime[357] for the construction of the chapel of St. John.[358] Prostrating themselves before him they begged him to inform <the saint> of their arrival so that they might see the man of God. And he said: "Gentlemen, remain where you are for the time being and be patient. For whoever should pass by after me is the man whom you seek. Prostrate yourselves before him." They did as instructed and not much later the saint passed through their midst,

---

[353] The term for blessed bread here (εὐλογία) is fundamentally a "blessing" or "benediction." For its application to bread sent as a gift, see *ODB* 2:745. It is odd that, while simply out for a walk, Theophilos apparently has in his possession bread to distribute.

[354] Ioannikios' gift of invisibility is also mentioned below in Chaps. 50 and 61. The same ability is mentioned in the *Life of Antony the Younger* (*AnalBoll* 62 [1944], 214.8–9), where the hermit Jacob indicates that one cannot be a real monk until one can make oneself invisible. The *Life of Ignatios* (PG 105:524D) refers to Elisha's smiting the Syrians with blindness (4 Ki. 6:18) as the biblical paradigm of the power. The same miraculous ability was also attributed to Peter of Atroa (see V. Laurent in *v. Petr. Atr.* 58 and 102 n. 2) and Ioannikios' power is mentioned again in *v. Iren. Chrysobalant.* 11 and n. 5.

[355] On the monastery of Antidion, see above, n. 106.

[356] Cf. Lk. 10:31.

[357] For examples of the use in lime in construction, see A.-M. Talbot, "The Posthumous Miracles of St. Photeine," *AnalBoll* 112 (1994), 98 n. 37. The word here for lime is ἄσβεστον.

[358] The construction of the chapel of St. John Prodromos in the monastery of Antidion is also mentioned by Sabas (chap. 38). In his version the monk is a certain John, not Paul, and he adds that Ioannikios had ordered construction of the chapel and had come to inspect the quality of the work. Janin (*Eglises Centres,* 136 and 157) briefly comments on the chapel.

<but> was not seen by them at all. They waited for many hours and suspected that they had been deceived; for the man they sought did not appear. The aforementioned Paul came back to the monastery and said to the men: "Behold, children, your desire has been fulfilled." But they asserted that they had seen no one up to now except him. The monk, who was astonished, was continuously importuned by the men; he agreed with them to inform <the saint> of their <arrival and then> returned to the saint. And making obeisance to him, he deferentially inquired and asked:[359] "How did you pass by without granting these visitors an audience?"[360] <The saint> replied: "I did not see them, but go now and tell them not to grieve any longer, but to have faith and return home rejoicing, as if they had already seen[361] me and received a blessing." And when this was done, the men received the message and, since they believed without doubt that they had obtained just what the saint had indicated, they returned to their homeland giving thanks and praising God.

51. One of the townspeople[362] had a habit of visiting the saint quite frequently to obtain his honored blessings, and he used to tell everyone about the miracles [p. 414] that <the saint> accomplished by the grace of God. For often when he went he would see wild animals tamed by him and taking food from his hands. And so one day as he was sitting in a crowded gathering and extolling the saint, someone arose in the midst of the meeting and said: "Sir, the <tales> you tell seem strange to me and exaggerated and I have no confidence in them. But if you want to <make> a believer of me, take me with you, if you have ready access to the saint, as you say, so that I too may see with my own eyes and no longer be hesitant, but believe without qualification." And so both men started out and went to the saint. After they saw him and obtained his blessings, they were invited to share a meal with him. In the

---

[359] Reading ἐρωτήσει for ἠρωτήσει.

[360] The word ἀπεριλόγητος is a *hapax;* Trapp (*Lexikon,* s.v.) translates it as "ignored," "neglected." But the translation "without an audience" seems justified, since περιλογή is used by Theophanes for "colloquy, conference"; cf. Lampe, *Lexicon,* s.v. περιλογή.

[361] Reading ἰδόντας for εἰδότας, as suggested by L. Rydén.

[362] The Greek term here, πολιτῶν, could, if capitalized, refer to a resident of Constantinople. Sabas (chap. 39) tells virtually the same story, but he refers to a "Theodore, monk and superior" instead of to "one of the townspeople" as the one narrating Ioannikios' miracles.

middle of the lunch,[363] behold, a huge bear[364] appeared and was eager to sprawl out near the guests. They were quite agitated and cried out in a loud voice: "Help <us>,[365] saint of God." He smiled rather gently,[366] and told them not to be afraid, but to be content with the miracles <already> recounted as trustworthy, and to have faith and not deny them as in any way unworthy of faith. Then he bade them feed the beast with their own hands. But they were paralyzed with fear and remained stunned. The saint said to the beast: "Since they are so lacking in judgment about you, go away for now and return again later." At his command the beast withdrew after making obeisance to the saint, and the men, coming to their senses, fell at the saint's feet. After he prayed for and blessed them, he dismissed them in peace.

52. The servant of God once ordered his disciple, the venerable Theo-doulos, to take a *magarikon*[367] of oil and give it to the poor and to carry an-other empty one with him. He was unwilling to do so, saying that he would carry this <empty one> to no purpose. The saint smiled and replied: "Take it nevertheless, in case you meet someone who needs it. And you will give it to him and obtain payment." He took both <vessels> as bidden. And indeed as he traveled along the road, he slipped badly and fell and the blow made a hole in the full vessel. He got up immediately and transferred <the oil> to the other empty <container>. And when he remembered the saint's words, he wept bitterly for his disobedient resistance. Then he completed his task and returned. He made obeisance and asked the saint to forgive him, explaining what had happened to him on the road. The <saint> spoke somewhat se-verely to him, <then> dismissed him with forgiveness and a blessing.

53. As our marvelous father Ioannikios was once passing through a cer-tain place in the company of the most blessed Daniel,[368] the former superior

---

[363] On the term ἄριστον, translated here as "lunch," see above, n. 275.

[364] For another saint feeding a bear, see *v. Theod. Syc.*, chap. 28:17–20.

[365] As the phrase βοήθει, ἅγιε is introduced by τό, presumably this is a reference to a known prayer. Perhaps the reference is to Mk. 9:24 or Mt. 15:25.

[366] Reading ἠρέμα for ἡμέρα; cf. n. 350 above.

[367] A μαγαρικόν (= μεγαρικόν) is "a large clay vessel, originally probably made in Megara"; see *ODB* 2:1329 and E. Schilbach, *Byzantinische Metrologie* (Munich, 1970), 100–102; 122.

[368] For Daniel and the island of Thasios, see above, Chap. 37.

of the holy monastery of the island of Thasios, they found caves that were quite terrifying and full of demons. For an *archon*[369] of demons inhabited these <caves> with his murderous army. Those who lived some distance away called them "the cave<s> at the *Toparch*" and no one could pass by that place. The venerable Ioannikios, who was so purified in his senses, perceived that demonic throng with the clairvoyant eye of his heart and said to the great Daniel: "Father, listen <to me>, and let us both agree to live separately for forty days in these caves. For I trust in the mercies of God that the grace of the all-holy Spirit will preserve us unharmed, but will expel and drive out the demonic multitude and manifest <the place> as an abode for men in search of salvation." And the most holy Daniel did not oppose the blessed man's word, but was persuaded. So the two men separated and went to live in the caves, [p. 415] earnestly entreating God for the expulsion of the unclean spirits. Near the end of the forty days a fearful man appeared, ugly, his head rising to a great height, his legs like huge columns. He moved quickly and attacked the saint with great anger. The saint armed himself with the sign of the cross, and stretching out his hand made the sign <of the cross> numerous times over the apparition. But <the giant> not only did not flee, but even continued to approach, acting quite shamelessly. And when that fearful apparition drew near and was close to the saint, the saint reached out with both hands and grabbed his feet; and crying out in a loud voice, "All-holy Mother of God, help <me>," he threw the <giant> to the ground with a fearful clatter. As he was being dragged down, he violently kicked the saint in the side, and for seven days the saint remained speeechless.[370] After a week our all-admirable father Ioannikios came to his senses and by God's grace regained complete health. He rejoined the God-bearing Daniel and they both joyfully sang God's praises for the total expulsion of the unclean spirits and completed their journey singing psalms.

54. Once the venerable man of God Eustratios (the one who earnestly

---

[369] *Archon,* a term for various magistrates (see *ODB* 1:160), and used also in patristic references to the "archon of darkness" (cf. Eph. 6:12), is apparently used here to explain the name of the cave below, "*at the top-arch.*" *Toparch,* lit., "archon of the place," is also a term for various magistrates (see *ODB* 3:2095).

[370] I.e., unconscious, a fairly common meaning for ἄφωνος; cf. *v. Stephan. Jun.* 1173в and *v. Andr. Sal.,* line 80.

and with faith composed <materials for> this wondrous and beneficial treatise[371] and left to the next generation an eternal memorial) suffered a severe
nosebleed. As a result of the great loss of blood the sanctified man grew quite
faint and almost lost his ability to speak. Since[372] the all-blessed Eustratios
was wondrous and well known to all, numerous physicians came and each
attempted by his skill to staunch that violent flow of blood. When they had
no success, but on the contrary did him harm, they finally left in despair. He
<then> summoned the most devout Nicholas and with difficulty, due to his
shortness of breath, supplicated this man to go with great speed to inform the
saint of his illness and supplicate him to pray earnestly on his behalf. For the
illustrious Eustratios quite rightly thought: "When the message is delivered
and the prayer is completed, I will assuredly obtain mercy," which indeed happened. For when the man went forth as bidden, that heavenly mind [i.e., Ioan-
nikios] <already> knew what had happened and went out to meet him. Upon
seeing the saint, <Nicholas> knelt on the ground and, after requesting and
receiving a blessing, he rose <to his feet>. The blessed <Ioannikios> spoke
to the man and asked him—although he <already> knew—why he had
troubled to come and what was this solicitous concern and if his faithful and
good friend the beloved Eustratios was in good health. When <Nicholas>
replied that he had come on this man's [Eustratios'] behalf, the blessed man
bade him sit down there on the spot and wait a little while. He did so and the
saint returned to his cell and petitioned God for a long time. Upon his return
he said to the man: "My <good> man, go back and say to my most beloved
Eustratios: 'For the time being do not be troubled, for you will not die, but
soon, when it pleases God, we will see one another.'" And with this word the
emissary took leave of the saint and gladly made his journey. Indeed the flow
of blood stopped at the same hour at which the saint said to the man, "He
will not die,"[373] and the illness was completely driven out through the saint's
entreaties. When the man arrived and conveyed that joyful message in the
presence of everyone, the sanctified Eustratios inquired the precise hour at
which the saint said this. And when he learned it, he knew in all truth that at
the hour at which the saint spoke he had regained his health, and together with
everyone <present> he sang a hymn to God and gave thanks to the saint.

---

[371] For Eustratios' role in the composition of the *vita,* see Introduction, 245–47.

[372] Reading ἅτε for ἄτε.

[373] Cf. Jn. 4:53.

A few [p. 416] days later, while the illustrious Eustratios was still incapacitated from his illness, the brothers living in the dependency named Leukades[374] entreated him to come for a visit, and to instruct and edify them in the <way of life> that leads to salvation. And indeed the sanctified Eustratios was persuaded—for he never hesitated in this matter, but you know how to this day he runs eagerly, if he is summoned by anyone for the salvation of his soul. For he is eager in this way to snatch by God's grace many and numberless souls from the mouth of the terrible dragon and lead them to God through repentance and make them the purest possessions and willing victims and *blameless sacrifices*.[375] And so he heeded <their appeal> and agreed to go <for the sake of> the salvation of the brothers, even if under some constraint on account of his illness, as has been said. When he set forth and arrived at the place I have already mentioned, he blessed the brothers and instructed each in the <way> of salvation. <But> he again fell ill due to the hardship of the trip. And so after he remained without food for four days, he became severely ill due to an increase in his raging fever. All the brothers stood around him in a circle and wept bitterly at his <imminent> demise and bewailed their orphanhood; he himself was also full of tears. The lamentation continued for many hours, as the disciples cried out "Alas!" and said: "Who will shepherd us from now on, O noble and most compassionate father? Woe, woe are we, who will guide and protect us as you <do>, who so cared for your children? Where will we wretched <souls> find such a pure spring of discernment? To whom shall we go, when we have heard words of life each day from you? Who will show us the road of our salvation? O, O for us, wretched sinners, that we are deprived of such a light and lamp; we are the cause of your death, noble father. For if we had not summoned you, but allowed you to rest a little from your illness, surely you would be alive,[376] earnestly caring for your flock." After the brothers had uttered these and other words of lamentation for some time, <Eustratios> signaled with his hand and said that their lament should stop; when he had blessed and prayed for all, he dismissed them. <Then> he himself turned to supplication and, beholding our miraculous father Ioannikios

---

[374] On Leukades, a dependency of the Agauroi monastery, see Janin, *Eglises Centres*, 164–65.

[375] Cf. P. Nautin, ed., *Jean Chrysostome. Homélies pascales* 2 (Paris, 1953), p. 69.18–19.

[376] Reading ἔζῃς for ἔξῃς.

as if in a mirror, <Eustratios> supplicated him to cure him and, as he [Ioan-nikios] promised, to see him [Ioannikios]. And indeed as he prayed he fell asleep and saw the saint standing beside him and saying to him: "Do not be at all fearful, O Eustratios, but quickly travel to such and such[377] place and to the sanctified monks so and so and tell them from us this and that." The sick man immediately made obeisance and set forth, as it seemed <in his dream>, and upon arrival at that place was met by the most lofty monks who were in hiding there and they all fell to the ground and asked for a blessing. Then in accordance with the custom of our blessed father Ioannikios when receiving visitors, there was a blessing. When the all-holy Eustratios had re-peated it, he seemed in his sleep to speak with them. And after a fervent[378] prayer, the brothers there heard the "Lord, have mercy" emitted for a long time <and> in a vibrant voice from the mouth of their divinely inspired supe-rior Eustratios. And indeed again in grief they asked him: "What is it, good[379] father, are you leaving us orphans?" He awoke and in a more confident voice replied: "I am not <leaving you>, children; do not grieve, for saint Ioannik-ios has visited me." And he immediately requested and took nourishment. On the next day <Eustratios>, who had already approached the very *gates of death,*[380] grew strong due to the saint's visit and departed to his own flock, and after walking fifteen stades[381] he came to his own monastery glorifying God and the saint. [p. 417]

55. At another time some men were having a discussion with one another, saying: "Is the great Ioannikios <really> honored with the word of faith as well as the gift of miracles? Or does he err somehow because of his simplicity and lack of <theological> erudition? If it were possible, we would <like to> hear about this and understand and have precise faith." And indeed they came

---

[377] Reading τόνδε τὸν for δὲ τὸν.

[378] The Greek here, ἐκτενοῦς, is presumably used in a nontechnical sense; cf. v. *Iren. Chrysobalant.* 56:4–6: τῆς ἐκτενοῦς δὲ ταύτης θερμῶς ἐπιτελουμένης προσευχῆς. The term can, however, refer formally to a litany (see Lampe, *Lexicon,* s.v.).

[379] Reading τί ἔν, καλὲ of the manuscript for τί, ἔγκαλε of the printed edition; cf. Sophocles, *Lexicon,* s.v. ἔν.

[380] Job 38:17.

[381] The stade was equal to 100 *orguiai* and could thus be either 187 or 210 m in length. The reference suggests the approximate distance between the metochion of Leu-kades and the Agauroi monastery to which Eustratios returns. See Janin, *Eglises Cen-tres,* 164 n. 9.

to an agreement and decided to go to him for a blessing and to inquire precisely concerning this <question>. So they went and were received by the saint. After they spoke at some length, that clairvoyant mind <of Ioannikios> realized their deceitful scheme and said: "Since oftentimes certain people raise objections concerning me and are badly scandalized, saying that I do not hold correct but erroneous beliefs, I wish to state publicly my faith in your revered presence." As the men rejoiced greatly at this, he opened his honored mouth and summarized his faith with the following words:[382] "I believe in one God the Father almighty, Maker and Lord of everything visible and invisible, Who has no beginning, is unseen, incomprehensible, unalterable, without end; and <I believe> in one Lord Jesus Christ, His only begotten Son, shining from the Father's essence without beginning and timelessly, and before all the ages; and in one Holy Spirit, Which proceeds from God and the Father and is regarded as equally divine with the Father and Son and is glorified together with them, as of like nature and co-eternal. I glorify the Trinity in hypostases[383] or persons, preserving the distinctive attributes in each of the aforementioned <persons> unmixed and without confusion, as never altering or changing; I attribute to the Father ingenerateness and the causation of the <things> that are from Him, generation to the Son, and procession to the Holy Spirit; and <I believe> that the One that is begotten and the One that proceeds shine forth from the Father as the cause and that each as light proceeds from light, one light, transcendent, shining with triple rays and like three suns. I worship the unity in essence and nature coming together in one supraessential and supernatural height of Divinity, possessing the same indivisible and inseparable glory and power [p. 418]; recognized in identical will and volition, in a single power and energy, and queen of all and mistress of everything, venerated and worshiped by every visible and invisible creation, as equally honored

---

[382] As noted by van den Gheyn (*AASS*, Nov. 2.1:17 n. 1, 424 note a), this statement of faith is taken virtually verbatim (verbs are changed from first person plural to first person singular or to participles) from Patriarch Nikephoros I, *Apologeticus pro sacris imaginibus* (PG 100:580D–592A; A. Mai, *Novae patrum bibliothecae* 5 [Rome, 1849], 22–27). For a theological analysis of portions of the text, see J. Travis, *In Defense of the Faith* (Brookline, Mass., 1984), esp. chaps. 2 and 7. I have followed Travis' translations of portions of the text.

[383] The complex term *hypostasis* (ὑπόστασις) is used here as equivalent to "person" (πρόσωπον), for an individual person of the Trinity. For the evolution of the word, see *ODB* 3:2117–18, s.v. "Trinity."

and co-enthroned. For <the Trinity> is one Godhead seen in three, united in the same essence, but three hypostases in one Godhead inseparably separate in the differentiation of the characteristics inhering in each. Nor do I dissociate the Son from the essence of the ingenerate Father on account of <His> generation, nor the <Holy> Spirit from the Father and Son on account of its procession. Nor do I acknowledge any confusion on account of the unitary coexistence and indivisibility, but I unite in the common nature what is distinct in each individual. *For they are divided without division and united in division. For the Godhead is one in three, and the three are one, in whom is the Godhead or, to speak more accurately, Who are the Godhead,* as the mightiest of theologians[384] has taught us, initiating us into the <divine> mysteries. Thus I revere God the Father, from Whom all things have been brought into existence from nothingness. I glorify God the Son, through Whom all things came to be and are preserved to essential permanence. I worship God the Holy Spirit, in Which all things are preserved and contained. I revere the three as one God, and I do not divide the one Godhead into three gods so as to avoid the great atheism of tritheism[385] or rather polytheism. And I know each of them <to be> perfect. For I do not confess one perfect <God> from three imperfect ones, but one *supremely perfect and beyond perfection*[386] from three perfect ones, as the theology of the divinely inspired fathers instructs. Nor do I propose the hypostases as alien and different natures, dividing them with inequalities and irregularities. Rather I separate them by reason of their characteristics, joining them into a single essence, rejecting superiority or inferiority in them. For as it is not possible to see greater or lesser in the essence, neither <is it possible to see greater or lesser> in the Trinity with respect to the essence or the divinity, in order that we may extinguish the Arian[387] madness, from which and against which is our present struggle. Nor indeed do I confound or confuse them into one hypostasis, but I introduce the distinction unified in the essence with existing persons and realities and names, in order to utterly oblit-

---

[384] Gregory of Nazianzos, *In sancta lumina,* PG 36:345.43–47.

[385] Tritheism was "an accusation often made . . . against those who emphasized the 'individuality' of the hypostaseis rather than the unity of the Trinity"; *ODB* 3:2121.

[386] Cf. pseudo-Dionysios, *De Divinis Nominibus* 2:10 (PG 3:648C): ὡς ὑπερτελὴς καὶ προτέλειος.

[387] Arius (ca. 250–336) distinguished the divine essence into greater and smaller; see Travis, *Defense,* 20.

erate the Sabellian[388] insanity. <These heresies, i.e., Arianism and Sabellianism> are opposite evils, but congruent in their impiety.[389] To sum up, I join while piously separating and I separate while joining as befits God. Therefore uniting in a common nature what is separate in the hypostases, but distinguishing what is united in essence and divinity by the difference of hypostases, I show piety and soundness in both <respects> regarding the great and most divine and highest mystery of our knowledge of God. Thus as one who worships the all-holy and supraessential Trinity in a spirit of truth, I venerate it in holiness and righteous faith, in pure and blameless belief all the days of my life.

"Consequently I confess also that One of the consubstantial and supraessential and superdivine Trinity, our Lord Jesus Christ, the Son of God and our God, the reflection of His Father's glory, [p. 419] the light from the light, the identical image of the Father and *the express image of His hypostasis,*[390] came down in the flesh to the earth and while among us fulfilled *oikonomia*[391] for us. For He Himself with ineffable love for humanity, moved by feelings of mercy and compassion, could not bear to see our nature enslaved to the end to the bitter tyranny <of the Devil>. But He willingly descended into the abasement <of the Incarnation>, with the approval of the Father and the cooperation of the all-holy and life-giving Spirit; He did so without ever abandoning the Father's glory or indeed in any way diminishing His own honors that are fitting for God. And He became flesh by the Holy Spirit and the all-holy, glorious and truly Theotokos and ever-virgin Mary, who was purified in advance by the Spirit in soul and body. He became human in all respects except sin, putting on this mortal and corruptible, depictable and circumscribable nature. He came forth one <and> the same from two, from divinity and humanity, and He remained perfect in all respects and unalterable in divinity and perfect likewise and immutable in humanity through which He shared

---

[388] Sabellianism opposed the doctrine of the Logos, suggesting that the persons of the Trinity are simply modes by which one God appears in the history of salvation; see *ODB* 2:1391, s.v. "Monarchianism." It thus blurred the real distinctions among the three persons; see Travis, *Defense,* 20.

[389] Cf. Gregory of Nazianzos, *In sancta lumina,* PG 36:348.4–5.

[390] Heb. 1:3.

[391] On the central theme here of *oikonomia,* "the eternal plan of God to save and restore fallen man from sin . . . by the incarnation of the Logos," see Travis, *Defense,* 66.

our life. He completely healed the transgression of Adam through His own innocence; He destroyed the corruption of sin and granted us incorruptibility by His voluntary suffering in the flesh and by His life-giving death and God-befitting resurrection. For He lived anew after three days, conquering death, and became the *first born from the dead*,[392] guiding human nature on the road to incorruptibility, depriving the unseen enemy of power over us. All He did and suffered is proclaimed in the holy Gospels and is believed by us. Thereby He reformed the ancient Adam, and renewed our nature, and brought <it> back to the original state of happiness. And He was taken up into the heavens and made the *first of our dough*[393] to sit with Him next to the Father's throne. For with such a confession <of faith>, to speak in a rather compressed manner, I maintain that the great and venerable mystery of the divine *oikonomia* has occurred.[394]

"I glorify also the dual existential quality of the essences coming together in Him together with their characteristics. For each of them [i.e., the essences] is perfect and complete, I proclaim it. I likewise confess the confluence of essences from these into a unity of person through unity in hypostasis, neither cutting or dividing the one Lord Jesus Christ into two sons, separately into man, separately into God, into parts, so that I may destroy the foolish distinction of the deranged and man-worshiping insanity of Nestorios.[395] Nor indeed do I lead the unity of the one Person into the same single nature by confounding or changing <the natures>, but I preserve unmixed and unconfounded the differences belonging to each nature, in order that I might totally destroy the conflation of the foolish and senseless Eutyches,[396] together with the fol-

---

[392] Col. 1:18.

[393] Cf. Num. 15:19, 21; Rom. 11:16. The metaphor suggests that, with the offering of the first loaf, the entire remaining dough is consecrated, i.e., Christ is the offering Who saves humanity. The text of Paul reads (in the Revised Standard Version translation): "If the dough offered as first fruits is holy, so is the whole lump."

[394] The text here omits chap. 20 (PG 100:585.1–588.8) of Nikephoros' *Apologeticus.*

[395] Nestorios, bishop of Constantinople (428–431), stressed the human principle in Christology, denying the hypostatic unity of Christ; see *ODB* 2:1459–60, s.v. "Nestorianism."

[396] Eutyches (ca. 370–454), a supporter of Cyril of Alexandria and Monophysitism, denied that Christ had two natures after the Incarnation and refused to accept that Christ was consubstantial with mankind; see *ODB* 2:759.

lowers of Severos,[397] who are rightly called Akephaloi.[398] For these wrongly conflate, while <Nestorios> impiously divides, so that Eutyches stood in the same <relationship> to Nestorios regarding the Incarnation, as Sabellios <was> to Arius regarding divinity.[399] And so <if> one confesses to the two perfect natures in Christ, [p. 420] both in their existence and in the natural qualities relating to them, it will consequently be necessary to confess as well the natural wills and energies inherent in each nature. For it is necessary, if one believes in two essences, to proclaim as well that these <qualities>[400] are <also> double. For otherwise the perfect purity in these <essences> will not be preserved, since these are the characteristics of the natures, and it is not possible to find a nature without will or energy. And so inasmuch as He willed and acted as God, so also He willed and acted as man, both in the miracles and also the other activities of the Incarnation. But He did not possess these in opposition to one another. For those <characteristics> that He assumed yielded to and were subject to those of the One Who assumed them. And just as nothing in Him is considered as opposite and antithetical on account of the concurrent natures, even though <the natures> are opposite (the proof is <that> where essences are different and the basis of existence is different— which indeed is apparent in things of different natures—it is also necessary for the essential qualities of will and energy to be different; and through them we acquire knowledge of the natures; for where the energies are the same,

---

[397] I.e., Severos, bishop of Antioch (512–518), a moderate Monophysite for whom Christ's humanity "did not form a nature . . . or hypostasis but only an annex of the single divine" nature; see *ODB* 3:1884–85.

[398] That is, "Headless." The term was used of extremist Monophysites who were "leaderless"; see *ODB* 3:1638, s.v. "Peter Mongos."

[399] I.e., at opposite ends of the heretical spectrum. Eutyches emphasized the unity in Christ, Nestorios the duality; Sabellios emphasized the unity in God (making the persons in the Trinity aspects or modes of being in one God), Arius reduced the Son and Spirit to the status of separate and subordinate beings. For another saint's (Euthymios the Great's) similar defense of his orthodoxy, see E. Schwartz, *Kyrillos von Skythopolis* (Leipzig, 1939), 40:2 ff, Eng. trans. R. M. Price, *The Lives of the Monks of Palestine* (Kalamazoo, Mich., 1991), 36–37, where the evils of Arius and Sabellios are said to be ἐκ διαμέτρου, while Nestorios' and Eutyches' heresies are characterized with the terms διαίρεσις and σύγχυσις.

[400] I.e., will and energy.

natures are alike), so also the mode of the *theandric energy*[401] in Christ, as He lived with us, will be clarified, understood indeed periphrastically, signifying the duality of the energy through the appropriate appellation of the two natures.[402] For the mode of unity contains the basis of the difference preserved in itself. For would one thus concede that *each form acts with the cooperation of the other?*[403] And so we do not proclaim one will and <one> energy in the divine Incarnation, taking away the naturally occurring <qualities> in each of the essences, unless we intend to do away completely also with the nature itself, so that we may not fall into the sickness of the mad and insane Apollinaris,[404] but so that we may at the same time condemn the faction of Sergios[405] and Pyrrhos[406] concerning the lack of energy and lack of volition of the true Word. And this mystery of the revered and salvific Incarnation is glorified by us; *what is to be understood of it remains ineffable and what is to be said of it remains unknowable,* according to the aforementioned God-bearing <father>.[407]

"And so we confess that we are saved through the visit <of the Incarnate>, and we honor and embrace also the holy and venerable symbols and tokens of this <Incarnation>, together with all the <other> holy objects of veneration among us. Through these it is portrayed and signified to us as in the gospel story, if indeed they stimulate us to remember the descent effected by the Savior for us. We have received them piously from above and from the beginning, like children receiving from fathers. Treating them with care we

[401] Pseudo-Dionysios, *Epist.* 4 (PG 3:1072c).

[402] That is, the dual term "God-man" or θεανδρικός.

[403] Leo I the Great, *Epistula (Tomus) ad Flavianum,* PL 54:768B.

[404] Apollinaris, bishop of Laodikeia (ca. 310–390), stressed the divine element in Christ and subsequently argued that, while Christ had a human soul and body, He had a heavenly "reason"; see *ODB* 1:136.

[405] Sergios I, patriarch of Constantinople (610–638), developed the formula of Monoenergism, which suggested that Christ had a single "energy" attributable to His individual hypostasis. This then developed into Monotheletism, the view that there was a single "will" in Christ; see *ODB* 2:1396–97, 3:1878, and 2:1400–401.

[406] Pyrrhos, patriarch of Constantinople (638–641 and 654), supported and developed the Monotheletism of Sergios I; see *ODB* 3:1761.

[407] Pseudo-Dionysios, *Epist.* 3 (PG 3:1069B): ἀλλὰ καὶ λεγόμενον ἄρρητον μένει, καὶ νοούμενον ἄγνωστον.

assign <to them> the reverence that is appropriate; we do not indeed (God forbid!) offer <them> worship befitting divinity, which is appropriate only to the God Who rules over all. For all disciples of God in the Spirit know the difference in reverence and <understand> what kind of veneration should be rendered to Christ and our God and assign fitting reverence to the holy icons and through them refer honor to the archetype.[408] In addition we honor also the revered icons of our all-holy, undefiled mistress and true patron, the ever-virgin Theotokos, who bore our Lord Jesus Christ God, without seed, [p. 421] ineffably and beyond nature; <we honor> also <the icons> of the holy angels, and all the saints who have pleased Him from the beginning, whose memory we piously honor and whose intercessions we request. For they live in God and act in Him and are able by the power and grace of God residing in them to aid and assist those who approach them and make petition."

The theological mouth, filled with the Holy Spirit, spoke <thus> of God with piety, and amazed all who heard. And those who had come <to him> fell at his feet and confessed their act of deceit. They begged forgiveness, and upon receiving it returned with joy, glorifying God Who gave[409] His saint such words of wisdom.

56. Once an intolerable <swarm> of caterpillars[410] descended on the dependency of the Agauroi <monastery> where the all-sacred church of the miracle-working saints Kosmas and Damian[411] is honored. And this constituted a great pestilence[412] on the vegetables cultivated there by the brothers. When the brothers living there saw this, they reported it to their superior, I mean the venerable Eustratios. And indeed as was his custom, he consoled them with sweet-sounding words and dismissed them. A little later the sanctified Eustratios went up to the saint and told him what had happened. The <saint> said to him: "Go and gather all the brothers; after you pray in the church of the saints, you will see the disappearance of these <caterpillars>."

---

[408] Cf. B. Pruche, *Basile de Césarée: Sur le Saint-Esprit,* 2d ed. (Paris, 1968), 18:45.19: ἡ τῆς εἰκόνος τιμὴ ἐπὶ τὸ πρωτότυπον διαβαίνει.

[409] Reading τὸν δόντα for τῷ δόντι.

[410] For another saint dealing with a swarm of caterpillars in a garden, see the *Vita of Niketas Patrikios,* ed. D. Papachryssanthou, *TM* 3 (1968), 335, chap. 11.

[411] On this dependency, see above, n. 113.

[412] Perhaps one should read λύμη, "damage," instead of λοίμη.

He said this because he was of humble spirit and sought to avoid *the praise of men*.[413] <Eustratios> begged the saint to come in person and make these <caterpillars> disappear by his command and prayers, but the <saint> replied: "Go and do as I have said, and I will come at dawn." And indeed at this the two men parted. After the sanctified Eustratios summoned the community and told of the saint's coming, they prayed and went to sleep; for it was night. When they went out together at dawn, they saw the saint standing in the middle of the garden and that multitude of caterpillars being expelled and leaving the garden. At the sight of this, they fell at his feet and asked for his blessing. After receiving it, they returned joyfully glorifying God.

57. A man named Isaac, who was *kourator*[414] of the monastery called Kloubion,[415] went up to the blessed man to obtain his blessings. There happened to be with the saint at that time the most devout men Dositheos and Eustratios. Then the blessed man said to the *kourator:* "Did you not promise to become a monk?" He said: "Yes, father, but I am held fast by the mother superior <of Kloubion> and as a result am delayed." The father gave instruction to this man and made the sign <of the cross> over his head, enigmatically suggesting that his end would be sudden. He <then> dismissed him with these words: "The<se> two most devout men Eustratios and Dositheos are going to the city <of Constantinople> on business; they will assuredly persuade the mother superior to release you." Both men received the saint's blessings and went to the city. The aforementioned *kourator* took only lord Dositheos to the mother superior to relay the saint's message. When she heard it she was greatly upset, and indeed even fiercely assailed the most devout Dositheos. For she considered the <*kourator*> her best adviser[416] in all matters that pertained to her. Nevertheless, in the end she was stung by her own conscience—for she was a devout woman—and sought out the most devout Eus-

---

[413] Cf. Jn. 12:43.

[414] The term was used of managers of imperial estates, but here refers to those of a monastic establishment; see *ODB* 2:1155–56. Sabas (chap. 33) says he was "*kourator* of the *proasteia* of one of the famous women's monasteries around the imperial city."

[415] The version of Sabas (chap. 33) indicates that Kloubion was a nunnery near Constantinople. It is not otherwise known; see Janin, *Eglises CP,* 282.

[416] The term translated "adviser" is φροντιστήριον, which in classical usage was a "think tank" and in Byzantine Greek a "monastery." Its application to a human adviser is unusual.

tratios, desiring [p. 422] to learn the truth from him. For she knew that he was a genuine friend of the blessed <Ioannikios>. So he went and informed her about everything, saying: "You will get no benefit, if you should decide to hold onto him, since he will die shortly." <Thus> he persuaded the most devout woman to assent to release <the *kourator* from his duties>.

When the man said farewell and departed, lo and behold, the Stoudites who were followers[417] of Athanasios and Naukratios[418] arrived. It is the habit of these men to stir up trouble and to shake up not only the church of God, but also everyone who is dedicated to God; they cleverly wield their venomous tongue in the criticism of sainthood,[419] and recommend only themselves[420] and proclaim their barking <as> inspired by God. So those deceitful <monks> fooled also that woman; and, in addition, these <people> who should be spat upon and hated by all, who are weights on the world, so to speak, *graceless creations, fabrications of the Devil,*[421] turned upside down and spat upon the saint's words; they <tried to> hinder, so they thought, the salvation of the man who was about to depart to God. And he would already have been delivered over to death unrepentant if the saint's prayer had not come to the ears of the Lord and furnished <the *kourator*> the briefest <additional> measure

[417] The Greek here, οἱ περὶ Ἀθανάσιον καὶ Ναυκράτιον, could also refer to Athanasios and Naukratios themselves; see below, Chap. 69 and n. 498, where τοὺς ἀμφὶ Ἀθανάσιον καὶ Ναυκράτιον almost certainly does so.

[418] Naukratios succeeded Theodore as superior of Stoudios, while Athanasios was superior of Sakkoudion at this time. See C. van den Vorst, "La translation de S. Théodore Studite et de S. Joseph de Thessalonique," *AnalBoll* 32 (1913), esp. 27–28. They led the bitter opposition to the patriarch Methodios. See also I. Doens, Ch. Hannick, "Das Periorismos-Dekret des Patriarchen Methodios I. gegen die Studiten Naukratios und Athanasios," *JÖB* 22 (1973), 93–102, and Darrouzès, "Le patriarche Méthode," 15–57. The two abbots are mentioned again below in Chap. 69.

[419] The Greek here is ἁγιοκατηγορία, a rare term found in a variant form, ἁγιοκατήγοροι, in the acts of the Second Council of Nicaea against iconoclasts; see Dagron, "L'ombre," 66. Trapp (*Lexikon,* s.v. ἁγιοκατηγορία) cites only this passage.

[420] Reading αὐτοὺς for αὐτούς. Cf. von Dobschütz' translation, "Methodios und die Studiten," 96: "sich allein zu empfehlen," and below, Chap. 69 (431A): οἱ δοκοῦντες συνιστᾶν τοὺς ῥηθέντας Στουδίτας. An alternative translation, retaining αὐτοὺς (as subject of the infinitive), might be "and to proclaim that only *they* have understanding and that their barkings are inspired by God."

[421] Cf. Gregory of Nazianzos, *In sanctum pascha* (*or.* 45), PG 36:657.44; idem, *In theophania* (*or.* 38), PG 36:328.6–7.

of life. For the mother superior, as mentioned <above>, who had been deceived <by the Stoudites>, sent the man to one of her *proasteia*,[422] where he suddenly fell ill. One of the most devout monks[423] was sent, by God so to speak, to visit him; he tonsured him and dedicated him to God. And two days afterwards he departed to the Lord. *Let them be clothed with shame, therefore, and cover themselves with shame as with a mantle*[424] who set aside the prophetic pronouncements of the saints and say "Bravo!" to their own barkings.

58. The aforementioned mother superior once came with her daughter to the blessed man to obtain his blessing. The sanctified Eustratios also accompanied them. After our most blessed father gave them his blessing, he ordered one of his subordinates to bring him one of the staffs[425] <he used> for support. When the father received it, with the perception of prophetic grace he gave the pastoral staff to the mother superior's daughter. Vexed at this, the mother said: "You have not done rightly, father. For your holiness should have given it to me because of my advanced age and the honor <due me> as a mother." Our father answered her in a gentle voice: "You have spoken rightly, mother. But it has been given to the one for whom it was predestined." Then he dismissed them with a blessing. As they were going down to the *proasteion* called Mandrai,[426] the aforementioned mother superior was still aggrieved and

---

[422] *Proasteia* in this period were allotments of land located away from inhabited centers; see *ODB* 3:1724. A. Alexakis notes (in a private communication) that in the *v. Eustrat.* 377.24 and 380.26 the term προάστειον is used of a monastic dependency (μετόχιον) and that may be the sense of the word here.

[423] As the same superlative adjective, "most devout" (εὐλαβέστατος), is used of Dositheos and Eustratios three times earlier in this chapter, it may be that one of them is designated here.

[424] Ps. 108 (109):29.

[425] Reading ὑπερειστικῶν for ὑπηριστικῶν. Cf. *v. Ant. Jun.* 199.18–19: φέρων τε ἐπὶ κεφαλῆς τιάραν ἔνδοξον καὶ ῥάβδον ἐπὶ χεῖρα τὴν ὑπερειστικὴν . . . ; and Gregory of Nazianzos, *or.* 45, chap. 19 (PG 36:649B–C): περὶ δὲ τῆς βακτηρίας οὕτως ἔχω, καὶ τοῦ περὶ ταύτην αἰνίγματος. τὴν μὲν ὑπερειστικὴν οἶδα, τὴν δὲ ποιμαντικήν τε καὶ διδασκαλικήν, καὶ τὰ λογικὰ πρόβατα ἐπιστρέφουσαν.

[426] The term *mandra* (μάνδρα) is literally a "sheepfold," then a "monastery." Van den Gheyn (*AASS*, Nov. 2.1:424 note o) takes it as referring to a suburb of Constantinople, specifically one containing monasteries. This would require taking προάστειον in the classical sense ("suburb") rather than in the Byzantine usage (see n. 422 above). Janin (*CP byz.*, 515), citing this passage, characterizes it as of unknown location. If the word can refer to a *metochion* (see above, n. 252), perhaps that is the usage here.

said to lord Eustratios: "I adjure you by the great God to tell me why the saint dishonored me, and took <what should have been> my honor and gave it to my daughter." He replied with frankness: "My <good> woman, our divine father did not, as you think, <do this to> insult and dishonor you, but because he foresaw that you will <soon> depart to God and that your daughter will succeed to your pastoral office; for this reason he gave preference to her." Upon hearing these <words>, the woman glorified God. And in accord with the saint's foreknowledge, as soon as the mother went into the city she departed from this <life>, while her office was given to her daughter who even now leads a good life and carries out her <duties> of leadership.

59. The most saintly superior of the Agauroi[427] <monastery>, who was mentioned earlier,[428] was <once> going to the city <of Constantinople> on some business. But as he was about to leave from there [i.e., Agauroi], he sent word to the saint to come down for the sake of the Lord and pray for him. And so they both met in one of the dependencies of the Agauroi <monastery>, in which the all-sacred [p. 423] church of the great martyr Saint George[429] is honored. After a prayer, they sat and discussed the journey.[430] Our father Ioannikios enigmatically said to that God-honored man: "Be[431] aware, father, that the land is already pale <with ripe grain> and the reapers are already present, and the emperor is about to summon one of us to Himself." The blessed man [Ioannikios] was speaking about his [i.e., the superior of Agauroi] death—for he had foreknowledge that after he went into the city and completed his business, the <superior> would die there; but the most gentle superior, as he was a simple man, did not comprehend the statement. And so after a prayer and embrace, they parted from one another. The superior went into the city and after completing his business fell ill; on the eleventh day he departed to the Lord. His nephew[432] succeeded him as superior and, after he

---

[427] The same story is also briefly told by Sabas (chap. 32), who indicates that this was Gregory, who was superior of Agauroi when Ioannikios first arrived there. Peter nowhere mentions him by name.

[428] See above, nn. 103 and 104.

[429] The dependency is not otherwise known; see Janin, *Eglises Centres,* 141.

[430] The sentence lacks a main verb.

[431] Reading ἔσο for ἔστω.

[432] For another example of a nephew succeeding to the superiorship of a monastery, see V. Laurent, *La vita retractata et les miracles posthumes de saint Pierre d'Atroa* (Brus-

died in turn, the most blessed Eustratios succeeded to the leadership in accord with our angelic father's true prophecy. Even to this day, like a shining sun, he illuminates all those being guided by him.

60. <Thus> the servant of Christ [Ioannikios] distinguished himself with these extraordinary and wondrous gifts. By the providence of God he moved from the regions of Trichalix, already mentioned above,[433] and traveled with the beloved Eustratios to the mountains called Crow's Head.[434] When he was near the village of Merillon,[435] our heavenly minded father said to the all-wondrous Eustratios: "Do not be afraid, lord Eustratios, if you see dogs." He replied: "No, father." "Let us stop, then," said the saint, "upon this rock that juts into <the road> and rest a little, and then resume the rest of the journey." When they both stopped, the most excellent Eustratios raised his eyes and saw a large herd of sheep grazing and fearful-looking guard dogs running about the sheep. When the dogs noticed their presence, they <began> barking frightfully and loudly and, urging one another on and opening their mouths like lions, attacked the saint in a frenzied manner. But as soon as they drew near and caught the scent[436] of their holy and fragrant and most sweet skin, they turned quite gentle and fell at the saint's feet in charming fashion. The saint <then> said to the most devout Eustratios: "Call the shepherds." "How can I call them, father," he replied, "when I have no idea at all of their names?" The saint said: "Call out, 'Theophylaktos!'" When he called out this name, there was for the moment no word of response, no <sign> that anyone heard. Again the saint <said>: "Now call out, 'Christopher!'" When he shouted out this name, some men who were standing some distance away responded and at once the two shepherds Theophylaktos and Christopher came to the saint. The saint bade them to be their guides on the road leading to Trapeza.[437] But

---

sels, 1958), chap. 103.39 and his note, 157 n. 1. Cf. also above, Chap. 58, where a daughter replaces her mother as head of a nunnery.

[433] See n. 122.

[434] Sabas (chap. 9) comments τὸ ὑπεράνωθεν τῆς μονῆς (i.e., Antidion) ὄρος, Κόρακος προσαγορευόμενον Κεφαλήν, hence a part of Mt. Olympos. Sabas also refers to it in chap. 34.

[435] The text of Sabas (chap. 34) has Μεριλουκώμεως for Peter's Μερίλλου κώμης.

[436] On the "odor of sanctity," see R. Browning, "'Low-Level' Saint's Life," 126 and, for bibliography on the phenomenon, v. Phantin. Jun. 47 n. 44.

[437] The name is also found in Sabas (chap. 34); Menthon (L'Olympe de Bithynie, 49) lists Trapeza among the villages in the plain of Atroa. The name also appears in an

<the shepherds> replied: "As there are <just> two of us, we cannot do this. For one of us is assigned to watch and guard the flock and cannot leave it, while the other has to leave and search for <the sheep> we have lost." "Talk about it no longer," said the saint, "but show us the road and you will find the little lamb safe with its mother. For it has not been seized by wild beasts, as you think, nor stolen by anyone, but is standing unharmed in a thicket." When they heard this they fell to the ground in great astonishment. The saint blessed them and had them rise. He took one of them with him and indicated that he should guide them for a certain distance, <then> dismissed him. [p. 424]

61. After they had proceeded a short distance, the prophet of God again <said> to lord Eustratios: "Beyond the hill some men are traveling toward us, and we toward them. We are about to meet one another, and I strongly wish, lord Eustratios, not to be seen by them at all." He said: "If you do not wish to be seen by them at all, father, you will not be seen. For it is possible for you, *through the grace dwelling within you*,[438] to do this or not."[439] But <Ioannikios> bade him to walk quickly, and he followed behind me.[440] When the <two parties> came to the ridge, that is the hill separating them, they easily saw one another. Both groups converged, and as was customary said: "Bless <us>, saints." The <other> men asked lord Eustratios, "From what monastery are you?" When he replied, "Agauroi," these men said, "How can you travel in the<se> pathless mountains without a companion?" He said, "He who has God and all the angelic powers to assist him is not alone, as you say." The saint, who was standing behind the revered Eustratios, was seen by no one. After some further conversation they parted from one another. The humble-minded saint said to the all-admirable Eustratios: "Truly, most beloved Eustratios, I was not seen by them at all, since I was concealed by your prayers as if by a curtain." [p. 425]

62. And so when they completed the entire journey, they arrived at the

---

11th-century letter of Michael Psellos as a monastery, perhaps in Opsikion or Bithynia (see E. Kurtz, F. Drexl, *Michaelis Pselli scripta minora* 2 [Milan, 1941], *ep.* 39, p. 63.3; Janin, *Eglises Centres,* 184–85); whether a connection with this later monastery is possible remains uncertain.

[438] Gregory of Nyssa, *In Basilium fratrem,* 10 (PG 46:796D).

[439] On Ioannikios' gift of invisibility, see above, n. 354.

[440] If the text is correct, the "me" should refer to Eustratios, not to the writer Peter. This may reflect Peter's use of a written account by Eustratios. For a similar slip between narrator and source, see *v. Eliae Spel.* 873A.

monastery named Antidion[441] and in the harshest thickets of the mountains constructed a cell, a kind of delightful palace, as it were. The saint said farewell to the revered Eustratios and went to live <there>. Was he <then>, as he planned, hidden from men or forgotten by those who indeed desired and sought him out? By no means, but even there he became more visible through the grace dwelling within him and God worked very many miracles through him. And lest time overtake me as I narrate these <miracles>, or I impose a burden on you my listeners, if I should <write> an excessive amount, I will call to mind <only> a few miracles and leave the rest to more industrious <souls>. For since you have heard most of them from many <others> here and there, not doubting them—heaven forbid!—but even with great faith, I have decided to record only those narrated to me by the sanctified Eustratios,[442] who was with him and saw them with his own eyes. Well then, surely I must also tell, to the best of my ability,[443] the remaining miracles of the angelic and God-imitating father, to which I am obligated, as has been mentioned.[444] Let me begin here.

A certain man living in a village called Elos, who was a nephew of the *notarios*[445] Eugantres, left his home and went to another place on some business. Suddenly the Hagarenes[446] attacked the place; they took him prisoner and he was led away to Syria bound in iron chains and put in prison. At that <same> time Leo,[447] the imperial *patrikios*[448] and *sakellarios,*[449] and Aga-

---

[441] See above, n. 106.

[442] For the roles of Peter and Eustratios in the composition of the *vita,* see Introduction, 245–47.

[443] For this translation see above, n. 206.

[444] Peter uses the same terminology (ὑπόχρεων) of his obligation in Chap. 3; see n. 77 above.

[445] An official who served in various government departments as a scribe or secretary; see *ODB* 3:1495.

[446] Descendants of Agar or Hagar (Gen. 16:1), another name for Arabs; see *ODB* 1:149.

[447] A Leo, *patrikios* and *sakellarios,* is mentioned in the letters of Theodore the Stoudite. Identification of that Leo with the one mentioned here is not certain; see Efthymiadis, "Correspondence of Theodore," no. 11 ("Leo patrician and sacellarios"), 157–58.

[448] A high-ranking dignity; see *ODB* 3:1600 and n. 278 in the Life of David, Symeon, and George, above.

[449] Here the title of the imperial official who by the 8th century apparently had fiscal responsibilities; see *ODB* 3:1828–29.

petos, the imperial *koubikoularios*[450] and *protovestiarios,*[451] happened to come to the saint for his blessing. When the captive's relatives learned of the <impending> arrival of these distinguished personages, they ran quickly and presented themselves first to the saint. Falling at his feet, they tearfully supplicated him to bid the men to make a petition to the most pious and Christ-loving and orthodox empress Theodora,[452] that one of the Hagarenes[453] be dispatched to be exchanged for the captive, so that he might be preserved from the hands of the infidels. Subsequently, when the distinguished men arrived, after a prayer they all sat down and began to converse. The petitioner stood opposite the saint and with importuning nods begged the blessed man to fulfill his petition. After much talk among them, mention was made of the capture of Amorion,[454] that took place because of our sins, and the innumerable number of captives. And so after the saint prayed for <the captives from Amorion>, the petitioner gazed at that honored mouth <to see> whether he would also speak on his behalf. When the saint saw this man in such anxiety, [p. 426] his <eyes> filled with tears and he raised his hands to heaven. While all were still there, he uttered the following sweet words: "I trust in God," he said, "that the man who is held by the foreigners will be quickly returned." After praying for and blessing the aforementioned distinguished men, he dismissed them. The petitioner was consumed by grief that his request was not accomplished, and indeed in his mind he berated the saint and called him a person given to favoritism. That theological mind [Ioannikios] was aware of this; he summoned the man to himself and said to him in a gentle voice: "O child, it is not good or just that we abandon God, the ruler of all, and have

---

[450] A general term to designate palace eunuchs who waited on the emperor and fulfilled a variety of functions; see *ODB* 2:1154.

[451] Initially a post for a palace eunuch, "in the 9th–11th C. *protovestiarioi* commanded armies, conducted peace negotiations, investigated conspiracies," etc. See *ODB* 3:1749.

[452] The wife of the emperor Theophilos and after his death empress (842–856); see General Introduction, xvi, and the final *vita* in this volume.

[453] Reading Ἀγαρηνῶν for Ἀγαυρινῶν. Cf. Sabas (chap. 50): δοῦναι αὐτοῖς Σαρακηνὸν ἀντ' αἰχμάλωτον (lege αἰχμαλώτου). If Ἀγαυρινῶν is retained, Peter, a monk and advocate of the Agauroi monastery, may be suggesting that one of his fellow monks be sent to negotiate an exchange.

[454] Amorion, capital of the Anatolikon, was captured and destroyed by the Arabs in 838. For the captives who were subsequently executed in 845, see *ODB* 2:800–801.

hope in <secular> rulers,[455] in whom there is no salvation. For it is better to place trust in the Lord than in <secular> rulers. But, O child, have unhesitating *belief and you will see the glory of God*."[456] And after he encouraged him with many other words of advice, he dismissed him.

On that <very> night one of the captives, in the guise of the saint, stood before his fellow captive and condemned man; he urged him to arise and follow him. He <in turn> roused the man next to him and said: "Come, brother, arise; let us follow the saint and be delivered from the misfortune that besets us." And he asked in wonder, "Who is this saint? How is it possible for us all to be released from our bonds and pass through the securely locked gates, or to escape the notice of the multitude of watchful guards, and to flee through their midst? For this is totally beyond hope." He [the captive from Elos] replied: "Come, come, brother,[457] let us have absolute trust in and follow our blessed father Ioannikios who urges us on. And *the God of miracles*,[458] Who through an angel spontaneously opened the locks of the doors for the chief of His apostles Peter[459] and brought him unharmed through the midst of the guards, will show mercy to us too through His servant." As soon as they arose in faith, the bonds fell from their feet. And with the guidance of the saint, they passed through the midst of their fellow condemned <prisoners>. When they reached the gates of the prison, miraculously they found them open. And since the guards were fast asleep, they ran through <the gates in a manner> beyond human belief. They <then> followed the saint who led and transported them safely away from all the sentry posts and watchtowers that the most wicked Hagarenes are accustomed to place on all the essential roads.[460]

---

[455] Cf. Ps. 117 (118):9.

[456] Cf. Jn. 11:40.

[457] Reading ἀδελφέ for ἀδελφοί. Two prisoners apparently follow Ioannikios through their fellow prisoners and out of the prison, although the narrative is somewhat unclear on this point. The version of Sabas (chap. 50) also suggests that only two escaped and adds the name of the captive, Evandrios.

[458] See above, n. 210.

[459] Acts 12:10.

[460] For an earlier example of guarded roads to prevent escape of Christians, see the *vita* of Euthymios the Great (ed. E. Schwartz, *Kyrillos von Skythopolis* [Leipzig, 1939], 18:22–25): βουλόμενοι οἱ μάγοι πάντας θηρεῦσαι τοὺς Χριστιανοὺς τοὺς φυλάρχους τῶν ὑπ᾽ αὐτοὺς Σαρακηνῶν ἐπέστησαν πανταχοῦ ταῖς ὁδοῖς πρὸς τὸ μηδένα τῶν ἐν Περσίδι Χριστιανῶν Ῥωμαίοις προσφεύγειν.

<This was> to prevent escape, if any of their captives should somehow happen to flee, for even if <a captive> should find a way to escape the place in which he was held, he would be unable to get out in any direction and would be caught there. And so after they miraculously passed these <guard posts>, as has been said, since a clear day was now dawning, they lay down <to sleep>[461] in a thicket.

On the same day Saracen shepherds happened to be passing through the same thicket, shepherding their flock. When the dogs noticed the footprints of the captives, they tracked them and found their hiding place. And so they [the captives] stood opposite in silence and dared not approach them [i.e., the Saracen shepherds],[462] but were smeared abundantly[463] with the dogs' foaming saliva. As the <fugitives> trembled in fear and already had death before their eyes (for they thought that they would surely be betrayed by the dogs' attack), the saint suddenly appeared to them and drove the dogs away. He encouraged them and told them to have no fear at all and guided them as far as the very mountain passes without leaving them. And when they had passed over and left them behind, he pointed out their route and vanished from their <sight>. They tearfully glorified God and after some days completed their entire journey.

When they reached the saint [p. 427] and appeared before him, they related the powers and miracles of God, that God worked through him [i.e., Ioannikios]. Let no one doubt the wondrous miracle, but let all believe purely and without hesitation. *For things which are impossible with men are possible with God.*[464] Moreover the <captive> who received the assistance of God through the pure entreaties of our blessed father is still alive and, if some people should have some doubt about this miracle (may God not allow it!), let them make a journey to the man who was saved and, when they have heard from him the great works of God, let the darkness of their doubt be dissolved and let them together with us glorify God, Who is wondrous in His saints.[465]

---

[461] For this meaning of καταπίπτω, see n. 250 above.

[462] The sentence is unclear as the subjects of the verbs are not expressed directly in the Greek text.

[463] Reading καταχρηστικῶς with the manuscript rather than καταχριστικῶς, as emended by van der Gheyn; cf. n. 111 above.

[464] Lk. 18:27.

[465] Cf. Ps. 67 (68):35.

63. The wife of Stephen,[466] the former *magistros,*[467] was envied by her maidservants due to diabolic jealousy. And she took poison from them and drank it, without knowing <what it was>, and with God's permission became deranged in her senses. After spending a great deal of money on doctors and *receiving no benefit,*[468] she finally went to the saint and, throwing herself at his feet, begged to obtain mercy. Since the saint knew that she was a victim of magical practice, he said: "Woman, if you wish to obtain a cure, agree to do no harm to any of those who wished to kill you and the Lord will quickly cure you." When she agreed to this under oath, the saint blessed her and sealed her three times with the sign of the life-giving cross. He restored her to a sound mind and dismissed her in good health glorifying God.

64. The most devout monk Stephen, who was once *protonotarios*[469] of the general Olbianos,[470] used to visit the saint frequently and was ruled by his illuminating[471] injunctions. One day when he came to the saint, the saint said to him enigmatically, as was his custom: "The emperor is going to summon one of the two of us to himself. And so let us take thought, brother Stephen, and prepare ourselves that we become pleasing to Him and not on the contrary, like useless and careless servants, provoke His indignation against us and be cast out from His glory." He said many other things as well and em-

---

[466] This Stephen *magistros,* called by Sabas (chap. 35) "*patrikios* and *magistros,*" may be the same Stephen *magistros* to whom Theodore of Stoudios wrote a letter of consolation (*ep.* 420) on the death of his wife, but there are chronological problems with this identification. See Fatouros, *Theod. Stud. Epist.* 1:400 n. 781 and Efthymiadis, "Correspondence of Theodore," no. 13 ("Stephanos *magistros*"), 160–62.

[467] A high-ranking dignity; see *ODB* 2:1267.

[468] Cf. Mk. 5:26–27.

[469] The *protonotarioi* of the themes were responsible for civil administration, under the general (as the terminology here suggests), but also sometimes reporting directly to Constantinople; see Oikonomidès, *Listes,* 315. For the seal of "Anastasios, imperial *kandidatos* and *protonotarios* of the general of the Thrakesioi," see J. Nesbitt, N. Oikonomides, *Catalog of Lead Seals in Dumbarton Oaks and the Fogg Museum* 3 (Washington, D.C., 1996), p. 15, no. 2.35. Sabas (chap. 35) says that he was a *notarios,* not a *protonotarios.*

[470] General of the Armeniakon under Leo V and Michael II; see Treadgold, *Byz. Revival,* 228–30.

[471] Reading φωτοποιαῖς for φυτοποιαῖς, as suggested by L. Rydén. φωτοποιός is also found in the *v. Ioannic. a Petr.* at 430C, while the Greek word φυτοποιός is unattested in the *TLG.*

braced and dismissed him. <Stephen> went out and left and then, after living for <only> eight <more> days, departed to the Lord. Even to this day many cures take place at his tomb through the grace of God.

65. The most devout monk Thomas went up to the saint to receive his blessings, accompanied by Euthymios,[472] son of the *magistros*[473] and former *spatharios*,[474] who now nobly distinguishes himself in the monastic ranks. After they saw him and received his blessing, our divine father said to the most devout Thomas as they were about to depart: "Take care for your soul and make ready your affairs for your departure, because you will soon leave this <life>." And indeed after he <said> a prayer and they were dismissed, the most devout Thomas took most diligent care in accord with the saint's prophecy. And after he nobly distributed all his possessions to the poor, he lived another fifteen days and died in peace.

66. A monk Antony,[475] who was neglectful of his soul and often fell into heresy, was appointed to the superiorship of the <monastery of> Agauroi by the heretical exarchs[476] who were sent out at that time. This man, after being chastised once and a second time by the saint, but then returning again to his former state, like *a dog to its own vomit*,[477] importuned the saint to give him a penance that would cure <him>. Our truly most compassionate [p. 428] fa-

---

[472] Sabas (chap. 35) indicates that Euthymios was a "monastic superior" (ἡγούμενος).

[473] Euthymios' father is not named by either Peter or Sabas. Sabas (chap. 35) says the father was a "*patrikios* and *magistros*."

[474] A dignity originally associated with bodyguards, but by the 8th century it had probably become a title; see *ODB* 3:1935–36 and Life of Nikephoros, above, n. 339.

[475] The promotion of this Antony to the superiorship of the monastery of Agauroi is also reported by Sabas (chap. 36). Sabas adds that Eustratios, like many bishops and superiors, had left his post (i.e., as superior of Agauroi) to lead a wandering existence under threat of the persecution. He also notes that this Antony was chastised by Ioannikios for falling into iconoclasm. Van den Gheyn suggests (*AASS*, Nov. 2.1:369 note f) that Antony may be the Antony mentioned by Theodore the Stoudite (see Fatouros, *Theod. Stud. Epist., ep.* 490.30); on the iconoclastic leanings of superiors of Agauroi, see K. Ringrose, "Monks and Society in Iconoclastic Byzantium," *BSlEB* 6 (1979), 130–51, esp. 147.

[476] The term is presumably here used in the ecclesiastical sense, and may refer to a metropolitan bishop or to a patriarchal functionary; see *ODB* 2:767. The same term is also used by Sabas (chap. 36).

[477] Prov. 26:11; cf. 2 Pet. 2:22.

ther Ioannikios said to him: "Antony, not once but twice have I given you a helping hand to the best of my ability.[478] But you have again fallen into the same wickedness and brought your own destruction upon yourself. But still, with confidence in the mercies of God, I will offer you this cure. I do not urge you to abstain from wine and oil or anything else, but to bear patiently for forty days the punishment that is going to befall you, and to supplicate and glorify God. And I trust in His ineffable love of humanity that He will give you His compassion, forgiving you all <your> transgressions." <Antony> made obeisance and said: "As you bid, father, only assist me." No sooner had he spoken than his limbs on one side were paralyzed from top to bottom. And he was lifted up, almost dead, by bystanders and lay <on his bed> in the monastery, nobly enduring the punishment and giving thanks to the Lord. After the forty days were fulfilled, he virtuously fell asleep [i.e., died] in God.

67. The *spatharios*[479] Drosos, who was once *anagrapheus*[480] of the Opsikion,[481] while still involved in fiscal administration, went up to the blessed man wishing to obtain a blessing. Our father received him and said: "Prepare yourself, *spatharios*, and put your records in precise order, because the emperor is about to require an accounting from you." He did not understand that this was said in a spiritual sense, but assumed a material one and said: "I am ready, father, even if this <very> hour he should wish to examine me." Then the father replied: "We have told you what seems likely and are not responsible <for what happens>; for our warning was not in reference to physical records or a physical emperor, as you think, <my> child, but about the Emperor of emperors[482] Who is going to examine everyone's hidden acts and thoughts. And He will either judge favorably if you have acted rightly and beneficently

---

[478] Cf. n. 206 in Chap. 23.

[479] See above, n. 474.

[480] Reading ἀναγραφεύς, the reading found in Sabas (chap. 42) who calls him τοῦ Ὀψικίου πρωτονοτάριος ἀναγραφεὺς καὶ σπαθάριος Δρόσος, for the ἀντιγραφεύς given in the printed text of Peter's version. The latter function belonged to the central administration and is not elsewhere associated with a theme, as here. Also the term translated "fiscal administration" is ἀναγραφῇ in the printed text of Peter. See Zacos, *Seals,* 1.2, no. 2095 for a "Leo, imperial *balnitor* and *anagrapheus* of the Opsikion." For the *anagrapheus,* who was a fiscal official, see *ODB* 1:84.

[481] One of the four original themes of Asia Minor; see *ODB* 3:1528–29.

[482] Cf. 1 Tim. 6:15 and Rev. 19:16:2. The King James Version has "King of Kings."

and justly, or condemn for failure to do so." With these <words Ioannikios> prayed for and dismissed the man. After <Drosos> went down <the mountain> and came to Metata,[483] he fell ill and expired, leaving us uncertain with regard to his repentance.

68. Your humble <servant Peter>, the one who has compiled[484] this treatise in unlearned fashion and with such ability as I have, was once sitting in my humble cell, when the thought occurred to me to go to the saint and obtain his blessings. So I took with me brother Plato, who was sharing my life of solitary contemplation, and we went to the blessed man. After we were deemed worthy to behold that angelic sight and enjoy his very many beneficial words of advice, the brother who accompanied me said to the saint: "I beseech you, father, that for the sake of the Lord, you give us permission to come to your reverence once a year and to delight in your holy prayers and to return <home> joyfully." I stood <there> trembling severely, so that I did not dare to raise my eyes at all to look upon that divine sight nor to utter any sound at all. But fearful on account of the multitude of my sins I accused my conscience and wept in my mind, saying, "Even though I am unclean and *have unclean lips* and deeds, *I dwell in the midst of the people*[485] and land of the Lord and I am deemed worthy to see and embrace His servant." And with lamentation I condemned myself in many other ways. As I was tormented in these silent lamentations, the blessed man opened his honored mouth and said to the brother with me: "I want you to know, O magnanimous Plato, that you will not see me again in this life." I was completely astonished at this statement and even more greatly consumed with fear, [p. 429] so that I dared say nothing

---

[483] The Greek here is τὰ μητάτα, and the corresponding passage in Sabas (chap. 42) has τὰ μητάτα Λυδίας. Sabas (chap. 13) also mentions τὰ Μητάτα καλούμενα. Mango ("Ioannikios," 402 and n. 25) notes "Metata or Lakkou Metata is associated with Achyraous (Hadrianoutherae) and a locality called Pteleai." It appears in the *Life of Theodore of Stoudios* (ed. B. Latyschev, "Vita s. Theodori Studitae in codice Mosquensi musei Rumianzoviani no. 520," *Vizantijskij vremennik* 21 [1914], 292:28–29) as ἐν τοῖς λεγομένοις τοῦ Λάκκου Μιτάτοις. Another possibility in this passage might be to see the reference not as a place name, but as a noun used here in the sense of "lodgings," on which see *ODB* 2:1385.

[484] For the role of Peter in the composition of the *vita,* see Introduction, 245–47.

[485] Cf. Is. 6:5. The text of Isaiah continues "in the midst of a people having unclean lips"; Peter alters it to a positive statement.

at all. The blessed man gave us blessed bread from the twice-baked loaves[486] customarily given to him and in addition a wooden cross made by his own hands and most beautifully carved. After a prayer he dismissed us. And so as that year passed and the next one was beginning, we decided to go down to visit the most holy Peter,[487] who is now metropolitan of Sylaion. He welcomed us and urged us to take a meal with him. As we ate, the aforementioned Peter said to us: "If it pleases the Lord, I plan to journey to our father, lord Ioannikios, and to communicate to him all my thoughts and be blessed by him." When we replied, "And we will travel with you," the man was overjoyed. And so after we rose from the table, we busily concerned ourselves to find horses because of the length of the route and the fact that we were not accustomed to make <such a long> journey on foot. The metropolitan, encouraged in his heart by God, so to speak, said to me: "Why are you so disturbed and troubled? Take one of my horses. Stop your worrying, and come with me. Seek above all the good blessing of our most lofty father and pray to obtain it absolutely, for it will not be taken from you in eternity." Then I thanked the metropolitan, but was perplexed because, despite the fact that the metropolitan had other horses and we begged him to give one also to brother Plato, he refused to relent though we praised him [Plato] and adorned <the metropolitan> with words of thanks. So I turned to the brother and urged him to search <for a horse> among nearby friends and monasteries. Although he did so, he did not obtain what he desired, and the brother was left completely at a loss and filled with deepest grief. And so when I turned and saw this man deeply grieved, I empathized with him and suffered terribly. For the brother was much beloved by me in the spirit of the Lord and we were seen by all as a *single pair*

---

[486] The Greek term here is παξαμάτια, which refers to loaves of bread baked twice and dried in the sun. It was used particularly by soldiers on campaign; see *ODB* 1:321, s.v. "Bread." Sabas (chap. 43) calls it "dry bread" (ἄρτου ξηροῦ).

[487] The version of Sabas (chap. 43) indicates that this Peter was formerly superior of the Herakleion monastery in Bithynia and appointed bishop of Syl(l)aion following the restoration of orthodoxy. For Sylaion in Pamphylia, see *ODB* 3:1980, s.v. "Syllaion," and V. Ruggieri, F. Nethercott, "The Metropolitan City of Syllion and Its Churches," *JÖB* 36 (1986), 133–56, esp. 147 where this passage is briefly discussed in the context of appointment of monastic superiors as bishops following the restoration of orthodoxy. For a similar point, see also von Dobschütz, "Methodios und die Studiten," esp. 98–99 and 99 n. 1.

and there was no better way to see *one soul in two bodies*[488] than is Peter in Plato and Plato in Peter. Nevertheless I made an end to our conversation[489] and after reminding him of that prophetic statement,[490] I then bestowed on him joy and the victory of patience. Bidding farewell to him, I traveled with the metropolitan and John,[491] who is now bishop of Prusa.

After we went up to the saint and enjoyed the illuminating sight of him, we were also privileged to share a meal <with him>, and filled with his word<s> and divine law and discussions of grace, rather than with food, we got up from the luxurious banquet. Thus each <of us> separately and privately, in order of his rank, went in and revealed, or on the other hand shamefully <confessed>, his thoughts and deeds, and was somewhat enigmatically criticized by that most luminous man, and then took our departure, after receiving the customary blessed bread. When it was the turn of my rank, I was afraid to enter and terrified and, debating with myself, said: "O humble Peter, how will you, who are darkness, approach the sun? How will you touch or even grasp those holy feet as you have defiled lips and are thoroughly besmirched with most shameful passions? How will you look upon those holy eyes, you who have directed <the gaze> of your eyes to every evil and indeed have looked not rightly to roads that are not straight, but have directed them to *distorted byways.*[492] What defense at all will you offer, since you are totally unable to make any defense due to the victory of passions?" Then some power gave me strength. I went in to the saint and, throwing myself on the ground and grasping his holy feet, I washed them abundantly[493] with tears. He touched

---

[488] See Gregory of Nazianzos, *De Vita Sua* (ed. C. Jungck, *Gregor von Nazianz. De Vita Sua* [Heidelberg, 1974]), lines 228–30, describing his relation with Basil the Great: ξυνωρὶς ἦμεν οὐκ ἄσημος Ἑλλάδι. τὰ πάντα μὲν δὴ κοινά, καὶ ψυχὴ μία δυοῖν δέουσα σωμάτων διάστασιν.

[489] L. Rydén has proposed emending προσηγορικοῖς λόγοις to παρηγορικοῖς λόγοις, and translating "my consoling words."

[490] I.e., Ioannikios' statement that Plato would not again see him in this life.

[491] This John, bishop of Prusa, is not known from other sources. Van den Gheyn (*AASS,* Nov. 2.1:430 note r) comments that he does not appear in the list of bishops of Prusa given by M. Le Quien, *Oriens Christianus* 1 (Paris, 1740), 617.

[492] Cf. Prov. 11:20, etc. Peter uses ἄνοδοι for ὁδοί in Proverbs.

[493] Reading καταχρηστικῶς with the manuscript instead of καταχριστικῶς, as emended by van den Gheyn; cf. n. 111 above.

my head and made the sign of the cross; <then> he had me rise and [p. 430] most peacefully gave me an embrace in the Lord. And taking twelve pieces of the blessed bread, he gave them to me and said: "Take these and give them to brother Plato with these words: 'Do not grieve, for God has accepted your resolve.'" Then taking twelve other pieces of blessed bread, he gave them to me and said: "Take these for the preservation of your soul." As I thought to myself: "May God advise him to give some also for my mother," he looked again and stretching[494] his hand to the place where the blessed bread <was kept>, he drew it back full. And so he urged me to spread out[495] both my hands and gave me thirty-six <pieces of bread>, saying, "Take these and give six each to your mother and to your five sisters." When I was left quite at a loss at this wondrous statement, again touching my head he blessed me, and making the sign of the cross dismissed me. And so we all returned in peace, glorifying God.

69. And so it is just that everyone marvel at the illuminating and lofty marvels that were performed and accomplished by the saint, but especially the divine and prophetic utterances of his deepest and honored old age by which he heralded what would come about and happen [p. 431] for Methodios,[496] the most blessed and loftiest among patriarchs and martyrs. For while the heresy still rose in swells, the oft-mentioned most devout Eustratios happened to go up <to visit> the blessed man. He heard in turn from his holy mouth of the coming resurrection of orthodoxy and the total destruction of the heresy. <Eustratios> was filled with joy at such a proclamation and, as was his custom, said boldly to the saint: "Would that it were possible, honored father, through the grace of the all-holy Spirit that has been given to you, <for you> to tell[497] us the man who will, with orthodoxy and nobility, control and steer the rudder of the church [i.e., the future patriarch]. For opinion among men is much divided and one person is eager to proclaim and promote one man, another another. For some strive to glorify Athanasios and Naukrat-

---

[494] Reading τετανυκὼς for τετανικῶς.

[495] Reading ἁπλοῦν for ἁπλεῖν.

[496] Patriarch of Constantinople (4 March 843–14 June 847) following the death of Theophilos; see ODB 2:1355 and nn. 285 and 289 in the Life of David, Symeon, and George.

[497] Reading λέξαι for ἕλξαι in the printed edition (ἔλξας in the manuscript), as suggested by A. Alexakis and L. Rydén.

ios[498] and John, called Katasambas,[499] while some <support> Methodios who is preeminent in words and most wise, some <yet> others." And our father said: "O Eustratios, they labor in vain who think fit to recommend the aforementioned Stoudites and their colleague John. But if indeed they should vote for Methodios, who is *poor in spirit*[500] and most *meek*,[501] in the words of the divine David, they will cry out this <name> with the inspiration of the Holy Spirit." When the most devout Eustratios heard these <words>, he gave glory to God. And after he asked for and received a prayer, he departed. By the grace of God the heresy abated and by the decree of God and angels and men the most holy Methodios was elevated to the patriarchal throne, in accordance with our father's divine proclamation. He restored fitting splendor[502] to the churches of God, the ancient beauty of the incarnate life and deeds[503] of Christ. And there was deep peace in all the world through the grace of Christ and the concern of the great patriarch Methodios and the honored prayers of

---

[498] The Greek here, τοὺς ἀμφὶ Ἀθανάσιον καὶ Ναυκράτιον, literally means "those about Athanasios and Naukratios." In the translation I follow Liddell-Scott, *Lexicon* (ἀμφὶ C.3), which indicates that such phrasing can be a circumlocution for the individual(s) mentioned. See also W. R. Knorr, *Textual Studies in Ancient and Medieval Geometry* (Boston, Mass., 1989), 25 n. 3, and R. Kühner, B. Gerth, *Ausführliche Grammatik der griechischen Sprache*, 3d ed., Teil II, Bd. 1 (Hannover-Leipzig, 1898; repr. Hannover, 1966), 270. For a possible parallel construction, see n. 417 in Chap. 57 above. On the two Stoudite abbots, see above, n. 418.

[499] Reading, with the manuscript, Κατασάμβαν. His nickname Κακοσάμβας is used later in the text (432в). Van den Gheyn (433 note c) apparently identifies this John with John VII Grammatikos, the iconoclast patriarch appointed by Theophilos and deposed in 843. His note, however ("Patriarcha haereticus Constantinopolitanus, a Theophilo loco S. Nicephori suffectus"), is strange in that the patriarch Nikephoros was replaced with Theodotos in 815 by Leo V. von Dobschütz ("Methodios und die Studiten," 96 n. 2) shows that such identification is highly implausible. On the wordplay Κατασάμβας/ Κακοσάμβας and possible connection with the monastery of Kata Saba, see von Dobschütz, "Methodios und die Studiten," 96 n. 2, and Darrouzès, "Le patriarche Méthode," esp. 21 n. 16 and 42 n. 16. John Katasambas is also mentioned in the Life of David, Symeon, and George, above, 216.

[500] Mt. 5:3.

[501] Cf. Ps. 36 (37):11; Mt. 5:5.

[502] I.e., the use of images.

[503] Taking *oikonomia* here as referring to the fact of the Incarnation (Lampe, *Lexicon*, s.v. C.6).

our miracle-working father Ioannikios. But the evil demon who hates the good could not bear to behold the peaceful state restored to the churches of God. So he entered into some glory-seekers, men of aged appearance who were deluded in their minds, the aforementioned jealous Stoudites and their colleague Kakosambas, whom you all know to be *vessels fitted to destruction*.[504] When he found them, he turned their unjust and profane tongues to babbling nonsense and through them won over a very large faction and stirred up disorder in the church of God. You all know the shameless face of the men and their opposition to that great light and martyr Methodios. <What befell him> was no different from what happened to that great and wondrous Athanasios[505] at the hands of schismatics and Arians. While the church of God was in these lamentable conditions, in that it could not bear to see its teacher unjustly assailed by arrogant attacks and there was great turmoil, report of the grievous occurrences in the church reached even our most holy father Ioannikios. Inspired by the Holy Spirit he told his dear friend Eustratios to come to him and wrote a letter[506] of consolation to the shepherd and teacher of the church. He ordered that the consolatory letter be dispatched with great speed by one of the most esteemed subordinates of the beloved Eustratios. <In it> he urged <Methodios> not to be at all dispirited amid his afflictions, in the knowledge that he suffered the same <abuse> as Christ and His saints at the hands of similar apostates from the church. At the same time he urged him also to come to him, somewhat enigmatically hinting at his <own> demise. [p. 432]

70. The most divine Methodios was full of joy at this encouragement. Without delay he showed the letter to the emperors and after those profane calumniators were convicted, like the old men <who accused> Susanna,[507] he

---

[504] Cf. Rom. 9:22.

[505] St. Athanasios (295–373), archbishop of Alexandria, who was deposed and exiled five times due to Arian influence; see *ODB* 1:217–18.

[506] The text of a letter from Ioannikios to Methodios is given in the version of Sabas (chap. 47). It differs particularly from the summary given here by Peter in also advocating (373A) that Methodios not accept iconoclast bishops and priests in the priesthood. For a view of the differences between Peter's and Sabas' presentations of Ioannikios' role in supporting Methodios with respect to the Stoudites and iconoclasts, see Afinogenov, "Great Purge," 84–87.

[507] The story of Susanna, the woman wrongly accused of adultery by two elders who had unsuccessfully tried to seduce her, is told in the apocryphal book of the Septuagint that bears her name. The analogy of Methodios to Susanna indicates that the calumny

handed them over to just and canonical exile and anathematization.[508] This done, he then hurried quickly to the blessed man. After the great patriarch and the God-bearing Ioannikios embraced each other in the Lord, Ioannikios, the citizen of the desert,[509] said to the saintly[510] patriarch: "Master, I never

Peter is referring to here is the story that a woman was bribed to denounce Methodios for having violated her, a charge he was able to refute by demonstrating his impotence; for an English summary of the Byzantine sources (Genesios, Symeon the Logothete, Theophanes Continuatus, and Skylitzes) of the story, see C. Walters, "Saints of Second Iconoclasm in the Madrid Scylitzes," *REB* 39 (1981), 307–18, specifically 314. Peter's allusion to the story is perhaps the earliest extant reference to it.

The sources attribute the plot to the heretics generally and to the deposed patriarch John VII Grammatikos specifically. F. Dvornik (*Les Slaves, Byzance et Rome au IXe siècle* [Paris, 1926; repr. Hattiesburg, Miss., 1970], 129) suggests that, while Peter includes the Stoudites with the iconoclasts in this plot against the patriarch, their involvement is doubtful. Von Dobschütz ("Methodios und die Studiten," 46) suggests that the accusation would not have been taken so seriously without Stoudite participation, and Afinogenov ("Κωνσταντινούπολις ἐπίσκοπον ἔχει: Part II," 66) argues that the personalities of the accuser (the mother of Metrophanes, later metropolitan of Smyrna) and the investigator (the *protomagistros* Manuel) support von Dobschütz' view.

[508] The anathema was "the highest form of ecclesiastical censure directed at unrepentant heretics"; see *ODB* 1:89. Bury (*Eastern Roman Empire,* 151) paraphrases the sources on the outcome: "the heretics who had invented the lie received the mild punishment of being compelled every year, at the feast of orthodoxy, to join the procession from Blachernae to St. Sophia with torches in their hands, and hear with their own ears anathema pronounced upon them."

Peter's statement that they were exiled (ἐξορία) is not readily verified from the other sources, even allowing for his inclusion of the Stoudites in the plot, as the action taken by the patriarch against the Stoudites for their own opposition to him was confinement (περιορισμός) in their own monastery, on which see the article by Doens and Hannick referred to in n. 418, above. Perhaps Peter is referring to the deposed iconoclastic patriarch, John VII Grammatikos, who is said to have been relegated (ὑπερόριος) after his deposition to a monastery on the Bosporos at Kleidion and also confined (περιορισθείς) in his *proasteion* at Psicha, although his exile, in the monastery at least, seems to have preceded this plot against Methodios. For a useful summary of the conflicting sources on the fate of John VII Grammatikos following his deposition, see Lemerle, *Byz. Humanism,* 165–66 n. 151.

[509] This expression is reminiscent of the description of Antony the Great; cf. *v. Ant.,* chap. 14 (PG 26:865B) and *v. Davidis, Sym. et Georg.* 214.30–31. Ioannikios compares himself to Antony in the next paragraph.

[510] The Greek here, ἐν ἁγίοις, lit., "among the saints," is generally used of the deceased, for example by Sabas (chap. 47, 373A): Ταρασίου, τοῦ ἐν ἁγίοις. V. Laurent (in *v. Petr. Atr.* 14) and M. Cunningham (in *v. Mich. Sync.* 144 n. 64) note similar usages.

<previously> dared to invite you to come <visit> my unworthiness. It was your virtuous act, when you were called by the all-holy Spirit Which moved you to visit our unworthiness and to advise us with words of encouragement to virtue.[511] But now, compelled by great necessity and moved by God, I myself was driven to write to my holy master, <asking him> to make the weary journey to my rustic self, so that I may obtain your prayers and depart in peace. For <my impending death> has been clearly revealed to me. But since numerous *tares*,[512] <that is> those who calumniate your holy sanctity, have sprung up in the holy church of God and certain people did not shrink to offer my humble self as a co-defender[513] of their blasphemies, behold, I wish to declare freely God's revelation to me concerning your holiness."

And so he bade all the people who had come up with the venerable patriarch to gather; there were about seventy <of them>, bishops, clerics, and monks. The great man of God Ioannikios spoke to their assembly with his angelic mouth as follows: "Hear ye, all who stand here in this wilderness and herald it to those in the cities and villages. Of old the great Antony[514] bade his disciples to have no communion with Arians, nor with Meletian schismatics, nor with their anti-Christian faction. And now behold, I, unworthy <as I am> and lowly and uneducated, am likewise moved by God and say to you: separate yourselves, all of you, from impious heretics, and the most abominable Stoudites and their colleague Kakosambas and the lapsed bishop of Niko-

---

It is perhaps with similar import that Methodios is referred to as ἐν μάρτυσι at 431A. On the question of whether Methodios was still alive when Peter wrote, see Introduction, 247.

[511] The phrasing here seems to imply that Methodios had, on his own initiative, previously come to visit Ioannikios on Olympos. So Afinogenov, "Great Purge," 85–86, against Darrouzès ("Le patriarche Méthode," 17) who concludes that the *vitae* of Ioannikios give evidence of only this one meeting on Mt. Olympos.

[512] Mt. 13:25–30.

[513] Ioannikios apparently indicates here that opponents of Methodios had falsely claimed Ioannikios' support for their position.

[514] Antony the Great (ca. 251–356); see *ODB* 1:125–26. For Antony's speech against Arians and Meletians, see R. T. Meyer, *St. Athanasius: The Life of Saint Antony* (Westminster, Md., 1950), chap. 89: "Do not go near the Meletian schismatics . . . . Have nothing to do with the Arians . . . ," with Meyer's notes on the two heresies, 127 nn. 231 and 234. On Arianism and Meletianism see also *ODB* 1:167 and 2:1333.

medeia,[515] Monomachos[516] or rather opponent of God, and the most irrational eunuch of the church of Kyzikos.[517] For they spoke great nonsense against God and against our father the preeminent patriarch. They are not afraid nor do they shudder in fear of God. For you know that for this reason I brought you <here> so that I might pour forth my words to you. For behold, certain people will try to lead some astray with deceitful missives and words, as if through us,[518] as the great apostle says.[519] But I now say to you with my mouth: separate yourselves from those who dare such <outrages> against the church of God and are not afraid *to rend the tunic*[520] of the word of God, and have even torn it into many pieces. Those who did not shudder to do these things to the fathers and the holy patriarchs[521] who have gone before, have themselves become therefore by their own action a scandal to the church of God, and

[515] On the Bithynian city see *ODB* 3:1483–84 and Janin, *Eglises Centres,* 77–104. I do not find the individual referred to here otherwise attested.

[516] The Greek μονομάχος literally means "fighting in single combat." C. Mango, "Observations on the Correspondence of Ignatius, Metropolitan of Nicaea," *Texte und Untersuchungen zur Geschichte der altchristlichen Literatur* 125 (1981), 403–10, specifically 409 and n. 2, indicates that it is a family name here, giving rise to the subsequent pun with θεομάχος. He also suggests a possible identification with the Ignatius, metropolitan of Nikomedeia, who is known from other sources. See also A. Kazhdan, *ODB* 2:1398.

[517] For this city on the southern coast of the Sea of Marmara, see *ODB* 2:1164–65. On the "eunuch of Kyzikos," see Afinogenov ("Κωνσταντινούπολις ἐπίσκοπον ἔχει: Part II," 65 n. 98) who suggests, "It is not improbable that he is identical with John of Cyzicus, the addressee of the letter of the Graptoi brothers: *Vita Theodoris* [*sic*] *Grapti,* PG 116, 669D." The comments in M. Le Quien, *Oriens Christianus* 1 (Paris, 1740), 756, are derived from this passage in the *vita* by Peter.

[518] Ioannikios again seems to suggest that he has been claimed as a supporter of the opponents of Methodios; see above, n. 513.

[519] Cf. Eph. 5:6.

[520] Cf. Mk. 14:63; Jn. 19:23–24. Rending the tunic of Christ was a metaphorical expression for fomenting schism in the Church; thus Arius was accused of such an action in a letter of Alexander of Alexandria; cf. *Theodoret. Kirchengeschichte,* ed. L. Parmentier, 2d ed. (Berlin, 1954), 9.23–10.2.

[521] F. Dvornik, *Les Slaves, Byzance et Rome au IXe* siècle (Paris, 1926; repr. Hattiesburg, Miss., 1970), 130 suggests that this is an allusion to the patriarchs Tarasios and Nikephoros.

sons of the wicked one and *tares.*[522] If anyone, therefore, does not accept the great Methodios as patriarch, like the great Basil,[523] and the theologian Gregory[524] and the divine Chrysostom,[525] let him be anathema. And if anyone cuts himself off from communion with him [Methodios], he will be cut off from the glory of God on the Day of Judgment, and he who rends the catholic and apostolic church *will be cut asunder,* as the gospel[526] <says>, and *his portion appointed with the unfaithful.*" After he spoke these <words> and others in addition, <Methodios>, together with all the most holy gathering there, heralded the saint and subjected those profane and corrupt men to many anathemas, and made his farewell to the saint.

71. And so they parted, cheered with very many spiritual words and saying farewell to one another in the Holy Spirit. And that patriarch, the expert theologian, went down from the mountain initiated into the mysteries, carrying back, as if from a second Moses, spiritual tablets written by God, <that is> the teachings of the saint. Ioannikios, the most divine light of the wilderness, lived for three days more and then, *lifting* his blessed *feet* with fitting piety, like the blessed Jacob,[527] he departed to the Lord. *He fought the good fight,*[528] spending fifty-two years in the wilderness and living a total life span of eighty-four years.[529] He died on the third day of the month of November, the tenth <year of the> indiction,[530] during the reign of our orthodox emper-

---

[522] Cf. Mt. 13:38.

[523] Basil the Great, bishop of Caesarea (370/1–379); see *ODB* 1:269.

[524] Gregory of Nazianzos, bishop of Constantinople (27 Nov. 380–381); see *ODB* 2:880–82.

[525] John Chrysostom, bishop of Constantinople (26 Feb. 398–20 June 404); see *ODB* 2:1057–58.

[526] Lk. 12:46.

[527] Gen. 49:33.

[528] Cf. 1 Tim. 6:12.

[529] Sabas (chap. 53) says that Ioannikios died in his 94th year. Van den Gheyn suggested (*AASS,* Nov. 2.1:433 note o) that Peter's "84" may be the result of a scribal error. Peter's chronology, however, is internally consistent and Mango ("Ioannikios," 398–401) plausibly argues that Sabas may be trying to obscure Ioannikios' desertion from the army after only twelve years of service.

[530] On the indiction, a fifteen-year cycle, the first of which began in the year A.D. 312, see *ODB* 2:993. For the day of Ioannikios' death, see J. Pargoire, "Quel jour Saint

ors, Michael,[531] the young and most meek nursling of orthodoxy, and the aptly named Theodora,[532] she who was truly bestowed on the world by God as a divine gift of orthodoxy and who awarded total peace to the church, together with their relatives[533] who are guarded by God and crowned.

These were the accomplishments of our divine father, these were the valorous acts of the most blessed man, these were the virtuous deeds of the venerable man, these were the victories of the contestant, these were the struggles of the noble soldier. When <news of> his holy death was spread about everywhere, there gathered a large multitude from the surrounding monasteries and regions. And all escorted him as their champion to the emperor on high and conducted his funeral with psalms and hymns and spiritual odes. They deposited his honored remains in a sarcophagus and placed it in the monastery called Antidion, in which by the grace of Christ many cures and miracles are effected[534] up to this day. For all who come to that holy coffin ill or

---

Joannice est-il mort?" *EO* 4 (1900–1901), 75–80. Pargoire notes that Sabas (chap. 54) says Ioannikios ἐξάρας αὐτοῦ σεμνοπρεπῶς τοὺς πόδας . . . νοεμβρίῳ τρίτῃ, ἡμέρᾳ τετάρτῃ πρὸς Κύριον ἐξεδήμησεν. He plausibly suggests that this does not mean Ioannikios became ill on November third and died on the fourth, but, agreeing with Peter, that Ioannikios died on 3 November, on Wednesday, the fourth day of the week.

[531] Michael III, emperor (842–867); see *ODB* 2:1364.

[532] On Michael III's mother, the empress Theodora, whose name means "gift of God," see the final *vita* in this volume.

[533] The Greek here, αὐτῶν κλάδοις, lit., "*their* offspring," is difficult to interpret. Κλάδος is a "branch <of a tree>," but in Byzantine usage may be used metaphorically for "offspring" (Sophocles, *Lexicon*, s.v.). As Michael was born in 842, is here described as "young" and the "nursling of piety," and as Peter is presumably writing not long after Ioannikios' death in 846, Michael had no "offspring" at this time; whether he subsequently had children is uncertain (see *ODB* 2:739, s.v. "Eudokia Ingerina"). Presumably the phrase refers to his sisters, Theodora's daughters, of whom the eldest, Thekla, was portrayed wearing a crown on coins with Michael and Theodora and is mentioned as sharing imperial rank with them in a *martyrion* of the Forty-Two Martyrs of Amorion, ed. V. Vasil'evskij and P. Nikitin, *Skazanija o 42 amorijskich mučenikach* (St. Petersburg, 1905), 52.8–9: βασιλεύοντος τῆς Ῥωμαίων ἀρχῆς Μιχαὴλ καὶ Θεοδώρας καὶ Θέκλης (see P. Grierson, *A Catalogue of the Byzantine Coins in the Dumbarton Oaks Collection* 3:1 [Washington, D.C., 1973], 407 and 454).

[534] The 9th-century hymn composed to Ioannikios by Theodosia the Melode also mentions miracles worked at his grave (see J. Schiro, *Analecta Hymnica Graeca III:*

possessed or paralyzed or otherwise beset with disease return home healthy. [p. 434]

72. Such was the conduct of our divine father Ioannikios, a <true> citizen of heaven. This man loved God insatiably and was worthily loved by Him. He honored and was honored, for <as> He said, "*I will honor those who honor Me.*"[535] This Ioannikios was <truly> *the defender of the Trinity,*[536] the shield of the church, the ally of the orthodox, the subduer and opponent of schismatics and the impious, the champion of the faithful people, the house of wisdom, the charioteer who courses the heavens, the ethereal runner, the unsleeping *light of the world,*[537] *the gleaming morning star,*[538] *the guide of wanderers,*[539] *the chosen vessel,*[540] the sanctified tabernacle, the most holy treasure, the dwelling place of the Spirit, the habitation of the Trinity, the residence of virtues, the workshop of the commandments, *the ornament of the world,*[541] the splendor of monks, the paradigm of courage, the triumph of purity, <the source> of our pride,[542] *the bulwark of the faith, the mainstay of the church,*[543] the finest nursling of the wilderness. Ioannikios <was also> the Christ-imitating teacher, gentle and most peaceful, the God-bearing man, the model of ascetics, the enlightened mind, the burning lamp, *the vigilant eye,*[544] *the mediator between God and men,*[545] the guide of the repentant, the corrector of those returning <to right conduct>, the banisher of demons, the destroyer of the passions,

---

Canones Novembris [Rome, 1972], 126:71–77 and 132:198–202), as does that of Joseph the Hymnographer (see Μηναῖα τοῦ ὅλου ἐνιαυτοῦ [Rome, 1889], 46–47).

[535] 1 Ki. 2:30.

[536] Cf. Gregory of Nazianzos, *In laudem Heronis philosophi* (*or.* 25), PG 35:1201A and pseudo-John Chrysostom, *In Joannem Theologum,* PG 59:614.13.

[537] Cf. Gregory of Nyssa, *Laudatio S. Stephani Protomartyris,* PG 46:721A.

[538] Acts of the Council of Ephesus, *Acta conciliorum oecumenicorum,* ed. E. Schwartz, 1.1.4 (Berlin-Leipzig, 1928), 50.26.

[539] Cf. pseudo-John Chrysostom, *De poenitentia sermo* 1, PG 60:688.16–17, and pseudo-John Chrysostom, *In adorationem venerandae crucis,* PG 62:748.69.

[540] Acts 9:15.

[541] Pseudo-John Chrysostom, *In Petrum et Paulum,* PG 59:493.71–72.

[542] Cf. 2 Cor. 1:14.

[543] Gregory of Nazianzos, *Funebris Oratio in patrem* (*or.* 18), PG 35:985A.

[544] Gregory of Nyssa, *In sanctum Ephraim,* PG 46:829.50.

[545] 1 Tim. 2:5.

the good shepherd,[546] the hunter of wild beasts, *the unsleeping guardian,*[547] the foundation of endurance, the fruitful palm,[548] the contemplator of the mysteries,[549] the disdainer of the mundane, the ethereal rider, *the high-flying eagle,*[550] the associate of angels, the comrade of the apostles, the companion of the prize winners,[551] the inhabitant of the kingdom, *the heir of God, sharing the inheritance of Christ,*[552] the defender of the Trinity, who together with the angels incessantly intercedes for the universe.

But, *O divine and holy head,*[553] you who have *Christ as the head*[554] of all, brightest light, lover of God and thrice blessed, you conducted yourself nobly, you practiced virtue diligently, and were proclaimed the best soldier of Christ, after leaving the temporal army. You kept the nobility of your soul unsullied by mortification of the body and preserved its honor from enslavement by study of the Holy Scriptures. By the purity of your mind you became wholly Godlike and comprehended, in so far as is possible for men, the One Who is beyond all comprehension. You lifted the cross upon your shoulders and followed Christ[555] unswervingly and found an inviolate treasure[556] preserved in the heavens. You sold all earthly <goods> and purchased the highly honored pearl,[557] I mean the kingdom of heaven. You did not construct your house on the sand of careless laziness and vanity, but you built its foundation on the solid rock of faith in Christ; and thus it remained unshaken even by gusting winds, or the spirits of evil, and even the rivers of impiety.[558] *You have borne*

---

[546] Jn. 10:11, 14.

[547] Pseudo-John Chrysostom, *In annuntiationem Deiparae,* PG 62:763.65.

[548] Cf. Ps. 91 (92):12.

[549] Cf. J. Daniélou, *Grégoire de Nysse. La Vie de Moïse,* 2d ed. (Paris, 1955), pt. 2.181.8, and *Liber in hexaemeron,* PG 44:65.34 (both references are to Moses).

[550] Cf. Gregory of Nazianzos, *Ad patrem (or. 12),* PG 35:849A; pseudo-John Chrysostom, *In Psalmum 102,* PG 55:642.58–59.

[551] I.e., martyrs.

[552] Rom. 8:17.

[553] Gregory of Nazianzos, *or.* 7, chap. 17 (PG 35:776B); *or.* 43, chap. 82 (PG 36:604D).

[554] Cf. 1 Cor. 11:3, and John Chrysostom, *Adversus Judaeos* 1, PG 48:848.25–26.

[555] Cf. Mt. 16:24; Mk. 8:34.

[556] Cf. Mt. 13:44, 19:21; John Chrysostom, *De verbis apostoli,* PG 51:278.55, et al.

[557] Mt. 13:45–46.

[558] Cf. Mt. 7:26–27; Lk. 6:48–49.

the whole day's burden and heat[559] through all your life, but you received your reward from the Creator and Generator of nature. You have multiplied with generosity *the talent*[560] of gifts given to you by God and you heard those blessed words: "*Well done, thou good and faithful servant, enter thou into the joy of thy Lord.*"[561] You kept alight the lamp of your soul through the oil of beneficence and now you have readily entered with Christ [p. 435] into the heavenly bridal chamber.[562] You traversed the narrow and rough road and now you enjoy life above. You carried out the commandments of the Lord, you preserved the archetypal beauty of the icon.[563] You traded away[564] all your <earthly> life in *the practice of death*[565] and mortified the passions of the flesh by the toils of piety and subjected all thought of the flesh[566] to the spirit. You reached the highest point of freedom from the passions,[567] and by the loftiest virtues, I mean of love and faith and hope and compassion, were raised up, in a chariot like Elijah,[568] to the height of the mysteries. You also were wholly *beside yourself for God*[569] and became one with Him through divine purity and pure illumination and, to sum up, you imitated the virtues of all the saints <who have existed> from the beginning <of time>.

You brought forth the unblemished oblation of Abel[570] through your

---

[559] Mt. 20:12.

[560] Mt. 25:24.

[561] Mt. 25:21.

[562] Mt. 25:1–13.

[563] Cf. Basil of Caesarea, *De spiritu sancto,* chap. 9.23 (PG 32:109B).

[564] The translation of τὸν βίον διήλλαξας here is difficult. At 2 Macc. 6:27, διαλλάξας τὸν βίον is taken as "parting with my life," while at Plato, *Republic* 620 b5, ἀετοῦ διαλλάξαι βίον, Agamemnon is said to "substitute the life of an eagle <for his own>." Presumably Ioannikios has by his asceticism traded away earthly existence for life hereafter.

[565] Plato, *Phaedo* 81 a2; cf. P. Gallay, *Saint Grégoire de Nazianze. Lettres* 1 (Paris, 1964), *ep.* 31.4: καὶ ζῆν ἀντὶ τοῦ παρόντος τῷ μέλλοντι, θανάτου μελέτην—τοῦτο ὅ φησι Πλάτων—τὸν τῇδε βίον ποιούμενον. . .

[566] Cf. Rom. 8:5.

[567] On ἀπάθεια, the goal of spiritual purification, see *v. Phantin. Jun.* 45 n. 37.

[568] 4 Ki. 2:11.

[569] 2 Cor. 5:13.

[570] Gen. 4:4–5.

blameless prayers; the hope of Enos[571] in the invisible; Enoch's pleasingness to God,[572] through which your soul too was transferred to the heavens, <while> your body lies here as a manifest spring of miracles for the cure of the sick. <You imitated> the *justice* of Noah, like him *before God;*[573] the hospitality of Abraham, through which he entertained the Trinity,[574] while you served <the Trinity> through your <hospitality>; the simplicity[575] of Jacob, through which you were blessed and loved by God as <Jacob> was by his father Isaac. And so not in visible symbols, but rather by the unseen gifts of the Spirit you procured many children in the wilderness. <You imitated> the self-control of Joseph through which, after shedding the garment of all material <attractions>, you fled the shameless behavior of the frenzied Egyptian woman,[576] that is, of the flesh. <You imitated> the gentleness[577] of Moses, through which you yourself entered into the *darkness*[578] of the virtues and truly received spiritual tablets written by God by which you gave us the spiritual law. <You imitated> the dedication of Samuel[579] to God and <the ability> to speak of and foresee the future, as he <did>. <You emulated> the innocence of David,[580] whereby you yourself warded off your pursuers through blessings; the zeal of Elijah,[581] whereby you, like he, shamed the heretical emperor and profane priest, proclaiming them *prophets of shame;*[582] the solitary life and self-control of John <the Baptist>, through which you purified the senses and *lived purely with the pure.*[583] You spoke out freely with the prophets,

---

[571] Gen. 4:26.

[572] Gen. 5:22.

[573] Gen. 6:9–10.

[574] Gen. 18.

[575] Gen. 25:27.

[576] I.e., Potiphar's wife; cf. Gen. 39.

[577] Num. 12:3.

[578] On the *darkness,* see above, n. 68.

[579] 1 Ki. 1:11, 28.

[580] Ps. 25 (26):11.

[581] 3 Ki. 19:10.

[582] Cf. 3 Ki. 18:19, 25.

[583] John of Damascus, *Homilia in sabbatum sanctum,* PG 96:640.45.

preached with the apostles,[584] confessed with the martyrs,[585] conquered with Christ. Wherefore you also heard the great words: *Come, ye blessed of my father, inherit the kingdom prepared for you.*[586]

Wherefore we importune you, holy father and guide of our salvation— you are not forgotten by us, even if you have departed from us and by the law of nature passed beyond life, but your memory remains with us eternally—do you yourself not forget my humble self, but remember me your *unprofitable servant*[587] and accept from me this most brief funerary[588] composition. Even if <it is> unworthy, may you accept what is offered to you in faith—for you are also an imitator of Christ[589]—as He <accepted> the two mites of the widow.[590] For like that <widow>, I had nothing else to offer to you. Accept <this>, honored father, and in exchange grant me release from passions by your intercessions and restrain *sin's tyranny*[591] over me, which, as you see, is very great and a crushing <burden>. Release me from *hardness*[592] of soul by your entreaties to the Lord. For I know well that you are empowered by God for Whom you endured the labors of asceticism. Grant that He may be very merciful toward us, beneficent and easily reconcilable, so that He may deem us worthy to share in your lot, purifying us through repentance and illuminating our mind for the keeping of His commandments, in order that through a

---

[584] Cf. Mk. 3:14.

[585] Cf. 1 Tim. 6:12.

[586] Mt. 25:34.

[587] Lk. 17:10; Mt. 25:30.

[588] The claim that this composition was "very brief" was a standard "topos of modesty" in hagiography; cf. the similar protestation at the end of the lengthy *vita* of the patriarch Nikephoros, above, 141. The term ἐπιτάφιος may refer to a eulogy composed soon after the death of its subject or one written later, sometimes in connection with the translation of a saint's relics. Given the length of Peter's work and his reference in Chap. 71 to cures and miracles worked at Ioannikios' tomb at Antidion μέχρι τῆς σήμερον, it seems unlikely that the work was composed immediately upon Ioannikios' death. For the ἐπιτάφιος, see *ODB* 1:720–22 and A. Sideras, *Die byzantinischen Grabreden* (Vienna, 1994).

[589] Cf. 1 Cor. 11:1.

[590] Mk. 12:42; Lk. 21:2.

[591] Cf. John Chrysostom, *In epistulam ad Romanos, hom.* 13.4 (PG 60:512).

[592] Cf. Mk. 3:5.

pious life[593] here <on earth> and right conduct, we may obtain blessedness in heaven, in Christ Himself, our Lord, in Whom is the glory and power, together with the Father Who is without beginning, and the all-holy and life-giving Spirit, now and always, and unto the ages, Amen.

---

[593] Reading here εὐσεβοῦς βιώσεως for the otherwise unattested εὐβιώσεως; cf. above 384c.

8. LIFE OF ST. THEODORA THE EMPRESS

introduction and translation by Martha P. Vinson

Introduction

The Life and Encomium of the Blessed and Holy Empress Theodora recounts the story of a woman who rose from provincial origins to become the wife of the iconoclast emperor Theophilos (829–842) and who, after his death, presided over the restoration of orthodoxy as regent for her son Michael III (843–867). Theodora eventually withdrew from court life and died in a convent. The precise dates of her birth and death are unknown. Since she married in 830, she was probably born around 815. It is generally accepted that she survived her son, who was assassinated on 24 September 867, but one should note that in the Life of Theodora Michael III is alive and present at his mother's death.[1]

In both form and content, the Life and Encomium of the Blessed and Holy Empress Theodora differs markedly from a traditional saint's life. Although hagiography typically includes encomiastic elements, this Life is unusual in that it is a *basilikos logos,* that is, an imperial oration or encomium of an emperor, and conforms quite closely to the compositional guidelines for this genre as set forth in a third-century treatise on epideictic oratory ascribed to Menander Rhetor.[2] The author's use of a rhetorical form specifically designed to give scope to a ruler's accomplishments not only helps to explain certain otherwise puzzling features of the Life but also suggests that Theodora's sainthood was essentially political rather than religious in nature. For example, although saints' lives typically abound in supernatural occurrences,

[1] P. Karlin-Hayter, "La mort de Théodora," *JÖB* 40 (1990), 205–8, but see n. 99 below for further discussion of this problem.

[2] *Menander Rhetor,* ed. with trans. and comm. by D. A. Russell and N. G. Wilson (Oxford, 1981), 76–95; for the date, see p. xl. Ph. Bourboulis in *Studies in the History of Modern Greek Story-Motives* (Thessalonike, 1953), 7, identified the Life as "a sort of ῥητορικὸς ἔπαινος," but did not specify the form or attempt to incorporate rhetorical strategy into her analysis.

Theodora's Life contains only two, the prediction that she would become empress and the miraculous defeat of an Arab naval expedition shortly after the death of Theophilos. It is significant that neither prophecy nor miracle is attributed to Theodora.

In fact, the Life consistently portrays Theodora as a pious laywoman rather than a traditional saint. One notes, for example, that even after her retirement to a convent, this mother of seven does not seem to have embraced the ascetic life or to have taken monastic vows.[3] It is also striking that even during her tenure as empress, when she was ostensibly at the forefront of the movement to restore icons, Theodora is often relegated to the status of a minor character in her own Life. This is most noticeable in Chapters 5–10, which read more like a chronicle of the iconoclastic period than the hagiography of an iconodule heroine. Not only is Theodora frequently thrust from center stage by politically powerful men, notably her son, Michael III, and her husband's chamberlain, Theoktistos, but at times she even disappears from view altogether as the struggle against iconoclasm is waged by the male champions of orthodoxy. In sum, the portrait of Theodora that emerges from the Life is that of an exemplary wife and mother, whose defining virtue, moreover, appears to be her deference to male authority, be it civil, religious, or domestic.

The political character of Theodora's sainthood is underscored by the rhetorical form of the Life and the probable circumstances of its composition. There are indications that the Life was not only intended for oral delivery but was written in relatively close proximity to the events described. For example, the heading of the principal manuscript, B.M. Add. 28270,[4] indicates that the Life is "For the Sunday of (the feast of) Orthodoxy," that is, the first Sunday in Lent, the day on which the restoration of icons was, and is, commemorated

---

[3] Three children, a boy and two girls, died young. See P. Grierson, "The Tombs and Obits of the Byzantine Emperors (337–1042)," with an additional note by C. Mango and I. Ševčenko, *DOP* 16 (1962), 26–27. On Theodora's tonsure, see n. 82.

[4] The Life of Theodora is found in only three manuscripts: British Museum Add. 28270, completed on 3 August 1111; Messina Biblioteca Universitaria, San Salvatore 30, written in 1307; and, the 13th-century Vaticanus graecus 2014, which contains an incomplete version of the Life. Another version of the Life, called "the second redaction" by Regel, *Analecta,* p. x, and containing sections 5–8 in their entirety and parts of 9–10, was published by F. Combefis, *Historia haeresis monothelitarum sanctaeque in eam sextae synodi actorum vindiciae* (Paris, 1648), 715ε–743ΑΑ.

in the Greek church. In the proem, the author uses the second person ("you have assembled here") and refers to the "audience" in explaining that he has undertaken the composition of this work for purely altruistic reasons. Further, although the morphology and diction are representative of the high or classicizing style, the syntax is relatively simple in that it is characterized by a low incidence of subordination, thus making the encomium easy for a listener to follow. Finally, not only does the author reveal a close familiarity with the persons and events described, but his elaborate disclaimer of any ulterior personal motive, while conventional, would be completely pointless if all the principals involved were long dead.

The reference in the proem to the death of "the man who is being praised," that is, Michael III, provides a terminus post quem of 867 for the composition of the Life, since Michael died in September of that year. Other internal evidence points to a date of composition in the early years of the Macedonian dynasty, either during the reign of Basil I (867–886) or that of his son Leo VI (886–912),[5] and suggests that the Life may in fact be an inaugural sermon introducing Theodora's feast into the church calendar. One notes, for example, that the author introduces his narrative with the words, "Let us enjoy the account . . . and her passing . . . will be observed on our part as a feastday," instead of saying, "Today we are celebrating . . ." or "Now it is time once again to commemorate . . . ," which are more traditional ways of opening a panegyric for a saint whose cult is already well established. Given Theodora's role in the restoration of icons and the prominence this event receives in our Life, it would not be inappropriate for her sainthood to be proclaimed on the Feast of Orthodoxy. Such a move would be consistent with imperial policy in the latter part of the ninth century since Theodora played an important role in pro-Macedonian propaganda designed to legitimize the new regime. One may note as well that the Life's positive portrayal of Michael III, who is elsewhere represented as a womanizing drunkard, accords well with his status during the reign of Leo VI, for Leo's first official act after his accession was to

---

[5] Regel, *Analecta,* xiii; Karlin-Hayter, "Théodora," 208. A. Markopoulos, in the introduction to his edition of the Life (Markopoulos, "Theodora," 251–55), and at greater length in his "Συμβολὴ στὴ χρονολόγηση τοῦ Γεωργίου Μοναχοῦ," *Symmeikta* 6 (1985), 223–31, argues that the Life was composed after the death of Michael III in 867 and before the Chronicle of George the Monk, which he assigns to a period after 871, noting that the evidence does not permit greater chronological precision. See also n. 14 below.

rehabilitate the emperor whose assassination brought his father to the throne.[6] Considered collectively, the evidence provided by both the form and content of the Life indicates that this work was authorized at the very highest level of the political and religious establishment. It suggests moreover that the cult of Theodora was instituted as a means of demonstrating the orthodoxy, and hence the legitimacy, of a regime which overthrew the dynasty that conquered iconoclasm.

The political nature of Theodora's sanctity is further demonstrated by the official rather than popular character of her cult. She is commemorated in the *Synaxarion of Constantinople* on 11 February, in the *Menologion of Basil II,* and in the *Synodikon of Orthodoxy.*[7] Yet she developed no popular following and nothing is known of her relics or any posthumous miracles. Many fewer hymns are dedicated to her than to her homonyms from Alexandria and Thessalonike.[8] Most astonishing, in view of her role as restorer of image veneration, is her virtual absence from the very sacred art that she made possible. Only three Byzantine iconic images of her are preserved: in the *Menologion of Basil II,*[9] in a fresco in the 14th-century Cretan church of the Virgin Gouverniotissa,[10] and in the Feast of Orthodoxy icon of ca. 1400 recently acquired by the British Museum.[11] In the menologion she is dressed in impe-

---

[6] P. Karlin-Hayter, "L'enjeu d'une rumeur," *JÖB* 41 (1991), 85–111, and esp. 103–8 on the role of Theodora and Michael III in Macedonian propaganda. Leo VI's affinity with his father's predecessor is further attested by his promotion of the cult of the archangel Michael; see P. Magdalino, "Observations on the Nea Ekklesia of Basil I," *JÖB* 37 (1987), 56 and n. 26.

[7] *SynaxCP* 458–60; *Il Menologio di Basilio II* (Turin, 1907), fol. 392; Gouillard, "Synodikon," 93.768–69, 97.801–2.

[8] Cf. E. Follieri, *Initia hymnorum ecclesiae graecae* 5.2 (Vatican City, 1966), 124.

[9] Fol. 392; cf. A. Grabar, *L'Iconoclasme byzantin. Le dossier archéologique,* 2d ed. (Paris, 1984), pl. 138.

[10] M. Vassilakis-Mavrakakis, "The Church of the Virgin Gouverniotissa at Potamies, Crete," Ph. D. dissertation, Courtauld Institute of Art, University of London, 1986, 247–48. I am grateful to S. Gerstel for providing this reference.

[11] D. Buckton, *Byzantium: Treasures of Byzantine Art and Culture from British Collections* (London, 1994), no. 140. It should be noted that in the 18th-century Painter's Manual of Dionysios of Fourna, there is no description of an individual iconography for Theodora; she is included only in the group scene of the Restoration of Holy Images; cf. P. Hetherington, *The 'Painter's Manual' of Dionysius of Fourna* (London, 1974),

rial garb and holds an icon of Christ; in the icon she stands with her young son Michael next to an icon of the Virgin Hodegetria.

It remains to consider the value of the Life of Theodora as a historical source and its relation to other sources for the iconoclastic period. In this regard, two events recounted by the Life, the defeat of the Arab naval expedition and the bride show in which Theodora was chosen as Theophilos' consort, are of particular importance. Since, however, an understanding of the conventions governing the composition of an imperial oration is crucial to analyzing these events and locating them within the historiographical tradition, it will be useful to provide a summary of the rhetorical structure of the Life:[12]

Chap. 1	Proem
Chap. 2.1–4	Country
Chap. 2.4–41	Family
Chap. 3.1–3	Birth and Upbringing
Chap. 3.3–14	Nature
Chap. 3.14–Chap. 4	Accomplishments
Chap. 5–Chap. 12.18	Actions
	a. War (Chaps. 5–8)
	b. Peace (Chaps. 9–12.18)
Chap. 12.19–40	Synkrisis (Comparison)
Chap. 12.40–98	Fortune
Chap. 12.98–107	Epilogue

At the outset, one may observe that objective truth is not the goal of encomium generally or the encomium of an emperor in particular. In fact, in his discussion of the topic "Birth," Menander actually encourages the prospective encomiast to use fabrication if it can be done convincingly; as he puts it, "the audience has no choice but to accept the encomium without examination."[13] There are reasons to believe that the abortive Arab assault on Con-

---

64–65. A search of the Princeton Index of Christian Art and *LCI* 8:452–53 has revealed no further examples.

[12] The chapter and line numbers refer to the edition of Markopoulos.

[13] Russell-Wilson, *Menander Rhetor,* 83.

stantinople shortly after the accession of Theodora and Michael represents such a fabrication. What makes this incident suspect is that no Arab source mentions it and the only other Greek reference occurs in the Chronicle of George the Monk, which is itself dependent on our Life for information.[14] The victory over the Arab naval forces appears as the first item in the subheading "Peace," where it effectively marks the transition from the preceding topic "War." This military triumph not only invites comparison with the crushing defeat dealt to Theophilos by the Arabs at Amorion in 838 but, since virtually the entire Arab fleet of four hundred ships was destroyed, thus guaranteeing national security for some time to come, it also highlights in a more general way the contrast between the universal strife that characterized the reign of Theophilos and the peace that is the hallmark of Theodora's rule. That this episode is so obviously tailor-made for its rhetorical context both undermines its credibility and supports the priority of the Life as a source in relation to the Chronicle of George the Monk.[15] That in all probability the Arab invasion of 842 never actually happened should in no way diminish our appreciation of the Life of Theodora. Rather, the handling of this event, in particular the ascription of victory to divine forces rather than direct military intervention on Theodora's part, attests to the author's skill in adapting what is essentially a male genre to a female subject.[16]

[14] After examining the parallel passages found in the Life of Theodora and the Chronicle of George the Monk, Regel (*Analecta,* v–xiii) concluded that the Life was composed during the reign of Basil I (867–886) and served as a source for the Chronicle, which he assigned to the reign of Leo VI (886–912). Markopoulos ("Theodora" [1983], 251–55 and "Georgios Monachos" [1985], 223–31), after a thorough review of the evidence and scholarship, followed Regel in accepting the priority of the Life, but revised the dating of the Chronicle upward from the generally accepted date of 866–867 to a period after 872 ("Theodora" [1983]) or 871 ("Georgios Monachos" [1985]).

[15] A. Kazhdan ("Chronika Simeona Logofeta," *Vizantijskij vremennik* 15 [1959], 126–27) suggested that the portions of George's Chronicle that duplicate the contents of the Life of Theodora are interpolated, that is, additions inserted into the text at a later date; see also Karlin-Hayter, "Etudes," 455, n. 1. Against this view, Markopoulos ("Georgios Monachos" [1985], 228–29) adduces persuasive new evidence to show that the passages in question are not interpolations but rather integral parts of the Chronicle.

[16] It is the subdivision of accomplishments into war and peace that primarily distinguishes an imperial oration from a "normal" encomium of the sort described by Aph-

The bride show which results in Theodora's marriage to Theophilos appears to belong to the category of fiction as well.[17] The account begins under the heading "Nature" (Chap. 3.3–14), exemplified by Theodora's "natural beauty," that wins her a summons to Constantinople, and continues under the next topic, "Accomplishments" (Chaps. 3.14–4), defined by Menander as character traits, where the events leading up to and surrounding Theodora's marriage provide a venue for illustrating her moral qualities of wisdom, temperance, courage, and piety. Here again, the rhetorical structure of the Life holds the key to interpretation. Technically, the topic "Nature" ought to fall between the two preceding ones, "Birth" and "Upbringing," which are treated together in an extremely perfunctory manner (Chap. 3.1–3). By contrast, the bride show is given expansive treatment and this fact, together with its position in the rhetorical framework of the Life, has the effect not only of diminishing the significance of the account of Theodora's birth but even of supplanting this topic altogether. If one views the marriage as a substitute for birth, the implications are twofold. First, it is possible to see in the elaborate treatment of the bride show the sort of fictionalized account of a monarch's origins that Menander urges upon his reader. Second, by treating marriage as the equivalent of birth, the author asserts that Theodora's claim to the throne is as valid, indeed as "natural," as that of her husband.

This latter point is of crucial importance for the simple reason that the legitimacy of Theodora's official acts, in particular, the restoration of orthodoxy, hinges upon the legitimacy of her political status. But since Theodora's claim to sovereignty rests not on birth but marriage, the process by which she became an emperor's wife is the essential element in demonstrating the legitimacy of her claim. The bride show is the means to this end. By representing Theodora as the absolute flower of her generation, culled after an exhaustive and wide-ranging search, it confirms beyond all question Theodora's right to wield power. Once Theodora's political position is secured, it follows that her theological position on the question of icons is secured as well. Hence,

---

thonios, where the corresponding categories are body and soul. See G. A. Kennedy, *Greek Rhetoric under Christian Emperors* (Princeton, N.J., 1983), 63.

[17] The historicity of the Byzantine bride show is the subject of much scholarly debate. For a discussion of this phenomenon with bibliography, see J. Herrin, "Bride Shows," *ODB* 1: 323–24.

while the bride show in the Life of Theodora may not reflect objective reality, it does serve the rhetorical objectives of the Life for, by validating Theodora's sovereignty, it validates the sovereignty of orthodoxy and with it Theodora's claim to sainthood.

BIBLIOGRAPHY

Edition Used for Translation
(*BHG* 1731) A. Markopoulos, "Βίος τῆς αὐτοκρατείρας Θεοδώρας (*BHG* 1731)," *Symmeikta* 5 (1983), 249–85.

Other Editions
F. Combefis, *Historia haeresis monothelitarum sanctaeque in eam sextae synodi actorum vindiciae* (Paris, 1648), 715–50.
W. Regel, *Analecta Byzantino-Russica* (St. Petersburg, 1891–98; repr. New York, 1964), iii–xix (introduction) and 1–19 (text).

Translations
(modern Greek) P. Baïtse in Tsames, *Meterikon* 3:368–405.

Secondary Literature
P. A. Hollingsworth, "Theodora," *ODB* 3:2037–38.
P. Karlin-Hayter, "Etudes sur les deux histoires du règne de Michel III," *Byzantion* 41 (1971), 452–96.
———, "La mort de Théodora," *JÖB* 40 (1990), 205–8
L. Rydén, "The Bride Shows at the Byzantine Court—History or Fiction?" *Eranos* 83 (1985), 175–91.
D. Stiernon, *Bibl.sanct.* 12 (1969), 222–24.
W. Treadgold, "The Bride-Shows of the Byzantine Emperors," *Byzantion* 49 (1979), 395–413, esp. 402–6.

LIFE WITH ENCOMIUM OF THE BLESSED AND HOLY EMPRESS THEODORA

Lord, give your blessing.[18]

1. We are going to praise the empress Theodora even if some unscrupulous person is liable to subject us to the greatest possible disparagement for having undertaken these words of praise for the sake of personal aggrandizement and not as a way[19] of benefitting others. After all, the present praise cannot possibly curry favor with her, since this encomium <comes> after her death, nor will my account have in its audience the man who is being praised.[20] There is thus no advantage to be gained nor material reward to be had from <relating> events that are worthy of praise and narration.[21] She, of course, has now taken her place with the heavenly choir above, adorned and illuminated with the beauty of the Godhead, while he is tuning his life to the strain of his past triumphs[22] and summoning to piety and salvation[23] those who praise piety and virtue. But let us enjoy the account, all those of us who have the highest admiration for her <accomplishments>, and her passing, that is, her death, will be observed on our part as a feastday. Since you have assembled with such enthusiasm and request an account because of your yearning, I shall set before you the story of her life so that together you may well enjoy the account, while I will have the very great satisfaction of having benefitted you.

2. Now then, the homeland of Theodora, that truly blessed and holy

---

[18] For this invocation, see n. 20 at the beginning of the *Acta* of David, Symeon, and George.

[19] The variant τρόπῳ is read here.

[20] That is, Theodora's son and co-emperor, Michael III.

[21] Regel's text (διηγήματος) is read instead of διηγήματα (Markopoulos).

[22] Regel's correction (κατωρθωμένοις for κάτω ρεωμένοις) is read instead of that of Markopoulos (κατηρημένοις), but the precise meaning of the text remains uncertain.

[23] Markopoulos obelizes the words †ἀλλὰ καὶ σωτηρίαν† to indicate the uncertainty of the reading. Regel is even more cautious, printing ἐναγλα[ΐζεται . . .], which indicates loss or severe damage to the text.

queen, was Paphlagonia[24] that provides the Queen of Cities with the necessities <of life> and all the other parts of the world with its own special bounty, bestowing useful items of various kinds upon various <regions>. Her parents, the most blessed Marinos and Theoktiste, expended a great, indeed endless, amount of effort in their pursuit of goodness and mercy. Many are the tales of their goodness and great was their zeal on behalf of piety, but out of this multitude I shall give only a few brief examples. There was a great persecution[25] and the champions were not ignoble nor was the contest over trivial issues or for small prizes but rather about the kingdom of heaven and the good things that last forever. To be sure, the stadium [p. 258] and the track streamed with blood from the contest, but it was piety that was at stake and the prize was the kingdom of heaven and the good things there prepared for those who have suffered or are suffering or will suffer for their sake. The religious issue involved nothing less than the destruction of images and the abolition of icons. These were not <images> of the kind whose destruction results in no great peril or even little harm; on the contrary, they were the <images> whose installation was a mark of pious zeal and whose abolition was a bitter form of tyranny. As a result, church thought was perverted, books were altered, sanctuaries demolished, churches were stripped of decoration, priests replaced, innocent men subjected to legal investigation, criminals placed in positions of power and the most illustrious sees. Nor was this all: whole regions were torn by civil strife, monasteries were deserted, people took to the hills, their family property confiscated by the state. This is how far the heresy of the iconoclasts went. Some people were intimidated by <this climate of> fear and looked to play it safe on the question of their religious belief, while others were subjected to harassment by[26] members of their own families. For a great many individuals chased even their own relatives away and refused to share the same roof with people who would not obey the imperial decree. But in the face of such cruel and inhuman behavior, what did they do, that truly

---

[24] Paphlagonia was a theme or province located on the southern coast of the Black Sea in north-central Asia Minor. According to *TheophCont* 89.15–22, Theodora came from a town called Ebissa and her father Marinos was an army officer, either a *droungarios* or a *tourmarches*.

[25] This was the second phase of iconoclastic persecution, which began in 815.

[26] Regel's reading "by" (ὑπό) is accepted here instead of Markopoulos' "because of" (περί).

noble and divine couple who gave birth to the blessed Theodora in both body and piety? When they saw people endangered because of their piety—some lacking the necessities <of life>, others worn out by the multitude of their sufferings, others still gasping for breath like those who are harried and terrified by their opponents in the arena—they opened up the storerooms of their heart and, *becoming all things to all men,*[27] some they skillfully anointed for the contests in the arena, while they tended to the wounds of others and filled the bellies of yet other unfortunates with the necessities <of life>. And as for those who lost their cities and homelands against their will, one home willingly took them in and welcomed complete strangers like members of the family. This is how some people, after receiving a helping hand, survived the persecution, while others not only found new courage to face their persecutors but also inspired piety in the rest. This was the first triumph of the religious devotion of the blessed Theodora's parents; this is the very first of the famous stories about them.

3. And so, having obtained both her birth and her education from these righteous and thrice-blessed <parents>, the holy and blessed Theodora was brought up [p. 259] in all piety and *admonition of the Lord.*[28] But when she reached marriageable age, her parents began to consider when and to whom she should be given in marriage since she was much sought after because of her natural beauty. In fact, she was so <beautiful> that she was fit even for marriage to an emperor. <And so> Theophilos, the emperor of the Romans at that time,[29] sent couriers to bring her to the Queen of Cities. And not just Theodora, but many other <girls> who were noted at that time for their youthful beauty and figures were also summoned to the palace for inspection. The emperor lined them all up to inspect and judge their beauty. Then the emperor Theophilos, after evaluating them in this way and picking out seven of the girls, gave each of them an apple and sent them off to their rooms. The next day the emperor had them brought back for an audience and, to test their virtue, asked each one of them for the imperial apples but they were nowhere to be found. What a disgrace! Such a disaster! At that moment by

---

[27] 1 Cor. 9:22.

[28] Eph. 6:4.

[29] Theophilos had been crowned co-emperor with his father in the spring of 821 at the age of eight and succeeded as sole ruler upon his father's death on 2 October 829. See Treadgold, "Chronological Accuracy," 167.

the will of God the blessed Theodora, who was standing behind the <other> six like a rose among thorns, cupped her hands like a lily and gave the emperor Theophilos a second apple in addition to the imperial one.[30] The emperor conducted a careful inquiry into this miraculous development in an effort to learn the truth. One could not help but notice the confidence in her voice, coming as it did from a pure heart, when she spoke of her success in <winning> the imperial crown. "The first apple, my lord, the talent entrusted to me by God, I give back to you undamaged and intact: it is my virginity and chastity. The second one is like the denarius and <represents> the son I will bear for you: do not refuse it."[31] But the emperor and his courtiers pressed on in their effort to know the truth. "Where did you get this prophecy from? What is the source of this mysterious revelation?"[32] To the emperor she replied, "My lord, the whole way here I was continually subjected to cutting remarks from brazen tongues. I was terribly upset, but endured it with never a word to anyone. Instead, I steeled my soul with tears that welled up within me and prayers

---

[30] In a different but essentially parallel version of the episode recounted by the sources known collectively as Symeon the Logothete (Leo Gramm. 213, ps.-Sym. Mag. 624–25, and George Mon. Cont. 790), there is only a single golden apple; Leo and George add the anachronistic detail that the contest was held in the Triclinium of the Pearl. In this variant, the center stage is held not by Theodora but by Kassia, who, in the course of a verbal exchange likewise based on biblical allusions (to Eve and Mary), so humiliates Theophilos with her witty retort that he immediately proceeds to choose Theodora in her place. Unlike our Life where the bride show serves to glorify Theodora, the object of the chroniclers is to denigrate or blame Theophilos by having a woman get the better of him. Kassia, who subsequently became a nun and poet of some renown, is used because her name is easily recognizable. For an exhaustive review of the literature on this question with a similarly skeptical conclusion, see I. Rochow, *Studien zu der Person, den Werken, und dem Nachleben der Dichterin Kassia* (Berlin, 1967), 5–19. For an English translation of Kassia's poetry, see *Kassia: The Legend, the Woman, and Her Work,* trans. and ed. A. Tripolitis (New York, 1992).

[31] Theodora alludes first to the parable of the talents found in Mt. 25:14–39; the choice is not particularly apt since the servant who received the single talent was sharply criticized for burying it in the ground instead of lending it out at interest. The denarius, or "penny" of the King James Version, figures in the lesson on taxation at Mt. 22:15–22, Mk. 12:13–17, and Lk. 20:20–26, which concludes with the famous line, "Render to Caesar the things that are Caesar's, and to God the things that are God's." Here again the allusion is of questionable taste since it emphasizes the great gulf that exists between the emperor and God.

[32] Cf. Rom. 16:25.

to the Lord our God. And when I learned of a certain holy man[33] who was enclosed in the tower at Nikomedeia—after all, his lofty and virtuous way of life was famous everywhere—when I drew near the place, I went up to him, for a star shone upon me as of old on the Magi in Bethlehem[34] making <me> feel worthy to pay homage to him there. [p. 260] That holy and thrice-blessed man looked at me and said, "Be of good courage, my daughter, and do not be upset by the tribulations you have suffered on your journey; for an angel of the glory of the Lord is crowning you empress of the Christians and *the hand of the Lord is upon*[35] your head. Take the apple that I give you in addition to the one you are going to receive from the emperor's hand. Then, after the <girls> who say mean things about you have been driven out of the palace doors in tears, give them <both> to the emperor. <In this way>, clad in purple you will be seated above all women on the imperial throne in a golden-roofed chamber."[36] The emperor Theophilos then took the two apples from the hand of Theodora who is held in everlasting remembrance and, in full view of the senate, gave her a gold ring to mark the imperial betrothal. Immediately after this, the ladies-in-waiting of the empress Euphrosyne, the emperor's mother,[37] whose lives were a model of propriety, took her <into their

---

[33] The saint Theodora visited was the Isaiah mentioned by the *De Theophili imperatoris absolutione* (ed. Regel, *Analecta,* 25), as living in the tower of St. Diomedes in Nikomedeia. Our Life specifies that he was "ἐγκεκλεισμένος," that is, an *enkleistos* or secluded monk. Isaiah is alleged to have subsequently played a role in the restoration of Orthodoxy. See also Janin, *Eglises Centres,* 89, and n. 77 below. A similar motif of a young virgin visiting a holy man en route to Constantinople for a bride show is found in the *vita* of Irene of Chrysobalanton; cf. *v. Iren. Chrysobalant.* 8–10.

[34] Mt. 2:1–12.

[35] Acts 13:11.

[36] The "golden-roofed chamber" or Chrysotriklinos was the throne room of the Great Palace located in the southeastern part of Constantinople. Theophilos is famous for "redecorating" this room with mechanical birds and lions made of gold, which appeared to sing and roar when their movements were coordinated with the playing of two massive organs, also made of gold. See Treadgold, *Byz. Revival,* 283–85.

[37] Euphrosyne was actually Theophilos' stepmother; his real mother was Thekla, his father's first wife. After her death, Michael II married Euphrosyne, a daughter of Constantine VI and Maria who, like Theodora, is also said to have become empress by means of a bride show. In order to marry, Euphrosyne first had to be released from her convent on the island of Prinkipo near Constantinople where she had been living as a nun with her mother. See Bury, *Eastern Roman Empire,* 80 and 111.

care> and attended her with decency, decorum, and the respect that was her due. Twenty-two days later, the aforementioned Theodora was crowned along with the emperor Theophilos by Antony the falsely named and accursed patriarch, or should I say chief conspirator,[38] who ought to have been strung up for miserably and insanely dishonoring the holy and venerable images.[39] The same Theodora became the emperor's consort and ruled piously after being crowned in the all-holy and venerable church of St. Stephen the Protomartyr in Daphne.[40] Large numbers of clergy and government officials joined in applauding and congratulating the imperial couple on their coronation. To show her generosity, the empress gave fifteen pounds of gold to the patriarch, fifty pounds to the senate, and fifteen pounds to the clergy, while those who had helped with or participated in the coronation itself she received in a fit and gracious manner.

4. After these events had taken place in the manner described, the Augusta Euphrosyne, the mother of Theophilos, having spent ten months living in the palace, felt a desire to be relieved of her many cares and worries and longed for the untroubled and contemplative way of life. And so by her own choice and not under any compulsion, she left the palace voluntarily and of her own free will and entered the Gastria monastery.[41]

[38] The term "chief conspirator" (φατριάρχης) contains a pun on the word "patriarch," which literally means chief father in the sense of head of a family or people. The hagiographer also puns on the name of Antony (Ἀντώνιος), calling him ἀγχώνιος, or "fit to be hanged."

[39] Antony I Kassymatas was instrumental in laying the theological groundwork for the iconoclastic synod organized by Leo V in 815. He was appointed patriarch of Constantinople by Michael II in 821 and died sometime before 21 April 838, when he was succeeded in office by John VII Grammatikos. On the date of John's accession to the patriarchate, see Treadgold, "Chronological Accuracy," 178–79.

[40] Since Theophilos had already been crowned emperor by his father in 821, the "crowning" of Theophilos and Theodora must refer to the marriage ceremony that took place on 5 June 830 (Pentecost), when Theophilos was seventeen (?) years old. Theodora's coronation will have followed shortly thereafter. For the date, see W. T. Treadgold, "The Problem of the Marriage of the Emperor Theophilos," *GRBS* 16 (1975), 327–28. The church of St. Stephen, located within the Great Palace complex, was the traditional site of imperial weddings and coronations; see Janin, *Eglises CP,* 473–74.

[41] Euphrosyne left the palace in the summer of 830 but there is some debate as to whether she voluntarily went to the Gastria monastery as indicated by our Life, Leo

5. And so the emperor Theophilos, once he began to wield imperial power, took up in turn the unlawful, wicked, cruel, and soul-destroying heresy of the triply damned and insane Kopronymos[42] [p. 261] and his beastly and bestial <cohorts>.[43] Furthermore, once he took up this <heresy>, he proved to be every bit their equal in sheer wickedness and tyrannical behavior. For, in a display of evil-mindedness and mental derangement, the fool revived this <heresy> and, imitating the madness of the previous empty-headed and murderous iconoclasts, a form of insanity with roots stretching back to the pernicious tyranny of Manes, he personally rekindled a relentless persecution against the church of God.[44] He had as his adviser, confederate, and accomplice in the soul-destroying heresy and guide to perdition John,[45] the chief conspirator or rather chief sorcerer and chief demon, in actual point of fact a new Apollonios or Balaam[46] who evilly reappeared in our own day to work

---

Gramm. 214.6–8, George Mon. Cont. 790.21–23, and ps.-Sym. Mag. 628.8–11, or whether she was forcibly returned to her original convent on the island of Prinkipo as alleged by *TheophCont* 86.9–11. What has given credibility to the account of *TheophCont* is that the Gastria convent was reportedly founded by Theodora's mother Theoktiste (*TheophCont* 90.2–4), thus making it, in the eyes of some scholars, a highly unlikely destination for the empress' mother-in-law. Whatever the truth may be, it is undisputed that Theodora and her family enjoyed a special relationship with the Gastria monastery: it was to this convent that Theodora retired after leaving the court and it was here that she was buried along with her mother, her brother Petronas, and her daughters Thekla, Anastasia, and Pulcheria. See Const. Porph., *De cer.* 1:647–48 (bk. 2.42), and Grierson, "Tombs and Obits," 27, n. 85. The Gastria convent was located in the southwestern part of Constantinople, on the site of the Sancaktar mosque. For further discussion and bibliography, see Janin, *Eglises CP,* 67–68, Markopoulos, "Theodora," 276, and Treadgold, *Byz. Revival,* 271 and 310.

[42] On Constantine V Kopronymos (741–775), see General Introduction, x–xi.

[43] The literal meaning of this phrase is "those who both bore the name of and acted like beasts." It is no doubt an allusion to the iconoclast emperors Leo III and Leo V, whose name means "lion"; cf. n. 185 to the Life of David, Symeon, and George, above.

[44] Manes was the founder of Manicheanism, a dualist heresy that originated in Persia during the 3d century A.D. The persecution of Theophilos began in late 832–early 833.

[45] On John VII Grammatikos, patriarch of Constantinople from 838 to 843, see n. 299 in the Life of David, Symeon, and George, above.

[46] Apollonios of Tyana was a pagan wonder-worker and Neopythagorean philosopher of the 1st century A.D. whose travels and adventures are chronicled in a biography written by Philostratos. Apollonios' ability to perform miracles, especially healing, invited comparison with Christ and he eventually came to be regarded in the Christian tradition as

wickedness and perform divination from dishes of water.[47] For once the wretch had been undeservedly put at the helm of the patriarchal throne, he proceeded to scuttle the ship of the church of God. It was this crafty expert and author of monstrous lies and every act hateful to God who taught poor, simple-minded Theophilos his letters and, by treacherously bombarding his mind with bad advice, wormed his way in and turned him into a true and loyal servant and fit instrument of the devil. The sheer perversity of it! The stupidity and everything else of the kind! The ridiculous fantasies of the impious and unholy iconoclasts including the rulers themselves had no grounding in reality whatever; on the contrary, their writings and rejoinders were chock full of gibberish, thoroughly fictitious nonsense[48] and irrelevant quibbling. Dangling <this stuff> like bait on a hook the sorry wretches hauled in the simpler and less educated folk; in fact, *their throat was an open sepulcher* and smoky haze, and their words *darkened the eyes*[49] of their unwitting victims. For, priding themselves on the baselessness of their lies, they became strangers to the truth. But while the enemies of truth were thus engaged in this presumptuous course of action, the venerable and holy congregation of the orthodox saw what was going on, and the fact that people considered to be Christians were acting like this made them angry and very upset. They said to one another, "What kind of impious and depraved person could reach such a height of willful arrogance as to presume to undermine the principles <of our faith> laid down by the most eloquent, divinely instructed, and far-famed holy Apostles and the seven holy ecumenical councils [p. 262] or to tamper with just *one* tiny *jot,*[50] as these accursed iconoclasts are doing, when he ought rather to embrace and gladly

---

an evil sorcerer. The story of Balaam is told in Num. 22–24, where he is rebuked by his ass as he makes his way to curse the Israelites at the behest of the Moabite king Balak. At Rev. 2:14 he is held up as a prototype of the false teacher for inducing the Israelites to eat sacrificial meat and commit fornication; cf. also 2 Pet. 2:15 and Jude 11.

[47] This allusion to the practice of *lekanomanteia* combines the twin insults of paganism and sorcery. John is elsewhere alleged to have engaged in this (and other forms of) black magic; see, for example, Georg. Mon. 2:798.22; Duffy-Parker, *Synodicon Vetus,* chap. 155.6; and John Scylitzes, *Synopsis historiarum,* ed. H. Thurn (Berlin-New York, 1973), 72.66, 85.3 and 9, 86.44. Accusations of sorcery were often made against highly educated individuals in both the Byzantine East and Latin West. See Lemerle, *Byz. Humanism,* 154 and n. 106.

[48] Regel's correction (ψευδεπιπλάστου εἰκαιομυθίας) is read here.

[49] Ps. 5:9; cf. Ps. 68 (69):23.

[50] Mt. 5:18.

keep quiet in the face of their divinely inspired and soul-saving teaching? Anyone who presumes to do such a thing or to teach another should be excommunicated from the Church and estranged from the kingdom of heaven." So high did feelings run on this issue. Meanwhile, the sorry wretch Theophilos remained incorrigible and condemned many of the orthodox to exile after subjecting them to countless cruel punishments, tortures, and abuse. At the sight of this, those who were conducting themselves in an upright and pious manner and pursuing a dignified way of life that is pleasing to God and who were adorned with virtue and orthodoxy, bore it nobly and with good grace, asking God for deliverance from their misfortunes. For orthodox belief is the prime virtue.

6. In those days there shone forth remarkable, God-fearing men who were filled with divine zeal and wisdom. Among them were Ioannikios, the great standard-bearer,[51] a marvelous and thrice-blessed man, who was found worthy to receive from God the great and truly remarkable gift of seeing and knowing the future through the illumination of the all-holy and lifegiving Spirit and when asked often foretold what was to be. There were as well Nikephoros,[52] the sanctified patriarch honored by God; Theodore,[53] the famous superior of the Stoudios monastery; Methodios,[54] the thrice-blessed and divine confessor and fervent supporter of the orthodox faith; Michael,[55] the great confessor and equal of the angels; the admirable and sanctified confessor

---

[51] For the *vita* of Ioannikios, see above, 243–351. The word *semeiophoros,* here translated as "standard-bearer," may also mean "thaumaturge" or miracle-worker. See *v. Ioannic. a Petr.* 401A, 403C, and 409B, and *v. Petr. Atr.,* chaps. 59.11 and 85.29.

[52] For the *vita* of the patriarch Nikephoros I, see above, 25–142.

[53] Theodore (759–826), the hegoumenos or superior of the famous Stoudios monastery in Constantinople, led the monastic opposition to iconoclasm.

[54] On Methodios I, patriarch of Constantinople from 4 March 843 until his death on 14 June 847, see nn. 285 and 289 in the Life of David, Symeon, and George, above.

[55] Michael was the *synkellos,* or adjutant, first of the patriarch of Jerusalem and later of Methodios I. Sent to Constantinople on a diplomatic mission around 815, he was persecuted along with Theodore and Theophanes, fellow monks from the Lavra or monastery of St. Sabas outside of Jerusalem, during the reigns of both Leo V and Theophilos. In 836, Theodore and Theophanes suffered the additional indignity of having their foreheads tattooed with scurrilous verses, thus earning them the nickname "Graptoi." See the *vita* of David, Symeon, and George, above, Chap. 23, for a description of this event.

Theophanes,[56] <founder> of the Megas Agros monastery; the brothers Theodore and Theophanes whose foreheads were tattooed,[57] and many, many more champions of virtue and the orthodox faith. All of these were manning their positions in defense of the truth and faith of their forefathers and beating back the enemy onslaughts and taking up their positions against the entire phalanx of heretics. For to offset <this> great tide, the governor of the universe, Christ our true God, had provided captains and guardsmen, and positioned them to resist the violence of the enemy forces, <and> from His goodness and bounty provided a healing remedy for the evil temper of the times. The venerable and most pious lady Theodora, on the one hand, secretly honored the orthodox and received them graciously, while on the other she despised and rejected the empty-headed iconoclasts who were despised by God. She was deeply troubled and worried [p. 263] and felt sick at heart over her subterfuge.[58] Yet she feared her husband's angry and irascible disposition, his foul moods, his implacability in matters of punishment, the vehemence of his anger, the harshness of his voice, how very ferocious he looked when little by little he screwed his face up into a knot. So, in terror of him, she held her tongue. Still, she kept looking for a suitable opportunity to reveal and bring out into the open her devout character and pure orthodox faith. But God the humane and merciful, Who ever and always cares for the salvation of mankind and in His providence manages everything for the good, did not overlook her good intention but soon revealed through her the blameless and soul-saving orthodox religion and restoration of the holy and venerable images as will be shown more clearly below.

7. In the fifth year of the reign of Theophilos, who was no friend to God,[59] the utterly abominable and unclean Hagarenes[60] came in full force to

[56] On Theophanes the Confessor, see n. 208 in the Life of David, Symeon, and George, above.

[57] See n. 55.

[58] Combefis' text (διαπράξαιτο) is read instead of Regel's correction (διαπράξοιτο for διαπράξυτο).

[59] The Greek text contains a pun on Theophilos' name, which means "dear" or "friendly to God." The invasion actually took place in 838, or the tenth year of Theophilos' reign.

[60] The term Hagarene (or Agarene) originally denoted a descendant of Hagar, whose story is recounted in Gen. 16:1–16 and Gal. 4:21–31, and later came to mean Saracen or Arab, in the present case, those of the Abbasid dynasty.

his homeland, I mean Amorion.[61] Finding the city well secured by massive fortifications and defended by eight generals along with their elite units and regular infantry forces, they captured it in the month of August after a fifteen-day siege and took everyone prisoner. A vast multitude of Christians was executed while a second multitude of prisoners of war, including the holy and glorious forty-two new martyrs for Christ,[62] was transported to Syria. Similarly, multitudes of their ships came out and laid waste to the islands of the Cyclades and took over Crete and Sicily.[63] Constantinople suffered intensely from the cold and the lengthy and very hard winter.[64] It was indeed a long winter, extremely brutal and harsh, and there was a terrible famine; no rain fell, flames appeared in the sky, atmospheric conditions were unhealthy, and the weather was unpredictable. On top of all this, there was a succession of horrible earthquakes that provided tangible proof of the emperor's great, indeed unlimited, depravity and heresy. For the emperor drifted into such great hostility toward God[65] and mindless folly that he surpassed even the thrice-accursed Kopronymos and his beastly <cohorts>[66] in the wickedness that is hated by God.

8. And so the wicked sinner Theophilos, after acting and behaving like this for the twelve years and three months that he reigned, [p. 264] came down

[61] Amorion in central Asia Minor was the birthplace of Michael II, the founder of the Amorian dynasty, whose last representative was Michael III. Hence its capture, on 15 August 838, was particularly humiliating for Theophilos, especially since he had barely escaped with his life after a previous defeat at Dazimon in Armenia on 22 July. See Treadgold, *Byz. Revival,* 297–305.

[62] The Forty-Two Martyrs of Amorion were actually taken to Iraq rather than Syria. They were put to death in 845, after a long period of captivity during which they resisted conversion to Islam. See *ODB* 2:800–801.

[63] There was actually a ten-year interval between the Arab raids on Sicily, Crete, and the Cyclades (which began in the period between 824–828) and the capture of Amorion in 838. The conflation of these events also occurs in Georg. Mon. 2:798. Crete was in Arab hands by 828 but the conquest of Sicily was not completed until the early 10th century; cf. Treadgold, *Byz. Revival,* 248–58, 333, and 452, n. 454, and *ODB* 1:546 and 3:1892.

[64] The unusually cold winter was that of 832–833. See Treadgold, *Byz. Revival,* 279 and 435, n. 385.

[65] The Greek again contains a pun on the name of Theophilos.

[66] See n. 43 above.

with dysentery and departed this life in the following manner.[67] As he was dying, his mouth gaped so wide you could see all the way down his gullet, and while he lay painfully struggling to breathe, the Augusta Theodora lamented over him. Then, she dozed off for a while and saw the supremely holy Mother of God holding in her arms the infant <Christ> with His cross and a terrifying ring of beautiful angels violently reproaching the emperor Theophilos and beating him without cessation because of the holy and venerable icons. This went on for some time. Meanwhile, the emperor Theophilos babbled, tossing his head endlessly from one side to the other and saying over and over in his anguish, "Woe is me, wretch that I am! Because of the icons I am being beaten, because of the icons I am being flogged." The sound of it was a fearful and strange thing for the mourners there to witness. The emperor spent the whole night crying out and saying things like this while the empress kept vigil, dedicating her heart and mind to tearful intercession with the supremely holy Mother of God. Then Theoktistos, who served as *kanikleios*,[68] hurriedly put on the *enkolpion*[69] that he had been keeping hidden out of fear of the emperor. The emperor was in great distress, being subjected for a long time to incessant

[67] The chronology of the Life is accurate on this point, as Theophilos acceded to the throne on 2 October 829 and died on 20 January 842.

[68] Theoktistos illustrates the powerful role played by eunuchs in the Byzantine court. The *kanikleios* kept the pen and purple ink used to sign imperial decrees. Theoktistos also held the very important position of *logothetes tou dromou*, the official in charge of the imperial post whose responsibilities included oversight of foreign relations and internal security. Theophilos appointed Theoktistos to serve as regent during Michael III's minority (*TheophCont* 148.9–11). After Theophilos' death, Theoktistos played a vital role in the restoration of orthodoxy: the (preliminary) meeting of the Council of 843 is said to have taken place in his home. See Duffy-Parker, *Synodicon Vetus,* chap. 156.4; C. Mango, "The Liquidation of Iconoclasm and the Patriarch Photius," in Bryer-Herrin, *Iconoclasm,* 133–34; and n. 367 in the Life of David, Symeon, and George, above.

[69] In both form and function an *enkolpion* was much like a religious medal or crucifix. During the 9th century, image-bearing *enkolpia* served as a vehicle for expressing anti-iconoclastic sentiments. Theoktistos' *enkolpion* is suspended from around his neck by means of a *tenantion,* here translated as "necklace." This *tenantion* comes from the Greek τείνω and should be distinguished from the *tenantion* that is a loanword from the Latin *tenere* and means a pin to fasten clothes. See A. Kartsonis, *Anastasis. The Making of an Image* (Princeton, N.J., 1986), 116–25, and M. P. Vinson, "The Terms ἐγκόλπιον and τενάντιον and the Conversion of Theophilos in the *Life of Theodora* (BHG 1731)," *GRBS* 36 (1995), 89–99.

beating[70] in full view of the mourners on every side. He saw the necklace with the *enkolpion* bearing[71] the holy and unchanging image of the Most High on his [Theoktistos'] neck. The emperor repeatedly pointed his finger at him and vigorously nodded at him, commanding <Theoktistos> to come toward him. Although he [Theoktistos] tried to flee in terror because of the holy icon, he was overpowered by other hands and, with no opportunity to cover up the sacred object, was brought before the emperor in a state of great terror. The others decided that <the emperor> was asking to tear out his [Theoktistos'] hair so they put strands of it in his hands. Meanwhile, he [Theoktistos] thought that he was going to lose his head, but instead the emperor touched the necklace with his finger and drew it to his lips. Well, when the necklace, that bore, as was said, the holy and venerable image of our Savior and God, had been put to his lips and mouth, suddenly—what an unexpected miracle!—those lips of his that had gaped wide apart, the ones that had debased the teachings of the Church and babbled a lot of nonsense against the holy and venerable images, came together and were closed. After this extraordinary and astonishing miracle occurred, the wild, guttural noises he had been making abruptly stopped and the emperor's physical appearance and features returned to normal. His screams fell silent [p. 265] as did the unbearably painful torments and punishments. Whereupon he fell asleep at once, firmly convinced that it was a very good and spiritually beneficial thing to adore and honor and venerate the holy and venerable image of the Lord our God and Savior Jesus Christ and His all-holy mother and all His saints as the first step on a journey to Godhead that ends in revelation.

9. A few days after these developments, the emperor Theophilos breathed his last and died peacefully. Following the death of Theophilos, his son Michael, who was five and a half years old, became emperor along with his mother Theodora.[72] During Michael's reign, Apodinar, the tribal chieftain of

---

[70] Combefis' text (συνεχομένῳ τῷ τύπτεσθαι) is read here instead of συνέχοντι . . . τυπτομένῳ (Markopoulos).

[71] Combefis' text (ἐμφέροντος) is read here instead of ἐμφαίνοντα.

[72] Michael III was actually born on 19 January 840, thus making him two years old, not five and a half, at the time of his father's death on 20 January 842. Our Life (Chap. 11) also misstates Michael's age at his assassination: he was twenty-seven, not twenty-nine. See C. Mango, "When was Michael III Born?" *DOP* 21 (1967), 253–58, and L. Rydén, "The Bride-Shows at the Byzantine Court—Fact or Fiction?" *Eranos* 83 (1985), 182 n. 30.

the accursed and God-forsaken Hagarenes, after many years' preparation launched an all-out assault on the divinely protected city of Constantinople with a fleet of four hundred awesome and terrifying ships.[73] In the end, though, this miserable wretch was completely wiped out and destroyed thanks to the mighty and invincible Trinity, omnipotent and consubstantial, the single God-head and sovereign authority through Whom all things, both visible and invisible, are not only brought safely through danger but are also managed for the best in a masterful way, and through the power and effective intercessions of Mary, the ever-virgin Mother of God. All those awesome and terrifying ships were wrecked together with all their crews off the cape of Kibyrrhaiotai, in the so-called Chelidonia.[74] Only seven safely reached Syria where they reported the victory that saved the Romans and the defeat that brought their own ruination.

10. And so the emperor Michael, after succeeding to his father's throne with his mother Theodora, as was mentioned above, abolished and condemned on the one hand the accursed and soul-destroying heresy of the iconoclasts that was hateful to God, while on the other he strengthened and confirmed the divinely ordained, holy, soul-saving, and most orthodox faith that has long been dear to God by openly proclaiming his strong support for it at the urging, encouragement, and instruction of his venerable and holy mother Theodora. For even though in chronological age the emperor Michael was

---

[73] On this incident, recorded by no other Greek or Arab source except George the Monk (Georg. Mon. 2:801.7–14), see the introduction to this Life. A. A. Vasiliev accepts the historicity of the attack, dating it to 842, and attributes the silence of the Arab sources to the relative unimportance of the expedition. See his *Byz. Arabes*, 1:192–93; in the "Notes complémentaires," 407, M. Canard suggests that the tribal chieftain Apodinar may have been Ahmad-ibn-Dinar. Markopoulos ("Theodora," 250) is more sceptical about this episode, characterizing it as the only miracle (of which saints were supposed to perform many) in the entire Life. Even so, the miraculous defeat of the Arab forces is not specifically attributed to Theodora, but rather to the Trinity and the Virgin Mary.

[74] Kibyrrhaiotai was a naval theme or province located on the southern coast of modern Turkey. The Chelidonia, also known as the Chelidoniae, were a group of rocky islands off the ancient Hiera Akra or Sacred Promontory in Lycia; this is the modern Cape Gelidonya, southeast of Finike, at the entrance to the Gulf of Antalya. The Chelidonian islands are mentioned in both Lucian, *Navigium,* chap. 7, and Pliny, *Natural History* 5.35.131, as posing a serious hazard to navigation. Cf. G. F. Bass, *Cape Gelidonya: A Bronze Age Shipwreck* (Philadelphia, 1967).

still a babe—after all, as mentioned above, he was only five and a half years old—still God Himself, Who *out of the mouth of babes and sucklings hath furnished praise,*[75] enabled <one even so young as> this [p. 266] to celebrate and demonstrate and affirm with brilliant clarity the truth of the divine doctrine to the praise and glory of the Word of God Who became flesh because of His infinite mercy and loving kindness and was seen on earth and lived among mankind. Consequently, thanks to an imperial decree and divinely guided decision of all the holy and orthodox fathers acting in concert with God's advocates the monks and confessors, the thoroughly wicked and evil heresy of the ungodly and impious iconoclasts was refuted and their vacuous and disgusting ravings were demolished point by point, and religious freedom and orthodoxy shone forth throughout the entire universe. And the pernicious beasts were obliterated and throughout the entire world there sprang up as if from dark holes and corners and virtually inescapable labyrinths a definitive statement of orthodoxy; and, on the first Sunday of Holy Lent, orthodoxy became a reality for all who piously honor and venerate the holy and revered images.[76] For the grace of the true knowledge of God sprang up throughout the whole world and a period of justice, peace, and kindness to others was ushered in for everyone everywhere, and it was decreed by the great and orthodox rulers and by the holy and thrice-blessed fathers, I mean Ioannikios and Arsakios, Isaiah and Methodios,[77] and many others who met for this purpose at that time, that tranquillity and calm should dwell in the land for all time to come.

It was then, too, that the aforementioned John, the prime leader and exponent of the ill-famed and soul-destroying heresy, that miserable and wretched chief sorcerer, was deposed from the patriarchal throne in disgrace

---

[75] Ps. 8:2.

[76] The formal restoration of icons took place in the church of St. Sophia on 11 March 843. The Feast of Orthodoxy is still commemorated in the Greek Church on the first Sunday in Lent. For further details, see n. 398 in the Life of David, Symeon, and George.

[77] According to the *De Theophili imperatoris absolutione* (ed. Regel, *Analecta,* 24–27), Arsakios and Ioannikios (on whom see previous *vita*), hermits from Mt. Olympos in Bithynia, were prompted by a divine revelation to visit the same Isaiah of Nikomedeia that Theodora had previously stopped to see. Isaiah, at the direction of the Holy Spirit, enlisted their aid in successfully urging Theodora and Methodios to restore the veneration of icons. See also Bury, *Eastern Roman Empire,* 147, n. 1 and n. 33 above.

and anathematized, rightly and in accordance with the judgment of God, along with his like-minded henchmen and agents of persecution who ravaged the flock like savage and destructive beasts. By the grace of God and the providence of Christ our true God and by unanimous vote of all the orthodox he was succeeded by Methodios, the famous confessor and defender of orthodoxy; he confirmed and proclaimed our blameless orthodox faith after demolishing in its entirety, using the clearest and most forceful arguments, the pernicious scheme against the holy images (the work of the devil, who is always casting a malignant eye over our people) and the unholy drivel of the heresiarchs and their disciples in viciousness[78] and insanity. It was for this that he had in the past endured many other persecutions and dangers as well as many painful situations and punitive tortures at the hands of the unholy iconoclasts and the wicked Theophilos. These things he bore with noble patience as befits a martyr, [p. 267] giving thanks to the merciful God. For who could count the many different persecutions and ordeals that he endured one right after the other, the bottomless pits, the dark and filthy conditions of solitary confinement, the stifling and hellish prison cells,[79] the deprivation not only of the necessities of life but of friends, family, and fellow-believers as well? All of this the blessed man endured nobly and even eagerly, providing for those experiencing hardship a conspicuous example of patient endurance and silent encouragement. In this way, then, Methodios, the marvelous and sainted man of the church, by the favor of the merciful God and with the assistance of the most pious empress Theodora and, as we said, the holy fathers, took into his keeping the flock of Christ and led it to the pastures of eternal life. And the house of God and the community of the orthodox began its forward progress, rejoicing in holiness, justice, and the power of God and was clearly strengthened and shone forth. But as for the assemblage of impious and ungodly heretics, in point of fact a Jewish sect and clique, it was discredited and completely stripped of power, being conspicuously muzzled and refuted on a daily basis. Whereupon by imperial decree all the fathers who had been exiled or subjected to harsh imprisonment were immediately recalled and released from their chains, together with large numbers of monks and further, quite a few pious

---

[78] Regel's correction (κακονοίας) is read instead of κακονίας.

[79] Regel's correction (κατακλείσεις) is read here. On Methodios' imprisonment, see the Life of David, Symeon, and George, above, 199–200 and n. 289.

laymen whom the impious Theophilos had banished after high-handedly confiscating their property and mutilating them, not to mention others whom he ordered to be punished with harsh confinement for refusing to obey his treacherous and insulting commands. All of these lived forever after in peace and joy, praising and glorifying God.

The venerable and virtuous empress Theodora, seeing the orthodox faith of the Christians shining forth in full flower, was happy and perfectly delighted, and was filled with joy and gladness. The *logothetes* Theoktistos, who also served as *kanikleios,* shared the empress' happiness and joined her in applauding these <developments> since he was a fervent supporter of the orthodox faith. But Bardas, the caesar and brother of the most pious empress Theodora crowned of God, hated him and killed him unjustly.[80] So after that the holy and religious empress Theodora took pity on a number of men who came to her for protection and helped them out of her natural goodness and virtuous character and compassionate nature, a woman resplendent with virtue in many forms.

11. And so the blessed Theodora lived in the palace for fourteen years[81] after she assumed imperial power with her son Michael, managing the affairs of her subjects in this meet and fitting manner. [p. 268] She fell out with Bardas, her aforementioned brother, who had become caesar, because of his unjust murder of the likewise aforementioned *logothetes* Theoktistos, and involuntarily and against her will left the palace for the Gastria monastery with her four daughters Pulcheria, Thekla, Anastasia, and Anna. The emperor Michael tonsured three of her daughters and clothed them in the holy garb of monastic life, assigning them to the Karianos monastery. His mother, on the other hand, the most pious lady Theodora, along with her daughter Pulcheria he ordered to take up residence in the previously mentioned Gastria monastery.[82] This is

[80] Theoktistos was murdered on 20 November 855, a casualty of the alliance formed between Bardas and Michael III to depose Theodora and establish Michael as sole ruler. Normally, only the sons of a reigning monarch held the rank of caesar, the highest dignity or honorific title after that of emperor. Bardas became caesar in April 862, several years after Theodora's deposition in 856. See also nn. 367–68 in the Life of David, Symeon, and George, above.

[81] That is, from 842–856.

[82] Both the location of the Karianos monastery and the sequence of events here are problematic. For a discussion of the convent's location, see Janin, *Eglises CP,* 278, who

what happened during those years. Michael ruled alone for fourteen years and
was murdered at the age of twenty-nine in the palace of St. Mamas by his
parakoimomenos, Basil the *patrikios.*[83]

12. But how did that truly good mother and wise preceptor <respond>
to these <developments>? She did not delay her retirement from imperial
life, nor did she seek to regain the sovereignty that her husband had entrusted
to her even though a substantial portion of the senatorial order wanted her
to. On the contrary, she asked her son to come see her and expressed to him
the following views with regard to the state and provided her son with expedient advice as well. "Child of mine and gift of God," she said, "now that I am
free from the responsibility of providing for the people, I shall be content to
keep to myself, praying for you and my other children. As for you, consider
how you have been found worthy by God of the dominion <you have> over
the people, and understand quite clearly that we are called for their sakes
rather than they for ours, and generously grant appropriate rewards to the
deserving while at the same time piously passing judgment on the guilty. This
is all I have to say. Now may God on high, Who is the source of your sovereignty, grant that this sovereign voyage be brought well and safely to port,
with you at the helm, guiding this earthly ship with the rudder of righteous-

---

places it in Blachernai, a region in the northwestern part of Constantinople, and more
recently Treadgold, *Byz. Revival,* 310 and 446, n. 426, who considers it part of the
Great Palace complex. As for the chronology, Bury (*Eastern Roman Empire,* 469–71)
and Karlin-Hayter ("Etudes," 469–74) posit an interval during which Theodora remained in the palace after her deposition from power, an event dated to 856 by our
Life and further specified by Bury as 15 March. Karlin-Hayter (473–74) posits a second
interval between Theodora's expulsion from the palace and her tonsure as a nun, which
resulted from her complicity in a plot against Bardas. See *TheophCont* 174, ps.-Sym.
Mag. 658, and Leo Gramm. 237. On Theodora's tonsure, see also Theognostos, *Libellus,* PG 105:857A and *v. Ignat.,* PG 105:505B. One should note that in both sources
the emphasis is on the patriarch Ignatios' refusal to tonsure the empress rather than
on the actual tonsure itself, which is explicitly attested only by *TheophCont* 174. On the
Gastria convent, see above, n. 41.

[83] On the chronology, see above, n. 72. After the death of Michael III on 23–24
September 867, Basil became emperor and founder of the Macedonian dynasty. *Patrikios* was a dignity or honorific title indicating very high status. *Parakoimomenos* literally
means someone who "sleeps at the (emperor's) side," but by the late 9th century this
office had expanded far beyond its original function of imperial bodyguard. The palace
of St. Mamas was located on the European side of the Bosporos, across the Golden
Horn from Constantinople.

ness, filling <its sails> with the fair wind of salvation." After fortifying her
son with this maternal advice and endowing him with prayers as with any
other maternal legacy, she made her home outside the palace as a private citizen. Then, after she was free from the cares of empire—the marvel of it!—
just as she had once set an example for emperors, so now too she served as an
example for everyone else and won renown after leaving imperial life. What
lady was so widely esteemed as she for her service to the monastic community
[p. 269] or participated with her children so fully in their [the monks'] prayers?
Who set a richer table for the poor than she or graced the sick with visits or
emptied more prisons or clothed with tunics a greater number of the naked
or forgave more loans or recalled her own people from a foreign land? Who
devoted her eyes and ears and her other senses more completely to God and,
like Israel, prepared her mind to see God[84] and raised herself up as a deathless
monument and living icon?[85] For the young, she set up the image[86] of her own
youthfulness, while for those of middle age, the image of her final years, and
again for the elderly and those advanced in age, her own wisdom mature beyond her years. She provides corn with Joseph,[87] and guards her chastity and
receives with Abraham the Trinity,[88] that does not overshadow the dwelling
but dwells within her heart, with Job[89] she opens her doors, and with David
she hymns night and day the ordinances of the Lord,[90] and she washes the feet
of the disciples[91] and preaches the gospel with the apostles,[92] and participates
in the struggles of the martyrs, sharing the martyrs' suffering without bloodshed, and she is justified by Christ,[93] and she obtains the incorruptible crown
in heaven, having gained Christ in the end.

But now that I have mentioned the end of her life, it would be good to

---

[84] Cf. Clement of Alexandria, *Paedagogus* 1.9, PG 8:341c.

[85] Regel's text, which includes "and" (καί), is used here.

[86] The textual variant ἀναστηλοῦσα is read here.

[87] Gen. 47:12.

[88] Gen. 18:1–15. The emendation proposed by A.-M. Talbot (ἐνοικιζομένην) is accepted here.

[89] Job 31:32.

[90] Ps. 17 (18):22 and 118 (119):54.

[91] Jn. 13:5. Regel's text (νίπτει) is read here.

[92] Mk. 16:15.

[93] Gal. 2:16.

include as well some mention of what was said at the time, all the words of advice she offered her children and all the edifying remarks she made to the members of her household at the very hour of her passing. She spoke to her children[94] first. "My children and glorious offspring of my womb," she says, "Lo! *the time of my departure is at hand.*[95] Lend me your ears and hear now my last words. For my tomb is ready and my burial garments are in the hands of those who are going to lay me to rest. A tear of sympathy wells up, shed before my very eyes, and choirs of loved ones stand around in a circle tragically lamenting my death. The whole household has stationed itself at my bedside, wailing bitterly and beating the breast at my imminent departure. Dearest children, remember my many efforts and exertions and the daily teachings with which I brought you up. Remember the moans from my heart in its deep distress, how many tears I shed propitiating God, how many times I stayed up all night in prayerful supplication that you might go forward in God. I kissed the feet of saints and I never stopped sending out prayers of intercession in all directions [p. 270] in order that you might obtain the intercession of the elect. And, just as you were bound by your birth to obey me while I still remained in this life, so now I entreat you to abide[96] by my words and instructions after my death as well. Do not fail in your love for God nor abandon your customary prayers. Do not neglect your relationship with your neighbor; do not lift up against your neighbor your hands to do wrong nor your tongue to revile. Even if you have had your fill of every advantage and have enjoyed the pleasures of imperial life while at the same time you were resplendent with gold and decked out with precious jewels and vast sums of money and slaves have been given to you for your personal use, know that this present life comes to an end for every individual, but that the everlasting pleasures of the angels are promised to us if only we carry out God's ordinances. For this reason, turn your gaze upward and seek the kingdom of heaven, scattering your wealth among the needy so that you may have the wealth that is gathered in heaven. For the previous kingdom with its empty glory and glittering wealth has conferred no benefit on us at all; indeed, it has rather subjected us to tyranny and distracted our minds from divine contem-

---

[94] The use of feminine adjectival forms in the passage that follows indicates that Theodora is addressing her daughters.

[95] 2 Tim. 4:6.

[96] Regel's text (ἐμμείνατε) is read here.

plation and on numerous occasions may very well have even brought misfortunes upon us. You yourselves are witnesses to this. But what I never stopped saying in the past, I urge upon you now as well: be at peace with yourselves and with all mankind, the peace given by God that I have cherished above all else. Strengthen one another, rouse one another to the good, carry one another's burdens so that a desire for glory does not destroy your unity. Through peace let the last be more exalted than those ahead of him and through love let the first be more lowly than those behind him.[97] Let there be one law among you, the will and fear of God, neglecting none of His undefiled commandments so that you may *bring forth fruit unto God,*[98] being offered up to Him as the most appropriate kind of gift and first fruits of my fertile womb, endowed with reason. It is my hope that, if you follow the words of advice I have given you and live your lives accordingly, you may obtain Christ in the end and will become heirs of the bliss in that other realm, to the renown of myself, the mother who bore you and brought you up, and to the glory of God Who put you into my arms." With these words and more the blessed lady strengthened her children. "May God," she continued, "grant that you, too, manage your affairs in this life aright and obtain the object of your hopes in the other. This shall be the reward for your ready obedience to His people; this is why you were put on this earth as our sons and daughters and for the same reason we, too, became a mother."

Now Michael himself, her son and emperor, [p. 271] paid a visit with his consort to express their sympathy at her death.[99] To them, too, she made a

[97] Cf. Mt. 19:30, 20:16; Mk. 9:35, 10:31; Lk. 13:30.

[98] Rom. 7:4.

[99] The visit of Michael III and his wife Eudokia of Dekapolis to Theodora's deathbed presents a serious problem, since in the tradition represented by Symeon the Logothete (Leo Gramm. 252.20, ps.-Sym. Mag. 686.7) it is Theodora who survives to lament over her son's corpse after his assassination. Karlin-Hayter ("Théodora," 207–8) has recently attempted to resolve the difficulty by positing the following interpolation: "<Michael> himself <her son and> emperor." The "emperor himself" would then be Basil I, who was married to Eudokia Ingerina. This is a truly ingenious suggestion, but the rationale behind it, namely that it is odd for Theodora to address the "emperor" separately from her other "children" as she does a little further on in the passage, does not take into account the rhetorical context of the Life. For example, the distinction between emperor and (female) children is not meant to reflect a lack of maternal feeling on Theodora's part, but rather her deference to proper, that is, male, authority. As such, it is of a piece with her earlier refusal of the senate's invitation to resume power and

dying bequest, praying that they should govern their subjects in the best possible way and obtain the kingdom in heaven. Then, after speaking individually with each of her children, the emperor, and her household staff, on 11 February she gave her holy soul into the hands of the God Who made her. Her last words were, "*Lord, into Thy hands I commend my spirit.*"[100]

How noble the birth and upbringing that produced such a flower! How praiseworthy her marriage and admirable her widowhood! How edifying her sound advice and words of wisdom! She honored virginity, glorified marriage, preserved her husband, led a multitude of humanity into the light, ascended to heaven, through hope gained the object of her hopes, was illumined by the light of heavenly radiance, became a light unto God in every respect, gained free access to God, intercedes on behalf of those below, purified by God, perfected by God, giving thanks to God, praising and glorifying Him in Father, Son, and Holy Spirit, because to Him belongs glory, power, honor, now and forever, and unto ages of ages. Amen.

---

the way she subsequently limits her involvement in Michael's life to praying for him and urging him to seek the kingdom of God through his just rule on earth. This is the behavior of an exemplary woman, one who knows her place and does not interfere in the affairs of men except under the most extraordinary circumstances, such as when the emperor is a child of two (or five). Hence, despite Karlin-Hayter's ingenuity, the discrepancy between our Life and the Logothete does not seem to admit of an easy solution. Rhetorical analysis is of limited value here since in the end the question boils down to whether a dutiful but grieving mother is more credible than a dutiful but grieving son: there is little to choose between them. A secure date for the Life might help, but one should caution that mere proximity to events is no guarantee of an author's veracity. One suspects that final resolution of this question will come only from "hard," that is, nonliterary evidence of the kind that Mango used so successfully to establish the date of Michael III's birth in the face of similarly contradictory evidence (see above, n. 72). For a discussion of Michael III, Basil I, their consorts, and concubines, including Thekla who was allegedly given to Basil for this purpose by her brother, see C. Mango, "Eudocia Ingerina, the Normans, and the Macedonian Dynasty," *ZRVI* 14–15 (1973), 17–27 and more recently the extremely perceptive analysis of Karlin-Hayter in "L'enjeu d'une rumeur," *JÖB* 41 (1991), 85–111.

[100] Ps. 30 (31):5; Lk. 23:46.

INDEX OF PEOPLE AND PLACES

Entries on churches, monasteries, monuments, etc. of Constantinople are found under the listing for that city.

GENERAL INDEX

abbess (mother superior), 13, 14, 322–25
abbot (father superior), x–xi, xv, 27, 149 n. 20, 151 n. 31, 158 n. 72, 173, 174, 192, 201, 278, 279, 292
acorns, 156
adventus ceremony, 232 n. 436
Amomos (Ps. 118 [119]), 181 and n. 199
anagrapheus, 334
anathema, x, 112, 114–15, 122, 123, 124, 202 n. 294, 214 and n. 353, 218, 221, 226 n. 411, 248, 341, 344, 376
angels, 58, 141, 158–59, 182, 234, 235, 236, 237, 238, 265, 291, 305, 347, 365, 369, 372, 380; images of, 98–100; dressed in white, 239 and n. 472, 279 and n. 201
animals: images of, 91–92; irruption into churches of, 177–78
Antichrist, 76
apples, 363–65
archdeacon, 199
arithmetic, 26, 53 and n. 105, 54
Ark of the Covenant, 88–89
armor, iron, 276
army, xii, xv, 18, 23 n. 13, 29, 71, 189, 201 n. 291, 240, 243, 257, 259–60, 271 n. 153, 289 n. 259, 329 n. 451, 347; desertion from, 243 and n. 6, 244 n. 7, 245, 257, 344 n. 529
arrows, 276
art, secular, xi, 91–92
asekretis, 25, 26, 44 and n. 66, 46, 50, 105, 197 n. 278. *See also protasekretis*
astronomy, 26, 53 and n. 105, 54, 194 n. 260

asylum, 72
axes, 6, 125; pick-axes, iron, 297, 298

banquets, 45, 52 n. 103, 198, 224 n. 401, 233 n. 441, 337
baptism, x n. 14, 9, 116, 224 n. 404
basilikos logos, 353, 357–58
baths, 153
bears, 284, 310
beggar, 221–22
betrothal, 365
birds, 91, 96, 269, 306 n. 349, 365 n. 36
birth, predictions of, 14, 18, 19, 21–22, 153–54
bishop, installation of, 233–34
blankets, 228, 229, 230, 233
blinding: as divine punishment for iconoclastic views, 291; as punishment, xi, 23 n. 13, 26, 119 and n. 409, 190, 199 and n. 284
boars, wild, 91
boats, 37, 118, 156, 193, 195, 211, 231 n. 433, 239. *See also* ships
bolts, 301
books, 75, 102, 362; burning of, 75
bows (and arrows), 190, 272, 276
bread, 141, 167, 173, 174, 206, 207 n. 318, 222 n. 393, 300; twice-baked, 174, 206, 336; blessed (εὐλογία), 69 n. 187, 126 n. 444, 308, 336, 337, 338
bride shows, 357, 359–60, 363–65 and nn. 30, 33, and 37
bridges, 171–72 and n. 171
buffalo, water, 178 n. 183
builders, 298–99, 303
buildings: construction of, 160, 298, 303, 308; design of, 298
bulls, 76 n. 213, 85, 88, 90

libelli, 200 n. 289, 201 nn. 292 and 294
lice, 90 n. 279, 200
lime, 125; burning of, 308
lions, 88, 89 n. 272, 91, 116–17, 138, 365 n. 36
locks, 301, 330
locusts, plague of, 198–99
logothetes, 105 n. 336; *tou dromou,* 202 n. 295, 216 n. 367, 372 n. 68, 377; *tou genikou,* 227

magarikon, 310
Magi (New Testament), 365
magic, 275–78, 332, 368 n. 47. *See also* sorcerer
magistrianos, 17 n. 22
magistros, 216 n. 367, 332, 333
maidservants, 332
marketplaces, 84, 92
marriage, 156 n. 61, 359, 363, 366 n. 40, 382; forced, xi, 23, 194; second, xiv, 27, 28, 68, 249, 260 n. 96, 292 n. 272
mathematics, 53
mattocks, 307
meals, 123, 206, 230, 237, 287, 293, 302, 309–10, 336, 337. *See also* banquets
Menologion of Basil II, 4, 251, 252, 356
mice, 178 n. 183, 200
milk, 277
mills, 173
miracles, healing: broken nose, 172; deafness and muteness, 3, 196; deliverance from poison potion, 278; demonic possession, 39, 302; fever, 313–14; hernia, 205–6; insanity caused by poison potion, 332; liver pains, 168–69; nosebleed, 312; paralysis, 198 n. 283, 289–90; severe illness, 209–10, 236–37; sexual dementia, 282–83, 304–5; snakebite, 89, 298–99

miracles, non-healing: control over animals, 244, 246 n. 18, 267, 305–6, 309, 326, 331; disappearance of writing from document, 208–9; expulsion of caterpillars, 321–22; expulsion of demons, 205, 289, 311; expulsion of dragon, 294–5; expulsion of locusts, 198–99; expulsion of snakes, 295 n. 283, 298; invisibility of saint, 244, 307–9, 327; killing of dragons, 244, 285–86, 297–98, 303–4; killing of snakes, 244; knowledge of future events, 35, 73, 114, 119, 144, 177, 183, 192, 229–30, 265, 269, 270, 271–72, 284, 338, 349, 369; levitation of iron cross, 289; levitation of saint, 244, 280–81; miraculous escape of prisoners of war, 330–31; multiplication of grapes, 234–35; multiplication of wine, 198, 235; salvation of child from demons, 281–82; salvation of church from fire, 279–80; spontaneous appearance of spring, 303; spontaneous opening of locked doors, 301, 330; spontaneous unlocking of shackles, 330; transfiguration of saint, 244, 251, 280–81, 299; walking on water, 211, 212, 300. *See also* birth, predictions of; death, predictions of
miracles, posthumous, xx, 3, 19, 39, 333, 345–46, 349, 350 n. 588, 356
modesty, topos of, 41–42 and n. 47, 47, 142, 150–51 and n. 31, 266, 328, 350 n. 588
modios (measure of grain), 174, 175
Moechian controversy, 27, 28, 35, 249 and n. 29, 260 n. 96, 292 n. 272
monasteries, double, 13, 14, 18 n. 26, 28, 35, 66–67, 134 n. 493
monasteries, parts of: cell, 19, 172, 206, 239, 266, 267, 271, 276, 287,

INDEX OF NOTABLE GREEK WORDS